Forward in Flight

The History of Aviation in Wisconsin

by
Michael J. Goc

Wisconsin Aviation Hall of Fame

New Past Press, Inc.,
Friendship, Wisconsin

Forward in Flight

The History of Aviation in Wisconsin

by
Michael J. Goc

Wisconsin Aviation Hall of Fame

History Book Committee
Earl Pingel, Chair, West Allis; Carl Guell, Madison; Duane Esse, Waunakee;
Brig. Gen. Ralph Jensen (USAF, ret.), Madison; Irene Lotzer, Arbor Vitae; Tom Thomas, Madson;
Marge Van Galdler, Beloit; Charles Marotske, Greenfield; Michael Goc, Friendship.

New Past Press, Inc.
Friendship, Wisconsin
Research: Kathy Wendorff
Publishing Assistants: Christy Ciecko, Carol Ann Podoll and Erika Hall
Cover and Page Design: Jay Jocham

Printed in the United States of America

Library of Congress Cataloging in Publication Data

Goc, Michael J.
        Forward in Flight : the history of aviation in Wisconsin / Michael J. Goc.
           p. cm.
        Includes bibliographical references and index.
        ISBN 0-938627-40-6 (alk. paper)
         1. Aeronautics--Wisconsin--History.   I. Title.
TL522.W6G63 1998
629.13'09775--dc21
                                       98-16701
                                        CIP

Howard Morey, Madison, 1948.

Art Scholl and his Super Chipmunk, 1980s.

ACKNOWLEDGEMENTS

American Waco Club; Bette Arey, Hales Corners; John Ashley, Madison; Murtice Aukema, Boyceville; Stan Badzinski, Milwaukee Area Technical College; Ardith McEldowney Bahr, West Salem; Matthew Bainbridge, Menomonie; Larry Bartell, Waukesha; Fred W. Baumgartner, La Grange, Illinois; Delores Beaudette, Chippewa Falls; Richard Bedzinski, Oak Creek; Herb and Laverne Behl, Clintonville; Goodwin Berquist, Washington Island; Ken Bigelow, Stevens Point; George Bindl, Waunakee; Sue Bodilly, Green Bay; Greg Bosak, Blackhawk Technical College; Donald N. Botsford, Racine; Ina Marple Bousselot, Naples, Florida (Hayward); Joseph J. Brauer, Rhinelander; William Brennand, Neenah; James Bresina, Blair; Barb Bretting, Ashland; Harry Brewer, Palm Harbor, FL (Richland Center); Barb Brunner, Elroy; Ed Bruso, Rhinelander; Gregg Bruso, Rhinelander; Marshall Buehler, Alexander House, Port Edwards; Richard Cairns, Richland Center; Don Cammack, Madison; Cessna Owner Organization; Marion Chaput, Kenosha; Jack Conant, Eagle River; Steve Conway, Crandon; Jo Cooper, Pasadena, California; Corporate Angel Network, Inc.; Wendy Cramer, New Holstein; Dean Crites, Waukesha; Marcia Crothers, Granton; Doris Cruckson, Portage; Cumberland Municipal Airport; Dodge County Historical Society, Beaver Dam; Greg Dorcey, Wisconsin DNR; John Dorcey, Aeronautics Bureau, Madison; Richard H. Driessel, West Bend; Robert Driver, Monroe EAA Chapter; David L.F. Duax, Eau Claire; Vera and Don Duesterbeck, New London; Gerald Earleywine, Brodhead; Merton Eberlein, Mauston; John Ebert, Fond du Lac Jack Eder, Indianapolis, Indiana; June J. Edwards, Brooks, Alberta, Canada; Luella Edwards, Richland Center; Bob Egan, Eagle River; Dave Engel,

Wisconsin Aero Club, Milwaukee, 1914.

Rudolph; Charles Ercegovac, Merrill; Joyce Bong Erickson, Poplar; Jack Faas, CAP Wisconsin Wing Headquarters; Chuck Faber, Waukesha; Robert Fay, Manitowoc; Alden Ferguson, EAA Ultralight Chapter 41, Oshkosh; Peter J. Fetterer, Kohler Company, Kohler; Fern Fisher, Racine; Andrea Freitag, Aeronautics Bureau, Madison; Ray Freiwold, Warner Electric, South Beloit; Jerry Friermood, Barnes; Robert Gall, Wisconsin Valley Improvement Company, Wausau; Gary Gatton, West Allis; David M. Greene, Madison; Debra Giuffre, Appleton; Greg Gorak, Milwaukee; Don Gunderson, Wild Rose; Mack Gunnlaugsson, Washington Island EAA Chapter; Thomas Guntly, Franksville; George Hardie, Hales Corners; Chan Harris, Sturgeon Bay; Daniel L. Haulman, Maxwell Air Force Base, Alabama; Jerry Hawkins, Oshkosh; Virginia Knapp Healy, Racine; Brig. General Donne C. Harned, Madison; Bob Heffner, Rice Lake; Dale Heikkinen, Prentice; Mary Jane Heittinga, Marathon County Historical Society; Jackie Hermann, New Berlin; Isla Hetzel, Almond; Marc Higgs, Spring Green; Mary Ellen Hodge, Janesville; Pete Horton, Madison; Lloyd Hougdahl, Deer Park; Kirk W. House, Curtiss Museum, Hammondsport, New York; John Ingalls, Walworth; Gerald Inman, Woodruff; Iowa County Historical Society; Dave Jankoski, Stanley; Martin L. Janssen, M.D., Friendship; Newell Jasperson, Wisconsin Rapids; Brig. General Ralph C. "Bud" Jensen (Ret), Madison; Jean Jerred, Pardeeville; Paul Johns, Racine; Leroy Jonas, Mosinee; Tom Kalina, SC Johnson Wax; Karen Kalmanson, Appleton; Keith R. Kasbohm, Sturgeon Bay; Marlo Keller, Fremont, Ohio (Hayes Presidential Center); Paul Kerr, Beloit; Karl Kerscher, Land

Pheasant Traveler, Fond du Lac, 1930s.

O'Lakes; Carl Kerstetter, Antigo; Dan Kilpatrick, Fox Valley Technical College; Connie King, CAP South East Wisconsin ; Dorothy Kittleson, Brown Deer; Bob Klager, Land O'Lakes; Nate Klassey, Monroe; Michael Kohrs, Aeronautics Bureau, Madison; Gilbert Korth, Juneau; Robert Krause, Kewaunee; Bernice Krippene, Ripon, California; Steve Krog, Hartford; Tom Kuchenberg, Fond du Lac; Robert Kunkel, Aeronautics Bureau, Madison; Charles Lang, Cassville; Marie Langham, Stone Lake; Viola Larson, Larsen; Dan Leslie, Hayward; Ralph C. Lester, Martinsville, Virginia; Dawn Letson, Texas Women's University; Phil Leyda, Richland Center; Debbie Salmon LoGuercio, Frazier Park, California; Eric Londt, ANG museum, Volk Field; Fred W. Lueneburg, Worden, Montana(Brown Deer Airport); Susan Lurvey, EAA, Oshkosh; Dennis McCann, Milwaukee Journal-Sentinel; Roderick McLean, Dane County Regional Airport, Madison; Kent McMakin, Brodhead; Madeline Island Historical Preservation Association; Jeanne Mahony, Mazomanie; Dale Mann, Fountain City; David Mann, Racine; James Marshall, East Providence, Rhode Island; Major General Ray Matera; Dan Maurer, Marshfield; Chuck Mayer, Sheboygan Falls; George Meade, Glendale; Mellon Area Historical Society; Tom Miller, Green Bay; Steven R. Milquet, Green Bay; Wally and Lois Mitchell, Brookfield; Mrs. Robert Mohr, Wausau; Field Morey, Middleton; Joanne Murphy, Waukesha; Nathanial Nez, Phillips; Ben Olson, Wisconsin Dells; Ted Osenga, Plover; Geoffrey S. Parker, Easton, Maryland; George Parker, Virginia Beach, Virginia; Bill Paul, UW Stevens Point; Piper Owner Society; Bonnie Poberezny, EAA, Oshkosh; Paul Poberezny, EAA, Oshkosh; Chuck Pollard, Tomah; Pearl B. (Toddy) Porath, Black River Falls; Elinore Pyle, Merrill; Tip Randolph, National World War II Glider Pilots Assn., Inc.; Claire Rayford, Flight for Life, Milwaukee; Jeffrey Reabe, Plainfield; Tom Reise, Adams; Charlotte Reynolds, Cable; Norman G. Richards, Washington, D.C.; Owen Richardson, Spring Grove; Allen Robinson, Two Rivers; Ed Russell, Maxwell Air Force Base, Alabama; Dorothy Rylander, Shell Lake; David Sandberg, Grantsburg; Mary Sather, New Richmond; Francis Edwards Saunders, Brodhead; Renee Scheidecker, Med Flight, Madison; William C. Schuette, Reedsburg; Elizabeth Schuetze, Waukesha; Russell Schuetze, Waukesha; Thomas Schuller, Kewaunee; Jim Schumacher, Watertown; Arnold Schwarz, Manitowoc; Ron Scott, Waukesha; Bonnie E. Selmer, Cornell; Jan Severson, Aeronautics Bureau, Madison; Tom Sheppard, West Bend; Paul L. Shultz, Menominee, Michigan; John Simenstad, M.D., Osceola; William Sisson, Greenwood; Rod Slotten, Verona; Jane Smith, Ashland;

Thomas Smith, Society of Experimental Test Pilots; Forest Sommers, Wisconsin Dells; Deb Spaeth, West Bend; John Spellman, Hartford; Fran Sprain, Westfield; John Sullivan, Kenosha; Fran Susor, Wausau; Dick Sweeney, Hillsboro James A. Taylor, Milwaukee; Michael Tegtmeier, Juneau; Tom Thomas, Aeronautics Bureau, Madison; Art Vredenburg, Waukesha; Marge Van Galder, Beloit; Terri Vetter, Medford; Ted Vogel, Milwaukee; Scott Volberding, Siren; Eleanor Wagner, Early Birds of Aviation; Bob Washburn, East Troy; Tom Weigt, Basler Turbo Conversions, LLC., Oshkosh; Dave Weiman, Midwest Flyer Magazine, Oregon; Joanne Wells, Beaver Dam; Don Winkler, Madison; Andrea Marple Witter, Hayward ; Joanne Wixom, Janesville; Marty Wyall, Fort Wayne, Indiana; Bob Wylie, Wausau; Donna Zech, Prairie du Sac; Jim Zuelsdorf, Mayville

Pitcairn Autogyro, Wausau, 1930.

INTRODUCTION

Wisconsin people have been taking to the air for almost as long as Wisconsin has been a state. "Smoke" balloonists in the 1850s, adventurous homebuilders in the 1900s, barnstormers and wingwalkers in the 1920s, airline founders and airport builders in the 1950s, corporate flyers and sport aviators in all the years since, have created a hangar full of stories for the historian to recount. This book is the first attempt at a comprehensive recounting of those stories.

Work began almost fifty years ago, when Wisconsin took part in the national celebration of the fiftieth anniversary of the Wright Brothers' flight. In 1953, Clifford Lord, the director of the State Historical Society and a former Navy pilot, worked with Aeronautics Commission education chief—and former Army pilot—Carl Guell, to collect information on the history of flight in this state. Lord went on to other work, but Guell made Wisconsin's aviation history his private passion.

Throughout a busy 40-year career of public and community service, Guell gathered aviation history. Upon his retirement from the Aeronautics Bureau in 1985, he made the publication of a book on Wisconsin aviation his goal. For nearly a decade, Guell continued to collect information, including an invaluable and exclusive set of taped interviews with pioneer aviators from all over the state. Ill health prevented Carl from completing his mission on his own, but the goal was not forgotten. In fact, it was shared by the many others who joined him to organize and maintain the Wisconsin Aviation Hall of Fame.

In 1994, the directors of the WAHF voted to raise the funds to complete Carl's research, and to write and publish a history book. WAHF President Dave Duax named a history book committee chaired by Earl Pingel. Its members were Irene Lotzer, Ralph "Bud" Jensen, Duane Esse, Tom Thomas, Carl Guell and Michael Goc, who were later joined by Marge Van Galder and Charles Marotske.

In short time the committee decided to publish enough books so that one could be presented free of charge to each school and community library in Wisconsin. They initiated a fund-raising program that attracted major gifts from SC Johnson Wax and the Jeffris Family Foundation. The Jeffris grant funded the research and writing of this book. Fund-raising also began at the grass roots level, with individuals asked to purchase a book—sight unseen—for eventual presentation to a library of their choice. Led by the tirelessly enthusiastic Earl Pingel, a corps of volunteers was organized at the county level.

By mid-1997, most of the research on and writing of the book was completed, and a considerable portion of the fund-raising, when the opportunity arose to apply for a Wisconsin Sesquicentennial Commission grant. The application was successful, the Commission supported the project and made it possible for the WAHF to achieve its initial goal of placing a book in every Wisconsin community and school library. Thanks to the efforts of the history book committee and the funds it raised, no one who wants to learn the history of aviation in Wisconsin will be denied the opportunity.

Researching the story was also the work of many hands. It started with the materials Carl Guell had been collecting for decades. In the course of two years, virtually every related scholarly institution, government agency, local historical society, library, airport, aviation organization and interested individual was contacted. Many people—and not all of them located in Wisconsin—donated hours of work to gather and share information about special subjects. Many others sat for interviews or shared personal photos. The list is long and easily fills two pages with small type.

Although all deserve special recognition, a few stand out: Kirk House, of the Curtiss Museum in Hammondsport, New York, for information on A. P. Warner and other early Curtiss aviators; Marty Wyall of Fort Wayne, Indiana, for her guidance on woman aviators of the World War II era; Fred Lueneberg of Worden, Montana, who wrote and sent a history of the Brown Deer airport; George Hardie, the dean of Wisconsin aviation historians, who shared his knowledge of aviation in the Milwaukee area; Dean Crites of Waukesha, for his memorable recounting of how to fly a Jenny; Fran Susor, Wausau, who seems to know everyone who ever flew an airplane in north central Wisconsin; and Robert Wylie of Wausau, who shared his sixty-volume set of scrapbooks, his hundreds of photos, as well as his considerable knowledge of aviation in Wausau and northern Wisconsin.

A special word of thanks is also owed to the men and women of the WAHF History Book Committee, who acted as an editorial board to read, comment on and correct the manuscript; also to Christy Ciecko and Kathy Wendorff, of the New Past Press, for diligence and dedication to quality and accuracy.

A final expression of gratitude is owed to Carl Guell, who hoped this book would be his but who shared it nonetheless, and to Earl Pingel whose leadership and hard work helped make it possible.

Although all these people and many others helped produce this book, all errors are my own.

Michael J. Goc
March, 1998

CURTISS

"There were no directions with it, but I finally got it together." Inadvertently, with help from a wind strong enough to keep him aloft, but not too rough to send him crashing to earth, Arthur P. Warner brought Wisconsin into the age of aviation.
(WAHF)

First Flights

WISCONSIN'S FIRST AVIATOR

In 1906, Arthur P. Warner, inventor and entrepreneur, left his home town of Beloit, Wisconsin to meet with "a little group in New York City composed of people who were interested in building flying machines." At dinner with the group one evening, Warner listened attentively to an eminent mathematician from Harvard University hold forth on the subject of aviation. Filling a small blackboard with diagrams and equations, the professor proved categorically that a heavier-than-air machine could not fly. Surprised at this conclusion, Warner asked one of his dinner partners what he thought of it. The gentleman replied that he'd put more stock in the professor's words if he had not already seen a fellow named Wright fly.

Orville and Wilbur Wright had made the first controlled flight of a heavier than air machine in North Carolina on December 17, 1903 and wire service reports appeared in newspapers—including Milwaukee's—on the 19th. Although the Wrights continued to fly in North Carolina and in Dayton, Ohio, it was not until Orville's dramatic demonstration for the army in September, 1908 that their accomplishments were widely acknowledged in the United States, including Harvard.

Warner's New York group consisted of ambitious backyard tinkerers, curious men of means and a few bona fide geniuses, all aware of the Wrights' success, all hoping to duplicate it. Among them was August Herring, one of aviation's most experienced experimenters. In the mid-1890s, he had assisted Chicago engineer Octave Chanute, whose biplane glider design had been adopted by Orville and Wilbur Wright for their own successful flying machine.

Herring had also been on hand in 1903 when Samuel Langley of the Smithsonian Institution attempted to fly what he called "the aerodrome" off a barge anchored in the Potomac River.

Now he was in New York working on engines and "planes" to make a machine that would fly.

Glenn Curtiss was also in Warner's group. He was a member of Alexander Graham Bell's Aerial Experiment Association and had flown gliders and the cigar-shaped balloons known as dirigibles near his home at Hammondsport, New York. Curtiss had also designed and built engines for high speed motorcycles, one of which set a record of 136.3 miles per hour, and for dirigibles, one of which made a sensational flight over Milwaukee in 1906.

Arthur P. Warner felt right at home with these inventive men. Born in 1870 in Jacksonville, Florida, Warner grew up in Beloit and studied electricity at Beloit College. At age 18, he built a water-powered dynamo that churned out the first electric power in Beloit.

By 1893, his Warner-Wiley company was providing electric service throughout the city. Ten years later Warner and his brother Charles developed a magnetic device that became the first commercially successful automobile speedometer. By 1906, with customers like Willys-Overland, Cadillac and other American and foreign car makers, the Warner Instrument Company was the largest manufacturer of speedometers in the United States. In a few years, Warner's speedometer would make him a millionaire.

He had yet to strike it rich when he came to New York in 1906, but Warner was comfortable enough to indulge in his "mechanical hobby" of aviation. Whenever he came east, he investigated the latest developments in the field and was elated when he heard that Glenn Curtiss had built and demonstrated a machine that could fly. On July 4,

1908 in Hammondsport, Curtiss and his "June Bug" machine met the challenge issued by *Scientific American Magazine* calling for an aeroplane to demonstrate that it could fly for a distance of one kilometer. This flight put Glenn Curtiss on the front page of newspapers across the country and convinced Arthur Warner to buy a flying machine of his own.

About a year later, Warner saw an advertisement in a New York newspaper placed by the Wyckoff, Church and Partridge agency, dealers for Stearns automobiles. The dealer had announced that it was also the exclusive American agent for the newly-organized Herring-Curtiss aeroplane manufacturing company. Since the Herring-Curtiss Company had yet to build any aircraft, the ad was certainly guilty of overstatement—but just the kind of overstatement that would lure automobile buyers into the show room.

The ad proved to be more successful than the car dealer expected.

"It was a surprise to him when he sold a plane the very day after his first advertisement appeared," said Warner.

"I bought it."

The contract was signed on June 23, 1909. The cost was $6,000 and Warner later recalled that it was the first aeroplane in the United States sold to an individual consumer.

A few days later, Curtiss made the first genuine aeroplane flights in the New York City area at the Morris Park race track in Yonkers. Warner was there and, although the longest flight consisted of a circuit around the track at a maximum altitude of 150 feet, he was deeply affected. "I never afterwards saw a flight which impressed me as that one did."

Soon after, Curtiss went to France to fly his newest machine— powered by an equally-new, eight-cylinder, 50-horsepower engine—and won the world championship air races in Rheims. Herring remained in New York and, through the Wyckoff, Church and Partridge agency, continued to sell aeroplanes based on the older Curtiss June Bug design and powered by a 4-cylinder Curtiss engine. Since Curtiss and Herring were being sued for patent infringement by the Wright Brothers, these sales were of pending legality, which might explain why records are incomplete and sometimes contradictory.

As Arthur Warner remembered it, delivery of

his aeroplane was postponed because Curtiss needed a plane to fly at the big Aero Club exhibition in St. Louis in October, 1909.

Warner was there for his "first sight of my own plane," and watched Curtiss make the initial flight of an aeroplane west of the Mississippi River. Afterwards, Curtiss dismantled the machine, crated it and loaded it on a train bound for Beloit, Wisconsin, "at a $200 express charge."

Another version of the story holds that Curtiss flew this machine in Chicago immediately after the St. Louis show and then took it back to New York. In any event, a Herring-Curtiss, four-cylinder machine did arrive in Beloit in late October or very early November, 1909.

"I had to reassemble the pieces," said Warner. "There were no directions with it, but I finally got it together."

On November 4, 1909, he took his "box-kite" to the Morgan Farm on the east side of Beloit. It was a sunny day with mild, steady breezes. With no intention of actually getting off the ground, Warner started the engine and began to taxi around the field.

"I thought I would keep it on the ground until I became familiar with it, but on account of the wind, I unexpectedly took to the air, and the first thing I knew, I was flying."

Inadvertently, with help from a wind strong enough to keep him aloft, but not too rough to send him crashing to earth, Arthur P. Warner brought Wisconsin into the age of aviation.

He made at least six, perhaps nine flights that day, the most impressive for a distance of about one-quarter mile at an altitude of fifty feet. If he tried to bank, turn or fly faster than the minimum to maintain altitude, he did not report it. He would have kept at it, but one of his steering cables worked loose and forced a rough landing during which two spars snapped.

Since the nearest source of replacements was in Chicago, Warner was grounded for a few days. Despite the mishap, Wisconsin's first aviator told the Beloit newspaper that driving an automobile or anything else he had ever done for sport could not compare with flying.

Nearly forty years old, Arthur Warner was a bit older than the majority of pioneer pilots, who tended to be in their twenties or teen years. Flying was a young man's game, too risky for adults with

Arthur P. Warner, Wisconsin's first aviator, about the time of his flight in 1909. (Curtiss Museum)

PAGE OF HONOR

Wisconsin Aviation Hall of Fame Underwriters

Benefactors

The Jeffris Family Foundation, Janesville

The Wisconsin Sesquicentennial Commission

SC Johnson Wax, Racine

Sponsors

Archie Becher Memorial, Wausau

Stoughton Trailers, Stoughton

Theodore J. Bachhuber, Mayville

Supporters

James P. Coughlin, Winneconne

Eckrose/Green Associates, Inc., Madison

KC Aviation, Inc., Appleton

Robert & Carrol Kunkel, Middleton

Rayovac Corporation, Madison

Wagner Foundation, Ltd., Lyons

CONTENTS

a stake in the world, and Arthur Warner was a successful businessman He took an intellectual and perhaps a business interest in aviation, and enjoyed flying as a pastime, but he did not consider it his life's work. Warner did share the typical pioneer aviator's love of mechanics—the desire to take apart a machine, put it back together and make it run faster, smoother, better, and he probably enjoyed building and tinkering with the Curtiss as much as flying it. He also shared the aviator's love of motion, of being carried along at great speed, whether on land or in the air.

Warner kept his aeroplane for a few years and made great use of it as a drawing card at auto shows where he exhibited and sold his speedometer. He flew it often enough to polish his piloting skills to the extent that he could boast to Glenn Curtiss of having made a successful dead stick landing after an engine stall.

Ever the inventor, Warner also fitted his machine with an "Aerometer," a device he had built to measure air speed that resembled his auto speedometer. It was one of the first instruments developed for aviation use and the first developed in Wisconsin. Warner remained active in aviation,

attending, if not flying in, the most significant national air meets of the pre-World War I period. In Los Angeles in 1910, he recalled meeting a young balloon pilot named Lincoln Beachey who asked Warner for an introduction to Glenn Curtiss. Warner obliged and Beachey soon became the most famous and daring pilot of his day.

After a few years, Arthur Warner sold his aeroplane to an exhibition pilot who flew it on the air show tour. The last word he had of it said that Wisconsin's first flying machine ended its days parked in a shed in New Orleans where it was destroyed by fire.[1]

"AMAZEMENT AT THE MARVEL"

Arthur Warner was only one of many Wisconsin people interested in aviation at the turn of the 19th Century. Aviation was in the air, so to speak. It was one of a cluster of technological advancements based on electricity and the internal combustion engine that made the decades bracketing 1900 one of human kind's great periods of invention. Electrically-powered motors, electric

Ever the inventor, Arthur Warner fitted his airplane with an "Aerometer" to measure air speed and advertised in aviation journals. The Aerometer was one of the first instruments developed for aviation in the United States. (WAHF)

lighting, motion pictures, sound recordings and radio emerged.

Gasoline and diesel powered engines transformed bicycles into motorcycles, steamboats into ocean liners, horse-drawn carriages into motorcars and gliders into flying machines.

Descriptions, photos and drawings of the newest breakthroughs appeared regularly in the press, which had itself just undergone a technological revolution that made the penny newspaper the first medium of mass communication. All these advancements were founded on progress in education. In the United States, the national commitment to universal public education made in the mid-1800s had, by the end of the century, created the world's largest population of people who could read, write and cipher basic mathematics. As a result, the first successful flying machines were not built in the lab of an exclusive university or in a pricey industrial research department, but by public school graduates—two brothers who repaired bicycles in Dayton, Ohio, and a young fellow from Hammondsport, New York, who liked to tinker with gas engines.

The Wright Brothers and Glenn Curtiss had their counterparts in Wisconsin, where an incredible number of aeronautically-minded people were

dreaming, scheming and building machines they hoped would fly. Some were crackpots, a few were con men, a few more were surprisingly able craftsmen who could assemble machines that actually took off, flew a respectable distance and landed with no serious mishap.

It is not surprising that no sooner had word spread of the Wright Brothers first success than a publicity seeker should step forward and claim that he had, could or would accomplish the same feat. In Wisconsin, that role fell to a Fond du Lac machinist named Tom Abel who, a few days after the Wrights' flight, told a reporter that he had been working on a flying machine for "twelve years" and that it would "be in readiness for the test of flying through space propelled by motive power, controlled by the operator." Abel said he wanted to exhibit his creation at the St. Louis World's Fair in 1904 and collect a cash prize for it. When the reporter asked to see Abel's machine, however, the mechanic refused, so there is no record of whether it was a motorized balloon, an aeroplane or a figment of the imagination. There is also no record of its ever having flown.

John Stierle was more open about his work than Tom Abel. Stierle was a Milwaukee inventor who, in the spring of 1904, hauled his machine out to a vacant lot at 37th and Vliet Street and tried to take off. Descriptions of the device and its ability to fly are unclear but a news report says that Stierle's machine got off the ground and "showed signs of flight" before struggling to earth and staying there. Had he made a sustained flight, Stierle would have entered the books as second only to the Wright Brothers as a builder and pilot of a heavier-than-air machine. However, Stierle's machine didn't do much more than execute what Wilbur Wright called a "jump" and, as Wilbur also said, "There is all the difference in the world between jumping and flying."

Stierle's failure to span the gap between "jumping" and "flying" did not deter another Milwaukeean, the courageous Albert Dufour. A "constructing engineer" for the Chain Belt Company, who said he was familiar with the work of Octave Chanute, Dufour started work on gliders in 1906. He developed a machine that he said was built on the lines of the Wright Flyer and, like the Wrights, tested it as a glider by launching it off an inclined plane. By 1908, he was ready to give it a real road test. He recruited the aid of R. C. Chidester, who boasted that his 60-horse power Packard was the most powerful auto in Milwaukee.

Accompanied by a reporter and a photographer for the Sunday Sentinel, they took the Packard and the glider out to a country road near Whitefish Bay. After assembling the flying machine, they secured it to the bumper of Chidester's Packard with a stout fifty-foot line.

Dufour climbed aboard his aircraft, Chidester shifted the Packard into gear. After taxiing down the dirt road for about fifty feet, Dufour set his "lateral rudder to cause the ascent" and rose to an altitude of ten feet. A gust of wind pushed the plane dangerously close to the barbed wire fence that lined the road, but Chidester came to the rescue by stepping on the gas. The big Packard shot forward and the glider soared upwards about 25 feet. It hung in the air for an instant until, with a final swoop, it nosedived into the wire fence. Although his invention was reduced to a tangle of sticks, wire and canvas, and he himself was injured, Dufour was still able to talk to the reporter. "The great problem is to find some means of maintaining the equilibrium," he said. Dufour never did solve it and that is what separated him and many others from Orville Wright, Wilbur Wright and Glenn Curtiss.

Dufour continued to work on his machine and hoped to fly it at the State Fair in 1910.

He was not successful and, if he ever did make a flight, it was not recorded. Instead, in 1913, he placed an ad in *Aero and Hydro* magazine offering for sale a biplane with motor, two propellers, hangar and tools, "cheap."

Not all the would-be aviators were big-city boys. In the Clark County community of Granton, a young sawmill operator named Walter Moldenhauer was building a flying machine of his own. A word-of-mouth report in the Marshfield News in December 1909, states that Moldenhauer had "great success." He "went several hundred feet and had the machine under perfect control." In 1911, he exhibited a biplane with a 25-foot wingspread mounted on a tricycle landing gear and powered by a two-cylinder engine at county fairs in Marshfield and Neillsville. The Moldenhauer Flyer did not fly at either fair. Back at home, he did get his machine to "jump" into the air before making a final and conclusive dive into a rock pile.

Fifty years later, Moldenhauer told a Marshfield reporter that he wanted to continue trying to perfect his flying machine but his parents, understandably concerned for his safety, talked him out of it.

Perhaps no one in Wisconsin placed more fanciful hope in aviation than "Doctor" A. Rudolph Silverston. He appeared in Milwaukee in the spring of 1907, after spending time either in the

airdromes of Europe or in the Chicago city lock-up. He took rooms in Milwaukee's elite Hotel Pfister and, dressed in stylish suits and speaking with an elegant European accent, made the acquaintance of the city's leading families.

He also petitioned the State Board of Agriculture for permission to use the horse barn at the State Fair Grounds in West Allis to construct an "airship." He needed a large building because— as he let it be known—Silverston had solved the problem of "aerial navigation." His airship would

fly by utilizing "the force of a vacuum created by [the] rapid motion of a propeller inside of a huge tube." While work was underway, the aircraft would be exhibited at the Fairgrounds and, when completed, fly. In the meantime, investors were welcome to buy stock in the Vacu-Aerial Navigation and Manufacturing Company of America, A. Rudolph Silverston, president and sales agent.

Rear View

SILVERSTON'S MILWAUKEE N°2 PENDULUM SYSTEM 120 H·P ENGINE

"Doctor" A. Rudolph Silverston's Vacu-Aerial Flying Machine was a concept that fanned a lot of air but never got off the ground. (George Hardie, UW-Milwaukee)

According to one newspaper report, Silverston was able to convince a member of Milwaukee's prominent Plankinton family to invest $20,000 in his scheme. He also convinced the owner of a Milwaukee hairdressing salon to put her life's savings of $5,000 in Vacu-Aerial stock and sweetened the deal with a promise of marriage. The proposed nuptials went sour when Mrs. Eleanor Silverston arrived in town with two children and the whole family moved to a comfortable apartment on Grand Avenue.

So that as many investors as possible might buy in, work progressed slowly on Silverston's flying machine. In its final form it consisted of a ten-foot tube housing a large propeller driven by a motor on a platform beneath, plus two v-shaped wings suspended above the pipe in biplane fashion. Approximately thirty feet from top to bottom, the machine grew too tall for the state fair horse barn. Since they could not raise the roof, workers were forced to excavate the dirt floor beneath it.

The moment of truth came at the State Fair in September, 1908, when Dr. Silverston promised that his machine would soar into the heavens. While a crowd of spectators watched, the inventor turned on the motor and set the huge propeller spinning. After a few moments however, the crankshaft broke, forcing a postponement. At first, Silverston promised to try again the next day, then announced that he did not know just when he would be able to find a replacement shaft.

In the meantime, the Vacu-Aerial Flying Machine would be on exhibit at the fair—to paying customers only. After the state fair ended, the Doctor returned custody of the horse barn to the fair board and in turn obtained permission to construct a building for his machine at the edge of the race track. He also promised to exhibit the Vacu-Aerial again at the 1909 Fair and climax the event by flying the machine in front of a packed grandstand.

Before a year could pass, however, word leaked that Silverston and the Vacu-Aerial might be a scam. The Doctor defended himself by pointing out that his work was experimental and—outlandish as it may seem—he was not the only inventor working in vacu-navigation. He could produce published accounts with photos of other experimenters who were putting a propeller into a tube, mounting a wing or two on it, and claiming that the contraption might fly. The proof would come at the State Fair of 1909, if the fair board would only give the Doctor another chance. They did not. In the spring of 1909, the fair board rescinded its permission for Silverston's new building and ordered his machine off the grounds.

Although the Vacu-Aerial machine failed to soar at the State Fair, Doctor Silverston did not abandon it, aviation or West Allis. Forced to vacate the state fairgrounds, he located a patch of vacant ground near 70th and Main in West Allis and founded the Milwaukee College and School of Aviation. It was the first flight school in Wisconsin and—since more than one aeroplane was on the grounds for more than a day or two—arguably the first airport in Wisconsin. A 1912 guide to West Allis touts the "hangar" of the College as home to a "French model of a monoplane, a Curtiss practice machine, a model of a Curtiss built by students of the school and a large Curtiss aeroplane for flying." Also on hand was another version of the Vacu-Aerial machine christened "Milwaukee Number 2." The first flight instructor was Ignace Semenionk, "a Russian aviator who learned to fly in France." He was soon replaced by Harry W. Powers of Chicago, who had the advantage of owning his own Curtiss machine. On the list of students was Jack Knight of Waukesha, William Simmons of Minneapolis and T. Matsu of Japan, the first two of whom are known to have actually learned to fly an aeroplane.

The lifespan of the Milwaukee College and School of Aviation ran no longer than the summer of 1912—long enough for Doctor Silverston to find a new vocation. Leaving his Vacu-Aerial machine to its fate, he found a new pool of investors and started a flight school, airfield, and aircraft manufacturing operation at Cuyahoga Falls, Ohio.

Among the disappointed Milwaukeeans Rudolph Silverston left in his wake were the thousands who genuinely desired to see an aircraft of some sort actually fly. The balloon and dirigible acts that appeared at the State Fair in the 1900s were extremely popular and in July 1909, after evicting Doctor Silverston, the State Agriculture Board instructed its secretary "to correspond with noted aviators" to exhibit at the fair.

Finding an aeroplane to perform at the State Fair in 1909 was all but impossible, but the situation was different one year later. Both the Wright Brothers and Glenn Curtiss had organized aerial exhibition companies in time for the 1910 summer flying season. The Wisconsin fair board signed a contract with the Wright Exhibition Company stipulating five flights at the State Fair. They would be of no less than fifteen minutes duration and include a passenger weighing no more than 150 pounds, if a game volunteer stepped forth. When not in use the plane was to be exhibited, with admission proceeds returned to the fair board. The total charge was $5,000, with $2,000 paid after the first flight and lesser amounts after each succeeding flight. It was one of the most expensive attractions yet offered at a Wisconsin State Fair. The board also tried to hire Barney Oldfield to race the Wright Flyer at the fair but the most famous auto racer of his day was already booked. The fair board had to settle for "Wild Bill" Reuss and his Pope-Hartford race car.

The pilot the Wright Company sent to West Allis was Arch Hoxsey who, with Ralph Johnstone, made up the "Heavenly Twins" of the Wright Exhibition Company. Rivals in aerial derring-do, the pair competed to set records in speed, altitude and risky maneuvers.

Arch Hoxsey made Milwaukee County's first aeroplane flight, and the second in Wisconsin, at the State Fair on Tuesday, September 13, 1910. He launched the Wright Model B from the race track right in front of the crowded grandstand and slowly circled to a height of about 700 feet. "Now it darted like a hawk," reads one report, "now it moved in the air like a boat on a rough sea and again it went higher and ever higher in circles." The flight lasted for 17 minutes, and seemed to stun the crowd, which maintained a hushed quiet throughout. Excitement was evident, though, and led the Milwaukee Journal to predict a crowd of

100,000 for the aeroplane-auto race on the following day.

Whether 100,000 strong or not, the crowd was many times larger for Hoxsey's second flight and his race with the automobile. At the starter's signal, both Hoxsey and Reuss took off, one into the air, the other down the race track. The plane circled the field once at about 45 miles per hour, not fast enough to beat the Pope-Hartford, which won the race by several car lengths. Once again the crowd was largely silent, a phenomenon well explained by one spectator who said, "I was so surprised to see the aeroplane make such evolutions that I was spellbound and my mind was held by amazement at the marvel that I saw."

Controlled, mechanically-powered flight by an aeroplane truly was a marvel. The flight of a dirigible, which was nothing more than a cigar-shaped balloon with an engine mounted on it, was easy to

---

Chicago's First Pilot, Otto Brodie

In the fall of 1909, a few months after Arthur Warner purchased his Curtiss aeroplane, a Chicago auto dealer named James E. Plew ordered one for himself. When word spread that a flying machine was coming to Chicago, a city ambulance driver named Otto Brodie approached Plew and said he wanted to be its pilot—even if it meant a cut in pay, which it did.

Plew sent Brodie to the Curtiss factory in Hammondsport, New York, where he took flying lessons. Early in 1910, he accompanied the machine back to Chicago, where he became the first resident of that city to pilot an aeroplane. Brodie would have been the first person to fly in Chicago had not Glenn Curtiss already flown his machine there in October, 1909.

Aviation became Otto Brodie's livelihood. After Plew sold his Curtiss, the pilot purchased a Farnam hiplane which had previously been owned by famed French pilot Louis Paulhan. He gave exhibitions, instructed and carried passengers for hire in the Chicago area and also briefly operated a flight school in St. Augustine, Florida. He continued to fly until April 1913, when his Farnam clipped a treetop that severed its control wires and nosedived to earth. Brodie did not survive the crash.

His death certificate states that Otto Brodie was born at an unspecified place in Wisconsin. Other records give "Cheboygan" or "Cheyboygan" Wisconsin as his birth place, probably misprints for Sheboygan. If these records are correct, Chicago's first pilot was a native of Wisconsin.[3]

---

understand. The balloon floated and the propeller pushed it along.

The flight of an aeroplane was harder to comprehend. What kept the flimsy framework of bamboo, spruce, wire and cloth in the air? How did the pilot actually control it? What a marvel!

Hoxsey's next flight was scheduled for Friday, September 16 and the largest crowd of the year turned out to witness the marvelous sight. Winds were troublesome, varying from calm to gusty, so

Hoxsey postponed his takeoff as long as he could, always aware that he had a grandstand full of impatient spectators and a contract that decreed he would not be paid unless he flew.

The pilot and the fair managers had decided that, instead of using the infield or the race-track across the infield from the grandstand, Hoxsey would take off and land on the stretch of race track directly in front of the grandstand. The spectators would have the best view of the machine—and derive the greatest thrill from the flight—if Hoxsey flew directly in front of them. So, even though he was concerned about the wind, Hoxsey began his take off on the track in front of the stands. Soon after he was airborne, a freak gust of wind tipped his wing, banking the plane and veering it towards the stands. After flying exhibitions all summer, Arch Hoxsey was one of the most experienced pilots in the country, if any pilot could he called experienced in 1910. He reacted quickly. Instead of letting the plane approach the stands at an angle where it might rake through hundreds of spectators, he made an abrupt turn directly towards the seats. He also had enough presence of mind to shut off his engine. The machine glided over the picket fence in front of the stands and crashed head on into the first rows of seats.

The spectators scrambled back as fast as they could, but "a score of persons" were caught under the machine. Nine men and women were seriously injured, with an early and inaccurate report stating that one was near death. All recovered without permanent injury. The aeroplane was destroyed, but Hoxsey was unharmed, except by the recriminations, which began almost immediately. Fair managers absolved themselves of responsibility by saying that Hoxsey should not have flown if he thought conditions were unfavorable. The pilot retorted by stating the fair board had agreed to provide him with a safe place to land and take off but had failed to deliver. In fact, both sides wanted to put on the best show they could and neither wanted to cancel the flight, nor use any runway other than the racetrack only a few feet in front of the spectators. Hoxsey also had another incentive. If he did not fly, his company would not be paid. As it turned out, the board paid the Wright Exhibition Company only $3,500 of the $5,000 stipulated in the contract.

Four years later, the Wrights lost more money because of Wisconsin's first aeroplane crash. Emily Morrison, one of the persons seriously injured, sued for damages and, in 1914, received a payment of $4,000. It was the first award of cash in a civil suit resulting from an aviation accident.

The West Allis exhibition vividly demonstrated the excitement generated by the mere sight of a machine in flight. It also vividly demonstrated the danger of flying to please a crowd and earn a dollar in aviation's earliest days. Spectators took risks, but no life was more at risk than that of the pilot. Arch Hoxsey survived the West Allis crash, but not the year. He died after his aeroplane came apart and fell to earth at the Los Angeles air meet in December, 1910.[4]

WISCONSIN'S FIRST HOME-BUILT AEROPLANE

While Milwaukeeans were contemplating the marvel of aviation as demonstrated at the 1910 State Fair, John Schwister was building an aeroplane. Born in Wausau in 1882, Schwister was a natural mechanic, the kind of man who may have come into this world not with a silver spoon in his mouth, but with a crescent wrench in his hand. In the early 1900s he went to work as chauffeur for the C. J. Winton family, who had business interests in Wausau and Minneapolis. The Wintons were an adventurous clan and their driver did more than just ferry the boss to and from work. Instead, the Wintons toured the United States, with Schwister at the wheel, and also under the hood, or by the side of the road repairing a flat tire. In the 1900s, any trip outside a city was a challenge. Paved roads were as rare as skyscrapers, potholes more common than cows. Gasoline and usable motor oil might be found at country stores, but spare tires and parts surely could not. If he didn't already have it, long distance motoring in the 1900s would have given John Schwister a taste for adventure and an interest in alternative modes of travel. Flying couldn't be more difficult than motoring, could it?

By the summer of 1910, Schwister was in Minneapolis and using a livery stable on Lyndale Avenue South for a workshop. Perhaps he had witnessed the first attempts by Ashley Bennett and others to fly on Lake Minnetonka in early 1910. More likely, he saw descriptions of flying machines in newspapers and magazines, then relied on his own mechanical acumen and a cautious experimental approach. The earliest account of his work appeared in a Wausau newspaper in July 1910 and stated that he was building an aeroplane "almost eighty feet wide and forty feet in length" powered by an "aluminum gasoline engine."

Schwister may have been building such a giant

The Minnesota-Badger Biplane John Schwister Wausau Wis.

COPYRIGHT 1911 BY W.I. LaCRATE

KIRKHAM MOTOR

of a machine—more than twice as large as the Wright Flyer or Curtiss June Bug—but it was unlikely. The machine he brought to Wausau at the end of 1910 was a biplane similar to a Curtiss, measuring thirty-two feet nose-to-tail, with a thirty-foot wingspan, and powered by a customized 35-horsepower automobile engine. It weighed about 650 pounds, a good 100 pounds heavier than a Curtiss, which Schwister attributed to his use of heavier gauge wire and other materials. It cost about $3,000, well above the annual wage for a mechanic, but apparently within Schwister's range, since he did not have any investors supporting his experiments. Although his machine was ready to fly in the winter of 1910-11, Schwister was not. He said he preferred "to be a lawnmower rather than a snowplow," and would wait until spring.

Spring came and Schwister built a "hangar" for his machine near the village park in Rothschild, a few miles south of Wausau. He selected the site because it offered "a clean sweep over land of about three-quarters of a mile," with more clear airspace near at hand over the Wisconsin River and Lake Wausau. Rib Mountain was close enough to enhance the view, but too far

away to pose a hazard. John Schwister's hangar was the first building in Wisconsin specifically erected for an aeroplane. The concept was so new it required the editor of the Wausau News-Herald to explain that "a hangar is to an aircraft, what a garage is to an automobile."

With his hangar completed, Schwister began to experiment with flight, first towing the machine as a glider behind a 40-horsepower Chalmers auto owned by Wausau car dealer L. H. Hall. Unlike the ill-fated Albert Dufour, Schwister had solved the problem of "equilibrium" and made many "tow-flights" behind the Chalmers without mishap in April and May. On one occasion he soared to seventy feet and on another he carried a passenger named August Kickbusch, who said the flight was "a thriller." Schwister did not try to fly his machine under its own power until he felt comfortable with his ability to control it and also because he was waiting for a new, 50-horsepower engine he had ordered from the Kirkham Company in New York.

The Kirkham arrived on June 21, 1911 and was soon mounted amidships on the machine, directly behind the pilot. On June 23, "the power

John Schwister, Wisconsin's first successful home-builder, at the controls of his Minnesota-Badger in Wausau. (Robert Wylie)

Right: Like many pioneer aviators, John Schwister tested his plane as a glider towed like a kite behind an auto. Sometimes the auto was also used to bring home the wreckage after a flight test failed. (Robert Wylie)

Ready for the start
Antigo Wis

When he flew at the Langlade County Fair in Antigo in 1911, John Schwister earned $50 and thereby became Wisconsin's first "professional" pilot paid to fly. (Robert Wylie)

feet, hit a "hole" in the air and started to fall. At treetop level he regained enough control to level off and rise again, but clipped a branch with a wing and went down.

Just as the nose wheel struck the ground, he jumped off the machine, thereby saving himself from serious injury. When the plane hit the ground, the motor, which was mounted directly behind the pilot's seat, broke its moorings and rocketed forward. Had he remained aboard, Schwister would have been hit square in the back and possibly pinned to the earth. Since he jumped free, the pilot escaped with a sprained knee and plenty of bruises, but remained intact.

Undeterred, Schwister spent the month of July rebuilding his machine and started to fly again in August. He still made his familiar straight-line hops from Rothschild to the golf course and back again, working towards an exhibition flight at the Marathon County Fair in September. He also planned a flight across Lake Wausau with the plane equipped with floats of his own design and a flotilla of rowboats on the water "in case he should become obliged to alight on the lake." Also in August, Schwister attended the international aviation meet in Chicago, where Arthur Warner acted as official timer. In the big city, the Wausau flyer was thrilled to see three aeroplanes in the air at one time and to shake hands with Wilbur Wright.

Back at work in Wisconsin, Wausau's first aviator missed his home county's fair but did sign a contract to perform at the Langlade County Fair in September. Before agreeing to the deal, the Langlade fair board required proof that Schwister and his machine could really fly, so they dispatched board secretary L. G. Armstrong to make a flight. Schwister had now mastered the art of turning his machine in the air and soared as high as 200 feet to give the tight-lipped fair secretary an experience he claimed to enjoy "greatly." He probably did not know it, but this flight gave bragging rights to L. G. Armstrong as one of the first Wisconsinites to fly as a passenger in an aeroplane. The following month, when he made one flight at the county fair in Antigo for which he was paid, John Schwister became Wisconsin's first "professional" pilot and made Langlade the first county in the state to feature an aviator at its fair.

Schwister continued to grow more confident in the air. In October he stayed aloft for 34 min-

was turned on, the machine was started and it arose gracefully into the air, skimming along at an elevation of about twenty feet for quite a distance." This was the first flight of an aeroplane designed and built by a Wisconsin native. Since he had begun work on it in Minneapolis, but first flew it in Wisconsin, Schwister christened his machine, "The Minnesota Badger."

The machine worked fine, but the pilot needed some training and, since no one in Wausau knew any more than he did, Schwister taught himself. Over and again he made straight line flights from the park in Rothschild northeast to the Wausau Country Club golf course, landed, turned the machine around and flew straight back to Rothschild. After two weeks on the straight and level, the cautious pilot announced that he planned to celebrate Independence Day by flying over the big celebration in Rothschild Park and then "if the wind is right" actually turn the machine while still in the air and land back at his hangar.

He didn't make it. On July 3, while flying over the park, Schwister soared to an altitude of 200

utes to make a 27-mile flight from Rothschild to the north edge of Wausau and back.

He was reported to have reached an altitude of 2,000 feet, which meant he flew slightly higher than the summit of Rib Mountain. The flight was not only the first flight of more than a few miles, it was also the first flight higher than a few hundred feet made by a Wisconsin pilot. Appropriately, as he made his way over Wausau, "thousands" of people came out into the streets to see the first flying machine to appear over their city. This greatest flight of the Minnesota Badger brought John Schwister's first season as an aircraft designer, builder and pilot to a fitting close.

The following year was not as good. In the winter of 1911-12, Schwister returned to Minneapolis and built a new machine. Larger than the Minnesota Badger and with a seat for a passenger, the new plane was designed for professional use at air shows and to carry passengers for a fee. The new design seemed to work well until a flight in June, when the engine stalled in the air. Accounts of Schwister's altitude at the time of the stall differ, but it is clear that, although he struggled to make a dead stick glide to a safe landing, he came down hard. The $4,000 plane was a total loss, and the pilot was severely injured, breaking an arm and shattering several ribs.

John Schwister recovered enough to occasionally fly again, but never with the same vigor and enthusiasm. Indeed, when he died at age 45 in 1927, his demise was attributed to the injuries suffered in 1912.[5]

WISCONSIN'S FIRST GREAT YEAR OF AVIATION

By the start of summer of 1911, three pilots had flown aeroplanes in Wisconsin: Arthur Warner at Beloit in November, 1909; Arch Hoxsey at West Allis in September, 1910; John Schwister at Rothschild in June, 1911. In the next few months, aeroplanes would make their first appearances over many of Wisconsin's largest cities and a few small ones. Late summer was the prime flying season in this part of the country. The weather was as favorable as it ever would be, while state and county fairs offered exhibition pilots a steady series of venues.

The air meet at Chicago in August that John Schwister and Arthur Warner attended had attracted most of the nation's leading pilots, many of whom moved on to Wisconsin in the next two months. These pilots were the "early-birds" of legend, America's first heroes of flight, as famous in their day as Charles Lindbergh, Jacqueline Cochran and Chuck Yeager would be in theirs. They were soon joined by Wisconsin people who, both at home and in other places, gave the state its own distinguished flock of "early-birds."

KIRKHAM MOTOR.   SCHWISTER FLYING OVER COUNTRY CLUB AUG. 6-11

John Schwister flying at the Wausau Country Club in 1911. On one of his flights that year, Schwister reached an altitude of 2,000 feet, higher than Rib Mountain, visible in the background here. (Robert Wylie)

The event billed as "the first aviation meet in the state" took place in Kenosha at the end of August, 1911. Two aviators flying Curtiss machines, Cromwell Dixon and Jimmy Ward, promised three big days of flying. They would make cross-country flights from Kenosha to points as far away as Waukegan, Illinois, and Racine. They would make high-altitude flights and race a big Buick at the fairgrounds. As it turned out, Dixon and Ward did get off the ground, and not much more. Ward would later attract a crowd of Wisconsinites to Rockford, Illinois; Ironwood, Michigan; and Madison, but 1911 was not his year in this state.

The state's "first aviation meet" at Kenosha turned out to be an aviation bust.

At the same time, the first "hydro-aeroplane" to appear in Wisconsin was experiencing difficulties of its own. Another Curtiss exhibition pilot, Charles "C.C." Wittmer, brought one of the first flying machines able to land and take off on the water to the Brown County Fair in De Pere. Hydro-aviation was brand new, with Glenn Curtiss having just made the first successful float plane flight the previous January. Wittmer's machine was advertised as one of only three in the nation.

The hydro-aeroplane was an modified version of the land-based Curtiss machines flown by Warner, Dixon and Ward. It had a larger, eight-cylinder engine that mustered sixty horse power and, of course, it was mounted on a single pontoon that measured twelve feet long, two wide and one foot deep. As on other Curtiss models, the pilot sat in front of the wings and handled the plane with a steering wheel and body harness arrangement. Connected to the front elevators and the rudders, the wheel allowed the piloted to lift or drop the nose and to pivot the rudder. The shoulder harness was linked to the ailerons mounted between the wings and allowed the pilot to bank the plane by leaning in the desired direction. The most difficult problem the designers of early hydro-aeroplanes faced was to design a pontoon that would allow the machine to break the surface tension of the water and get into the air in a reasonable amount of time. Speed on takeoff was the crucial variable. If the pilot revved the engine too fast, it kicked up water that choked the engine, yet if the engine ran too slow, the plane would have to have to run on the water for a great distance before it could get airborne.

C. C. Wittmer would well illustrate this dilemma at De Pere.

Wright Model B

Brown County was ready to see any kind of aeroplane get into the air. The fair association had made an "eleventh-hour" deal to obtain a Curtiss machine and Green Bay businessmen had hurriedly pledged $2,000 to cover the cost of the initial flight. Although announced only four days before it was to take place, the flight brought nearly 15,000 people to the river side park in De Pere. "People came in swarms," with the electric trolley line bringing a carload of 100 spectators from Green Bay every fifteen minutes between 11:00 AM and 4:00 PM. Others rode the line from Appleton, Oshkosh and Fond du Lac. Still more came via special North Western Railroad trains, Fox River steamboats, automobiles, horses and their own two feet. A "mosquito fleet" of sailboats and gasoline launches—"never before was such a fleet seen at any one point on the river"—lined the channel along Wittmer's flight path. Even though it was Tuesday and a work day, "There was a perfect jam at all the gates."

At about 5:00 PM, with the park packed with spectators, Wittmer nodded to his assistants and the hydro-aeroplane slid gracefully into the Fox. The pilot climbed aboard, switched on the engine and, with the crowd cheering, horns blaring and whistles blowing, headed downstream to Green Bay.

"He went so fast the spectators hardly realized he was gone," wrote one reporter.

Just about as fast, he was back, still on the water, with his engine running rough. He tinkered and tuned, while the crowd murmured and shuffled. A few folks went home because they thought that Wittmer's fast run up and down the river was all the new-fangled machine was supposed to do.

With his engine running better, Wittmer tried again. He streaked down the river past the bend. In front of the state reformatory, but out of sight of the crowd in the park, he rose from the water and flew to about 150 feet. Still the engine ran rough, so he set down in the river and taxied back to the park. He tinkered and tuned, the crowd continued to dwindle.

Three was the charm, at least for getting a few feet into the air. Not until his fourth try did Wittmer actually fly. He raced downriver and round the bend, turned quickly and sped back towards the park. In full view of the spectators, who gave out "a great shout of joy," the hydro-aeroplane lifted off the water. Rising to about 50 feet, Wittmer soared up the Fox for "several hundred feet" then banked into a turn. On its way back to the park, the plane "ran into one of those treacherous air currents" and dropped towards the water. The pontoon hit first, then the right wing. It caught in the water, flipping the machine completely over and into the Fox. Wittmer was uninjured, since he had jumped off the plane just before it flipped, but the aeroplane was seriously damaged, with wings and rudder broken and the

County. Not until the Curtiss company posted a bond for $10,000 would he release the machine so it could be shipped to Green Bay for Wittmer to fly.

The sheriff should have kept it. On September 17, Wittmer tried again to lift his machine off the

Jimmy Ward, an exhibition pilot, flew his Curtiss at the Dane County Fairgrounds in Madison in 1912. (SHSW)

engine stuck fast in the mud of the Fox. With night falling and the plane not about to go anywhere, Wittmer decided to defer salvage until the following morning. And so, the first floatplane to fly off Wisconsin waters also spent its first night in Wisconsin waters, the Fox River at De Pere.

Charles Wittmer went on to become one of the most successful of the Curtiss exhibition pilots. A few weeks after his bad luck in De Pere, he made several fine land-based flights in Portage and Sheboygan. The following winter he would pilot a hydro-aeroplane across Florida's Biscayne Bay, but the Fox River was bad medicine for him. Hoping to make up for Wittmer's failure in De Pere in August and see something for the $2,000 it had raised, the Brown County fair association went to great lengths to bring the pilot back in September.

With Wittmer's machine smashed, the only other Curtiss they could find in Wisconsin was in Lancaster, impounded by the sheriff of Grant

surface of the Fox. After several attempts, he rose about ten feet into the air, then settled back into the water, and did not rise again.

Cal Rodgers had better luck in Appleton. He flew a Wright Model B with great success in the upriver city only a few days after Charles Wittmer's Curtiss landed in the drink downstream. There were two familiar rivalries at work here—Wright Brothers versus Curtiss and Appleton versus Green Bay—and Appleton came out on top in each case.

In Chicago, Cal Rodgers had set a world record for endurance flying of two hours, fifty-five minutes and thirty-three seconds. No one had ever kept an aeroplane aloft for so long. Since he also won over $11,000 in prize money, Rodgers saw a future in long distance flight. He was not the only one. Newspaper publisher William Randolph Hearst had offered a prize of $50,000 to any aviator who could fly across the United States in 30 days or less.

Since no one had flown anywhere near that distance, meeting Hearst's challenge would be quite an accomplishment. Rodgers said he could do it and scheduled the start of his flight from New York to California for September 15.

Meanwhile, he accepted an invitation to fly in Appleton that his manager Fred Felix Wettengel arranged. If Green Bay could supply 15,000 spectators for an aviator, why couldn't Appleton? Wettengel scheduled an "Aviation Meet" to take place at the Appleton Baseball Park on September 3-4 and announced that he would put up the going rate of $1,000 in expenses that Rodgers required for his first flight and an additional $500 for subsequent flights. Since Wettengel worked for Rodgers, it is doubtful that his costs were actually that great, which meant that a good sale of tickets would bring a nice profit. Rodgers could use the money for his transcontinental trip, but he also had another reason to visit Appleton.

His wife, Mabel, was the sister of Elizabeth Graves Whiting, wife of Frank Whiting and daughter-in-law of George Whiting. A prominent Fox Valley industrialist, George had made his fortune as one of Wisconsin's first wood pulp papermakers and owned mills on the Fox and the Wisconsin Rivers, where he left his name on the city of Whiting, near Stevens Point. Although they lived in Neenah, the Whitings were happy to welcome their adventurous in-law to Appleton and were all in attendance at the Aviation Meet.

The day "was perfect for cloud inspection work," reported the Appleton Daily Post, "and the aviator was fearless in his flights, having no treacherous air currents or alternating winds to battle with while exploring the infinite regions

Cal Rodgers and his Wright Flyer soared out of the baseball field at Appleton on their way to win a race with an auto down College Avenue. (Neenah Historical Society)

known to man as space."

Rodgers rose to the infinite regions from the infield of the ball diamond and over the remains of the outfield wall, which Wettengel had recognized as a hazard and had hastily-dismantled. During a twenty-minute flight, he performed "the Dutch roll, the spiral glide and a few other dangerous aerial turns," before flying to a smooth landing in front of the grandstand.

Now Rodgers was ready for passengers. First up was brother-in-law Frank Whiting, who accompanied the pilot for a few spins above the grandstand, then hung on tight while the machine swung over to Appleton's main street, College Avenue. Parked on College was a Baldwin automobile, warmed up and ready to race the Wright Flyer. It was no contest, even with the passenger. Rodgers swooped down the wide street, easily defeating the auto in a race from one end of the business district to the other. This race can go on record as the first auto-aeroplane race in Wisconsin that the aeroplane won—while carrying a passenger to boot.

Rodgers than returned to the park and a line of waiting passengers. First was George Whiting who, at age sixty-seven, was informed by Rodgers' manager that he was the "oldest man" to yet fly in an aeroplane. Next came Rodgers' sister-in-law, Elizabeth Graves Whiting, who made a twenty-minute flight and thereby became the first woman to fly in an aeroplane in Wisconsin. Since she was not an Appleton resident, the Daily Post did not record her reaction to the flight, but the reporter did chronicle the impressions of two other women who flew that day. Bernice Howard Van Nortwick said, "I enjoyed every second of the trip and am disappointed only in its brevity," while Mrs. Joseph Steele said "It was an experience of a lifetime...fear of altitude never entered my mind."

Since Rodgers charged these two women $25 each for a ride, they were paying customers. Along with Appleton resident John Scheer, who had gone up before the women, they were the first Wisconsin residents to pay for an aeroplane ride in Wisconsin. In all, Rodgers gave about a dozen paying customers aeroplane rides that Sunday and the following Monday. With these flights, he inaugurated in Wisconsin the tradition followed by every barnstormer in the 1920s and '30s, and continuing today, of earning money to fly by taking passengers aloft.

Rodgers reserved his longest flight for Fred Felix Wettengel. On Monday, September 4, he took the Wright Flyer out over Lake Winnebago then turned north towards Kaukauna. Neenah,

Menasha, Appleton, Kimberly and Little Chute, all came into view. Automobiles on the highways attempted to race along with the plane, people came out from their homes to cheer and wave. On the way back, the generous Wettengel directed Rodgers to fly over the north side of Appleton so those who did not live near the ball park on the south side could see the machine. The flight took about twenty-five minutes and covered about twenty-five miles. It was the first cross-country flight in Wisconsin made by a machine designed and built by Orville and Wilbur Wright.

Wettengel had hoped to cover expenses and show a profit in Appleton by charging an admission fee to the grandstand of fifty cents for adults and twenty-five cents for children.

"Let there be no pikers," read an ad in the Daily Post that urged Appletonians to pay the half-dollar to come into the ball park even though they could stay outside and see the machine fly for free. Human nature being what it was and is, there were quite a few pikers in Appleton.

Wettengel lost about $750 dollars.

It did not trouble him. "I'm not complaining a bit," he said. "I wouldn't miss that trip to Kaukauna and back for all I lost and more too."

Fred Wettengel's Aviation Meet in Appleton on the first weekend of September in 1911 was the first truly successful aviation exhibition to take place in Wisconsin. The plane got into the air safely and did not crash on landing. Passengers experienced the thrill of flight and returned safely to earth. Thousands of people, the paying and the pikers, saw their first flying machine. If Fred Wettengel and Cal Rodgers lost, it was the state's gain.

Wettengel and Rodgers left Appleton after the meet and journeyed to Chicago where they found the financial support they needed for the transcontinental flight at the Armour meat packing company. Armour was marketing a new brand of soda pop called "Vin Fiz" and saw the transcontinental flight as a good promotion. With the brand trademark, a bunch of grapes, painted on the rudder, and the aeroplane itself rechristened in honor of the product, Cal Rodgers and the "Vin Fiz" began

their long and bumpy voyage to California.

The journey took fifty arduous days. Of that no more than 82 hours were spent in the air. Rodgers spent the rest of the time waiting out bad weather, repairing damage inflicted by numerous crashes, scrounging for parts in the outback and nursing assorted abrasions, contusions and broken bones. Mabel Rodgers accompanied her husband by train in the special Vin Fiz "hanger car," a workshop on rails in which the Vin Fiz was all but rebuilt several times. Her family back in Neenah kept track of the flight through wire service reports

in the newspaper. Although he didn't reach California in time to collect William Randolph Hearst's $50,000, Cal Rodgers—the first person to fly down Appleton's College Avenue—was also the first person to fly across the United States.

While Cal Rodgers was content to make his name as an endurance pilot, Lincoln Beachey required instant gratification. In June 1911, with his trusty Curtiss engine sputtering in the spray, he made his landmark flight over and into the gorge of Niagara Falls, New York. Already known as a daredevil dirigible pilot, Beachey was on his way to becoming the most daring and famous flyer of aviation's early days.

After setting an altitude record of 11,642 feet at Chicago, Beachey toured Wisconsin. He started

Cal Rodgers with Bernice Howard Van Nortwick, one of the first women to ride in an aeroplane in Wisconsin (Neenah Historical Society)

Lincoln Beachy

World's Greatest Aeronaut

PROGRAM

Subject to change on account of atmospheric conditions or accidents.

1. An exhibition flight, in which the spiral, the dip, the ocean wave and similar thrilling maneuvers will be demonstrated.
2. Will make a glide for life with his motor "dead."
3. A demonstration of accuracy in landing, in which the aviator will make a flight and return to the same spot from which he started the flight.
4. An exhibition of bomb throwing.

5. A five-mile flight against time, illustrating the great speed of an aeroplane.
6. A race with a motorcycle or automombile.
7. An altitude flight, in which the aviator will rise to an altitude of 5,000 feet or more.

Concert by Cone's 4th Regiment Band
Aeroplane on exhibition at Fair Grounds from 1 to 2 p.m. Program commences at 2 p.m.
Adults 50 cents.   Children 25 cents.

Sunday September 15, 1912   FAIR GROUNDS
WAUSAU, WIS.

Lincoln Beachey was as famous in his day as any American aviator who ever flew. He thrilled spectators with loops, bombing runs and his famous high-altitude "Death Drop." (Robert Wylie)

at the State Fair in September 1911, where he performed his signature "Death Dip." He would fly his Curtiss in an ascending spiral to gain as much altitude as possible and switch off the engine. He would then silently dive as low as he possibly could and, just when the spectators were convinced he would crash, pull up and make a safe landing, not necessarily switching on the engine again. At a time when a flight of a few hundred feet was considered unbelievably daring, merely ascending to 10,000 feet, as Beachey did at West Allis, was a death-defying, crowd-pleasing stunt.

Beachey also repeated the balloonist's feat of flying from West Allis to downtown Milwaukee and circling City Hall. Going to Milwaukee was not as exciting as the Death Dip, but the flight made Lincoln Beachey the first pilot to fly an aeroplane over Wisconsin's largest city. In the wake of Rudolph Silverston and Arch Hoxsey performances at West Allis, Beachey's three days of derring-do constitute the first successful aerial exhibition in Milwaukee County.

After completing his performance at the State Fair, Beachey moved on to the Grant County Fair in Lancaster. Although his career had yet to peak,

the pilot who had conquered Niagara Falls and buzzed the Capitol in Washington, D. C. was bound to find Grant County, Wisconsin, a very minor venue. In addition to being all but fearless, Beachey was independent-minded. After making one of the three flights called for in his contract, he judged the weather bad and refused to fly anymore, no matter how many people were in the grandstand and no matter how far over the hills and dales of Grant County they had traveled to see him.

The county sheriff argued that Beachey and the county fair association had a contract and the flyer must honor it. Situations such as this one, with the pilot concerned about flying conditions and the fair's management sticking to the letter of their agreement, had already put many an exhibition flyer at risk. Beachey was nervy enough to back out of his contract and out of Grant County, but the aeroplane, which belonged to the Curtiss Company, was stuck in Lancaster. It remained impounded until the Curtiss Company, which was also in trouble in Brown County after C. C. Wittmer's crash into the Fox, posted a $10,000 bond. The machine was shipped to Green Bay and fitted with floats but Wittmer still could not make it fly.

Lincoln Beachey continued on tour and at the end of September joined Wittmer and the Curtiss machine for a successful exhibition at Sheboygan. He would return to Wisconsin several times over the next few years, but never to Grant County.

The hazards of flying in these early days made uneventful exhibitions the exception rather than the rule, and often led to unintended consequences. When Harry Powers, the pilot the Dunn County fair association hired to appear at the fair in Menominee in 1911 had to cancel because he was injured when his Curtiss cracked up, the association hired Rene Simon. He was a French pilot who had set a record for climbing speed in a Bleriot monoplane at Chicago. Later in the meet, Simon dumped his Bleriot into Lake Michigan and was rescued by Cal Rodgers. He then signed on with another French monoplane builder, Moisant, and went on tour.

Simon appeared at the Dunn County Fair and his seven minute flight on September 13, gave Menominee the right to claim, "the honor of having carried out the first ascent of a heavier-than-air machine in Northwest Wisconsin and probably the first by a monoplane in the entire state."

In the years prior to World War I, French designers crafted the most advanced-looking aeroplanes. While the Wright and Curtiss machines still resembled motorized box kites, the Bleriot and Moisant models featured a single wing and tail, a fabric-covered fuselage, a front-engine mount, and a half-cockpit for the pilot. Although the more stable biplanes would continue to dominate aircraft design until after World War I, the French "monocoques" of the prewar years presented a view of the future.

They liked that view in Menominee, where a record crowd of 12,000 people came to the fairgrounds to watch Simon circle the racetrack three times, swing out over Red Cedar Lake, then return to make a precision landing in the infield. The pilot had planned to touch ground only briefly at the end of his flight and take off again but, as soon as he landed, the crowd rushed onto the field and mobbed the machine. For his own safety and that of the crowd, Simon switched off his engine and, as quickly as possible, rolled the plane into a tent. Hiding the machine in a tent meant that only paying customers could view it up close and, while there, listen to the lecturer who explained its construction. The tent also protected the machine from the overly-curious who, accidentally or not, might scrape the "dope" or poke holes in the fabric of the machine. Especially on the wings, a scrape in the dope was more than a cosmetic problem. Without it, the fabric covering was not air tight. Wind flowed through instead of around the wings and reduced the lift they were designed to provide. So Rene Simon was right to protect his machine from the probing fingers of the public.

"Simon is a pilot who is known to be a stranger to fear," wrote a satisfied reporter for the Dunn County News. The "master of aerial navigation" had done his job well. He planned to make two more flights the following day in Menominee before leaving the state with the first monoplane to fly in Wisconsin.

Of the touring aviators to go aloft in Wisconsin in 1911, none was more successful than Beckwith Havens, who flew in Manitowoc, Ashland and Chippewa Falls. He made a total of six flights over two days with his Curtiss machine in Manitowoc, reaching an altitude of 2,000 feet

and enjoying a splendid view of Lake Michigan. The sponsor of the event was the local streetcar magnate, Thomas Higgins, whose trolley cars were filled with spectators traveling to see the flights.

A few days later Havens was in Ashland, where he brought aviation to the shores of Lake Superior. "Well I remember how excited the crowd was to be introduced to this handsome young hero from the east at a reception held for him at the Elks Club," recalled Edith Dodd Culver, who was a teenager in Ashland when Havens arrived. She also remembered how he flew "graceful figure eights" above the race track at the county fairgrounds and how he was "the drawing card of the fair."

Though he might be the idol of the local teenagers and the well-paid star of the show, an

Lincoln Beachey at Wausau, 1912. (Robert Wylie)

exhibition pilot was still a working man. Havens recalled how he rode the trolley from his downtown Ashland hotel to the fairgrounds, unpacked his machine from its special railroad freight crates, assembled it, tested the motor, pushed it out to the head of what served as a runway in the fairgrounds infield and stood ready to fly at the appointed time. His contract called for one flight a day, usually of no more than twenty minutes, for three days. The rest of the time was spent sharing guard duty over the plane with his mechanic.

In Ashland, Havens met a college student named Walter Lees who begged him for ride. Havens refused, and his caution helps to explain why he was one of the minority of early birds who lived to a ripe old age. He told Lees that the fairgrounds infield was too short for his plane to take off with the added weight of a passenger and his Curtiss wasn't equipped with a seat anyway. So even if Lees could pay the going rate of at least $5, which he probably couldn't, Havens would not take him up. Lees reluctantly accepted Havens refusal, but the bug had bit. He would soon leave Ashland and take up aviation as his life's work.

Havens moved on to Chippewa Falls where he performed at the big Northern Wisconsin State Fair. After six smooth flights that thrilled the spectators, his luck ran out. He was circling over the fair grounds on the northern edge of the city when his engine coughed and sputtered to a stop. He had enough altitude to glide away from the grandstand and saw a clear spot to land on what turned out to be a school playground. No sooner did the aeroplane appear over the trees than the playground

Lincoln Beachey's Curtiss and shipping crates at Sheboygan, 1912. The age of aviation had begun, but aircraft still traveled from city to city by rail. (Sheboygan County Historical Society)

filled with children. Havens was pilot enough to find a favorable air current that enabled him to glide up and away from the playground and on towards a vacant lot. As he glided in for his landing, the tail of the Curtiss snagged a power line. The plane tripped onto its nose and fell to the ground. Fortunately, the motor remained in its mountings and, although he was tangled in the wreckage of split struts, wire and torn canvas, Havens was uninjured. It is testimony to his ability

as a pilot and the gliding ability of the Curtiss machine that he was able to steer away from the schoolyard full of children. Not one to brag on his heroics, the following day Havens crated up the remains of his machine and was on his way to the next stop on his tour.

The 1911 exhibition season—Wisconsin's first great season of flight—ended with a grand flourish that included an attempted transcontinental flight, the first delivery of mail by air and the boldest example of aerial derring-do yet seen in the state.

Long-distance flights for large cash prizes captured the imagination of flyers, advertisers and the public in 1911. Harry Atwood flew from St. Louis to New York. Cal Rodgers was on his way from New York to California. Now, Hugh K. Robinson was set to fly down the Mississippi River from the Twin Cities to New Orleans.

The scheme originated with St. Louis and Minneapolis boosters who saw the flight as a way to promote their cities and the Mississippi Valley. Robinson was a mechanic-turned-pilot for the Curtiss company who had invented the first arresting equipment to enable an aeroplane to land on a ship at sea and an author who wrote the instruction manual shipped with Curtiss hydro-aeroplanes. He was certainly ready and able to fly a Curtiss hydro-aeroplane along the longest floatplane runway in America, stopping at promotional events from the Mississippi headwaters to the delta, and collecting the $20,000 prize that the promoters confidentially predicted would be raised by business groups in the cities of the Valley. To add interest, Robinson would also also carry fifty pounds of mail with each envelope duly bearing two cents of United States postage and stamped "Aerial Route." It would be the first delivery of air mail to the river cities.

Telegrams flashed up and down river and the money was pledged to keep Robinson fed and fuelled at least as far as St. Louis. In order to raise their share, boosters in La Crosse sponsored the city's first aviation meet. The event featured Robinson flying his Curtiss, minus its float, off the racetrack at the Inter-County Fairgrounds. The show netted $300 for the Mississippi River flight, a fair share of the $20,000 for a city the size of La Crosse. Afterwards, Robinson loaded his machine on the train and shipped it to Minneapolis where it was mounted on its pontoon again and ready for take off as scheduled on October 9. With the hardwoods turning color and the river sparkling on clear autumn days, Hugh Robinson would be the first person to view the Upper Mississippi Valley at its most beautiful from the seat of an aeroplane.

The Minnesota weather did not cooperate. Rain and cold delayed the initial take-off until October 17 and a forced landing on the river caused another delay. Instead of making a triumphant flight into Winona, Minnesota, Robinson and his plane were ignominiously towed into town by a steam launch. He was scheduled to appear at a grand reception on the river in La Crosse on October 18 where local aviation booster John Salzer, the comely Miss Mae Williams and, presumably, thousands of others, would turn out to greet him. Instead, he was bottled up in Winona.

The following morning at 8:00 AM, Robinson redeemed himself. The highway bridge crossing the river at Winona was a venerable, timber and stone span with nearly 700 feet between the main pilings and a deck that sat at least 50 feet above the surface of the water. It was flanked by an equally formidable railroad bridge. When he took off from the Winona dock, and headed upstream into the wind Robinson had to swerve to avoid a spectator's boat, lost speed and could not gain enough altitude to clear the bridges, so he flew under them. He turned around on the upstream side, but still did not have enough power to rise above the bridges, so he flew under them again. Finally headed downstream, he was on his way to La Crosse.

Robinson completed the quick hop to La Crosse where a crowd of 10,000 lined the downtown bridge and filled Levee Park on the waterfront. He steered the Curtiss down river to the south city limits then turned back and headed for the Mississippi River bridge. This structure was a center pivot span, about as long but not as high as Winona's. While the spectators watched in awe the dauntless pilot dived under the bridge, cleared the water, and soared upwards. With this gesture, Hugh Robinson inaugurated the dubious practice of flying beneath bridges in Wisconsin.

He continued up the Mississippi to the mouth

Pilot Hugh Robins... at Prairie du Chien with first mail carr...

of the Black River, passing over the future site of the La Crosse Municipal Airport on French Island, then circled back to land downtown at Levee Park. He taxied to the dock and delivered letters from his Minnesota sponsors to La Crosse Tribune Editor A. M. Brayton and businessman J. M. Fuerber. This was the first delivery of mail by air in Wisconsin.

Robinson was the toast of La Crosse. He had flown from one end of the city to the other, giving anyone who cared to look up a good view of an aeroplane. The crowd at Levee Park had seen a fine example of aerial derring-do beneath the downtown bridge. The pilot was treated to the best breakfast the city could offer then dispatched to New Orleans with waves and cheers.

In little more than an hour, Robinson landed at Prairie du Chien where he received another enthusiastic greeting. The Prairie du Chien highway bridge had yet to be built so Robinson did not have a chance to thread the needle beneath a sixth bridge that day. He merely stopped for lunch, photos and refueling before taking off again.

When he arrived at Rock Island, Illinois Robinson received word that St. Louis and points south had lost interest in his flight. Not only could he forget his $20,000 award for reaching New Orleans, he would not even receive expense money to reach St. Louis. Having flown 375 miles from Minneapolis, Robinson quit and the great flight down the Mississippi Valley was concluded.

Hugh Robinson at Prairie du Chien. Robinson attempted to fly his Curtiss hydroaeroplane down the entire length of the Mississippi River in 1911. At La Crosse he delivered a sack of "air mail" from Winona and flew under the bridge, then continued down river until halting his flight in Illinois. (WAHF)

Also concluded was Wisconsin's first great season of flight. Throughout the state, aviators had demonstrated to believers and skeptics that what they had been hearing and reading about flying machines was true. The initial reaction of most spectators, as reported in newspapers from Kenosha to Chippewa Falls, was a combination of amazement and enthusiasm. As Delavan pilot Jesse Brabazon recalled, so many folks had stared open-mouthed into the sky in 1911 that Wisconsin doctors reported an epidemic of sun-burned tonsils.

More significant than the sensational effect, and more enduring than the sunburn, was the impression the exhibition pilots had on the young people who watched them struggle with machinery, wrestle with weather, yet still soar into the heavens—at least most of the time. A seed was planted that bore fruit all over the state. Although many similar stories remain to be told, perhaps the most vivid example of the effect the exhibition flyers had on the future of aviation is found in Ashland.

A boy named Harold Bretting watched Beckwith Havens fly on the county fair weekend in September. Taken with flying, Bretting became an army pilot during World War I. While on leave in 1918, he wanted to visit home, so he flew a Curtiss JN model from Illinois all the way across Wisconsin—probably the first person to do so. Paul Culver also saw Havens fly in Ashland. A few years later, he also entered the army flying corps and was chosen to be one of the first of four army pilots who inaugurated regular air mail service in the United States. After seeing Havens fly in Ashland, Walter Lees was so impatient to get himself in the air that he left classes at the University of Wisconsin in January 1912 and scraped together $150 to pay for flight instruction with Otto Brodie in St. Augustine, Florida. He later became one of Billy Mitchell's flight instructors and, as a test pilot, set a record for endurance flying that lasted over fifty years. Such was the 1911 harvest of aviators from only one Wisconsin city of 20,000 people.

There were others, of course. In Green Bay, young people were interested enough in aviation for the high school graduation class to title their Commencement Day program book "The Aeroplane." A century earlier it might have been called "The Steamboat," a century later, "The Starship." In 1911, "The Aeroplane" was right and fitting. It conveyed an up-to-date message to and about young people ready to launch themselves into adulthood at the dawn of the age of flight.

One of the most forward-looking graduates of this forward-looking class was Harry Tees. He wanted more than just a booklet called The Aeroplane. He wanted the real thing. With help from his Dad and a friend named Earl Knowland, Harry built an aeroplane. Like many other home-builts of its time, including John Schwister's, it resembled a Curtiss machine. Unlike the Wright Brothers, Glenn Curtiss was willing to share and publicize his work. All Harry Tees had to do was use his high school education to read articles about

Harry Houdini, First In Australia

Early in the aviation age, Harry Houdini, the Appleton-raised master illusionist and escape artist, looked for ways to incorporate an aeroplane into his act. He proposed making a parachute jump from a Wright Flyer while wearing handcuffs and would have tried it too, but no one could figure out how a parachutist could leap from the machine without damaging it or injuring himself in the rear-facing propellers.

Instead, Houdini, who was touring Europe at the time, purchased a French-built Voisin machine and learned to fly it in Germany. In November, 1909, a few weeks after Arthur Warner became the first person to fly an aeroplane in Wisconsin, Houdini flew his own machine in Germany.

Merely being one of the world's first aircraft pilots was not enough for the great illusionist. He had to be the first in at least one category. He scanned the globe and realized that by early 1910, Europe, North America, Africa and Asia had all had their first flights, but Australia and South America were still aviation's terra incognita.

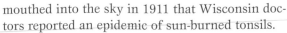

He packed his Voisin, which somewhat resembled a Wright Flyer, onto an ocean liner and set off on a 29-day voyage for Australia. Houdini and his entourage landed at Melbourne in February, 1910 and—in between performances—looked for a suitable landing field. He found a likely site at Digger's Rest about 20 miles outside of Melbourne and told his crew to assemble the plane.

Not willing to let a foreigner triumph on their turf, a group of Australians headed by Ralph Banks challenged Houdini. Banks had earlier imported a Wright Flyer to Australia, but had yet to figure out how to fly it. Now the pressure was on to defend Australia's honor. Banks took his machine out to Digger's Rest and prepared to fly.

On March 1, 1910, Ralph Banks turned the nose of his machine into the wind, started his engine, rose twelve feet into the air, then dived to the ground. His Wright Flyer was seriously damaged and would take weeks to repair. The Australian air was now clear for Houdini. On March 16, 1910, he launched his Houdini No. 1 flying machine into the air, made a wide circle around the field and returned for a safe landing. Harry Houdini had become the first person to fly an aeroplane in Australia.

He never piloted a plane again and, when he left Australia, did not take his machine with him. He had made the mark he wanted to leave. "Even if history forgets Houdini, the "Handcuff King," he wrote before he left Australia, "it must write my name as the first man to fly here." And so it has.[6]

(Photo, Outagamie County Historical Society)

and examine drawings of Curtiss machines to produce a copy that could fly. Of course, going from a printed description or a magazine sketch to a real aircraft was no mean feat, but at least Tees and other home-builders had plans of machines that they knew worked and could duplicate.

Starting inside the Tees home on Walnut Street in Green Bay, then moving to the back yard, Harry and his friends built a real flying machine. As Albert Dufour, John Schwister and other backyard builders learned, assembling an aeroplane was one thing, flying it safely was another. Harry Tees learned the same lesson. When his machine was ready to fly in the summer of 1912, he took it to a clearing near the Oak Circle area in Green Bay for its maiden flight. The Tees Flyer got into the air and reportedly stayed aloft for a few minutes, but Harry was not pilot enough to make a smooth landing and damaged the machine. Repairs were made and, in a week or so, Harry flew again, but once again cracked up the machine on landing. Repairing the damage took a lot more time and, while he was working, Harry noticed an ad in an aviation magazine placed by an exhibition pilot from Tennessee named Johnny Green. He needed a mechanic to accompany him on tour and Tees certainly met the requirements. If he could build a plane, he certainly could maintain one. Harry left Wisconsin and traveled with Green on the air show circuit throughout the southeastern states until the United States entered World War I. He served in the army and although he tried very hard to join the Air Corps, even writing President Woodrow Wilson and asking for a transfer, he stayed in the infantry. After the war, he played no active role in aviation.

The Tees Flyer remained in pieces on Walnut Street in Green Bay, but its legacy is larger than its lifespan. Although it is not clear how far and long the Tees machine actually flew, if it really did make more than a "jump," it was the first successful home-built aeroplane designed and built entirely in Wisconsin. Parts of the machine, and its design, were borrowed by Earl Knowland who built his own hydro-aeroplane and flew it over Green Bay and up the Fox Valley in 1913. This machine can make a good claim as being the first home-built floatplane designed and built in Wisconsin.

Coincidentally, Earl Knowland was part of the

Harry Tees (Aviator) Curtiss Biplane 40 H.P. Green Bay Wis 1912

Young Harry Tees at the controls of his homebuilt flyer in Green Bay, 1912. (WAHF)

Hoberg family of prosperous Green Bay papermakers. In 1917, when an eccentric, charismatic, aviation magazine publisher named Alfred Lawson appeared in Green Bay with a government order to build a prototype military trainer, the Hobergs invested in his new company. It was a risky investment, and it is worth asking if the Hobergs would have made it if one of them had not had some experience in aviation. There is a link connecting Wisconsin's first aircraft factory to two teenagers who wanted to fly and the high school that nurtured their desire.

Jesse Brabazon didn't need a high school to nurture his desire. He was the "yokel farm boy from Delavan, home of the bull frogs," whose fondest wish was "to do something that the yokels wouldn't dare attempt." In 1911, he attended the Chicago air meet and described it as "a sight never to be forgotten for the country boy to see real aeroplanes being operated and maneuvered in the air by plain human beings, just ordinary men."

After thinking about it over the winter, the twenty-six year-old Brabazon sold his farm implement shop in Delavan and moved to Max Lillie's airfield in Cicero on the edge of Chicago. In August 1912, he registered with Lillie for a maximum of five hours of in-the-air lessons for $300 and soon soloed in a Wright Flyer. He then went on tour in Illinois and Indiana and would have been Wisconsin's first professional exhibition pilot had not John Kaminiski started flying for pay a few months earlier.

He may have called himself a yokel, but Brabazon was shrewd enough to concoct a plan that kept him flying—and getting paid—every weekend of the season. When booking an exhibition in a new town, he would contact the local motorcycle club and challenge them to a race—and offer to split the one-dollar admission fee. The motorcyclists and their friends would turn out in force and pack the grandstand to see the local champion take on the flying machine from out of town. According to his formula for success, Brabazon would soar ahead of the motorcycle at the start of the race and maintain a lead until the last turn of the last lap. Then he would take a wide bank, fall behind and let the cycle win, which brought the expected "roars from the crowd." With

---

First Female Pilot In Wisconsin

The first woman on record to fly a aeroplane in Wisconsin was Blanche Stuart Scott. Born and raised in Rochester, New York and trained by a reluctant Glenn Curtiss, Scott became the first American female pilot in September 1910. She joined the Curtiss exhibition touring team and appeared at the Dane County fairgrounds in Madison on Memorial Day in 1913.

With the grandstand in front of the racetrack full of spectators anxious to see the "woman driver," Scott took off in her "Red Devil" Curtiss. The engine was sputtering but she got into the air and began to circle the racetrack. As she rounded the curve into the backstretch, the motor continued to cough and she decided to land. Unable to touch down on the smooth track, she landed in a field of tall grass nearby. The front wheel snagged and the plane started to flip, but Scott had enough presence of mind to jump off before the machine upended.

When they saw the plane go down in the grass, many in the crowd raced across the infield to the crash site. They found Scott bruised and dirty from her fall in the mud, but standing.

"I'm all right," she said, "not a bit hurt, don't worry."

She was a bit hurt, though, having suffered a broken arm that put her flying on hold for a while. However, Scott did return to the air and continued to tour with the Curtiss team until 1916. She quit because she could find "no place for the woman engineer, mechanic or flyer. Too often people paid money to see me risk my neck more as a freak—a woman freak pilot—than as a skilled aviator."

Nonetheless Scott had opened the door for other women in Wisconsin and elsewhere.[7]

---

this kind of showmanship Brabazon could net over $1,000 a week— "a real bank roll," for a yokel or anyone else.

The plane Brabazon flew in the autumn of 1912 was already a historical artifact. It was not especially old, but it was significant, since it was Cal Rodgers' machine, the Vin Fiz. In April 1912, six months after surviving the long flight from New York to California, Rodgers died in a crash at Long Beach. His widow sold the damaged, but reparable, Vin Fiz to Brabazon for $3,500. In the as yet small world of aviation, coincidences and connections like this one were not uncommon.

Brabazon put down $3300 of his own money for the Vin Fiz, then asked the banker in Delavan, with whom he and his family had been doing business for years, for a $200 loan. The banker was friendly and favorable until Brabazon told him the loan was for an aeroplane. Then "they wouldn't let me have a dime."

Brabazon bought the Vin Fiz without the loan and had perhaps his proudest moment as an aviator when he flew it at the 1912 Chicago Air Meet. Glenn Martin, Katherine Stinson, Hugh Robinson and dozens of other top-rated pilots were also on the program. He might have stayed in Chicago, but Max Lillie said the Vin Fiz was bad luck and didn't want it on his airfield. Brabazon then formed a partnership with his good friend Andy Drew and the two pilots opened a flying school in Lima, Ohio. They continued to fly exhibitions during the 1913 season and were doing well until Drew died in a fiery crash. The Vin Fiz proved to be a bad luck machine, after all.

After Drew's death, Jesse Brabazon lost his taste for flying. He returned to Delavan, then moved to Beloit where he bought an auto dealership. He lived there until his death in 1956. He had said that his ambition was to head the list among his brother aviators in careful and sane flying. He also wanted to return to Delavan and give some of his "nervy" friends a ride through the air. He met his ambition to be careful and sane but, after Drew's death, he no longer cared about returning to Delavan to give his fellow "yokels" a ride.[8]

The Boy Aviator And Wisconsin's First Licensed Pilot

The pilot who created the biggest splash in the early days of aviation in Milwaukee was aptly-named Farnum Fish. He was a precocious California teenager who graduated from high school in 1910 at age 14. Young Farnum had the parents every aspiring aviator dreams of having. About a year after their boy graduated, Mom and Pop Fish sent him to aviation school with the Wright Brothers in Dayton, Ohio. When he learned to fly, they bought him a $5,000 Wright Model B Flyer. When he said he wanted to tour on the exhibition circuit, they said yes. Could a teenage flyer ask for anything more?

In the spring of 1912, Farnum Fish and his machine were at the Cicero Flying Field. He was approached by a representative of the *Milwaukee*

Journal, whose circulation people had decided that aeroplanes could help sell newspapers, and who was hiring aviators for "Milwaukee's first air meet" on Memorial Day weekend at the State Fairgrounds.

An air meet was a good idea, but then the promotional people thought they could do better. They brainstormed a bit, had a few meetings, talked to a few advertisers. The plan began to grow. Why not have Fish fly all the way from Chicago to Milwaukee? Wouldn't that be some kind of record? And, since his Wright Flyer can carry the weight of a pilot and a passenger, why not have young Farnum bring some cargo? What about some ad leaflets or mail? Will he do that?

"You bet I will," said the pilot.

So, on May 25 1912, Farnum Fish strapped into the passenger seat of his plane a few thousand leaflets announcing the air meet, a few hundred letters to be delivered "via airship," a 300-yard bolt of silk cloth, plus more leaflets advertising its sale at Milwaukee's largest retailer and leading Journal advertiser, The Boston Store.

Cicero Field was located on 22nd Street and Cicero Avenue on the Chicago city limits, about seven miles due west of Lake Michigan. It seems that when he asked for directions to Milwaukee, Fish was told to just head for the lake and turn left. He took off, steered east down 22nd Street, hit the lake at the point where the McCormick Place Exposition Center was later built, and turned left. He made it a point to keep out over the water, but still within close sight of land. His mechanic, the aptly named Herb Hazzard, and a Journal newsman waving a large white flag, kept pace in an auto so Fish wouldn't get lost.

On the boy aviator flew, past the Chicago north shore suburbs, past Kenosha and Racine, where he had to veer out over the lake to weather Wind Point. In about two hours, he arrived over the center of Milwaukee, circled the downtown area several times at an altitude of 1,000 feet and dropped his cargo of leaflets. It was the first time printed advertising "flyers" rained on Wisconsin from an aeroplane. He tried to stay at 1,000 feet, but smoke, steam and exhaust from a city that fuelled its industries with coal and oil blocked his visibility. Rather than fly into a smokestack, he rose to 6,000 feet and headed for Lake Park, where fairway space on the golf course was reserved for his landing. As he approached the park, a "bomb"

was fired to tell the crowds lining the lakefront from Juneau Park north that it was time to look up.

He touched down perfectly at Lake Park, jumped out of his plane and, with all the bravado of youth, announced that, "It was nothing."

It was a little more than nothing. Farnum Fish had made the first aeroplane flight from Chicago to Milwaukee. He had delivered the first aerial advertising messages to appear in the city. He also delivered the first air freight in the form of the silk cloth that was rushed to the Boston Store and put on sale. Fish also brought the first "air mail" in the form of the few hundred notes of greeting to good customers from Herman Black, advertising manager of the Journal. They bore postage, were authenticated by a stamp that read, "Carried by Farnum T. Fish In Record Breaking Aeroplane Trip between Chicago and Milwaukee," and were rushed to the post office by auto as soon as they landed.

Fish also claimed that his 90-mile flight up the shore had set a world's record for over-the-water travel. It is true that he did stay over the lake, but Fish was never out of easy-gliding distance from shore. Although longer in terms of miles, his trip was hardly comparable to Louis Bleriot's first crossing of the English Channel in 1909. In terms of danger and piloting skills required, Fish's flight over the smokestacks of industrial Milwaukee was probably more demanding than his run up the lake.

The young pilot was duly feted and celebrated, but the business and social leaders of Milwaukee

The "boy aviator" 16-year-old Farnum Fish, who claimed a record for "over the water" aviation when he flew up the lake from Chicago to Milwaukee in 1912. (George Hardie)

really did not have much to say to a 15-year old boy, even if he was a pilot. It was easier to put him to work delivering newspapers. On May 27, Fish loaded up his machine with hundreds of copies of the special aviation issue of the Milwaukee Journal for Wisconsin's first aerial delivery of the daily news. It was a regular issue of the paper bearing the imprint of a flying machine resembling a Wright Flyer on page one that Fish would carry to Waukesha, Oconomowoc and Watertown. The Journal announced that it was the first special aeroplane edition of a newspaper ever printed.

The pilot was ready to go, but heavy clouds, rain and wind grounded him for one day. On the next afternoon, he got into the air, but heavy winds forced him to land his machine at McKinley Park and wait for better weather.

On May 29, the sky cleared and bundles of newspapers were again loaded on Fish's Flyer. He took off from McKinley Park, circled over the lake to gain altitude, then headed west, his departure heralded by the boom of a loud gun. Telegrams were sent ahead with his estimated time of arrival, but Fish got to his first destination, Waukesha, ahead of schedule and had to circle the business district several times before anyone noticed he had arrived. Then the brewery whistle blew, work stopped, businesses closed and all Waukesha headed for the grounds of Carroll College. As he dropped to three hundred feet, Fish reached for the sheath knife fastened beneath his seat, cut the line on the first bundle of papers and the Aeroplane Edition of the Milwaukee Journal fell upon Waukesha. Also in the bundle was a letter from Milwaukee Mayor G. A. Bading to Mayor Hawley Wilbur of Waukesha. "This is the first time, I believe," wrote Bading, "that it has been the privilege of one mayor of a Wisconsin city to send greetings to another Badger mayor by aeroplane."

Fish continued on and, in another twenty minutes, delivered the second mayoral greeting and more newspapers. As he approached Oconomowoc, "A pandemonium of whistles, bells and cheers greeted the boy flyer," reported the Journal. So many people had been camped out at the drop point that "For the past two days there hadn't been a regular meal cooked in the town. Druggists had run out of liniment for necks stiffened by craning."

Fish flew over the circus grounds and cut loose his second bundle. Mayor Edward Solversen received his letter from Milwaukee and "was so tickled, he could only say again and again, 'That's fine. That's fine'."

The final delivery was another twenty minutes away in Watertown. Fish flew over the campus of Northwestern College there and glided in for a smooth landing. He delivered his newspapers and the third mayoral message to an enthusiastic crowd consisting of "professor after professor, all the city officials and hundreds of students." Farnum Fish had completed his mission, delivered his papers, flying fifty-miles in sixty-five minutes. He then settled in for the night with the students at Northwestern, who were about the same age as he.

The next morning he took off for the State Fairgrounds with the passenger seat occupied by Herb Hazzard. The flight back to West Allis was perhaps the longest yet made in Wisconsin by a pilot and a passenger. Fish also carried a special message for the distributor of Rambler autos in Milwaukee. Auto dealer D. B. Roach of Watertown wanted to place an order for the Kenosha-built Rambler car as soon as possible and thought that Fish's aeroplane would get it to the distributor in Milwaukee faster than anyone else. If the order was placed, Fish didn't do it, because he landed at the State Fairgrounds to fly in the Memorial Day Weekend Air Meet.

For the Journal it was a 3-Ring Aerial Circus that would take place "Rain, Shine or Cyclone." For an admission fee of fifty cents, spectators would see Farnum, the "Flying Fish;" Julia Clarke, "The Birdgirl" who was also the first female pilot to appear in Wisconsin; Horace "Peck's Bad Boy" Kearney, who would make a special delivery of air mail; M. Callen, "The Daring Frenchman"; Lieutenant Motohisa Kondo, a Japanese pilot, whose nationality alone made him an exotic attraction; and, for the first time in his home town, "Milwaukee Boy" John Kaminski. With two Wright Flyers and two or three Curtiss machines, this event was the largest gathering of aeroplanes yet to take place in Wisconsin. They would perform "Many Stunts You Never Dreamed Were Possible With An Aeroplane."

As was often the case with air meets, the promises of the Milwaukee event exceeded its reality. With the more experienced Kearney and Fish doing most of the flying, the now standard auto and motorcycle races, aerobatic displays and altitude flights came off without a hitch. The newer pilots had their problems. Clarke and Callen did

not fly at all. Lieutenant Kondo cracked up his machine on the first day and did not fly again. In his home town debut, John Kaminski ran into the racetrack fence on his first take off attempt and damaged an aileron. He got into the air on his second try, but lost control just as he cleared the fairgrounds fence and had to make a forced landing in the infield. That was all on the first day.

The second day of the meet, which was also the Memorial Day holiday, attracted 10,000 spectators. The main event was Horace Kearney's "air mail" delivery. The post office had set up a temporary counter in the grandstand and cancelled letters and cards with a special "Aeroplane Station" stamp. The mail was then loaded in a sturdy bag and placed onto Kearney's Wright Flyer which, like Farnum Fish's, had a passenger seat. Kearney took off, circled the grandstand, then headed off for the West Allis post office about one-half-mile away from the fairgrounds. Kearney got over the post office and, still in sight of the crowd, dropped the mail bag. Instead of falling free and completing the "air mail" delivery, the bag snagged on the machine. Kearney wiggled and waggled, dived and climbed, banked and rolled—giving the spectators an extra exhibition of fancy flying—but could not dislodge the bag. He was forced to return to the fairgrounds and land to free it. Farnum Fish then took the bag up and made the drop on the West Allis post office, where the "air mail" delivery was

At the Memorial Day aero meet at the state fairgrounds in 1912, Farnum Fish delivered the "air mail" from the fairgrounds all the way to the West Allis post office. (WAHF)

completed the old-fashioned way, by railroad, horse cart and on foot.

The Journal Air Meet peaked with the mail drop on May 31. The pilots flew again on June 1, but the performance was marred by four accidents that led the sponsors to cancel the final events. Making matters worse, June 1 was a working day and few Milwaukeeans could take a day off for an air show, so no more than 500 spectators turned out to see the flying machines. Compared to the big bang Farnum Fish had created the week before, the air meet concluded with a whimper.

The 1912 flying season was just beginning so the aviators traveled to other bookings out of town. Farnum Fish came back to Milwaukee in October, 1912 and took a photographer aloft who made pictures of the Vanderbilt Cup auto races that the Milwaukee Journal claimed were the first aerial photos of an auto race. Fish continued to fly exhibitions until he entered the military for World War I. Although he was one of the most experienced pilots in the country, he failed to qualify as an army flight instructor. It is possible that he deliberately tanked the program, so he wouldn't have to spend the war instructing in the United States when he could be flying in Europe. Instead he entered the French air corps, saw combat action and is credited with an aerial victory. After the war he flew in the Mexican Revolution where

Wisconsin's first "boy aviator" lost his life.

Wisconsin's other "boy aviator" was just beginning his career when the Milwaukee air meet ended. John Kaminski was sixteen years old and had been a pilot for all of three months when he returned to his home town.

As a boy growing up on the 800 block of Racine Street in Milwaukee's Polish neighborhood, Kaminski used to take walks with his grandfather along Lake Michigan in Juneau Park. "We would sit on top of the bluff and watch the wild ducks and sea gulls flying over the water," he recalled. "One day as my grandfather and I were watching the maneuvers of the sea gulls flying over the lake, I told him that soon I would be flying like them." It was about as accurate a prediction as a boy could make.

The first flying machine Kaminski saw "was at a so-called aviation school near Milwaukee and it was a decided disappointment....The plane was so poorly designed and inadequately motored it couldn't leave the ground." Kaminski is referring to Rudolph Silverton's Vacu-Aerial Navigation Machine which was then parked at his flying school in West Allis. Fortunately, young Kaminski had read enough about aviation to know that there was more to it than the Vacu-Aerial. He wrote to both the Wrights and Curtiss for information on pilot training and, in December 1911, set off for the Curtiss school on North Island in San Diego Bay, California.

Glenn Curtiss had opened a winter flying facility at North Island the previous year primarily to continue experimental work on hydro-aeroplanes and flying boats in cooperation with the United States Navy. With as many as ten aircraft on the ground or in the water at one time, North Island was one of the largest aviation facilities in the country. The flight school was part of the operation and here John Kaminski entered the already-international world of aviation. Among his classmates were Lansing Callan of New York, Mohan Singh of India, Motohisa Kondo of Japan and a young heiress from Colorado, Julia Clarke. Although he had signed up for lessons he had not seen an aeroplane fly until he arrived at North Island. It was a Curtiss machine piloted by none other than Lincoln Beachey. The famous pilot so impressed the Milwaukee boy that Kaminski got himself a checkered cap identical to Beachey's signature headgear and wore it whenever he flew.

At North Island, Kaminski began flight training in the standard manner with "grass-cutting" trips around the field. Dual-control machines were few and far between then, so Curtiss controlled the throttle on his trainers with a set-screw that allowed the plane to taxi around the field but did not power it enough to fly. One day Kaminski started grass-cutting but, "before I knew it, I was flying in the air at about 50 feet above the ground."

The set-screw had worked loose and the engine accelerated to take off speed. "I was too surprised to feel any sense of fear, and after a straight away flight of a few minutes, I landed the machine without mishap."

Kaminski may not have been afraid during his accidental solo, but after he landed, Glen Curtiss told him that the teenager had scared the life out of him.

The young man got another opportunity to scare the life out of Glenn Curtiss during a test of a flying boat. Not a float plane, the flying boat was just that, a boat with wings and a motor in which the pilot sat and which itself sat in the water. As with the hydro-aeroplane, the first design problem with a flying boat was to find the right combination of power and hull design to break the surface tension of the water and lift the machine into the air.

On one occasion, Kaminski and Lieutenant Theodore Ellyson, the first American naval aviator, were watching Curtiss unsuccessfully attempt to break a flying boat free of the water. After Curtiss docked, Ellyson said, "Johnny why don't you stand on the tail of the flying boat?"

"Sure," said Johnny.

Curtiss asked if Kaminski was scared, but the young man didn't answer until he climbed on the tail of the flying boat, took hold of the outriggers and said "Let's go."

Down the bay they went and, with the added weight on the tail, the nose of the boat lifted and the ship took off. Curtiss made a straight-away flight for about two miles over San Diego Bay with Kaminski standing on the tail. When he landed, Curtiss said, "Johnny this is the second time that

you scared the life out of me."

Johnny didn't reply, but he remembered the story.

Kaminski completed his pilot training in the spring of 1912 and went right to work with three days of exhibition flying at nearby Coronado Beach. On April 17, 1912, he met the requirements of the International Aeronautics Federation and became the first Wisconsinite to hold a pilot's license. He then leased a plane from the Curtiss Exhibition Company and came home to Wisconsin.

Not long after he arrived Kaminski landed his machine at Rudolph Silverston's school of aviation in West Allis. The trim little Curtiss, with its Gnome engine, made a striking contrast with the lumbering Vacu-Aerial machine. It was about this time that Kaminski named his machine, "Sweetheart" and painted the sentiment on its tail—no surprise from a young man in love with flying. He also met Jack Knight, a Silverston student, and moved his plane to the Knight family farm near Stone Bank in Waukesha County. When Kaminski went on tour in 1913, Knight joined him as a mechanic to form the first all-Wisconsin professional flying team.

Kaminski's exhibition flying was limited in 1912. In August, he loaned his plane to a pilot named John Brown who was filling a date at a community fair in Sun Prairie. Brown lost control of "Sweetheart," landed rough and ran the machine through a wire fence, around a tree and into a large stone. Losing his plane in August was a major disappointment to the young pilot. The

John Kaminski, second from left with classmates at North Island flight school. Among his classmates were Lansing Callan of New York, Mohan Singh of India, Motohisa Kondo of Japan and Julia Clarke.
(George Hardie, UW-Milwaukee)

Above: Milwaukee's John Kaminski wearing his "Lincoln Beachey" checkered hat in West Allis, 1912.

Right: Kaminski christened his plane "Sweetheart," mounted it on a float and flew off the beach at Milwaukee. (George Hardie)

Curtiss Company was not able to replace the plane in time, so Kaminiski had to bow out of a scheduled exhibition at the State Fair where he would have flown with his idol Lincoln Beachey.

Kaminski did make one frigid flight from Chicago to Milwaukee at the end of November that demonstrates one of the other hazards of flight in the days not just before aeroplanes had cabins, but before they had cockpits as well. Engine failure forced Kaminski to set down in a corn field just north of Racine, much to the astonishment of a farm woman who was husking corn at the time.

"When the ship struck the earth a young Pole fell out and he was so numb with the cold that he was unable to talk for some time," reported the *Racine Journal-Times*. The young man, who was of Polish heritage, was bundled off to the farm house where he thawed out and arranged for his machine to be shipped to Milwaukee by rail.

Kaminski also got to know Rudolph Silverston, which must have been an education of another sort for the square-dealing grocer's son whose father's advice was to "promise nothing which could not be fulfilled." In the spring of 1913, Silverston moved to Cuyahoga Falls, Ohio to start an aviation operation that included a flying school with Kaminski as flight instructor. The pilot stayed with Silverston for a few months, but by July of 1913 was again on the exhibition tour.

He was billed as the "only Polish and the youngest licensed aviator in the world," nudging out Farnum Fish on the latter point by about six months. To be sure, Kaminski's parents were Polish immigrants, although one Ohio news reporter announced that Kaminski was "the famous Japanese aviator."

Neither his age nor his nationality mattered when he was in the air. Skill and courage did. On one flight in Ohio a freak gust of wind blew him out of his seat and he struggled for what seemed like "ages" to get back into place and regain control of the aeroplane. In North Carolina, his engine stalled at 2,000 feet and the only "landing field" he could find was in an orchard. On glide, he put the machine down precisely between the rows of trees. Only afterwards did he learn that he had landed a plane with a 26-foot wingspan between trees planted thirty-five feet apart.

He came home to Wisconsin many times. In 1914, he flew at the Independence Day celebration in Tomahawk where his runway was the main street of the business district and lined with spectators. He made one trouble-free flight, but ran into difficulties on the second after the Tomahawk fire department hosed down the street to settle the dust. Kaminski's runway was now slick concrete and he could not take off quick enough to rise over a set of wires crossing the street. He tried to get under them and accelerated to 70 MPH. As he crossed an intersection, a cross wind caught his plane and pushed it towards the spectators. To avoid hitting them, he banked the plane and caught an aileron on a telegraph pole, tipped his nose towards the ground, and crashed. "Sweetheart" was seriously damaged and Kaminski was knocked unconscious. He recovered and continued to fly, returning to Milwaukee in 1915 to fly hydroplanes on Lake Michigan. He estimated that he logged 800 hours for the Curtiss Company at exhibitions throughout the eastern half of the United States and Canada until he entered military service in 1917.

A young man full of bluff and bravado in these days, Kaminski once told a reporter that his motto was, "Fly when you say you will fly, and laugh at the wind if it begins to blow a cyclone... I will live to be at least 76 years old and I will probably be flying a 500 horse-power aeroplane..."

It was an optimistic prediction, but a suitable one for an accomplished teenager pursuing the life that he loved.[9]

EVEN IN FRIENDSHIP

As aviation developed in the years between 1910 and World War I aeroplanes appeared in ever-smaller Wisconsin communities and more Wisconsin people assembled their own aircraft and took to the skies.

"This is history," said the *Stevens Point Daily Journal,* as it recounted "the first aeroplane flight ever attempted in this city." Franco Castory took off in his Curtiss machine at the Portage County Fairgrounds in July, 1912 and boxed the compass over Stevens Point and the surrounding countryside.

Harry Powers, erstwhile flight instructor at West Allis, took off in his Curtiss hydro-aeroplane at Oshkosh's Electric Park and, accompanied by his mechanic, made the first flight across Lake Winnebago to Waverly Beach. His Curtiss was not a two-place plane, so Powers' mechanic, who went unnamed in the news reports, made what must have been an exciting 19-minute passage over the lake perched on the pontoon.

The hardest-working aviator in Wisconsin that season must have been Nels Nelson, whose name gave him a guarantee of popularity among Wisconsin's large Scandinavian community. Nelson flew his Curtiss at Lancaster, Monroe, Ashland, Chilton and Janesville.

Horace Kearney, who starred at the Milwaukee Journal Air Meet on Memorial Day, appeared in October at the year's smallest venue when he flew at the Central Agricultural Association Fair in the Crawford County community of Gays Mills. The local correspondent for the nearest newspaper, in Prairie du Chien, was so proud the little community raised the money for an aviator that he crowed

AERO CLUB OF AMERICA
297 MADISON AVENUE
NEW YORK CITY

This certifies that John J. Kaminski

Aviator's Certificate No 121 of the Aero Club of America is licensed under Article 70 of the regulations of the F. A. I. for the year 1913.

This certificate expires on December 31st, 1913.

Secretary.

This license must be exhibited whenever required.

John Kaminski's pilot's license, issued by the International Aeronautics Federation in April 1912, made him Wisconsin's first licensed pilot. (George Hardie, UW-Milwaukee)

WRECK OF THE AEROPLANE
AT TOMAHAWK—WIS.
JULY 4th 1914
PHOTO BY DOWNIE

Above: Wreck of John Kaminski's Curtiss at Tomahawk, 1912. (George Hardie)

Right: The crash that killed exhibition pilot P.C. Davis at Mauston in 1913. (Juneau County Historical Society)

"for a little city of less than a thousand souls, you can't find a two thousand city anywhere to beat them."

As aeroplanes became more commonplace, exhibition pilots not only had to seek out smaller communities where machines had yet to fly, they also had to concoct ever more thrilling and dangerous stunts.

In Janesville, Nels Nelson took up a hand-cranked movie camera to film the grand parade at the Eagles Convention. Flying his Curtiss already required that he keep at least one hand on the steering wheel, while if he leaned too far to the left or right his shoulders bumped the aileron controls. So, how did he hold a camera as big as a breadbox, turn the crank and fly the aeroplane?

Nelson, whose ads said he flew a "wonderful piece of mechanism which obeys the will of mighty man," also announced that he would give a free ride to "honeymoon" couples.

He must have had a mighty will to keep that promise, since he flew a single-seat Curtiss.

Louis Mitchell was more traditional. He relied on man's favorite promotional asset, a young woman. He gave a ride to Anna Kuelz, "one of Evansville's popular young ladies," who reported that "the sensation of being carried through the air so swiftly and smoothly was one impossible of description." Therefore, something that any man, woman or child should try—for a fee.

WRECK OF AEROPLANE
AT JUNEAU COUNTY FAIRGROUNDS
SEPT. 5. 1913 — MAUSTON. WIS.

Mr. and Mrs. Clair G. Horton took Mitchell and Nelson one step further. They were the first pilots who were also a married couple to tour Wisconsin. They flew a Curtiss hydro-aeroplane with dual controls on Lake Mendota in 1914. They offered to take riders up for a flight to see the lakes, the city and the recently-completed state Capitol. Among their passengers was University of Wisconsin President Charles Van Hise.

Like many pilots, Floyd Barlow promised to fly "Rain, Shine or Cyclone" but a tour he made through the small towns of west central Wisconsin was derailed when he "bumped into a bluff" at Durand. One of the exhibitions Barlow had to cancel was at the Adams County Fair in Friendship. One of the smallest counties in Wisconsin, with one of the smallest fairs, in one of the smallest of county seats, Adams was hardly a prime venue for an aviator. The fact that a pilot planned to fly even in Friendship is testimony to the speed at which aviation had grown throughout the state. Although he didn't fly in Friendship, Barlow came back from his tangle with the bluff for two days of flying at Sparta, then wowed the spectators at the Elroy Fair where he looped the plane over the grandstand.

The list of pilots and performances continued into 1914, 1915, 1916. Convinced that the show must go on no matter what, George Mestach defied the weather and flew in the rain on a cold October day in Mondovi. On an even colder January day, Joe De Riemer took off on the ice of the Marinette-Menominee harbor in his Curtiss-powered Wright Flyer and made the first of several flights over the ice of Green Bay.

Louis Gertson flew at Watertown, Portage, Fond du Lac and Sturgeon Bay. He charged the Door County Fair Association an unheard of $1,050 and, although eyebrows were raised over the fair board's extravagance, Gertson was praised and a record crowd attended his exhibitions. Katherine Stinson and Ruth Law, whose gender made them attractions no matter how they flew, appeared in Wisconsin: Stinson at La Crosse and Law at the State Fair in 1915.

After the start of World War I in Europe in 1914, American aviators added "aerial wars" or "battles in the skies" to their repertoire. As the number and variety of aeroplanes increased, different models "battled" each other for control of the skies. In heavily-Germanic Wisconsin, spice was added to the battles by advertising one of the pilots as "The German Aviator" and one of his opponents as a "Frenchman."

Races between aeroplanes and autos were about as old as exhibition flying, but Fred Hoover, "The German Flyer" added a daredevilish twist for the 1914 Sheboygan County Fair. He promised not only to race an auto, but also to fly close enough to the driver to touch his head with the forward landing gear of the Curtiss. Hoover never kept his promise because he crashed shortly after take-off—which might have been a stroke of good luck for the autodriver.

In September 1913, the inevitable happened. A Chicago-based exhibition pilot named P. C. Davis was filling in for the busy Nels Nelson at the

Juneau County Fair in Mauston. He made two fine flights on September 13 and 14, but ran into trouble on the 15th. He was completing his landing when, for some reason, his engine would not shut off. The machine roared down the fairgrounds racetrack, skipped over the curb and headed straight for a wire fence. The machine struck the fence, turned completely over, and rammed Davis into the wire. The pilot suffered a broken leg and collar bone and sliced up his feet horribly, with two toes amputated. He was hospitalized in Mauston, then transferred to his home in Chicago. A tetanus infection set in and, in three days, P. C. Davis was dead. His passing was the first aviation fatality due to an accident in Wisconsin.

Flying was a dangerous profession and the increasing demands of exhibition flying only added to the death toll. John Kaminski pointed out that of the 13 people who took flight instruction at North Island with him in the first half of 1912, six died in aeroplane accidents before a year had passed. At Oshkosh in 1916, Charles "Do Anything" Niles, seemingly responding to goading from spectators, drew on the Lincoln Beachey bag of aerobatic tricks. He looped his monoplane three times in front of the grandstand, flew down the fairgrounds race track upside down, then rose for a final dive. At 2,000 feet, a wingtip cracked off and Niles lost control. Fighting all the way down, he steered the machine away from the grandstand before it crashed on an Oshkosh street. Niles did not survive.

"We are living in a fast age," said John Kaminski in his flying days, "and the aviator who is willing to sacrifice his bones and gore on the altar of a highly seasoned and chance-taking sport, is going to be the one to draw the crowds." So they did, and many of them died.

The fact that flying was a dangerous profession did not deter an increasing number of Wisconsin people from building and flying their own planes. In 1910, Beloit native Trenton Fry

An adaptation of a notice that appeared in Ashland after John Kaminski's crash in Tomahawk resulted in the cancellation of his flight there.

ASHLAND DAILY PRESS
JULY 15.1912

KILLED

John Kaminski, the daring aviator who was to make the flight in the Aeroplane today, wrecked his machine and narrowly escaped death.

AS A RESULT THERE WILL BE
NO AVIATION MEET

Flying is a dangerous profession and the increasing demands of exhibition flying only adds to the death toll. John Kaminski pointed out that of the 13 people who took flight instruction at North Island with him in the first half of 1912, six died in aeroplane accidents before a year had passed. At Oshkosh in 1916, Charles "Do Anything" Niles, seemingly responding to goading from spectators, drew on the Lincoln Beachey bag of aerobatic tricks. He looped his monoplane three times in front of the grandstand, flew down the fairgrounds race track upside down, then rose for a final dive. At 2,000 feet, a wingtip cracked off and Niles lost control. Fighting all the way down, he steered the machine away from the grandstand before it crashed on an Oshkosh street. Niles did not survive.

"We are living in a fast age," said John Kaminski in his flying days, "and the aviator who is willing to sacrifice his bones and gore on the altar of a highly seasoned and chance-taking sport, is going to be the one to draw the crowds." So they did, and many of them died.

was in Chicago working for Eddie Heath, whose E.
B. Heath Aviation Vehicle Company was only one
year old. Heath was already selling aeroplane parts
and kits, including one kit for a copy of a $5,000
Curtiss machine for $125—minus fabric, engine
and propeller. Fry also worked at Cicero Field,
which was already billing itself as the busiest airport in the United States, and where Fry could see
just about every new development in aviation as it
came down the runway.

He came home to Beloit in 1912 and went to
work for the Warner Instrument Company where
he met Tom Timmons. The two young men
became friends and decided to build an aeroplane.
In 1914, they completed and flew an advanced-
looking, small biplane with the engine mounted in
"tractor" fashion at the front of the fuselage.
Although the term is rarely used today, nearly all
modern aircraft are "tractors," as opposed to the
pioneer "pusher" models with rear-facing engines.
In another modern touch, the pilot of Timmons
and Fry's machine sat half-in, half-out of a cockpit
placed behind the engine and in between the
wings. Timmons and Fry were also very proud
that they had borrowed rubber shock absorbers
from a farm tractor and installed them on their
plane, which
enabled them to
claim that theirs
was the first flying
machine equipped
with a suspension
system.

It flew, too. The
partners made
straight-line flights
from hay field to
hay field in the
Beloit area through-

out the spring and summer of 1914. When the
weather turned cold, they sold the machine and
lost track of it. Timmons drifted away from aviation and eventually became a police detective in
Beloit. Fry stayed in aviation, went back to the
Heath Company and later served in the air corps
during World War I. After the war, he became one
of the first United States Post Office pilots and
helped pioneer the first transcontinental air mail
route, flying the Chicago-Cleveland leg in 1919.

One of those Heath-kit Curtisses that Trenton
Fry was helping to sell in Chicago might have
turned up in West Salem, Wisconsin, where a trio
of home builders assembled a dead ringer for a
genuine Curtiss in 1916. Abel Jostad, Selmar
Gjestvang and Wendell McEldowney assembled
their plane from plans and materials they purchased by mail. Like so many would-be flyers, they
had been impressed by exhibition pilots—in this
case, Lincoln Beachey and Hugh Robinson in
1911—and set out to build their own machine.
They put it together beneath the shade of some tall
oaks near to the closest thing to a level spot they
could find in the Coulee country and were ready to
fly when they realized that none of them knew the
first thing about it.

Selmar Gjestvang was more interested in actually flying than his partners so he taxied around
the field, "grass-cutting" just like John Kaminksi at
the Curtiss flight school. And just like John
Kaminski, Selmar Gjestvang inadvertently found
himself in the air. He made a quick hop that could
barely be called a flight, then landed as quickly as
possible. Perhaps it was Nordic reserve, or just his
own cautious nature, but Gjestvang decided to
park the plane in McEldowney's shed until he
learned a bit more about piloting.

Before he could get back to the West Salem
Flyer, the United States enter World War I.
Gjestevang took pilot training and was on his way
to fly in Europe via the ill-fated troopship
Tuscania when a German submarine torpedoed
the ship. He was seriously
wounded, contracted
tuberculosis in the hospital
and died only a few days
after the war ended in
1918.

Although he never
piloted a plane himself,
Wendell McEldowney
became the number one
booster of aviation in the
La Crosse area. In 1919, he
invested in the Lawson

Aircraft Company in Milwaukee. When air mail service began through La Crosse in 1926, his was the phone number pilots called if they couldn't make the airport and had to set down in a farm field. He was a lifelong advocate of airport construction and airline service in La Crosse, even though his only experience behind the controls of an aeroplane was with the imitation Curtiss he and his friends steered around a hayfield in 1916.

As the largest community in the state, Milwaukee naturally had a good share of experimental aviators in the years prior to World War I. Perhaps no group was more ambitious than Paul Gnauck and his friends in the Wisconsin Aero Club. Late in 1913, they started meeting in the basement of Wally Schmidt's tavern on the corner of North and Fond du Lac Avenues. They thought they could build a "flying boat" using plans and materials purchased from a Chicago supplier, perhaps the Heath Company. In so doing, the aptly-named Wisconsin Aero Club can make a strong claim to being the first experimental aircraft club in Wisconsin.

Gnauck was the sparkplug of the group which also included Wally Schmidt, Jr., Frank Mullenbach, Klaus Bergenthal, Otto Hagemann, the four Hoerst brothers and, the only non-German, a Chicagoan named Logan R. Vilas, "Jack" to his friends. Although sharing their name, Jack was not a close relative of the Milwaukee Vilas's, who included William Freeman Vilas, the United States Senator who left his name on the lake-studded northern Wisconsin county or Edward P. Vilas, an enthusiastic balloonist and founder of the Milwaukee Aero Club. Jack Vilas was a wealthy Chicagoan and an early purchaser of one of those flying boats that John Kaminski helped Glenn Curtiss perfect in the spring of 1912. A year later, while practicing for the proposed 900-mile Great Lakes Reliability Tour from Chicago to Detroit via the shores of Lakes Michigan and Huron, Jack Vilas used his flying boat to make the first aerial crossing of Lake Michigan. His thrilling voyage of 64 miles, much of it out-of-sight of land and at altitudes above 5,000 feet, set a record for over-the-water flight.

With experience as a pilot of flying boats, Jack Vilas was certainly welcome in Wally Schmidt's

horse barn, to which the aeroplane builders had moved after their flying boat kit arrived and proved to be too big for the basement doors of the tavern. They worked through the crisp days and cold nights of early 1914, assembling a fuselage copied from the two-place Curtiss design. They had ordered a hefty 85 horsepower motor, but received two smaller engines accompanied by a note from the supplier stating that twin engines were now

the cutting edge of aircraft motive power and superior to a single power plant.

The new engines required a redesign of the wings, with the services of neighborhood blacksmith Emil Krause necessary to refashion turnbuckles and end-holes for the wires. Re-engineering help came from Wally Schmidt's mother, who volunteered to cover the frames with 100 yards of aeroplane linen, provided the boys followed her advice to fasten the fabric to the frames with staples every two inches, which they did. After completing the redesign and mounting the twin engines, the team discovered that, despite the endorsement of the supplier, the motors would not run very well. Gnauck then volunteered to finance the purchase of a new Maximotor aircraft engine, which arrived in late April, 1914.

In the early hours of April 27, the Wisconsin Aero Club Flyer was wheeled down to McKinley Park Beach and, with Paul Gnauck at the controls, made its maiden flight over the waters of Lake Michigan. Although he had never built an aeroplane before, Gnauck had flown and received his pilot's license the previous year in New York City. He apparently had little trouble getting aloft. According to one account, the flying boat became so popular that the Aero Club established a going business taking riders up over the lake at three dollars a head, even flying to and from Chicago for $25 a round trip.

Wisconsin Aero Club members and the flying boat that they attempted to fly across Lake Michigan in 1914. The engine failed and the plane sank, but the crew was rescued by friendly yachtsmen. (Waukesha Aviation Club)

By Memorial Day they were ready to challenge Lake Michigan. The influence of Jack Vilas was present, although he was not. Instead, on Memorial Day morning, Gnauck and an unidentified crew member aimed their machine into the sunrise and took off for Michigan. They had taken the precaution of asking members of the Milwaukee Yacht Club for an escort across the lake, and a fortunate decision it was. About five miles out, the Maximotor maxxed out and the flying boat, which did not possess the good gliding capabilities typical of Curtiss designs, fell like a rock into the lake. The crew was soon rescued by a Yacht Club boat, but the Wisconsin Aero Club Flyer, the first Wisconsin aeroplane to attempt a Lake Michigan crossing, was lost.

After watching the harvest of their winter's labor slip beneath the waves, most of the Wisconsin Aero Club members gave up on aviation. Vilas stayed in and, in the summer of 1915, flew his Curtiss flying boat on fire patrol in northern Wisconsin for the State Forestry Board. It was the first use of an aeroplane for conservation work in the world.

Paul Gnauck acquired another aeroplane and, after listening to a few words of advice on flying

from John Kaminski, performed exhibitions in the Milwaukee area. The highlight of his career occurred at the State Fair in 1915, when he shared the program with Ruth Law.

Only a few years had passed since 1910, when 10,000 State Fair spectators had watched in amazement at the marvel of Arch Hoxsey merely getting his machine into the air. Now a team of Wisconsin home builders had set out to conquer Lake Michigan by air. That they failed is less important than that they felt confident enough to try.

To say that aviation had become old hat by 1914 is an exaggeration, but flyers and flying machines had become very familiar and less exciting than they once had been. In 1913, after Nels Nelson flew at the Grant County Fair in Lancaster, the newspaper reported that interest in the air show had waned "Thousands were present this year, however, who had seen the same aviator make equally as fine flights last year, and like the child with a used toy the novelty was gone and much of the interest lost."

Public indifference pushed exhibition flyers to deliver more thrills and no one worked harder at it than Lincoln Beachey. He made his final tour of Wisconsin in the summer of 1914 with an act that included the aerial bombing and detonation of a miniature battleship; the Death Drop; the loop-the-loop; and several aeroplane versus auto races against Barney Oldfield and his 120 horsepower Fiat during which Beachey would circle over Oldfield and gently tap him on the head with his front landing gear.

In Beloit a crowd of 2,500 saw Beachey give "everyone their money's worth," by flying, "upside down, almost on edge and the crowd does not put it a bit above him to fly backwards." Nonetheless, one spectator remarked that "Beachey is welcome to his $2,000 a day if he wants to earn it that way. I'll sell shoes for ten a week for mine."

Flying would never become as routine as selling shoes, but it had to develop into something more than a county fair thrill show, or a pastime for boys to dabble in until they grew up and pursued real careers. Aviation would have to find a practical use for itself, and soon it would. In the very same summer of 1914, while Lincoln Beachey exhibited his Death Drop above the grandstands in Wisconsin, the armies of Europe began a genuine drop into death on the battle fields of World War I. In short time, the aeroplane would pass from carnival show stopper to practical instrument of war and Wisconsin would play a part in the transition.[10]

Ballooning In Wisconsin

In the summer of 1863, while American soldiers wearing uniforms of blue and grey were engaged in the bloody Civil War campaigns of Vickburg and Gettysburg, a young lieutenant of the Royal Army of Wurttemberg in Germany disembarked from a lake steamer at the raw frontier village of Superior, Wisconsin. He was Ferdinand, eldest son of the Graf von Zeppelin, commissioned by his father to observe the fighting between the Union and Confederate armies, and also to explore the wilder reaches of the United States. In no time after he landed, the sandy-haired young soldier, with his European wardrobe and manners, so charmed the inhabitants of Superior that many begged him to stay and settle in their community. A few of his more enthusiastic fans started a movement to rename the village in honor of their guest. Had they succeeded, the largest Wisconsin city on the shore of Lake Superior would have been called Zeppelin.

The young lieutenant politely refused the honor and set off to explore the interior. Accompanied by two other Europeans and a crew of Ojibwas, Zeppelin canoed up the St. Louis River, portaged to the Upper Mississippi and proceeded downstream. Two weeks later he emerged from the wilderness at St. Paul, Minnesota and found lodgings at the Hotel International. One morning Lieutenant Zeppelin looked out of his hotel window and saw a large, gas-filled balloon slowly rise into the heavens. With a pilot in a basket suspended below, the airship rose several hundred feet into the air until it reached the end of the rope tethering it to the ground. There the balloon paused, gently buffeted by the wind, until the pilot signaled the ground crew to carefully reel the ship back to earth.

Zeppelin had to try this new experience. He introduced himself to the pilot, a German immigrant named John Steiner, and scheduled a flight. Since the St. Paul gas works was hard-pressed to furnish the full 41,000 cubic feet of gas required to fill the balloon to capacity, Steiner had to keep a close watch on the amount of weight he allowed in the gondola. He learned to be observant when Alexander Ramsey, the hefty United States Senator from Minnesota, tried to make a flight and the balloon could not get off the ground.

Weighing about one-half as much as the Senator, young Zeppelin had better luck. He and Steiner rose to the end of the tethering line, surveyed the scenery as long as they liked, then descended. Since he was a military observer and the son of a strict father, Zeppelin later penned a report detailing how an invading army might assault St. Paul and how there might be a future in military reconnaissance via balloon. A few days later, he boarded an eastbound train for La Crosse and Milwaukee, where he caught a ship and began his voyage home.

About three decades later, after he inherited his father's title, Ferdinand, Graf von Zeppelin, began his experiments with "dirigible" airships. He became so identified with the cigar-shaped craft that his family name was bestowed on them—instead of on a lakeshore city in Wisconsin. Zeppelin later reminisced that his tethered ascension in St. Paul first inspired his interest in "aerial navigation." It was there, he said, "that the first idea of my Zeppelins came to me."

The pilot whose balloon so inspired the young lieutenant was Milwaukee's most popular balloonist, John Steiner. He was one of the first professional balloon pilots in the United States and, starting in 1859, made regular flights in Wisconsin for nearly twenty years.

Steiner followed his first Wisconsin ascension with a hair-raising crossing of Lake Michigan on July 4, 1860. He made the voyage in the Europa, an 18,000-cubic foot balloon made of finely-woven linen cloth. Lifting off from the end of Main Street in Milwaukee, Steiner and his balloon quickly rose to 12,000 feet. From that altitude the pilot saw that, "The Milwaukee River seemed like the silver string of a violin...and to the south and west the farms and streams were visible for at least forty miles."

Forty minutes into the voyage, the Europa was engulfed in a violent thunderstorm that Steiner found gorgeous and terrifying. "The lightning darted up and down the sides, and the thunder peals were loud and continuous." Masses of snowy white clouds towered above the dark rainclouds and patches of blue sky and sunlight broke through the gloom. The reverberating echo of his own voice sounded as loud and as clear as a church bell.

Steiner was not alarmed by the lightning and thunder, but the rain that followed was dangerous. The Europa was made of water-absorbent linen cloth and, as more rain fell, the balloon gained weight. Losing altitude, Steiner drifted eastwards and when the storm broke and the sky cleared, he found himself about ten miles from the Michigan shore, a few hundred feet above the water, and dropping fast. He had to gain altitude at any cost so, over the side went sandbags, grappling hook, food and drink, even his overcoat. Still the water-logged balloon failed to rise. Finally, with the floor of the gondola brushing the wavetops, Steiner climbed into the rigging connecting the basket to the balloon. He pulled out his pocket knife and sliced away at the lines until the gondola dropped off into the water. Freed of this weight, the balloon shot up to 5,000 feet, with the pilot precariously perched in the rigging. In about fifteen minutes the balloon reached the Michigan shore and Steiner slowly released gas to

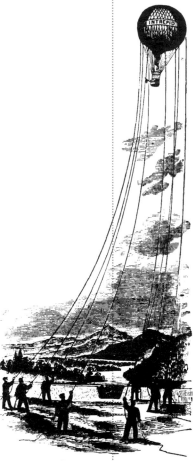

WAR BALLOON.

make a safe landing in knee-deep water. The flight had covered 103 miles and lasted two hours, thirty minutes. It was the first recorded crossing of Lake Michigan by an airship launched in Wisconsin.

Back in Milwaukee, Steiner's friends were understandably concerned about the aeronaut. Word of his fate did not reach them until he returned safe and sound on July 6 with his balloon intact and safely stored in the hold of a tugboat, but minus the lost gondola. His Milwaukee friends went to work and, a few weeks later, presented the balloonist with a new gondola designed for lake crossings. It was an artfully woven wicker "boat," that weighed only fifty pounds, yet was light and strong enough to keep two passengers afloat in the water. Steiner promised to use it soon at an ascension he planned to make in Canada in honor of the visiting Prince of Wales.

The following spring the Civil War began and, about a year into the conflict, the first balloonists entered military service. Steiner served briefly as an observer for the Union Army on the Mississippi River and perhaps he used his Milwaukee-made wicker boat to spot the rebels. Almost certainly, the many Wisconsin soldiers who fought on at Island Number 10 saw the balloonist and maybe a few remembered his Milwaukee appearances. Be that as it may, the American military was not really ready for an air force and only briefly experimented with balloons. In 1863, Steiner was back in Milwaukee with a balloon called the Hercules. On a fine summer's evening he and passenger William Strickland made a nice flight from downtown to North Point beach. Then Steiner moved

on to St. Paul, where he met Ferdinand von Zeppelin, and to La Crosse, where he flew his balloon over the Mississippi.

In 1871, Steiner returned again and this time with a balloon christened "The City of Milwaukee," probably the first aircraft named in honor of the city. Ascending from State Fair Park in West Allis, he made another harrowing crossing of Lake Michigan. He floated at high altitudes in near-freezing temperatures for six hours and 150 miles across the widest part of the lake and did not land until after dark when his grappling hook snagged a tree root near Kalamazoo, Michigan.

It was all in a day's work for a 19th century balloonist in Wisconsin or elsewhere. Ballooning was an uncertain profession and not just because of the vagaries of wind, weather and public gas works. Building a balloon, transporting it around the country and purchasing gas all cost money, yet no one had found much use for the airships except as entertainment at county and state fairs. Like the pioneer pilots of heavier-than-air craft, balloonists tended to be an adventurous, inventive lot. John Steiner, for example, developed a device using scrap iron and sulphuric acid to generate hydrogen gas so he would not have to rely on and pay for the "coal gas" produced at public gas works. Perhaps because of such cleverness balloonists were commonly referred to as "Professor," or perhaps it was because, like their balloons, they were often filled with hot air.

While balloon events were reported in the 1840s, the first confirmed balloon flight in Wisconsin took place in 1856 when "Professor" Joshua Pusey agreed to a flight at Milwaukee accompanied by Mrs. Theodore Reis. No fool she, Mrs. Reis agreed to go up only if the wind blew from the lake. On the day of the flight, the wind was barely discernable, but Mrs. Reis still refused to fly, because the sky was as foggy as soup. Pusey was less cautious, but lucky. He launched and fortunately drifted three-and-a-half miles to the southwest before alighting in rural Milwaukee county.

For the rest of the 1850s, and into the 1860s and '70s ballooning in the state was dominated by John Steiner, who felt quite at home among Milwaukee's German community.

He made his last visit in 1875, with a gigantic 100,000-cubic foot balloon that he proposed to fly across the Atlantic Ocean—if he could find investors to finance the trip. Hoping that his Milwaukee connection would pay off, he proposed launching what can be called a shakedown cruise from the city and not putting down until he reached the Atlantic Coast. The flight would, he hoped, generate enough publicity to attract investors to back a transoceanic hop. All he asked was that the people of Milwaukee pledge money enough to "guarantee against loss to himself," which meant paying for the gas to fill the balloon and providing whatever provisions the pilot would need on his trip east. This was probably the first time Wisconsinites had been asked to finance a trans-Atlantic flight, but certainly not the last. Sad to say, the people of Milwaukee were forthcoming enough only to finance a flight for Steiner and three passengers from the grounds of East High School to Waukesha. Although the balloon passed within sight of Pewaukee Lake, the flight was hardly a sufficient warm-up for the North Atlantic. Steiner did not attempt his transcontinental or his trans-Atlantic voyages, nor did he ever fly again in Wisconsin.

Another would-be trans-Atlantic balloonist visited Wisconsin in 1881. Samuel King, who had made his first flight in the 1850s and would continue ballooning until the 1900s, was one of the most experienced pilots in the United States. Like John Steiner, he had tried for years to attract backers for a flight to Europe, especially the United States Army Signal Corps. Carrying a gondola full of meteorological and scientific instruments supplied by the Corps and by inventor Thomas Edison, plus a Signal Corps weatherman, King launched the 100,000 cubic-foot Great Northwest at Minneapolis in September, 1881. Like John Steiner, his goal was to fly the balloon over Wisconsin and other northeastern states to a spot on the Atlantic coast as a warm-up for an Atlantic crossing. It was not to be. The balloon ran into trouble soon after lift off, had to make a forced landing, and was damaged seriously enough for King to cancel the voyage.

A month later, King tried again. For this voyage the Great Northwest was re-named the A. J. Nutting and the launch site was Chicago. Once again the gondola carried scientific instruments and a Signal Corpsman, Private J. G. Hashagan. Although they planned to travel east after they launched, King and Hashagan caught contrary currents that carried them across Illinois and into Wisconsin. They flew over the southwestern counties, and on to Sparta, Durand, Eau Claire and up the Chippewa River. After 20 hours and 550 miles, King slashed open the balloon and put down in the logged-over country of northern Chippewa County. They were a long way from civilization—five days, in fact. Hardly dressed for an outdoors journey on the Chippewa in October, the balloonists struggled through the cedar swamps and marsh meadows until they

reached Bruno Vinette's lumber camp on the Chippewa. Vinette fed them a lumberjack's meal of salt pork, biscuits and tea, which tasted mighty good after five days in which the only provision they had consisted of old sandwiches and a young porcupine they had trapped and cooked on a campfire. The hospitable Vinette also put the balloonists on a boat bound for Chippewa Falls, where they returned to civilization, casualties of yet another failed attempt at long-distance ballooning.

PLEASE POST THIS IN A CONSPICUOUS PLACE.

SPECIAL ATTRACTIONS.

Grand Balloon Ascension!

—AND—

RUNNING RACES,

—DURING THE—

WISCONSIN STATE FAIR,

At Madison, Wis.

Prof. Gimmer, of Cincinnati, in his Monster Balloon, will make a __ Ascension, filling his Balloon from the Gas Main that supplies the __ consin State University, and going far up beyond the clouds and __ of sight, on

Tuesday, September 9th, at 2:30 P. M.

After the Balloon Ascension there will be a Running Race of a mile and a half by a whole field of Horses which is destined to be

THE GREATEST RUNNING RACE

Ever Held in the West.

Old Camp Randall is one of the *most delightful Fair Grounds in the World.* Everybody should go to the Farmer's Show at Camp Randall, Madison, Wis.,

September 8th to 12th, 1879.

"AMERICA"

Holding 80,000 ft. of Gas, and capable of carrying five persons.

M. J. Cantwell, Printer, Madison, Wis.

Poster advertising the "Grand Balloon Ascension" at Madison in 1870. The balloon was inflated with coal gas generated by the plant at the university. (SHSW)

Ballooning was a precarious profession, but sometimes balloonists seemed to ask for trouble. "Professor" Denniston was one of them. After falling out of his gondola and crashing onto a Milwaukee rooftop in 1870, he went on tour with an unusual co-pilot. In Eau Claire, he advertised that he would fly his balloon accompanied in the gondola by a live black bear. The customary crowd of thrill-seekers showed up at the time the flight was scheduled, but Denniston did not. With the gate receipts carefully tucked into his pocket, he tried not to fly, but to flee, via a fast carriage. Waylaid by the crowd, he was forced into the basket and the balloon cut free of the ground. Denniston rose about one hundred feet, then released the gas and settled down to a quiet landing. The bear never did appear, but the crowd was appeased enough to stop talking about tar and feathers.

With bears coming into ballooning, other circus acts could not be far behind. Trapeze acts were popular over cities situated on large bodies of water, since a lake or river offered a softer cushion than the earth in the event of a slip-up. At Oshkosh, in 1878, "Signor Pedanto" performed acrobatics from a trapeze suspended beneath his balloon as he floated south along Lake Winnebago. He kept at it for about five miles, with spectators trailing along in carriages on shore and in boats on the lake. When the show was over, Pedanto opened the gas valve and gracefully settled to a landing in shallow water.

It was only a small jump, so to speak, from the balloon to the parachute, which "Captain" Thomas Scott Baldwin first successfully demonstrated in a jump from a balloon at San Francisco in 1887. In no more than five years, parachute jumping from balloons became a familiar county and state fair act in Wisconsin. One of the state's most spectacular balloon-parachute drops took place at the State Fair in 1899 when Ida LeRoy, "the daring young aeronaut from Mt. Vernon, Ohio," mounted her trapeze and took off in front of thousands of spectators in West Allis.

"Higher and higher went the big grey ball, smaller and smaller it grew," reported the Milwaukee Sentinel. When she reached an altitude of about 2500 feet, LeRoy slid off the trapeze and "shot down toward the earth for several hundred feet." During her free fall, which a future generation might call a sky dive, "thousands and thousands of people on the ground held their breath." Just when they thought the young woman would plummet all the way to the ground, the parachute opened and "the rapid descent of the brave little woman was checked and she began to flutter gradually to the ground."

LeRoy disappeared out of sight behind the fairgrounds fence and the spectators thought all the thrills were over. However, as she dropped to about 100 feet Le Roy noticed, "coming down the railroad track, in the middle of which I was going to land, a freight train." She judged that "by the distance between me and the train that I would land there just about in time to be run over." LeRoy tried to steer the chute away from the tracks but was unable to swing or kick to safety. Since she had time to think about it, she decided that as soon

as she touched ground—if she touched ground in front of the train—she would leap off the tracks. Then all she would have to worry about was whether the train would snag her parachute and drag her down the right of way until she slid under the wheels.

Fortunately for LeRoy, the locomotive engineer was alert. As the parachutist "fell just a few feet in front of the engine," he braked the train.

"A second more and I would have been ground to pieces," said LeRoy.

Unharmed by her near brush with death she continued to jump from balloons at low altitudes. She was one of a corps of touring balloonists who made hundreds of parachute jumps and, in fact, established the sport long before the military adopted it and even before the aeroplane was developed.

One of Wisconsin's first home-grown parachutists was Ed Freeman of Beaver Dam. Starting in 1898 and continuing until 1915, he put in an annual appearance at the Dodge County Fair. Unable to afford coal gas or hydrogen, Freeman lofted his balloon the old-fashioned way— with hot air. On the day he planned to make an ascension, he spread the bag out in a grassy spot with its narrow, open end draped over the mouth of a covered trench. At the other end of the trench he built a fire. When the initial smoke subsided and the coals were hot, a youthful assistant or two would fan the hot air up the trench and into the balloon. The trench technique, as a few balloonists had learned the hard way, was safer than building a fire directly beneath the airship.

In time, Freeman's balloon would fill and start to rise, requiring the aid of more young assistants for anchor duty. When the ground crew could hang on no longer, Freeman mounted the trapeze hanging below the balloon, signaled the boys to let go, and took off. When he had risen to what he deemed a safe height, he slid off the trapeze, opened his parachute and made a safe landing. There is no record of how and why Freeman took up balloon parachuting, nor if he ever jumped anywhere other than at fairs and carnivals in Beaver Dam, where he was the star attraction for 17 years.

Balloons and ballooning underwent a dramatic change at the turn of the century. The development of light and powerful gasoline engines—the same kind of engines that put heavier-than-air-machines aloft—also created new opportunities for the designers of lighter-than-air ships. Ferdinand von Zeppelin was one of the first, making his initial flight in an airship of his own

design in 1900. Four years later, after visiting Zeppelin in Europe, parachutist Thomas Baldwin mounted a second-hand Curtiss motorcycle engine on his own balloon and made the first successful flight in the United States of a steerable or "dirigible" balloon. Baldwin's dirigible, and others that followed, featured not a round but a cigar-shaped balloon with a catwalk instead of a gondola suspended below. An engine was mounted either at the forward end or in the middle of the catwalk, with a propeller in front and a rudder at the stern. To ascend, the pilot revved the engine to full speed and lifted the nose of the balloon by walking to the stern of the catwalk. To descend, he walked to the front. To steer he pulled on lines that ran the length of the catwalk and were attached to the rudder at the rear.

Two years after Baldwin's first American flight, a pair of dirigibles appeared in Wisconsin. The first was piloted by "Captain" William Matteray and was booked

for an exhibition flight on September 6, 1906 in Oconto. The second made a sensational flight over West Allis and Milwaukee a few days later.

Matteray's flight lasted much longer than he had intended. After waiting all day for the wind to moderate in front of a crowd of increasingly unfriendly spectators at the Oconto fairgrounds, he ignored his better judgment and, at 6:00 PM, launched his airship. No sooner was he aloft than he was in trouble. Strong westerlies pushed him out over Green Bay and, with his underpowered engine, he could make no headway against the wind to return to land. A Frenchman who had already flown a dirigible across the English Channel, Matteray was no stranger to over-the-water flying, so he was not alarmed until night began to fall. Hoping to make a safe landing on the ground, he released gas but found nothing below but the dark waters of Green Bay. He dropped ballast to gain altitude then rose into a cloud bank in which he

The "dirigible" or steerible airship flown by Jack Dallas from West Allis to Milwaukee in 1906. Two years earlier, pilot Charles Hamilton flew an identical dirigible to make the first controlled flight of an airship in Wisconsin. (WAHF)

A re-creation of a newspaper graphic displaying "The Perils of the Aeronaut" at Milwaukee.
(Milwaukee Journal-Sentinel)

lost visibility and floated right over the Door peninsula without seeing it. He was over Lake Michigan when he spotted the lights of "several big vessels" and dropped to within fifty feet of one ship. Believing he was rescued, he lowered his anchor rope and hailed a crewman on deck to catch the line, only to have the sailor ignore it and say that he was not "in the catching business."

Matteray floated on and tried to land again, but this time succeeded only in dunking himself to the waist in cold lake water. In order to rise out of the water, he dumped the last of his ballast, cut away the engine, then gained so much altitude that the air temperature around the balloon dropped below freezing. Ice formed on the damp silk and turned the catwalk into a treacherous, slippery, ramp. Cold, miserable and exhausted, with his

wet clothes frozen to his body, Matteray now found himself falling asleep—a potentially fatal condition in his circumstances. Exhausted as he was, he still possessed enough presence of mind to lash himself to the framework of the catwalk before letting himself doze. While the pilot slept, the balloon drifted east northeast across Lake Michigan, past Traverse City and Grand Traverse Bay and half way across the Lower Peninsula of Michigan until it lost altitude and bumped into a tree northwest of Gaylord. Roused from his sleep, Matteray made a lasso in the end of his mooring rope, looped it around a treetop and anchored the airship. He shinnied down the tree, made a bed out of his canvas rudder and, exhausted, fell asleep, only to be rudely awakened by a curious black bear who came nuzzling nearby. Happily for the stunned Matteray, the bear ambled off and the pilot fell back to sleep until dawn. He awoke to find himself lost in the woods, but not completely out of luck. After only a few hours of wandering, he found the tiny village of Wolverine, which had a railroad depot and a telegraph line which he could use to inform the world of his whereabouts. Then all he had to do was figure out how to transport his stranded airship out of the wilderness.

While William Matteray struggled in Michigan, Charlie Hamilton was flying high in Milwaukee. Equipped with a state-of-the-art dirigible designed by Tom Baldwin and powered with a dependable Curtiss engine, he was the center of interest at the 1906 State Fair. Wisconsin fair-goers had seen many a balloon ascension and parachute jump. They had even seen a few circus performers shot out of cannons, but they had never seen any device that could fly and carry a pilot who actually controlled the flight.

On September 10, 1906, Hamilton launched his airship at the fair grounds, ascended effortlessly to 700 feet and "sent the ship sailing through the air in every direction he desired" He then landed—not in Waukesha or Lake Michigan—but right back where he started. This flight was sensational, not because of the flight, but because it was controlled. Recognizing a good thing when they saw it, the fair managers asked Hamilton if he would go up again and fly to downtown Milwaukee. He willingly agreed and, as the Journal reported, "made the most sensational aerial flight ever seen in Milwaukee."

He took off from the fairgrounds and headed east, "with thousands of sky-gazing Milwaukeeans," looking up. He cruised effortlessly over the city, on course for its most notable civic landmark, city hall. On the way, he spotted the tall spire of Trinity Church on Ninth and Prairie Streets, flew for it and circled it several times. Then it was on over the business district to city hall, whose tower he also circled, before once again heading west. The flight was nearly silent, punctuated only by the rhythmic clicking of the Curtiss engine at 225 revolutions per minute and the spontaneous applause of the citizens of Milwaukee, who clapped for the pilot and his machine as they passed overhead.

Hamilton planned to return to the state fairgrounds and make a safe landing in the generous open space there. He would have made it too, had he not run out of gasoline. With the engine sputtering, the pilot was forced to set down on the west side of Milwaukee near Mount Calvary Cemetery, much to the delight of the neighborhood residents, who crowded around the airship and peppered Hamilton with questions until well past dark. The next morning Hamilton's crew arrived, gassed the engine, and the airship made its way back to the fairgrounds. Charlie Hamilton's simple flight from West Allis to Milwaukee and back, so routine and timid in terms of future developments, was astounding in comparison to what had come before. Instead of trusting to winds that could blow him anywhere from Minnesota to Michigan, Charlie Hamilton had been able to fly north, south, east and west. When trouble arose in the form of an empty gas tank he had been able to land safely and take off again to complete his journey. It was powered, controlled flight, the first ever witnessed in Wisconsin.

Charlie Hamilton's flight over Milwaukee was only one of many events that stimulated interest in aviation in the 1900s. In 1905, their interest had prompted a number of wealthy, prominent New York men to organize the first Aero Club in the United States. Although primarily interested in traditional ballooning, Aero Club members also supported the development of dirigible balloons and aeroplanes. In 1910, the Aero Club of America, became the first organization to license pilots in the United States.

The first Aero Club chapter in Wisconsin was organized in Milwaukee in March of 1908. Quite typically, its membership consisted of men of wealth and influence with names such as Smith, Plankinton, Watrous, Vilas and Pabst. The Club also had one of the few experienced, licensed balloon pilots in Wisconsin, Major Henry B. Hersey, who also headed the local office of the U. S. Weather Bureau. In 1906, Hersey and U. S. Army Lieutenant Frank P. Lahm won the first Gordon Bennett Trophy race, in a balloon that flew over 400 miles from Paris to Scotland.

In July of 1908, August Pabst authorized Hersey to purchase a 16,000 cubic foot balloon for the club. It did not arrive in time for the Milwaukeeans to fly in the big balloon race sponsored by the Chicago Aero Club on July 4, but Wisconsin was still represented there. Doctor Frederick Fielding, a summer resident of the village of Winneconne, near Oshkosh, did quite well in the Chicago race. Locally famous as a racer of automobiles

and motor boats, Fielding co-piloted a balloon that won the race by flying over 786 miles from Chicago in less than 24 hours.

While the balloon races sponsored by local clubs were interesting, none stimulated more excitement than the international Gordon Bennett Race. First organized by newspaper magnate James Gordon Bennett himself in 1906, the races were held in St. Louis in 1911. While the Milwaukee Aero Club did not launch a balloon in that race, Wisconsin played a part. On the day of the launch in October 1911, the weather pattern saw winds blow up the Mississippi River Valley. The balloon that flew the farthest was the Berlin II. Piloted by two German army officers, the Berlin II glided for 468 miles before landing in the woodland north of the Chippewa County village of Holcombe. This landing took place no more than twenty miles away from where Samuel King had set down with his balloon in 1881. The German pilots were more fortunate than their predecessors. They landed only about four miles outside of Holcombe and made their way to the village after a short hike through the underbrush. The balloon that placed second in the 1911 race was the Buckeye, piloted by two Americans, Lieutenant Frank P. Lahm and J. H. Wade. They landed near La Crosse after a 365 mile flight, packed up their gear and were on their way. Incidentally, although he had a long and successful career as a balloonist, Lieutenant Lahm is better-known as the United States Army's first aeroplane pilot.

As the aeroplane developed in the years after 1908, traditional ballooning waned. Balloons were much more costly and—more importantly—much less controllable than aeroplanes. Floating free at the mercy of the wind and weather was certainly not as attractive as a direct flight at the controls of a flying machine. Although balloon ascensions, trapeze artists and parachutists continued to appear in Wisconsin until World War I, they were increasingly supplanted by aviators and aeroplanes. Indeed, as late as 1922, the Milwaukee Aero Club sponsored a race in which thirteen balloons participated, including U. S. Army and Navy airships, but it was a rare event and the final one of its kind in Wisconsin.

The great contribution of the balloon to the history of aviation was as the precursor of things to come. Balloonists demonstrated that people could ascend to the heavens and survive. They showed that the rules of wind and weather could be observed, learned and used to navigate through the air and that aerial observation could be useful in scientific, economic and military endeavors. As the inventors of the dirigible demonstrated even before the Wright Brothers flew, controlled flight did not require wings or "planes," but it did require dependable engines. Even as carnival acts, balloons prepared the way for aeroplanes. A direct line runs from John Steiner, who first ballooned over Milwaukee in 1859 to John Kaminski and his Curtiss pusher in 1912, and continues on to the men and women who flew in their wake.[11]

OX-5-POWERED JENNY

Maximum speed 75 mph
Rate of climb 200 Feet/minute

1926

Above: Fueling a Jenny with a chamois cloth filter at a lakefront air show in Milwaukee in 1926. (WAHF)
Opposite: Young Brian Meisenheimer enjoying the view from the nose of his father's Curtiss Canuck at the first Milwaukee County Airport on Lisbon Road. (George Hardie)

Golden Age of Aviation

1919 -1941

WISCONSIN'S FIRST AIRPORTS, 1919 - 1926

If an airport is defined as a patch of ground exclusively designated as a place for aircraft to land and take off and where aircraft are fuelled, maintained and stored on a regular basis, the first airport in Wisconsin was at Rudolph Silverston's School and College of Aviation in West Allis in 1912. Several pilots kept flying machines there and several mechanics maintained them for about six months in 1912. They made Silverston's field a short-lived but real airport.

Another patch of ground that fits the definition of an airport early on is the farm acreage the Lawson Aircraft Company leased from the Francis Blesch family in Ashwaubenon. Here Lawson tested its MT-1 and MT-2 machines in 1917 and '18. With only two planes and no hangar, the Lawson operation was small, but still large enough to spawn an airport. After Lawson moved to Milwaukee late in 1918, the newly-organized Green Bay Aero Club took over the landing field, which was already known as Blesch Field. The Aero Club, which its organizers hoped would evolve into an aviation business, kept a Jenny at Blesch's for about five years. Then a private company called Brown County Airport Inc. moved in, built a hangar and maintained two runways. The airport remained under private management until 1933, when it was purchased and managed by Brown County. Blesch Field continued as

the Brown County Airport and Green Bay's main air field until 1948.

As the only airplane factory in the state, Lawson Aircraft had a special need for an airport. However, with so few airplanes and pilots before and during the war, the rest of the state could do quite well without one. When the war ended though, the situation changed. Due to military production and training programs, airplanes and pilots were available by the thousands and aviation offered commercial opportunities beyond the county fair thrill show. As Billy Mitchell said in a luncheon address to the Milwaukee City Club only a few months after the war, "You're going to have an entirely new era in world affairs as the result of aerial development. It will lead to new ways of doing things."

Milwaukee was ready for the new ways. The day after Mitchell spoke to the City Club, pilot Giles Meisenheimer landed a Jenny on the golf course at Lake Park. A Milwaukee native and Air Service veteran, Meisenheimer flew the plane up from Chicago for the George Browne Auto Agency, which was now selling Curtiss airplanes. Meisenheimer's plane was called "the first commercial aeroplane to enter Wisconsin" and its arrival heralded the state's entry into the general aviation business.

Earlier in the year, Milwaukee Mayor Daniel Hoan had met with the county park commission to discuss the urgent request of Alfred Lawson for a publicly-financed airport. Lawson was already

building what he called the "world's first airliner" in the auto pavilion of the State Fairgrounds and, as he told Mayor Hoan, he was not interested in trucking his plane all the way to Chicago merely for a test flight. Also, the perpetually under-capitalized Lawson venture could not afford to purchase or lease land for an air field. The county park commission was the logical department to develop an airport, since it already owned and managed large tracts of green space on the edge of the city, including a likely site on Lisbon Road in New Butler.

A legal hitch arose in the form of a state statute limiting the purposes to which county park land could be put, but this obstacle was overcome by an act of the legislature in July, 1919. In a few days, the county park commission set aside a portion of the New Butler property for an airport and authorized $5,000 for improvements. In August, Alfred Lawson used the field for the first flights of his 20-passenger airliner and Giles Meisenheimer, who had been using a farm field on the Beloit Road near National Avenue for a landing strip, moved to the county property. He built a hangar for his Jenny and became Milwaukee's first airport manager and fixed based operator. Sometimes called Zimmermann Field after the farmer who sold it to the county, Lisbon Road or Butler Field because of its location, or Currie Park because of the use to which the land was put after the county airport moved in 1926, this plot of ground was the first Milwaukee County Airport. It was also the first publicly-financed airport in the state and the

first facility in Wisconsin created specifically as a general purpose, municipal airport.

Milwaukee County Airport was open in time to host two of the most significant transcontinental flights of the early postwar period. Both flights were initiated by Billy Mitchell, who came home from the war determined to stimulate interest in and support for both civilian and military aviation. From his position as second in command of the Army Air Service, he launched army planes on highly-visible flights around the country. One of these missions was the "Round-The-Rim" flight of an army Martin Bomber in the summer and fall of 1919. A behemoth for its day, the twin-engined Martin and its crew of four took off from Washington, D. C. and flew up the East Coast to Maine, then headed west to the Pacific Coast via Cleveland, Chicago, Milwaukee, Minneapolis, Bismarck, and Spokane. The flight continued down the Pacific Coast then east along the southern border, turned north through the South Atlantic states and came back to Washington, for a total of 114 hours of flying time in 108 days to cover 9,823 miles.

The Martin spent six of those days parked at the Milwaukee County Airport. While attempting to take off from the new field, the 12,000-pound Martin blew two of its four of its tires. The runway may not have been graded as well as it might have been, or maybe the Martin's tires had taken too much wear. Either way, the flight was grounded for a week until replacement tires could arrive by rail.

While stranded in Milwaukee the Round-the-Rim crew was on hand to observe another Army flight as it passed through town. The "All-American Pathfinder" expedition was the extravaganza of American military aviation in 1919. Starting from Mineola, New York, nine Army JNs were dispatched to tour 171 cities across the country. They were accompanied by 87 crewmen in 39 army trucks, one of which weighed twelve tons and carried a complete airplane repair shop. Also part of the show was a "radio telephone" which kept one of the planes in close contact with the ground and a three hundred million candlepower searchlight whose beam was reported as visible for 110 miles.

The Pathfinders' mission was to show off army air power and also to assess the suitability of American airports for civil transport and air mail. In these beginning days of federal aviation regulation, the War Department was the supervising agency, which made the work of the Pathfinders important to every community they visited.

The Pathfinders arrived over Milwaukee at about one

MAP FOR PILOTS, 1920

hour before sunset on September 15, 1919. They had difficulty finding the new county airport and circled the city and suburbs searching for it. With night starting to fall, bonfires were lit to guide the planes, but only the commanding officer, Major. O. J. Baldinger, was able to find the airport and make a landing there. The rest of the squadron touched ground in farm fields and vacant lots around the north and western edge of Milwaukee and did not assemble at the airport until the next day.

Once they found it, the Pathfinders were quite pleased with the county airport. "Milwaukee has the best flying field in the airport at New Butler that we have seen since we left Mineola," said Captain H. J. Vogel, who commanded the Pathfinder ground crew. "Not only is the field excellent for its four-way take-off, but it shows evidence of having money liberally spent on it to perfect it in every respect."

So impressed was Major Baldinger that he said he thought Milwaukee was likely to beat out Chicago as a stopping point for the new air mail route the Post Office was considering. In the enthusiasm of the moment, the Major overlooked one geographic and aeronautical fact Milwaukee could not overcome. The city was located about

A map to guide "Sky Pilots" to the new Milwaukee County Airport published by the Curtiss-Wisconsin Aeroplane Company, the state's first fixed base operator. (George Hardie)

one-third up the length of Lake Michigan. Since land-based planes were not considered reliable enough to fly over the lake in 1919, air mail coming from the east would have to be transferred to seaplanes to reach Milwaukee. The alternative was to fly around the lake, which meant landing in Chicago, which is what the air mail pilots did when the route was established in 1920.

While the Pathfinders were in town, Mayor Hoan was notified that the War Department had officially designated the Milwaukee airport as air station W 33. Remembering the difficulty his pilots had in finding the field, Major Baldinger suggested that the W 33 title be painted on a rooftop or two at or near the airport so incoming pilots would not have to rely on bonfires.

The Pathfinders usually topped off a visit to a community with an exciting military air show. The Jennies would buzz each other in mock combat and dodge dummy anti-aircraft fire while the beam of the giant searchlight chased them around the sky. It would have been a great show in Milwaukee but rainy weather forced the army to cancel. After being grounded for two days at the airport, the squadron took off for its scheduled date in the Twin Cities.

On their way west, the Pathfinders stopped at another early Wisconsin airport. In the summer of 1919, Air Service veteran Captain Norman Moll brought his Jenny to La Crosse. He was able to persuade the city government to lease a farm field from the John Salzer Feed Company on the far southern edge of the city for a landing field. Moll then pitched an army surplus tent for a hangar,

parked his machine and announced the birth of the La Crosse Airport. Moll was fortunate that La Crosse was the home of John Salzer. One of the first aviation boosters in La Crosse, Salzer served on the welcoming committee for Hugh Robinson's Mississippi River flight in 1911.

The flying business was good for Moll in the summer of 1919. Paying customers showed up for rides nearly every good flying day and the newspaper supported his efforts with favorable articles. "I'd trade my flivver for it—if I had one," remarked La Crosse Tribune reporter Cora Bangsberg after flying in the passenger seat of Moll's Jenny. With that type of support, Moll decided to stay in town and, in 1920, opened a flying school and agency for Curtiss airplanes.

Moll inaugurated air freight in the La Crosse area when a local appliance dealer asked him to make a delivery in Onalaska. The pilot strapped a washing machine between the wings of his Jenny, flew to Onalaska and landed at the high school to deliver the merchandise without a scratch. He also inaugurated air mail delivery of newspapers when he dropped bags containing the La Crosse Tribune at West Salem and Bangor.

While dropping mailbags on West Salem was fun, Norman Moll made a more significant contribution to the growth of air mail in Wisconsin by setting up Salzer Field. The Army Pathfinders recommended the La Crosse airport as a refueling stop for the proposed Chicago-Milwaukee-Twin Cities mail route. What they would have said if Norman Moll hadn't created an airport is open to conjecture.

In August of 1920, a Martin Bomber making an experimental run on the air mail route landed at Salzer. Although it could carry up to 80,000 pieces of mail, the Martin's cargo consisted of only 86 pounds of mail plus its crew. Even with the light load the plane made slow progress against strong headwinds, and needed three hours and forty-five minutes to complete the trip from Chicago. After spending more than an hour on the ground in La Crosse, the Martin took off for Minneapolis/St. Paul, where it landed to much fanfare. Total air time from Chicago was five hours, twenty minutes.

After the flight of the Martin Bomber, La Crosse's status as a regular air mail stop was confirmed. Regular U. S. Post Office air mail service began on the Chicago-Milwaukee-La Crosse-Twin Cities route in November 1920, but it did not last long. While the federal government was ready to support air mail, it was not sure if it wanted a nationalized system with the Post Office hiring pilots and owning its own planes. In March 1921, while Congress debated the issue, service on the Chicago-Twin Cities route was suspended, then discontinued indefinitely in July when Congress slashed funding for the Post Office's air mail. Not until the summer of 1926, after the contract system was established, would air mail return to the Chicago-Milwaukee-Twin Cities route and La Crosse once again become a regular refueling stop.

Salzer Field continued to be the La Crosse airport until 1933, when it became too small and hazardous for the airplanes of the day.

Milwaukee, Green Bay and La Crosse were among Wisconsin's largest cities and logical sites for airport development in the first years after World War I, but airports were also being built in a few smaller communities.

Military service ended for Rellis Conant in January 1919, but flying did not. He came home to the Marquette County village of Westfield determined to spend as much time as possible in the cockpit of an airplane. In partnership with his brother John Conant, brother-in-law Bruce Hamilton and William Moss, who managed a woodworking firm in Westfield, Rellis began purchasing unused and slightly-dam-

aged war-surplus machines and refurbishing them for sale to other pilots. His landing field at the Marquette Country Fairgrounds in Westfield attracted pilots from all over the state who were looking for a good deal on a Jenny or a Canuck, as Canadian-made Jennies were called. In 1919, a new OX-5 powered Jenny still cost about $5,000, but a re-conditioned Canuck could be had for less than $3,000, which is why the Canadian planes were very popular in Wisconsin.

The little Westfield landing field soon became home to a small aircraft rebuilding shop. A crew of local men repaired frames, stretched and doped canvas, repaired old motors and installed new ones. They also customized planes for barnstormers by replacing the single seat in the front cockpit of the Jenny or Canuck with a double seat, so the plane could carry more paying passengers.

Rellis Conant, who never needed much of an excuse to get into the air,

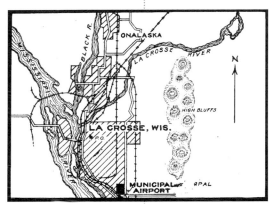

A U.S. Army Martin bomber on an experimental air mail run at La Crosse's Salzer Field in 1920 and the 1927 Aeronautics Commission Map locating the airport on the south side of the city. (UW-La Crosse and WAHF)

soon became one of the most well-known pilots in Wisconsin. One of the first Wisconsin barnstormers of the post war years, he would turn up in Madison one day, Phillips the next, then Waukesha or Milwaukee, where he sold airplanes in partnership with East Side Auto. In September 1919, John Conant became the first Wisconsin legislator to fly

to a legislative session in Madison, thanks to his brother Rellis.

When Rellis married Marjorie Hamilton in 1920, the ceremony took place in an airplane on its way from Florida to Cuba. Later on that year, Conant entered the field of political advertising when he used his plane to promote the candidacy of Roy P. Wilcox in the Wisconsin governor's race. In 1923, Conant and Marty Warshauer became the first pilots to fly a land-based plane across Lake Michigan. Although their Jenny was about as reliable as an airplane could be in 1923, Conant's and Warshauer's lake hop was a courageous endeavor.

The flying would have continued for many more years and it is likely that Rellis Conant would have made a large contribution to aviation in Wisconsin. In 1925, however, a student he was instructing froze at the controls of a Standard biplane and crashed the machine into the ground, nose first at full speed. Neither the student nor Rellis Conant survived.

One of the fields that Conant probably landed on early in his career was in Black River Falls. War veteran James Pugh landed a Jenny at the Jackson County Fairgrounds there in the summer of 1920 and along with Dr. Eugene Kroh, founded the Jackson County Aero Company. Pugh was the pilot, Krogh the president, with the plane available for exhibitions and "probably for flights for hire by the hour or trip." The airport remained at the Fairgrounds for about five years before it was moved to Vaudreuil on the edge of Black River Falls.

Marshfield was also one of Wisconsin's airport pioneers. In the summer of 1920, Jake Blum, owner of the Palace garage announced that he would buy a Curtiss machine that touring pilot Don Bennett would fly at air shows and exhibitions. It would be kept at the Weber farm on the edge of the city. About the same time, M.B. Brunkalla of Athens bought a OX-5, J-1 Standard from the George Browne agency in Milwaukee at the "flyaway" price of $2,750. Brunkalla later formed a partnership with Max Berghammer who completed nearly sixteen hours of flight instruc-

tion at Dave Behncke's Checkerboard Field near Chicago in 1921. Two years later another airplane arrived at Marshfield when auto dealers Walter Miner and Henry Peil bought their Curtiss and established an airport on Highway 13 at the Wood-Marathon County line. In 1925, just about everyone involved in aviation in Marshfield—Brunkalla, Berghammer, Miner, Peil—incorporated Ski-Hi Airways. This combination came apart after a few years and, in 1928, Berghammer joined Herman Dickoff to organize the Marshfield Aerial Service Company, which purchased 79 acres from the Gessert family on the southeast edge of the city. This property served as Marshfield's airport until the municipal airport was established in 1945.

The most famous rural airport in Wisconsin was built by the four Larson Brothers in the Winnebago Town of Winchester in 1922. It was the creation of eldest brother Roy, who had spent his tour in the World War looking up at flying machines from the bottom of a trench. He resolved to become a pilot when he came home, even though he knew it would not be easy. The Larsons were a traditional Norwegian-American family with strong ties to farming. Roy's father had died young and Roy knew that his mother, who had never seen a flying machine, would not understand his desire to risk his life as a pilot. When the subject came up, she tried to keep Roy on the ground by making him promise that she would never see him fly an airplane. Roy put a literal interpretation on his mother's words and told himself that she did not say he could not fly in so many words, only that she did not want to see him do it.

On the pretext of spending a week at the State Fair in September 1920, Roy boarded a southbound train, but rode right by West Allis and on to the Ralph Diggins Flying School in Chicago. He passed the short course for pilots, soloed in a Jenny and returned home on schedule.

Roy was now ready and able to fly, but would not openly defy his mother. Early in 1921, after seeing her four sons reach manhood and working together on the farm, Mrs. Larson passed away. Roy waited about one year then moved to Duluth, Minnesota, where he had heard of a Jenny for sale, cheap. He bought the plane in partnership with another flyer and started earning a few dollars carrying passengers and taking aerial photographs that he sold to businesses in Duluth and Superior. In the winter, Roy and his brother Leonard took a course in aircraft mechanics in Kansas City and in the spring of 1922, they were ready to return home. One morning in May, Roy's brothers—Clarence, Newell and Leonard—drove the farm wagon down to the depot in the crossroads village of Larsen where the night freight had deposited several large wooden crates. Inside the crates were two Standard J-1 airplanes and their Hall-Scott motors.

Roy returned home at the end of the summer and, with his brothers, assembled the two Standards and laid out a runway on their father's best hayfield. It was a symbolic gesture that showed how the times were changing in Winchester, Wisconsin and America.

In January 1923, with no field work or milking to do, the Larson boys took their axes to the farm woodlot and felled some trees. A neighbor with a portable sawmill came round and turned the logs into boards, which were stacked to dry until summer. When the weather warmed, the Larsons and their neighbors built a hangar with space for four airplanes. It was a fine, solid building that earned a backhanded compliment from one of the neighbors who said that the Larson hangar was a better building than their dairy barn. A good Wisconsin dairyman, he couldn't fathom how any farmer could think an airplane deserved better quarters than a cow. Roy Larson had no trouble with that assumption. He was already flying exhibitions in Winnebago, Outagamie and other nearby counties and had taught Leonard how to fly. When winter brought the flying season to a close the Larsons stored their two Standards in the hangar along with a third that Roy was rebuilding.

About this time, Elwyn West, a young pilot from Lind Center in Waupaca County, landed his Canuck at the Larson Airport and rolled it into the hangar for the winter. West was the first of hundreds of pilots to land at Larson's, which became the gathering place for flyers in east-central Wisconsin. If you had been to Larson's, and could call Roy and later Leonard a friend, you were a real pilot. Youngsters like Steve Wittman from Fond du Lac and Howard Morey from Madison landed at Larson's. Noel Wien parked his Standard there before heading off to establish Alaska Airways. A Larson cousin, wild Clyde Lee from Oshkosh, badgered Roy to teach him how to fly at Larson's. It was the first step in a journey that concluded with Lee's attempting a trans-ocean flight as bold as Charles Lindbergh's.

Larson's has been called the first airport in Wisconsin, but others were operating earlier. Instead it should be identified as the longest continuously operated private airport in the state. Remaining in use as Leonard Larson's landing strip until 1990, the Larson Airport remained active on its original site longer than any other airport in Wisconsin.

About the same

time the Larson Brothers were felling timber for their hangar in Winchester, Anton Brotz was building his airport in Sheboygan. Work started on a 48' x 48' foot hangar on the 31-acre site Brotz had selected adjacent to a cemetery on the south-

Roy Larson in the cockpit at the family airport in Larsen, a few miles west of Neenah. (Betty Eckstein)

Bottom: Anton Brotz's hangar and airplane at the first Sheboygan County Airport. (WAHF)

west side of the city.
Born in Sheboygan
in the 1878, Brotz
had built his own
automobile in
1902 and, twenty
years later, took up
flying as the middle-
aged father of a
teenaged son. Like Roy
Larson, Anton Sr. went to
Chicago to learn how to fly from Ralph
Diggins. He then came home to show Anton Jr. the
ropes. "Tony" Brotz became an avid flyer who participated in air races in the 1920s and pursued his
own career as an aircraft engineer who helped
design the B-25 Bomber.

Anton Sr. worked in the research department
at the Kohler Company and brought a methodical,
cautious approach to his aviation efforts. He
emphasized that airplanes stopping at his airport
would "secure the right kind of fuel, oil or minor
repairs." Dependability of this sort, when pilots
routinely carried a patch of chamois cloth to filter
gasoline which came from uncertain sources, was
new to aviation. Daredeviltry was still part of the
game, but would play a smaller part in it as more
people of Anton Brotz's
persuasion entered the
field. If ever there was a
pilot who resolved to be
old instead of bold, it
was the engineer from
Sheboygan.

After his hangar was
completed in the spring
of 1923, Brotz brought
an OX-5-powered, JN4-D
(the most common Jenny
model) and a Curtiss J-1

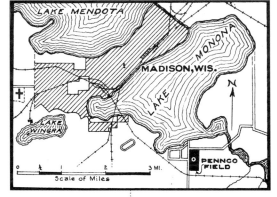

lage. The Woodson
had a 260
Horsepower
Salmson power
plant and must
have moved like a
rocket compared to
Brotz's other planes.
Typically cautious,
he parked the Woodson in a
new, fireproof, metal hangar.
Fireproof, but not windproof. In the
spring of 1927, a big wind lifted the building off its
foundation and collapsed it on top of the Woodson.

Brotz rebuilt his Woodson and then decided
that the airport could be replaced as well. He
accepted the invitation of Walter Kohler to move
his operation and supervise the construction of the
new village airport in Kohler. With Anton Brotz,
Tony Brotz, Walter Kohler, Werner Bunge, Mel
Thompson and many others on hand, the Kohler
airport would soon become one of the most active
aviation centers in the state.

A landing field remained in use at the site of
the old Brotz Field, but it was overshadowed by
Kohler throughout the 1930s and '40s. Kohler
remained the leading airport in the Sheboygan area
until the Sheboygan County Airport was built in
1959.

Other airports were also beginning in the mid-
1920s. In Eau Claire, Guy Wood, Leo McDonald
and M. A. Sine organized the Eau Claire Airplane
Corporation in 1923. They leased 80 acres for an
airport on the bluff about a mile and a quarter
south of the business district on State Street. Like
Rellis Conant, the Eau Claire men purchased war-
surplus Canucks and Standards, refurbished them
and sold them to pilots. The south side airport continued to serve Eau Claire until after World War II.

Wausau's first airport began on the northern
edge of the city in May of 1926.
Wausau native George Turner, who
had been flying in Virginia, returned
home with veteran flyer John P.
Wood and organized the Wausau
Airplane Service. They brought three
planes to a landing strip they laid out
on old Highway 10 north of the city:
a Curtiss Jenny, a "Hisso"-Standard
powered by a 130 horsepower
Hispano-Suiza motor and a brand
new Waco 9 that was one of the first
of its kind in the state.

The partners set up a "general
commercial aviation business,"

Standard to the airport. He planned
to use the planes to take up passengers and fly exhibitions, but Brotz
was not really a barnstormer of the
Rellis Conant school of flying.
Indeed, at a time when crashes were
common, he could claim the dubious
distinction of having his planes
destroyed while they were on the
ground in the hangar. A fire caused
by a bolt of lightning claimed the
Jenny, the Standard and the hangar
in 1925. Brotz came back by purchasing a Woodson Express, one of the
first airplanes with an all-wood fuse-

which included airplane sales and service, flight instruction, passenger charters, advertising, exhibitions and aerial photography. They got off to a good start, selling two planes in their first month of operation. John Wood and his Waco went on to have one the most distinguished—but brief—aviation careers in Wisconsin. Also brief was the lifespan of the first Wausau airport he founded. It was

the days of the Wright Flyer, youngsters during World War I, Wittman and his cohorts would take aviation from the Jenny to the jet in three decades. He began his journey in Byron in 1924.

Another member of aviation's second generation began his career in 1924 when 19-year-old Howard Morey decided that life was far too tame behind the counter of his father's lumberyard in

replaced by Alexander Field in 1928.

The Oshkosh airport that would become the home of Steve Wittman and the Experimental Aircraft Association Fly-In began in 1925. Richard Lutz who, along with Army Air Service veteran Florian Manor, had been flying a Jenny out of a landing strip on the Fourth Street Road since 1920, organized a company called The Oshkosh Airport, Incorporated. Francis Lamb, Albert March and Arthur Leupold were Lutz's partners in the original purchase of 100 acres on the southwestern fringe of the city. The airport remained privately-owned until 1940, when it became the Winnebago County Airport. Steve Wittman moved north from Fond du Lac to manage the Oshkosh airport in 1931.

Wittman had taught himself to fly in a J-1 Standard he and a friend purchased and assembled at his family's home in Byron, a few miles southeast of Fond du Lac. It was 1924 and the 18-year old Wittman was a member of what can be called American aviation's second generation. Babies in

the Washburn County village of Birchwood. He went off to the Heath Flying School in Chicago and mastered the ways of the JN-4. In partnership with a wealthy young Texan, Morey bought a Jenny and barnstormed in Illinois until the fall of 1925. With winter coming they thought they would move to Birchwood and continue to fly the plane off the frozen lakes of northern Wisconsin. On the way, the pilots stopped overnight in Madison, where they woke to find their Jenny buried by a snowstorm. Morey's Texas partner decided that winter flying in Wisconsin was not for him and abandoned his half-interest in the Jenny, but the boy from Birchwood didn't think a Madison snowstorm amounted to all that much.

He staked down his plane on the lee side of a barn and went home for the winter, but came back ready to fly in the spring of 1926. Morey then met Daniel P. Egan, an auto salesman and aviation enthusiast who had earmarked the Weber farm south of Lake Monona as a good site for an airport. Egan and restaurateur Edgar Quinn put up operat-

Howard Morey's Pennco Flyer at the Madison Airport. The local Pennsylvania Oil distributor paid Morey $150 per month for advertising painted on his JN-4. (WAHF)

ing cash, Morey put up his airplane, and the trio established the Madison Airways Corporation. The company took out a lease on farmer Weber's field, made a deal with the Pennsylvania Oil Company and, for a monthly fee of $150, named their new airport Pennco Field. It was the first airport worthy of the name in Madison. After the owners of the Royal Transit Bus Company invested in Madison Airways, the field was renamed Royal Airport. It would remain Madison's busiest air field until the late 1930s.

While airports were opening all around the state in the early and mid-1920s, activity was continuing where it all started, in Milwaukee. Thomas Hamilton, who had turned the Matthews Brothers Woodworking Company into a defense contractor supplying propellers to the army air service in World War I, made a very successful transition to peacetime production after the war. In 1920, he established the Hamilton Aero Manufacturing Company to build wood and metal propellers and pontoons. Hamilton was a pilot himself as well as a designer with new inventions to test. He also had many customers who wanted to fly to his factory so he needed an airport. In 1920, he purchased 56 acres of farmland on East Layton Avenue west of Cudahy and opened Hamilton Field. Activity at Hamilton's increased every year, culminating in 1926, when Hamilton's became the Milwaukee stop on the Ford Reliability Air Tour.

While Hamilton's Airport was thriving, the Milwaukee County Airport on Lisbon Road was having its difficulties. Adequate for the air traffic of 1919, the airport's shortcomings became evident in only a few years. Bracketed by a cemetery on the north, railroad tracks and high-tension power lines on the west, and the Menominee River on the east, it was sandwiched into a narrow north-south corridor and could not easily expand. In addition, pilots did not appreciate the flooded quarry that sat at the end of the 1500 foot-long east-west runway.

The county airport's inadequacies reached the crisis stage after it became a regular air mail stop in the summer of 1926. On one night the farmer the county hired to mow the airport grass left his hayrake parked in the middle of the runway, unaware that the air mail plane from Chicago was scheduled to arrive shortly after dawn the next morning. When pilot Nimmo Black arrived in his Laird Biplane he had to make a white-knuckle landing between the hayrake and the hangars. Along for the ride that morning was Black's boss, air mail contractor Charlie Dickenson, who had quite a few colorful words to say to the airport manager. He also told the County Park Commission that unless Milwaukee improved its airport facilities, his air mail planes would not land there. As is often the case, a crisis event points out a larger, chronic problem, and the hayrake on the runway acted as the indicator of the inadequacies of Milwaukee's airport. On the other hand, Milwaukee's was not the only airport to bedevil air mail pilots in 1926. Livestock straying onto the Minneapolis/St. Paul landing field was such a nuisance in 1926 that the police cited neighboring farmers nineteen times for trespass of cows, sheep, horses and goats.

In October 1926, the Milwaukee County Park Commission purchased the Hamilton Airport. It was renamed Milwaukee County Airport in January 1927 and, with many changes and additions, has remained in the same location ever since. The timing was right, for 1927 was a seminal year for aviation and the development of airports in Wisconsin. After Charles Lindbergh's solo flight across the Atlantic, a sort of airport-mania would take hold in communities large and small throughout the state. Places slow to jump on the airport bandwagon would catch up with the pioneers and, by 1931, Wisconsin would have sixty-one entries listed in a federal Department of Commerce directory of airports and landing fields.[1]

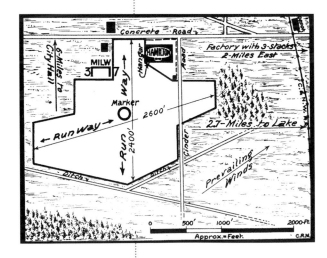

AIR WAYS, AIRLINES
AND AIR MAIL

On the morning of February 9, 1921, a Junkers-Larson J.L.6 monoplane took off from Checkerboard Field near Chicago to fly the mail route to Minneapolis/St. Paul. The flight to Milwaukee was uneventful, but a snowstorm west of Madison forced pilot William Carroll to land on the sandy flats of the Wisconsin River near Lone Rock. An all-aluminum, low-wing model with a crew of three and twice the cargo capacity of the older D.H. 4 mail plane, the J.L.6 was, so the Post Office hoped, its airplane of the future.

After the weather cleared at Lone Rock, Carroll took off for his scheduled refueling stop at La Crosse's Salzer Field. As the airplane came over the bluff east of the field, it suddenly dropped into a dive, crashed and burst into flames. Carroll, a

war veteran who had made the inaugural air mail flight on the Chicago-Twin Cities route in August 1920, died, along with co-pilot Arthur Rowe and mechanic Robert Hill.

The tragedy in La Crosse had reverberations throughout American aviation. It occurred in the midst of a debate on the government's role in aviation and was used by those who opposed a nationalized air mail system as yet another example of why the government should not be in the aviation business. When the Republican administration of Warren Harding came into office in March of 1921, the air mail budget was slashed and feeder lines, including the Chicago-Twin Cities route, were discontinued. Air Mail service survived only on the transcontinental route that ran from New York to San Francisco via Chicago and Denver.

The debate did not end with the shutdown of air mail feeder lines. Concerned with safety, efficiency and, ultimately, financial aid, the fledgling

Loading the mail into a made-in-Milwaukee Hamilton Metalplane flown by Northwest Airways at Milwaukee County Airport, 1928. Air mail subsidies helped fledgling airlines grow in their early years. (WAHF)

Billy Mitchell and Anthony Fokker at Milwaukee in 1922. Faithful to his home town, Mitchell flew Fokker to Milwaukee so the aircraft builder could look it over as a factory site. (George Hardie)

aviation industry sought federal involvement in its affairs. It was, as Secretary of Commerce Herbert Hoover pointed out in 1921, "the only industry that favors having itself regulated by government." Ironically, in light of the repercussions following the crash in La Crosse, in a few years, one of the most powerful arguments for federal regulation was the safety record of the only regulated air service in the country, the United States Air Mail. In 1924, though it flew a regular transcontinental schedule in all kinds of weather, the Air Mail had one fatal accident for every 463,000 miles flown, as compared to commercial aviation with one fatality for every 13,500 miles. The lesson was obvious but the discussion continued and Wisconsin played a role.

One of the first arguments against federal regulation of aviation was constitutional. Many legal scholars believed that an amendment to the constitution was necessary before the federal government could set rules for aviation. The point was settled in February, 1922 when the United States Supreme Court ruled on the case of the Wisconsin Railroad Commission, the predecessor of the modern Department of Transportation, versus the Chicago, Burlington and Quincy Railroad. The Court determined that the federal government's power to regulate interstate commerce also gave it power to regulate intrastate commerce. In other words, if the federal government could regulate a railroad that runs across state lines, it could also regulate the operations of that railroad within state

lines. By extension, if the federal government could regulate railroad operations inside a state, it could also regulate aviation operations there. Ultimately, the Wisconsin ruling would enable the federal government to license pilots and aircraft, draw up uniform rules for airport design and construction and establish communication systems compatible throughout the land no matter how small the airport and even if the pilots who used it never fly out of state.

Once it was established that the federal government could regulate aviation, the question of how to do it entered the public forum. In the early 1920s, aviation had no more prominent a spokesman than General Billy Mitchell, whose public profile was at its height after Air Service bombers under his command sank the confiscated German battleship Ostfriesland in July 1921. Mitchell extended his call for a unified command of all military aviation to the civilian sector by proposing that a single government agency oversee army, navy, commercial and general aviation in the United States. As his opponents pointed out, the General was proposing the aeronautical equivalent of a combined department of the Navy, Coast Guard, merchant marine, ocean passenger service and recreational boating all in one.

Nonetheless, Mitchell had supporters in Congress, including Progressive Republican Representatives John Nelson of Madison and Florian Lampert of Oshkosh. Nelson had gained a brief measure of fame by opposing federal legislation proposed by President Calvin Coolidge in 1924. Employing the rhetoric of the Progressive tradition, Nelson charged that an "aircraft trust" was at work in the Congress and exercising undue influence on the new air mail legislation that was passed as the Kelly Act in 1925. Since the Kelly Act resulted in regular subsidies that all but created the American airline industry, Nelson's point of view may have had some validity.

The Kelly Act ordered the Post Office to contract for air mail service with privately-owned air carriers and, along with the Air Commerce Act of 1926, is credited as the midwife of modern American aviation. However, a hazardous route was traversed between the initial authorization of mail contracts in the Kelly Act and the establishment of aviation regulation under the Air

Commerce Act, including the roadblock thrown up by Billy Mitchell.

Mitchell's proposal for a unified aviation agency gained support during hearings conducted by Congressman Lampert, who headed a special committee investigating military aviation contracts in the summer of 1925. At the Lampert hearings, General Mitchell expressed some of his most severe and well-publicized criticisms of the army's and the navy's management of American aviation. However, after Mitchell's searing public criticism of the high command in September 1925, the tide turned. President Coolidge ordered Mitchell court-martialed and established his own aviation board, headed by Wall Street banker Dwight Morrow. With his court-martial looming on the horizon, Mitchell made an uncharacteristically subdued presentation before Morrow's committee.

Dwight Morrow's panel recommended that civilian and military aviation remain separate and Congressman Lampert agreed. His committee also declared that it could find no "aircraft trust" and recommended that a "bureau of Air Navigation" be created within the Commerce Department. It was another defeat for Billy Mitchell, and its announcement during his court-martial helped to neutralize public opinion on Mitchell's case. Too late to help Mitchell, the Lampert Committee also recommended that the army and navy air forces be combined into a unified "department of defense." Like many of Mitchell's ideas, this proposal was implemented, but not until many years after he first made it.

The Air Commerce Act of 1926 established federal regulation of aviation in the United States. Among its most important provisions were the certificate system for regulating aircraft construction, the licensing of pilots and aircraft, minimum standards of health monitored by exams for pilots, the creation of the airway system of air traffic control and the expansion of air mail.

The first manifestation of aviation's new regime came to Wisconsin with the restoration of the Chicago-Milwaukee-La Crosse-Twin Cities air mail route, now identified as Contract Air Mail #9, or CAM-9. The first contractor for CAM-9 was Charles "Pop" Dickinson, a retired Chicago seed dealer who, when asked why he wanted to "lose money in aviation," declared that he was "trying to open the way for commercial aviation" and that he "might as well spend my money for Uncle Sam."

He opened the way in June 1926, with Dickinson Airways, whose flight line consisted of three Laird biplanes powered by Wright J-4 engines, plus two home-built, open cockpit

The Court-Martial of Billy Mitchell

"The battleship is obsolete. This is the day of the airplane and submarine. In these two forces will lie the strength in the next war," said Billy Mitchell in August of 1925. The occasion was a statement to the press marking the publication of his book Winged Defense, which was a summation of the opinions he had been voicing with increasing vehemence on the state of the nation's aerial defenses since the end of World War I.

Mitchell's most dramatic public moment occurred in 1921 when a squad of Martin Bombers under his command demonstrated the power and the future of aerial warfare by sinking the captured German armored battleship Ostfriesland and several other naval vessels, at sea off the coast of Virginia. One reporter described Mitchell's feat as "the victory of the air force against the craft which has been for centuries the chief power of empires...one seemed to be watching the end of an era."

Historical eras die neither cleanly nor swiftly, and they often claim the messenger of the new era as the price of their passing. So it was with Billy Mitchell.

A few weeks before the publication of Winged Defense, Mitchell's term as assistant chief of the air service had expired and he had been "demoted and exiled" to the command of air forces at Fort Sam Houston near San Antonio, Texas. Mitchell was out of Washington, D.C., but not out of the spotlight. The Select Committee chaired by Oshkosh Congressman Florian Lampert and the Morrow Commission appointed by President Coolidge were both in session and Mitchell's views were much in evidence even if he was not.

Mitchell was already near the precipice of dismissal from the army for his outspoken and public criticism of the War Department and the army and navy establishment when his reaction to two aviation mishaps pushed him over the edge.

On August 31, 1925 two Navy P-N9 Flying Boats, each with five crew members on board, lifted off from San Francisco Bay to make the first attempt to fly from the mainland to Hawaii. P-N9-2 was forced down by an engine oil leak shortly after take-off, but P-N9-1, piloted by Commander John Rodgers, cleared the Golden Gate and set its course for Oahu. Twenty-two hours later, on September 1, the P-N9-1 missed a rendezvous with the seaplane tender Aroostock, and was lost somewhere in the Pacific.

On September 2, the Navy airship Shenandoah, with a crew of forty-three, slipped its mooring at Lakehurst, New Jersey, to begin a tour of the Great Lake states that would include a flight across Wisconsin from Milwaukee to Minneapolis/St. Paul. While over southern Ohio, the Shenandoah encountered an electrical storm. The airship broke apart, drifted in pieces and crashed to earth, with all officers and men lost.

Mitchell believed that the War Department had authorized the flights of the P-N9s and the Shenandoah in response to his criticisms of the navy's reliance on obsolete airplanes and air ships. More than once he had stated that the United States no longer needed to rely on sea-based defenses. The battleships should be mothballed, the blimps deflated, and the U.S. should defend its shores and overseas possessions with a land-based air force of up-to-date pursuit airplanes and bombers under independent command. With nearly fifty aviators lost with the P-N9 and the Shenandoah, and in response to a self-serving public statement by Navy Secretary Curtis Wilbur, Mitchell penned a 6,000 word indictment that charged "these accidents are the direct results of incompetency, criminal negligence and almost treasonable administration of the national defense by the war and navy departments."

The reaction was swift and telling. Upon orders of President Coolidge, Mitchell was relieved of duty and charged for insubordination under the 96th Article of War. It was the first event of one of the most eventful months in the history of American aviation. The Lampert and Morrow investigations of civil and military aviation were underway, along with an inquiry into the Shenandoah disaster, all accompanied by avid press coverage. Good news came on September 9, when the downed P-N9-1 met a submarine on routine patrol just off the island of Kauai. The plane had run out of gas four hundred miles short of the Hawaiian Islands, made a forced landing in mid-ocean and had drifted through the Navy's search net until the crew jury-rigged a sail and navigated the plane to Kauai.

continued on page 67

machines and a cabin job supplied by his pilots. "Celerity, Certainty, Security," read the motto Dickinson emblazoned on the fuselages of his planes, a worthy aspiration difficult to achieve from the very first day of service.

The weather was threatening on June 7, 1926, when four of Dickinson's pilots took off from Chicago's Maywood Field and two more took off from Wold-Chamberlain Field at Minneapolis. Of the Chicago quartet, two made forced landings in southern Wisconsin, one got as far as La Crosse, while only one, Nimmo Black and his Laird, made the Twin Cities, eight hours behind schedule. Of the Minneapolis crew, William Brock flew in front of the gale and made Chicago in four hours, including stops in La Crosse and Milwaukee. Elmer Partridge flew no more than ten miles from the airport before the wind forced him down in a fatal crash.

Dickinson continued to struggle with adverse conditions until August when, reduced to only one pilot and one surviving Laird plane, he sent his contract back to the Post Office. He was still game for aviation so, at age 67, he took up air racing and stayed in it for another decade.

Despite Charlie Dickinson's unfortunate start, the terms of the CAM-9 contract were attractive to at least one new bidder. Lewis H. Brittin, an engineer working for the St. Paul Association, a business and civic organization, had assembled a group of investors from Detroit and St. Paul to incorporate Northwest Airways. With $300,000 in capital, the new company had deeper pockets than Charlie Dickinson and better luck as well. In September 1926, the Post Office accepted Northwest's uncontested bid of $2.75 per pound of mail and service returned to CAM-9 on October 1.

Northwest hired three pilots, Robert W. Radall, Charles "Speed" Holman and Dave Behncke at $75 per week, and leased two Curtiss OX-5 Orioles and a Thomas Morse Scout for them to fly. Planes were scheduled to fly to and from Chicago and St. Paul daily in time to meet the morning and afternoon mail trains. The Oriole and the Scout were open-cockpit planes meant to carry a pilot and the mail but not any passengers, although it would have been a rare and hardy passenger willing to fly in an open plane over Wisconsin in the winter. Indeed, with paying passengers in mind, and after only one month, Northwest took delivery of its first cabin planes. Holman, Behncke and Eddie Stinson himself each piloted a Stinson Detroiter biplane from the factory in Detroit to St. Paul. The Detroiters could carry the mail, a pilot and three passengers at a cruising speed of 85 MPH. They went into regular service between St. Paul and Chicago, with stops at La Crosse and Milwaukee in July 1927. Air fare was $50, one way.

Northwest quickly expanded throughout Wisconsin, with service extended from Milwaukee to Fond du Lac, Oshkosh, Appleton and Green Bay in 1928 and to Madison in 1929. The one-way fare between Milwaukee and Green Bay was six dollars. A year later flights began from Madison to Chicago with stops in Janesville and Beloit. Northwest airplanes also flew over Wisconsin on the non-stop Chicago-to-Rochester, Minnesota, route.

Northwest did a good job of living up to Charlie Dickinson's motto of "Celerity, Certainty, Security." In the first six months of 1929 on the CAM-9 route, Northwest flew 299,336 of 328,157 scheduled miles, an excellent record considering the weather in a typical Minnesota-Wisconsin-Illinois winter, not to mention the equally unpredictable spring and summer. Northwest flew a greater percentage of its scheduled air mail miles than carriers working in comparable weather on the Chicago-Kansas City, the New York-Chicago and the New York-Boston routes. In the air mail business, reliability paid off, with Northwest carrying 65,610 pounds of mail for which it earned $180,378 in the first six months of 1929. Although it was one of the shorter air mail routes, CAM-9 proved to be a solid foundation for the company that became Northwest Airlines.

While the story of the early days of Northwest Airlines in Wisconsin can be told in terms of airports, equipment and earnings, another perspective is offered by Joe Bednar of La Crosse. He served as ground crew, traffic controller, weather observer and ticket agent for the six years, 1926-1932, when Northwest landed at Salzar Field.

Bednar began his aviation career informally as a service station operator for Cities Service Oil, the company that supplied Northwest in St. Paul. Bednar also lived conveniently adjacent to Salzar Field and could meet planes with his fuel truck on short notice. He started refueling planes with a gas can and a funnel as soon as Northwest started using Salzar, and progressed with the airline as it moved from Curtiss Orioles and Stinson Detroiters to Hamilton Metalplanes and Ford Tri-Motors.

"I took care of the oil and gas, I sold tickets and not only that I had to be weatherman too," Bednar recalled. "[My wife] would answer the telephone a lot of times. Call from Madison, 'Mrs. Bednar, can you see the divide'?"

The "divide" was a notch between two of the

The Court-Martial of Billy Mitchell continued

The court-martial of Billy Mitchell began on October 22, 1925. Twelve generals and one colonel were named as judges, among them Douglas MacArthur, who said not one word during the course of the proceedings. Mitchell's attorney, Congressman Frank Reid, challenged three of the judges, leaving ten officers to decide the case. The trial went on for seven weeks, longer than any court-martial the American military had yet held, with Mitchell and Reid determined to shift the focus of the proceedings from the defendant to an examination of the aerial defense policy of the United States.

They succeeded with the assistance of a stream of witnesses for the defense including future Air Force commanders H. A. "Hap" Arnold and Carl Spaatz, as well as Martha Lansdowne, widow of the Commander of the Shenandoah. However, Mitchell was not on trial for his ideas—at least ostensibly—only for his outspoken advocacy and his criticism of superior officers and civilian appointees who disagreed with him. Of these charges alone, as Mitchell himself would agree, he had little hope of acquittal. He could only hope that by airing his ideas—and exposing the failings of his adversaries—in the very public forum of a trial he would be exonerated, first by the public and, perhaps, by the military as well.

It was not to be. A majority of two-thirds or seven of the ten judge panel was required for a verdict. After deliberating for thirty minutes, one of the judges asked if Mitchell had any "previous" convictions, which the audience assumed meant that they had already found him guilty. After nearly another three hours of deliberation, the judges returned to the court room and declared Mitchell guilty. He would be suspended from "rank, command and duty," and forfeit all pay for five years. A reporter who retrieved from the trash can the slips of paper on which the judges balloted found that MacArthur had voted for acquittal.

After nearly twenty-eight years in the army, Billy Mitchell returned to civilian life. He continued to express his arguments in favor of an air force independent of the army and navy but under the supervision of a unified national aviation agency. The American Legion, the Air Force Association and other veterans groups endorsed his position. In 1928, friends in Wisconsin mentioned him as a candidate for the United States Senate seat once held by Robert La Follette, but went no further. The son of a Democratic Senator, Mitchell campaigned for Democrat Presidential candidate Al Smith in hope that he would be named Smith's running-mate, without success. After Franklin Roosevelt was inaugurated in 1933, many political and military leaders were confident that Mitchell would be placed in charge of a sweeping reorganization of both military and civilian aviation. True to character, Mitchell continued to be an outspoken critic of aerial defense policy and of the scandal-ridden administration of civil aviation. Despite his prominence and his clearly-stated vision, or perhaps because of it, Mitchell's participation in aviation policy making was limited to testimony before executive and legislative commissions. He was too controversial for Franklin Roosevelt and the New Deal. In his last statement to Congress Mitchell warned of the growing threat in the Pacific and of the vulnerability of American bases there to attack from the air.

Late in 1935, legislation to reinstate Mitchell in the army was introduced into Congress, but it died in the House Military Affairs Committee. The same morning news broke of the Committee's action, Mitchell entered the hospital. His condition deteriorated steadily and on February 19, 1936, he died.

"Although I should like to be with the pilots and my comrades in Arlington," he told his wife before passing on, "I feel that it is better for me to go back to Wisconsin, the home of my family."

Billy Mitchell was buried in the family plot at Forest Home Cemetery in Milwaukee. Among the mourners were Mayor Daniel Hoan, four members of the House Military Affairs Committee, a representative of the President, and Colonel George C. Marshall representing no one but himself.

In January 1942, less than one month after the Japanese attack on American bases in the Pacific that Mitchell had predicted nearly two decades earlier, the Congress posthumously raised Mitchell to the rank of Major-General. In July 1946, Congress awarded him a special medal of honor (not the Congressional Medal of Honor). In 1958, the Secretary of the Air Force whose creation Mitchell had argued for many decades earlier rejected an appeal by Mitchell's son William and Wisconsin Senator Alexander Wiley to reverse the verdict of the 1925 court-martial. Billy Mitchell, hero of American military aviation, was still guilty of insubordination.[2]

Joe Bednar fueling a Northwest Airways Hamilton at La Crosse after the airline took over the air mail/passenger route from Chicago to the Twin Cities in 1927. (UW-La Crosse)

Below: Beacons lighted the airway to guide pilots across Wisconsin and the world. In remote locations world wide many beacons were powered by generators made by the Kohler Company of Kohler, Wisconsin. (Kohler Co. Archives)

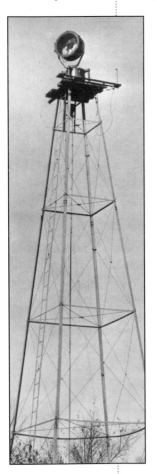

bluffs visible from the airport. If he was worried about foggy conditions, a Northwest pilot waiting to take off from Madison, Rochester or St. Paul would call the Bednars. If they could see the divide, then Salzar Field was clear for landing.

After Northwest added flights that were not scheduled to stop at LaCrosse, the weather warning system improved. It still required a telephone, so the airline paid to install and maintain a private line—rare in the 1920s—at the Bednar home. The airline also installed a set of lights, one red, one green, on the roof of Bednar's gas station at the corner of Ward Avenue and Losey Boulevard.

As Bednar recalled, "They told me, we'll call you...tell you whether it's bad weather [in St. Paul, Rochester or Milwaukee]. If so, Bednar would turn on the red lights and the planes would land and wait out the weather. If the weather was good, "nobody called, I turned on the green lights." Such was the state of advanced weather reporting and air traffic control in 1930.

Before Northwest mounted the red and green lights, Bednar was in the habit of keeping a yard light switched on all night. Pilots came to know the light and, if they needed fuel, buzzed the house. The only airport ground crewman in La Crosse would then get out of bed, drive his fuel truck to the landing strip and gas the plane. If a plane was socked in for the night, the Bednars would drive the passengers to a downtown hotel, but solitary air mail pilots stayed in their spare bedroom. Hospitable people, the Bednars always tried to make their guests feel at home. In the case of Northwest's most famous pilot, Charles "Speed" Holman, feeling at home meant being able to consume a vast quantity

of peanut butter and tomato preserve sandwiches, whose ingredients the Bednars kept in the cupboard.

Holman had to while away the hours with sandwiches in La Crosse because pilots had few navigational aids for flying after dark or in rainy or foggy weather. Cities and villages were smaller than in the 1990s, were not as well-lit in the evenings and often not lit at all after midnight. Commercial lighting was dim, residential lighting dimmer, and switched off at bedtime. Since electric power lines had yet to reach most rural areas, the countryside beyond the city limits was as dark as a coal mine at midnight.

The Air Commerce Act of 1926 created the national Airway System and in less than a year, Wisconsin newspapers reported the birth and development of a "Great Aerial White Way." The original airway followed the air mail route north from Chicago to Milwaukee then turned west and north through Watertown, Portage, Tomah and La Crosse. In February 1927, the first chain of revolving beacons and "emergency" landing fields was laid out, starting at Somers in Kenosha County, then proceeding north to Franksville and the Milwaukee County Airport. "Emergency" fields were established in those stretches of territory where no suitable commercial or municipal airport already existed.

By the end of the year, the line of beacons stretched from Milwaukee to Waukesha, New Berlin, Watertown, Reeseville, Columbus, Otsego, Wyocena, Portage, Wisconsin Dells, Mauston, Camp Douglas, Tomah, Fort McCoy, Sparta, Bangor, West Salem and La Crosse. As initially surveyed, the Milwaukee-La Crosse Airway ran for 398 miles.

Not long after it was laid out, the airway was expanded to include Madison. Unhappy that the state capital had been bypassed, civic leaders requested that the Aeronautics Branch add a 74-mile dog-leg on the Milwaukee-La Crosse Airway to run from Watertown to Madison and then to Portage. About the same time, Madison took an option on 410 acres of "smooth land" northeast of the city and expressed serious interest in an additional 290 acres. The state showed its support by promising to construct a new paved highway on the eastern border of the new airport. Despite this promising start, progress was slow at the new Madison Municipal Airport. It did not replace Howard Morey's Pennco Field, which soon became the Madison terminal for Northwest Airways air mail and passenger service.

The extension of Northwest Airways service to Madison all but stifled Wisconsin's first home-grown airline. Howard Morey's Royal Airlines began scheduled service from Madison to Chicago in July, 1928. Without an air mail subsidy, Royal had to survive solely on ticket sales and freight fees, a very difficult feat that few airlines had been able to accomplish. Royal was no exception. While its other aviation services continued, Royal halted regularly scheduled passenger service in less than one year.

The airway beacons that made up the lighted airway were erected at ten mile intervals on towers ranging from 20 to 87 feet tall. The main beam revolved and course lights mounted lower on the tower flashed identifying numbers to help pilots fix their locations while directional lights helped to keep pilots on course. The towers were numbered with smaller numbers running to Chicago, larger to the Twin Cities, and for day time identification, a 50-foot long concrete arrow sat at the base of each tower, its head pointing to the beacon with the higher number.

By the end of 1929, another lighted airway extended from Milwaukee to West Bend, Fond du Lac, Oshkosh, Appleton and Green Bay. To guide pilots on non-stop flights from Chicago to the Twin Cities, another line of lights ran from Rockford, Illinois, northwest to Brodhead, New Glarus, Ridgeway, Lone Rock, La Crosse and up the Mississippi River. Yet another chain of beacons branched off from Lone Rock to reach Rochester via "the Boscobel cutoff" across northeastern Iowa and southern Minnesota.

The intersection of these airways made Lone Rock a very important spot on the aeronautical

map. Since no suitable airport existed within the 30-mile sector required for safe flying, the Aeronautics Bureau of the Department of Commerce designated the Lone Rock airstrip as an Intermediate Field and improved it accordingly. Three landing strips, each about 2,500 feet long, running north/south, east/west and northwest/southeast, a disk-and-circle ground marker and special boundary lights were constructed. Lone Rock also received a flashing white beacon to distinguish it from the standard rotating airway beacon, plus a weather station and a "radiophone." When requested, Lone Rock radio would act as "a miniature type radio range beacon...for field localizing."

While the airway was extended to Madison, it did not continue on to Janesville or Beloit, where Northwest planes also landed briefly in the early 1930s. Since they were served neither by air mail nor by a scheduled airline, Sheboygan, Manitowoc, Sturgeon Bay, Eau Claire, Wausau, Stevens Point and smaller Wisconsin cities were not on lighted airways, while Superior was served by the airway that connected Duluth to the Twin Cities. Instead, beacons were mounted at airports in these cities to mark their place in the night and guide pilots home.

Cities also mounted beacons on prominent

Aeronautics Commission map of Lone Rock Airport, 1927. Lone Rock was designated as an emergency air mail landing field because it was at the intersection of both airways that crossed Wisconsin in the 1920s. (WAHF)

Below: The Travel Air cabin plane that Howard Morey used to established Royal Airways which flew from Madison to Chicago. (WAHF)

buildings and landmarks. Wausau's 1,000 watt beacon on Rib Mountain was the highest in the state. Sheboygan, Green Bay and Milwaukee mounted

A Kohler
Aviation Loening
Amphibian at
Milwaukee's
lakefront airport.

Below: A Loening
on the ramp into
the water prior to
take off.
(George Hardie
and WAHF)

24-inch diameter, eight million candlepower beacons downtown that were accompanied by directional beams pointing flyers to nearby airports. Considering its involvement in Milwaukee's early ventures in aviation, the Boston Store appropriately played host to the city's first beacon in 1928. Two years later, the Boston Store light was  replaced by a smaller beacon mounted on the Mariner Tower at Eighth Street and Wisconsin Avenue. Mounted adjacent to the rotating beacon was an eight-million candlepower "directional projector" pointing to nearby Maitland Field.

The beacon at Milwaukee was of prime importance to pilots and passengers of the Kohler Aviation Company. This Kohler Company was not connected to the Wisconsin Kohlers, who made their own significant contribution to business, politics and aviation in this state. Kohler Aviation was based in Grand Rapids, Michigan and named after its founder, John T. Kohler.

Billing itself as the "Bridge Across The Lake," the airline began passenger and transport service from Milwaukee to Grand Rapids and Detroit in September 1929. By the end of the year, 371 passengers made the crossing.

Since regular travel over a body of water as large as Lake Michigan was still considered extremely hazardous, Kohler flew Loening Amphibians, affectionately known as "Ducks." These aircraft, with their prominent banana-shaped floats mounted under the fuselage, were larger versions of the Loening OA-1A Amphibians that had shown their reliability in 1926 when army pilots took four of them on a "Goodwill Flight" from the United States to Argentina. Kohler presumed—and hoped its passengers would agree—that a company that could build an airplane reliable enough to fly from San Antonio, Texas to Buenos Aires, Argentina, could build a plane capable of carrying passengers from Milwaukee to Michigan.

The six-passenger, single-engine Loenings made three flights a day from Maitland Field in downtown Milwaukee. Tucked between Erie Street and the lake, Maitland Field occupied ground that would later become the site of Milwaukee's SummerFest Park. It had two runways for land-based planes, but its most distinctive feature was a ramp that enabled the "Ducks" to taxi off the field and into the lake.

Placing faith in its pilots and its planes, Kohler

Dave Behncke was born near Cambria in east central Wisconsin's Dodge County in 1897. Bored with farm life he joined the army infantry in 1915 and, the following summer, found himself stationed at San Diego, across the bay from Glenn Curtiss's old school of aviation on North Island. Behncke was able to transfer to the Air Service and learned how to fly, thereby becoming one of the army's first non-commissioned pilots. When the United States entered World War I, Behncke was promoted to lieutenant and served briefly in France.

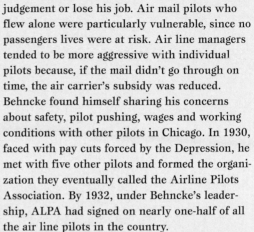

After the war, he was just another unemployed pilot looking for a way to stay in the cockpit and make a living. He landed at Checkerboard Field in the Chicago suburb of Maywood and started an air express service that delivered tailored clothes to men's stores in Illinois and neighboring states. He entered and won the Chicago Air Derby race, which led to a job as pilot for the actors playing in the most popular radio show of the day, Amos and Andy. He barnstormed, flew charters, ran a flight school and managed the airport.

He flew the air mail for Charley Dickenson and, when Dickenson's contract passed to Northwest Airways in 1927, Behncke was hired as one of the new carrier's first three pilots. He would have been content to fly for Northwest for the rest of his working life, but he quarreled with Northwest's chief pilot, Charles "Speed" Holman, after Holman "warmed up" the Stinson Detroiter Behncke was about to carry passengers in by flying loops and other aerobatics over the airport. Unusual in his day, Behncke was a stickler for safety and he thought daredevils like Holman belonged at air shows and not at air lines. Holman, who later died in a crash while stunting, disagreed and Behncke was fired.

After a stint on active duty in the army in which he shared housing with Werner Bunge, the Sheboygan native who became Walter Kohler's first pilot, Behncke went to work for Boeing Air Transport out of Chicago. The lot of an air line pilot in the late 1920s was not easy. Aircraft were primitive; navigational aids, both onboard and on the ground, were equally so. Yet schedules had to be maintained for the struggling air lines to build credibility with passengers and collect the federal air mail subsidy which kept them financially afloat.

In 1928, Northwest Airways pilots flying the Chicago-Twin Cities route over Wisconsin were paid $350 per month to fly five trips per week. There were no hourly limitations on the flight, no overtime pay and no vacations. "The speed of the J-4 Stinsons we flew was only 83.5 miles per hour, so that made for some long days," recalled Northwest pilot Walter Bullock.

While long hours and low pay were important issues for pilots,

they were not as important as the practice known as "pilot pushing." It occurred when a pilot was forced to fly against his better judgement or lose his job. Air mail pilots who flew alone were particularly vulnerable, since no passengers lives were at risk. Air line managers tended to be more aggressive with individual pilots because, if the mail didn't go through on time, the air carrier's subsidy was reduced. Behncke found himself sharing his concerns about safety, pilot pushing, wages and working conditions with other pilots in Chicago. In 1930, faced with pay cuts forced by the Depression, he met with five other pilots and formed the organization they eventually called the Airline Pilots Association. By 1932, under Behncke's leadership, ALPA had signed on nearly one-half of all the air line pilots in the country.

ALPA went on to score a major victory over E. L. Cord, whose Century Airlines offered reduced air fares by cutting pilots' wages nearly in half. The resulting strike and lock out, scarred by highly-publicized crashes in which strikebreaking pilots died, saw Cord defeated and ALPA established. In 1934, Behncke was one of few aviation leaders who supported Franklin Roosevelt's cancellation of air mail contracts. He had to stand firm against a firestorm of criticism, especially the fire coming from the one-third of ALPA members who had lost their jobs when the contracts were cancelled.

Behncke asked his members for patience and trust, for he knew that the air mail contracts would be renewed again and that Franklin Roosevelt would remember his friends. In fact, when the contracts were rewritten they included a guaranteed minimum wage for pilots and a clear statement of working conditions. The precedent of fair treatment for pilots was set on these questions, but Behncke was still concerned about safety.

He tackled the safety issue by pointing out that only pilots could speak for air line safety because only pilots—not air line executives or federal regulators—had the same interest as the flying public, i.e. a safe, accident-free flight. At hearings conducted after Senator Bronson Cutting of New Mexico died in a plane crash in 1937, Behncke raised the old question of "pilot-pushing." Air line executives William Patterson and Eddie Rickenbacker vehemently denied it ever occurred, but Behncke produced categorical evidence to the contrary. The new regulations resulting from the hearings constituted another victory for ALPA.

"Schedule with Safety," was the motto Dave Behncke gave to his organization shortly after its birth. It was still one of the guiding principles of the organization when Dave Behncke resigned as president of ALPA in 1951.[3] (Photo: WAHF)

did its best to maintain a year-round schedule, and that confidence was well placed. Milwaukee pilot Joe Doerfflinger, a World War veteran of the German Air Force, made over 2,000 lake crossings for Kohler. When a Loening carrying pilots Pat Gossett and B. W. Craycraft, but no passengers, went down in the lake on the frigid night of December 28, 1933, the aircraft remained afloat for eight hours until it was sighted by a rescue vessel. The Duck floated even though one of its wing pontoons had been torn off when the plane crashed.

After struggling financially for three years, Kohler was awarded a mail contract in February 1933. The airline would enjoy one last year of solid earnings before the federal government suspended all air mail contracts. Already struggling because of the national economic downturn, Kohler Aviation could not rebound from the loss of the air mail subsidy. The company was sold to Pennsylvania Airlines, which later merged with Central Airlines and maintained Kohler Aviation's "Bridge Across The Lake."

The lighted airway that Kohler, Northwest and other airlines relied on was only one result of the new federal involvement in aviation. Standards were set for airport design and construction, for inspection and certification of aircraft and improvements made in weather forecasting and ground-to-air communication. With federal encouragement, and sometimes with federal aid, Wisconsin invested over $1.4 million in airport construction between 1927 and 1931.

The development of radio provides a good example of how aviation progressed. Ground-to-air radio had been used on airplanes as a novelty even before World War I and turned up often in the years after the war. The Ford Reliability Tour of 1930 was on the cutting edge of radio technology since it featured a radio-equipped airplane that could send a signal to the ground which a commercial station could pick up and broadcast to all its listeners. When the Tour passed through Wisconsin, the local station in Eau Claire broadcast greetings from the pilot to all its listeners. However, progress was slow and uneven. The Kohler airliner that went down in Lake Michigan in 1933 was not radio-equipped. Indeed, by the end of 1934, the Aeronautics Bureau reported that only 775 privately-owned aircraft in the United States had radios and only about one-half of them were two-way devices. Wisconsin itself had three radio-equipped airplanes, all of them one-way. Although they became increasingly common in the later 1930s, radios did not become standard equipment in airplanes until after World War II.

The use of radio for weather and range finding on the Chicago-Twin Cities Airway over Wisconsin began in La Crosse in the summer of 1929. The chain of stations ran from Chicago to Rockford, Illinois, La Crosse, Wisconsin, and St. Paul Minnesota. The range of each station overlapped, so a plane was never out of radio contact, although the overlap was small and reception could

be spotty between La Crosse and Rockford. Weather reports were broadcast hourly from each station on a fixed schedule, with La Crosse first transmitting at 15 minutes before the hour. By 1931, two-way radio communication was available, but so new that the Aeronautics Bureau felt obliged to remind pilots who wanted to talk to the ground that they had to have both a "sender" and a "receiver" on board their planes.

The Aeronautics Bureau issued its first aircraft and pilot's licenses in the spring of 1927. Two years later the Bureau reported that Wisconsin had 121 licensed aircraft, with another 82 unlicensed but identified. Licensed pilots numbered 112, with 52 mechanics owning their cards. Even though not every person or airplane able to fly had a license, the numbers reveal that aviation was restricted to a small segment of the population. It would remain so throughout the 1930s. In 1933, the Aeronautics Bureau counted 231 aircraft in Wisconsin and 304 pilots. Due to the Great Depression, the number of licensed pilots and aircraft declined in the mid-1930s and did not begin to rebound until 1937. In that year the Aeronautics Bureau counted 130 licensed and 74 unlicensed aircraft in the state, plus seven gliders. Licensed pilots numbered 208, with 92 holding transport licenses, 76 private pilots, 25 limited commercial, and 15 amateur.

The relatively small number of pilots and aircraft in Wisconsin was due to a number of circumstances. Comparatively small in population and size, Wisconsin also possessed excellent rail and highway transportation networks that made stiff competition for air travel. Geography played a role in that the state was located off the main east-west air corridor, bounded by two of the largest lakes on earth, and experienced the full blast of a northern

climate. Milwaukee, the state's largest city, was not an aviation hub, yet two nearby out-of-state cities, Chicago and Minneapolis/St. Paul, were important air transportation centers that siphoned off interest and people. Nor was the state home to an army or navy base that would have brought flyers here and bolstered interest in aviation. While Wisconsin had many manufacturers of industrial products, few were involved in aviation or related fields, which meant very few jobs for those interested in flight. The large majority of people looking for aviation careers had to look out of state.

While all the negatives points help explain why Wisconsin did not rival California or Washington as a leader in aviation in the 1920s and '30s, they do not tell the entire story. Aviation in Wisconsin was vital, vibrant and eventful in the golden decades of flight.[4]

WISCONSIN AVIATION EVENTS, 1919 - 1941

When Lieutenant Dave Behncke was discharged from the Army Air Service at Chanute Field, Illinois, in 1919, he knew aviation was in his blood. Since he wasn't likely to find much to engage this interest in his home town of Cambria, Wisconsin, he made his way to Chicago and went to work as an independent flyer out of Checkerboard Field in the west Chicago suburb of Maywood.

The sight of an airplane in the sky was, if no longer rare, still an unusual event in 1919 and would remain unusual until World War II. This special nature of flight made airplanes prime tools for advertising and promotion. By 1919, airplanes

U. S. Army Loening "Duck" at Wausau, 1927. After flying from the United States to the southern tip of South America the Army Loening named after the city of New York toured the United States, including Wisconsin. (Robert Wylie)

Right: Madison newspaper ad announcing delivery of clothes by airplane.

Below: Dave Behncke, pilot of the "World's First Aero Express." (WAHF)

had been used as much for marketing, entertainment, politics and patriotic displays as they had for actual travel between two points, and the end of the war only offered new possibilities.

Dave Behncke signed a contract with the marketing people at Society Brand Clothes in Chicago to deliver their goods to retailers within easy flying range of the JN-4 which the company had recently purchased. Relatively lightweight and compact, suits, shirts, pants and socks made a handy cargo for the front cockpit of a Jenny. Behncke scheduled stops in Janesville and Madison, Wisconsin and, of course, merely delivering clothing by air without some promotional hoopla would not do.

When the first air shipment of Society Brand clothes came to Madison in June, 1919, Mayor George C. Sayle and Association of Commerce President Louis F. Schoelkopf were on hand to greet "the huge checkered plane," whose underside had been painted to resemble a checkerboard. A good-sized crowd of spectators was also present at Vilas Park, which the Madison Park and Pleasure

Drive Association had just developed into an airport for both "aero and hydro" machines.

The clothes were delivered to the Baillie-Hedquist Co on East Main Street, "The Neckwear House of Madison," which advertised that its stock now arrived via the "World's First Aero Express." The Society Brand "Aero Express" made several flights from Chicago to Janesville and Madison in the summer of 1919 and attracted large crowds to Vilas Park. On one flight in August, Pilot Behncke found "the crowd of children on the field too large" and after buzzing the field twice, flew off and landed in a farm field on Verona Road.

While Society Clothes Aero Express always had something to carry to Madison, the front cockpit was usually empty on the way back. Aviation promoters were quick to fill the vacuum. World War I had given many young woman an opportunity to enter the work force. Publishing was a field many women entered and just about every newspaper of size in Wisconsin still had a "girl reporter" on staff in 1919. Also, the war years had seen the women's suffrage movement succeed in convincing Congress to pass the 20th Amendment and American women would cast their first votes in national elections in 1920. The promotional possibilities of an airplane and an emancipated woman were too great to ignore and a touring pilot often found the front cockpit of his Jenny occupied by a "girl reporter."

Harriette Wheaton, formerly of the Capital Times, worked for the Janesville Gazette when she accepted an offer to fly from Janesville to Chicago on the first return flight of the "Aero Express" in June 1919. She penned an account of her flight which appeared in both Madison and Janesville newspapers that serves as a good description of what it was like to fly in a Jenny:

"Clouds, winds...bumps...views, gasps, wonder, surprise, consternation, speed, are some of the outstanding features."

"Breathe through your nose, they said. No one needed to tell me to keep my mouth shut. I didn't find an earthly chance to open it...But even then there are means of communication."

"He [the pilot] punched me in the back of the head and pointed down, way way down, to two little ponds, which looked about a block apart...Geneva and Delavan lakes...only 3,800 feet below us."

Wheaton's flight from Janesville to Maywood took one-hour, forty minutes, only a few minutes longer than the taxi ride the reporter took to downtown Chicago to catch the train home.

Harriette Wheaton was not the first women to occupy the front cockpit of the Aero Express Jenny. Mrs. Susie Mae Potter had preceded her there on the first flight down from Madison to Janesville. Although she was not a reporter, Potter was no stranger to aviation. When a crew of army flyers performed an aerobatic show in Madison a few months earlier, she had ridden along, and the pilot reported that she was the "coolest passenger" he had ever flown.

Potter, whose husband Harry managed Madison's Valvoline Oil distributorship, was quick to recognize the business potential in aviation. No sooner did she return to Madison from the Aero Express flight to Janesville then she bought a Jenny. She had to look no farther than the University of Wisconsin to find a former army pilot, Robert Erickson, and no farther than the July 4 celebration in Mount Horeb for an air show booking. Susie Potter soon became one of Wisconsin's first air show impresarios of the post-war period.

She was also known as a sportswoman, a crack shot with a rifle, and one of the first females in Wisconsin to drive an automobile, so it was no surprise when after her first flight, she told a reporter that "a straight cross-country flight is not at all exciting and I was not even strapped in."

She also declared that, "Sure, I'm going to fly," but the record is not clear on whether or not she was as good as her words. One of her Jennies crashed during the 1919 season, but she replaced it and continued to book air shows throughout Wisconsin and Minnesota. In 1920, Susie Mae Potter may have taken the the controls of a Jenny and flown the plane. If so, she was Wisconsin's first female pilot.

Clothes were not the only products pilots were marketing in Wisconsin in 1919. The Wrigley Company sent two Jennies, Spearmint 1 and Spearmint 2, on a tour of the state in September to promote sales of chewing gum. Appleton was their first scheduled stop but, "Fences, high voltage wires, patches of trees and cultivated fields," as well as the absence of an airport, made it impossible for the planes to land "within a five mile radius of the city." The "Wrigley Flying Squadron" was

forced to set down in a field on the south limits of Neenah.

The Wrigley Flyers planned to fly over the Fox Cities and drop small parachutes bearing packages of Spearmint gum. The Appleton Crescent joined the act by persuading the Wrigleys to drop newspapers along with the gum and to take along two "girl reporters," who would pen accounts of the trip. The flight went off as scheduled, with gum and newspapers delivered to Kimberly, Little Chute, Kaukauna and Black Creek and with reporters Ella Benyas and Viola Cavert filing stories.

Benyas wrote that "I had always imagined the joyous freedom of flying in the air like a bird, but I felt hardly birdlike nor did I experience any sense of freedom when every time I moved I felt the retaining grip of the belt around my waist."

Cavert was more upbeat, saying that, "When up in the air it was fine sailing, the wind whistling past as in a fierce gale, sometimes cooling, again with gusts of hot air from the engine as the plane turned."

Appleton was the first stop on the Spearmint Tour, and it lasted longer than the Wrigleys intended. A heavy rain turned the impromptu air field into a quagmire and stranded the planes. As "officers and gentlemen," the pilots found lodgings in a hotel, but the mechanics, whose job was to follow the planes by truck and stay with them at all times when they were not in the air, camped out in the muddy field. After three days, the weather cleared and the ground dried enough for the pilots to return and take off for their next stop in Madison.

Gum-laden parachutes were dropped on the capital city along with tickets good for an airplane

Left: One of Wisconsin's first post-World War I air show promoters, Madison's Suzy Potter, purchased war surplus airplanes, hired pilots and organized exhibitions in 1919.

Below: Ad for the 1919 State Fair where war-veteran pilots would reenact the air war over the grandstand. (WAHF)

ride. John Hammond, manager of the tour, assured the State Journal that passengers in the Wrigley planes were "just as safe in the air as you would be traveling down Madison's State Street in an auto-mobile." Nonetheless, only two Madisonians stepped forth to claim a free ride.

The Wrigley Flyers then left the city for their next stop in La Crosse, but not before urging Madisonians to "Have another stick of Spearmint."

Wisconsin's biggest aviation event of 1919 was the Milwaukee Journal's Flying Circus. Here the Journal combined the services of its automobile writer, "Brownie," with its newly hired aviator, "The Flying Squirrel." The anonymous "Brownie" was a familiar figure to Journal readers. He had been providing first-hand reports on motoring in Wisconsin, offering advice on road conditions, and producing detailed maps and guides for easy travel

by car. The Journal hoped that "The Flying Squirrel", who went by name of Glen Otis, or sometimes Giles Meisenheimer when out of the cockpit, might be equally popular.

For the summer of 1919, the Squirrel with his Jenny and Brownie with his Kissel "Gold Bug" auto toured the state to race each other at county fairgrounds, and sell newspapers. In fact, the Journal would send the car and the plane gratis to any community that could provide two hundred new subscribers to the paper. Included in the pack-age were free rides to the "most popular" man and woman in each community.

The Circus performed at the Brown County Fair in De Pere, where it was upstaged by Green Bay Aero Club pilot John Moore, who looped his Jenny, side slipped, tail spun and dove, much to the delight of the paying customers. A race between an auto and a Jenny around a quarter-mile or half-mile track was not exciting compared to a good aerobatic show, or the triple parachute drop that balloonist Lucille Belmont also per-formed at De Pere.

The Flying Circus continued to tour, mak-ing dates at Sturgeon Bay, Oconto Falls, Wausau, Antigo, Rice Lake, Neillsville, Friendship, Bloomington, Watertown and Marshfield. The auto, whether it was Brownie's Kissel or the Ford that occasionally substituted for it, usually won the race, since the Jenny was not designed to maneuver in the tight space of a county fairgrounds. The popularity contest winners enjoyed their rides, however, as summed up by Marshfield winner Olive Lange who said, "I wouldn't miss it for the world."

To highlight the tour, the Circus made a long distance race from Marshfield to the state fairgrounds in West Allis. The Gold Bug was given a three-hour handicap since it had to travel 214 miles over long stretches of unpaved road, while the airplane could make a straight-line flight of 170 miles. The Gold Bug got off to a rough start and had to nego-tiate nearly one-half the distance on muddy roads but the airplane was delayed by a detour to Wausau to take aerial photos and by down time at Ripon, where it landed to refuel.

After the dust settled, the judges deter-mined that the auto arrived in West Allis after four hours, fifty minutes, and the air-plane in less than three hours, which made the Kissel, with its three-hour handicap, the winner. This contest was one of the

last instances in which an auto would outrace an airplane, even with a generous handicap.

The Wisconsin Air Derby of 1920 was more typical of the air races of the future. Sponsored by the Milwaukee Journal, Hamilton Aero Manufacturing and the Green Bay Aero Club, it was the first long-distance air race of the postwar years in Wisconsin. The 264 mile course ran from Milwaukee County Airport to Kenosha, then back to Milwaukee, up the lakeshore and west to Green Bay. The return leg ran up the Fox River Valley and Lake Winnebago past Fond du Lac to Milwaukee. The presence of adequate landing fields was factor in determining the course. Kenosha could provide a marker, but had no airport, so the race could not stop. Green Bay had an airport and an aviation group to support the Derby.

Entered in the race were Florian Manor and his JN-4 from Oshkosh, Lester Younghusband in a Curtiss Oriole, Dwight Morrow and Grant Smith in Canucks and M.K. Riddick in a Standard J.L. Also contesting were the two new Lincoln-Standard machines the Journal had just purchased. Edward Gardner flew a Lincoln-Standard Tourabout and Glen Otis, "The Flying Squirrel," piloted a Lincoln-Standard Speedster. The Lincoln-Standards were fresh off the assembly line in Lincoln, Nebraska and had just flown 600 miles to Milwaukee a few days before the race.

Since the Wisconsin State Fair was under way, the Journal couldn't resist the temptation to create news. Since Nebraska was well-known as a producer of hogs, pilot Gardner flew his new open-cockpit Tourabout from Lincoln accompanied by a 50-pound pig. The animal was delivered intact to the fairgrounds where it was exhibited as a prime example of Nebraska porkritude. As far as can be determined, this is the first pig to fly in Wisconsin. In fairness, the Dairy State should have shipped a heifer to Nebraska and someone probably suggested it, but the scheme was not carried out.

Instead Gardner flew his Tourabout in the Wisconsin Air Derby with the front cockpit occupied by the inevitable "girl reporter," Muriel Kelly, also billed as "the only woman ever to ride in an air derby in America." Otis, the other Journal flyer was accompanied by "Brownie," and a sack of mail authorized for delivery to Green Bay by the Milwaukee postmaster.

The planes took off for Kenosha, circled the marker there after about fifteen minutes, then returned to Milwaukee County Airport to refuel. Then it was off on the roughly seventy minute flight to Green Bay, where the racers stopped for

Calvin Coolidge on the Brule

In the summer of 1928, President Calvin Coolidge sought relief from the heat and humidity of Washington, D. C. by vacationing in northern Wisconsin. A fly fisherman and member of the Isaak Walton League, Coolidge knew the Brule River in Douglas County as a good place to wet a line for trout. When he needed a "Summer White House" in 1928, he selected the Cedar Island Lodge on the Brule about midway between Solon Springs and Iron River.

The business of the country still had to be tended and, even if he wasn't running, Coolidge also had to pay some attention to the November Presidential election, but he didn't feel the need to be right on top of the action. Accordingly, a contingent of Presidential aides and assistants moved the administrative branch of the federal government to the Central High School in Superior, fifteen miles away from Cedar Island. In order to keep the President and his staff briefed on government business, the Army Air Corps arranged regular delivery of mail by air from the transcontinental stop in Chicago.

In the spring of 1928, two Army pilots arrived at Superior to site an airport. They landed at the Billings Park air field which local pilots had been using for a few years but decided that a 60-acre plot across the road from the county asylum in the Town of Parkland would better meet their needs. The War Department contracted to build a hangar for several planes at Parkland, graded and levelled runways and moved a detachment of eighty officers and men to lodgings near by.

The months of May and June are often very rainy in Douglas County and May and June of 1928 were two of the rainiest. The newly churned up red clay at Parkland Field became a morass that nearly claimed the life of one Army pilot. Conditions grew so bad that the Army abandoned the field, leaving the President to rely on the railroad and the auto for his mail. A few special dispatches were flown in, but the Army pilots landed at Billings Park, where the ground was more firm.

At the end of the summer, the Army wanted to sell the hangar at Parkland to the highest bidder, but instead presented it to Douglas County as partial payment for grading work the county had performed on the field. A few civic leaders wanted to keep the Parkland site for a city airport, but the cost of maintaining that soft clay surface and its distance from the heart of Superior militated against it. President Coolidge's up-to-date communications link to the rest of the world and the first army air field in northern Wisconsin reverted to trees and shrubs.

The life of Parkland Field was brief, but not without lasting consequence. As the army pursuit planes flew overhead a boy living on a farm near the village of Poplar kept watch as they passed. It was then that young Richard Bong thought he might be an army aviator himself some day.[5]

lunch served by the Association of Commerce at Blesch Field. The downwind run back to Milwaukee via Fond du Lac was a little faster than the flight to Green Bay.

The winner was Ed Gardner in the Tourabout, who flew the course in three hours, twenty-five minutes and forty-eight seconds. "We won the race on altitude on the trip from Milwaukee to Green Bay," he said. "Going to Green Bay we got above the strong air currents blowing southward and speeded up. Coming back we flew low and took advantage of the wind."

Tom Hamilton's "Maiden Milwaukee" open cockpit metalplane mounted on Hamilton floats after its success in the Reliability Tour of 1927. (George Hardie)

Gardner took the first prize of $700. The $400 for second place went to Morrow and his Canuck, with $200 for Younghusband and his Oriole, and $100 to Smith, who also flew a Canuck. Florian Manor was awarded a new Hamilton propeller.

As more pilots and aircraft appeared in the state, long distance air races became more popular. One big race in the mid-1920s was the *Wisconsin News* Air Derby. Part of the Hearst chain, the *News* was a lesser rival of Milwaukee's major papers, the *Journal* and the *Sentinel*, and was just as willing as the other papers to use aviation to build circulation. For the Air Derby of 1925, the *News* pulled out the promotional stops. Letters of support were solicited and received from Milwaukee-area business leaders, from World War I ace Eddie Rickenbacker, Air Service Chief General Mason Patrick, Assistant Chief Billy Mitchell, who was very consistent in his support of aviation events in his home town, and President Calvin Coolidge, who telegraphed that he was "glad to know of this helpful plan to stimulate aviation and hoped it may be a success." Considering the state of relations between Coolidge and Mitchell in the summer of 1925, supporting the Wisconsin Air Derby was one of few aeronautical matters they could agree on.

The Derby itself was scheduled for July 19 with two races, a 100-mile handicap and a 125-mile open, for a total prize of $2,750. The course was a circle from the Milwaukee County Airport in New Butler, to Lincoln Park in Milwaukee, then down the lakefront past Cudahy, Racine harbor and Kenosha. At Kenosha harbor, the planes turned northwest towards the Resthaven Sanitarium in Waukesha then back to the finish line at Milwaukee County Airport. The entry list reads like a who's-who of aviation in southeastern Wisconsin in the 1920s. Dan Kiser, Chris Setvate, George Weins, Dwight Morrow, Monty Warshauer, Les Holoubek and Giles Meisenheimer were Milwaukee veterans. New to Milwaukee was Austin Bettac, who entered a new Waco biplane in the race. Other out-of-towners included Pewaukee's Ed LaParle, Madison's John Grab and Henry Overley, Manitowoc's Frank Shoblaska, and Kohler's Anton Brotz, Jr. Nearly all the pilots flew Jennies or Canucks, except for Bettac in his Waco and Meisenheimer who flew an E.1. Scout that belonged to St. John's Military Academy in Delafield.

"The meet was, without question, the greatest and most successful air festival participated in by civilian flyers ever held in America," reported the News, with typical Hearstian exaggeration. If not the greatest, the Derby was a success, with no accidents and a close finish. Tens of thousands of people watched as Monty Warshauer and his Canuck won the open race with a winning time of one hour, fourteen minutes, seventeen seconds. Only four seconds behind was the "23 year-old lad from Kohler," Anton Brotz, Jr. and his JN-4 Meisenheimer won the handicap, with Warshauer placing second.

In 1926, *Wisconsin News* sponsored its second Air Derby. This was a smaller event, part of Milwaukee's lakefront "Neptune Festival," and accompanied by much less hoopla than the 1925 contest. The single race covered a 60 mile circuit, with Frank Shoblaska and Dan Kiser finishing in a dead heat and splitting the $550 first prize. The 1926 Air Derby was notable not for what happened but for those who participated: German air force veteran Fred Holterhoff, who would later establish the Brown Deer Airport; Wausau's John P. Wood, on his way to winning the 1928 Ford Reliability Tour; Roy Larson, the Norwegian bachelor farmer pilot from Winnebago County. The "kid" of the 1926 race was Fond du Lac's Steve Wittman, flying a J-1 Standard in his first air race and finishing no higher than third.

While a majority of individual pilots were still flying World War vintage Jennies, Canucks and Standards in 1926, the American aircraft industry was producing airplanes far superior to these venerable models. Travel Air, Stinson, Waco, Ryan, Buhl, Eaglerock, Pitcairn, Fairchild, Fokker and Ford were all turning out machines bigger, faster and safer than the older craft. Wisconsinites looking for progress in aircraft design had to look no farther than Keefe Avenue in Milwaukee to see the first models of Tom Hamilton's Metalplanes roll out the factory doors.

Hamilton and other airplane builders looked for venues to exhibit their products to prospective purchasers and the public at large. In 1925, after introducing its new Tri-Motor airliner, the Ford Company sponsored its first "Commercial Airplane Reliability Tour." The tour was designed, as its name indicated, to demonstrate that modern airplanes were dependable, safe and, yes, reliable. Tour sponsors hoped to dispel the barnstorming image of aviation as a pastime reserved for daring young fools willing to risk their necks, and replace it with an image of confident technology providing comfort and safety, with a little glamour thrown in. The course of the Ford Tour, which altered every year, was determined by the willingness and capability of individual cities to play host to dozens of contesting airplanes, their crews and the press.

The Second Ford Tour passed through Wisconsin in August, 1926 and stopped briefly at Hamilton Field. An estimated 10,000 Wisconsinites "looked on and cheered" as two dozen airplanes, "Swooping low across the field in a glittering procession of blue, red, orange and silver...passed in review above the heads of the crowds, whirled in graceful semi-circles and settled down daintily to the ground to taxi across the finish line."

Many of those spectators got their first look at a Ford Tri-Motor, Stinson Detroiter, Waco-9, Travel Air 2000, Pitcairn Fleetwing and many other new airplanes. The Tour stopped at Milwaukee on its way around the lake from Dearborn, Michigan via Chicago as a courtesy to Tom Hamilton, whose propellers were mounted on many of the planes. Among the famous flyers in Milwaukee that day were Walter Beech in his Travel Air 4000, Eddie Stinson in a Detroiter SB-1, John Riddle and Susan Embry in a Waco 9 and Harold Pitcairn in an Orowing PA-2. The "glittering procession" paused in Milwaukee for a few hours, then took off to continue its 2500 mile tour.

The 1927 Ford Tour did not stop in Milwaukee, but Milwaukee entered the Tour. In April of '27, seven year-old Ethel Hamilton used a bottle of Prohibition champagne to christen the "Maiden Milwaukee." It was the first model all-metal airplane built by the Hamilton Aero Manufacturing Company. Hamilton's plane was adapted from the company's successful metal pontoon design and featured a rounded, corrugated fuselage and a thick airfoil on its single high wing.

The plane carried four passengers plus the pilot, who rode perched above in an open cockpit. Passengers traveled in the shiny aluminum fuselage and looked out windows built into the underside of the wings. The Metalplane was powered by a 225-horsepower Wright J5 Whirlwind rotary motor, the same model engine that would take Charles Lindbergh across the Atlantic in May, 1927. Since the plane was a first model and Hamilton had yet to decide if more should be produced, the company did not apply for a Type Certificate. Yet to fly in the Ford Tour, it had to be licensed, so the Aeronautics Bureau issued number C235, which authorized the Maiden to fly across state lines. With this certificate, the Hamilton became the first all-metal plane licensed in the United States.

With Randy Page as pilot, Ernie Engelbert as mechanic, and a few Hamiltons and friends aboard, the Metalplane lined up for the start of the 4,000-mile tour at Dearborn, Michigan on June 27, 1927. The planes started by flying east to Buffalo,

on the design of the Boeing 247 Airliner. Boeing's first successful airliner and an aviation landmark, the 247 had it roots in Tom Hamilton's shop in Milwaukee.

With all the attention drawn to the success of the Hamilton Metalplane in the Ford Tour of 1927, the other winner from Wisconsin was overlooked. Flying a Wright J5-powered Taperwing Waco 10, John P. Wood placed fifth.

A World War I Air Service veteran, Wood was flying in Virginia in the mid-1920s when he met Wausau native George Turner. Also a pilot, Turner convinced Wood that his home town in

Wausau's John Wood with the new car and the Edsel Ford Trophy that became his after he flew his Waco 10 to victory in the Ford Reliability Tour of 1928. (Robert Wylie)

Boston, New York and other major eastern cities. They turned west and south to Louisville, Memphis, Dallas, Oklahoma City and Wichita before circling back to arrive at Dearborn on July 12. After all the planes landed and the handicaps were calculated, the Maiden Milwaukee was declared the second-place winner.

The victory established Hamilton Aero Manufacturing as a builder not just of props and pontoons but of a top quality airplane. The Maiden Milwaukee continued its winning ways in 1927, taking a third for speed and efficiency at the National Air Races in Spokane and a first for efficiency in races in New York and Detroit. The funny little plane, which resembled a corrugated road culvert shaped into a flying machine, was the foundation for Wisconsin's most successful airplane manufacturing company. In the fall of 1927, investors Clarence Falk, William F. Pabst, Philip Koehring, S. B. Way and Rudy Hokanson joined Tom Hamilton to incorporate the Hamilton Metalplane Company to make planes based on the Maiden prototype.

With a new factory and 150 employees at 530 Park Street in Milwaukee, Hamilton Metalplane soon turned out larger eight-passenger "airliners." Northwest Airways purchased nine of them and for the first and only time airplanes made in Wisconsin went into regular service flying to and from destinations in Wisconsin. Hamilton Metalplane continued to manufacture airplanes in Milwaukee until 1929, when it was purchased by Boeing. Tom Hamilton moved with his company to Seattle and became one of the principals working

Wisconsin was virgin territory for aviation. They came to Wausau, leased a farm field for a landing strip and organized Northern Airways. Wood brought his new Waco with him and raced it in the 1926 Wisconsin Air Derby, where the Canucks and Jennies showed their lack of respect for the new plane by finishing ahead of it. The following year Wood signed up for the Ford Tour and came home with $1,500 in prize money.

He was ready to do even better in 1928. The course was the longest yet for a Ford Tour, running from Dearborn to San Antonio, Los Angeles, and Tacoma, Washington before turning east across the northern Rockies and the Great Plains to St. Paul. Literally, aviation had come a long way since 1919, when the Wisconsin Air Derby ran the distance between Kenosha and Green Bay, and no farther.

The smallest city with a stop on the 1928 Ford Tour was Wausau, Wisconsin, whose municipal airport, Alexander Field, was barely one year old. With up to thirty examples of the latest in commercial aircraft, accompanied by national press coverage, the Ford Tour would be the biggest aviation event ever to land at Wausau. A Monocoupe 70, Bellanca CH, Stearman C2B, Mahoney-Ryan B-1, Fokker Tri-Motor, Ford Tri-Motor, and probably the first Lockheed Vega to fly in Wisconsin, were in the race. Nearly all the planes were powered by Wright Whirlwinds, with only one Curtiss Robin still using an OX-5.

Wood named his plane the "Waco From Wausau," and attracted a lot of attention on the Tour, especially as he built a lead in the point system that would determine the winner. Regular news reports from the Tour kept the folks in Wausau briefed, with the news from John Wood uniformly good. From Los Angeles, he wired, "everything perfect condition. Fabric and finish on ship perfect and kept thoroughly clean."

Los Angeles was the half-way mark for the Tour and Wood continued to build his lead on the return leg. Frank Hawks and his Ford Tri-Motor were second, with Randy Page, now flying a Stinson instead of a Hamilton, placing third.

As the bulletins continued to reach Wausau, excitement built. "Wood Piling Up Air Tour Points," was the word from Portland. "Wood Continues to Increase Margin in National Air Tour," said Missoula, Montana, "Wood 2,000 Points Ahead of Next Man," reported Minot, North Dakota.

Wausau planned a knockout of a reception for the tour and its first-place favorite son when the planes landed on July 26. A band would play, a choir would sing, a crowd would line the rails at Alexander Field, children would release hundreds of rubber-band-powered balsa wood planes. "Whistles Will Shriek, Bells Will Clang, Bombs Will Be Exploded," predicted the newspaper.

The excitement did not diminish when the Tour landed in St. Paul, the last stop before Wausau, and the judges announced that John Wood had won. He had amassed so many points that, no matter how well they flew, the other pilots would not be able to overtake him.

When he arrived in Wausau, Wood was already the winner of one of the longest and most publicized aerial races held in the United States. To greet him, in addition to the 27 planes on the Tour, another forty Wisconsin machines were expected to converge on Alexander Field. Roy Larson, Stuart Auer, "Speed" Holman and Harold Westphal would be there, so would Walter Miner with his Jenny from Marshfield and Frank Koehn from Green Bay. Milwaukee's Lee Mulzer would bring the Wadhams Oil Fairchild and the Knaup brothers would arrive with two Ryan Broughams.

While the crowd waited for the Tour to arrive, Wausau's Russell McNown performed aerobatics, then relinquished the air space to "Speed" Holman who "gave the crowd the works" in his Laird biplane.

After making a dramatic high speed approach over the top of Rib Mountain Holman, "flew on his back, tail spinned, dropped sideways, made nose dives, side dives, and on many occasions stopped his motor at a high altitude and after dropping some distance toward the field, started it in full blast, bringing the plane on a beautiful

straight-a-way," said the news report.

At approximately 11:00 AM, "Waco of Wausau could be seen flying over the edge of Rib Mountain...All eyes were strained toward the west when the word was passed that 'Wood is coming.' He made a beautiful landing on the field, displaying to the thousands how it is that he is able to be in the lead of the flyers on the tour."

When Wood and the other Ford flyers landed they were treated to a luncheon with local dignitaries in the new Alexander Field hangar. Speeches were made, with Wood, who was a man of few words, briefly thanking his neighbors for the great progress that had been made in aviation in Wausau since he arrived in 1926. After three hours the flyers were off for Milwaukee where they would spend the night.

While he had already won the race on points, it would not do if Wood did not complete the course back to Dearborn. Just to be sure, he left Alexander Field accompanied by a Ryan Brougham carrying a set of parts for the Waco and an entire new Whirlwind engine, with expenses covered by Wausau businesses.

Wood completed the Tour, won $3500 in prize money and temporary custody of the four-foot tall silver and marble trophy named in honor of Edsel Ford. A Ford representative formally presented the trophy to him at a Wausau Chamber of Commerce dinner in August, after which it was displayed in a jewelry store window downtown.

John Wood dressed for open-cockpit flying and his Waco 10 in 1928. (Robert Wylie)

John Wood and his durable Waco continued to race successfully. In September 1928, they placed third in a transcontinental endurance race that covered 8,000 miles. While on the west coast, they bagged $3,575 in prize money at races in California. A celebrity in Wisconsin, Wood flew in the first Wisconsin Air Tour, went on a lecture tour of the larger cities, was promoted to Captain in the Air Reserve and joined Lester Maitland as Aviation Aide to Governor Walter Kohler. His Northern Airways Company was growing, and would briefly manage the Oshkosh Airport in 1929.

A Bellanca
PM300 Airbus on
the Ford
Reliability Tour
which stopped in
Eau Claire and
Wausau in 1930.
Aircraft designers
used events like
the Ford
Reliability Tour
to test new ideas.
(Robert Wylie)

He enjoyed his greatest success at the stick of a Waco 10 Taperwing and, ironically, died trying to replace it. In August 1929, Wood and his Wausau partners purchased a new Lockheed Vega at the plant in southern California that he hoped to fly in the Cleveland Air Races. Conveniently, a Los-Angeles-Cleveland race was scheduled to start in a few days, and Wood had a speedy new plane, so he signed up for it. Wood and mechanic Ward Miller took off from Los Angeles in the afternoon of September 2. As they were crossing the desert near Needles, California, they encountered a thunderstorm. Lightning stuck the Vega and the gas tank exploded. Miller was blown out of the plane but remained conscious long enough to pull the ripcord of his parachute. When he awoke he found himself bruised and battered—but alive—on the floor of the desert. John Wood was not as fortunate. His remains were discovered with the wreckage of the plane. With him ended one of Wisconsin's most promising aviation careers.

John Wood's triumph in 1928 was the highlight of the Ford Tours in Wisconsin, but the races and the state's participation in them survived his passing. In 1929 and 1930, both Wausau and Eau Claire were stopping points on what turned out to be a less prestigious event. The 1930 Tour covered 4,800 miles, but most of the stops were in small cities like Wausau, Eau Claire, Davenport, Iowa and Duluth, Minnesota. The Ford Tour was a victim of its own success at demonstrating the relia-

bility of modern aviation. Business and civic leaders in major cities no longer felt the need to promote aviation through the Tour. While New York, St. Louis and Los Angeles were no longer interested, the Ford Tour still held luster for aviation enthusiasts in small cities. Duluth, for example, used the occasion of the Tour's arrival to dedicate its new airport on September 13, 1930.

The only Wisconsin flyer taking part that year was Walter Lees. Billy Mitchell's erstwhile flight instructor was now employed as a test pilot for the Packard Motor Company, which had installed one of its new diesel aircraft engines in a Waco HTO. Although anxious to test its new engine, Packard did not enter the Ford Tour as a contestant. Instead, the diesel Waco became an "Official Tour Plane" in which Lees ferried Tour Manager Ray Collins from city to city, always making sure that he arrived at the next air field ahead of the racers.

Two thousand cars circled the landing field, seven thousand cheering people—most of them youngsters—pushed against the fences, and the Elks Club Concert Band raised its trumpets in salute when the Ford Tri-Motor in the lead winged its way into Eau Claire Airport on the morning of September 13, 1930. After all the contestants and escorts landed safely and the crews were escorted to a hangar luncheon, the spectators were allowed on the field to inspect the plane. Ford Tri-Motors were always popular attractions and three of them were at Eau Claire. The crowd also inspected a 12-

passenger Bellanca PM300 "Airbus" with its long, slim nose and diagonal air foil landing carriage, a Sikorsky S39A amphibian and the so-called "Mystery Ship", a Travel Air R, which pilot Frank Hawks had recently used to set a transcontinental speed record.

Also creating a stir was the "broadcast plane," a Lockheed Vega that circled the field and sent a radio signal to Eau Claire station WTAQ. The local station then rebroadcast the conversations between the announcer on the ground and the airplane, "and most of them were clear enough to be audible," as the newspaper reported.

After a stay of three hours, the pilots returned to their planes and took off for Duluth, where they would spend the night. The organizers of the Tour congratulated Eau Claire, but said that "The only drawback...and few if any failed to mention the fact, was the immense number of sand burs which adhered to the shoes, stockings and clothing of everyone who ventured out upon the field."

The Ford Reliability Tours were not the only events of their kind in which Wisconsin aviators played a part in the 1920s and '30s. In 1927, the Alonzo Cudworth Post of the American Legion in Milwaukee organized the first Wisconsin Commercial Airplane Tour. Believing that a healthy civilian aviation industry was vital to the national defense and that it could provide employment for Air Service veterans who were also its members, the Legion had been a prominent and active promoter of aviation in the United States since the end of the war.

Twelve airplanes took part in the 1927 Commercial Tour of Wisconsin in October 1927. Participants included Howard Morey and the Royal Airways six-passenger Travel Air as well as John Wood in his Waco 10. The course the planes flew offers a snapshot of airport development in the state as of autumn, 1927.

The Tour started at Milwaukee County Airport, then flew to Brotz Field in Sheboygan and Arnie Schwarz's new airport at Manitowoc. Blesch Field in Green Bay was the next stop, followed by the Neenah landing field once used by the Spearmint Flyers. Oshkosh was a highlight of the Tour since airport owner Richard Lutz and his partners at Oshkosh Airport, Inc., combined the visit with a dedication of their new field on 20th Street. Then it was on to a quick stop at Portage's "intermediate field" with a beacon and marker on the Milwaukee-La Crosse Airway. Madison was

next, where promotional efforts on the part of the Legion and Royal Airways brought 2,000 people out to Pennco Field. Bright and early the next morning the flyers took off for Monroe, where they were greeted by the Mayor with coffee and donuts. One hour later they were at Herman Krause's landing strip at Janesville, where the mayor and the newspaper editor greeted them, then on to Kenosha's airport on South 22th Street followed by lunch with the Kiwanis, Rotary and Optimists. The Tour concluded with a stop at Racine's new Air City and the return to Milwaukee.

In the evening, the Legion Post held a dinner for the flyers and Milwaukee business leaders. Colonel L. H. Brittin, president of Northwest Airways, was there, but the featured speaker was

A Sikorsky S-39 Amphibian on the 1930 Ford Tour. (Robert Wylie)

William P. McCracken, head of the federal Aeronautics Bureau who pointed out the value of air tours to small cities.

"The department of commerce aims primarily to promote aviation and we are emphasizing the air mail," he said.

"To the small cities in the country which cannot hope to be stations on the air mail route for some years, we must bring the message of commercial aviation.

"We want airports in every city of 10,000 and we want better ports in the larger cities."

At the time, Wisconsin had twenty-six cities with populations greater than 10,000, but—as the Legion Tour showed—not all of them had airports.

The Wisconsin Department of the American Legion continued to support aviation with another Air Tour in 1928, then switched to another tactic in 1929.

Each year the Legion ran a major drive for membership renewals with a deadline date of November 11, Armistice Day. For 1929, Legion

"I believe that private initiative and support of aviation through private ownership of planes not only will assist in the development of the industry but may, in an emergency, be of tremendous value to the nation as a factor in national defense. For these reasons and for business purposes, I bought an airplane..." (Walter J. Kohler)

Pilot Werner Bunge with his hand on the Hamilton propeller with Flying Governor Walter J. Kohler, 1928. (Kohler Co. Archives)

Walter J. Kohler bought his airplane at the start of his campaign for governor of Wisconsin in 1928. He was President of the Kohler Company, the manufactuer of plumbing fixtures and gasoline engines located in the Sheboygan County village of Kohler, which Walter Kohler had designed to be the perfect planned corporate community. Once in the Governor's chair, Kohler of Kohler became the public champion of aviation in Wisconsin, leaving his mark in the business, politics, policy and the promotion of flight itself. He ordered his first airplane in the spring of 1928 from the Knaup brothers' Midwest Airways of Milwaukee. It was a Mahoney-Ryan Brougham, the same model that Charles Lindbergh had flown across the Atlantic in 1927 and already the most widely recognized airplane in the world. Six days after his Ryan arrived at Milwaukee County Airport from San Diego, Kohler put it to work. With Elmer H. Leighton at the stick, Kohler took the plane to the National Convention of the Republican Party in Kansas City, Missouri. Soon after his return, he learned that he had been nominated for Governor by the Stalwart or conservative wing of the Republican Party. Wisconsin had not elected a Democratic Governor since the early days of the Progressive movement in 1893 and was not likely to elect one in 1928. Consequently, the Republican primary was the race that mattered and Kohler had to defeat three other candidates, including incumbent Fred Zimmerman, before he could walk over the Democrat in the regular election. Kohler began his journey in his airplane.

Other Wisconsin politicians had used airplanes in campaigns, starting with Roy Wilcox in Rellis Conant's Jenny in 1920. Robert M. La Follette was one of the first, if not the first, Presidential candidate to use an airplane when he hired Roy Larson to fly him to Progressive Party rallies during the campaign of 1924. Fred Zimmerman had occasionally used an airplane supplied by business supporters and had himself been called "The Flying Governor," but no Wisconsin candidate had made such extensive use of an airplane as Walter Kohler. With its link to Charles Lindbergh, and with the Kohler name emblazoned in bold black letters on the underside of its silver wings, the Ryan was an instantly recognizable and persuasive campaign poster.

In eighty days, starting on July 4, 1928, Walter Kohler and his pilot, Sheboygan war vet Werner Bunge, covered 7,200 miles and visited forty-six of Wisconsin's seventy-one counties. He touched down in fifty-five or more communities and was especially proud of one 200-mile flight from La Crosse to Kohler that "was made in two hours." Many of their landings were made in farm fields and meadows that Bunge had spotted from the air after rejecting a hazardous site selected by a local campaign committee. A good campaigner, candidate Kohler always invited the farmer who owned the field up for a flight, thereby enabling the farmer to tell all the neighbors that he had flown in the same kind of plane that took Lindbergh to Paris.

Walter Kohler was the first and only Wisconsin Governor to enter office as a licensed pilot but he usually left the controls of the Ryan in the hands of others. Werner Bunge stayed with Kohler until the end of 1928 when he left to fly the air mail in Utah. He later became a pilot on the trans-Pacific route for the Royal Dutch Airlines, KLM. After Bunge left, Kohler hired Mel Thompson who continued as his personal pilot until the Governor sold Thompson the Ryan in 1937.

As Governor, Kohler used his airplane "to save time and meet my engagements." On Friday afternoons he left his desk at the Capitol at 5:00 PM, drove to the airport, took off in the Ryan, landed at the new village airport in Kohler and was home to carve the roast for supper at 7:00. Kohler usually kept on working during his flights since, in the plane, "One can write with pen and ink just as well as at a desk." The very public aerial commutes of the "Flying Governor" were an endorsement of aviation and an illustration of how a future generation of commuting executives would spend their time in the air.

Thanks to his airplane, he was able to attend events in parts of the state—such as the dedication of the airport in Superior—that he probably would not have made because of the time lost to travel. Although Ripon wasn't as far away as Superior, Kohler flew there for the 75th anniversary celebration of the Republican Party in June, 1929. Accompanying him was his newly-appointed military aviation aide, John P. Wood, who Kohler commissioned as a Major in the Wisconsin National Guard. Wood and Lester Maitland, who Kohler commissioned as a Colonel, joined Howard Morey, who was appointed by Governor Zimmerman, as the first aviators to serve as military aides to a Wisconsin Governor.

Governor Kohler also did his best to make the village of Kohler airport a model facility. He hired Anton Brotz as manager and supported his efforts to maintain well-marked and lighted runways and a service center capable of, for example, preparing Felix Waitkus's Lockheed Vega for its trans-Atlantic flight. In 1930, Kohler hosted the annual convention of the Wisconsin American Legion and made it an aviation event. Colonel Frederick H. Payne, the assistant secretary of war, arrived in an Army Ford Tri-Motor accompanied by nine Army pursuit planes from Selfridge Field. An air race from Superior to Sheboygan for civilian pilots was also held, with Howard Morey, Frank Dean and Leonard Larson the top three finishers.

While Kohler was a conservative who believed in limited government, his administration drew up and submitted to the legislature the state's first comprehensive aviation code. It was passed and Kohler signed it into law. He also saw the need for coordination between state and federal government. In 1930, he called for a conference of governors and other officials from midwestern states and the federal government. The Mid-West Air Parley was held in Milwaukee. It adopted Kohler's recommendation for a federal and state aviation construction finance program similar to the successful federal-state highway program and called for a national conference.

Word of the "Flying Governor" spread beyond Wisconsin. At the National Air Races in Chicago in September 1930, where Steve Wittman competed with his Pheasant H-10, Kohler was honored on "Wisconsin Day." He was presented with a silver plaque inscribed, "In appreciation of his outstanding participation in the field of aeronautics and for his indomitable enthusiasm in the cause of aviation." It was signed by Charles and Anne Lindbergh, Art Goebel, Jimmy Doolittle and other aviation luminaries.

Despite his renown among aviators in Chicago, Walter Kohler ran afoul of the voters in his home state. In the Republican primary of September 1930, they chose Philip La Follette as their candidate and elected him governor in November. Kohler ran again in 1932, but the electoral tide had turned so strongly against conservatives that Albert Schedeman, the former mayor of Madison and a Democrat, was elected governor. Wisconsin's Flying Governor withdrew from politics to manage his family's business during the tough years of the 1930s. He passed away in 1940, at sixty-five years of age.

The Kohler name continued to make headlines in aviation after Governor Kohler left office. The company had been producing gasoline-powered electrical generators to power beacons in remote sites on the lighted airways since 1925. By 1929, over 600 Kohler units were in operation on nearly 11,000 miles of airway, including most of the transcontinental route from New York to San Francisco and on the Atlantic and Pacific coastal routes, but not on the CAM-9 air mail route through Wisconsin. By 1931, the number of units in service had more than doubled.

Throughout the 1930s, beacons and radios powered by Kohler generators played a role in the development of aviation around the globe. Pan-American and Panagra airline routes through Central and South America were lighted by Kohler-powered beacons. When Admiral Richard Byrd made his daring flight over the South Pole in 1930, radio contact with his base at Little America was maintained by Kohler generators. Pan-American Airlines launched its first China Clipper Airplane across the Pacific in 1935 guided by Kohler-powered radio beacons on Hawaii, Midway, Wake, Guam, the Philippines, and at Canton, China.

Perhaps the proudest moment for Kohler's aviation equipment occurred in November 1932, when a 150-foot tall stone monument was erected on the sandy bank of Kill Devil Hill, near Kitty Hawk, North Carolina, to commemorate the first flight of Orville and Wilbur Wright. Atop the tower was a 1000-watt beacon, similar to many used on the lighted airways. It was to serve as an eternal flame to preserve the memory of the flight. So that the beacon would not fail, even if the regular power line went down, a Kohler generator stood in the powerhouse nearby, ready to switch on. It was part of the Wright Brothers monument but also a memorial to the contributions of Wisconsin's "Flying Governor." [6]

Aviation Chairman Russell Wilcox of Horicon organized a squadron of aviators to tour the state and collect membership cards and dues. "The planes will take to the air shortly after dawn on November 11 and at night when they come to rest at the end of their journeys at Milwaukee County Airport, campaign officials expect that they will carry cards and 1930 dues for 28,000 Legionnaires and for 16,000 Auxiliary members."

Carlyle Godske and his Great Lakes Trainer at Racine. (Elmo Halverson)

Pilots from all over the state took part, with expenses covered by business sponsors. Among them were, Ed Hedeen, Racine; Mel Thompson flying Governor Walter Kohler's Ryan Brougham, Kohler; Russell Wilcox, Horicon; C. L. Wheeler, Monroe; Ed Nelson, Manitowoc; Verne Williams, Rice Lake; Archie Towle, Wausau; Frank Muth, La Crosse; Collins Murray, Green Bay; Elmer Rudolph, Medford; John Rossey, Menasha. Although only a little more than 20,000 memberships were delivered, the Legion resolved to repeat the aerial drive the following year.

The 1930 membership drive was another success but 1931 was marred by bad weather and a tragic accident. Twelve machines were ready for takeoff on November 11, but much of the state was blanketed by fog. Harold Westphal left Rhinelander, made a pickup at Menominee but was socked in at Appleton. Frank Petrusha set out from Rice Lake, made Chippewa Falls, but got no farther south than Tomah. Archie Towle left Wausau and stopped at Oshkosh, as did Ed Nelson from Manitowoc. In the southern part of the state the fog was too heavy for any pilots to fly. Mel Thompson, Pat Trier, Frank Ernst, Dick Kartheiser, Herman Krause, Ed Hedeen and Charlie Gittner were all

FIRST FLIGHT OF
AIR MAIL
FROM
WISCONSIN RAPIDS
WISCONSIN 5-19-38

grounded. At Wisconsin Rapids pilot Rodger Davy took off in one of the Fairchilds belonging to the Tri-City Flying School, lost his bearings in the fog and crashed about thirty miles away at Coloma.

In response to Davy's death, but also affected by the economic downturn, which had prompted a sharp drop in membership, the Legion cancelled the air round-up for 1932. One pilot could not accept the cancellation. Carlyle Godske of Racine delivered his community's memberships to Milwaukee in his own machine. A World War I Air Service veteran, Godske had already opened Racine's second airport on Highway 11 west of Sturtevant and would soon become the leading figure in Racine aviation. His solitary flight in 1932 began a decade-long commitment to organizing and expanding the Legion Round-up.

In 1933, Former Governor Kohler loaned his Ryan Brougham and Thompson covered a route in the northern half of the state. The southern half was covered by Carlyle Godske, who also flew a Ryan. For 1935, Godske recruited Lee Promen, Jim King, Henry Robinson and Archie Towle to fan out over the state and collect memberships. Every year until World War II suspended civilian flying, Godske organized the Legion Air Round-Up and, by 1938, had ten planes participating. Wausau's Archie Towle, Racine's P.J. Landreman and

Milwaukee's Jim King participated almost every year. Other pilots who flew in one or more Round-Ups were Kewaunee's Leo Salkowsky, Eau Claire's Arch Ward, Madison's Henry Robinson, Eagle River's Ora McMurray, Racine's Frank Lovell, and Waupun's Lloyd Graves.

In 1940, the planes were grounded by the Armistice Day ice storm that shut down travel of all kind throughout the state. In 1941, a total of eighteen planes flew in the drive, including those piloted by Bloomer's Alten Kenz, Boyceville's Art Allseth, River Falls' A.L. Moody and Eau Claire's B.M. Hammond. They covered virtually every corner of Wisconsin, from Washington Island to Superior, Lancaster and Kenosha.

The size of the roster of pilots taking part in the Legion Round-Ups mirrors the effects of the Great Depression on aviation. In the late 1920s, the Round-Ups and aviation got off to a good start. In the early 1930s, when the Depression was at its worst, the fewest number of pilots volunteered to fly for the Legion. By the end of the 1930s, the recovery had begun and, in 1941, more flyers than ever took part.

Other Air Tours followed a similar curve: up in the late 1920s, down in early 1930s, up again in the late 1930s and early '40s.[7]

Famous Flights, Famous Flyers

Marc Mitscher

Transoceanic hops, endurance trials, races across the country and from pylon to pylon—these are the events that put luster on the golden age of aviation in the years between the World Wars. Wisconsin is linked to many of the golden moments of flight in these years, starting in 1919.

As soon as World War I concluded aviators on both sides of the Atlantic contested to make the first flight across the water. In the United States, the Navy put forth the most promising effort, having commissioned the Curtiss Company to design an airplane capable of making the 1,300 mile jump from Newfoundland to the Azores Islands in the mid-Atlantic. From the Azores, Portugal and the rest of Europe were only 1,000 miles away. Curtiss came up with the NC Flying boat, an airplane powered by four Liberty engines, with a 126-foot wingspan, and a watertight fuselage able to weather heavy seas,

Three NC aircraft left Newfoundland on May 8, 1919, headed for England via the Azores and Lisbon, Portugal. The co-pilot of NC-1 was Lieutenant Marc Mitscher, Annapolis grad and a native of Hillsboro, Wisconsin. The planes separated shortly after take off and encountered dense fog

over much of their course. The NC-1 was about 100 miles off the Azores when, in order to determine his bearings, pilot P. N. Bellinger decided to land the plane in the ocean. Bellinger got his bearings, but thirty-foot swells so damaged the plane that it could not lift off from the water. The NC-1 was in no immediate danger of sinking and its engines still ran, so Bellinger, Mitscher and crew started to taxi the 100 miles to land. They were spotted by a steamship and the crew transferred but, after a towing cable parted, the swamped NC-1 was lost at sea.

Of the three Navy planes that started the voyage, only the NC-4, piloted by A.C. Read, completed the flight to the Azores and Lisbon. They were the first Americans to fly across the Atlantic. Among the sailors at Lisbon to greet the NC-4 was Walter Loehndorf, who later became a pilot at Waukesha. Marc Mitscher remained in naval aviation and, starting as commander of the aircraft carrier Hornet and concluding in command of Task Force 58—"the most powerful naval striking force ever assembled in the Pacific"—became one of the most distinguished naval air commanders of World War II.

Lester Maitland

While the U.S. Navy won laurels for flying the Atlantic, pilots of the U.S. Army Air Service dispatched by Billy Mitchell racked up their own list of aeronautical accomplishments. Army flyers set speed records for transcontinental travel, circumnavigated the globe and completed other long-distance flights to Alaska, South America and the Hawaiian Islands. The flight with the strongest Wisconsin connection was Lester Maitland's journey between California and Hawaii in 1927.

Maitland was born in Milwaukee in 1899 and graduated from Riverside High School the same month in which the United States entered World War I. He enlisted in the Army Air Service, did not serve in Europe, but liked the Army well enough to stay in uniform during the peace. The Army also liked Maitland well enough to keep him at a time when it was discharging all but a few of its Air Service personnel. It helped that Maitland caught the eye of General Mitchell, whose aide he became and with whom he returned to Milwaukee on many occasions,

As early as 1919, Lester Maitland requested Army authorization to fly a Martin Bomber from California to the Hawaiian Islands. Had it

occurred, Maitland's flight would have been the longest over-the-water air journey yet made. He wanted to use the same model Martin that had made the "Round-the-Rim" flight in 1919 and the experimental air mail run through La Crosse in 1920. Dependable as the Martin was, it was strictly a land-based plane and, unlike the Navy's NCs, would sink like a brick if forced down in the ocean.

Maitland's request was denied but he did not abandon his idea. "For seven years I studied and hoped," he wrote. "Whenever a new type of transport or bomber was purchased by the army I considered it from every angle to see if it might be the ship." In 1922, as Mitchell's aide, he had met the German airplane designer Anthony Fokker, who was touring the United States looking for a site for an airplane factory. Four years later, the Army purchased a Fokker Tri-Motor and Maitland saw that it was "the ship."

Easily mistaken for the more familiar Ford Tri-Motor, the Fokker was, like the Hamilton Metalplane, a "thick-winged monoplane." Unlike the smaller Hamilton, it had a wingspan of 72 feet and was powered by three 200 horsepower Wright Whirlwind engines. Within a year of its purchase, the Army authorized Maitland to fly the Fokker to Hawaii in the spring or summer of 1927. In a passage revealing the state of contemporary military thought, Maitland wrote that, "it was highly valuable to ascertain if Hawaii could be linked to the coast by air...In the case of war it might be necessary to send a valuable staff officer with the least possible delay from the United States to Hawaii..." The notion that transport or combat aircraft might routinely make the 2,400 mile hop was an idea whose time had not arrived.

Maitland was named pilot for the flight and Lieutenant Albert Hegenberger navigator. While all of the great flights of this era required a solid airplane with a dependable motor, the California-Hawaii hop also required navigational expertise. Finding the Islands in the vast expanse of the ocean was of first importance so the Army

equipped Maithland's Fokker with just about every navigational instrument available at the time: "radio beacon receiving installation, an Air Corps radio set for receiving and transmitting messages, an aperiodic compass, earth inductor compass, a bubble sextant and three dozen smoke bombs for measuring drift." The radio beacon technology was so new that the Hawaiian expedition was its first real flight test. If all the equipment failed, the fate of the mission rested with Lieutenant Hegenberger, who was selected for the flight because of his reputation as the finest navigator in the Army.

In the midst of their preparations, the Army flyers learned of Charles Lindbergh's solo flight across the Atlantic. Although Lindbergh is not mentioned in Maitland's many recountings of his flight, comparisons are inevitable. While Lindbergh flew approximately 3,500 miles from New York to Paris, the longest over-the-water portion was the 1,900 miles from Newfoundland to Ireland. Lindbergh also knew that as long as he continued to head east he would strike land. Maitland and Hegenberger would take off from Oakland and fly 2,400 miles in hope of finding a string of islands in a vast ocean before they ran out of gas. Lindbergh had flown solo for 33 hours, while Maitland and Hegenberger had each other's company for their 26 hours aloft. However, the Fokker's engine was so loud the army flyers could not hear each other talk and communicated by means of notes scribbled on a chalkboard.

On June 27, 1927, Air Corps Commander General Lyman Patrick visited the Oakland Airport and inspected the Fokker which the crew had christened the "Bird of Paradise." As the sun lightened the eastern sky, he shook hands with Maitland and Hegenberger, and said, "I know you boys will make it."

The weather was "glorious" as Maitland rolled the Fokker down the runway, quickly rose to 2,000 feet and set out on the southwesterly course for Hawaii. "I had perfect faith in the ship, in

Hegenberger, and in myself," Maitland recalled, "and if there was any worry in my head it was that for the first time since 1922, I was flying without a parachute." The army had determined that if an emergency arose it would be better for Maitland and Hegenberger to ride the plane down to the water and launch their inflatable life raft, with its good supply of emergency rations, instead of simply parachuting into the sea.

Despite all the preparations they had made and the quantity of navigational instruments on board, the Hawaii aviators were in trouble shortly after take-off. "First of all we could not use the smoke bombs for measuring drift because of high winds and heavy seas, then the induction compass called it a day, next the radio beacon failed, and on top of all this, to make our bubble sextant virtually worthless, the clouds obscured the sun. All this occurred within the first hour and a half..."

Maitland dropped below the clouds to enable Hegenberger to set his course with an ordinary compass. He corrected for drift by peering through a trapdoor in the floor of the plane and observing the "spume" on the waves below. Based on those observations, Hegenberger reckoned that he had to make a seventeen degree correction to the course. Maitland revealed the boldness of this decision when he called it "a considerable correction.... because we could make a possible error of only 3.5 degrees on either side....and still reach Hawaii."

In the course of the day, they gleaned estimates of their position by spotting steamships whose course they had been informed of before they left Oakland. They could spot the ships, even send a signal to them, but their malfunctioning radio could not pick up the return broadcasts. They made their best estimate and flew on through the afternoon. In the evening, hoping that Hegenberger would be able to fix their position by shooting the sun as it set, Maitland dropped the Fokker to 200 feet, but the clouds still muddied the horizon. After dark, Maitland took the "Bird" through the clouds, up to 11,000 feet so Hegenberger could get a fix on the stars but, before the navigator could align his sextant the Fokker's middle engine started to falter. It coughed, sputtered, then wound down to idling speed, where it stuck. Maitland then let the plane lose altitude and drop through the clouds to 3,000 feet, when the ice that built up in the carburetor thawed and the

engine kicked to life again.

Shooting the stars was still their best hope for finding Hawaii, so Maitland decided to risk icing-up. Cautiously, he pulled the nose of the Fokker up to 7,000 feet, where he found breaks in the clouds. Hegenberger was able to fix on Polaris a number of times and reported that the Bird of Paradise was right on course for Hawaii. His seventeen-degree course correction had proven accurate.

Now Maitland and Hegenberger faced the problem caused by their success. If they stayed on course and maintained their cruising speed of 108 miles per hour, they would strike land in the dark in the rain—no small problem since Wheeler Field, their destination on Oahu, was unlighted.

A Fokker Tri-Motor of the type Maitland piloted on his flight. (WAHF)

Accordingly, Maitland throttled down to the stately speed of seventy miles per hour and held his course. After twenty-two hours in the air, the flyers spotted Kilauea Lighthouse on the northern shore of the island of Kauai, northwest of Oahu. The Army flyers had reached the Hawaiian Islands.

They circled Kauai through the final minutes of darkness. At dawn they turned into the sun and flew across Kauai Channel to Oahu. They touched down at Wheeler Field after twenty-five hours and forty-nine minutes in the air after having set a record for the longest non-stop, over-the-water flight yet made.

On Oahu, the army pilots were congratulated by their superiors, hailed by the press, and decorated with flowered leis from grass-skirted dancers. A month later, Maitland and Hegenberger came to Milwaukee and, although no grass-skirted dancers appeared, they received a triumphant welcome.

The Bird of Paradise landed at county airport where a crowd of military, civic and business dignitaries were on hand. Governor Fred Zimmerman and Mayor Daniel Hoan were present. Mark Forrest, Milwaukee's "Poet Laureate" read a verse in their honor that began, "Sons of Eagles, Boldy Daring, Lords of the Lanes of the Limitless Air." With his wavy blond hair, solid jaw and broad shoulders, Maitland could have played the role of a lord of the "limitless air," at least in the Hollywood version, and the newspapers duly reported the favorable reaction of the young women in the crowd.

The welcoming ceremony climaxed after Milwaukee Alderman Cornelius Corcoran announced that the city had just purchased a tract of lakefront property for a downtown airport. Then keynote speaker Oscar Stotzer stepped forward and addressed Maitland:

"In order to show in some lasting and permanent way our appreciation of what you have done for our city, our state and our nation, we do here and now solemnly and reverently dedicate in your honor and in your name this beautiful lakefront airport."

Maitland responded by pointing out that the Hawaiian flight was a 50-50 proposition and that Lieutenant Hegenberger deserved equal attention. The Milwaukeeans responded by cheering the navigator as heartily as they had the pilot.

"I simply have to get out and do something else worthwhile in order to live up to all this," Maitland declared before saying farewell to Milwaukee on the following day. He kept that promise as an Army Air Force general in World

War II, as the first director of the Wisconsin Aeronautics Commission and finally, as a priest of the Episcopal church.

Charles Lindbergh

At the time Maitland and Hegenberger made their flight to Hawaii, the United States and much of the civilized world was experiencing the first outbreak of its mania for Charles Lindbergh. He had made his flight across the Atlantic only five weeks before the Army flyers' Pacific hop.

Lindbergh's Wisconsin connection began in September 1920 when he left his family home in Little Falls, Minnesota to study engineering at the University of Wisconsin. An indifferent student who would have preferred farming to "the dreary prospects of college," Lindbergh later recalled that, "It did not take my instructors long to discover my deficiencies in knowledge and my inability to concentrate on studying." Instead of attending lectures, the tall, slim Minnesotan preferred to spend his time on the ROTC rifle range where he led the Wisconsin team to a national title, racing his motorcycle up and down campus hills and hanging out with his friends Richard Plummer and Delos Dudley. The trio built a motorized iceboat which they piloted on hair-raising romps over frozen Lake Mendota.

Midway into his second year in Madison, Lindbergh concluded that he was not cut out for the university; nor, like many 20-year-olds, did he know what he was cut out for. His friend Delos Dudley had a better handle on the future and he shared it with his friend. "As a young boy I had been attracted by airplanes and built many models," Dudley recalled. "I also knew that Lindbergh had the right stuff to make him an exceptionally good pilot."

Dudley then asked the fateful question, "Why don't you learn to fly an airplane and go into the flying business." Lindbergh replied that once he'd learned how to fly, it wouldn't be much different, or more exciting, than driving a car, but he did like the idea of parachute jumping.

After Dudley produced a selection of aviation school catalogs, Lindbergh picked out the Nebraska Aircraft Corporation of Lincoln, Nebraska—home

port of Wisconsin's flying pig—and enrolled. Over the next five years, Lindbergh pursued the life of a 1920's free lance pilot. He purchased an OX-Jenny and barnstormed for dollar bills and pocket change. He trained as an Army flight cadet in the hope of a Regular Army commission, but left the military without it to become the chief pilot on the air mail route between Chicago and St. Louis. Here he was able to get his fill of parachute-jumping, not for fun, but to save his life when the inadequate aircraft he was obliged to fly were about to crash. Eventually, he made the most famous airplane flight ever—3,500 miles solo from New York to Paris.

The official record states that after he left Madison in 1922, Charles Lindbergh did not return to Wisconsin until his triumphal tour of the country in the summer of 1927. In Lone Rock, however, they tell another story. One spring, perhaps in 1923 or '24, maybe even later, the Lower Wisconsin River was at an unusually high flood stage. The Lone Rock highway bridge had yet to be built and the river was too wild for the ferry boat to venture out. At this inopportune moment, Dr. Bertha Reynolds, the physician who tended the sick in the area, received a call from a patient in the Town of Clyde across the river from Lone Rock.

Dr. Reynolds was well-remembered in the stretch of river valley between Iowa, Sauk and Richland counties as a good doctor who served her people for over thirty years. If there was a sick person in Clyde, a mere flood on the Wisconsin was not likely to keep her away. She had heard that a barnstorming pilot had parked a plane at the farm field that became the Lone Rock Airport and was killing time waiting for something to turn up. Reynolds tracked the fellow down and hired him to fly her over the river to Clyde. In the meantime, another patient at Plain, on the ridge in Sauk County, called for help. So Dr. Reynolds climbed in the plane. The pilot hopped it across the river to Clyde, waited while she made her call, then hopped over the river again to Plain and back to Lone Rock.

A few years later, when Charles Lindbergh became a world celebrity, folks in Lone Rock remembered that he was the same pilot who had flown Dr. Reynolds over the flooding Wisconsin River to Clyde and Plain.

Be that as it may, Charles Lindbergh did return to Wisconsin after his Paris flight in the summer of 1927. He was the most popular man in America and every city, large and small, wanted to see him in person. Of the 82 cities on his itinerary that summer, Milwaukee and Madison were the only Wisconsin stops.

The weather was threatening on August 20,

The *Spirit of St. Louis* at Milwaukee County Airport after the Paris flight in 1927. (George Hardie)

but Lindbergh landed the *Spirit of St. Louis* at the Milwaukee County Airport on schedule. He was greeted by business leader and aviation enthusiast Clarence Falk, Mayor Dan Hoan and other officials, then traveled by motorcade to Juneau Park. The lakefront park could not contain the estimated 100,000 spectators who came to see and cheer "Lucky Lindy." If the estimate was accurate, no aviation event in Wisconsin would attract as many people until the EAA Conventions of the 1970s. Lindbergh's crowd was larger than the mass of people that welcomed Maitland and Hegenberger one month earlier.

The officials gave the customary speeches, followed by a brief address by Lindbergh, who spoke of aviation's bright future and the necessity for cities and citizens to support it. The pilot spent the night in Milwaukee and all of the next day, then took off for his scheduled stop in Madison. On the

appreciation of your interest in the tour and the promotion and expansion of commercial aviation."

From Oshkosh he circled back to land at Pennco Field in Madison, where he was greeted by Howard Morey, Governor Fred Zimmerman, Mayor A. G. Schmedeman and University President Glenn Frank, who warmly greeted his university's world-renowned dropout. Delos Dudley was also present to provide some relief from the weighty words for the 25-year-old pilot, who was noted for his aww-shucks simplicity and dislike for pretense. A motorcade of 100 cars escorted Lindbergh to Camp Randall stadium, where 40,000 people stopped cheering just long enough to listen to the young man deliver his message in support of aviation.

"It is essential that each city provide an airport for commercial purposes," he said. Then it was on to another banquet with dignitaries, followed by another night in a strange hotel bed followed by another flight and more of the same in the next town.

Lindbergh endured the schedule because he believed that he had been granted a unique opportunity to speak for aviation. As a barnstormer and an air mail pilot, he had flown inferior airplanes on uncharted routes to land at "airports" that could be distinguished from cow pastures only because the word "airport" was scribbled on a sign at the gate. Lindbergh and the people who funded it viewed his tour as a "bully pulpit" from which he could urge Americans to build the aviation infrastructure the nation needed. Coming on the heels of the Kelly Act of 1925 and the Air Commerce Act of 1926, Lindbergh's message had a positive effect in Wisconsin and throughout the country.

Charles Lindbergh came back to Madison in 1928 to collect the degree he had opted out of in 1922. Wisconsin presented Charles Lindbergh with

Paul Collins, air mail pilot. (UW-Stevens Point)

way he flew over the veterans home in Waukesha and dropped a message stating his regret at not being able to visit in person.

Lindbergh was scheduled to fly directly to Madison but, apparently at the urging of Congressman Lampert, detoured to Fond du Lac and Oshkosh, where he dropped specially-prepared packages bearing messages expressing his "sincere

a doctorate "as a rival in friendship to Benjamin Franklin."

"Since the days of Dr. Franklin no other American has reached his eminence in friendship," said Professor Frederic Paxson at the presentation. "But he has mastered the currents of the air, giving to mankind a new dimension: and he has done it with restraint and power that have enhanced the dignity of our manhood. As a representative of American good will to all the world he has served us well. And Wisconsin takes real pride in the feeling that he is one of us."

Lindbergh made his customary brief and humble speech, then left the ceremonies to attend a reunion of the class he would have graduated with had he stayed at the university. He enjoyed the informal party and stayed around with the other men to help wash the dishes afterwards. The following day, he flew down to Janesville to look up his old friend Delos Dudley who, along with partner Will Kempton, was pursuing the career Lindbergh might have followed himself if he hadn't made that trip to Paris. Dudley and Kempton were running a small airport and having a great time of it.

Paul Collins

Of Wisconsin flyers having a great time of it, none seemed to be enjoying aviation more than Paul Collins. The Stevens Point native who had enlisted for World War I left the service knowing that flying was his future. On the day of his discharge, he hired on with the Curtiss Aeroplane Company and was soon in Washington, D. C. giving demonstration flights in a Curtiss Oriole two-seater to Congressional leaders. Curtiss hoped to woo the lawmakers into appropriating a suitably large sum of money for the Post Office to purchase replacement planes for the DH 4's then in air mail service. Collins took several hundred Representatives, aides and assistants up for flights around the Washington Monument and over the Capitol. He got a taste of politics that would serve him well in the future, but failed in his immediate mission. Congress cut air mail funding.

In the summer of 1920 Collins left politics for the movies. He signed up as "director" of what he remembered as "the first real aviation full-length feature picture." It was called "Flying Pat" and starred Mabel Normand and Lillian Gish with the dashing James Rennie as the pilot. D. W. Griffith was the producer. As director, Collins' first job was to find an airplane that would "fly" on wires ten-

feet above the ground. He volunteered his own OX-5 Jenny and strung it between two telephone poles. When a scene called for a crack-up, Collins had a tree cut and mounted on a cart, off camera. At the right dramatic moment, Collins directed the tree into the nose of the Jenny, with cameras rolling. In the next scene the camera panned to a wrecked machine Collins had scrounged from a crash site. "The continuity of shooting was quite realistic," he recalled, "and surprised me, the director, most of all."

Despite this success, Collins' movie career was short-lived. After a short period of unemployment, he ran into Randy Page, future pilot of the Hamilton Metalplane. Page was an old Army buddy of Collins now flying in the Air Mail Service. He put in a word for his friend and Collins found himself employed by the post office and assigned to fly the mail on the transcontinental route from Chicago to Cleveland.

"I've never been over the route," he told his supervisor on his first day on the job at Checkerboard Field in Chicago.

"You won't have any trouble," he replied. "Just follow the east and west section lines straight east from the foot of Lake Michigan to the foot of Lake Erie and just fly around Cleveland. The field is on the east side along a railroad track."

With directions like that, how could he miss? In fact, Collins did make the Cleveland air field, even though a snowstorm half-blinded him, cold weather half-froze him, and his crash on landing half-killed him. It was all in a day's work for an air mail pilot in 1921.

Paul Collins would remain an Air Mail pilot until August 1927. During most of this period the only air mail route in operation was the transcontinental from New York to San Francisco and most of Collins' flying was on the Chicago-Cleveland leg. In those six years he logged 3,587 hours and flew more than 360,000 miles.

Newspaper and movie newsreel editors soon learned that the Air Mail could make deliveries faster than the railroad or the auto and came to rely on Collins and his fellow pilots to deliver film of news events in time to meet deadlines. Thanks to the Air Mail, print news coverage became more graphic and weekly newsreels more timely.

The dedication of the Tomb of the Unknown Soldier in Washington in 1921 was a major news event and Collins flew film of the ceremony to Chicago, where the major newsreel production companies were then located. He also delivered film of the state funeral of President Warren Harding in 1923, but not after overcoming a few obstacles. As he was approaching Gary, Indiana, the oil gauge on the engine of his Curtiss Oriole hit bottom, so Collins switched off and prepared to glide in for a landing. Guided by the headlights of automobiles on an adjacent highway, he selected a patch of dark and what he hoped was uninhabited terrain to make a landing. He touched down safely, but caught in a rut and flipped the plane. He was on the ground, upside down but unharmed. That is, until he released his seat belt and dropped head first into a swamp. He clambered to his feet, pulled the can of film out of the front cockpit and struggled up to the highway.

Few drivers were willing to stop and pick up a sopping wet hitch-hiker dressed in pilot's clothes and carrying a parcel on a dark road outside Gary, Indiana. Trying his best to look sane and friendly, Collins was able to stop a car that took him to a street car that took him to a taxi, that took him to a train, that delivered him within walking distance of the newspaper office. He made the delivery before the deadline, but not without the editor cracking wise about the undependability of the U.S. Air Mail.

In 1926, when Congress established the contract air mail system, Collins and some of his fellow pilots organized North American Airways and bid for the Cleveland-Chicago run. They failed, but the experience showed Paul Collins where his future should lie. A year later, he received a message from C. M. Keyes, who was looking for the right person to manage his new airline, Transcontinental Air Transport. Collins accepted and began setting up operations from New York to Los Angeles via Indianapolis, Wichita and Alberquerque. Keyes also hired Charles Lindbergh as Technical Advisor and purchased a fleet of Ford Tri-Motors that were christened in honor of the cities on the route. By the end of 1929, TAT was established and growing—but without Paul Collins, who had failed to survive a management shake-up. Charles Lindbergh fared better. After a series of mergers and acquisitions TAT evolved into Trans World Airlines which advertised itself as "The Lindbergh Line."

With financial backing from a wealthy Washington, D. C. family, who gave their name to the operation, Collins then formed Ludington Airline, which he dubbed as "revolutionary," because it was committed to fly between New York, Philadelphia, Baltimore and Washington, "Every Hour on the Hour — Your Watch is Your Timetable." Keeping this operation aloft—literally—was Collins' chore. His system was simple and clearly explained to an executive from the German

airline Lufthansa who was visiting a Ludington hangar.

"Where are the airplanes?" he asked.

"In the air, where they should be, to make money."

"Ja wohl, sehr gut," said the German.

With Ludington Airlines, Paul Collins can make a good claim to being the inventor of the commuter airline. Ludington was, however, a casualty of the air mail controversy of 1934, when the federal government's cancellation of all contracts forced another industry-wide shake-up. Collins had already moved on to organize another airline. He teamed up with Gene Vidal, S. J. Solomon and Amelia Earhart to form National Airways. This airline would fly Stinson Tri-Motors to connect cities in the New England states and New York. Collins, Earhart and her husband George Putnam became fast friends while touring New England to promote the new line. In the late 1930s, National Airways evolved into Northeast Airlines and Paul Collins became company president.

During World War II and under Collin's management, Northeast pioneered air routes across the North Atlantic to deliver war supplies to Europe and support Allied air forces on anti-submarine patrol along the convoy route to the Soviet Union. In the process, Collins helped spot airport locations in Newfoundland, Northern Labrador, Baffin Island and Greenland as links in the chain to Reykjavik, Iceland and Prestwick, Scotland.

Paul Collins was a successful airline executive, but his heart belonged to the old United States Air Mail. In 1968, the Air Mail Pioneers Association, of which Collins was president, presented a fully restored DH 4 U. S. Air Mail Plane, "Old No. 249," to the Smithsonian Institution. Paul Collins was acknowledged as the "inspiration" of the project. It was the final public act of his half-century in aviation. He passed away in 1971.

Robert Reeve

As a young man in 1917, Paul Collins left Wisconsin and ultimately charted the northeastern air route to the Arctic Circle and Europe. The same year, Robert Reeve also left the state to follow a round-about course that carried him in the other direction, northwest to the Arctic and Alaska.

Reeve was born in the Dane County village of Waunakee in 1902. When the U.S. entered World War I, the fifteen-year-old youngster was able to persuade a recruiter to enlist him in the Army.

Discharged at war's end and still only 17 years old, Reeve returned to Waunakee where, at his father's urgent request, he completed high school, probably the only graduate of Waunakee High who had already been a sergeant of the infantry.

His father wanted Bob to attend the University of Wisconsin, but the young man had other plans. He left home and signed on as a merchant seaman in the Orient. Back home in 1924, he did register at Madison but instead of hitting the books he "learned to make gin and not bet into a one-card draw." He also hung around with George Gardner, Monk MacKinnon, ex-World War I pilot Ora McMurray and barnstormer Cash Chamberlain, who parked his Jenny in a farm field on the edge of town. Gardner and MacKinnon took up flying and ended up working for Paul Collins at Northeast Airlines. With Eagle River as his base, McMurray became the flying physician of northern Wisconsin, while Chamberlain barnstormed and flew the air mail out of Milwaukee until he died in a crash in 1927. With friends like these, what else could Bob Reeve do, but fly?

He did not object when his dean asked him to leave the University. After knocking around the country, he stopped in Texas, where he found work as a grease-monkey and gopher for a pair of barnstormers aptly named Maverick and Hazard. In return they gave him three hours of flying lessons and said he was ready to solo. Reeve later recalled that "I was what you could call a natural-born flyer," and he must have been. When the Aeronautics Bureau began licensing pilots in 1927, Bob Reeve qualified for both the commercial pilot's and mechanic's tickets.

He also returned briefly to the Army and trained as a Flight Cadet at Brooks Field, Texas. His instructor was Lieutenant Nathan Twining, born in Monroe, Wisconsin. Instructor and cadet became life-long friends, but Army discipline and Robert Reeve were not compatible. He did not object when an Army doctor discovered that his blood pressure was too high for military service.

Reeve walked out of the Army and into the opportunity of a life time. Pan-American Airways, with backing from the W.R. Grace steamship company and a United States Air Mail contract, had organized Panagra Airlines to serve Central and South America. After a small start with Loening "Ducks" and Fairchild 71s, Panagra stepped up and ordered a fleet of Ford Tri-Motors. Ford was look-

Robert Reeve, Waunakee's and Alaska's "Glacier Pilot." (WAHF)

ing for men who could fly the planes to South America, set them up, train and check out native pilots and mechanics. This was no small order and it is testimony to Bob Reeve's ability that, among the hundreds of pilots vying for a Ford job, he was accepted, passed the training courses and parked in the pilot's seat of a spanking new Ford Tri-Motor with its nose pointed south.

He delivered the first Ford Tri-Motor to enter regular service in Peru then pioneered the extension of Foreign Air Mail Route Number 9 from Lima, Peru to Santiago, Chile, Buenos Aires, Argentina and Montevideo, Uruguay. It was the longest aviation route in the world and, with its 23,000 foot jump over the Andes, one of the most hazardous. The stretch between Lima and Santiago was equivalent to the 1900-mile trans-Atlantic route from Newfoundland to Ireland. The difference was that, while flying the North Atlantic was considered to be an extraordinary feat until the late 1930s, flying the equivalent route over the Pacific between Lima and Santiago became a regular weekly job for Bob Reeve in 1930.

While the Panagra Fords flew the mail-and-passenger hop from Lima to Santiago, planes flying the Andes carried only the mail. Here Reeve flew a Fairchild 71 powered by a new 600 horsepower Curtiss-Wright supercharged engine that would not conk out in the cold, oxygen-thin air. Even with a dependable plane, flying the Andes was no joy-ride.

"Until my crossing of the Hump, as we called the southern Andes," Reeve recalled, "I felt a certain amount of skepticism about...deathly air pockets or downdrafts that snatched your ship out of control...and having their planes literally thrown thousands of feet down in the space of a few seconds." He was skeptical until he encountered one. After ascending to 20,000 feet, without air tanks, Reeve struggled to stay conscious and find a fog-free pass through the mountains. He made it over the top and onto the lee side of the mountains, when a downdraft knocked him straight down 5,000 feet. "A vision of mail, Fairchild and Reeve scattered over those crags below flashed through my brain," he said. He was just about to meet the rocks, when an updraft pushed the plane skyward and prevented the crash.

His thousands of hours of flying in South America, from the fogbound coasts of the Pacific, to the dusty plains of the Argentine and the peaks of the Andes made Bob Reeve one of the most experienced pilots in the world. He was also one of the richest, until he lost what he hadn't already spent in the bear stock market of 1930. He was also a little bit bored by the long flights over the water and the plains, followed by the intense hops over the mountains.

He had been reading about Alaska, which a pilot he had met in Madison, Carl Ben Eielson, had opened for aviation in 1924, and contracted a case of gold fever. He quit his job with Panagra and came home to Waunakee, where the pilot who had survived the Andes at 22,000 feet fell into a frozen creek and contracted a non-crippling, but serious case of polio. After a month in bed, he got up, said good bye to his family once again, and hopped a freight for Seattle. Flat broke, with not much more than the clothes on his back, he stowed away on a freighter and landed at the port of Valdez. Old-timers saw him as another down-and-outer at the end of his rope who had come to the end of the earth to finish out his days.

Reeve had a different view. He located the airport, found a battered Eaglerock biplane with a Wright Whirlwind motor in fairly good shape, and talked the owner into hiring him to repair it. Once he repaired the plane, Reeve would lease it back and hire out as a bush pilot.

Alaska had more than its fair share of bush pilots when Robert Reeve arrived there in 1932. They were territorial and competitive and resentful of newcomers looking for a piece of a diminish-

ing pie. The easy pickings of the 1890s gold rush days were over in the 1930s. Gold and other mineral riches were still present, but hard to reach. Transporting supplies and equipment to mountainous mining sites was slow and expensive and could be done only in the brief summer months. In the winter, the diggings were buried by glacial snow and ice.

The oldtimers patiently explained this hopeless situation to the newcomer and expected him to be just as accepting as they were. Then Reeve asked if anyone had ever flown supplies into a mine? Had anyone landed on a glacier?

Reeve said he could and he would, if a mining company paid him for it. He waited a year to get an answer. In the meantime he made a few dollars ferrying passengers and freight as all the other bush pilots did. He earned enough money to put $1500 down on a used Fairchild 51 four-passenger cabin plane, and promised to come back with the $2,000 balance due in two years. The Fairchild was very similar to the planes he had flown over the Andes. Now all he needed was a job for it.

The Big Four gold mine was 6,000 feet up the Brevier Glacier only about 30 miles from Valdez but all but closed in the winter because the pack trains could not make their way in with supplies. Reeve offered to supply the mine by air at the rate of a nickel a pound if he could land there. The manager of the mine told him not to worry, that there was a "thousand-foot fine flat surface."

When he arrived over the mine in his Fairchild, Reeve saw a bowl-shaped ice shelf, about 100 feet wide and 500 long bounded by thick walls of snow. The surface was uniformly white, with no marks or horizon to judge altitude. He thought he would make a low pass from top to bottom to check the terrain, but lost all perspective and, without knowing it, started to land. The plane glided over the surface, slowed as it slid uphill, then slammed into the wall of snow on the edge of the bowl.

"The propeller was picking up the whole side of the mountain. It was just like an Arctic blizzard outside. I had to shut off my motor quick, so we could see what shape we were in," Bob recalled.

In good shape, as it turned out. The snow wall stopped the plane but did no damage, not even to the propeller. Bob Reeve had made a successful landing on a glacier. Now all he had to do was spend the day digging the plane out, turn it around and see if he could take off. As it turned out, getting off the glacier was easier than landing. Rob revved his engine, headed down the slope and was airborne in about fifty feet.

This first successful landing on the glacier at the Big Four Mine opened up a whole new set of opportunities for Bob Reeve and for Alaska. Mines that had sat dormant in the winter could now run. Mines that had closed years before could reopen. "For the first time in the history of Valdez an airplane was used today as an aid to opening up the vast treasure vaults in the hills," reported the Valdez Miner newspaper. The bush pilot was now the key to economic development.

For the rest of the 1930s, Reeve continued to supply mines by air in the winter and the summer. Since some mines were located on sites where the snow did not melt in summer, Reeve kept the skis on his plane all year and used a mud-flat near Valdez for a landing strip instead of the airport. The skis glided over the wetland grass and mud just as they did over the snow. Other mines were in country inaccessible to any plane, so Reeve supplied them via airdrops. Drums of gasoline and oil, sacks of food, crates of tools, even a small electrical generator cushioned by a mattress, were shoved out the door of the Fairchild—no parachutes used.

World War II brought unprecedented aviation development to Alaska. The Territory that did not have one genuine airport in 1941, had over 60 by 1945. Reeve was ready to capitalize on this windfall thanks to General Lee Mulzer, wartime commander of Elmendorf Airfield who Bob had met back in Wisconsin in the 1920s when Mulzer was flying a Ford Tri-Motor for the Nekoosa Edwards Paper Company. Mulzer told Reeve that the C-47

that he had used for his command plane was now war surplus and would go on sale at Anchorage for $20,000, with only $3,000 down. Reeve was the first bidder and got the plane. He flew it himself to Seattle, picked up a load of passengers and brought them back to Anchorage. By the end of 1946, Reeve had a total of four C-47s, once again known by their civilian designation as DC-3s.

These planes were the nucleus of Reeve Aleutian Airlines, the first regularly scheduled airline to connect the string of islands that reaches half-way across the northern Pacific to the mainland of North America. Bob Reeve, the glacier pilot, died in 1980, but his airline continues to operate today.

Clyde Lee & Felix Waitkus

Making a flight to Europe was the Holy Grail of American aviation throughout the 1920s and early 1930s. Even after the solo flights of Charles Lindbergh in 1927 and Amelia Earhart in 1928, aviators had little trouble finding a reason to risk a cold death in the North Atlantic. Prize money was an incentive for some, especially during the hard times of the early 1930s. A desire for fame and glory pushed a few more to try "hopping the pond." Ethnic or national pride—the desire to be the first native son of the New World to return to the European motherland—was also a com-

Clyde Lee and co-pilot Julius Robertson with the Stinson they hoped to fly across the Atlantic to Norway in 1932. Hoping to find a sponsor in his home town Lee originally named his plane the "Oshkosh B'gosh." When business people in Vermont offered backing, the plane became the "Green Mountain Boy." Shortly before the flight, Robertson was replaced by John Bochkon, who was lost at sea with Lee. (Bernice Lee Krippene)

Clyde Lee waves farewell just prior to takeoff. (Bernice Lee Krippene)

1930s and about the kind of people involved in it.

"Our success," wrote Lester Maitland of his California-Hawaii flight in 1927, "was dependent upon that important thing called Preparation." Important it was, but preparation alone did not get the Bird of Paradise to Hawaii. Maitland and Hegenberger prepared and packed a half-dozen different navigational devices on their plane. All of them failed under the actual conditions of the flight, leaving navigator Hegenberger to rely on one of the human traveler's oldest navigational practices—a fix on the North Star. A successful aviator strikes a balance among the complimentary forces of preparation, equipment, training and ability to fly across the county or the Atlantic Ocean.

Clyde Lee was born in 1908 on a farm near Rozellville in Wood County, but in a year or so his parents returned to the the Winnebago Town of Winchester where they had both been raised. Clyde grew up on a farm just across the road from the Larson Brothers and was a young teenager when the Larsons turned their farm into an airport. Lee was sixteen years old when Roy Larson trained him to fly his OX-Standard. By the time he was twenty, Clyde was a stunt pilot, wingwalker and parachute jumper prone to push the envelope of safety. He squeezed his plane under bridges with low clearances, made parachute jumps from planes flying below minimum altitude, hung with his teeth on a rope suspended beneath an airplane, and minus a safety harness. No one ever questioned Clyde Lee's courage, but more than a few people wondered about his common sense.

In 1928, Roy Larson died when a student he was instructing froze at the stick and drove his Swallow biplane nose into the ground. The accident had a sobering, maturing effect on Clyde Lee who had looked on Roy as an older brother. He continued to barnstorm but took fewer chances and started to think beyond the next day's stunt. When a group of businessmen in the Upper Peninsula of Michigan purchased a Stinson cabin plane, Lee hired on as their pilot. He ferried the executives across the Upper Midwest until the business downturn of the early 1930s made the plane a luxury they could not afford. They also owed Clyde a few thousand dollars in back pay that they made good by giving him the Stinson. He now had a plane, but no source of income, a common situation for pilots in 1931.

He returned to Oshkosh and flew when he could, including one memorable trip to Milwaukee

pelling factor. Usually a combination of reasons was involved, as in the famous case of "Wrong Way Corrigan" who, in order to evade a government ban on trans-Atlantic flights by ill-prepared aviators, filed a flight plan from New York to California, then flew to Ireland "by mistake." His subsequent denials that he had always intended to be the first American son of Eire to alight on the "auld sod" were blarney, but had little impact on Corrigan's reputation, his lasting fame, or the number of pints his admirers ponied up for in 1938.

Wrong Way Corrigan never found his way to Wisconsin but the state was involved in several trans-Atlantic flights with ethnic links in the post-Lindbergh/Earhart years. In the early 1930s, the Adamowicz brothers wanted to be the first Polish-American aviators to fly non-stop from the United States to Poland. Wisconsin's participation in their successful 1934 flight was limited to fund-raising appeals by the aviators and their supporters in the substantial Polish-American communities of Milwaukee and central Wisconsin.

The state was more closely connected to two other ethnic flights. In 1932, Oshkosh pilot Clyde Lee tried to capture the $10,000 prize offered by an Oslo newspaper and go down in history as the first American son of Norway to return to the homeland by air. In 1935, Felix Waitkus used the facilities at Kohler Airport to prepare his Lockheed Vega to realize his dream of becoming the first American son of Lithuania to fly non-stop to the old country.

The two flights differed in the preparation the pilots made, the resources available to each one and the outcome. Yet each one reveals much about the state of aviation in Wisconsin in the early

to fetch a load of cash ordered by a Oshkosh bank to stave off a run by nervous depositors. That cargo would have kept the Stinson in gas forever, had Clyde chosen not to deliver it. He wasn't tempted even though obtaining money was very much on his mind.

Lee had given himself the mission of fulfilling Roy Larson's dream of flying across the Atlantic, "maybe back to Norway." Clyde's Stinson had the same model Wright Whirlwind engine as Lindbergh's *Spirit of St. Louis* and with a few modifications could make the Atlantic hop. Clyde also had a mechanic, Fred Sensiba, and a co-pilot, 20-year-old Julius Robertson, whom he had met and flown with in the Upper Peninsula. All Clyde needed was a sponsor to underwrite the cost of rebuilding the Stinson's motor, installing new gas tanks and purchasing the 450 gallons of gas required for the 35-40 hours of flying to Norway.

He approached businesses in Oshkosh but found no backers. When the management of Oshkosh B'Gosh clothing expressed interest Clyde went so far as to paint the company name on the fuselage of his plane, but then they backed out. He had all but given up on the flight when an publicity agent he had hired told him that businessmen in the Vermont communities of Barre and Montpelier would back him. A check for $500 arrived from Barre, with another $500 promised from Montpelier. Clyde and his crew went to work rebuilding the motor, installing a 100 gallon gas tank in the cabin of the Stinson and a fifty-gallon wing tank. They also ordered 50 five-gallon gas cans and stacked them in the plane. In the course of the flight Robertson would top up the big tank as needed and drop the five-gallon cans into the sea. With all this gas in unsealed containers the Stinson was a flying bomb which any stray spark could turn into a firebomb. Alarmed, Lee had decided not to install a radio, lest a spark from its battery accidentally ignite the gas.

On August 5, 1932, Clyde Lee and Julius Robertson climbed behind the controls of their plane and lifted off from Oshkosh Airport. Among the family members and friends bidding them farewell was Steve Wittman, who shot a home movie of the take off.

They landed in Vermont and repainted the Stinson a bright red with white lettering. It was now the "Green Mountain Boy," advertising Barre/Montpelier as "The Granite Center of the World" instead of Oshkosh as the "Overall" capital. On a promotional flight to Bennett Field on Long Island, where Lindbergh had taken off for Europe, Clyde met John Bochkon, a veteran of the

Norwegian air force who wanted a ride home. Bochkon offered to pay for the honor of accompanying Clyde on what would be the fourth attempt to fly from North America to Norway. The cash-strapped Lee accepted and bumped Julius Robertson as co-pilot.

Back in Vermont, the flyers received word that another pair of Scandinavian pilots—Thor Solberg and Carl Peterson—were about to head off for Norway. Although not a Wisconsin native, Solberg did spend about a year as a flight instructor and pilot at the Holterhoff Airport in Brown Deer in the late 1920s, about the same time Clyde Lee was there. Also competing in what was turning out to a be a North Atlantic sweepstakes were "The Flying Hutchinsons," husband, wife and two small daughters hoping to make a "leisurely jaunt" to London.

The Hutchinsons were delayed, but Solberg and Peterson took off in a Bellanca CH-300 from Bennett Field in the early hours of August 23, 1932. They were headed for Harbor Grace, Newfoundland, the jumping off point for the Atlantic crossing. Clyde Lee and John Bochkon were bottled up by fog in Vermont until mid-morning and scrambled to catch up.

Both planes ran into a storm on the way to Newfoundland. Clyde and Bochkon reluctantly set down on a rainswept beach near Burgeo on Newfoundland's south shore about 150 miles from Harbor Grace. They spent a miserable night in the wet and cold, convinced that Solberg and Peterson had the jump on them and would beat them to Norway.

Solberg and Peterson were ahead of their rivals when they met the storm. They attempted to fly above the rain, but as they rose into the clouds, the moisture turned to snow and the Bellanca's engine stalled. It would not start again and the Bellanca nose-dived into the icy waters of Placentia Bay about twenty miles short of Harbor Grace. The flyers were rescued by fishermen and the plane towed to shore, but none would fly again for many days.

At dawn on August 24 the sky was clear and Lee and Bochkon struggled to take off from the soft sand of Burgeo Bay. After releasing air to soften the tires, they got the Stinson off the sand and made Harbor Grace, where they learned that they were the only competitors left in the race to Norway. They could pause at Harbor Grace, make repairs to the wing damaged on landing at Burgeo, change the spark plugs, top up the fuel tanks. Since gasoline was more expensive than anticipated, Clyde had to wire home to his cousin Leighton Hough in Oshkosh, who sent more money.

Fully-loaded and fuelled, the Stinson weighed

5,400 pounds. Getting that weight into the air would be a challenge for the Whirlwind engine and, once aloft, its top speed would be 80-90 MPH. As fuel was burned and weight decreased, the plane would gradually increase its speed to the maximum of 130 MPH. Clyde estimated it would take about thirty hours to reach the British Isles and seven more to reach Oslo. The Stinson carried fuel for forty hours of flying. At the last minute Clyde decided to lighten the load by discarding a rubber liferaft that weighed thirty-five pounds.

Shortly after 4:00 AM on August 25, 1932, Clyde Lee and John Bochkon took off from Harbor Bennett Field, Long Island.

They almost made it. After thirty-seven hours and 4,100 miles they made a forced and fatal landing at night in rough, forested terrain 120 miles east of Berlin in Germany. The death of the two flyers triggered a wave of nationalistic feeling in Lithuanian communities in the United States. Girenas and Darius would not die in vain, vowed the leaders of the Lithuanian community. Another plane would be purchased, another pilot found and another flight made.

Back in 1930, Wisconsin Governor Walter Kohler had hosted the state convention of the

Felix W. Waitkus at Kohler preparing his Lockheed Vega to fly across the Atlantic and Europe to Lithuania. (Kohler Co. Archives)

Grace, circled the field once and headed into the sunrise. The weather forecast in Newfoundland was for two days of clear weather over the North Atlantic, but ships at sea later reported a severe storm west of Ireland. At the time the Stinson was scheduled to arrive, all the British Isles were socked in with a thick fog and no local planes were flying. One observer on the coast of Wales reported hearing the sound of an airplane engine approaching from the west. Then it abruptly stopped. No trace of John Bochkon or Clyde Lee has ever been found.

About one year after the disappearance of Bochkon and Lee, two other pilots, Stanley Girenas and Stephen Darius, were racing across the North Atlantic in a Bellanca CH-300. Their goal was to be the first Lithuanian-Americans to fly non-stop to their ethnic homeland, 4,500 miles from

American Legion in his home village of Kohler, near Sheboygan. Sixteen hundred Legionaires and family members turned out for a big picnic and celebration. Part of the entertainment was a visit by a nine-plane squadron of Army pursuit planes from Selfridge Field, Michigan. One of the pilots was Lieutenant Austin Straubel, who would leave his name on the Green Bay airport in a few years, another was Lieutenant Felix Waitkus, a Chicago-born son of Lithuanian immigrants.

The folks in Kohler threw out the welcome mat for the pilots and Lt. Waitkus was pleased to meet young Martha Brotz, daughter of airport manager Anton Brotz. Waitkus left with his squadron at the end of the day, but had found a reason to return to Kohler. In 1931, he was discharged from the Army to join the ranks of the Depression unemployed. He moved to Kohler, where a pilot with an engineering degree was a welcome addition to the airport crew.

Early in 1934, the committee organizing the second flight to Lithuania named Felix Waitkus as their pilot. They had already purchased a Lockheed Vega 5B from the Shell Oil Company that had been piloted by Jimmy Doolittle and had spent over $7,000 for Lockheed to rebuild it. The final preparations for the flight would be made by Waitkus and Brotz at Kohler over the winter of 1934-35. Waitkus later wrote that Brotz was "the most qualified person I could have chosen to supervise the designing and construction of the vital parts."

They installed a new 550 horsepower Pratt and Whitney engine and tanks to hold 670 gallons of fuel. A new set of instruments went into the cabin, so did a radio compass and a directional radio receiver. He would be flying solo so Waitkus put great stock in the directional receiver which operated "independent of visibility or roughness of the air." Although sea-going ships had been using directional radio for years, the devices were new to aviation. "Since there were no such radios commercially available at the time it was necessary to have one specially built," Waitkus recalled, at a cost of $900. Also, since a receiver wasn't of much use unless someone was sending a signal, Waitkus and Brotz arranged for a radio station in Athlone, Ireland to broadcast weather and music every fifteen minutes during the flight.

Waitkus and the Vega left Kohler on May 23, 1935 to conduct final flight tests at Bennett Field, Long Island. The crucial problem was getting a plane carrying 670 gallons of gasoline into the air within an explosion. Starting with a 450 gallon load, Waitkus added more gasoline on each take off until he tested the Vega with a full load of fuel. Then, before landing the Vega on a bumpy grass field at 80 MPH, safety dictated that Waitkus switch off all electrical switches, ignition included, and dump unused fuel.

"I often wish that I were on the ground to witness the dumping," Waitkus wrote, "as they say the white Lockheed seemed to be waving a long white plume of gasoline. It must have been beautiful in the sparkling sunlight." It was beautiful, but also an expensive and necessary procedure.

On September 21, 1935, with a forecast of clear weather over the Atlantic, Felix Waitkus took off from Bennett Field, headed for Newfoundland. He encountered fog over Nova Scotia, but was able to fix his position with a radio signal from St. John's, Newfoundland. Thanks to the radio, he kept on course even though the fog did not lift over

Newfoundland nor did it lift after he turned east over the Atlantic. He continued flying east until after about three hours and three hundred miles out, his radio picked up Athlone radio and he corrected his course on it.

Hoping to fly out of the fog, Waitkus rose to 12,000 feet, but ice in the carburetor forced him to stay in the soup at 3,000 feet. When he tried to fly above the clouds again, the fog turned to snow and ice that built up on the prop and wings. About 150 miles out from Ireland, he found holes in the fog through which he got his first sight of the ocean below and the stars above. In seventeen hours he had flow nearly all the way across the North Atlantic without seeing the water.

Soon he was over Ireland, but he still had more than 2,000 miles of flying to reach Lithuania. He had burned more fuel than anticipated and the radio reported heavy fog ahead over Britain, the North Sea and Germany. Awake, alert and tense at the controls for a long day, Waitkus found that "the instruments were beginning to fairly dance before my eyes."

He decided to find a level, clear Irish meadow and land for a rest and refueling. "After searching for a pasture large enough in which to land the Lockheed, I proceeded to frighten the cattle away...but in coming in for a landing and passing within a foot or two of a haystack and one of those Irish stone fences, an unexpected gust of wind picked up one wing and dug the other into the ground. The ship spun around, washed out the

A cartoon celebrating Felix Waitkus, who damaged his plane landing in Ireland and could not complete the flight to Lithuania. (Kohler Co. Archives)

landing gear, right wing front section of the fuselage and propeller."

The flight to Lithuania looked like it would end in Ireland, and so it did. The Vega was crated up and shipped by rail to Kaunas, Lithuania where Waitkus and his wife Martha met up with it. They received a royal greeting in the capital city and the rest of the country where "for two months our time was not our own." To the Lithuanians who, after 200 years of Russian rule had just achieved independence at the end of World War I, any expression of national accomplishment was worth celebrating, Felix Waitkus was a hero whether or not he actually completed his flight.

He didn't reach Lithuania, but Waitkus was the sixth person to fly solo across the Atlantic in a single engine plane. His thoughts on the flight were typically low-key. "The chief value in most ocean flights is the good will attained between nations and national publicity. They also tend to

Walter Lees at the controls of a Benoist shortly after leaving Wisconsin in 1912. (Jo Lees Cooper)

develop air consciousness and air confidence..." Not much more could be said.

After the cheering stopped, Waitkus returned to Kohler to work with Anton Brotz, then studied aeronautical engineering at the University of Wisconsin and the Massachusetts Institute of Technology. He served in the Army Air Force during World War II as a test pilot for Boeing B17s and B29s. He remained in the military until his death of a heart attack in 1955 at age 49.

The Lockheed Vega that he and Anton Brotz had so diligently rebuilt into a airplane that could find its way across the Atlantic in a fog became part of the Lithuanian air force. When the Soviet Army occupied the country in 1940, the Vega disappeared.

Walter Lees

When Walter Lees left the United States Army Air Service in 1919, his aviation career was already one of the longest in the world. The Mazomanie native had soloed in a Benoist XII with dual stick controls at St. Louis in November, 1912. That he was still alive and flying in 1919 placed him among a select group of aviators—one that did not include Cal Rodgers, Lincoln Beachey or Wilbur Wright.

He may have been flying longer than all but a few pilots but, in 1919, Lees was just another war vet flyer looking for a job. He barnstormed in Illinois, Ohio and Oregon, spent time in and out of the Army and the Navy, tested one of the first commercial-model parachutes—all so he could fly as much as possible. In 1922, he flew one of the last airplanes manufactured by the Wright Company. It was a four-place cabin biplane powered by two Liberty engines and mounted on floats that Lees flew off of lakes in central Ontario, Canada. Two years later, in Michigan, he flight-tested William Stout's single-engine metal plane out of which the Ford Tri-Motor evolved.

In 1925, he became a service representative/test pilot for the Packard Motor Company and traveled the country to work on Packard aircraft engines. The company was a serious and innovative competitor in the aircraft engine field and Lees checked every model it made and flew just about every plane in which a Packard was installed.

The engineer driving Packard's aircraft engine department and who hired Walter Lees was Lionel M. Woolson. In the mid-1920s, Woolson and Hermann Dorner, a German inventor, developed a 225-horsepower diesel engine for airplanes. They installed it in a Stinson SM-1DX "Detroiter" and told Lees to make the world's first flight powered by a diesel engine, which he did. The engine ran well but revealed its experimental status when it wouldn't throttle down for Lees to land. After pulling up on his first approach, he circled the runway, shut off the fuel pump to kill the motor and glided in for a safe landing.

In May 1929, Lees made a much-publicized 600-mile flight from Detroit to Langley Field, near Washington, D. C. The diesel used a mere $4.68 worth of fuel, about one-tenth of the cost of regular aviation gasoline. Fuel economy was the diesel's

selling point and Packard hoped that it would make up for the motor's extra weight, which was considerably more than a conventional power-plant. Lees also flew the plane in the 1930 Ford Reliability Tour which stopped in Wausau and Eau Claire.

By 1931, Woolson and Packard knew they had a good product, but felt it needed some marketing "sizzle" to close sales. For example, after Lindbergh flew to Paris, the Wright Company couldn't manu-facture the Whirlwind model engine fast enough to meet demand. That was a situation Packard would be happy to experience.

Instead of risking a long-distance flight, which was just as likely to be a spectacular failure as a success, Packard settled for an endurance test. If an airplane powered by a Packard diesel could stay aloft longer than any other plane ever had, the marketing people would have something to crow over.

The record Packard hoped its diesel would

beat was 74 hours, 29 minutes in the air without refueling. The airplane they chose was a new Bellanca two-place cabin plane, a model used in many trans-Atlantic and other long distance flights. Packard installed its diesel motor in the Bellanca and made other modifications. Fuel tanks of 91-gallon capacity were mounted inside each wing and space cleared so fifty-two custom-made five-gallon fuel cans could be stacked behind the seats. In addition, fifty cans of lubricating oil that could also be burned for fuel were crammed into the plane. In the course of the flight, the small cans would be emptied first and discarded, thus lighten-ing the load and freeing space in the plane so the pilots could leave their seats.

For Walter Lees, the endurance test was his best shot at becoming a big name aviator. He was one of few people on earth with twenty years expe-rience as a pilot, yet he was no more well known than the kid who washed his plane at Packard's airport. At the same time, pilots with much less

Fred Brossy and Walter Lees with the auxiliary fuel cans that would enable them to stay aloft in their Packard-diesel-powered Bellanca long enough to set an endurance record that held for over fifty years. (Jo Lees Cooper)

experience and—in Lee's view—a lot more luck, were world famous. Lees hoped the Packard diesel would do for him what the *Spirit of St. Louis* had done for Lindbergh.

No one could be expected to fly solo for the three days-plus it would take to break the endurance record so Lees shared piloting duties with Packard's other pilot, a young man named Fred Brossy. They took the Bellanca from Detroit to the test site at Jacksonville Beach, Florida in March, 1931. Jacksonville Beach was selected for its mild Florida climate, its miles of sand beach open for emergency landings and because a good airport was only a few miles inland. The endurance test would begin as soon as the weather forecaster predicted three days of good weather and consisted of Lees and Brossy flying the Bellanca back and forth over the beach. The pilots could select their course but at least once every half hour they had to be sighted by the judges from the National Aeronautical Association, who manned an observation post on the beach on a twenty-four-hour basis. If a storm blew the Bellanca out of sight, if fog took the airplane out of sight or sound of the observers for thirty minutes, the clocked stopped running and the test was over. It was deceptively simple aerial expedition, requiring only that the pilots keep the plane in the air, the fuel tanks topped up and themselves alert and sane for better than three days and nights.

On March 11, the weather report was favorable. The crew fueled the Bellanca's inboard tanks and the additional cans of gas and lubricants were stacked in the tail, along with thermos jugs of coffee and soup, ten gallons of water, five southern-fried chicken dinners and thirty-six peanut-butter and jelly sandwiches. The total weight of the plane, including pilots, fuel and chicken dinners, was 6750 pounds. Lees and Brossy had never tried to get the Bellanca off the ground while it was carrying such a heavy load.

As Lees recorded in his journal, "I slowly opened the throttle. Fred had the stabilizer wheeled way forward so as to help lift the heavily loaded tail...My main concern was to keep the plane straight, because the least deviation from a straight line might put a strain on the side of the tires and cause them to blow out...We went faster and faster, up to 70 MPH. The tail came up in the flying position...Then the machine became light..."

The Bellanca needed 3,000 feet of runway to get off the ground. Lees ascended slowly, not reaching 800 feet until he had covered five miles straight ahead. He rose at the rate of about 1,000 feet an hour, leveled off at 3,000 feet, throttled back and flew the plane over the course. He had begun the flight that he hoped would put make him America's most famous aviator.

Near sunset on the first day, Lees and Brossy noticed oil running down the fire wall in front of them. They searched but could not find a leak, and the oil gauge was steady, so they kept flying. About 3:00 AM they noticed that the oil gauge read zero, but the engine wasn't running any hotter, so they guessed the oil gauge was off, and kept flying. At 9:00 AM on the second day, more oil was dripping down the fire wall and the oil temperature gauge conked out. With both their oil gauges out and a leak they could neither find nor fix, they decided to abort the flight before the engine was damaged. Their first attempt to set an endurance record failed after 30 hours, 13 minutes.

While quitting wasn't easy, the plane was still intact, the pilots ready, and the Packard management still supportive. On April 12, Lees and Brossy took off again after the record, but since the first flight, two French pilots had stretched the endurance time to 75 hours, 23 minutes. This time Lees and Brossy took off with more fuel—468 gallons—and minus the chicken dinners. They had been too tense to eat much of anything on the first flight and even the "finest Southern fried chicken in Florida," was inedible.

Their second take off was smooth and first day of flight uneventful. After 45 hours in the air, they had emptied and discarded enough of the five-gallon fuel cans to hang a string hammock behind their seats. They could move about a bit and take

Walter Lees showing how a discarded fuel can lodged in the tail brace nearly aborted his record endurance flight. To free it, Lees crawled to the tail of the Bellanca, slit the fabric and reached out to dislodge the can. (Jo Lees Cooper)

turns napping out of their seats. All was going well, as Lees recorded, "Nothing exciting happened on this flight until the morning of the fourth day..."

At 4:30 AM, a thunderstorm broke and dumped buckets of rain. The ground crew switched on a bank of floodlights so the plane could continue to circle above the observers, but visibility was fast diminishing. The Bellanca did not have any windshield wipers so, to keep on course, Lees and Brossy had to stick their heads out the side windows into the soaking rain. They flew this way until 11:00 AM, when fog started to roll in. They flew down the beach, away from the fog, and hoped the observers would realize their predicament and move with them, but the judges did not follow.

As they flew away from the fog, Lees and Brossy had been aloft for over 70 hours. The engine was running fine, they had all the fuel they needed to break the record, but in order to return to the observation point they would have to fly blind into the fog. The Jacksonville-Miami stretch of the airway, with airliners bearing passengers, ran only a few miles to the west of the beach and the area below was populated. Rather than risk their own lives and the lives of others, Lees and Brossy aborted the flight.

"It was the hardest decision I ever had to make," Lees wrote. "Maybe I should have taken the chance and flew into that fog, but my better judgment said no and down we came."

Instead, after having flown for 74 hours, 12 minutes, they landed on a clear stretch of beach. They had been 72 minutes away from breaking the record.

Another month passed and they tried again, certain they could make it and determined to set a record that would last not just for days, but for years. Since taking off with a heavy load was not as difficult as feared, they mounted a sixty-gallon tank on the belly of the fuselage and made further modifications inside that enabled the Bellanca to carry twenty-five more gallons of fuel there. They culled their supplies and equipment to reduce the load, laid off the fried chicken and dieted so each man lost ten pounds.

On May 25, 1931 the Packard Bellanca lifted off the beach once again. Even with the new belly tank, the plane rose into the air, if not easily, at least smoothly. Lees and Brossy resumed their monotonous course over the glistening sand of the beach and the blue waves of the ocean. They were past the fifty hour mark when Brossy glanced at the tail and noticed that one of the five-gallon gas cans they had been discarding in the night had lodged in the tail brace. No damage was evident yet, but they could not leave the can there. Wriggling the tail would not shake loose the can and the maneuver wasted fuel so Lees agreed to crawl back to the tail and see what he could do from there. He used his pocket knife to slit the fabric of the fuselage, pushed his arm through to the outside and was just able to grab the handle of the can. On Lees signal, Brossy then dropped the nose slightly so Lees could drop the can without fear of damaging the tail. Then, using needle and thread from a repair kit they had decided not to discard, he sewed the fabric shut and climbed back into the pilot's seat.

Into the third day of the flight, they started mixing the remainder of their lubricating oil with the gasoline. The diesel would handle the thinned oil and burning it would keep the Bellanca aloft longer. At 10:10 AM on their fourth day, May 28, 1931, Lees and Brossy passed the record mark. They were in fine spirits and resolved to keep flying as long as they had oil or gasoline to keep pouring into the fuel tank. Early in the evening, a storm front appeared on the horizon and, even though they had fuel for about four more hours, they decided to land. When they touched ground at 7:19 PM they had set a record of 84 hours, 32 minutes. It was the longest non-refueled duration flight yet made.

Although the Packard people were duly grateful, and the flight received its full share of publicity, there were no ticker tape parades for Fred Brossy and Walter Lees. Flying circles over Florida did not have the sizzle of Lindbergh's jaunt to Paris or Wiley Post's round-the-world trip. Walter Lees did not find the fame he had sought even though the flight earned the Collier Trophy from the National Aeronautical Association. Lees continued to work for Packard until World War II, when he entered the Navy. At the end of war he took up farming in California and stayed on the land until he passed away in 1957. The Packard diesel, although proven powerful and dependable, was not able to compete with newer conventional engines and was soon phased out.

The record that Walter Lees and Fred Brossy set lasted much longer than their fame. Except for military flights and space shots, of course, no non-refueled airplane stayed aloft for more than 84 hours and 32 minutes until 1986, when Dick Rutan and Jeana Yeager, in preparation for their round the world flight, kept their Voyager aircraft aloft for 111 hours over California.[8]

Brothers Airport, for example, became the neighborhood social center for the men and boys of the Larsen-Winchester area. On any Sunday when an airplane was parked on the field, the neighbors hurried to finish their chores so they could be at the field when the paying customers arrived.

When the novelty wore off and the neighbors took for granted the presence of an aviator in their midst, the pilots had to take off for greener pastures. In the early days that meant setting off on a pleasant Sunday morning in summer, flying to a farm field or county fairgrounds and charging passengers for rides. Usually, a pilot could not land just anywhere and expect to attract a crowd of paying customers, although many tried it and were content just to make gas money. However, on just about every weekend in Wisconsin there was a community picnic, celebration or fair whose organizers welcomed pilots. They became part of the show along with the parade, the baseball tournament, and the ice cream sold by the village ladies club.

Although summer was the prime flying season, winter didn't bring an end to barnstorming in Wisconsin, where thousands of lakes froze into smooth, hard landing strips and people were hardy enough to ride in an open cockpit.

As more flyers entered the game, they had to organize, send out an advance person to place ads in the local paper, mount posters in town and get permission from a farmer to use his land. Relations with landowners could get sticky, as when Marge Van Galder, who did advance work for her husband Russ in southern Wisconsin, got permission from one farmer only to see Russ land on the field belonging to the farmer across the road that she had not visited.

After the first thrill of seeing a plane set down on their land wore off, farmers started to worry about crop damage. When Bill Leithold set down in a beautiful field of wing-high winter rye near Wilton in Monroe County, the farmer stormed out of the house ready to do battle. He had given

Elizabeth Lathrop at Madeline Island in 1919. Air mail of a sort came to Madeline Island when barnstorming pilot Harold Russell gave Postmaster Lathrop her first airplane ride. (Madeline Island Historical Society)

BARNSTORMING MEMORIES

In the 1920s and '30s, virtually every pilot in Wisconsin, whether World War vet or starry-eyed farm boy new to the cockpit, was a barnstormer. The term developed out of a pilot's need for an open field to land and take off. Most fields were farm fields and—at least in Wisconsin—just about every farm had a barn which the pilot "stormed" over—much to the consternation of the Holsteins inside.

In its simplest version, barnstorming meant giving airplane rides for a fee—first to neighbors, then to anyone else who happened down the road and saw the plane parked in the yard. The Larson

Leithold permission to land two months earlier when the rye was inches high and could easily recover. Now Leithold had gone through it like a small steam roller, flattening the crop just as it was about to ripen. Even worse, since the grain was so high, it hampered Leithold's take off, which meant he had to make several attempts to get into the air, mashing more rye with each pass.

Leithold made peace with the rye farmer who, like most landowners, was happy to get a free ride or two in exchange for use of his field. Other farmers let the flyer use the field but wouldn't go near the airplane. Others still, after they saw what looked like the large wad of cash the pilot was collecting, demanded a share of the take—which often led to a quick exit by the pilot.

Not that barnstorming put a pilot on easy street. Rellis Conant was the hit of the Waupaca County fair in 1920, even though he charged $15 for a ride that lasted about ten minutes. The length of the ride usually depended on the number of passengers waiting in line, but other variables also mattered, such as the weather or outbreaks of airsickness. Since many pilots were young and unmarried, they were likely to give an attractive young woman a longer ride than an aged grandfather. However, giving preferential treatment to pretty faces was not always the most profitable practice, as Roy Larson learned when he took up an ancient veteran of the Civil War and was rewarded with a $5 gold piece.

As time passed and more pilots got into the air, rates fell. By 1922, Russell McNown was charging $5 for "straight rides" at Wausau and "$7.50" for "stunt rides." Three years later, Roy and Leonard Larson had to cut their price to $2.50 and, in the down years of the Great

Above: Mel Thompson (standing hatless next to prop) really did storm over the barn when he landed on the family farm near Quarry and a crowd of prospective customers came out.

Left: Starting with his home-built plane in 1919, barnstormer Thompson was a genuine "Joy Hop Merchant." (WAHF)

Above: In her white shirt and jodhpurs, young Ruth Harman was a hit at air shows in southeast Wisconsin in the mid 1930s. (WAC) Below: Russ Van Galder flew and Marge Van Galder managed air shows for their "Flying Circus" in south central Wisconsin in the late 1930s. (Marge Van Galder)

Van Galder's Flying Circus

Sunday, Sept. 25, 2:00 P. M.

at Brodhead U.S. Emergency Field

About 5 miles west of Brodhead (Follow the arrows)

Smoke Riding   Stunting
Ribbon Cutting   Balloon Busting
Trick Flying   Parachute Jump
Motorcycle Board Wall Crash

Thrills   Chills   Spills

Sponsored by Albany American Legion

that we always spent all of the money we made repairing the airplanes when we got back home."

As competition increased, a pilot had to develop a gimmick or two to get riders into the plane. For Howard Morey, who barnstormed with a Ford Tri-Motor in the mid-1930s, merely advertising night flights was enough to fill the plane with paying customers—provided he was flying out of a lighted airport. Few Wisconsin flyers had Tri-Motors like Morey's, but many started taking more than one passenger aloft as soon as they could. In fact, one selling point for the Wacos, American Eagles, Travel Airs and other popular aircraft of the late 1930s was that they had room for two paying customers in the front cockpit.

Wisconsin was a popular vacation destination even during the Depression, and it is a truism that folks on vacation spend money they wouldn't spend at home. Therefore, La Crosse's Les Borer made it a habit to spend summer weekends with his Waco 10 in the northern Wisconsin resort country, because if people could afford a vacation, "you know they had money."

Borer's regular fee was $3 for ten minutes. "But if the clouds were low, fleecy, there was nice big cumulus...maybe 1500 feet, you'd change your sales pitch, say 'beautiful clouds, we'll take you up above the clouds for fifteen dollars'." Even if he didn't get the fifteen, Borer would sometimes fly through the clouds, and get his money without asking when he landed.

Some passengers wanted more than a simple jaunt over the countryside or a pass through the clouds and used a five-dollar bill to induce a pilot to perform a roll, a loop or a spin. Elwyn West was flying his Waco 10 over a lake in Waupaca County when a passenger handed back a five dollar bill and made a spinning motion with his hand. In response, West planned to rise "to probably twelve, fifteen hundred feet" make a loop and spin down to a landing. However, he miscalculated his altitude and, as he spun down, his tail flicked the surface of the lake, giving both the passenger and the spectators a thrill greater than they expected. "If I had spun down over the field, I would have hit," he recalled.

Gambling with money instead of with lives also provided a thrill in western Wisconsin where Les Borer flew with a "punchboard" raffle card. "You could get people's mind off paying $2.50 or $3.00 for a ride," by selling them six chances on the board. The prize for punching out the winning hole was an airplane ride.

Borer was also one of many flyers who carried bathroom scales, "the gimmick which was the most fun." He would gather a group of women around the scales and ask them to check their weight. "You'd get somebody, and they'd fight you for a while, they didn't want no part of it, they were bashful. Pretty soon you'd hit on the right word or something and they'd jump on the scale...137 pounds, well, you're going to go for a dollar and thirty-seven cents." Once the ice was broken, "everybody was happy and that would get the ball rolling."

The scales were also used to lure men into the plane. The trick was to find the heaviest man in the crowd, weigh him, and offer him a free ride. Once the pilot proved that his plane could fly with

plane. The trick was to find the heaviest man in the crowd, weigh him, and offer him a free ride. Once the pilot proved that his plane could fly with the "big man" in the passenger seat, other riders would follow.

Gimmicks worked out in the fields, but flyers soon learned that they could get paying customers to come to them by putting on an air show. They started with simple stunts—rolls, loops and spins—and mock dogfights reminiscent of World War I. Happily, few spectators knew enough about military aircraft to be upset about the use of a Jenny, Canuck or Standard airplane in a dogfight. The lumbering training planes were not flown in combat, but most of the folks on the ground didn't know the difference between the slow glide of a Canuck in the "flying circus" at the county fairgrounds and the quick dive of the Fokker flown by the genuine Red Baron and his Flying Circus in France. As with any performance, the air show required the audience to suspend disbelief, at least briefly.

When faster, more maneuverable planes came along, pilots grounded their JNs and flew more exciting machines. In the days before regulations prevented it, Janesville's Stiles Whipple was fond of announcing that he was in town for a show with his Aeromarine Klemm by making a full, wing-wailing power drive followed by a steep climb over the town. On one such dive, he lost his ailerons. "My wings were jumping up and down. The side window broke out because of the vibration. The stick was like a demon pounding on my legs. I held it with both hands. It took all my strength...When I climbed out I had to sit on the wheel of the plane. My legs were so weak I couldn't walk." Whipple survived the barnstorming days of the 1930s and then flew commercial air liners for thirty years without a comparable experience.

Above: "Nothing" was too difficult for Waukesha photographer Warren O'Brien. One of Wisconsin's first aerial photographers, O'Brien was also good in the dark room, where he could make an airplane "fly" without it ever leaving the ground. (WAC)

If Stiles Whipple pushed the speed envelope on the fast end, Russell Schuetze of Waukesha nudged the slow side. Although he did most of his flying in a Swallow christened the Sky Rider, Schuetze did his best air show trick in a Curtiss Robin pusher, which resembled a motorcycle sidecar on wings with a rear-facing prop perched overhead. He would fly into the wind and throttle down until the thrust of the engine matched that of the wind and the Robin hung poised as if dead in the air. Then he would throttle down a little more and let the wind push the plane backwards, which looked doubly odd since the Robin's engine faced its tail. A little less throttle and Schuetze would set the Robin down vertically, as if it were a helicopter or autogyro.

On the other extreme from the tiny Robin was the metal-hulled Ford Tri-Motor. With room for fourteen passengers, the Ford was hardly the cheeky barnstormer's dream plane, yet Buck Leighton of Milwaukee, Howard Morey of Madison, and Lee Mulzer of Wisconsin Rapids, all stunted with them. Both Leighton and Mulzer,

Left: For the 1924 Presidential campaign of Senator Robert M. La Follette, Roy Larson barnstormed around the upper Midwest. (Bernice Lee Krippene)

who later became Army Air Force officers, were particularly proud of their ability to loop a Ford over the heads of a disbelieving crowd.

Mulzer seemed determined to maintain the Wisconsin tradition of air showmanship that started with Susie Mae Potter and Dave Behncke in the first years after World War I. In the early and mid-1930s Mulzer's air show toured Wisconsin with parachutist Dick Hunter and "Central Wisconsin's Only Girl Pilot," Virginia Whittesley. In Madison, Whittesley shared top billing with Steve Wittman and performed "intricate acrobatic [sic] stunts including Immelmans, tail spins, barrel rolls, slow rolls and inverted flying" in her Stinson Junior.

Whittesley had learned to fly with Mulzer at Wisconsin Rapids in 1929 and, in 1930, became the first female in the state to qualify for a transport license. She went on the road with Mulzer's show in Wisconsin, Minnesota and Iowa in the summer and, in 1929, made her first winter flight to Florida. After she arrived there, the St. Petersburg paper printed her account of the flight in Mulzer's Tri-Motor from Wisconsin Rapids, where the temperature at time of departure was -12, to sunny Florida with readings in the 80s. "This has been a journey unique. Everything has happened that could take place on such a trip. We have had rain, snow, sleet, fog, forced landings, tears, laughter, tranquility, excitement, all of which, when molded into one, produces the great-

est of all teachers, experience," she wrote.

In Florida, Whittesley used her experience to perfect her balloon-busting act. For this stunt a balloon was placed on a post in front of the grandstand about eighteen inches off the ground and a fish hook was mounted on the wingtip of Whittesley's Stinson. She would dive on the post and, in a excellent example of precision flying, tip her wing downwards and pop the balloon. She performed the act throughout Florida and back home in Wisconsin.

Whittesley returned to Wisconsin Rapids in 1930 and continued to appear in air shows until 1935. Then she stopped flying and moved to a farm near Waupaca where she lived until her death in 1979.

While Whittesley was popping balloons with her wingtip, Dean Crites used his wing to pluck a handkerchief off the ground. He developed this stunt at Waukesha in the mid-1930s in his Monocoupe, then switched to his Waco 10. He started by mounting a foot-long piece of wire on the wingtip that was thick enough to hook and hold the handkerchief yet thin enough to be invisible to the spectators. When Crites swept down on the kerchief, tipped his wing and plucked the bright cloth off the ground, it looked to all the world that he had actually touched the ground with his wingtip.

"It looks dangerous," said an aeronautics bureau inspector who visited the airport when Crites was practicing.

"Not much," deadpanned Crites, who was fond of understatement.

The handkerchief lift became Dean Crites' sig

nature stunt and one he performed at air shows with a variety of aircraft for three decades.

While later model planes were better suited for aerobatic and other flying stunts, the slow and steady, war surplus, biplane trainers of the early 1920s were admirably suited for wingwalking, parachute jumping and other acts that required a stunter to climb out of the cockpit. In fact, wing-walking, trapeze acts, transfers from one plane to another or to a car or boat as well as most of the stunts of the day were easier on the solid old Jenny, with its rack of wires and cross-braces to hang onto to, its broad wings, and dependable OX-5 engine.

Of Wisconsin wingwalkers, young Clyde Lee was among the most daring. As a teenager in the mid-1920s, he rode atop Roy Larson's Canuck while Larson stunted in front of grandstands throughout east-central Wisconsin. After riding the pedestal above the cockpit, Lee would climb onto a ladder suspended below the plane. There he would hang while the plane flew at 75 MPH, first with two hands, then with one hand, then only by his teeth—without a parachute. When he took up parachuting, which he learned by reading the instructions that accompanied his mail order 'chute, Lee continued to tempt fate, and suffered at least one serious injury because of it.

Clyde Lee was more fortunate than Mae Rox, the jumper who used the stage name "Peaches La Mar." She was performing at the Independence Day celebration in Reedsburg in 1930, when her chute failed to open and she plunged to her death almost faster than the audience could comprehend. Although only 19 years old, Rox/La Mar was an experienced parachutist and not likely to be careless, but accidents happen in risky situations.

Accidents and risk did not stop stunters from walking on wings or hanging beneath them, nor did it stop pilots from flying with them. To promote Goodyear tubes and tires, Howard Morey circled the state Capitol with a stunt man hanging on

Dean Crites performing his signature handkerchief pickup. He perfected this stunt with a Monocoupe and a Waco 10 at Waukesha in the 1930s. (Dean Crites)

a inner tube beneath the plane. After completing the circuit, the stunter was supposed to climb up the tube into the plane, but the new tube had come out its box covered with slippery talcum powder. While Morey circled the city watching his gas gauge and wondering if he should fly over Lake Monona so the stunt man could drop off there, the

stunter struggled to climb the tube. Finally, just as Morey reached the point where he had to make a decision, the stunter's head popped over the lip of the cockpit and he scrambled inside.

Art Hodge of Janesville recalled a similar experience with a stunter whose act was to transfer himself from a speeding motorboat to an airplane. Floyd Stone was the pilot of a 45-horse Szekely-powered American Eaglet for the stunt as it was performed on the Rock River at Newville, where the Interstate 90-94 bridge was later built. Starting well upriver of the old Newville railroad bridge, Stone flew the Eaglet with its trailing rope ladder over the motorboat. The stunter grabbed the ladder on cue, scrambled up to the first rung, then waved and bowed to the spectators. "He was quite a grandstander," Hodge recalled, "and he had to stay down there and show off and wave to the crowd and he wasn't paying too much attention to what was going on flying-wise. Stoney was flying the airplane and he could see that he couldn't climb with this guy hanging onto the rope ladder...He said he would have given anything for a hatchet...Finally the fellow on the rope started to

realize what was happening and he climbed up real fast and got into the airplane...and just barely oozed over the bridge."

Of the stunters who performed in Wisconsin in the 1930s, none seemed to perform more often and more successfully than Milwaukee's Herman Salmon, who had to be nicknamed "Fish." Born in 1913, Fish started flying at Curtiss-Wright Airport in 1931, but gravitated to parachute jumping. In 1935, he signed on with Manitowoc barnstormer Frank Shoblaska to make two jumps per weekend for $100 plus a five percent share of the gate. It was good money for a working man in 1935.

Salmon made one of his first jumps at Curtiss-Wright Airport in July, 1935. It was a twilight jump in which Fish was expected to make a dramatic appearance out of the darkened sky and into the beam of a searchlight which would follow him down to the ground. The wind was heavier than expected and the inexperienced Salmon missed the airport by over a mile. When the spectators saw him drift out of the range of the searchlight, they feared the worst. Crowding into about two hundred autos, they rushed out of the airport gate and down the back roads, expecting to find the parachutist stuck in a tree or strung out on a power line. Good fortune follows the foolhardy—sometimes—and Fish Salmon was fortunate this time. He made a soft landing in the dark in an aromatic field of cabbages, which his rescuers soon trampled into cole slaw, thereby irritating the cabbage farmer, who declared, "You guys are getting to be a public nuisance."

He was a nuisance that night, but Fish Salmon perfected his skill as a parachute jumper. He developed what he called the "Delayed Drop," or "Detroit Plummet" from an altitude of 10,000 feet. He would start with a free fall of 8,500 feet, than pull the cord and float down for the remaining 1,500 feet to hit his mark in the center of the airport.

In 1935 and '36, Fish Salmon's "Delayed Drop" was a featured event at airshows all across Wisconsin. With Frank Shoblaska, Buck Leighton or Howard Morey as his pilots, Salmon jumped at Curtiss-Wright near Milwaukee, at Maitland Field downtown, at Markesan near Green Lake, at Eagle River, Sturgeon Bay, Fond du Lac, Beaver Dam, Waupaca, Stevens Point, Merrill, Lake Delton, Racine, Kenosha, Kewaunee, Manitowoc, Gillette and Lena. Fish was due to jump in Livingston when Frank Shoblaska crashed and died in August 1936. He did not jump that day, but he made his show the following weekend.

Salmon found a pilot's job and moved to Detroit at the end of the 1936 season, after making well over 400 successful parachute jumps. Convinced a war was on the horizon, he moved to California in 1938 because he wanted "to join a big aircraft company." He worked first for Phillips Aviation and for Lockheed, where he tested P-38s and B-17s. When the U.S. entered World War II, he failed the Air Corps physical exam and enlisted in the Ferry Command, but his supervisors at Lockheed persuaded him to return as a test pilot. In 1944, Salmon became one of the first Americans to fly a jet aircraft. Other planes he tested included the F-90, F94C, F104A, T-33, XF vertical takeoff turbo-prop, the Constellation 649 and Superconstellation 1049. Also an air racer, he won the Goodyear Race in Cleveland in 1948.

One of the stunts Fish Salmon shared billing with in Wisconsin was the "Flying Farmer." In this act, a seemingly-careless pilot leaves his plane untended with the engine running and a "Farmer" dressed and acting like a hick climbs into the cockpit, accidentally hits the throttle and takes off. In some versions, the "Farmer" is replaced by a "Little Old Lady" or a "drunk" who swigs from a bottle throughout the show. No matter which costume he wears, the "Farmer" then performs a series of stunts both humorous and dangerous.

Done well, the "Flying Farmer" convinces the spectators that he really does not know how to fly. At minimum he raises a spector of doubt about his identity in the minds of the skeptical and keeps them interested. While the "Farmer" has to be good, the announcer can make or break the show.

Marge Van Galder tells the story of one "Farmer" act that she, her husband Russ and Stiles

Whipple took to an American Legion air show in southern Wisconsin in the late 1930s. Whipple was the "Farmer," Russ was the careless pilot who left his plane untended, while Marge was the business manager who set up the show with the Legion Post.

Whipple was ready to go when Van Galder noticed that the announcer was missing. After searching behind the grandstand, Marge found him, pickled to the gills. He was the only announcer they had, and the act was ready to go, so she pushed him up to the microphone. The act was supposed to start after Russ walked away from his airplane and reached the grandstand. In his befuddlement, however, the announcer didn't wait until Russ got to the grandstand before he said, "Ish that farmer taking off?" This alerted the Legionaires lining the field who then rushed to get the "Farmer" out of the plane. Fearing they would be hurt, Van Galder's ground crew, began to block them—really block them as in a football game. With the field littered with limping Legionaires, Whipple began to taxi. He zigged and zagged down the runway and struggled unsteadily into the air.

He flew in front of the spectators and shouted, "Help me. Get me out of here." He disappeared over a nearby hill and the crowd was sure he crashed only to see him pop over the horizon and make a fitful climb. Then he turned and headed

Above: Air show poster announcing the "delayed jump" or sky dive by George Moffat. (Marge Van Galder)

Left: Waukesha's parachutist Jack Miller, who made his first jump in 1930. (WAC)

straight for the spectators.

"He'sh gonna kill us. Lay flat on your belly," shouted the announcer. Man and woman and child, they dropped flat into the dirt and sandburs while the plane struggled overhead and disappeared over a hill on the other side of the field.

When Whipple returned and once again steered towards the crowd, the announcer shouted, "Save the woman and children first, Get them out of here!"

Women screamed, children cried, men shouted. Everyone ran for their cars. Whipple made one more pass over the now empty field and fluttered into a bumpy landing. As the plane halted, the announcer revealed, "Hey that'sh no farmer, that'sh Stiles Whipple, the best damn pilot in these parts."

Realizing that they had been duped, the spectators were angry and the Legion Commander was

Stiles Whipple, airline pilot. After the excitement of stunt flying ended, most barnstormers who survived turned to less adventurous flying. (Marge Van Galder)

livid. Russ grabbed the announcer and hurriedly stuffed him into Whipple's plane, then took off himself, leaving Marge to contend with the unhappy Legionaires.

"Don't forget to ask them about next year," Russ reminded Marge, just before he took off.

That was barnstorming in Wisconsin.[9]

AIRPLANE BUILDERS

THE LAWSON AIRPLANE COMPANY

The Armistice of November 11, 1918 brought an end to hostilities on the Western Front in Europe and an abrupt conclusion to the build-up of war industries in the United States. For the Lawson Aircraft Corporation of Green Bay, the declaration of peace meant that the long-awaited government order for military trainers would not arrive. Alfred Lawson's Green Bay backers were willing to write off their investment as a patriotic gesture for the war effort, but they balked when Lawson suggested that they put more money into the company so it could build civilian aircraft. The Green Bay plant closed and Alfred Lawson looked for a new place to realize his latest dream.

Lawson and his chief designer Lee Wallace had conceived a plan to build "airliners"— passenger planes larger than any non-military airplane ever built. Although he is often credited with coining the terms "airline" and "airliner", Lawson could have borrowed them from pioneer American railroads, many of which were called "airlines" in order to emphasis the speed and smoothness of their ride in contrast to travel on bumpy wagon roads. Indeed, south central Wisconsin was once served by the "Baraboo Air Line Railroad."

Lawson had a new and promising idea and a staff of talented people to implement it but, as usual, his pockets were empty. He returned to New York City in search of investors, even knocked on the doors of some of his old professional baseball cronies, none of whom saw Lawson as a financial slugger who would hit a home run with their money. He had better luck in Milwaukee where, with Burnelli's assistance, Lawson found investors willing to put up $100,000 to start a new Lawson Airplane Company. Once again, Lawson was ahead of his time in terminology. For him, flying machines were airplanes, as they would be in the future, not aeroplanes, as they had been in the past.

From the very beginning of his Milwaukee venture, Lawson found himself in a tight financial spot. Since a company that built airplanes had to

sell airplanes for its investors to see a return, Lawson promised his backers that the Lawson Airplane Company would be able to sell its planes as soon as they were built. The purchaser would be another new venture with neither capital nor assets, the Lawson Airline Transportation Company. Not only did Lawson have to organize one company to build an airplane unlike any yet seen, he also had to create a second company to deliver a service unlike any yet in use.

He contracted with the Cream City Sash and Door Company on West Pierce Street in Milwaukee and began construction of the first airplane in the United States expressly designed and built to carry a large number of passengers on a scheduled, commercial basis. It would be the first airliner in the United States.

Lawson, who was notorious for taking credit for work performed by others, claimed to be the designer of the plane but Lee Wallace and many of the other men who worked on it contributed as much or more. No matter who designed it, the Lawson airliner was a creditable and innovative

effort. Running fifty feet from nose to tail, with a wingspan of ninety-five feet, the plane was powered by two 400-horsepower Liberty engines. The fuselage was constructed of new material—plywood—which gave it relatively lightweight, structural rigidity without interior bracing. The cabin had seven feet of headroom, celluloid windows, and space for eight double rows of wicker chairs to carry 16 passengers. The pilot and co-pilot sat at the front of the cabin—inside—contrary to the conventional wind-in-your-face school of thought which held that a pilot could not really fly an airplane unless he was exposed to the full fury of the elements. The U. S. Army, for example, kept its bomber pilots in open cockpits until the early 1930s.

In five months—April-August 1919—Lawson and his crew built an airplane that flew over 2,000 miles, survived several hard landings and more than a little rough handling. It was solid testimony to the quality of the design and the craftsmanship of the Milwaukee work force. On August 22 1919, after removing the wings so they and the fuselage

Alfred Lawson in a characteristically heroic pose in the doorway of his first airliner. Lawson would have been awarded a large air mail contract that would have established his operations if his "Midnight Liner" airliner had survived its first take off. (George Hardie)

The interior of the first Lawson airliner which featured innovations such as inside seating for pilot and co-pilot as well as wicker seats for sixteen-passengers. (George Hardie)

could be hauled to the new Milwaukee County Airport in a wagon drawn by brewery horses, Lawson was ready to test his Airliner. With Mayor Hoan and other civic dignitaries on hand, Lawson and co-pilot Charles L. Cox, with Burnelli and other staff on board, started the engines. The announced plan was to test the motors by taxiing around the field, but Lawson had his own agenda. Before the engines were fully warm he slammed down the throttles and directed Cox to head for the trees at the end of the runway and "clear them by fifty feet."

A Royal Air Force veteran with, so he said, nine combat credits, Cox was hired because he was willing to take orders from "Captain in Command" Lawson, and he did. If not by fifty feet, Cox did clear the trees and the Lawson Airliner was airborne. Circling over Milwaukee, it proved to be a good flyer and Lawson kept it aloft until the gas gauges approached empty. No one on board had kept track of where they had flown or how to get back to the airport, which had little to distinguish it from a hay field anyway, so Lawson ordered Cox to land in a pasture. The plane came down nicely and the landing would have been perfect except that all four of the tires blew out on the rough ground. After the dust settled, Lawson and his relieved crew decided that they had built a real airplane.

Five days later, with new tires and full tanks, the Airliner was ready to fly again. On this flight Lawson was accompanied by Cox, Burnelli and mechanics Andrew Surini and Carl Schory. They

lifted off smoothly from the pasture and began one of the longest and strangest aerial odysseys yet flown. First they headed north, but after about ten miles, Lawson suddenly ordered Cox to turn around and fly to Chicago. In less than one hour, they landed at Ashburn Field on Chicago's far south side and were soon discovered by the press. Inspired by the attention, Lawson then announced that he was on his way to New York and Washington, D. C. Since his passengers thought they were only going up for a test flight over Milwaukee, they had to wire home for spending money and a change of underwear.

For the next three months, Lawson and his Airliner flew to Toledo, Cleveland, Buffalo, Syracuse, New York City, Washington, D. C., Dayton, Indianapolis and Chicago. In Washington the plane was inspected by Colonel Billy Mitchell, who was interested in big planes for use as bombers, Speaker of the House Joe Cannon, Secretary of War Newton Baker and a half-dozen United States Senators. While Baker, his wife and daughter, the Senators and a few others were on board, Lawson abruptly shut the cabin door, rushed to the cockpit before anyone could react and taxied the plane down the runway, once again before the engine oil was warm. Despite protests from his kidnapped passengers, Lawson gave them an aerial tour of the capital city and agreed to land only after Father John Cavanaugh, former President of Notre Dame University, pleaded with him to halt. When he made his landing, Cox miscalculated his approach, prompting Lawson to slam down the throttles again and nearly kill the engines. When they finally did land, the passengers fled as quickly as they could, except for Hoke Smith, the three-hundred pound Senator from Georgia, who had fainted and could be extricated from his seat only with great difficulty.

At each stop on the flight Lawson worked the press to the maximum, declaring at one point that he would have 100 airplanes flying from New York to San Francisco by the spring of 1920. He also laid out his plan for an airline to connect those cities with civic leaders far-thinking enough to provide air fields and investors possessed of vision enough to buy Lawson Airline stock. Once again Lawson was borrowing from the pioneer railroad executives, who promised to lay track only to cities willing to provide land for right-of-way, depot

buildings, cash grants and loans. Cities wanting to be served by the Lawson Airliner had to pony up for infra-structure. At nearly every stop he found mayors and council members willing to spend public money on airports, but far fewer investors willing to put up their own cash for Airline stock.

On November 15, 1919, Lawson, Cox, Burnelli, Surini and Schory returned to

Milwaukee, where they were received as heroes, treated to a motorcade downtown and a welcome home banquet. Here Lawson announced his plans to be the "Columbus of the Air," by bringing airline service to cities across America and building so many airplanes that Milwaukee would be the Detroit of the aviation industry. "It is now up to the people of Milwaukee to continue to support the enterprise," he said, and asked for another $100,000. He planned to build at least ten new and

better airplanes and put them into transcontinental service by July 10, 1920.

His corps of investors in Milwaukee was relatively small so Lawson's sales force fanned out across the hinterlands and struck gold—at least a little—in the La Crosse area, when Wendell McEldowney and others put up a few thousand dollars. In the spring of 1920, the newspapers announced that the Lawson Airplane Company had received orders for ten new airliners but the news release neglected to mention that the order came from the Lawson Airline Transportation Company, whose ledgers had only goose eggs in the asset column.

In the midst of the hype, during which deadlines passed and promises went unmet, Lawson purchased the old Fisk Rubber factory and three adjoining acres in Milwaukee. He hired more workers, purchased tools and materials, and began to build his next plane.

Although the first Lawson Airliner had performed well, the engineers agreed that it was underpowered. It was also too humble a vehicle for Lawson's grandiose plans. The new design called for a third motor and stretched the wingspan to one-hundred and twenty feet. The fuselage was also lengthened to accommodate 24 passengers plus cargo space for air mail and a chute for mid-air transfers to smaller planes of mailbags or passengers. Since it was designed to fly passengers overnight from Chicago

Above: Lawson's Midnight Liner, with a wingspan of 120 feet, sleeping berths and seats for twenty-four passengers, a bathroom and the first shower-bath ever installed on an airplane.

Left: The Lawson work force and the Midnight Liner at the old Fisk Rubber Plant on the south side of Milwaukee, 1920. (George Hardie)

to New York, Lawson's new plane was called the "Midnight Liner." It had Pullman-like sleeping berths, a bathroom and the first shower-bath ever installed on an airplane.

Merely building this aircraft was an accomplishment and one well described by Milwaukee aviation historian George Hardie:

Consider for a moment the task faced by Lawson and his crew. Airplanes of that day were built with a wooden framework covered with fabric and sheet metal. Douglas spruce was purchased as 50 foot logs and brought to the plant from the state of Washington in box cars. The logs were sawed into strips of desired dimensions on a large bandsaw and then dried in a crude kiln constructed in a corner of the shop. All of the fittings were of steel or brass, hand formed and welded or brazed to individual specification. Even special bolts were turned and threaded in the shop on a lathe and then heat treated.

Lawson had been promised the first long-distance federal air mail contract on routes running from Chicago to New York, New York to Atlanta via Washington, and Pittsburgh to St. Louis. If he began service by March 15, 1921, his company would receive $685,000 in government funds. March 15 came and passed, but the Midnight Liner was not ready, nor did Lawson have the $100,000 required for a post office bond. All but bankrupt, Lawson had made so many promises he did not keep that he had lost all credibility with his stockholders. They told him to get the Midnight Liner into the air or get himself out of town. There is some evidence that if he did get the plane off the ground, Lawson planned to fly it to the friendlier

confines of Salzer Field in La Crosse.

By the end of April, 1921, the Midnight Liner was ready to fly, but Lawson did not have the money to disassemble and transport it from the south side of Milwaukee to the airport on Lisbon Road. He then made the desperate choice to use the three acres of ground outside his factory door as an air field. He had 300 feet of runway on his property, plus a farm field adjoining to the south. With the lightest of loads and a brisk south wind, the Midnight Liner might make it into the air. Brisk south winds are not rare in a Wisconsin spring, but they were in April and May of 1921. Lawson waited in vain for the right wind to carry his airplane into the heavens. Finally, right wind or not, he had to fly the plane.

On May 8, 1921, Lawson, his new pilot Charles Wilcox, and mechanics Carl Schory and Andrew Surini climbed aboard the Midnight Liner. Wilcox began his takeoff and the 300 foot runway quickly passed beneath the landing gear. He continued into the farm field, which had just been plowed with deep furrows running across the path of the airplane. To clear the ruts, Wilcox pulled back on the stick and the plane rose slowly off the ground. It soon became apparent that the Liner would not clear the farm house ahead, so Wilcox banked. The left wing caught a tree branch and pivoted into a telephone pole. Carrying branches and pole, the Midnight Liner skidded a few hundred more yards down the field, spun round and came to rest with two wings shattered.

No one was injured, and Surini quickly snuffed out a small fire that had ignited near one of the engines. Ever the optimist, Lawson announced that the damage could be repaired and the plane made to fly again for only $10,000. He did not have it, nor did any new contributors step forth. With the Midnight Liner crashed the Lawson Airplane Company, the Lawson Airline, and Milwaukee's hopes of becoming the Detroit of American aviation.

Alfred Lawson left Milwaukee but he did not entirely abandon aviation. In 1926, in New Jersey, he started building a "Super-Airliner" designed to carry 100 passengers non-stop in double-decked seating from New York to San Francisco. With a

The Midnight Liner with wings shattered on take-off. Unable to hold off his creditors any longer and lacking the means to transport the giant airplane to Milwaukee County Airport, Lawson attempted a take-off from a hastily-prepared 300-foot runway near the factory. (George Hardie)

fuselage and tail measuring 150 feet, and powered by twelve 400-horsepower Liberty motors on loan from the Army, this plane would have been the largest airplane yet built—had it been built. In 1928, with little more than the giant fuselage completed, Lawson's backers withdrew their support. Lawson then withdrew himself from aviation to organize his Direct Credits Society and refine his philosophy of Lawsonomy. He passed away in Des Moines, Iowa in 1954. Adherents of his beliefs maintain the University of Lawsonomy near Sturtevant in Racine County.

It is easy to portray Alfred Lawson as a crack-

pot or a charlatan, to ridicule his eccentricities, play up his vices. It is not so easy to deny his accomplishments. Starting with little but his own wit and a monumental desire to succeed, he almost made it—twice. His military trainers were comparable to the Curtiss JN and had the war lasted longer, they might have gone into production and remained in use after the war. Given more time and money, the Lawson Airliner might have

become the prototypical passenger carrier that the Ford Tri-Motor and other early airliners became—except the Lawson would have had a five-year head start. Instead, the efforts of Alfred Lawson and his airplanes, are consigned to the historical file marked "What Might Have Been."[10]

THE HAMILTON AERO MANUFACTURING COMPANY

When Hamilton Aero produced the "Maiden Milwaukee" metal plane in time to compete and place second in the Ford Reliability Tour of 1927, Alfred Lawson's aborted promise to found an aviation manufacturing industry in Milwaukee was reborn. However, with a solid record as both an aeronautical engineer and a businessman, Tom Hamilton was not Alfred Lawson. He was marketing propellers and pontoons in a national market and had his own airport where he could test and display them. Unlike Lawson, who had to pitch his stock to any jittery purchaser who would listen, Hamilton was welcome in the offices of Milwaukee's business establishment. Clarence Falk, William Pabst, August Vogel, Rudy Hokanson and other solidly prosperous Milwaukeeans were on Hamilton's list of stockholders.

In March 1928, the Hamilton factory at 530 Park Street started to turn out eight-place all metal monoplanes powered by a single 400 horsepower Wright Whirlwind or Pratt and Whitney Wasp engine. Top speed of the "Metalplane" was 115 MPH and its cruising range 750 miles. With its 54-foot wingspan, square corners and flat surfaces, the Hamilton looked like a miniature, single-engine Ford Tri-Motor. The price was also smaller, with the Hamilton going for $21,000 - $25,000 compared to $45,000 - $50,000 for the Ford. The interior of the plane was described "as luxurious in its fittings as the most costly limousine. The cabin is lined with thick napped blue plush and paneled with walnut. A commodious double seat is at the back; in front of it are two swivel armchairs...upholstered in the same material as the body lining."

Hamilton played up the shiny corrugated aluminum finish of the planes with names like Silver

Tom Hamilton with a metal Hamilton prop. In 1928, the Hamilton propeller factory in Milwaukee produced 2,500 wooden and 1,100 metal propellers. The company later merged with the Standard Propeller Company, left town and became Hamilton Standard. (Robert Wylie)

Streak, Silver Eagle and, for the pontoon model, the Silver Swan. One of the company's first big sales was of six planes to Universal Airways for air mail and passenger duty on the Chicago-Cleveland route. Orders also came from Wien Alaska Airways, which wanted a Hamilton to carry the fur of mink and sable from Siberia to Anchorage, the Transatica airline flying from Rome to Venice, the Andian National Company, which wanted a Silver Hamilton to carry a payroll of silver coins to its oil and rubber workers in the interior of Venezuela, and from Neil Norris, a farmer who had a private airport near Big Bend in Waukesha County. Before it was delivered, the Norris plane was exhibited at the All-American Aircraft Show in Detroit.

Hamilton made a strong impression in Detroit, where 29 of the 57 planes on display bore Hamilton propellers. Company salemen came back from Detroit with seventeen orders for new planes and Hamilton soon announced that, with the props, pontoons and planes, the company would switch to round-the-clock operation and increase its work force from 150 to 300.

In the summer of 1928, four Hamiltons went into service on the nation's first air-to-rail passenger and mail route. Northwest Airways scheduled planes to meet trains arriving at St. Paul from Seattle. Passengers and mail were then flown to Chicago in time to meet the fast train to New York City. Northwest Hamiltons and Ford Tri-Motors also flew the reverse route from Chicago to St.

Paul, thereby cutting up to a day off a transcontinental trip.

In November the original Hamilton propeller plant on Keefe Avenue was severely damaged by a fire in its lumber room. The company was hardly

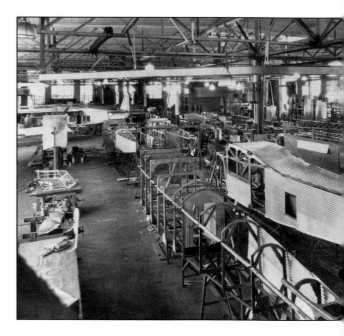

affected and instead purchased the former Edmonds Shoe factory, a 68,000 square foot plant on Bremen and Concordia Streets, where it would gear up to turn out 50 props a day. At the end of 1928, Hamilton reported that it had produced 1,100 metal and 2,500 wooden props resulting in sales of $650,000. Also in '28, its first full year of operation, Hamilton Metalplane sold 25 airplanes worth $600,000. In 1929, Hamilton expected to sell over one million dollars in propellers and fifty-to-one hundred airplanes to gross between one and two million dollars.

The rosy outlook of December, 1928 turned cloudy for Milwaukee after the turn of the year. In January, Hamilton announced that it was negotiating a merger with the United Aircraft and Transport Company. United's president, William Boeing, aspired to make his company "the General Motors of the Air" and was buying every aircraft company he could afford. In addition, Boeing and Tom Hamilton were old friends from the state of Washington where as a teenager Boeing had made his first flight in a plane built and piloted by Tom Hamilton.

United Aircraft already controlled the Boeing Company, Pratt and Whitney engines, Chance-Vought airplane manufacturing and the Pacific Air Transport airline. Hamilton Metalplane and Hamilton Aero, the nation's largest propeller maker, would nicely round out the growing conglomerate. United Aircraft and Hamilton merged in January 1929 by exchanging stock worth $1.4 million. Tom Hamilton left Milwaukee for a position in upper management in Seattle. He had a hand in designing the Boeing 247 but spent most of his career managing international sales for Boeing.

The initial announcement of the merger pointed out the "Probability that Milwaukee will become the nation's midwestern center for the manufacture of airplanes and airplane parts..." The report went on to say that up to $5 million might be spent to expand the Metalplane factory, with additional investments made in the propeller and pontoon plants. Other aviation industries would be born or move to the Milwaukee area and the city itself would become a center for "regional and national air transport lines." Subsequent articles talked about a new "airplane speed course...for performance tests on Hamilton propellers and planes..." with "five kilometer straightaway courses with electric timing facilities."

As the final reorganization developed, Hamilton Metalplane first became part of the Boeing Airplane Company, a subsidiary of United Aircraft. After United Aircraft acquired the Stearman Aircraft Company of Wichita, Kansas,

Hamilton Metalplane merged with Stearman. In June, 1929, Hamilton's Milwaukee plant shut down and remaining operations moved to Wichita. As the Milwaukee Sentinel reported, this move "is likely to end Milwaukee's dreams of becoming an airplane manufacturing center."

Hamilton Aero Manufacturing was still in town, but not for long. United Aircraft had also acquired the Standard Steel Adjustable Propeller Company of Pittsburgh, manufacturer of the prop that had taken Charles Lindbergh to Paris. United Aircraft merged Hamilton Aero and Standard Steel into the Hamilton-Standard Company. The Milwaukee plant was closed and operations concentrated at the Standard plant in Pittsburgh.

The Milwaukee Association of Commerce attempted to prevent the loss of the Hamilton operations but, with the local stockholders well compensated and corporate decisions made by managers with no link to the city, there were few grounds for hope. The aviation industry was going through the same process of consolidation that the automobile industry had passed through a decade earlier. Milwaukee was a casualty of the process. As the economy staggered in the 1930s, there was little hope that an aero manfacturer would be willing and able to take advantage of the skill and experience of the workers who had built Hamilton props, pontoons and Metalplanes.[11]

THE CORBEN ACE

In 1931, Madison had three airports, two real and one in the talking stage. The airport talked about was Madison

"A BABY IN SIZE – AN ACE IN PERFORMANCE"

The logo of the Corben Baby Ace airplane, Madison. (EAA)

Municipal which later developed into Truax Field. The real airports were Howard Morey's Royal Airport south of Lake Monona and the North Street or "Madison" Airport a few blocks east of the Oscar Mayer plant on the northeast side of town.

Opened in 1927, the North Street Airport became the home of the Corben Sport Plane Company in 1931, when Orland "Ace" Corben was hired as airport manager. He had been building and selling airplanes in kit and finished form in Peru, Indiana since 1923 and brought the operation with him when he moved to Madison. He set up shop in the hangar of the Mid-west Air Transport Company on Coolidge Street, which ran along the south edge of the landing field.

Corben had not been old enough to serve in World War I, but he had spent a few months flying for a Hollywood newsreel producer, so he knew how a pilot—at least a pilot in the movies—was supposed to look and act. He sported a clipped mustache, dressed in leather flying coat, riding breeches and knee-high boots and adopted the nickname "Ace" for himself and his planes.

He produced three basic models in Madison, the Baby Ace, Junior Ace and Super Ace. The Baby Ace was an open-cockpit, high-wing monoplane, with a wingspan of 25 feet and measuring just shy of 18 feet from nose to tail. As in all Corben models, the fuselage, tail and landing gear were framed of welded steel tubing, with spruce in the wings. Engine options included the Szekely 30 or 45 horsepower motor or the Continental A-40. A tachometer, altimeter, throttle, switch, oil temperature and pressure gauges were standard instruments, as were "black leatherette" seat cushions. In 1936, the "Flyaway Price" of a Baby Ace, equipped with an A-40 Continental motor, was $1,095, or $710 minus motor and prop.

The Junior Ace was a two-place, high-wing model, with a thirty-four foot wingspan and nineteen feet nose to tail. It was powered by a 45 horsepower Salmson or Szekely engine or a 50 horse Aeromarine and could be constructed either as a cabin or open-cockpit plane. With a Salmson AD-9 motor, the Junior Ace could be flown out of Madison for $1,265. Minus motor and prop, the price was $980.

The most exciting Corben plane was the Super Ace. Featured on the cover of *Popular Aviation* magazine when it was introduced in 1935, the new design offered, "the utmost in comfort, visibility, performance and stability even with the relatively high speed." About the same size as the Baby Ace, the single-seat, open-cockpit Super Ace featured a converted Model A Ford engine which—as the sales brochure claims—allowed it to reach speeds in excess of 100 MPH. The Super Ace sold for $895 minus engine and prop, with another $195

required for a converted Model A powerplant.

Corben offered kit versions of all his planes at reduced prices and a complete set of blueprints at $5 per model, two of his many adaptations to a Depression economy. Corben also filled his catalog with tips on how airplane owners could make money by painting advertisers' names on their planes, through aerial photography or by "dropping small hand bills." Corben owners could also turn a profit by renting their planes to other pilots for "$5 or $6 per hour." He thought Ford dealers would be particularly pleased to use a Super Ace powered by a Model A engine as an advertising tool.

Corben also attempted to make purchasing a plane easier by selling kits in stages. A home-builder could buy parts only as he needed them and his pocketbook allowed. Since Model A engines were so plentiful, Corben also sold conversion blue prints for homebuilders who could supply their own motors. Estimates of the number of Corbens sold in the 1930s run to several hundred for the Junior and Baby Ace model, and as few as a handful for the Super Ace.

Despite its low price, good design and imaginative marketing, the Corben Sport Plane Company was a victim of the Great Depression. Orland Corben left Madison sometime in 1936 or '37 after he purchased a Stinson Tri-Motor. He worked his way south as a barnstormer, ferried bombers to South America during World War II, was an airline pilot after the war, eventually ending his working days as a designer for Lockheed. He passed away in 1980. Corben planes continued to be made from blueprints and parts in Madison until World War II. Since they were relatively inexpensive home-built planes, more Corbens were built than any other airplane manufactured in Wisconsin.

WINNERS!

OF THE CONFIDENCE OF ALL
WHO SEE OR FLY

CORBEN
SPORT PLANES

CORBEN SPORT PLANE CO.
MADISON AIRPORT   MADISON, WISCONSIN

An afterword to the Corben story starts in 1953, when Paul Poberezny acquired the rights to Corben's designs. He modifed the plans to use Piper J-3 parts and, in 1955, *Mechanix Illustrated* magazine published them in a three-part article. Soon, hundreds of homebuilders were assembling Poberezny-modified Corbens, many of which still land at the EAA Fly-In today. In the early 1990s, the Madison Chapter of the EAA, named in honor of Orland Corben, built a Corben Super Ace from scratch. The plane was suspended in the atrium of Dane County Regional Airport's new terminal building in 1992.[12]

THE PHEASANT AIRCRAFT COMPANY

Steve Wittman started his racing career in a J-1 Standard in 1926. It was a ten-year old model, a close cousin of but older than the Curtiss JN, and Wittman was looking for a faster, more efficient machine. In 1927, he discovered the Pheasant, an OX-5 powered biplane manufactured in Memphis, Missouri, and brought one home to

Fond du Lac. Like the rest of the country, Fond du Lac was in the full flush of Lindbergh-inspired flying fever. A local Ford dealer, Tom Meiklejohn, was convinced that aviation was on the verge of a boom similar to that experienced by the auto industry in the 1910s and early 1920s. Such was the message Meiklejohn was getting from no less a source than Henry Ford himself. Meiklejohn had been instrumental in starting the first Fond du Lac airport and wanted to position himself and the city to take advantage of the aeronautical boom just over the horizon.

At first Meiklejohn thought he would start an airplane manufacturing operation from the ground up by designing and building an entirely new airplane. He consulted with Wittman who said that instead of starting from the drawing board, Meiklejohn ought to buy a company that already had a good plane and might be in financial trouble. Wittman also said he knew of just such a company and would be glad to fly Meiklejohn to it. Off they went to Memphis, Missouri and Tom Meiklejohn, along with Andre Bechaud and Florian Manor, bought an airplane company. Early in 1928, Steve Wittman ferried all seven machines in the inventory of the Pheasant Aircraft Company all or part way from Memphis to Fond du Lac. The company put up a cement block bulding at the Fond du Lac Airport and started making airplanes. The plan was to produce and sell enough of the older model Pheasant H-10 biplanes, which retailed for $2,895, to cover expenses and fund work on new models.

The Pheasant biplane was an improvement on the Jenny, Canuck and Standard, but it was not the plane of the future that Tom Meiklejohn hoped would launch the aviation industry at Fond du Lac. Florian Manor, the barnstormer from Oshkosh who also identified himself as an aviation engineer, said that the plane of the future should be a single-place, high-wing cabin model. It should be small, fast and economical to corner the sport plane market. This was the same niche that Orland Corben hoped his Baby Ace and Super Ace Models would fill. Steve Wittman, who hired on as test pilot at Pheasant, argued that the market would be far larger for a two-place trainer, but he was only a pilot, and what did he know? The company decided to build the Pheasant Traveler, a completely new single-place airplane with a completely new engine aimed at the sport plane market.

Meiklejohn and Manor hired Nick Rowinski, a engineer from the Harley Davidson Company, who designed a new four-cylinder motor that would run well—for ten minutes. It would then overheat and seize up, as Wittman experienced on more than one test flight. He had better success with a Pheasant H-10 using a redesigned Model A Ford engine, which Wittman flew in his first National Air Race in Cleveland in 1929, in the Chicago Nationals of 1930 and in two cross-country races.

Pheasant also made some mistakes in manufacturing H-10s. The federal government had been

A Pheasant H-10 at Fond du Lac. (WAHF)

inspecting aircraft for type certificates since 1926, but Pheasant built its first three biplanes in Fond du Lac and canvassed them over before contacting inspector George Vest. He was forced to order the planes uncovered for inspection before he could approve them. The delay cost money and was typical of the problems that plagued the company. Resources were also misplaced on an attempt to build a flying motorcycle. As Tom Meiklejohn, Jr., recalled, "They took a motorcycle, a Harley-Davidson, and they added wings and a tail....transferred power somehow to the propeller." The controls were on the handlebars, which pivoted back and forth like the stick of an airplane, while the throttle and brakes were operated by twisting the grips. As Meiklejohn remembered, "they finally got Gus Weigle on it because Gus only weighed about 100 pounds and we thought maybe with Gus it would fly. But it still wasn't able to fly, got to hop off the ground but that was about it."

Preoccupied with trying to make a motorcycle fly, the Pheasant easily fell prey to the hard knocks of the Depression. By the time Steve Wittman left the company to manage the Oshkosh airport in 1931, the company was well on the way to bankruptcy. In 1934, Fond du Lac pilot George Moersch was able to pick up a new Pheasant Traveler with a used engine for the bargain price of $375. The company was dissolved, but Wittman saved plans and blueprints and presented them to the Experimental Aircraft Association, where a Pheasant airplane is preserved today.[13]

THE INVINCIBLE CENTER-WING

Engineers who refused to take custom for granted have now developed one of the greatest contributions to the aircraft industry: the perfected center-wing."

So read the brochure announcing "The New Master of the Air," manufactured by the Invincible Metal Furniture Company of Manitowoc in 1929. The new plane, with its novel center-wing placement, was the brainchild of Manitowoc manufacturer John Schuette and his chief engineer and designer, Irl S. Beach.

Schuette was an Air Service veteran who came

Above: Designed by Florian Manor, the flying motorcycle was a diversion for Steve Wittman and other aviators at Fond du Lac around 1930. (Steve Wittman Collection, EAA)

Right: Promotional brochure for the Invincible Center Wing Cabin Plane. (Don Gruett)

home from World War I and purchased the Invincible Metal Furniture Company, a small but solid producer of office furniture and equipment. Aggressive and open to new ideas, Schuette improved and expanded the operation, with some unintended help from the federal government. About a year after he took over at Invincible, Schuette noticed that sales of a file cabinet with a built-in safe had jumped. Designed to provide secure storage of drugs in doctors' offices, clinics and hospitals, the cabinet was now selling to customers in all kinds of offices. It didn't take Schuette long to decipher that, with Prohibition enacted, his cabinets had become very popular storage places for illegal whiskey. The Invincible cabinet safe was the bootlegger's friend.

In 1927 A.L. (after Lindbergh) Schuette thought he should invest in aviation. He had observed the success of the Hamilton Metalplane and, like Tom Meiklejohn in Fond du Lac, saw a boom coming in aviation. He already had a manufacturing operation well-versed in metal working and knew that excellent aircraft engines were available for purchase. All he needed was a good design.

Irl S. Beach, no relation to Walter Beech, was "an accomplished designer and aeronautical engineer" who had worked for "leading aircraft manufacturers in Wichita." He drew up plans for three- and four-place cabin planes that could be used to carry air mail, light freight and passengers. That a market existed for these planes was evidenced by the 4-place Stinson Detroiters that Northwest Airways had just put into service in Wisconsin. What made the

Invincible stand out and, it was hoped, stand above its competitors, was its center-wing. "Wings are placed in alignment with the center of the propeller thrust, giving perfect balance and greater speed under all flying conditions. As definitely as a straight line is the shortest distance between two points, so surely does air leave a straight line

faster," said the sales brochure.

The Invincible had a thirty-eight foot wingspan and was twenty-five feet long. The three-place model was powered by a ninety horse-power LeBlond engine while the four-place used a 170 horse Curtiss Challenger. Top speed for the LeBlond model was 109 MPH, with the Curtiss Challenger reaching 140 MPH. The cabin was spacious and bright, with visibility above and forward unobstructed by the wing. A fully-equipped Challenger model Invincible, complete with wal-

nut-paneled instrument panel was priced at $7,800.

The Invincible made its first test flight at Manitowoc on February 5, 1929, with the "immaculately attired" Irl Beach at the controls. The plane sped down the snow-covered runway on skis, lifted off easily, then rose to circle the airport before heading over the city. After a brief flight, Beach brought the plane down to a perfect landing and taxied back to his starting point. Local officials praised the courage of the investors and promised to support them in their attempt to establish the aircraft industry in Manitowoc.

For the next two months the Invincible crew

tested and perfected their plane in preparation for its exhibition at the All-American Aircraft Show in Detroit in April. Unlike Hamilton's Maiden in Milwaukee, which flew to Detroit in 1928, the Invincible traveled by rail with its wings removed. Nonetheless, the Manitowoc newspaper reported that the Invincible won "high tribute" from Henry Ford, Edsel Ford, and William Mayo, Ford's chief engineer. Amelia Earhart and Viola Gentry, who had just set an altitude record for women, also expressed interest in the plane.

The Invincible's appparent success in Detroit led the city of Manitowoc to offer "all lands needed" for a factory adjacent to the airport. The *Manitowoc Herald-News* opined that "Manitowoc is in a way, through establishment of its airplane factory plant, to lead

the way to Wisconsin's advance in industry in the next few years..."

While all prospects appeared rosy, the Invincible Company produced only three planes in the summer of 1929. While Irl Beach and chief pilot Bill Williams flew the plane regularly, other pilots expressed doubts about the stability of the center-wing design. Already struggling to stay afloat even before the stock market crash of October 1929, the Invincible airplane became an early victim of the Great Depression. What was left of the company—pieces and parts—remained in Manitowoc until 1934 when it was purchased by Dean and Dale Crites, who then assembled an Invincible in Waukesha. The Crites flew the plane briefly, then sold it out of state, where it was destroyed in a crash.[14]

Left: The Invincible Center-Wing at Manitowoc, 1928.

Below: A prototype on its way to the All-American Aircraft Show at Detroit, via truck and train. (Don Gruett)

Note: Each airport history begins with the description of the airport as it appeared in U.S. Department of Commerce Aeronautics Branch Airway Bulletins "Descriptions of Airports and Landing Fields in the United States, September 1, 1931; June 1, 1933 or January 1, 1938. The dates in brackets after each listing indicate the year of the Bulletin, not the year the airport began.

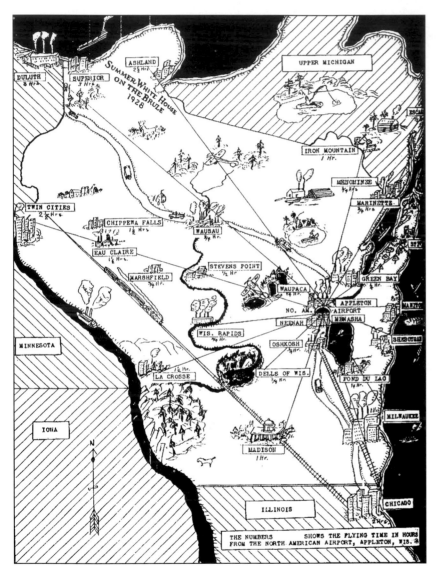

A fanciful promotional drawing featuring Appleton as the center of aviation in Wisconsin in 1928. (Robert Wylie)

Appleton/Neenah/Menasha

George A. Whiting Airport, commercial, rating —-. Three miles South on Menasha Highway. Altitude, 800 feet. Rectangular, 2,635 by 1,750 feet, sod, level, artificial drainage; three runways, 3,100 feet NE./SW., 2,100 feet NW./SE., 2,700 feet N./S., all 120 feet wide, remainder of field should be used with caution. GEORGE A. WHITING AIRPORT on hangar roof. Pole lines to E. Facilities for servicing aircraft, day only. [1931]

The Fox Cities area was the home of four airports in the 1920s and '30s. With populations smaller than Oshkosh and Green Bay,

the Fox Cities lagged behind their neighbors in airport development and did not catch up until the post-World War II years.

The immediate stimulus for Appleton's first airport was Charles Lindbergh's flight to Paris in 1927, but its roots go back to Cal Rodgers, who flew his Wright Flyer down College Avenue in 1911. One of Rodgers' passengers on that day was Frank Whiting of the Fox Valley paper-making family. In 1927, he put up $5,000 for the construction of a brick hangar on 100 acres of land leased from the Michael Wittmann family on the Appleton Road north of Menasha. The new landing field was named the George Whiting Airport in honor of Frank's father, who had also flown with Rodgers.

To use the airport, Eric Lindberg, Karl Hagen, H.A. De Baufer, George Schmidt and Fred Schlintz incorporated North American Airways and, with the help of a $2,000 grant from the city of Appleton, acquired a Stinson Tri-Motor. Christened the "The Pride of Appleton," the plane made its first landing at the airport in March, 1928. North American had high hopes of becoming the sole passenger and air mail carrier between Milwaukee and the Fox Cities. This was high-stakes gamble since, in order to survive, North American not only had to fill the 14-passenger plane with paying customers on a regular basis, the airline also had to acquire an air mail contract.

North American lost the gamble in December 1928, when the Fox Valley Air Mail contract was awarded to Northwest Airways. Northwest inaugurated mail service to the Fox River Valley in a ski-equipped Waco 10 on December 15. With a better handle than North American on what the traffic would bear, Northwest also began passenger service to Oshkosh, Appleton and Green Bay with 3-passenger Stinson Detroiters and 7-passenger Hamilton Metalplanes. By 1930, North American Airways was bankrupt and the "Pride of Appleton" sold out of town. When the Depression and the cancellation of air mail contracts in March, 1933 forced Northwest to pull out of Appleton, the Whiting Airport closed.

Taking advantage of a federal public works grant in 1934, Outagamie County purchased 110 acres on Ballard Road and constructed its first county airport. Federal money was not available to improve Whiting Airport since it was in Winnebago County and all of Winnebago's allotment was going to Oshkosh. However, once the airport moved across the county line, it was eligible for federal funding.

In 1938, with federal help, Outagamie County built three grass runways and a hangar, but the Ballard Road Airport was soon recognized as inadequate for commercial aviation. Many airport plans were considered in the 1940s, and '50s, but not until 1963, when the county purchased 1302 acres in the Town of Greenville, would the Outagamie County Airport leave Ballard Road.

The Neenah-Menasha area had been the site of several landing fields ever since the Spearmint Gum flyers landed on the south side of Neenah in 1919. In 1927, Neenah realtor H. H. Held set aside forty acres of ground and built a hangar on the corner of Commercial and Cecil streets. The airport was registered and listed

war, Bretting maintained his interest in aviation. In 1928, he organized the Ashland Aeronautical Association to build an airport. The Association purchased a strip of land two miles south of the city, east of Highway 13 and west of the Soo Line track. In July 1929, the Ashland Airport was dedicated with a fly-in that brought planes from Nekoosa, Wausau, Superior and Minneapolis. The biggest plane to arrive was the Ford Tri-Motor of Universal Airways from Minneapolis. A Minnesota airline, Universal hoped to extend service to Wisconsin, but never did much more than announce its intention. Also in Ashland for the dedication was Wilbur Haase and his Ryan Brougham from Superior, Verne Williams and his Waco 10 from Rice Lake and John Cawley with a OX-5 Challenger biplane from Nekoosa. Newspaper reports do not mention the presence of any aircraft from Ashland.

In 1931, the Ashland airport was visited by another native son serving in the military. Lieutenant Commander Arthur Gavin, who had left the city to become a naval aviator in World War I, returned at the controls of a Navy Tri-Motor escorted by five naval pursuit planes. The group was on its way to deliver Assistant Naval Secretary E. L. Jahnke to the American Legion Convention at Chippewa Falls and Gavin arranged a stop in his home town. Arthur Gavin was in the middle of a long and distinguished career in naval aviation that took him from Flying Boats in World War I to the command of the aircraft carrier *Ranger* in World War II.

Ashland was not a very active aviation center in the 1930s, in part because the original airport was poorly-sited between the highway and the Soo Line tracks. Nonetheless, it remained the city's landing field until the new John F. Kennedy Memorial Airport was completed in 1959.[16]

as open by the federal Aeronautics Bureau in November, 1927 and listed as closed in January 1930.

During its brief period of operation, the Neenah Airport was home to James Kimberly's Taperwing Waco 10, George Kroll's Waco 9 and Irving Stilp's Thomas-Morse Scout.

A few miles west of Neenah near the village of Larsen in the Town of Winchester, the Larson Brothers had their airport. After Roy Larson died in a crash in 1928, Leonard Larson took over the flying service, which included a flying school as well as aircraft sales, maintenance and storage.

The aviator most closely associated with the Fox Cities in the 1930s was Elwyn West. Born and raised in Lind Center, Waupaca County, West took up flying after Rellis Conant gave him a ride at the county fair in 1920. West learned to fly at the Diggins School in Chicago, acquired a Canuck airplane and parked it at Larson's. He became manager of the Whiting Airport, then moved to Ballard Road Airport when it opened. Sometimes sharing duties with his brother Luther and wife Esther, Elwyn stayed at Ballard Road until he moved to northern Minnesota in 1943.

By his own estimation West trained about 120 flyers at Whiting and Ballard Road, including George Apitz, who became one of the first pilots for American Airlines. Elwyn West said he could and would fly just "about anything, anywhere...but I wasn't doing any trick stuff or flying circus," which helps explains why he was a pilot for 62 years who logged over 30,000 hours of flying time.[15]

Ashland

Ashland Airport, municipal, rating —. Two miles S. of center of Ashland on Highway 13. Altitude, 700 feet. Rectangular, clay and sod, slight slope, artificial drainage; two graveled and oiled runways, N./S. 2,700 by 125 feet,, E./W. 1,800 by 200 feet; only runways available. Low pole line and trees across road on SE. boundary. Aviation fuel, day only. [1938]

Aviation in Ashland got off to a bang-up start in 1918 when Army Air Service Lieutenant Howard Bretting flew all the way from Chanute Field in south-central Illinois to his home town on Chequamegon Bay. It took ten hours, with stops for gas in Stevens Point and Phillips, to make what was probably the first aerial transit of the state from north to south.

Although he did not bring a Jenny or Canuck home from the

Athelstane

Schaf Airport, commercial, rating —. One half mile SW. and W. of main highway. Altitude, 500 feet. Available area, irregular in shape, 1,800 by 1,120 feet, sod, level, natural drainage. Pole lines to E. and 300 feet N., trees surround field. Aviation fuel, day only. [1931]

The members of the Wausakee Sportman's Club cleared a spot in the woods of Marinette County for Pilot Otto Schaf to land his Jenny in the mid-1920s. The airport was a private venture and served to bring out of town club members to fish and hunt in the area.[17]

Beloit/Janesville

Janesville City Airport, commercial, rating —. One half mile NE. of city limits, Rock River Three quarters mile W.; C. & N.W. Railroad 100 feet of W. boundary. Altitude, 600 feet. Irregular, 3,900 by 2,600 feet; surface, sod, level, natural drainage; entire field available except when NW. and NE. corners are sown with grain. JANESVILLE on hangar roof. Pole line on S. and trees to E. and S., beacon tower on E., windmills to E. Boundary, boundary, obstruction, and landing area flood lights. Boundary, 24-inch rotating clear. Facilities for servicing aircraft, day and night. [1931]

Rock County Airport, commercial, rating —. Three and one half miles

S. Altitude, 804 feet. Rectangular, 2,640 by 1,320 feet, sod, slopes from E. to W., natural drainage. AIRPORT on hangar roof. Pole line to W., ridge in field toward E. boundary. Facilities for servicing aircraft, day only. [1931]

Beloit Legion Civic Flying Field, commercial, rating —-. One and one half miles E. of city. Altitude, 750 feet. Irregular, sod, level, natural drainage; entire field available. BELOIT on hangar. Pole line to N.; trees to E., S., W., and NW. corner. Aviation fuel, day only. [1931]

In the 1920s, pilots had little trouble finding a place to land on the flat open fields of Rock County. Then Charles Lindbergh flew the Atlantic, the calendar turned to 1928 and three airports opened for business.

Janesville service station owner Herman Krause purchased an OX-powered Travel Air and opened a landing field behind his garage on the northeast edge of the city. The field soon came to be known as the Janesville City Airport and received the usual federally funded improvments that qualified it to be an air mail stop. Northwest Airways used it for regular air and passenger service from Madison in the early 1930s.

In 1931, the city airport hosted Wiley Post, Harold Gatty and the Lockheed Vega they had flown arround the world, the *Winnie Mae.* They pulled the plane into a hangar and roped off the entrance so the plane could be prepared for visitors. Neil Poland worked at the airport to earn flying time then so responsibility for washing the *Winnie Mae* fell to him. "Those engines were pretty dirty," he recalled. "It was a white airplane and the whole underside of the belly....was just black with oil... I had on a white pair of coveralls...By the time I got done you wouldn't know those coveralls were white." After Poland finished, a sparkling *Winnie Mae* was ready for company.

Post and Gatty were in Janesville at the invitation of Ken Parker, the pen company executive who, when all was said and done, would rather be flying. He kept the company Fairchild FC-2W2, christened the "Parker Duofold," at the city airport and used it regularly for business and pleasure. Well-known on the national aviation scene, Parker also flew his own Verville Air Coach, Stinson SM-2 and a Waco Cabin plane, to name a few. After he purchased his first

Stinson in 1931, Parker became fast friends with the plane's builder Eddie Stinson, who also became a regular visitor at Janesville. Ralph Tumelson, another youngster who learned to fly by hanging around City Airport, recalled that he "had the honor of flying with Eddie Stinson the day that he was killed." Stinson took Tumelson up for a ride in his "Detroiter," then dropped the boy off before heading to Chicago where he crashed and died. "I actually had the last ride with him in his own airplane," said Tumelson.

In 1932, tragedy struck the Janesville airport when a hangar housing nine planes and a glider—including Parker's Stinson—was destroyed by fire. "That left the area without much flying activity," Poland said, "and it was pretty dead."

After the fire Pete Tumelson, Joe Bozianne and a young Art Hodge revived the airport and organized the Janesville Flying Service. They started with an American Eaglet, but soon acquired a Piper Cub and an Aeronca K. Activity remained slow throughout the 1930s. Tumelson left Janesville and moved to the Beloit Airport. Bozianne and Hodge stayed at Janesville and flew as often as they could while still holding day jobs at Chevrolet. Not until 1940, when he established a flight school under the CPT program, was Hodge able to become a full-time aviator. He became manager of the Janesville City Airport and held the job until the airport closed in 1962.

The field known as the "old" Rock County Airport began life as the Wisconsin Air College when two University of Wisconsin graduates, Will Kempton and Delos Dudley, opened an airport about half-way between Beloit and Janesville in 1928. Dudley was a close friend of Charles Lindbergh during their student days in Madison and the Lone Eagle dropped in to visit him while touring the state in August 1928. Dudley was confined to a hospital bed in Watertown and did not know his friend was coming. Had he known and, if he was like most Americans at the time, he would have jumped out of his bed to see Lindbergh. Dudley's bad luck persisted and the Wisconsin Air College lasted for about one year before closing down.

At about the same time the Wisconsin Air College raised its windsock, the Beloit Commercial Club and the American Legion Post organized a corporation called Beloit Airways. The corporation leased eighty acres of land on the Morgan Farm east of the city, only a good stone's throw away from the hayfield where Arthur Warner made Wisconsin's first airplane flight in 1909. Beloit Airways hired Air Service veteran and pilot Roy Reed and purchased a Travel Air for him to fly out of their Beloit Legion-Civic Airport.

On dedication weekend Pilots Jerry Phillips, Harry Honsley and H. L. Johnson flew in from Madison and Al Padags came from Milwaukee. Phillips showed off with some aerobatics, and Reed took about sixty passengers up for rides. Beloiters showed a lot of enthusiasm for aviation then, but it did not last. In about one year, Beloit Airways was out of business and Roy Reed had moved on. Stiles

The illustration shows the speedy monoplane—Parker Duofold—owned and used by The Parker Pen Company in its business. The plane is a Fairchild Wasp, 410 H.P., 140 M.P.H.

Ken Parker's Fairchild FC-2W2 was used for pleasure and promotional work. (Geoffrey Parker)

Whipple reopened the Beloit Airport in 1931, but stayed only until 1933, when he moved to the Wisconsin Air College field and reopened it as the Rock County Airport. By then Pete Tumelson had moved from Janesville City to the Beloit airport and organized the Beloit Flying Club. The airport remained open under Club auspices until Tumelson, his brother Ralph, and other Beloit pilots entered the military for World War II.

Back at the Rock County Airport, Stiles Whipple, Si Smith and Russ Van Galder were the leading flyers. Whipple remembered that

Russ Van Galder and his Monocoach. (Marge Van Galder)

Art Hodge starting out with a glider at Janesville. (WAHF)

"We started operating the airport up there. I had the Warner Cessna....I picked up an OX 5 Pheasant...We had a Aeromarine Klemm that had a Salmson engine in it....A little later we purchased a Luscombe, about a year later we purchased another Luscombe.

"We were working the air show circuit...We did quite a lot of barnstorming around the country. It seemed like we always spent all of the money we made repairing the airplanes.

"We ended up getting quite a student business...We really got busy, we had people coming from Madison and Rockford, Illinois. We were getting really a good start." Despite his success as an instructor who even taught one student who couldn't make day lessons to fly at night, Whipple didn't hesitate to accept an offer to become an airline pilot in 1940. He spent thirty years in the cockpit of airliners before retiring in 1970.

Whipple's recollection describes airport life in the 1930s, when for most pilots aviation alone could not put bread on the table. The hard facts did not prevent men like Russell Van Galder from making aviation their lives' work. In 1934, Van Galder soloed in a Curtiss Wright Junior, a two-cockpit monoplane with a three cylinder engine mounted on the high wing, facing aft. The first plane "Van" owned was a Monoprep, than a J-5 Monocoach, which he used on barnstorming forays in Wisconsin, Illinois and Iowa.

While most flyers did their exhibition work in the warmer weather, Van Galder flew year round. On one winter's day he and a friend named Jake flew off to Delavan Lake and landed on the ice. In no time, folks began to line up for rides. The wind was gusty and the surface of the lake was very slick so Van Galder had to rely on Jake to turn the plane and hold the tail down for take off. While Van was in the air, Jake kept himself warm with swigs from a pocket flask. After a few more flights, Jake was very relaxed—relaxed enough to fall asleep while he sat on the tail, unbeknownst to Van Galder who began to taxi down the lake. Ice fishermen and skaters chased the plane, but Van didn't see them, nor did he see Jake. The Monocoach rose to about fifteen feet when Jake opened his eyes. He saw the surface of the lake dropping beneath him and so, without hesitating, slipped off the tail He fell into a lump on the hard ice, an uninjured and lucky man.

Despite his mishap with Jake and his flask, Van Galder kept fly-ing, and kept his job at Chevrolet. In 1939, he obtained his limited commerical license and joined Stiles Whipple as "co-manager" of the Rock County Airport. Russ Van Galder's entry into airport management was also the beginning of his wife's career at Rock County Airport. Marge became a ground school instructor, officer in the Blackhawk Chapter of the NAA, and of the Wisconsin Airport Owner's Association. In 1940, the Van Galders became the managers of the "old" Rock County Airport. They remained there until a few years after the Rock County board voted to build a public-funded county airport directly across the road in 1947. [18]

Black River Falls

Black River Falls—-Jackson County Airport, municipal, rating —-. One and one half miles E.; E. of railroad. Altitude, 830 feet. L shape, sod, level, natural drainage; two landing strips, 3,000 by 600 feet NW./SE. and 1,440 by 1,100 feet E./W. Pole lines to W. and E. Aviation fuel, day only. [1931]

The Jackson County Aeronautical Company brought the first airplane to Black River Falls in 1920. James Pugh, the community's first pilot, was a passenger in the Jenny on its inaugural flight from Milwaukee. Barnstorming pilots used the airport founded by the Aeronautical Company on the grounds of the old Vaudreuil School east of the city on Highway 54. Among the hazards the field presented were powerlines on two sides and the one-room school building in the center of the field.

Throughout the late 1920s and '30s James Pugh and Joe Reichenbach were the leading local flyers. The county took over the airport in the early 1930s. It remained at Vaudreuil until the new airport was constructed in 1969. [19]

Boscobel

Boscobel Airport, auxiliary. Two miles NE. of Boscobel. Altitude, 900 feet. Rectangular, sod, level, natural drainage; two landing strips, NE./SW., 2,650 feet, NW./SE., 1,770 feet, each 100 feet wide; entire field available. "CTC X-2" on shed roof. hort pole line to SW. Blinker in SW. corner, boundary, approach, and obstruction lights operated upon request. Beacon, 24-inch rotating, 1 mile S. No servicing facilities. [1933]

As the CTC X-2 painted on the shed roof there indicates, the Boscobel Airport was on the Chicago-Twin Cities airway that bypassed Milwaukee, Madison and La Crosse in favor of a more direct route via Rockford, Illinois and Rochester, Minnesota. Its location on the airway made Boscobel eligible for federal funding that paid for runway improvments, lighting and a rotating beacon.

Local aviation activity was slight until Kenneth Rogers brought a Waco 10 to Boscobel in 1935. Rogers was an auto mechanic by trade and an aviator by preference who started out by rebuilding his new plane from nose to tail. In addition to the Waco 10, he also restored a Waco 5, a 1917 Swallow trainer, an Aeronca and a Szekely-powered Curtiss Junior. He took up gliding in a home-built plane with a 39-foot wingspan. He also purchased a J-3-50 and became one of the first Piper dealers in southwestern Wisconsin.

Like most small town aviators, he did his share of barnstorming in and out of hayfields and pastures. While flying his J-3 over the Wisconsin River on a day with a low ceiling he found himself suddenly confronted by the Boscobel Bridge. A relic soon replaced by a modern span, the old Boscobel bridge was one of the last wooden-covered bridges in Wisconsin. Rogers thought he could fly over it until he noticed the high power lines mounted above its roof. Then he gritted his teeth and steered for the open spot between the piers and steered the J-3 through with inches to spare.

The Boscobel Airport closed during World War II, then reopened in 1946.[20]

Brodhead

Brodhead—-Department of Commerce intermediate field, site 10, Chicago-Twin Cities Airway. Six miles NW. Altitude, 832 feet. L shape, loam, level, natural drainage; three landing strips, N./S., 2,600 feet, E./W., 2,640 feet, NW./SE., 2,850 feet; entire field available; "10 C-TC" on shed. Trees to S.; low telephone line to N.; 40-foot windmill to S. Beacon, boundary, approach, and obstruction lights. Beacon, 36-inch rotating, clear with green course lights flashing characteristic "10" (—). No servicing facilities. [1933]

The Brodhead Airport was established as a service and communication stop on the Chicago-Twin Cities Airway. It continued to serve this function until World War II, but did not have a hangar nor did local aviators make much use of it until the postwar years.[21]

Brown Deer

Milwaukee—-Holterhoff Airport, commercial, rating —-. Five miles N. Altitude, 681 feet. T shaped, sod, level, natural drainage; landing strips 2,500 by 603 feet N./S., and 2,500 by 692 feet E./W. HOLTERHOFF FLYING SERVICE, INC., on hangar. Pole line along road on N. Facilities for servicing aircraft, day only. [1931]

The Brown Deer Airport began in August 1927, when Bill Williams force-landed his J-1 Standard on the Hunkel farm on Brown Deer Road in Milwaukee County. Williams thought the smooth and level Hunkel farm would make a good airport, but farmer Hunkel preferred to keep the ground in hay. Williams then moved down the road to Ed Gengler who was willing to lease some of his land for an air field. In 1928 Williams, who was flying his new OX-5 Swallow off the field, was joined by Fritz Holterhoff and his Canuck. Williams then left Brown Deer to become chief test pilot for the Invincible airplane in Manitowoc and Holterhoff Airport came into being.

Holterhoff was a veteran of the German air force, one of several Milwaukee-area pilots who had flown for the Kaiser in World War I. He built a maintenance shop, a hangar big enough for six planes and acquired the Wisconsin franchise for American Eagle Aircraft. The dual cockpit, OX-5-powered "Eagles" were billed as "The Fastest, Strongest and Safest Aeroplanes in Their Class." Holterhoff was able to sell at least six American Eagles before the Depression all but grounded the company.

Holterhoff started a flying school and among the instructors in 1928-29 were Clyde Lee and Thor Solberg, who later became rivals in the short-lived transAtlantic race to Norway. Starting on the same day, both Lee and Solberg made forced landings on the way to Newfoundland. Lee landed on the beach and was able to continue, but Solberg went down in the water and abandoned his flight without reaching the open sea.

Back in Wisconsin, Fred Holterhoff was joined by Carl Koeffler and together they formed a partnership with the Weeks Aircraft Company of Milwaukee. Holterhoff died in an automobile crash in 1932, but the Weeks-Holterhoff Company remained in business under Koeffler's management and added a franchise from the Great Lakes Aircraft Company. During the mid-and late-1930s, the operation was in the hands of "Sarge" Richter, Ralph Kofler and Roy Duggan, followed by Warren and James Stoll. By 1938, Ben Towle and his Badger Airways operated the field. He was one of Wisconsin's first Piper Cub dealers.

Badger sold a J-3 Cub to Jules and Max Sagunsky of Saukville. They put it to work delivering guitars and other musical instruments throughout the state. The Sagunskys sales approach was to place an ad for their insruments in a farm publication. When a farmer responded, Jules or Max would pinpoint the location, fly the

Cub there, and complete both the sale and delivery on landing. Max used this experience to prepare for his future career as manager of the Outagamie County Airport.

In the summer of 1938, Joe Jordan and Herman "Fish" Salmon made Brown Deer their base airport. Using a Spartan C-3 and a Ryan B-1, Jordan and Salmon made the air show tour, with Salmon making hundreds of jumps before leaving Wisconsin to become a test pilot for Lockheed. Other pilots connected with the Brown Deer Airport included Clarence Bates, Chuck Gardner, Garth Smith, Charles Christenson, Ed Weber, George Hathaway, and Miriam Edgerton Hathaway.

Fred and Rod Lueneberg were at the Brown Deer Airport right from the start. They were the farm boys leaning on the fence watching the planes land in the late 1920s. In short time, they were washing planes and running errands. By 1934, Fred was charging "fifteen minutes of flight instruction" as the price of a wash, and it took only until the summer of 1936 to get enough time to solo. Two more years and he had his Private Pilot's license, which then required fifty hours of solo time. Lueneberg continued to fly and earned his Commerical Certificate after two more years.

The Brown Deer Airport was closed to all but Civil Air Patrol aviation at the start of World War II. It opened briefly after the war, but closed when the Capitol Drive Airport opened.[22]

Delafield

Lake Nagawicka Seaplane Base, commercial, rating —-. Located just NE. of Delafield on Lake Nagawicka, 25 1/2 miles W. of Milwaukee. Altitude, 600 feet. Entire area of Lake Nagawicka available for operations. SEAPLANE BASE ST. JOHN'S MILITARY ACADEMY on hangar roof. Ramp and facilities for shoring seaplanes. Facilities for servicing, day and night. [1933]

In 1931, German air force pilot William Ehrengart incorporated Land O' Lakes Flying Service on Lake Nagawicka. He built a hangar on the lake and used two Kinner-powered fleet amphibians for flight instruction and charter work. The seaplane base was dedicated in June 1931, on a date to coincide with Governor's Day at St. John's Military Academy, so Governor Phillip La Follette and Adjutant General Ralph Immell attended. St. John's was already involved in aviation with a Ryan Brougham on floats flying off of Nagawicka.

A Sikorsky amphibian also took part in the event, but Waukesha Pilot Russell Schuetze stole the show by flying backwards in his

Curtiss-Pusher. Schuetze had perfected the stunt, which was always a crowd-pleaser.

The Land O'Lakes Flying Service got off to a good start, but was out of business after a few years.

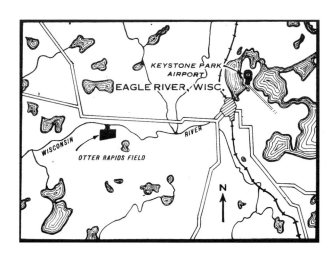

Eagle River

Eagle River Airport, municipal, rating —-. One and one half miles SE. Loon Lake borders field to NW. Altitude, 1,760 feet. Irregular, sod, level, natural drainage; three runways, 1,500 feet N./S., 2,700 feet NE./SW. and 1,765 feet NW./SE.; entire field available. Pole line to NE., scattered trees. Aviation fuel, day only. [1933]

Keystone Park Airport, commercial, rating —-. Two miles NE., bounded on three sides by lakes. Altitude, 1,760 feet. Oval shape, 2,200 by 900 feet, sod, level, natural drainage. Pole lines along E. and S., trees surround field. Aviation fuel, day only. [1931]

McCullough-Otter Rapids Field, commercial, rating —-. Six and one half miles West of Eagle River, Wisconsin River to N. Altitude, 1,800 feet. Rectangular, 1,800 feet E./W.; by 620 feet N./S.; sod, level, natural drainage; entire field available. Trees to N., E., and S.; water tank on north. Facilities for servicing aircraft, day only. [1933]

Eagle River was surrounded by small airports in the early late 1920s and early 1930s. The Keystone Park and Otter Rapids fields were private fields serving the tourist trade. The Otter Rapids field opened in 1928 as part of C. Gl. McCullough's Otter Rapids Golf Course.

The Eagle River Airport was also a private field on the farm of Edward and Lillian Brunswick. It received a first class airport and municipal rating in September, 1929.

The airport was popular with local and transient flyers because it was well maintained and had fuel available. Some local flyers were Dr. Ora McMurray, who flew in World War I; Colonel Jenkins, who brought his airplane from England; Fred Strong, Jim Hanson and Norm Warner. In 1929 Captain Westover flew in with the Universal Airline's Ford Tri-motor. Lieutenant Hamilton and Sergeant Rhodes made a number of visits with their Army Air Corps Douglas O-2-H while conducting aerial photographic surveys in the north country. The close proximity of Loon Lake was attractive to several Sikorsky and Loening amphibians which landed on the water and the airport turf.

A popular Sunday activity for the local people was to visit the airport to watch the flying, take a ride or drink a glass of lemonade at a refreshment stand provided by the six Brunswick daughters, whose first names began with the first six letters of the alphabet in the order of their birth. The current chairman of the Eagle River airport commission, Walt Mayo, has clear memories of his job, as a young man, delivering fuel to the airport and sometimes directly refueling Dr. McMurray's airplane.

The Municipal Airport in the Aeronautics Bureau Direcorty was replaced in 1936 by a new landing field. Located just north of the city on property purchased by the Mike Schmidt family, the airport was dedicated with an air show that featured Dr. Ora McMurray performing aerobatics in his Stinson Cabin plane and a "delayed" parachute jump by "Fish" Salmon.

Eau Claire

Eau Claire Airport, commercial, rating —. On bluff at S. boundary of city, 1 and 1/4 miles S. of business district. Altitude, 820 feet. Rectangular, 4,629 by 2,640 feet, sandy sod, slightly rolling, natural drainage. EAU CLAIRE on hangar roof. Pole lines on W. and half of S. boundary; trees around field except on W. Facilities for servicing aircraft, day only. [1931]

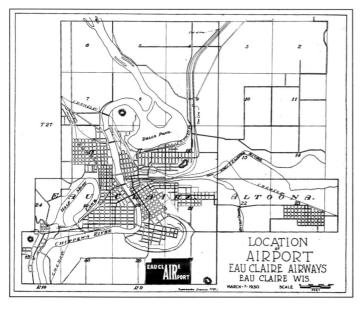

The Eau Claire Airport was located on the far south side of the city. (Chippewa Valley Museum)

Guy Wood, Leo McDonald and M. A. Sine organized the Eau Claire Airplane Corporation in 1923 and opened Eau Claire's first airport on 80 acres along State Street in what later became known as Putnam Heights. Their pilot was U. S. Navy veteran Virgil R. Grace who flew a J.1 Standard off the grass field.

Eau Claire was not exactly a hotbed of aviation activity in the 1920s and Grace soon moved on to find regular work as one of Hollywood's first stunt pilots. Among his credits was the 1926 movie "Wings." It featured the most dramatic and lifelike scenes of aerial combat yet produced and four spectacular crashes with Dick Grace at the controls. The most exciting, and life-threatening, required Grace to crash a German air force Fokker D-7 into the ground at 100 MPH and do it with enough finesse to finish with the plane standing on its nose. He succeeded and lived to do it again many times over. Grace set the standard for aerial drama in Hollywood. His piloting skills helped make "Wings" the recipient of the first Oscar awarded for Best Picture.

A Fairchild KR 54, press plane on the 1930 Reliability Tour, which landed at Eau Claire. (Robert Wylie)

Back in Eau Claire, the air field was quiet until 1929, when J.R. Davis, E. R. Hamilton and John Simpson organized Eau Claire Airways. The partners made a serious attempt to make it in aviation at Eau Claire. The new hangar of Eau Claire Airways housed a full-service operation, including a flight school that could take a pilot to his first solo and continue training for the private pilot, limited commercial and transport pilot's tickets. Fees were $475 for the private pilot license and $3500 for the 200 hour transport pilot card.

Eau Claire Airways offered round trip "taxi service" to the Twin Cities for $45, La Crosse for $40, Wausau for $47.50, Madison for $80, Milwaukee for $110 and Chicago for $130. The company also was a dealer for Travel Air, Curtiss Robin, De Havilland Moth, and Keystone-Loening Amphibian and Tri-Motor planes. Aerial photography and excursion flights were available, so was rental hangar space at $20 per month for "small planes."

The high point of Eau Claire Airways lifespan was its hosting of the Ford Reliability Tour in 1930. Despite this impressive success, the company struggled to survive and in 1935 pilot Alexander Ward bought the operation. He flew a Travel Air biplane and a Curtiss Junior until he left Eau Claire in 1939 and the State Street Airport all but closed.

With a large munitions plant and other defense-related industries in the area, Eau Claire and its inadequate airport attracted the attention of the federal government. Throughout the war years, the city of Eau Claire and several federal agencies shared the cost of purchasing land and building a new airport on the northern edge of the city. The steel hangar was moved from State Street, two runways were cleared of trees and George Pettit became airport manager. The new Eau Claire Municipal Airport was formally opened in 1945.[23]

Fifield

Fifield, Boyd's Airport, auxiliary. Twelve miles from Fifield, Long Lake immediately NW. Altitude, 1,200 feet. Square, light soil, level, natural drainage; entire field available. Small lakes on E.; 50-foot trees on W. Facilities for servicing aircraft, day only. [1933]

Boyd's Mason Lake Resort in Price County was one of the oldest resorts in the stretch of territory between Hayward and Minocqua. Opened in the early 1930s, the airport was a clear spot in the woods suitable for emergency landings. It was occasionally used by visitors to the resort until closing during World War II.

Fond du Lac

Fond du Lac Airport, commercial, rating —. One half mile E. of Fond du Lac on cement highway. Altitude, 600 feet. Rectangular, 2,600 by 1,800 feet, sod, level, artificial drainage. High-tension lines on N. and E., with red neon lights. Facilities for servicing aircraft, day and night. [1933]

In August 1927, Charles Lindbergh flew over Fond du Lac and dropped a message that landed on the roof of the Wilke Hardware building. It expressed Lindbergh's regrets that he could not land himself and encouraged citizens of the lake city to support aviation. Led by Tom Meiklejohn, the Fond du Lac Association of Commerce had already opened an airport and built a hangar on the east side of the city on Johnson Street with Steve Wittman and his J-1 Standard in residence. In 1928, the Pheasant Aircraft Company began operations at Fond du Lac, but was out of business by 1931 when Wittman moved on to Oshkosh. Also present in these years were Florian Manor and Nick Rowinski, who designed the Pheasant four-cylinder overhead valve engine and the almost-flying motorcycle. Rowinski had better luck with his low-octane-fueled Tank engine, which went into production in Milwaukee, but his center-wing airplane, which the Tank would supposedly push to speeds in excess of 185 MPH, never got off the drawing board.

Starting at the end of 1928, Fond du Lac was a stop on the Northwest Airways Fox Valley route from Milwaukee to Green Bay. Stinsons and Hamilton Metalplanes carried air mail and passengers until the federal government cancelled all air mail contracts in the spring of 1933.

In 1929, young Wilbur Moersch showed up at the airport and started flying lessons with Steve Wittman in a Pheasant biplane at $15 per hour. Moersch and some of his friends organized what they

Young Steve Wittman ready to switch on the Atwater-Kent radio displayed on the tail of his airplane at Fond du Lac. (EAA)

called the 3F - Fond du Lac Flying Club and pooled their quarters and dimes for a few years to make payments on one of the three Pheasant biplanes built in Fond du Lac. Moersch later acquired a Pheasant Traveler, which he described as "terrific." After Wittman

left for Oshkosh, Florian Manor became airport manager. He stayed until 1935 when Moersch and Al Devoe took over the job. With the help of federal grants and WPA labor, the airport was improved, with a lot of money going into drainage tiles to remove water from the low-lying site.

In 1938, Will Haase, Sr., landed his Fairchild 24 at Fond du Lac and, with this son Will, Jr., walked down the gravel road to the lake to look over the lakefront lot he had purchased in the Bechaud Beach subdivision. The Haases lived in Chicago but planned to build a summer house at Bechaud and commute to it in the Fairchild. Once they saw it, people were likely to remember the Fairchild, since painted on its fuselage was a burial vault surrounded by a mourning wreath. Haase ran the Wilbert Burial Vault Company and wasn't about to let jokes about flying coffins get in the way of free advertising. Haase's flying coffin continued to summer in Fond du Lac until World War II grounded it. After the war, Will Haase, Jr. came home and he and his father purchased the Fond du Lac Airport. A few years later they led the effort to relocate the operation to the west side of the city.[24]

Green Bay

Green Bay—-Brown County Airport, municipal, rating —. One and one half mile SW., one fourth mile W. of Fox River. Altitude, 900 feet. Rectangular, sod, level, natural drainage; four runways, all 1,500 by 100 feet; entire field also available. Pole lines to E. and N., woods to SE. GREEN BAY on hangar roof. Facilities for servicing aircraft, day only. [1931]

After Alfred Lawson left Green Bay for Milwaukee his landing strip at Blesch Field was taken over by the Green Bay Aero Club. a for-profit group of investors who hoped to see a return on their purchase of a war surplus Jenny. They would have turned a profit except, as President C. A Gross explained, "the pilots would crack up planes faster than we could buy them." Gross and his fellow investors—Edward K. Wagner, Carl Dreutzer, Perry S. Wagner, Andrew B. Turnbull—were philosophical about their loses. "We wound up a little in the hole, but it wasn't much and we had a lot of fun."

The Aero Club went out of business in 1923 and aviation all but dried up at Green Bay. Not until 1927 did local pilot Eddie Kersten bring a machine to Blesch Field and build a hangar. Still progress was slow until the end of 1928, when Northwest Airways took over Kersten's hangar and ran the Fox Valley air mail route north from Milwaukee and Appleton. In anticipation of the event, Brown County took over maintenance of the field, grading and mowing in the summer, plowing snow in the winter. Nonetheless, operations still had to halt for a few weeks in early spring until all the "tundra" thawed.

By 1931, Blesch Field counted 932 operations, including 600 air mail flights. The future looked bright despite the Depression, until the federal government cancelled the air mail in 1933. Northwest continued to provide passenger and freight service to the Fox Valley for about a month before it was forced to halt operations. Northwest did not consider restoring passenger service to Green Bay until 1940

Mel Thompson at Blesch Field with his "Green Bay" airplane in the 1920s. (WAHF)

and was about to begin when World War II intervened.

In the meantime Brown County purchased the airport property and received federal aid to improve the runways, build two hangars and pave the highway leading to the field. Still, activity was sparse throughout the decade and would remain so until the end of World War II. The county had already taken the first steps to leave Blesch Field by optioning the 950 acres that became the site of Austin Straubel Airport.[25]

Hager City

Hager City—-Department of Commerce intermediate field, site 31A, Chicago-Twin Cities Airway. One fourth mile SE. of Hager City; N. of Red Wing. Altitude, 713 feet. L shape, sod, rolling, natural drainage; two runways, 1,760 feet N./S., and 2,530 feet NW./SE. "31A, C-TC" on shed. Pole lines to N. and S.; trees to S. and W.; beacon tower to SW.; two railroad semaphores to NW. Beacon, boundary, approach, and obstruction lights. Beacon, 24-inch rotating, with green course lights flashing characteristic "1" (.—). No servicing facilities. Teletypewriter. [1933]

Just across the Mississippi from Red Wing, Minnesota the Hager Airport was built as a stopping point on the Chicago-Milwaukee-LaCrosse-Twin Cities Airway. It was graded, lighted and home to a beacon. Hager also had a weather station connected to the federal teletype weather reporting system. A pilot forced to land by threatening weather could find up to the hour bulletins printed out on the Hager teletype. By the mid-1930s a radio range finder beacon was in place to guide radio-equipped aircraft on the airway.

The Hager City field continued to serve as a guidepost on the airway until World War II when its services became obsolete.[26]

Kenosha

Kenosha Airport, municipal, rating —-. Two and one half miles SW. of business district. Altitude, 623 feet. Rectangular, 2,650 feet N./S., by 2,550 feet E./W.; sod, level, natural drainage; two runways, NW./SE., and NE./SW., 2,900 by 300 feet. Pole line on W.; trees to E.; buildings to S.; hangar in NE. corner. Facilities for servicing aircraft, day only. [1933]

In the years after World War I, Kenosha had as many as seven different landing strips on the western edge of town. One was used by Pete Galles, who brought the first Jenny to town in 1920 and held a christening ceremony where the Mayor and other officials

helped name Galles' plane "Kenosha." Ledger Reed and Hart Smith also had landing strips on 22nd Avenue and the Reverend Howe had the "Minister's Airport" on 39th Avenue, where he taught fledgling pastors how to fly on a wing and a prayer.

In 1928, after negotiations with Racine on the subject of building a joint airport failed, the city of Kenosha leased property for an airport on 22nd Avenue and 80th Street, at what later became Anderson Park. Smith served as airport manager until his death in 1932 and was succeeded by Ray Johnson. Other names in Kenosha aviation in these years were Floyd Bayless, John Sodlink, Herb Walraven, Howard Posselt, Harold and Carl Kaiser, Al Padags, Harold Erickson and many more.

The name most widely associated with Kenosha aviation is that of Ruth Harman. She was eighteen years old in 1931 when she saw a glider fly over the municipal airport and decided to give it a try. "I was the only woman who tried it, but it didn't seem to mean much to anybody that I was female. They just said, 'Do it' and I did." She did it three times, wrecking the glider on her last attempt.

Harman then signed up for flight instruction, selling her bicycle to pay for the first $8-an-hour lesson. She went to work in the mail room at Cooper's Inc. and used her pay to finance the six hours of training she needed to solo. In March, 1932 she earned her private license and in 1936 completed the hours for a transport and instructor's ratings. Coincidentally, on the same day Ruth Harman was licensed, Marian Stahl also received her private license, which she used to fly for pleasure for many years.

Aviators at the Kenosha Airport, late 1930s. (WAHF)

Harman went to work as a flyer, taking sightseers up for ten minutes flights and earning two dollars. She did charter work and promotional work for Cooper, with her plane identified as the Cooper "Masculiner." She and and another woman flew the "Masculiner" to Florida and raised eyebrows at airports all across the South. In Wisconsin she stunted at shows, where the "girl flyer" got extra billing. In 1936, she helped welcome Amelia Earhart when she came to Kenosha to speak at the high school.

The aspect of flying Harman most enjoyed was instructing. "I wanted to teach others to fly because I loved it so much myself," she recalled in 1988. "That was my objective in life."

In 1940, Kenosha balked on renewing its lease for the airport, so James Anderson bought the airport property, which enabled Harman to become the first woman to manage an airport in Wisconsin. She was also able to expand on her ambition to teach aviation. When local educators sponsored an industrial safety conference, Harman lectured on flight safety, the first time an aviator had been included in the program. She pointed out that "Ever since the day nearly 40 years ago when the Wright brothers flew their first airplane, aviators have been regarded as heroes....Daring and exhibitionism have been set up as standards...Little wonder that boy after boy and girl after girl goes to a flaming death...

"We must recognize that flying is no longer a romantic adventure, it is a business. We must build a new set of standards by which we judge and praise; standards of safety and conservatism."

Harman practiced what she preached. She eventually owned nine airplanes and ran a successful aviation business without mishaps. When the United States entered World War II, Harman became Kenosha's instructor in the CPT program and trained flight cadets for the Navy. She was one of fifty female CPT instructors in the United States and the only one in Wisconsin.

She married fellow pilot Herb Walraven in 1943 and continued as manager of the old Kenosha Airport until shortly after his death in 1950. The Kenosha airport remained at Anderson Park until it was replaced by the Kenosha Regional Airport.[27]

Herb Walraven. (WAHF)

Herbert Walraven and Ruth Harman, in the early 1940s. (WAHF)

Kewaunee

Kewaunee Airport, municipal. Two miles N. of city of W. side of Highway No. 42. Lat 44.30; long 87.30. Alt. 600 feet. Square, sod, rough, natural drainage; two gravel runways, 1,320 by 300 feet. N.S and E.W; use runways only. Pole lines to E. and N.; hangar to E.: buildings toNW. Facilities for servicing aircraft, day only. [1938]

Kewaunee made a brief entry into the aviation age in July of 1924 when local mechanic Eli Hessel purchased a Curtiss JN-4 from a dealer in Minneapolis for $1,000, delivered. The value of the venerable Jenny had plummeted from the $8,000 high that the Curtiss Company had charged the government back in 1917. Hessel had yet to learn how to fly a Jenny or any other kind of aircraft so his plane was delivered by Air Service veteran H. F. Cole, who made the three-hundred mile trip across Wisconsin in about three and one-half hours, including a stop for gas in Marshfield. Once Cole delivered the plane, Hessel was left to teach himself how to fly. The self-instruction lasted for about a year before the inexperienced pilot wrecked his plane while attempting to land across a set of telephone wires.

Aviation in Kewaunee was set back until 1931 when Leo Salkowski, who had already built the first modern Standard Oil service station in the city, purchased an airplane. He used aviation themes to advertise his gas station and began to lobby civic leaders to build an airport to replace the hayfield currently in use. He was unsuccessful until 1934, when the city of Kewaunee received a federal grant of $11,000 to improve the forty acres it had purchased north of the city from Henry Aude. Work on the field continued through 1934 and the airport was ready to open in the spring of 1935.

The new Kewaunee airport opened with a bang on the Memorial Day weekend of 1935. The U. S. Army had scheduled an exercise for the men of the 61st Company of the Coast Artillery and the 15th Aero Squadron of the Air Corps to take place in Kewaunee county for the week before Memorial Day. They would camp on farm land south of the city and "approximately 18 military airplanes" would use the new airport "as a base for sham battle flights....with actual artillery fire, searchlight drills and everything else that goes on with actual wartime fighting." The Coast Artillery would motor up from camp at Fort Sheridan, Illinois and the 15th Aero Squadron would fly across the lake from Scott Field, Ohio. Commanding the expedition, much to the pride of local people, was Kewaunee native Colonel Charles B. Meyer.

On Memorial Day, Kewaunee braced for its "greatest celebration." An estimated 25,000 people caused "the greatest traffic jam Northeastern Wisconsin has ever seen," as they filled the roads to the airport. Pilots reported that the roads were jammed as far south as Two Creeks, west to Pilsen and north to Sturgeon Bay. Many travelers on their way to see the cherry blossoms in Door County stopped to watch the airplanes in Kewaunee. Even a few Door County residents paid a neighborly visit.

Paul Koehn and his Travel Air at Kohler, 1928. (Kohler Co. Archives)

The roads, shoulders and adjacent fields were so crowded with horn-honking drivers and their cars that the ceremony was postponed for one hour and the Air Corps pilots were ordered not to perform their "famous power dives," because the grounds around the field were so jammed with spectators. With the horns sounding on the roads, the airplanes screaming overhead, the spectators shouting and clapping. Only the crisp slam bang of the eight-shot artillery volley fired at a target towed over the field silenced the clamor—at least momentarily.

The Air Corps' flying must have been contagious, because civilian pilots offering to take visitors up for rides reported record numbers of passengers. "I've carried passengers at a lot of celebrations," said one Milwaukee pilot up for the week, "but this one beats them all."

The Kewaunee airport was well-launched and would continue to serve its community until World War II. [28]

Kohler/Sheboygan

Kohler Airport, municipal, rating —. One half mile N. of Kohler, three and one half miles W. of Sheboygan. Altitude, 647 feet. Irregular, 2,600 by 1,800 feet, sod, level, artificial drainage. KOHLER on hangar. Pole line and factory building to S.; scattered trees. Beacon, boundary, approach, obstruction, and landing area flood lights. Beacon, 24-inch rotating, clear with green auxiliary beacon. Facilities for servicing aircraft, day and night. [1933]

Sheboygan

Sheboygan Airport, commercial, rating —. Two and one half miles SW. from center of city. Altitude, 662 feet. Irregular shape, 2,640 by 2,200 feet, sod, level, artificial drainage. Pole lines to N., E., and S., trees to NW. and SW. Facilities for servicing aircraft, day and night. [1933]

As home of the "Flying Governor" Walter Kohler, Anton Brotz, Tony Brotz, Felix Waitkus, and Mel Thompson, Kohler played a much greater role in Wisconsin aviation than its size would warrant. Especially in the early 1930s, no other Wisconsin village of 1800 people had as much air traffic, as many air shows, and witnessed as much aviation activity as Kohler. In 1929, over 100 different airplanes landed at the airport and more than 2,000 people embarked on flights. Air tours, air races, Legion activities, business

flights, preparation for a transAtlantic flight all occurred at the Kohler field. Although the Sheboygan airport remained open, it was all but inactive compared to its neighbor.

The airport was home to the Governor's Ryan Brougham, the Woodson Express owned by Anton Brotz, Mel Thompson's Waco 10, Joe Richardson's Travel Air, Carl Kohler's Aeronca, Paul Koehn's Curtiss OX-5 Swallow and a few homemade gliders. Part time and visiting flyers included Sheboygan's Ione Shaw, Dole Race winner Art Goebel and the nationally famous racing pilot, Nellie Zabel Willhite.

The first licensed female pilot in her home state of South Dakota, Willhite had married a Sheboygan man and briefly lived in the city. In June 1929, South Dakota Governor William Bulow commissioned her to deliver a letter to Governor Kohler by air. She did so by circling the Kohler airport and dropping a parachure bearing the letter with a genuine chip of granite from Mount Rushmore acting as a sinker.

Anton Brotz Sr., the professorial father of aviation in the Sheboygan-Kohler area, rebuilt his Woodson Express at Kohler and used it for experimental flights. In August, 1931 he took the open-cockpit Woodson up to 17,050 feet "to see the shores of the state of Michigan," without the aid of oxygen tanks. Anton Brotz, Jr., flew out of Kohler until the late 1930s, when he went to work at North American Aviation and helped design the P-51 fighter and the B-25 bomber.

As Walter Kohler and Anton Brotz grew older, activity at Kohler decreased, but Mel Thompson kept the flame alive. He became airport manager and acquired Brotz's Woodson and Kohler's Ryan in

Walter Kohler's Ryan Brougham and a Waco at Kohler, about 1930. (Kohler Co. Archives)

1937. He conducted a flight school, barnstormed and rebuilt airplanes for sale. He continued to manage the Kohler Airport until it was replaced by the Sheboygan County Airport in 1961. [29]

Land O'Lakes

Land O'Lakes Airport, municipal, rating —-. Six miles W. of city. Altitude, 1,760 feet. Irregular, 2,100 by 500 feet N./S. and 2,000 by 700 feet E./W.; gravel, loam, level, natural drainage; entire field available. Pole line 600 feet S. and one fourth mile E.; timber on all sides. Aviation fuel, day only. [1933]

The automobile and prosperity were boosting Northwoods tourism in the 1920s and many northern Wisconsin communities thought aviation could help. In 1925, a group of resort owners and real estate developers cleared 120 acres of stumpland about six miles west of the village of Land O' Lakes. Charles Bent, who owned Bent's Camp on nearby Mamie Lake, George St. Claire, who owned the Black Oak Lake Resort, and realtors George T. Halbert and Arthur Wenz presented the property to the Town of State Line, which would supply minimal maintenance.

Bent's interest in aviation was both professional and personal, since his daughter Mamie had married pilot George Fisher, who managed the Curtiss-Wright Airport in Winnetka, Illinois. Bent hoped that George would fly Mamie home to visit the folks and per-

The airport at King's Gateway Resort, Land O'Lakes, about 1940. (WAHF)

haps pump up some Illinois trade for the resort. It was an interesting use of aviation for economic development and one that would be duplicated many times in Wisconsin's tourist regions.

On the day the airport was dedicated, Fisher did fly up from Winnetka and spent the day taking up spectators for rides. While Fisher and others pilots used the field, it did not develop into a going commerical operation—at least not a legal one. Since it was relatively remote and less than one-hour's flight from the Canadian border, the Land O'Lakes Airport was reputed to be a good landing

spot for rum-runners delivering illegal whiskey from Canada. When Prohibition ended in 1933, traffic became uniformly legitimate.

The original Land O' Lakes Airport continued in operation until the 1940s, when it was replaced by the landing field at the King's Gateway Resort, which opened in 1939. King's Airport was located adjacent to the resort in the village just off of Highway 45. In the heyday of the Gateway, visitors, conventioneers and entertainers used its airport, while the older field slowly reverted to woods and brush.[30]

La Crosse

La Crosse Airport, municipal, rating, —-. Two and one-half miles SE. Altitude, 640 feet. Rectangular, 80 acres, 2,640 by 1,820 feet, sod, level, natural drainage; one oiled runway 2,000 by 500 feet N./S.; entire field available. LA CROSSE on hangar roof. Pole lines to E. and SW. Beacon, boundary, and landing area flood lights. Beacon, 24-inch rotating, clear. Facilities for servicing aircraft, day and night. Department of Commerce radio station WSG, operating frequency 254 kcs. [1931]

La Crosse County Airport, municipal. Five miles NW. of city, on W. side of U.S. Highway No. 35. Altitude, 640 feet. Cross-shape, sod, level, natural drainage; two landing strips, 3,400 feet NE./SW. 3,000 feet NW./SE., both 300 feet wide. Pole line to SW.; buildings to W.; trees to NE. and NW. LAX embedded in field, LA CROSSE on hangar. Boundary, approach, and obstruction lights operated upon request. Department of Commerce radio station WSG, frequency 371 kc, and radio range becon, identfiying signal "LE" (.- .. .), frequency 371 kc. Facilities for servicing aircraft, day only. Teletypewriter. [1938]

La Crosse's Salzer Field was a key link in the air mail and passenger service connecting Chicago, Milwaukee and the Twin Cities until 1932. Hemmed in by bluffs on the east, the river on the west and a growing city to the north, Salzer could no longer meet the needs of commercial aviation. Northwest Airways told city leaders either to remove hazardous telephone and gasoline tanks bordering the field, plow the runways reliably in winter and reseed the bare spots in spring or move the airport to a better site the airline had identified on French Island.

La Crosse, "won't spend another dime for aviation," said Mayor J. J. Verchota.

In May 1933, Northwest responded by pulling out of La Crosse. The federal aeronautics bureau soon followed and removed its weather, radio and other gear. La Crosse, one of the first cities in the state to have an airport and one of a handful to enjoy regular passenger and air mail service, technically spent the summer of 1933 minus an airport. While the city, the airline and the federal government wrangled, local flyers like Jack Fanta and Ken Reed continued to fly out of Salzer.

Another local pilot, Roy Pfafflin, filled the official vacuum by developing an airport on 160 acres northwest of the city on French Island. He obtained runway and boundary lighting from Salzer, along with three hangars, and moved them to French Island. After inspecting Pfafflin's work, Northwest manager Mal Freeberg agreed to let Northwest planes land and take off there.

With Pfafflin's airport seemingly established and with the prospect of federal funding on the horizon, county supervisor Ray

fund further airport improvements unless the county actually owned the property. This ruling set the stage for a dispute between Pfafflin and the county, for once the county agreed to buy the property, Pfafflin didn't want to sell. The county threatened condemnation, but was unwilling to actually confiscate the property and Pfafflin refused to negotiate further. By 1937, the level of frustration grew so high that the county board—includ-

Bice persuaded the La Crosse county board to lease the French Island airport from Pfafflin, then to hire Pfafflin as manager. The reason for this arrangement was not necessarily aeronautical. As the La Crosse Tribune reported, "An allocation of $31,839 was obtained...and will be spent not primarily to build an airport but to give work to a large number of men. The airport project is a buffer for unemployment." So out to French Island they went, 100 men with shovels and hoes to scrape and level and seed grass for an airport. A few of them were probably whistling the New Deal anthem, "Happy Days Are Here Again." They weren't getting rich, but they were working and getting paid.

By August 1935, the hand-made airport was in shape to be dedicated. Bice and the county airport committee arranged a ceremony and invited Governor Phil La Follette to attend. As Bice recalled, "When I told him how to find the airport by air he decided to come by car."

Nonetheless, the first La Crosse county airport was duly dedicated by Governor La Follette after he drove up from Madison. Local pilots also staged an air show but the committee felt that some out-of-town entertainment was needed. They hired a fellow who called himself, "The Bat Man," after the latest hero of the comic book world. His act was to jump from an airplane wearing a pair of mechanical wings that he used to half-flap and half-glide until he opened a parachute and descended to earth. Sad to say, at La Crosse, the wings malfunctioned and the Bat Man had to open his chute early, which meant he missed the airport and landed in the Black River—blessedly unharmed.

Bad luck and balky politicians continued to plague the La Crosse airport. The federal government looked askance at the arrangment between the county and Ray Pfafflin and refused to

ing number-one booster Ray Bice—voted to abandon the airport, bringing about the demise of the first La Crosse County Airport.

A few months later, after bad weather forced a Northwest Airlines plane to land at Pfafflin under emergency conditions, the

La Crosse aviators at the French Island Airport, 1941. (WAHF)

federal government leased the field and began to improve it. At the same time, another airport opened north of Onalaska on a fine piece of flat ground called Brice's Prairie. Both the French Island and Brice's Prairie airports continued to operate until the United States entered World War II. In 1942, once again led by Ray Bice, the city of La Crosse entered the fray. Bice headed a Citizen's Airport Committee that convinced city voters to pass a $100,000 bond issue authorizing La Crosse to buy the French Island Airport. As a municipal airport, French Island was now eligible for federal funding. The Brice's Prairie field was also a contender for federal funding, but only briefly, since at twelves miles away, it was considered to be too far away from La Crosse to well serve the city.

The La Crosse airport on French Island was improved with federal funding during the war and, after the war, Northwest Airlines and Parks Air Transport, a Chicago-based commuter line, used it. In 1947, another improvement program was completed and the La Crosse Municipal Airport was officially dedicated.

Fortunately, La Crosse's aviators were only minimally disturbed by the decade and one-half of political wrangling. One of the first was Barney Root, who was flying a Canuck out of Salzer in the mid-1920s. He was available as a flight instructor when a group of young men from La Crosse organized the Winneshiek Flying Club in 1927. Bill Leithold, then a student at Carroll College in Waukesha, placed an ad in the paper asking for volunteers to put in $250 each to buy an airplane. The ad was successful enough to raise $3800 to purchase an OX-5 Waco 10, plus wages for Root as flight instructor. Leithold, Les Borer, Ken Reed, Jack Fanta, Ray Schultz and Betty Leipelt put in their share, but the major backer was William Finn, who loved flying, but was hampered by poor eyesight. The club grew and became an incubator for aviation in the area.

Leithhold and Borer acquired another Waco and started the Winnishiek Flying Service, named after the nearby Mississippi River wetland known as the Winnishiek Bottoms. They mounted the plane on floats so they could fly anglers in and out of lakes in northern Wisconsin. They covered expenses in 1929, but by 1930 the depression was forcing La Crosse anglers to stay closer to home. Like other flyers during the lean years, Leithhold and Borer barnstormed or flew for pleasure on weekends, had a flying school, flew charters when they appeared, but held jobs not-related to aviation from Monday to Friday.

In 1934, Ken Reed and Jack Fanta started the Fanta-Reed Air Service, moved to Pfafflin Airport and built a hangar. Reed was the mechanic, Fanta the office manager, and both were pilots. They struggled to make ends meet until 1941, when they received the contract to start the La Crosse CPT program. The training program established the Fanta-Reed Air Service, which remained in business at La Crosse until the partners retired in 1966.[31]

Lone Rock

Department of Commerce intermediate field, site 15 Chicago-Twin Cities Airway. Two miles N. Altitude, 716 feet. L shape, three landing strips, 2,623 feet, N./S., 2,588 feet, E./W., 2,490 feet, NW./SE. Trees to NW., buildings NE./SE. "15 C-TC" on shed. Beacon, boundary, approach, and obstruction lights. Electric code beacon, green flashing characteristic "5" (.-.), in NW. corner. No servicing facilities. Marker beacon, directive, identifying signal "U" (..-), operating frequency 278 kc, (under construction). [1933]

An old railroad kerosene lamp of the type used to light the Lone Rock Airport for night landings. (Phil Leyda)

Madison

Madison Airport, commercial, rating —-. Adjoins city on NE. Altitude, 845 feet. Rectangular, 2,525 by 1,825 feet, sod, slight slope, artificial drainage. Pole line to N.; scattered trees to W. Landing-area flood lights. Beacon, 24-inch rotating, clear, operated on request. Facilities for servicing aircraft, day and night. [1933]

Royal Airport, commercial, rating —-. Three miles SE. of capitol. Altitude, 881 feet. Irregular, 5,700 feet N./S., 3,600 feet E./W., sod, level, natural drainage; entire field available except SE. corner and extreme E. Pole line to W. and S.; trees to N. and E. Facilities for servicing aircraft, day and night. Teletypewriter. [1933]

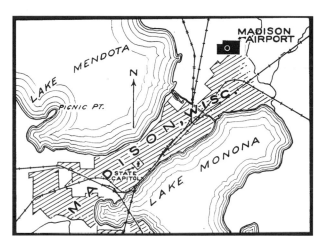

The first airport located on Madison's northeast side was on North Street east of the Oscar Meyer plant. (WAHF)

In 1926, young Louis Wuilleumier was driving on the south side of Monona when he saw a pilot land a Waco 9 biplane in the pasture that became Royal Airport. Wuilleumier stopped to talk to the pilot and ended up giving him a ride to a hotel in Madison. The next morning he picked up the pilot, drove him back to his plane and, for his trouble, got a five-minute ride in the Waco. Wuilleumier was hooked. By the summer of 1927, he and four other investors—Dr. John Bancroft, Mr. Stevenson, B.W. Hulskamp, W.A. Hansley and Joe Wuilleumier—organized Mid-west Air Transport Company. For an airport they rented a field from the Eakin family on North Street east of the Oscar Meyer plant and put up a good-sized hangar; for a plane, they purchased a Jenny. So began the North Street or Madison Airport.

The old Jenny was a good starter plane, but not much more. Wuilleumier and his partners purchased an "Air King" made in Lomax, Illinois, but soon replaced it with the Walter Beech-designed Travel Air. As the Wisconsin distributor for Travel Air, Mid-west sold Whirlwind-powered Travel Air two place biplanes and 5-place cabin monoplanes. "We sold quite a few of those," Wuilleumier recalled. Mid-west also offered flight instruction for $30 per hour, but would cut the rate to $10 if the student supplied the plane, gas and oil. Jerry Phillips was the chief pilot for Midwest, with Les Smith, Lee Smith and Travis Boggs also on hand to fly charters. The company did what Wuilleumier called "a fair business until the Depression." By 1933, Mid-west was out of business and the pilots were looking for work elsewhere. Although the Corben Aircraft Company continued to use it, aviation activity at the North Street Airport all but stopped.

Louis Wuilleumier was out of aviation until he bought a Waco

Howard Morey flying his Travel Air for air-to-air refueling in the 1930s. (WAHF)

10 in the summer of 1939 and started barnstorming in Dane and surrounding counties. Howard Morey had been named manager of the new Madison Municipal Airport located a few blocks north of the old North Street Airport so Wuilleumier moved to fill the vacancy at the Royal Airport. He, his wife Lois and Merrit Anderson organized Four Lakes aviation and became Wisconsin distributors for Taylorcraft. In 1940, Wuilleumier started a CPT program at Royal which he continued as the War Training Service during World War II. Four Lakes remained at Royal until 1951 when Wuilleumier became manager of Madison Municipal.

The course of Howard Morey's flying career intersected with Louis Wuilleumier's many times in the 1920s and '30s. A year after he established Pennco Field in 1926, Morey was approached by Madison's Royal Transit Company to begin regular air passenger service direct from Madison to Chicago. Royal saw an opportunity here since this route was bypassed by Northwest Airways, which flew from Chicago to Milwaukee and La Crosse. Royal also saw an opportunity to increase its bus business by carrying air passengers to and from its terminal and the airport. This was a true commuter service, with travelers leaving Madison's Union Bus Depot at 6:45 AM and arriving at Chicago's Sherman Hotel in time for business at 8:45 AM. Buses left the Sherman for the Chicago airport at 5:00 PM and arrived at the Madison bus depot at 7:00 PM. In between, they flew in the new Travel Air 5-seater piloted by Howard Morey.

Commuter air service was an idea ahead of its time. Royal couldn't find enough passengers to fill the plane and shut down after only a few months of operation in 1928. Morey was

philosophical. "This failure was a keen disappointment to those who had envisioned it and put money into it," he said many years later. "But to me, it was another venture that got me where I wanted to be—in the air. I looked upon aviation not as a money-making scheme, but as a way to satisfy my greatest desire."

Morey thought he found another way to satisfy his greatest desire when he linked up with the Velie Monocoupe Airplane Corporation of St. Louis. Velie was trying to set up a national network of aviation schools where students would learn to fly in and eventually purchase Monocupes. Morey volunteered to sell the assets of Royal Airways to Velie if the company would make his airport in Madison the site of their first school. The deal was closed just prior to the stock market crash of October, 1929. For three years Morey and Velie struggled along until Velie declared bankruptcy, which allowed Morey to buy back his assets and turn them into the Morey Airplane Company. Prospects were dim, but Morey still had an airport, a hangar and an airplane. Then he lost the hangar and the airplane to a fire in August, 1932.

"All my assets, uninsured, went up in smoke and a large part of my heart went with them."

He didn't give up and, with the help of a borrowed airplane, kept flying and slowly paid off his debts. In addition to barnstorming, instructing and charter work. Morey flew for Northwest Airlines. In 1934, when Madison city officials were slow to make the ten percent match for a federal grant to improve the airport property they had purchased years earlier, Morey designated "ramshackle buildings and a cabbage patch" as city improvements and garnered the federal support. Under the aegis of the WPA, con-

Aerial view of the airport that began as Pennco Field and was later known as Royal Airport. (WAHF)

struction of the new Madison Municipal Airport on the northeast edge of the city was completed in 1937. The following year, he became the new airport's first manager on the very same day that his son was born. "I couldn't call him airport, so I called him Field," Morey recalled.

He was already serving as one of five members of the first Wisconsin Aeronautics Board, which the legislature had just established to advise the state on aviation policy. He remained on the Board until it was discontinued and replaced by the Aeronautics Commission in 1944, of which he then became chairman.

Morey also continued to manage Madison Municipal Airport until 1942 when it was taken over by the Army Air Force for the duration of the war.[32]

Manitowoc

Manitowoc Airport, municipal, rating —-. Adjoins city to NW.; E. of railroad running N. and S. Altitude, 600 feet. Rectangular, 3,085 by 2,160 feet, sod, level, natural drainage. MANITOWOC embedded in field. Pole lines to W., S., and NE. corners. Facilities for servicing aircraft, day and night. [1933]

Louis Kakuk and his Waco at Manitowoc in the 1930s. (WAHF)

In 1926, Arnold Schwarz flew his Jenny from Manitowoc to the Milwaukee lakefront and took a spot on the starting line of the Wisconsin Air Derby. A prestigious group of Wisconsin flyers were on the line that day: Milwaukee's Gilles Meisenheimer, Dan Kiser and Fritz Holterhoff; John E. Wood of Wausau; Roy Larson of Larsen; Steve Wittman of Fond du Lac in his first air race. The gun was fired and the planes took off on the sixty-mile cross-country course. When the race ended in less than one hour, Schwarz clocked the fastest time, but since the race was handicapped, officials could rank him no higher than fourth behind Frank Shoblaska, Kiser and Wittman. The young man from Manitowoc, who had never flown in a race before, could be very proud of his effort and the $100 in prize money he had collected.

Steve Wittman and Manitowoc airport manager Frank Shoblaska. (WAHF)

Arnold Schwarz was a Lake Michigan fish mechant who had learned to fly at the first Milwaukee County Airport a year or two before the Air Derby. After his success in Milwaukee he went home to Manitowoc and, in August 1927, bought forty acres of land on the northwest edge of town to open the city's first airport. A good sportsman, he then hired Air Derby winner Frank Shoblaska as manager. It was the right time for an airport in Manitowoc, since the city was soon taken up with enthusiasm for the Invincible airplane. Business leaders were willing to back the venture and the city administration took over the airport and promised to supply land

for a factory next to the new airport. Despite the bright hopes and, even though it could fly, the Invincible never got off the ground commercially. The company folded and Dean and Dale Crites of Waukesha bought its assets, which consisted mainly of parts which they reassembled into a plane at Waukesha.

After the excitement over the Invincible died in Manitowoc, flyers settled into the routine of offering rides, teaching students and keeping their machines in shape. To make ends meet, Shoblaska and his friend "Fish" Salmon, hit the air show circuit together, with Shoblaska stunting in his 3 place Waco and Salmon making parachute jumps off the lower wing. They continued to perform together until the summer of 1936, when Shoblaska died while stunting at an air show in Livingston in southwestern Wisconsin.

Shoblaska was succeeded by the colorful Elmer "Buck" Leighton. The airport came came under municipal ownership in 1930 and has remained on the original site selected by Arnold Schwarz in 1927.[33]

Marshfield

Marshfield Airport, commercial, rating —-. One half mile SE., adjoining fairground; 70-foot chimney and reservoir five eighths mile W. of field good landmarks. Altitude, 400 feet. Rectangular, 2,640 by 1, 320 feet, sod, general slope from E. and W. to center, artificial drainage; four landing strips, 2,300 feet E./W., 1,300 feet N./S., and 1,750 feet NE./SW., and 1,650 feet NW./SE., all 75 feet wide; entire field available except 10 acres in SE. corner. MARSHFIELD AIRPORT on hangar. Beacon tower and high-tension line on W., stumps in SE. corner, trees to S. and SW.; fairgrounds buildings on N. Beacon and landing-area flood lights. Beacon, 24-inch rotating, clear. Facilities for servicing aircraft, day and night. [1933]

In the summer of 1920, Jake Blum, owner of the Palace garage in Marshfield, announced that he would buy a Curtiss airplane. Barnstorming pilot Don Bennett would fly it when it was not hangared at the Weber farm on the edge of the city. About the same time, M.B. Brunkalla of Athens bought a OX-5, J-1 Standard from the George Browne agency in Milwaukee at the "flyaway" price of

An American Eagle airplane outside the hangar at Marshfield, 1928. (Dan Maurer)

$2750. Brunkalla later formed a partnership with Max Berghammer, who completed nearly sixteen hours of flight instruction at Dave Behncke's Checkerboard Field near Chicago in 1921. Two years later another airplane arrived at Marshfield when auto dealers Walter Miner and Henry Peil bought a Curtiss and established a landing field on Highway 13 at the Wood-Marathon County line. In 1925, just about everyone involved in aviation in Marshfield— Brunkalla, Berghammer, Miner, Peil—incorporated Ski-Hi Airways. This combination came apart after a few years and, although pilots continued to use fields and meadows, Marshfield had no airport worthy of the name.

In 1928, Berghammer joined Herman Dickoff to organize the Marshfield Aerial Service Company and contracted to buy 79 acres from the Gessert family on the southeast edge of the city. Five years had passed since the city council had rejected a motion to buy this property for a municipal airport and pay for it through leases to Berghammer and other local pilots. Taking advantage of post-Lindberg euphoria and an announcement that Marshfield would be a refueling stop for the army planes delivering mail to President Coolidge while he vacationed in northern Wisconsin, Berghammer and Dickoff took the plunge. They erected a hangar with space for the three new American Eagle biplanes they had purchased, organized a flight school and advertised for aircraft sales, charters and exhibitions.

Flying up from Madison in a plane supplied by the Wadham's Oil Company, Governor Fred Zimmerman dedicated the new airport on June 24, 1928.

The OX-5 powered American Eagle was a solid if unspectacular barnstormer's plane with space in its front cockpit for not one, but two paying customers. Berghammer and Dickoff hoped to spend many a pleasant summer Sunday ferrying passengers in and out of pastures in central Wisconsin and lifting the mortgage on the Gessert farm. They were just about making it when Max Berghammer failed to pull his Eagle out of a tailspin, crashed and died.

As a commercial endeavor, Marshfield's airport now fell upon hard times. Landowner Guy Blodgett tried to interest the Commercial Club or the city government to operate the field and a series of managers appeared over the next few years: Lou Foote, Paul Wendlandt, O. A. Seim and Walter Miner. The Gessert farm remained the site of the Marshfield Airport until the city purchased

120 acres on the southwest side of the city in 1944.

While commercial operations struggled at Marshfield in the late 1920s and '30s, individual pilots were doing quite well. Walter Miner and Grant Johnson both took their Waco biplanes aloft as often as possible. Miner was a regular participant in the annual air races held at the Nepco/Tri-City Airport near Wisconsin Rapids while Johnson laid claim to the distinction of being the first pilot to fly non-stop from Marshfield to Chicago. He made the trip in his ski-equipped Waco 10 in December, 1928. When Governor Walter Kohler flew to nearby Pittsville to attend an Indian Pow-Wow in 1930, Johnson was called upon to test the condition of the landing strip by setting down first. If Johnson crashed, Kohler would know not to land.

Marshfield also hosted the American Legion Tour of 1930, which included nine aircraft ranging from Ole Anderson's Curtiss Robin to "Thunder" Johnson's Ford Tri-Motor. In 1932, when pilot Jimmy Mattern attempted a round-the-world flight and crashed in Alaska, aviators from all over the country rushed north to participate in the search and rescue. While on their way from New York to Alaska, four of Mattern's would-be rescuers were forced to land at Marshfield. After the weather cleared, they headed north to Duluth.[34]

Milwaukee

Maitland Airport, auxiliary. On E. central side of city, adjacent to mouth of Milwaukee River, extending 2,200 feet N. of same. Irregular, 2,200 feet N./S., by 750 feet E./W.; cinder surface, level, natural drainage, entire field available. No servicing facilities. [1933]

Air Marine Terminal, municipal, rating —. On lake front, 3,000 feet N. of harbor entrance, on E. side of business section of city, near C. & N.W. depot. Altitude, 587 feet. Rectangular, 1,000 feet N./S., 650 feet E./W.; earth, level, tile drainage; one macadam runway, 900 by 30 feet, ramp 60 by 70 feet, buoys for mooring amphibians, water area within breakwater 18,000 feet N./S., and 3,000 feet E./W., available for seaplane and amphibians. Pole line on N., and W. Facilities for servicing aircraft, day only. [1933]

`The airport directories of the federal Aeronautics Bureau for 1931 and 1933 list two airports in downtown Milwaukee. Maitland Airport was on the north bank at the mouth of the Milwaukee River. It was bordered on the west by Jackson and Erie Streets and on the east by the lake. Under construction in 1927, the airport took its name from Lester Maitland, the army pilot from Milwaukee who had made the first successful flight from California to Hawaii in July of that year.

By the end of 1927, Milwaukee city planners were redesigning the city's lakefront and sought to replace Maitland Airport. "Plans to provide Milwaukee with a lakefront airport that will rival any in the world have been drawn and are in possession of the board of harbor commissioners," reported the Sentinel in November. "The propoal is to fill in between the shore and breakwater in the vicinity of McKinley Beach and provide a seaplane haven and takeoff."

The new airport, which would be built on filled lakefront less than 1,000 feet north of Maitland and east of the old Milwaukee Road depot, was part of an ambitious lakefront development plan that included a yacht club marina, improved parks, beaches, and Lincoln Memorial Drive. The new airport, "would be ideal for air

Fueling up for an air show on the Milwaukee lakefront about 1920. (WAHF)

mail, air freight and passenger service because of its direct and easy connection with the downtown district," as its supporters stated. The site appeared to be ideal, only blocks away from downtown and the public transportation system that connected Milwaukee and its suburbs. At the same time, the lake was an all-directional runway that moved air traffic away from the heavily-populated urban center with its multi-story buildings and tall smokestacks. The lakefront airport offered the best of both worlds, bringing passengers close to downtown while keeping air traffic a safe distance away.

The Air Marine Terminal, later known as the Seadrome, was completed by the end of 1932, in time to be used briefly by Kohler Airways amphibian planes. However, and much to the disappointment of the suppporters of the downtown marine airport, Kohler

Milwaukee brewers commissioned the Knaup Brothers to repaint their Mahoney-Ryan-Brougham so it could be used to promote low-alcohol beer during Prohibition. (SHSW)

Fueling up for an air show on the Milwaukee lakefront about 1920.
(WAHF)

gradually shifted its operations to Milwaukee County Airport. In 1934, Kohler was absorbed by Pennsylvania Air Lines and the amphibians were replaced by Ford Tri-Motors and Boeing 247s which, of course, could not use a Seadrome.

The Seadrome did replace the original Maitland Airport. However, since the two facilities were all but adjacent to each other, Milwaukeeans commonly referred to both as "Maitland Airport." Although it lost commercial airline service, the Seadrome did see some air traffic. By the end of the 1930s an estimated 3,000 passengers used its charter seaplane service and small land-based planes used its north-south land runway. In his 1940 article, "Wisconsin's Future in Aviation," Wisconsin Adjutant General Ralph Immell was optimistic about air marine terminals. "Within a relatively few years every major Wisconsin metropolitan center having a waterfront may require a seaplane base even larger than the one with which Milwaukee has experimented," he said.

Although aviation expanded in the years after World War, seaplane bases were not in the mix. In the 1950s, Milwaukee's Seadrome became a site for Nike anti-aircraft missiles and in the 1980s, home of the city Summerfest event. [35]

Curtiss-Milwaukee Airport, commercial, rating —. Nine miles NW. Altitude, 750 feet. Irregular shape, 2,960 by 2,200 feet, sod, level, natural and artificial drainage. CURTISS-WRIGHT on hangar roof. Pole line to E. Obstruction and landing-area flood lights. Facilities for servicing aircraft, day and night. [1933]

One of the ironies of American aviation history is the merger of the Curtiss and Wright interests into a single company after nearly two decades of litigation and feuding that began when the Wright Brothers sued Glenn Curtiss back in 1909. The two adversaries got together as part of the general streamlining of the aviation industry that took place in the late 1920s. One of the Curtiss-Wright ventures was a chain of airports at major cities across the United States, including by the end of 1929, New York, Chicago, Cleveland, St. Louis, Houston, Los Angeles and Milwaukee.

Midwest Airways brought the first Mahoney-Ryan-Broughams to Wisconsin in 1927 and sold them widely around the state. (WAHF)

The Milwaukee Air Terminals Company was incorporated in 1929 as a Curtiss-Wright affiliate. The company purchased 150 acres about three and one half miles northwest of Milwaukee and hired Racine pilot Dan Kaiser as manager. News reports said $200,000 would be spent on construction of two twelve-plane hangars, an administration building and a passenger depot. Curtiss-Wright was making a serious bid to compete with Milwaukee County Airport for air mail and passenger service, but was set back by the Depression. Only one hangar with administrative offices was constructed and neither of the two airlines serving Milwaukee in the 1930s moved to the field.

Curtiss-Wright wasn't the leading commerical airport in the Milwaukee area, but a good case can be made for it as the leading air show airport in the state. Performing in a 1934 air show, for example, were Art Goebel, winner of the California-Hawaii Dole Race; Jimmy Haizlip and Frank Hawkes, cross-country speed record holders; Steve Wittman, who had taken firsts at the National Air races; and Roscoe Turner, the flamboyant air racer who would attempt to set a new air speed record on a 130 miles course from Curtiss-Wright to Green Bay. Also performing were Dick Granere, whose "Flying Farmer" act was nationally known, and Virginia Whittesley of Wisconsin Rapids, "the only licensed girl transport plane pilot."

Curtiss-Wright was also the airport where Herman "Fish" Salmon made his mark as parachute jumper, stunt pilot and old-fashioned daredevil of the Lincoln Beachey stripe. By the time he left Wisconsin at the end of the 1930s, Salmon would make over 400 parachute jumps at air shows around the state. His specialty, which he performed at Curtiss-Wright many times, was a 8,500-foot free fall he called the "Detroit Plummet."

Salmon was in good company at Curtiss-Wright, where the pilots seemed to take their cue from Elmer "Buck" Leighton, a one-time Kohler Airways pilot who started his career as a pilot flying for an oil company in Mexico in 1919. He joined the Mexican federal air force in 1921 and reconoitered "rebel" positions in the outback. He turned up in Milwaukee in time to deliver the first Ryan Brougham sold in the state. It was purchased by the Knaup Brothers' Midwest Airways and was displayed at Gimbel's department store in downtown Milwaukee. Leighton also flew charters for Midwest Airways and Northwest.

Always one to stir the pot when times were dull, Leighton convinced a baker's dozen of Curtiss-Wright pilots, including airport manager Ed Mulick and "Fish" Salmon, that they should volunteer to fly for the African nation of Ethiopia after it had been invaded by Italian forces in 1935. He put in a bid for $50 a day for observation work and $500 for combat pay, which he compared favorably with pilot's pay in Milwaukee.

"All of these fellows who have been starving on something like $15 a week consider even an African war a Godsend," he told reporters.

News reports said the Ethiopians were interested, but the scheme never got off the ground. Instead Leighton moved to Manitowoc and became airport manager there.

Curtiss-Wright retained ownership of the airport until 1945 then sold to Fliteways Inc. Two years later Milwaukee County acquired the field and Bill Lotzer's Gran-Aire Inc. became fixed base operator. True to its roots as the grand air show airport, Curtiss-Wright—renamed Timmermann Field—was the site of the first meeting of the Experimental Aircraft Association Fly-In in 1953. [36]

Milwaukee County Airport, municipal, rating —-. Six miles S. Altitude, 679 feet. Irregular, sod, level, artificial drainage; five runways, 2,500 by 100 feet N./S., E./W., NW./SE., 3,200 by 100 feet NE./SW., and 2,800 by 100 feet N./S., on W. side; entire field available. MILWAUKEE on hangar. Pole line on N., woods to E. Beacon, boundary, and landing-area flood lights. Beacon, 24-inch rotating, with green auxiliary code beacon flashing characteristic "MC" (— -.-.). Facilities for servicing aircraft, day and night. Department of Commerce radio range beacon, identifying signal "V" (...-), operating frequency 242 kc. (under construction). Teletypewriter. [1933]

Throughout the 1930s, the Milwaukee County Airport was the largest, most modern airport in the state. It was, as historian George Hardie described it, "a sort of community showcase for aviation," with a landscaped mini-park next to the administration building and dozens of park benches along the fence facing the runways so visitors by the hundred could enjoy special aviation events or merely observe the everyday goings-on.

Milwaukee County was the only airport in the state served by two regular air carriers. Passengers could board a Northwest Airlines Ford Tri-Motor or, in later years, a Lockheed 10A and disembark at the Pacific coast port of Seattle. Passengers traveling east could board a Pennsylvania Airlines Boeing 247 and reach Washington D. C. In 1939, Northwest Airlines begin service at Milwaukee with Douglas DC-3's that could carry 21 passengers and cruise at 170 MPH.

When the big names in flying came to Wisconsin, going back to the Pan-American Flyers, Lester Maitland and Charles Lindbergh in 1927, they came to Milwaukee. In the 1930s, Wiley Post, Harold Gatty and the *Winnie Mae*, Steve Wittman and *Chief Oshkosh*, Billy Mitchell home to visit family, all stopped at Milwaukee County.

With the aid of federal grants in the mid and late 1930s the airport was altered and expanded. Tom Hamilton's original hangar was razed in the mid-1930s. A two story brick administration building replaced the converted farm house in use since 1927 as part of a federal public works project that began in 1938 and was completed in 1940. By the time the United States entered World War II, Milwaukee County Airport had grown to 378 acres and was the base for the state's first Air National Guard unit. The first airport

manager was Leonard Ebert, followed by Milwaukee pilot Chris Setvate for 1928-29, and Major Stanley Piasecki, who ran the airport until his retirement in 1948.

While virtually everyone connected with Wisconsin aviation in the 1930s passed through Milwaukee County Airport, the three Knaup Brothers were present on a regular basis. Ed, Ray and Jim Knaup started Midwest Airways in 1927, as a charter service, flight school and dealer/distributor of Mahoney/Ryan airplanes, one of which they sold to Governor Kohler. They also held the dealership for Eastman Flying Boats, the Parks PT Trainer, Lockheed and Blackburn Engineering products.

Jim and Ed Knaup, along with Elmer Leighton were deputized by the county sheriff in 1928 to act as an "air patrol" to police the skies over Milwaukee and "search for bandits traveling the highways in high powered automobiles." Among those "bandits" were the bootleggers in the prohibition days, although the Knaup's also did promotional work for low-alcohol beer and christened one of their Ryans, "The Spirit of 3.2%." When Prohibition ended in March of 1933, and even though they were flying out of the beer city, the Knaups dispatched an aerial delivery of twenty-one cases of champagne to a party of revelers in La Crosse. In 1940, Midwest Airways became the first and one of the largest contractors in the state for the Civilian Pilot Training Program.

Practically on the eve of American entry in World War II, when many of his ideas about air power had been demonstrated as deadly accurate by the German and Japanese air forces, General Billy Mitchell was honored by the county board when they named his home town airport Billy Mitchell Field.[37]

Merrill

Merrill Airport, municipal, one and one-half miles N. of center of city. Lat. 45.15; long. 89.43. Alt. 1,285 feet. Rectangular, clay soil, level, natural drainage; 2 oiled runways, 2,300 feet NW/SE, 2,200 feet NE./SW., both 60 feet wide. Timver to NW. No servicing. [1938]

The city of Merrill opened its airport in 1936, but serious activity did not begin until 1939, when Ed Baesemann inaugurated the Merrill Flying Service. He kicked off operations with an air show that featured, "Stunts, Formation Flying, Spins, Loops, Inverted Flying, Wing Overs, Vertical Banks, Snap Rolls, Slow Rolls." Fifteen airplanes were advertised, with Wausau's Archie Towle supplying five of them. Other flyers on the bill were Lloyd Michelson, Roger Gilbertson, Ed McCarthy, Herb Spletztozer, Wausau; Ora McMurray, Eagle River; Robert Burt, Antigo; Wilfred Dotter, Tomahawk; Steve Shelbrock, Frances Barber, Rhinelander; Felix and Lucille Gauthier, Stevens Point; Max McCotter, Madison; Elmer Koch, Merrill.

Mosinee

Mosinee Airport, commercial, rating —-. One and one half miles SE. Altitude, 1,157 feet. Rectangular, 1,650 by 1,320 feet, sod, level, natural drainage. MOSINEE on hangar roof. Trees to NE. and E. Facilities for servicing aircraft, day only. [1931]

Howard Dessert, Warren Winn and J. J. Altenberg incorporated the Mosinee Airport Company with $5,000

Merrill's Ed Baesemann and an Aeronca C-3 at Wausau. (Robert Wylie)

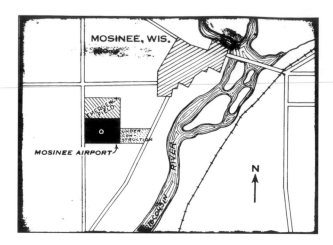

The Mosinee Airport was located southwest of the city. (WAHF)

in February, 1929. They leased 35 acres from Carl Rheinschmidt and Altenberg built a hangar. The airport was little used and not listed on the 1938 directory.

Oconomowoc

Oconomowoc—-Department of Commerce intermediate field, site 2, Milwaukee-La Crosse Airway. Three and one quarter miles SE. Altitude, 880 feet. T shape, sod, level, natural drainage; two landing strips, both 2,000 by 450 feet. Power shed marked "2 M-LC". Pole line to W. Beacon, boundary, approach, and obstruction lights. Beacon, 24-inch rotating, with green course lights flashing characteristic "2" (..-). No servicing facilities. [1933]

The Oconomowoc landing field was established by the federal Aeronautics Bureau as a stopping point on the Milwaukee-LaCrosse-Twin Cities Airway in 1927.

Oshkosh

Oshkosh Airport, commercial, rating —-. Two and one half miles SW. of post office. Altitude, 776 feet. Rectangular shaped, 2,640 feet N./S. by 1,800 feet E./W., sod surface, level, natural drainage; entire field available. OSHKOSH on hangar. Trees to W. and S.; pole line to NW.; approach between trees. Facilities for servicing aircraft, day only. [1931]

At the behest of Congressman Florian Lampert, Charles Lindbergh flew over Oshkosh in August 1927 and reinvigorated interest in aviation. The landing field on Fourth Street that Richard Lutz and Florian Manor had been using since 1920 had been all but abandoned by the time the Lone Eagle passed overhead. Now Richard Lutz was able to attract investors Arthur W. Leupold, Albert March and Francis Lamb to join him in putting up $5,000 to incorporate Oshkosh Airport and purchase 100 acres along Twentieth Street, on the southwest edge of the city.

Lutz had been trying to persuade the Oshkosh City Council to build an airport ever since he arrived in town, but now decided to spin the prop himself. Oshkosh Airport Inc. graded two runways, built a hangar, hired a mechanic, lighted and marked the field according to federal specifications. In the fall of 1928, with Northwest Airways about to begin regular air mail service at Oshkosh, Lutz again asked the council for help. He wanted $3,000 to equip and pay the salary of "a mechanic constantly on the ground to assist incoming and outgoing mail planes." The council passed on the request and left Lutz and Northwest to shift for themselves after air mail service began in December 1928. Northwest Wacos and

Hamiltons made regular stops at Oshkosh until the Fox Valley Air Mail line was cancelled in 1933.

By then, Steve Wittman, who had become airport manager in 1931, was making Oshkosh as famous for racing aircraft as it was for bibbed overalls. Wittman summarized how he spent the 1930s by saying, "I came to Oshkosh in 1931 to manage the airport. From 1931 to 1940, I ran a flying school, built racing ships, did a great deal of racing, and also built a conventional two-place experimental airplane." It was a typically brief and to-the-point Wittman statement to cover the years in which he built and rebuilt his racing planes *Chief Oshkosh, Bonzo I* and *Bonzo II*. He also designed and built his two-place sport plane, the *Buttercup*, designed and patented his flat spring landing gear; conducted a flight school and, with his wife Dorothy, operated an airport in the midst of the Great Depression.

One indicator of the conditions Wittman and other airport operators faced in the 1930s is reflected in the story of the Oshkosh beacon. As an air mail stop in the early 1930s, Oshkosh Airport kept a 24-inch rotating beacon lighted through the night. By 1936, the beacon was switched on only "on request." Air traffic was light and the budget was tight.

Although airports were recognized as potential sources of economic development, their immediate impact was often hard to detect. It became easier when Oshkosh banks faced a crisis early in 1932. Economic conditions were forcing many banks out of business and rumors had spread through Oshkosh that one of the city's two major banks was about to lock its doors and deny depositors access to their accounts. A run on the bank began with account holders lining up outside waiting to withdraw their money. The bank was sound, but did not have the cash on hand to meet the immediate demand. The money needed was in Milwaukee but could not be transferred in time by train or auto.

One bank manager remembered the airport and Clyde Lee, who had recently been in his office asking for money for his trans-Atlantic flight. Lee's reputation in his home town was that of a devil-may-care flyer who would never amount to much more than a hangar bum, so the bank did not contribute. Now the tables were turned and the bank needed the high speed delivery service that Lee and his Stinson cabin plane could provide. Promising to pay twenty dollars for his gas, the bank manager dispatched Lee to Milwaukee County Airport, where he was met on the runway by an armored car loaded with bags of cash. The money was loaded into the Stinson, Lee signed a receipt and took off for Oshkosh. Security precautions were more relaxed there than in Milwaukee and the bank wanted to keep the delivery as quiet as possible, so Lee arranged to have a friend meet him at the airport and drive him and approximately $500,000 in cash to the bank downtown. The money was delivered in time and the bank was able to meet depositors' demands. It was, however, unable to donate or loan the $1,000 Clyde Lee requested to purchase a new engine for his trans-Atlantic flight. The risk was too great.

Saving the bank was only one of the aerial adventures Clyde Lee and other Oshkosh aviators flew into in the 1920s and '30s. In the early 1920s, the Ku Klux Klan experienced a revival in the southern states and expanded north, even to the "progressive" state of Wisconsin. Thousands attended the state convention in Racine in 1923 and an even bigger crowd was expected for the meeting scheduled for Oshkosh in the summer of 1924. Not content with their customary cross-burning and race-baiting, Klan leaders looked for a pilot willing to fly over the convention city with the underside of his plane bearing electric lights in the shape of a cross. The only pilot in the area willing to make the flight was Elywn West, whose judgment must have been impaired by the fact that his wallet was empty. He agreed to make two flights over Oshkosh with the lighted cross rigged on his plane. After completing his second flight, the meaning of his actions dawned on West, as well as threats that he would be shot out of the sky, so he refused to fly again. Attendance at the Oshkosh convention was smaller than expected and the whole event turned out to be less than the Kluxers hoped, but the image of a small airplane circling over a Wisconsin city and bearing the Klan symbol of the lighted cross is surprising and memorable.

Most of the exploits of Oshkosh aviators were less significant. One male pilot, on the pretext of practicing "dead-stick" landings with an attractive female student, set down on the ice of Lake Winnebago. While the plane was parked, neither pilot nor student noticed that the chunk of ice beneath them had broken off from shore and was carrying them out to open water. Clyde Lee happened to be in the air that day, spotted the stranded flyers and alerted rescuers who picked up the embarrassed couple.

On another occasion pilot Dave Reed convinced a friend named Fritz to go "ice-skiing" behind Reed's airplane on the broad stretch of the Fox River upstream of Oshkosh. Although he had promised merely to taxi over the ice with the skier in tow, after he began, Reed accelerated to take off speed and pulled the skier into the air. With Fritz hanging on for dear life, plane and skier hopped into the air and skimmed the treetops over a small island in the river before Reed landed. Once he touched a solid surface again, Fritz dropped

the tow rope but his momentum carried him up the Fox for a few more miles. Risky hijinks such as these were in sharp contrast to the serious and also dangerous work that Steve Wittman was undertaking at the same airport. Aviation, like all human activities, has at least two faces, including that of the fool and that of the wise man.

As the 1930s came to a close, local government took more interest in the airport. Oshkosh Mayor Ed Oakes rivaled Superior's Bryn Ostby as one of Wisconsin's most aviation-minded public officials, but he was unable to convince his own city council to purchase the airport. When county officials debated the question in 1940, Oakes appeared before the county committee and made an eloquent argument in favor of establishing a county airport. It was in July, 1940 and the world had already seen much of China fall to Japanese army and air forces while Nazi army and air forces had conquered Poland, Belgium and France. Oakes, a Mayor of a small city in Wisconsin testifying before a minor committee of county supervisors, brought the world as changed by aviation to Oshkosh.

"Now...our thoughts are compelled to turn to plans for preparing ourselves against whatever danger the future may hold," he said.

"In order to prepare ourselves for air defense, we must have air fields. We must have planes and we must train pilots....Winnebago County has the resources. Has its supervisors the will?"

They did have the will. A month later the Winnebago County board voted to spend $34,000 to acquire the 100 acres of land and improvements of the Oshkosh Airport, Inc. They also voted to purchase an adjacent parcel of 57 acres for another $11,000 and established the Winnebago County Airport. Oakes was not content. After the county bought the land-based airport, he immediately began talking about how Oshkosh needed a seaplane airport in Lake Winnebago.[38]

Portage

Department of Commerce intermediate field, site 17, Chicago-Twin Cities Airway. One mile NE. Altitude, 800 feet. Rectangular, 60 acres, sod, rolling, natural drainage; two landing sytrips, 2.200 feet NE/SW, 1,895 feet NW/SE., both 400 feet wide. Directional arrow marked "17 C-TC." Pole line to S. Beacon, boundary, approach and obstruction lights. Beacon, 24-inch rotating, with green course lights flashing characteristic "7" No Servicing facilities. [1931]

The first airport in the Portage area was an Aeronautics Bureau landing field that was phased out by 1933. It was replaced by the landing strip opened north of the city by Bob and Chester Mael in 1930. Still teenagers, the Maels hoped to get into the budding aviation industry by building their own plane, dubbed the Mael Twin.

The Mael Airport must not have been a very active place since it appears on none of the Aeronautics Bureau directories for the 1930s. It did serve as the nucleus of the Portage Municipal Airport with the Maels and the city established in the years after World War II.[39]

Steve Wittman and Chief Oshkosh. (WAHF)

Ed Hedeen, at Racine's Air City in the 1930s. (Elmo Halverson)

Racine

Air City Flying Field, private, rating —-. Six miles due W., just SE. of Sturtevant. Altitude, 633 feet. Square, 2,640 by 2,640 feet, sod, level, natural drainage; two graded runways, N./S. and E./W., both 2,300 by 300 feet; entire field also available. RACINE on hangar roof. Pole line and buildings to N. Facilities for servicing aircraft, day only. [1931]

Racine Seaplane Base, commercial, rating —-. On lake front at foot of 6th Street. Take-off inside of sea wall harbor, 3,960 feet N./S. and 1, 320 feet E./W. Large ramp and hangar space. Facilities for servicing, day only. [1933]

Racine/Sturtevant

Racine Airport, commercial, rating —-. Eight and one half miles W. of Racine on Highway 120; one and one half miles W. of Sturtevant, Wisconsin; one half mile E. of U.S. Highway 41. Altitude, 650 feet. Rectangular, 2,500 by 2,112 feet, sod, level, artificial drainage; four landing strips, NE./SW., and SE./NW., 2,640 feet; E./W., 2,112 feet; N./S., 2,500 feet; entire field available. Name on hangar. Boundary, obstruction, and flood lights. Facilities for servicing aircraft, day and night. [1933]

Doctor George L. Ross began what business school students once called a vertically integrated company on the edge of Sturtevant in 1926. With Milwaukee aviator Dan Kaiser as manager, he set up a factory to build clones of the Curtiss Canuck, complete with OX-5 engines. Completed aircraft could be tested and demonstrated to potential buyers on the new landing strip Ross built next door to the factory. Buyers who didn't know how to fly could sign up for lessons at Dr. Ross's flight school. Finally, if a buyer wanted to live close to his airplane, Dr. Ross had a lot and house for sale in Wisconsin's first airport subdivision. It was Air City, home of Racine's first airport.

Dr. Ross was ahead of his time with his airport residential development, many of which would reappear in the years after World War II. He was behind the times with his airplane factory, where he was duplicating an already obsolete ten-year old airplane that would soon be grounded by the new Wacos, Eaglerocks, Travel Airs and other superior machines of the late 1920s. After about two years, Kaiser left to manage the new Curtiss-Wright field north of Milwaukee and the Air City airplane factory closed. The airport

The Sikorsky Amphibian Johnson's Wax used to fly up the Amazon River Valley in search of Carnauba palm trees in 1935. (S.C. Johnson Wax)

remained open and, with Ed Hedeen, as manager and flight instructor, soon developed into one of the largest flight schools in the state.

An Illinois native, Hedeen was a veteran of the Naval Air Service and a crackerjack pilot. He marked the tenth anniversary of the end of World War I by setting a world's record for barrel rolls. Flying an OX-5 Waco 10, he rolled the barrel a total of 283 times to break the record previously set by "Speed" Holman in Minnesota. The feat was testimony to the durability of the Waco and of Hedeen himself, as well as being a good publicity stunt.

In addition to stunting, instructing and managing Air City, Hedeen went to work for the S.C. Johnson Company. His first mission was to fly a case of Johnson's wax to St. Louis, where the aerial delivery produced a quick sell-out. He made many other promotional trips in Johnson's first plane, a Waco Taperwing, then moved on to the Waco Cabin model the company acquired in 1931. His traveling companion in the new "Johnson Waxwing" was model Jolietta McCready, the "Johnson's Wax Doll," who distributed samples of wax and electric floor polishers to lucky contest winners.

In 1935, Johnson purchased a Sikorsky S38 amphibian which Hedeen flew off the lake at Johnson's seaplane base inside Racine harbor. He was not along when Herbert F. Johnson and pilots E.H. Schlanser and J. A. Hoy took the Sikorsky up Brazil's Amazon River in search of carnauba palm forests. Carnauba was a basic ingredient in Johnson's waxes and the explorers conducted an aerial search for native stands and for sites where carnauba plantations could be located. The 22,000 mile flight resulted in the establishment of a Johnson plant in Brazil and worldwide distribution of Johnson's carnauba waxes.

Back home, H. F. Johnson was flying the Sikorsky and a Waco Cabin model on floats off the lake. He continued until a rough landing on the big lake persuaded him to let professional pilots man the company planes while he flew purely for pleasure. The Johnson family and corporate interest was a mainstay of aviation in the Racine area and key to the establishment of the John H. Batten Airport there.

The Batten Airport has its earliest roots on the far side of Sturtevant, where Carlyle Godske started the Racine Flying Service at his own airport in 1932. A Racine native and World War Air

Waco cabin plane and a load of floor polishers used to promote Johnson's Wax in the early 1930s. (S.C. Johnson Wax)

ELMO HALVERSON-FLT. INSTR.
N3N

Elmo Halverson, Racine. (Elmo Halverson)

Service veteran, Godske was known as "Racine's first pilot." It was at this airport that Johnson Wax kept its planes and young John Batten learned to fly. Batten, who later became president of the family's Twin-Disc Clutch Company flew a Waco Cabin plane out of Godske's airport in the late 1930s.

Godske was assisted by air show performer and parachutist Fig Landreman and mechanic Trygve Emilson, a Norwegian Air Force veteran who served on the crew of the first Norwegian aerial expedition over the North Pole. As the economy recovered in the late 1930s and aviation's prospects looked bright, Godske was able to act on his conviction that his airport was too far away from Racine and too small to meet the needs of the future. In 1941, with backing from Batten and Johnson, he leased acreage on the northwest edge of Racine from the A. J. Horlick Company and opened the Horlick-Racine Airport. When the United States entered World War II he opened a CPT training facility that established the airport in its new location. After the first blush of postwar prosperity faded and with neither the city nor the county of Racine interested in a publicly-owned airport, eleven Racine businesses invested in the Racine Commercial Airport Corporation. Godske then retired as manager, but continued to fly. In 1950, John Sullivan began his thirty-three year tenure as airport manager.

Of the other airports at Racine, Johnson Wax stopped using its seaplane base in the late 1930s. Air City continued under the ownership of Ludwig Wiese and Joseph Savage, who purchased it in 1943. Over the next twenty years, as Sturtevant and the Racine suburbs expanded, the property became more valuable for housing than for an airport. By the end of the 1960s, the last vestige of Doctor Ross's Air City was gone.[40]

Reedsburg

Reedsburg Airport, municipal, rating —. One mile E. on State Highway 33. Altitude, 876 feet. Rectangular, 2,500 by 1,200 feet; sod, rolling, natural drainage. REEDSBURG on hangar roof. Trees to S. and NE., pole line to N. Small hangar and aviation fuel, day only. [1931]

Cecil Hess was born in Richland County in 1901 and he saw his first airplane at the county fair there in 1912. Ten years later he attended the Sweeney Auto and Aviation School in Kansas City and graduated ready, willing and able to operate and repair both autos and aircraft.

He moved to Reedsburg, opened an auto repair shop and, in 1928, ordered an OX-5 Waco 10 from John Wood in Wausau. The plane, which Hess lovingly named *Miss Fortune*, cost $2,350, plus $1,000 for the motor and $75 for the prop. Hess's action prompted the Reedsburg city council to rent, then purchase sixty-nine acres northeast of the city. With this action Reedsburg, with a population of about 3,000, became one of the first small communities in the state to own an airport.

With Hess's Waco as the only plane present and his building the only hangar, the Reedsburg Airport was not crowded in the 1930s. The pilot enjoyed himself flying into picnics, offering rides and stunting. "The whip stall was the biggest thrill I got out of flying. You almost make the plane stand on its tail and drop down. Then you turn on the power and up she goes," he recalled in 1977.

"I never flew with a parachute, but I did a lot of stunting anyway. I didn't have enough power in the engine to do an outside loop., but everything else—that I could do."

Hess kept doing it for another fifty years and last flew his Waco with its original motor in 1978. Since Hess kept *Miss Fortune* and its motor in such fine shape over the years, many collectors of antique planes tried to purchase it. He resisted until after his fiftieth anniversary flight in 1978. It is currently the property of Dick Wagner at Burlington, Wisconsin.

The Reedsburg Airport has remained in its original location since 1928.[41]

Rhinelander

Legion Field, municipal, rating —. One mile SE. Altitude, 1,554 feet. Irregular shape, sod, slightly rolling, natural drainage; four runways, 1,800 feet E./W. and NW./SE., 1,435 feet NE./SW., and 1,150 feet N./S., all 200 feet wide; entire field available. Pole lines to N. and S., trees to W. Facilities for servicing aircraft, day only. [1931]

Aviation began in the Rhinelander area when local boy Ed Bruso acted on his boyhood passion and signed up for flying lessons with the Larson Brothers in the mid-1920s. He moved on to Appleton's Whiting Field where he worked as an instructor for a few years before returning home to Rhinelander.

His first landing strip was on the Louis Feiler farm south of the city on property which later became part of the Nicolet College campus. In 1927, the local American Legion Post and the city of Rhinelander started to maintain a landing field at the county fairgrounds. It served as the local airport until the 1940s.

Bruso soon found himself part of a growing aviation fraternity at Rhinelander. In 1928, he soloed Steve Shelbreck, who would manage the Rhinelander airport for more than three decades. Also on hand were Frank and Al Tank, who designed and built their own aircraft engine in their Rhinelander machine shop. The Tanks flight-tested their 90 horsepower motor in a biplane built by Chris

Priebe, also in Rhinelander. In July 1929, Priebe took off in his Tank-powered aircraft, which resembled a reduced-size Jenny, carrying a letter from the Rhinelander News to an engraving firm in Milwaukee. It was the first air mail shipment out of Rhinelander. Priebe carried the mail to Oshkosh where he met the Northwest Airways scheduled air mail plane, which carried the message on to Milwaukee.

Also in the summer of 1929, Chicago's Universal Airlines began regular weekend service to Rhinelander. Charles Rouse piloted Universal's six-passenger Fairchild north with a load of anglers on Fridays and brought them home to the big city on Sundays. On the same day that Universal began flying fishermen, the Chicago Daily News began to deliver reading material for them by air freighting daily editions of its newspaper into Rhinelander. The papers were then circulated throughout the resort area by auto.

Further development of aviation at Rhinelander was hobbled by the Depression. Universal was unable to continue passenger service beyond the summer of 1929 nor did it come back in 1930. The Tanks left the city to open an aircraft engine factory in Milwaukee. Ed Bruso's career came to an abrupt end when he and passenger Harry Baldwin died in a crash near Green Lake in June, 1930.

Steve Shelbreck stayed in Rhinelander and went on to fly, as he said, "everything from Piper Cubs right on up to DC-3's." His Rhinelander Airways was the premier flight operation at the airport and when the airport moved from the county fairgrounds in 1943, Shelbreck moved with it. He served as airport manager until 1960.[42]

Rice Lake

Rice Lake Airport, municipal, rating —. One mile S. of center of city. Altitude, 1,148 feet. Rectangular, 1,320 feet N./S., 1,275 feet E./W.; sod, level, natural drainage; entire field available. Building in NE. corner, highway and high-tension line, 1,000 feet E.; trees and river on W. Facilities for servicing aircraft, day only. [1933]

The city of Rice Lake entered the airport business, by renting 20 acres of the Ray Johnson family farm on the south edge of town. Visiting pilots, including future Northwest Airlines aviator Walter Bullock, had been using farm fields near the city since the end of World War I. The first airport manager was Jack Spaulding. He reported that 1,500 passengers had flown into or out of the Rice Lake field in its first two years of operation.

The first person to own an airplane at Rice Lake was Howard Bibbey, who purchased a Waco 10 in 1929. He hired pilot Vern Williams as flight instructor and a few local people learned to fly.

The original Rice Lake airport remained in use until a new site was chosen in 1944.

Stevens Point

Stevens Point Airport, commercial, rating —. One and six tenths miles E. of post office. Altitude, 1,000 feet. Rectangular, 1,866 by 1,507 feet; four runways, NW./SE. and NE./SW. 2,400 feet, N./S. 1,866 feet, E./W. 1,507 feet, all 100 feet wide; entire field available. Pole line to S. and small pond to NW. and SE. Hangar and aviation fuel available, day and night. [1933]

The first exhibition pilots to fly at Stevens Point in the years prior to World War I used the county fair grounds on east Main Street for a landing strip. The fairgrounds infield remained adequate for the light traffic of the early and mid-1920s, but as the decade drew to a close, it was clear that the city needed an airport unencumbered by grandstands, stock pens, and a race track.

Central Wisconsin aviators Gilbert Green, Archie Towle, Felix Gauthier, Ed Baesemann and Archie Becher, about 1937. (Robert Wylie)

Gauthiers had their transport licenses and were very active in the state department of the National Aeronautics Association. The biggest aviation event to occur at either Stevens Point or McDill was the NAA tour of 1939. A who's-who of Wisconsin aviation landed at McDill, including Archie Towle, Howard Morey, Carlyle Godske and Steve Wittman. The McDill airport continued to operate until World War II, when the Gauthiers shifted their operations to the new Stevens Point field.[43]

Sturgeon Bay

Cherryland Airport, commerical. Three and one-half miles NE. of Sturgeon Bay, at fork of Highways 42 and 57. Lat.44.55; long.87.23. Alt. 590 feet. Rectangular, 2,640 by 1,320 feet, sotd, level, natural drainage; entire field available. Trees to S. and NW. Hangar, aviation fuel from town. [1938]

In 1928, the Stevens Point Airways Corporation was organized by W. S. Delzell, E. B. Bach, G. A. Kenkel, F. A. Love, W.R. Gilbo, A. J. Schierl, Guy Rogers and J. H. Carriker. The partners purchased 67 acres of land off of Green Street in the far northeast corner of the city limits, cleared and graded four runways and built a hangar. Since Stevens Point was not on a federal airway, the field had neither boundary nor beacon lights. Vic Cartwright became the first local pilot to own a plane when he purchased a Pheasant in 1929.

The new airport was greeted by the aviation brotherhood in June 1928, when three airplanes taking part in the Second Wisconsin Commercial Airplane Tour landed with a cargo of Pabst Malt Syrup and Pabst-Ett, low alcohol beverages the Milwaukee brewer was promoting during Prohitibion. Two years later the Legion Air Tour brought Howard Morey, Noel Wien and Walter Miner to Stevens Point, where they put on a brief air show and were honored for their efforts at a "Skyriders Ball" at the Dreamland Ballroom in nearby Amherst Junction.

Stevens Point received a federal grant to build a hangar and make other improvements in 1935, in response to which the city purchased the airport real estate. However, Stevens Point made slow progress on the aviation front until 1941. Then, stimulated by the state government which wanted a Class 3 airport at Stevens Point, and the federal government, which wanted to take advantage of the college there for pilot training courses, the city purshased a new plot of ground about one mile east of its former airport. The Stevens Point Airport has remained there ever since.

While aviation at Stevens Point was in the doldrums in the late 1930s, it was more active at McDill. Established by Felix and Lucille Gauthier in 1938, the McDill Airport covered 78 acres southeast of Stevens Point. Both the

The first airport to serve the Sturgeon Bay area of Door County was the work of Karl Reynolds, cherry grower and owner of the largest cherry cannery in Wisconsin. He built a landing field, chiefly for his own use on his own land in 1928 and christened his single-plane operation Cherryland Airways. It was the beginning of a life-long commitment to aviation for Karl Reynolds, one that would take him from his grass field in Door County to the Aviation Commission in Madison.

Barnstormers and exhibition pilots used the Reynolds Airport and farm fields in Door County throughout the 1930s but, except for the Washington Island field, no other airports were built until 1939. In the late 1930s, Reynolds, Doctor Dan Dorchester, and other aviators and business people petitioned the Door County board to take advantage of federal funding and build an airport.

Although his office was nominally in Sturgeon Bay, Dorchester

Crop duster Les Smith and the plane he used to drop calcium arsenate on hemlock trees at Peninsula State Park in 1925. (SHSW)

A Waco at the first Superior Airport, about 1927. (WAHF)

order to inspect the booming shipbuilding industry, expressed their dismay at the inadequacy of the field, did the board act. In 1944, recognizing as its resolution read, that "the predicted Air Age has arrived in American and Wisconsin, and is bringing with it great opportunities for transportation," the board voted to spend $7,500 of county taxpayers money to purchase the 140-acres of land one mile west of County Trunk C "known as the Cherryland Airport." The Door County Airport was founded and has remained on this site ever since.[44]

Superior

Superior Airport, auxiliary. One mile W. on Lake. Altitude, 631 feet. Irregular, sod, level, natural drainage; three graded runways, 1,600 feet NW./SE., 1,600 feet NE./SW., and 1,600 feet E./W.; remainder of field should be used with caution. Pole lines to E. and N., ravines and low ground to W. Facilities for servicing aircraft, day only. [1933]

was a genuine "flying physician" who extended his practice to all of the county by landing his Aeronca C-3 on any patch of ground—or winter's ice—where it would fit. A dependable, well-maintained airport located near the county's largest community would make it easier for Dorchester to tend his patients. Reynolds and other business people wanted a good airport to promote business and tourism.

The county looked at several sites, including the Reynolds airport and a 120-acre plot inside Peninsula State Park. Putting the airport in the state park was an interesting idea, but one that the Wisconsin Conservation Department was sure to frown on, and did. In 1939, the board defeated a resolution to purchase a second "Cherryland Airport" established about one mile west of Sturgeon Bay on County Trunk C by the local chapter of the National Aeronautics Association that included Dorchester, Reynolds, George Draeb, Frank Ullsperger, Chester Teske, Earlin Smith, Art Cermak, Ed Ropson, Bob Kraus and T. C. West.

It was off this airport that glider pilot Ted Bellak made a record-setting 54-mile sailplane flight across lake Michigan. A New Jersey resident, Bellak was towed aloft to 18,000 feet by pilot Cass Smagha in his Waco. Charles Wood, Eau Claire, was the chief of Bellak's ground crew on the successful flight that commenced over Sturgeon Bay and concluded ninety miles away at Frankfort, Michigan. The 54-mile stretch over the lake set a record for over-the-water flight.

Lobbying continued into 1940, with local airport boosters reminding the county supervisors of the need for an airport and the availabililty of federal money to improve it. In 1940, they sponsored an air show at Cherryland that featured Elywn West's Stinson Tri-Motor, an old but still impressive flying machine. Bad weather forced a week's postponement of the event, but it also delayed the full-blossoming of the cherry trees. The 1,300 residents and vistors that West carried over the blossoming cherry orchards—at twelve per flight—saw the beautiful trees in their full floral glory.

The Stinson and the airshow turnout was not impressive enough to move the Door county board, nor was the American entry into World War II. In '42 the board agreed to supply land for an airport if the army, navy or other branch of the federal government would build, maintain and manage an airport. Finally, after a number of military procurement officials, who landed at Cherryland in

In the early 1920s, several pilots flew airplanes in the Duluth/Superior area, among them propeller builder and pilot Ole Fahlen, but it was not until 1926, when air mail contracts were awarded, that Superior looked seriously for an airport. It was logical to assume that CAM 9 would eventually be extended to the largest metropolitan area north of the Twin Cities. The question was where would the main airport for the Head of the Lakes be located, in Minnesota or Wisconsin?

Ole Fahlen, A. J. Hase, Ken Pettit, Leon Dahlem and other flyers had been using vacant land near the Arrowhead Bridge between Belknap Street and the Billings Park Golf Course for a landing strip. The site was close to downtown Duluth and Superior and on the St. Louis River for easy seaplane access. Hase built a hangar, opened a flight school and, as Arrowhead Airways, offered passenger service to the Twin Cities. On July 4, 1929, after deciding not to move to other sites south and east of town, the city officially dedicated the Billings Park field as the Superior Municipal Airport. The highlight of the ceremony occurred when B.A. Wright, flying a Ryan Brougham, dropped a bouquet of flowers on the field as he circled overhead.

At the same time, Duluth was developing an airport on the grounds of the St. Louis County poor farm and, with state aid, invested over $100,000 on grading, hangar and runway construction. In 1930, the field was dedicated as the Williamson-Johnson Airport

As expected, Northwest Airways extended air mail and passenger service to the area in 1930. Neither the Superior nor the Duluth Airport was used at first, since the plane Northwest designated for the route was a Sikorsky S 38 Flying Boat. Although Northwest continued to fly the Sikorsky until 1935, it made the fateful decision to use Duluth's instead of Superior's airport for its land-based planes. Superior had lost the contest for air mail port, but it was still served by four air carriers: Head of the Lakes, Great Lakes Airways, Mid-Plane Transit and Max Conrad's Flying Service.

1937, a turnaround was evident. Superior had elected aviation enthusiast Bryn Ostby as mayor. Under his leadership, the municipal airport moved from Billings Park to a larger, safer site on

Hammond Avenue. With federal aid, a large brick hangar was built with living quarters for the airport manager. Runways and taxiways were graded and surfaced with crushed rock and sand and modern lighting installed. On the day the new airport was dedicated, the official motto of the city of Superior was changed from "Where Sail Meets Rail" to "Where Air and Sail Meet Rail."

When the Twentieth Anniversary of Air Mail was celebrated in 1938 Superior pilot Jules Bernt started the run to pick up mail in other northern Wisconsin cities with Mayor Ostby as passenger.

A Laird Commercial at Superior, about 1927. (WAHF)

Enlisting the aid of U.S. Congressman Bernard Gehrmann and Senator Ryan Duffy, Ostby began to lobby the federal government for regular air mail service to northern Wisconsin. In a letter to postmaster General Farley, Ostby pointed out that northern Wisconsin did not have air mail service nor the scheduled passenger service that accompanied it. He also declared to all who would listen that Superior's new airport was actually closer than Duluth's, not only to Superior's post office, but to Duluth's as well. In addition, the clay surface of the Duluth airport could turn to mud soup in a wet spring, while Superior's gravel and sand was drained nicely dry. Two federal inspectors visited Superior and agreed that the new airport could handle air mail and passengers, but there could be only one air mail stop at Duluth/Superior. If Superior got air mail, Duluth would lose it.

The Post Office announced that it would leave the final choice to the air mail carrier, Northwest Airlines. Croil Hunter, president of Northwest, visited the Twin Ports, complimented the new Superior airport but let it be known that the WEBC radio broadcasting tower presented a hazard there. Mayor Ostby announced that the tower could be moved, but his words fell on deaf ears. Northwest opted to remain at the Duluth airport and so did the air mail. Superior could find some brief consolation in the spring of 1941, when the Duluth Airport was so muddy that Northwest's passengers and air mail service was shifted to Superior.

Bryn Ostby retired as Mayor in 1940 and the Superior airport

was renamed in his honor. It was a fitting tribute to one of the most aviation-minded civic leaders in Wisconsin. About this time a young man from Poplar, Richard Bong, was attending pilot training classes at Superior State College. Bong would, of course, become the most brilliant combat aviator of World War II. His death in 1945 was a tragedy for his family, friends and the nation at large. One of the minor tragedies associated with Bong's death is that the memory of Bryn Ostby was obscured when the Superior airport was rightfully renamed in honor of Richard Bong.[45]

Three Lakes

Three Lakes Airport, municipal, rating —. Adjoins city to S., W. of railroad. Altitude, 1,664 feet. Rectangular, 1,400 by 850 feet, sod, level, natural drainage. THREE LAKES on hangar. Pole line to W., trees to SE. and SW. Facilities for servicing aircraft, day only. [1931]

The sketchy records on the start of this airport state that pilots Harold Grandy, Norman Brewster and Ora McMurray started to use the Three Lakes Four Seasons Park for a landing field in the mid-1920s. By 1933, the village of Three Lakes was providing some funding.

Washington Island

Washington Island Airport, commercial, rating —. The island is about six miles square, and airport a little to the N. of center. Altitude, 20 feet. Rectangular, 1,980 by 1,320 feet, sod, level, natural drainage; entire field available. Pole line to E., trees and windmill tower to S., trees to SW. and W., 30-foot pole in field to NW. Facilities for servicing aircraft, day only. [1933]

Aviation came to Washington Island in the summer of 1927 when Arnie Arntzen flew over the bay from Escanaba, Michigan and put his Jenny down in an open field "between the lumber company and the Lutheran Church." Arntzen would make regular trips to and from Escanaba and Washington Island until World War II grounded such pleasure jaunts. A pilot first and last, he founded Upper Peninsula Airways in Escanaba, where he may have encountered Oshkosh's Clyde Lee. Like Lee, Arntzen was of Norwegian descent and, also like Lee, expressed his desire to be the first son of Norway to make a non-stop flight across the ocean to the ancestral home. Arntzen never made the big hop, just contented himself with shorter and regular flights across the water to Washington Island, where he was an all but honorary citizen.

Thanks to Arntzen, flying took a quick hold on the Island. In the summer of 1928, the Island Holstein Breeders Association held its annual picnic in the grove near the inland hayfield that became the airport. The Breeders were entertained by traditional Potawatomi dancers and the brand new airplane of the Cherryland Airways from Sturgeon Bay. Also that year the Tri-Motor of Appleton's North-American Airways flew over and dropped a note suggesting that the Islanders build an airport so planes of its size could land.

By the end of the year the Washington Island Airport Company was incorporated with $5,000 in capital. Officers were George Mann, William Jess, Dr. Charles Colebaugh, Tom Goodman and Ted

Gudmundsen. They put graders to work laying out two runways on a 55-acre plot of ground about two miles north of Detroit Harbor. The company did not purchase a plane but searched for a pilot who would inaugurate regular air service from the Island to the Door Peninsula to the south, Menominee/Marinette to the west or Escanaba to the north. When bad weather shut down the ferry passage across Death's Door to Gill's Rock, an airplane could maintain the link for mail, vital supplies and medical care.

In 1933, Islander Claude Cornell bought a Stinson four-passenger cabin plane to the Island. It was the first locally-owned airplane and suitably named, Washington Island. Like Arntzen, he landed at the airfield in the warmer seasons, but took advantage of the frozen waters around the Island in the winter. Between 1936 and 1938, Arntzen began regular air service from Washington Island to Escanaba and Green Bay, but was forced to stop for lack of passengers. In 1941, Door County's flying physician, Dr. Dan Dorchester started to make weekly flights to the Island. He was the first doctor to provide regular medical care to the Islanders—at least until his flights were suspended by the war.

In1940, the Town of Washington purchased the airport and has operated it ever since.[46]

Waukesha

Waukesha Aviation Club Airport, auxiliary. Two miles N. Altitude, 850 feet. Rectangular, 2,500 by 850 feet, sod, slope to W., natural drainage. Trees to E., pole lines to W. and S. No servicing facilities. [1931]

Waukesha County Airport, auxiliary. Two miles north of Waukesha at junction of Highways No. 30 and F. Lat. 43.02; long. 88.13. Alt. 904 feet. L-shaped, sod, level ,nautural and artificial drainage, two landing strips, 3,000 by 500 feet. N./S., and N.W./SE. Pole lines to N., E., and S.: water towers to SW. Hangar, no servicing. [1938]

Aviation in the post-World War I Waukesha area began at the Huggins family farm in the Town of Honey Creek. Young Bob Huggins built a glider and, much to his parents delight, flew it without breaking his neck. Huggins then got into powered flight by converting a JN-4D fuselage and an OX-5 engine into a high-wing monoplane. The goings-on at the Huggins place attracted two boys from a farm down the road, Dean and Dale Crites, twins in fact and in their attraction to aviation. When Huggins wanted a passenger for a

flight one day in 1927, Dean volunteered. It happened to be the very same day that Lindbergh had landed in Paris. Dale made his first flight a day or so later. Nonetheless, in a cobbled-together flying machine taking off from a field of oat stubble, two of Wisconsin's most memorable aviators began their careers.

By 1929, the Crites boys had rebuilt a clipped-wing Standard, which their father had reluctantly given them permission to acquire. They got around Dad's objections to flying by persuading their Mother to go up in a Canuck Huggins had refurbished. If Mom could fly, why couldn't the boys, they asked Dad? He couldn't answer that question and the Crites boys took to the air.

Of course, Dad Crites, and Mom too, must have had some reservations after Huggins and Dean landed the Standard in a tree on the farm house lawn.

Left: The Waukesha County Airport with its new hangar, 1938. (Dean Crites)

Below: Early members of the Waukesha Aviation Club, 1931: Charles Gittner, Russell Schuetze, Kathleen Eder, Margaret Hausser, Roy Weizenried, Walter Hausser, Ed Boehmke, Lee Barney, Joe Rombough, Warren O'Brien, Robert Huggins, Ellsworth Schuetze. (WAC)

"Nobody got hurt, the airplane was demolished," Dale matter-of factly recalled many years later.

He and Dean then found a Jenny in repairable condition in a shed near Sturteveant, brought it home and made it fit to fly. The next step was to teach themselves how to fly, which they did in a series of cautious flights near the home farm. "We never went far away from the field, we always stayed around and didn't dare get

Above: Dale and Dean Crites with two Wacos, and a Piper J3 at Waukesha. (WAC)
Right: Russ Schuetze built his first plane in the family furniture factory in 1928. (WAC)

away very far," said Dale. Since Dale was Dean's instructor, and Dean was Dale's, they each agreed that the other was ready to solo after two or three hours of flight time.

They kept flying off the family farm until 1933, when Dean moved to Waukesha. He had heard of a flying club there that he could join and whose members had planes he might be able to fly. In 1937, Dale joined his brother, although neither gave up his day job as mechanic and trucker. They did their flying on weekends in refurbished Jennys and Canucks, but also in modern EagleRocks, American Eagles, Wacos and a Velie Monocoupe that Dean was especially fond of.

Waukesha was the right place for two fellows like the Crites Brothers. The place was had been a beehive of aviation since the mid-1920s, with Cash Chamberlain, Stan La Parle, Fritz Holterhoff, Rellis Conant, Ed Hedeen and other out of town flyers mixing with the locals: Walter Liskowitz, who brought an OX-5 Standard to town in 1925; Warren O'Brien, the village photographer who started taking aerial shots while standing half-in and half-out of the cockpit of a Jenny in 1926; Harold Kippers, who built his Gnome Rotary-powered monoplane in 1928; Russ Schuetze, who built an "Irwin" biplane with a motorcycle engine at the family church pew factory in 1931; and Jack Miller, the parachutist who broke his ankle on his first jump at the county Gurnsey Breeder's picnic, but came back to jump many times again.

All these flyers and a few more met to organize the Waukesha Aeronautical Association in 1930, then reorganized as the Waukesha Aviation Club one year later. Starting with fifteen members its first season, the Club would grow to become the largest aviation club in the state by the end of the decade.

The Aviation Club was the driving force behind the creation of the Waukesha County Airport in 1934. Waukesha aviators had been flying off of farm fields south of the city, off the grounds of the state school for boys near Wales, and up at the Pabst Farm near Oconomowoc. Russ Schuetze, who lived in the city, kept his airplane in the family garage and used a big vacant lot out back for a landing strip. Russ's father, Charles Schuetze, served on the parks committee of the Waukesha County Board and, just by watching his son, could see that Waukesha needed an airport. The city government did not have the resources, so the county was the logical sponsor.

The Aviation Club conducted its own form of lobbying. In 1931, club members leased part of the A. J. Badinger farm just north of the city limits and sponsored a winter air show that attracted 1,000 spectators. In July they ran an "Air Circus," that brought 5,000 people to a grassy knoll adjacent to the landing strip and fifteen aircraft to the flight line. One month later, Lewis A. Yancey brought out another crowd when he made Waukesha a stop on the national exhibition tour for his Autogyro, or vertical take off flying machine. A year later, the Club took its message right to the top when it sponsored a visit by the famed air racer Jimmy Haizlip, who took county supervisors and business leaders aloft for rides in his airplane. The Club's efforts received a boost when Franklin Roosevelt was inaugurated as President in 1933. Airports were prominent recipients of his public works grants and the prospect of federal money coming to Waukesha raised political interest in a county airport.

At its meeting in December, 1933, the board of supervisors voted to use $5,000 of county taxpayers' money to match a federal grant of $14,796. The county would also take five acres of high ground and 125 acres of wetland from its asylum/poor farm acreage and build an airport. As in Milwaukee County in 1919, responsibility for the Waukesha County Airport was placed in the hands of the county parks committee, Charles Schuetze presiding. The first airport manager was World War I Air Service "ace" Rodney Williams.

Less than two years later, after the marsh was drained and runways laid out, marked and graded, the airport was dedicated with an air show in front of 6,000 spectators. Ruth Harman, Buck Leighton, Jimmy Hanson, Gillie Jackson and Dean Crites stunted, with Crites giving one of the first public exhibitions of the feat for which he would be most remembered—picking up a handkerchief with a wingtip. They did it again in 1938,

Wausau Airport, early 1930s, from the ground. (Robert Wylie)

Wausau Airport, early 1930s, from the air. (Robert Wylie)

when the airport hangar, funded by federal and county taxes, but also with a substantial contribution from the Waukesha Aviation Club, was dedicated.

In 1939, Dean and Dale Crites opened a Piper Cub dealership. The following year they organized the Spring City Flying Service and put in a bid for the job of airport manager that the county accepted. Both pilots became instructors in the CPT program and together they trained over 1,000 pilots by the end of World War II. Although Dean left Waukesha for a few years, Dale continued as airport manager until his retirement in 1969. The Waukesha County Airport was renamed Crites Field in 1980.[47]

Wausau

Alexander Airport, commercial, rating —-. Two and one half miles S. on Wisconsin River. Altitude, 1,122 feet. Triangular, sod, level, natural drainage; three runways, 2,500 feet NW./SE., 2,400 feet NE./SW., and 1,800 feet E./W.; entire field available. WAUSAU on hangar roof. Pole line and buildings to E., low trees to W. Beacon and landing-area flood lights. Beacon, 24-inch rotating, clear. Facilities for servicing aircraft, day and night. [1933]

In the summer of 1927, three trans-oceanic flyers visited Wisconsin: Charles Lindbergh, Lester Maitland and Herbert Dargue. Dargue is the least recognized today, but in the 1920s, he was as well-known as any celebrity aviator, except for Lindbergh, whose fame outshone them all. One of the first pilots to fly for the U. S. Army before World War I, Major Dargue commanded a squad of Loening Amphibians on a "good-will" mission to South America in 1926, a feat comparable to the other great flights of the period. He spent much of the following year touring the United States and in May, 1927—a few weeks before Lindbergh flew the Atlantic, and one month before Maitland made his hop to Hawaii—Dargue addressed the Chamber of Commerce in Wausau and told them that they needed an airport.

The response was swift. In less than one month, paper company executives Ben and Judd Alexander announced that they would lease the Radtke property south of the city for five years, level and grade the ground for runways and build a hangar. The site was on a high bank above the impounded stretch of the Wisconsin River known as Lake Wausau and accessible to both land and water-based aircraft. "An Airport For Wausau," as the headline read, concisely summarized the news.

In October, Governor Fred Zimmerman flew up from Madison in the "Stanolind" plane supplied by the Standard Oil Company of Indiana to lay a cornerstone of "Marathon County granite" for the hangar. There is no mention of John Schwister's attending the event, and it would have been appropriate for Wausau's first pilot and Wisconsin's first home builder to share the mason's trowel with the Governor, but Schwister was in his last month of life. His participation in events could go no farther than reading the glowing accounts in the newspaper. Perhaps he saw them and found some comfort for his last hours there.

Major Dargue ignited the airport fire but other pilots were already flying at Wausau. Irvin Hall, whose father had supplied the Chalmers auto that John Schwister used to pull his first homebuilt plane into the air in 1911, and Mark Hubbard, started flying out of a farm field north of Wausau in 1926. Hall, Hubbard and Russell McNown were already using the Radtke property south of town when the Alexanders turned it into an airport and the Hall Aircraft Corporation already held the Wisconsin franchise for Eaglerock airplanes.

John P. Wood was also on hand and his Northern Airways held the franchise for Waco aircraft. After flying in air races around the country and winning the 1928 Ford Reliability Tour, John Wood was the indisputable star of aviation in Wausau. Northern Airways sold fifty Waco airplanes in 1929, had added Ryan and Hamilton franchises, and contracted to manage the Oshkosh Airport as well as Wausau's. Wood was a celebrity throughout the state, called upon to speak at dinners, attend graduation ceremonies, and hold public appointments until his death in September 1929. His neighbors honored his memory by erecting a beacon bearing his name on Rib Mountain.

Part of Wood's legacy was an impressive awareness of aviation in Wausau. Civic groups hosted an impressive number of aviation luminaries in the 1930s: air speed recordholders Jimmy Haizlip and Frank Hawks; trans-Pacific flyers Art Goebel, Clyde Pangborn and Hugh Herndon. Invited more than once, Charles Lindbergh did not make it to Wausau, but Amelia Earhart did. The "First Lady of the Air" spoke to the students and faculty at the Teacher's College in 1936. In 1932, students at Wausau high designed their yearbook on an aeronautics theme in order to honor, "these daring aviators, who pilot the magic argosies" of flight. The students solicited and received letters from aviation notables, including Amelia Earhart and Dr. Hugo Eckener, the German engineer and builder of the Graf Zeppelin airship.

Wausau also was a stopping point for several army air corps expeditions. In 1929, two army men spent the summer flying out of Wausau and taking pictures of the northern lake country in order to test army air reconnaissance capability. The following January a squadron of army pursuit planes left Selfridge Field on a flight to Washington state to test the winter capabilities of men and machines. Flying across Wisconsin, Minnesota, the Northern Great Plains and the Rocky Mountains in January in an open-cockpit plane was certainly a test and it took the squadron a good three weeks to complete the swing to Spokane, Washington and return to Wausau. A few years later, the army "Arctic Patrol" passed through and landed their ski-equipped aircraft at Alexander Field.

Wausau also received regular visits from native son Sam Redetzke, who completed army flight training in July, 1929. Assigned to test army pursuit planes at Wright Field in Ohio,

Wausau Airport Manager Archie Towle checking the weather station in the late 1930s. (Robert Wylie)

Redetzke soon decided that the air over Wisconsin was just right for flight testing and that Wausau, with Ma Redetzke's home cooking ready and waiting, was just the right place to stop for refueling. As a result, Wausau saw more than its share of the latest military aircraft. In 1938, for example, Redetzke rocketed in with a Consolidated PB-2A, completing a 480 mile flight in two hours. He arrived just in time for lunch at Mom's before taking off for Wright Field. Redetzke, who had survived the air corps' disastrous attempt to deliver air mail in 1934, made his last test flight in June, 1939. He flew to St. Paul in a BC-1 aircraft, then stopped in Wausau on the return trip to Ohio. It was a rainy night and Wright Field was socked in with solid overcast at 1,000 feet. Redetzke missed the landing field, crashed about one-half mile away, and died.

The Wausau airport almost fell victim to the Great Depression. The Alexander family had made its initial investment with the understanding that the airport would eventually support itself or become municipally owned, neither of which happened. In January 1934, the Chamber of Commerce sent a letter to the city council saying that "we understand that the airport at Wausau is about to be discontinued," then went on to ask the city to purchase or lease the facility. Not only would city ownership keep the airport open, it would also make the landing field eligible for federal public works grants. The city did not act until 1936, after which Wausau Municipal Airport received about $200,000 in federal money, some of which went to build a seaplane dock and ramp on the lake adjacent to the field and some of which went to resurfacing the runways with the area's distinctive, reddish "rotten granite" gravel. Most pilots agreed that the hard, smooth Wausau granite made a fine runway but, when blown into the air, the tough, bullet-like pellets were rough on props.

In 1937, Archie Towle took over as airport manager. In the early '30s Towle was a mechanic at a local Ford garage and "a pretty sharp fellow," as recalled by Irv Hall. Towle then went to work at the Hall auto garage and took part of his pay in flight instruction. When the city took over the airport and built living quarters for the manager and his family, the Towles moved into the house and into flying. Two years later, 16-year-old Marie Towle earned her license. In 1942, both Archie's wife Marjorie and their son Larry, age 16, got their tickets.

By 1937, aviation was starting to shake off the depression blues and Towle made the best of it. He flew in Legion membership round-ups and air tours, started several chapters of the National Aeronautical Association in his part of the state, hosted fly-in conventions in Wausau and became a leader of the state organization. Towle joined his colleagues in other Wisconsin and Minnesota cities in an effort to bring regular airline service to link Chicago, Milwaukee, Sheboygan, Fond du Lac, Oshkosh, Green Bay, Wausau and Superior/Duluth. Northwest Airlines expressed interest and filed an application with the Civil Aeronautics Administration. The CAA rejected the proposal, and described the area to be served, as "of a rural nature and as such is not likely to benefit to any great extent from the inauguration of air transportation services." Not until after the war would north central Wisconsin receive airline service. The Towles continued to serve as airport managers until 1945, when Archie died and passed the job down to daughter Marie and her husband Lyle Grimm.[48]

West Bend

West Bend, municipal. Department of Commerce intermediate field, site 3, Milwaukee-Green Bay Airway. Two and one-half miles E along Highway 68. Altitude, 880 feet. L shape, 68 acres, sod, rolling in south portion, natural and tile drainage; three landing strips, 2,000 feet N?S., 1,733 feet E/W, and 2,400 feet NE/SW. Directional arrow marked "3 M-GB," Pole lines and beacone tower on N.; buildings to E. Beacon, boundary, approach and obstruction lights. Beacon 24-inch rotating, with green course lights flashing characteristic "3" (...-). No servicing facilities. [1931]

After it learned that the it would be on the Milwaukee-Green Bay Airway in 1929, the city of West Bend leased 96 acres of land for an airport. The federal government funded basic improvements and mounted a beacon to light the way between Milwaukee and Fond du Lac. West Bend was used occasionally by Northwest Airways planes flying the air mail route until the service was discontinued in 1933.

The West Bend Aero Club was organized in 1931, with Al Hilde, Walter Rempe, Al Hembel and Karl Guse as officers. They purchased one of those reliable Waco 10, OX-5-powered-three-seaters, complete with a red fuselage and silver wings. The club and the airport soon fell victim to the Depression, the one disbanding, the other becoming inactive. In 1937 Bud Fisher and Ray Zuelke flew a Fisher J-3 Cub off of West Bend and in 1938, Ed Spangler landed with his De Haviland Gypsy Moth. The following year Fred Lueneberg moved over from Brown Deer with his Cub and other pilots followed. By 1940, about 15 pilots were keeping planes at West Bend.

When World War II began, local flyers were able to stay in the air by organizing a chapter of the Civil Air Patrol. The West Bend airport has remained on its original site since its opening.

Wisconsin Dells

Berrys Dells Airport, commercial, rating —-. Two and one half miles N. of city on highway. Altitude, 895 feet. Irregular, sod, level, natural drainage; two landing strips, 2,000 by 1,300 feet NW./SE. and N./S.; entire field available. Trees to S. and NE. Department of Commerce beacon, 24-inch rotating. Aviation fuel, day only. [1933]

Air show at the Lake Delton Airport, about 1930. (Dells Country Historical Society)

Lake Delton Airport, commercial, rating —-. Three miles S. Altitude, 910 feet. Irregular shape, sod, level, natural drainage; landing strips, 1,500 feet NW./SE., 2,000 feet N./S., 1,800 feet NE./SW., and 950 feet E./W. LAKE DELTON AIRPORT on hangar. Trees to NW. and S. Facilities for servicing aircraft, day only. [1933]

Wisconsin Dells was well on its way to becoming the state's most popular vacation destination by the late 1920s when two airports were established there, both related to tourism.

Clinton Berry cleared a landing field on sixty acres of his Cold Water Canyon resort north of the city of Wisconsin Dells in May of 1928. Since it was on the original route of the Milwaukee-Twin Cities Airway, Berry's field had already been selected by the Aeronautics Bureau as a site for a beacon, so it was logical for the resort owner to build an airport around it. "The airstrip was the Number 2 fairway," recalled Marilyn and Audrey Berry, who were youngsters at the time. "The beacon light was behind the green. It circled every night relentlessly and kept us awake in our beds..."

Berry had been receiving "numerous requests for information regarding landing facilities," from pilots in Milwaukee, Chicago and St. Louis, but not much more than requests materialized. The beacon remained in place until 1932, but Berry's Airport was already closed and reverting back to golf course.

The Lake Delton Airport was part of the resort-entertainment-subdivision complex created south of the city of Wisconsin Dells by William Newman and Ralph Hines. Newman was a large-scale developer who dammed Dell Creek to build Lake Delton, plotted lots around it and built a resort on its shores. The airport was part of the package. Emulating Governor Walter Koher, Newman purchased a Mahoney-Ryan Brougham and painted "Lake Delton Recreation Company" on the fuselage. The familiar plane delivered Newman's advertising message at air shows in the early 1930s. In 1932, however, the Depression caught up with William Newman and drove him into bankruptcy. His associate Ralph Hines kept the Delton operations afloat and made improvements to the airport. It remained the leading airport in the area until after World War II. [49]

Wisconsin Rapids

Nepco Tri-City Airport, commercial, rating —-. Two miles S. of Wisconsin Rapids; E. of Wisconsin River. Altitude, 950 feet. Square, 5,280 by 5,280 feet, sod, level, natural drainage. WISCONSIN RAPIDS on hangar roof. Trees to S. and E. Beacon, boundary lights (E., N., and S., sides only), obstruction, and landing area flood lights, operated upon request. Beacon, 24-inch rotating, clear, with green auxiliary code beacon flashing 6 flashes per minute. Facilities for servicing aircraft, day and night. [1933]

By 1928, business leaders in the cities of Wisconsin Rapids, Port Edwards and Nekoosa had been raising funds to build an airport for several years when they realized they had to accelerate the pace of their efforts. The Nekoosa-Edwards Paper Company had ordered a Ford Tri-Motor in the summer of 1928 and needed a place to land it. The man behind the purchase, Nekoosa manager John E. Alexander, soon organized Tri-City Airways Corporation, and sold enough stock to acquire 330 acres on the southern edge of Wisconsin Rapids. News reports said the company invested $50,000 to lay out an excellent landing field with graded runways, lighted boundary markers, a rotating beacon and a 100-foot square hangar for the Ford.

The airport was dedicated in late October 1928, near the end of

The Nekoosa-Edwards hangar at Tri-City Airport. (Dave Engel)

the political campaign and both of Wisconsin's "flying" gubernatorial candidates—Fred Zimmermann and Walter Kohler—flew in for the event. They joined paper industry executives, 75 pilots and 4,000 spectators who took part in a two-day air show that featured balloon-busting, a dead stick landing contest, speed and long-distance air races, plus Roy Leavitz's Flying Circus.

The star performer of the day was the NEPCO Tri-Motor, with airport manager Lee Mulzer flying aerobatics. He was a showman who flew the Ford on a regular basis for Nekoosa-Edwards and made the airport a busy spot. Air races that attracted nearly all of Wisconsin's prominent pilots were held at Tri-City Airport every summer until Mulzer left in 1932. He welcomed fly-in visits by military pilots from Selfridge Field, Michigan and organized the "first" band concert ever broadcast from an airplane. While Mulzer and the Tri-Motor circled the airport on one September afternoon, ten members of the 120th Field Artillery Band played into a radio transmitter. The newspaper reported that the music sounded good on the radio, but one of the band members later recalled that the engine noise inside the Ford was so loud that he could not even hear what he was playing.

The fact that the Ford could carry twelve passengers proved very convenient when a local judge agreed to allow a jury deciding a case involving a land dispute to go aloft. Mulzer flew the jury over the land and, presumably, enabled them to make the right judgment. The Tri-Motor was also used in what was reported as the state's first aerial funeral transport and on forest fire patrol for the Conservation Department.

Mulzer also ran Tri-City Flying School, which opened in the spring of 1929, with a Travel Air purchased from Howard Morey in Madison. Delivery was delayed when the pilot Morey dispatched to fly the Travel Air followed the wrong railroad tracks out of Madison and ended up in Watertown. Once it arrived, the Travel Air was soon joined by six Fairchilds which, along with the Tri-Motor, gave the fifty students enrolled plenty of opportunities to get into the air. The school attracted students from throughout Wisconsin and

G36   JERE WITTER PLANE   MAY 1930

Jere Witter, Wisconsin Rapids, with the Krueger Challenger Aircraft he called "Scheherazade." (Dave Engel)

Minnesota, with a least one coming all the way from New York. Among the graduates of the Tri-City Flying School was "the first Wisconsin priest to learn flying," and Virginia Whittesley, who one of the first women in the United States to qualify for a transport pilot's license.

Aviation was developing nicely at the Tri-City Airport until the Great Depression all but grounded it. Nekoosa-Edwards sold the Tri-Motor to Mulzer, who struggled to keep it in gas and oil. He left Wisconsin with the plane in 1932 to weather the hard times as best

he could. A commissioned Reserve officer, Mulzer entered the Army Air Force in World War II and rose to the command of Elmendorf Air Force Base at Anchorage, Alaska. At war's end he alerted bush pilot Bob Reeve to the sale of the surplus C-47 that became the first plane in Reeve's Aleutian Airways.

Tri-City Airways continued to own and manage the airport until 1961, when John E. Alexander, founder and principal stockholder, presented the facility to the South WoodCounty Airport Commission.[50]

Forward in Flight

Less than ten years after the Wright Brothers' first airplane flight at Kitty Hawk, aviators were flying regularly in Wisconsin, as illustrated by the poster for Milwaukeen Paul Gnauck's exhibition flight in 1913.

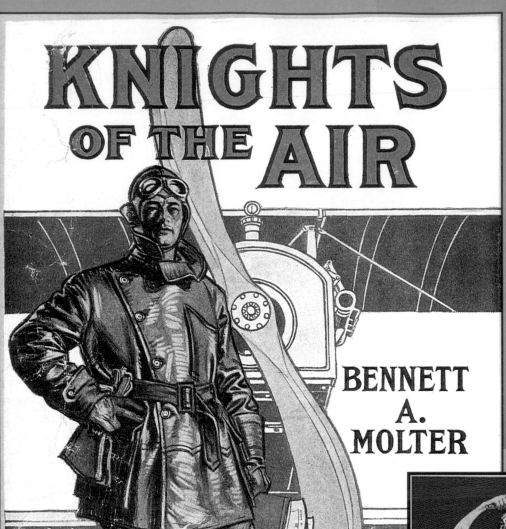

KNIGHTS
OF THE AIR

BENNETT A. MOLTER

Wisconsin in the War

An illustration from the 1919 University of Wisconsin yearbook, *Liberty Badger*, (Right) showed that Wisconsin went to war in airplanes for the first time in World War I. Wausau native Bennett Molter joined France's Lafayette Flying Corps and later wrote a book about it, while Milwaukee's William "Billy" Mitchell was the first American to fly over enemy lines and the top air force commander in the final months of the war.

A Wisconsin Air National Guard fighter roars off the runway at Madison, and a B-2 "Stealth" bomber is refueled by a Milwaukee-based Air Guard tanker. The Air Guard aspires to the standards set by World War II "Ace of Aces" Richard Bong of Poplar.

HELLO Lindy
MILWAUKEE GREETS YOU
COMPLIMENTS OF THE "MILWAUKEE HEROLD"

Wisconsin went wild for transoceanic flyers Lester Maitland and Charles Lindbergh in 1927. A Milwaukee native and army flyer, Maitland piloted the first plane to fly from California to Hawaii. Lindbergh made his famous flight from New York to Paris five years after leaving the University of Wisconsin. Before she made her fateful and final round-the-world flight, Amelia Earhart visited with Kenosha airport manager Ruth Harman.

LIGHT
for the
NIGHT AIR MAIL

KOHLER of KOHLER
AUTOMATIC ELECTRIC PLANTS

See Back Cover!
POPULAR
AVIATION

APRIL 25c
In Canada 30c

Corbin Super-Ace
See Page 247

In the 1920's and 30's Wisconsin's aviation industry produced electrical power plants made in Kohler that powered beacons on airways around the world. Among the airplanes built in the state were the Invincible mid-wing in Manitowoc, the Corben Ace in Madison and the fanciful flying motorcycle in Fond du Lac.

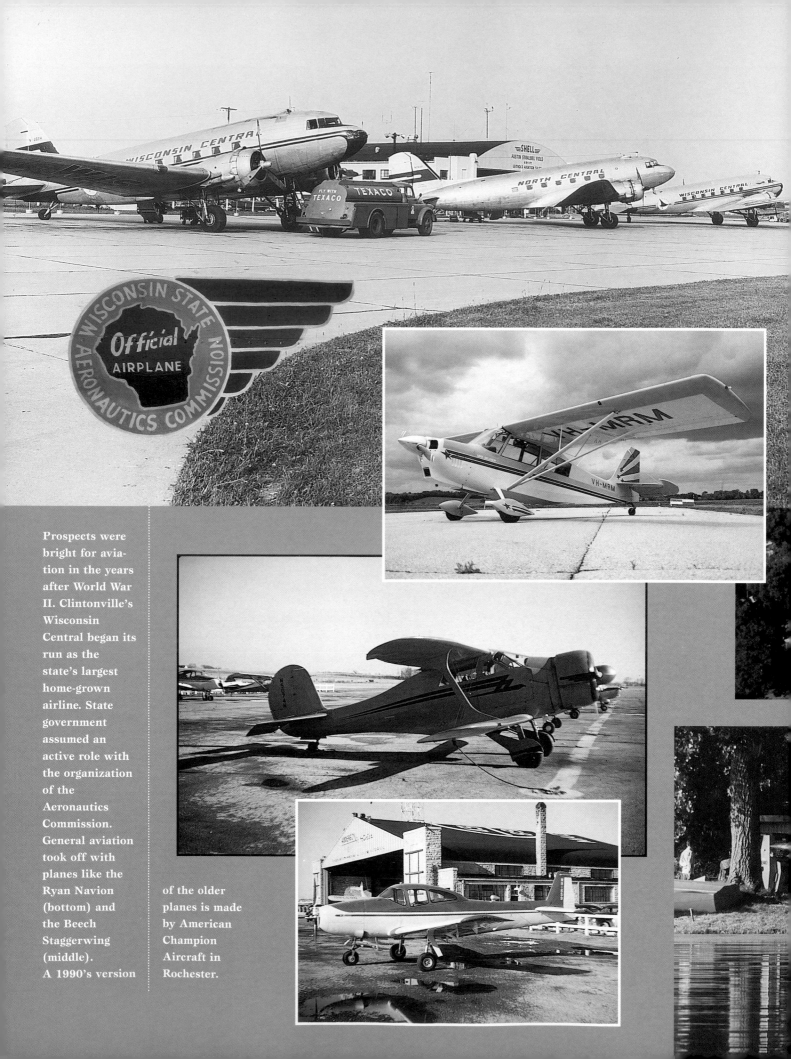

Official AIRPLANE

WISCONSIN STATE AERONAUTICS COMMISSION

Prospects were bright for aviation in the years after World War II. Clintonville's Wisconsin Central began its run as the state's largest home-grown airline. State government assumed an active role with the organization of the Aeronautics Commission. General aviation took off with planes like the Ryan Navion (bottom) and the Beech Staggerwing (middle). A 1990's version of the older planes is made by American Champion Aircraft in Rochester.

Organized by Milwaukeen Paul Poberezny in 1953, the Experimental Aircraft Association settled in Oshkosh in the 1970's. The annual fly-in convention, complete with seaplane base on Lake Winnebago, is one of the world's largest aviation events. Smaller fly-ins, like the antique airplane event at Brodhead, fill the summer weekend calendar.

Airports large and small serve Wisconsin aviators. A thunderstorm approaches Taylor County Airport, Medford. A state-of-the-art deicing facility lights the night at Rhinelander. Milwaukee's General Mitchell International, the state's largest and busiest airport.

Forward in Flight

M B · 1   M A R T I N   B O M B E R

Maximum speed 99 mph

Ceiling 8500 ft

1918

U.S. Army Air Service Martin MB-1 on the Milwaukee lakefront, 1919. The twin-engine, open-cockpit MB-1 was the first American-built bomber and the design predecessor of the aircraft Billy Mitchell used to bomb and sink heavily armored battleships. (WAHF)
Opposite: Brigadier General William "Billy" Mitchell, 1918. (WAHF)

CHAPTER III

Wisconsin Aviators at War

WORLD WAR I
THE LION OF THE AIR SERVICE

When the United States entered World War I in April 1917, the nation's air force ranked fourteenth in the world, behind that of Serbia, Bulgaria and the Ottoman Empire. It consisted of 1,100 enlisted men, 52 officers, 26 qualified pilots and about 150 aeroplanes, none suited for combat. On the positive side, the United States did have one Air Service officer on the ground in Europe when war was declared, Major William Mitchell of Milwaukee. If ever there was a coincidence of the right person being in the right place at the right historical moment, it occurred when "Billy" Mitchell turned up in France in April 1917. The man, the place and the times were made for each other. But maybe it was not a coincidence, since Mitchell had long argued that the United States would enter the conflict and should be prepared for it, and had asked his superiors to send him to the Western Front as an observer. To take charge of events, create his own coincidences, came naturally to Major Mitchell.

He belonged to one of Wisconsin's most prominent families. His grandfather, Alexander Mitchell, had emigrated from Scotland to frontier Wisconsin and made a fortune in banking, railroads and real estate. Billy's father, John Lendrum Mitchell, enjoyed a European education and lived the life of a cultured, wealthy Victorian gentleman, who did not need to toil for his daily bread. Drawn to politics in the 1890s, John L. Mitchell served one term as a United States Senator from Wisconsin. Young Billy, who was born in France in 1879, spent almost as much of his boyhood in Europe and Washington D. C. as in Milwaukee.

When the United States declared war on Spain in 1898, nineteen-year-old Billy Mitchell volunteered for service as a private with the Wisconsin Volunteers. He was assigned to Camp Cuba Libre in Jacksonville, Florida, but was soon transferred to Washington D. C. where he received a commission in the Signal Corps. It did not take long for the young Lieutenant to decide that the army would be his life's work. Over the next decade he served in Cuba, the Philippine Islands, Alaska and in many postings in the United States where he

consistently exhibited gifts of intelligence, hard work and resourceful inventiveness. In 1903, he completed two years of grueling, perilous labor to construct over 1,000 miles of telegraph line across Alaska. When he emerged from the wilderness after bringing the line to Nome on the Bering Sea, he was promoted and became the youngest Captain in the United States Army. An imaginative, intense personality, naturally curious and ready to question and learn, Mitchell was readily drawn to the new inventions of the age. It was no surprise that he was behind the wheel of the first automobile the U. S. Army owned and, although not officially assigned to be there, was present at Fort Myers, Virginia, in September 1908 when Orville Wright first demonstrated his aeroplane to the army.

In 1912, Mitchell became the youngest officer

yet assigned to serve on the army general staff. War had just broken out in the Balkans and he was placed in charge of all military intelligence on the conflict that has been called the opening act of World War I. In the packets of information Mitchell received and assessed were reports on the first uses of aircraft in offensive warfare, including the first bombing runs on both military and naval targets.

Mitchell had been aviation-minded for many years before he read reports about bombing in Bulgaria. "I had known the Wrights, had followed intently all aeronautical development," he recalled in his *Memoirs*. In the summer of 1916, while serving on the general staff in Washington, he decided to learn to fly an aeroplane. Since the army had no training facilities for aviators, he enrolled in the Curtiss school at Newport News, Virginia, and traveled by boat down the Potomac on Saturday evenings so he could "fly all day Sunday, and be back in the office on Monday." Here he met fellow Wisconsinites Paul and Edith Dodd Culver, who remembered that "his frequent arrivals would always create a sensation because he was a dynamic, dashing, handsome officer in Army uniform."

One of the flight instructors who took Mitchell up in the new Curtiss JN models in use at Newport News was Walter Lees, another Wisconsin native. He recorded in his log for September 1916 that as a pilot "Mitchell is very erratic. One day he would be OK and the next lousy..."

Flight training was brief in those days and, after "about four days of instruction," Mitchell was turned loose for his first solo flight. In the cockpit of Lees' machine, Mitchell took off smoothly and circled the field with ease. On landing, he made his approach too high and fast, hit the runway, bounced about twenty feet into the air, slammed into the ground again, stalled the engine and flipped over. Fortunately, the biplane framework held together and the future combat commander of the United States Army Air Service escaped injury to all but his ego. Suspended by his seatbelt, Mitchell calmly hung upside down until he was rescued by the ground crew. Afterwards at the Curtiss school, whenever a student pilot flipped a plane, he was told he had completed a "Mitchell."

Despite his rocky debut, Mitchell would become an excellent pilot and put his skills to good use in France less than a year after his mishap at Newport. Indeed, he was one of few army officers of rank who served in World War I, including those in the Air Service, who had actually flown in an aeroplane.

As soon as he received word that the U. S. was in the war, Mitchell rushed to Paris where he reinforced the two-man American military mission already there. He created two missions for himself. First, he would work with the Allies to draw up a plan to equip and train American air forces and bring them into combat as soon as possible. Second, he would gather intelligence on the war in general and aviation in particular.

The plan Mitchell formulated, in cooperation with the French military and aviation industry, called for American aviators to be in combat in the summer of 1917. They would be trained and equipped by the French, who had the largest Allied air force, and were already building two-thirds of all the aeroplanes flown on the Western Front. Acting with his usual swift dispatch, Mitchell drew up and cabled the plan to Washington in only two weeks. Although it was endorsed by the French government in a special missive to President Woodrow Wilson, Mitchell's plan was not implemented. Instead, the United States opted to train most of its pilots at home, concentrate on building its own version of the British DeHaviland machine and develop its own engine—the famous Liberty OX-5. As a result, the first American Air Service pilots—under Mitchell's command, by the way— did not go into combat in France until April, 1918.

Mitchell had better luck with his second mission, which depended almost solely on his own efforts. Instead of following the conventional practice of collecting information by meeting with staff and interviewing other intelligence officers, Mitchell went to the military airdromes, the training schools and the trenches. He flew every model of observation and pursuit plane from the Sopwith Camel to the French Spad. He saw German and Allied pilots in aerial combat while under anti-aircraft gunfire, observed troop movements from the gondola of a balloon, surveyed both day and night-time bombing missions, and experienced what it was like to be on the receiving end of a bombing run when the Germans attacked the city of Chalons during his visit there. He was particularly impressed when British bomber pilots told him that "given enough planes and explosives, there would be nothing left of Germany in a short while."

In a borrowed French machine, Mitchell became the first American to fly across enemy lines, then did it over and again. Even as Chief of Air Service for the First Army and a Brigadier General, Mitchell continued to fly into the combat zone. While flying alone over the Marne River in July 1917, he discovered a string of newly-built bridges teeming with German soldiers on their way to assault the Allies. He rushed back to report to both the American and French commanders who moved troops into place to counter the threat. The resulting Allied counter-attack, with full support of aircraft under Mitchell's command, played a vital role in the Battle of Chateau-Thierry, which proved to be the turning point after which the Germans switched from an offensive to a defensive posture.

Mitchell's observation flights yielded more than immediate battlefield gains. As he recorded in his Memoirs, "A very significant thing to me was that we could cross the lines of these contending armies in a few minutes in our aeroplane, whereas the armies have been locked in the struggle, immovable, powerless to advance for three years." He needed no further proof of the potential of military aviation. "An aeroplane is an offensive and not a defensive weapon," he wrote. It was a weapon of attack that could not be "too highly estimated." No matter how seriously ground forces might be locked in a defensive struggle, aircraft could always attack, "simply because the sky is too large to defend."

Mitchell was given the chance to implement his ideas on air power as commander of the largest air force yet mustered for a single action in the entire war. In the First Army's attack on the St. Mihiel Salient in September 1918, Brigadier General Mitchell was in command of 30,000 men and nearly 1,500 French, British, Italian and American aircraft. Although the actual number of machines in action was closer to 800, Mitchell's battle plan called for a continuous offensive in the air, with pursuit planes and bombers attacking enemy forces from the right, the left and the rear.

St. Mihiel was a swift and clear victory for the Allies, the American Air Service and Billy Mitchell. In congratulating Mitchell, General John J. Pershing, Commander-in-Chief of the American forces, said that "the organization and control of the tremendous concentration of Air Forces...is as fine a tribute to you personally as is the courage and nerve shown by your officers..."

After St. Mihiel, Mitchell did not stop formulating new tactics for air power. For the spring of 1919, he planned to combine an entire infantry division with "a great force of bombardment airplanes." He would equip the soldiers with machine guns and parachutes, load up to fifteen of them in a bomber and drop them behind enemy lines. Supported by pursuit aircraft, these shock troops would disrupt the enemy's rear echelon, also seize and hold strong points until concentrated armored units could break through the front lines. World

War I ended before Mitchell could test his system of coordinated offense in which air force, paratroop, infantry and armored units worked together to achieve victory. Known as "blitzkrieg" or lightning war, these tactics were adopted by the armed forces of the Third Reich with terrible and devastating effects in the opening years of World War II and used again by the Allies to defeat Germany in 1945.

The Other Mitchell

Lieutenant John Lendrum Mitchell was the younger brother of General Billy Mitchell. Born in 1892, and a graduate of the University of Wisconsin's class of 1917, the younger Mitchell attended ground school at the Massachusetts Institute of Technology and, in April 1918, was one of the first ten Air Service cadets to arrive in France. With an engineering background, he went to work building landing fields and ground support facilities for the fledgling Air Service but, of course, he wanted to fly in combat.

On May 27, 1918, Mitchell attempted to land his machine at a field near Air Service headquarters at Toul. He must have miscalculated his approach for the stern section of the fuselage slammed into the ground before the front landing gear and shattered. Mitchell was thrown from the plane and mortally injured. He was 26 years old.

His brother took it hard, confiding in his diary that he should not have let John enter the Air Service and that if any Mitchell should have been killed, "I should have been the one."

Billy Mitchell managed his grief in the best way he knew. On the day of his brother's funeral he got into his plane and flew up and down the front. Only in the air, could he assuage his grief and honor the memory of the brother he had lost.

In 1922, Billy Mitchell memorialized his brother John by offering the Mitchell Trophy as an award for aviation excellence at the National Air Races.[1]

Billy Mitchell returned from World War I a hero and—after Eddie Rickenbacker—was probably the most well-known American military aviator in the early postwar years. He never stopped arguing for the development of American air power and the creation not only of an independent air force, but of a command organization that would coordinate the efforts of each military arm. That he was a prophet there can be little doubt. Nor can there be little doubt that, like many another prophet, his proclamations were often unheeded. At the same time, there can be no doubt that he was one of the founding spirits of the United States air force, one of air power's first strategists and a creative battlefield tactician.

"Aggressive, assertive and abrupt, Mitchell belongs to the type of man who thinks fast, acts fast and talks fast," wrote Army Air Corps Captain Lester J. Maitland in 1929. "If he gets an idea he

Paul Collins with the Air Service in Germany, 1919. (University of Wisconsin, Stevens Point)

expects it to be carried out at once. He hates delay and scorns incompetence, is self-confident but ready to admit when he is wrong. He has initiative and intelligence, but is prone to jump at conclusions.

"Such is General Mitchell the man. No matter what life work he might be engaged in he would be the same. It would be as impossible for him to suppress his convictions as it would be for a lion to turn tail in an attack."

In the military climate of the 1920s, Mitchell's inability to "suppress his convictions" would lead to the tragedy of his court martial and resignation from the air service he had helped create and nurture.[2]

IN COMBAT WITH THE ALLIES

By the end of World War I, the United States had enrolled approximately 38,000 men in aviation training, 3,000 of whom were commissioned as pilots or observers. Roughly 750 pilots and 450 observers actually served in units that saw combat and nearly 200 of them died in action or of other causes.

The exact number of Wisconsin men among this first corps of American military aviators is not known. What is known is that Wisconsin men served in every kind of aviation unit mustered for the war and took part in combat action along the western front from Flanders in the north to Italy in the south.

The spirit in which Wisconsin men took to the air was well-expressed by Paul Collins of Stevens Point. He had already quit teaching school in Junction City, Wisconsin, to take flying lessons in Chicago when the United States entered the war. Then, "The spark became a bright flame," and Collins enlisted in the Army Air Service. Many other Wisconsin men would see the same spark as Paul Collins, feel the warmth of the same flame and enlist in army or navy aviation.

Perhaps the first aviator with a Wisconsin connection on duty in France was Bennett A. Molter. Although he left home in 1907 to spend four years in the Navy, Molter's parents lived in Wausau before and during the war years and he considered it his home town. As early as 1915, he tried to enlist in the French Ambulance Corps, but was not accepted. He worked in the motion picture industry in California until the fall of 1916, when he was accepted into France's Lafayette Flying Corps. The Corps included all the squadrons of American aviators flying in French service both before and after the United States entered the war. It is often confused with its most famous component squadron, the Lafayette Escadrille, but was much larger and included whole squadrons of Americans as well as individual American pilots who flew with predominantly French units.

Molter entered aviation school in France in November 1916, completed training in May 1917 and was flying in Spad Squadron 102 in July. The Spad was a speedy French-built observation plane with a 150 H.P. Hispano-Suiza engine and a single machine gun mounted in front of the cockpit.

Molter's first assignment was to fly missions over the front lines to drop counterfeit copies of German-language newspapers intended to misinform and demoralize German troops. On one flight his engine stalled at 12,000 feet and he was not able to start it again. Still on the wrong side of the lines, with anti-aircraft guns targeting his machine, the pilot started the long glide home. Unable to reach a landing field, he put down in a wheat field and flipped the machine. His seat belt broke and he was thrown forward out of the cockpit with his head pinned between the fuselage and the ground. Fortunately for the young American, the French required that their pilots wear hard, leather-covered helmets and Molter's helmet prevented his head from being crushed beneath his machine. Had he been wearing the more familiar soft leather headgear, he probably would not have survived the crash.

A news report later quoted Molter as saying, "The aerial service affords the least protection of any division and the driver [pilot] does not bring his machine safely home by scientific methods, it's just fool luck." To be sure luck always plays a role in flying, but training, skill and courage also make a difference.

The inevitable bruises and bumps healed quickly and in a few weeks, Molter was ready to fly again. He would have returned to combat had not France begun transferring Lafayette Flying Corps personnel to the American Air Service. The United States was building an air force and flight instructors were at a premium. As a pilot of at least three months experience who had actually flown at the front, Molter was choice material for a flight instructor. He returned to the United States and finished out the war training other pilots and boosting public support for the war effort. He toured the country, including Wausau, and wrote morale-boosting syndicated news articles on his war experiences—probably with the help of War Department public information people.

Bennett Molter also became the author of a book. In August 1918, his "Knights of the Air," was published and told, "of the thrilling experiences of an aviator in France, and vividly tells of the life and work of the birdmen in the war zone." It was the first book on aerial warfare published by a Wisconsinite.

Manderson Lehr could have been the subject of a novel with "knight" in the title. He was one of five idealistic Beloit College students who joined the French Ambulance Service in May 1917. The group cherished the ideals of democracy as pronounced by Woodrow Wilson and believed that World War I was a struggle between freedom and tyranny.

Once in France, the "Beloit unit" started to break up, and at Lehr's initiative. "I started it by going crazy over aviation," he wrote in a letter home to the Beloit College newspaper. He transferred to the French air corps and was sent to flight school at Avord. "Just imagine going up to 12,500 feet," he wrote, "then you start to loop the loop and when you get up and just before you turn over you cut your motor and cross your controls and nose dive about 1,800 feet just like a rock." He obviously loved to fly and was as ready for combat as any enthusiastic novice could be. By the sum-

mer of 1918, Lehr was in Breguet Squadron 117 piloting a two-man Breguet-14 bomber on low-altitude runs near Chateau-Thierry.

Equipped with a 300 horsepower Renault motor, the Breguet-14 was actually an observation plane with racks for up to three dozen light bombs mounted on the underside of the lower wing. The pilot was also the bombardier and the co-pilot/observer manned a pair of machine-guns swivel-mounted on the rear cockpit. Since they often flew lower than 1,000 feet over hostile territory, some Breguet crews attempted to armorplate at least part of their machines. They filled steel infantry helmets with sand and mounted them upside down beneath their seats in the cockpit.

After three years of aerial warfare, the French

John Kaminski Stops Flying

World War I was a global conflict and the first war in which the United States was obliged to defend territory overseas. The newly-opened Panama Canal was the most important American overseas possession and responsibility for its defense was shared by the army, the navy and the Army Air Service's 7th Aero Squadron.

One of the pilots in the 7th was Milwaukee's own John Kaminski. He had signed on as a civilian instructor at the Army's second flight school at Hazlehurst Field in Mineola, New York in 1916 where he trained National Guard and regular army pilots in brand-new Curtiss JN-4's. When the U.S. entered the war in Europe, Kaminski was offered a commission as a second lieutenant, but he opted instead to enter the air service as a non-commissioned "soldier" pilot.

He was assigned to the 7th Aero Squadron on duty in the Panama Canal Zone where he flew Curtiss Flying boats and amphibians on anti-submarine patrol over the ocean. Panama was in little danger of attack, but German submarines did threaten shipping through the Canal. Kaminski never saw a sub, but on one patrol he had to make a forced landing about sixty miles from shore. Fortunately the sea was relatively calm so pilot and observer waited until they were discovered by a sub-chaser and towed home. In December 1918, Kaminski also made the first air mail flight across the Isthmus.

John Kaminski was enjoying easy duty in a pleasant place, but all was not well. Even before he left for Panama he noticed that his eyesight was failing. He came home to Milwaukee where he had several pairs of special lenses made to fit inside his helmet. They gave him 20-20 vision, but also made him very protective of his helmet. It was common for pilots to share headgear in those days, but not Kaminski. Other fliers just presumed he was superstitious and humored him, so he continued to fly without his disability being discovered. He served out his enlistment even though his condition was further aggravated by an accident during refueling in which gasoline splashed into his eyes.

After the war ended, Kaminski was honorably discharged and came home to Milwaukee. His eyesight continued to deteriorate and on July 5, 1919, he went to work as a dispatcher for the United States Post Office. He would remain at the Post Office until his retirement in 1955. Wisconsin's first licensed pilot, the Milwaukee boy who dreamed of flying like a gull over Lake Michigan, and did it, was unable to take part in the golden and glorious days of aviation in the 1920s and '30s. After he came home from Panama, he never again piloted an airplane.[3]

Delafield native Rodney Williams was credited with five aerial victories and became Wisconsin's World War I ace. (WAC)

had learned that formations of at least four bombers stood a good chance of returning from a run with only minimal losses. Of course, this tactic was not flawless, as the story of Manderson Lehr proves. In July 1918, Lehr and his observer, Lieutenant T. Carles, were part of a formation of four Breguets returning from an attack in which each plane had dropped 32 bombs on the enemy. Crossing over the lines at about 3,000 feet they encountered ten German "chasses" or pursuit planes. As Carles recounted the action:

They first attacked us from the rear and at the left. I released a torrent of shot against them and it struck on the wing. I made a second on the rear and to the right. It made a nose dive and went exactly beneath our tail at 15 meters and gave us terrible shell fire. I released my machine guns in order to make Lehr see. It is only then that I noticed that the poor, dear friend must be wounded. He had given up his control and no longer moved.

Although his pilot was unconscious and his plane on fire, Carles still succeeded in landing intact. He survived, but Manderson Lehr experienced the swift, arbitrary death of a combat pilot at the controls of his machine.

Since he died flying for France, Lehr was awarded the Croix de Guerre and buried in the National Cemetery. His name is also inscribed on the Memorial erected in Paris to members of the Foreign Legion and the Lafayette Flying Corps. He was among the first Wisconsin pilots to die in aerial combat.

While the fame and glory connected with the Lafayette Flying attracted many Americans, others flew with British units. Delafield native Rodney Williams was a Carroll College student in April 1917. He became one of about 1,100 volunteers assigned to train with the Royal Flying Corps at Toronto that spring. With the onset of winter weather, the unit moved to Taliaferro Field, in Texas, where one of its flight instructors was the famous Broadway dancer Vernon Castle. By the spring of 1918, two squadrons of Americans—the 17th and 148th—were stationed with British units in Flanders. Williams was with the "17th Americans," flying a swift Sopwith Camel pursuit plane.

In July, Williams became the first member of the 17th to down an enemy aircraft. In the laconic style of the combat report, Williams wrote that he encountered two enemy Fokkers at 20,000 feet, damaged one so it was forced to land, then met the other:

One other Fokker dove on me firing short burst. Maneuvered so that I was only about twenty-five yards to his left rear, as he was making a slow climbing turn; gave him a burst of forty or fifty bullets which appeared to enter his machine at pilot's seat. He turned on his back and fell straight out of sight, apparently out of control.

It was the first of four enemy aeroplanes and one balloon that Williams was to destroy in one month of combat flying that saw him aloft nearly every day. It was during the bloody summer and fall of 1918, when American forces fought on the Marne, at Belleau Wood, Chateau-Thierry, St. Mihiel and the Meuse-Argonne.

"Low bombing and machine gun attacks on balloons and infantry were the order of the day, and we sent out two machines at a time all day long, from dawn to dark," wrote the historian of the 17th Aero Squadron. Before the end of August, Rodney Williams saw enough action to become Wisconsin's first "ace." He was the only pilot from this state to earn the distinction in World War I.

On one sortie an enemy plane attacked Williams from the rear. One bullet lodged in his back and another pierced the fuel tank mounted forward of the cockpit. A thin stream of gasoline began to leak from the tank so Williams acted on the first thought that came to mind. He stuck a finger in the hole and kept flying. Wounded, with one hand occupied in corking the leaky fuel tank, he was still able to return safely to his landing field, but not before he dropped to 100 feet and strafed a convoy of enemy trucks.

Since he continued to perform so well, it would seem that Williams was not seriously injured. However, the wound he suffered that day was grievous enough to keep him on the ground in the final three months of the war. Rodney Williams was a courageous man and a skilled pilot. He was also lucky. After he landed and the mechanics went to work on his plane, they discovered that the bullet that pierced Williams' gas tank was a phosphorous shell that should have ignited inside the tank. Had it gone off, the gas would have exploded into flames, incinerating plane and pilot.

Left: Photos from the Rodney Williams scrapbook of his Sopwith Camel pursuit plane, a captured German Albatross, and of Williams with his Sopwith "bus." (WAC)

Below: University of Wisconsin graduate and Caproni bomber pilot, Paton McGilvary. (Liberty Badger)

way down the Italian peninsula near the shore of the Adriatic Sea.

McGilvary was one of the first twenty Americans detailed to Italy, the vanguard, so the Italians hoped, of a steady stream of men and material from the United States. Accordingly, much attention was paid to the group, including a personal visit to the squadron from King Victor Emmanuel and a rousing welcoming ceremony in the Colosseum at Rome at which the commanding officer of the American aviators in Italy, Captain Fiorello LaGuardia, addressed the crowd in both English and Italian. LaGuardia, would be well-remembered as a Congressman who supported aviation and Billy Mitchell in the 1920s and as a colorful mayor of New York City in the 1930s.

After the greetings were over, McGilvary and the other trainees got down to work learning how to fly a Caproni bomber. It was a large biplane, with a wingspan of seventy feet and a chopped fuselage that extended about half the distance to the tail. Power came from three 400 horsepower Fiat motors, two mounted tractor fashion between the wings with the third mounted as a pusher at the rear of the fuselage. The crew consisted of a pilot/bombardier, co pilot and observer/gunner who all rode in an open cockpit in the nose of the plane. A second gun was

mounted in a turret mid-way on the fuselage which the gunner reached by climbing onto the wing and walking back to it. The Caproni could also carry up to two thousand pounds of bombs mounted on the underside of the wings which were released via a lever mechanism connected to the cockpit.

"Capronis were not built for acrobatics," reminisced the historian of McGilvary's unit, "but they rode the bumps in the air like ocean liners..."

Their mission was to bomb Austrian army

After the war Rodney Williams returned to Wisconsin and continued to fly. He was one of the founding members of the Waukesha Aviation Club and manager of the Waukesha Airport for many years.

While the large majority of American pilots flew in France and Belgium, a few were detailed to lesser known assignments. Paton McGilvary was a Madison native who completed ground school at the University of Illinois in the summer of 1917. He was sent to France and then on to training in Caproni Bombers with the Italian Air Service at Foggia, which is located about three-quarters of the

positions in the foothills of the Alps and threaten
the main Austrian naval base at Pola, on what is
now the Adriatic coast of Croatia. They were the
first bombers to fly over the Alps and across large
stretches of ocean on both day and night missions.
Accordingly the Capronis were also among the first
aircraft equipped with lights, both to facilitate
night landings and to flash warning signals so
friendly anti-aircraft batteries would hold their fire
when the planes returned to their airdromes at
night.

Lieutenant McGilvary made his first flight
over enemy lines in September, 1918 and later participated in a night raid that dropped sixty tons of
bombs on Pola. One of the largest single bombing
missions of the war, the Pola raid required the
bombing crew to navigate by the stars, find their
targets in the dark, release their bombs and return
safely to a darkened landing field.

Paton McGilvary survived his three months of
combat as one of the pioneers of aerial bombardment in one of the war's more obscure theaters
and came home to Wisconsin wearing the Italian
Cross of War.[4]

IN THE UNITED STATES ARMY AIR SERVICE

While many Wisconsin aviators served with
America's allies, most entered the United States
Air Service, trained and flew with American
squadrons. The Air Service actively recruited college students and even before the war established
aviation ground schools at colleges and universities
throughout the country. The University of
Wisconsin did not have a ground school, but many
Wisconsin men attended classes at the University
of Illinois in Champaign. The course lasted four to
eight weeks and theoretically prepared students for
training in an actual aeroplane. Many Wisconsin
students entered the Air Service via this route and
some of the state's most distinguished aviators
were also university alumni.

Other prospective pilots got in the air by
directly enlisting in the army and volunteering for
the Air Service. Because of the excitement and
romance connected with flying, and the grim reali-

ties of war in the trenches, the Air Service was very popular.

Although he was a healthy, athletic college graduate, Paul Collins of Stevens Point failed his first Air Service physical and was told to join the infantry. After he produced a report from his own doctor testifying to his superb health, the examining physician told Collins that, "It's quite apparent that flying is all important to you. I'll pass you." Later, Collins learned that since so many young men wanted to join the air corps army doctors routinely rejected one-half the applicants. Without his enthusiasm, his college degree and his previous medical exam, he would not have made it.

Paul Tobey of Wausau got past the physical and also a series of additional tests that included being spun around in a chair to test his equilibrium, focusing his eyes on a tiny dot on a far wall to test his vision and writing at a desk while, without warning, a gun was fired near the back of his head—apparently to test his nerve under fire. Then it was on to flight school at San Antonio, Texas, where he must have been a good student. In a letter home to his family, Tobey described his solo flight in the standard army trainer, a Curtiss JN-4:

It was a thrilling experience I can tell you...I taxied the ship to right and left, just turning it sufficiently to see no ship was ahead of me, looked all around, settled firmly in my seat, and gave her the gun, and I was off. The first trip around wasn't very exciting, except as the radiator sent a stream of water back onto my face and goggles so that I couldn't see...My first landing was about as bad as a landing can be without breaking anything, which means that it wasn't so bad after all.

My last trip around was the most exciting of all of them, for I had a dead motor... I was about eight hundred feet up over a patch of woods when I began to smell burning paint and oil, and the engine began to smoke, the big clouds enveloping me as we raced along. I didn't know whether I was in for a fire, or what, but the next instant the motor stopped completely...I had to look for a landing place, and that mighty soon....so I put her nose straight down, cocked her on her ear, and made a ninety degree turn toward the field...I just reached the field, leveled off and made a three point,

cross wind landing, coming down like a bundle of feathers. I couldn't have made a better one if I had tried for a month of Sundays...

If they survived flight training, the next step for aviators was to cross the North Atlantic. The trip onboard a troop transport was usually uneventful in the military sense, but often rough on the stomachs of Wisconsin boys who had little opportunity to acquire sea legs. The most serious tragedy involving aviators on the North Atlantic was the torpedoeing of the troopship Tuscania, with the personnel of three American Aero Squadrons on board. One Wisconsin pilot, Rellis Conant of Westfield, just missed being on the Tuscania. His squadron, the 168th, was scheduled to travel on the ill-fated ship but at the last-minute, and perhaps by error, the 158th Aero Squadron went in place of the 168th.

Once in Europe, training began with British or French squadrons, which offered its own hazards.

Above: Air Service Curtiss trainers lined up and ready at the flight school many Wisconsin aviators attended near San Antonio, Texas. (University of Wisconsin, Stevens Point)

Below: Air Service pilots in training at Wright Field, Ohio, including Ashland native, Harold Bretting. (Bretting Family)

John Buckley of Grand Rapids in Wood County, was training in a Spad with the 28th Pursuit Squadron when the German army advanced and forced his entire unit to retreat to safer ground. Buckley was later involved in a bizarre accident when he and a squadron mate, flying in clear weather over their airdrome, just missed colliding head on. At the last minute, each pilot turned to his right, but not soon enough to prevent sheering the left wings off of their planes. Buckley later went on to participate in the St. Mihiel air battle then transferred to an observation squadron. On November 8, three days before the war ended, he and his observer were aloft when a stabilizer crumpled and the plane plunged 2,000 feet to earth. Neither man survived.

Top: Paul Meyers
Bottom: Ora McMurray

Paul D. Meyers was more fortunate. A Milwaukee native who starred for the University of Wisconsin football and basketball teams in 1915 and '16. Meyers arrived in Europe in April 1918, trained with a French observation squadron, then was transferred to the First Observation Squadron of the American First Army, under the command of General Billy Mitchell.

The First Squadron was equipped with the French Salmson two-seater airplane, considered to be the finest reconnaissance airplane on the Western Front. With its 230 horsepower rotary engine, and one machine gun each for pilot and observer, the Salmson was well-equipped either to outfly or outfight most enemy aircraft.

Meyers flew his Salmson on a reconnaissance flight in April 1918 in the Chateau-Thierry offensive. The usual tactic was for observation planes to be accompanied by an escort of pursuit planes that took and held control of the sky long enough for the observers to do their jobs. However, ground forces needed aerial intelligence reports even when escort planes were not available. On one such day, Lieutenant Meyers received orders to go aloft and cross enemy lines. Although the weather was threatening, Meyers took off and headed for the enemy. Intelligence required that he fly low—no higher than 1,000 feet—vulnerable to attack from above and anti-aircraft fire from below. Indeed, a plane flying at such a low altitude was vulnerable not only to anti-aircraft batteries but to just about any gun that could be fired into the air.

Another Wisconsin observation pilot, Asher Kelty of Rice Lake, was killed while flying his Salmson with the 91st Aero Squadron when he was shot out of the sky on just such a low altitude reconnaissance.

Paul Meyers' luck held. He completed his mission, returned to his landing field, and made the necessary report. For this brief but harrowing mission, he was awarded the French Croix de Guerre.

Meyers was later promoted to Captain, served on the staff of the First Corps Observation Group and commanded the First Observation Squadron in October and November, 1918. He remained in aviation after the war and became the first commander of the Wisconsin Air National Guard when it was organized in 1940.

Another Wisconsin aviator who was awarded the Croix de Guerre was Ora McMurray. Born in Evansville and a University of Wisconsin student, he joined the French Ambulance Service in January 1917, served six months at the Front, then transferred to the United States Air Service. He trained with the French and made his first sorties into combat as the pilot of a Salmson observation plane. On one mission, McMurray and his observer were attacked by four enemy Fokkers. Taking advantage of the fighting qualities of their plane and their own abilities, McMurray and his observer drove off the enemy planes, crippling and perhaps downing two of them. On the way back to his own lines, McMurray spotted an enemy artillery column on the move, dove and strafed it. Wounded by enemy fire, he nonetheless piloted his machine and crew to a safe landing.

In August 1918, McMurray was flying a Spad with the American 49th Pursuit Squadron. In October he helped a wingmate shoot down one enemy Fokker then downed another by himself. He continued to fly with the 49th until the Armistice and is credited with another combat victory.

After the war ended Ora McMurray returned to Madison to complete medical studies at the University of Wisconsin. Here he palled around with a barnstormer named Cash Chamberlain and a pilot wanna-be from Waunakee named Bob Reeve. Later McMurray practiced medicine in Eagle River and became an active member of the American Legion who flew his own airplane in the big Legion membership drives of the late 1920s and 1930s.

American pilots relied on British or French machines because the pilots were ready to fly before the American airplanes were. The first American-made DeHaviland-models, equipped

the Air Service in the United States until February, 1918. Of the 6,200-plus machines delivered to the Air Service in Europe by the Armistice, only about 1,200 were American-made, nearly all of them DeHaviland DH 4s.

The DH 4 was a two-place observation plane with machine guns mounted fore and aft like the Salmson. Although it often suffered in comparison with the Salmson, and was later maligned as a "flying coffin" by air mail pilots, the D.H. 4 was flown with distinction by at least one Wisconsin pilot.

Rellis Conant was born and raised in tiny Westfield, in Marquette County and entered the Air Service in June, 1917. After training in Texas, he was assigned to fly a D.H. 4 with the 168th Observation Squadron and took part in the St. Mihiel and Meuse-Argonne offensives. Conant has unconfirmed credit for downing two enemy airplanes and a confirmed credit for an observation balloon.

Taking down a balloon was not as easy at it might appear. Although big, clumsy, stationary targets, the gasbags were protected by batteries of anti-aircraft guns and by pursuit planes in the air. It was also very difficult to surprise a balloon, since an alert observer could spot an airplane long before the plane was a threat and signal a warning to his defenders.

Of Wisconsin members of the Air Service, probably no one knew more about attacking and defending balloons than Alvin Reis. Starting as a Lieutenant in the First Balloon Company, he

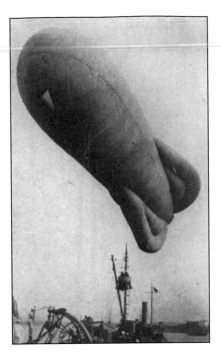

would spend 249 days at the Front, about half the total time the United States was in the war. In the final American offensive of the war at the Meuse-Argonne, Reis was promoted to the rank of Major and commanded a Balloon Group of six companies. He ended his tour of duty in the army of occupation, where on January 19, 1919, he rode in the gondola of the first American balloon to be launched on the German side of the Rhine River. Reis came home to Wisconsin after the war and pursued a successful career as an attorney, state legislator and circuit judge in Dane County.

The balloons under Reis' command were tethered or "kite" balloons and a company consisted of observers who rode in the gondola and ground crew who filled the balloon, dragged it into position near the trenches, tended the winch that controlled its altitude and manned the machine-guns that helped defend it. The observer's first job was as a spotter for the artillery. He kept track of when shells landed on target and when they didn't, communicating with the ground via a telephone line. He could also

report enemy troop movements and keep score on dogfights between friendly and enemy planes. World War I was an artillery war and balloon observers played an important role. They were also very vulnerable, as witnessed by Lieutenant L. B.

An unidentifed group on the campus of the University of Wisconsin. During World War I, the University's Forest Products Laboratory experimented with propeller construction, adhesives and lamination. (WAHF)

Rowe of Brodhead, who left a good account of the hazards the army balloonist faced:

"They [the Germans] have one aviator that is a pippin at getting our observation balloons. I've seen him get three close to us within a week. He soars high up over 15,000 feet or better, and his own anti-aircraft puts up a barrage as a blind...Then he circles over one of our balloons and dives straight down or at a slight angle. When he gets within about 200 yards of it, he lets go with a stream of explosive bullets, puncturing Mr. Gasbag...He flattens out after thirty or forty shots and...flies away as fast as his boat will take him...

Oh yes, the poor innocent aeronaut, the balloonist, was forgotten, but never mind, he has been out in his parachute for some time when the aviator dives, and about ten seconds after a stream of hot lead goes through the balloon, she bursts into flames, rapidly burns up and falls to the ground.

World War I was the last war in which manned balloons were used in combat. Although a better platform for artillery observation than an airplane, the balloon was far too vulnerable to attack, especially as airplanes and armaments

improved in the 1920s and '30s. Like the battle ax and the cavalry charge, the manned balloon became a relic of a bygone war.[5]

THE WAR AT HOME

Prior to World War I, the aviation industry in Wisconsin consisted of homebuilders and a few manufacturers who built airplane parts on custom order for them. For example, the Matthews Brothers woodworking company of Milwaukee, could and would turn out wooden propellers on order. There is some evidence that the J. I. Case Company of Racine considered building airplanes as early as 1912, but production did not begin and, even though it was the company trademark, the Case eagle did not go airborne.

If it was slow to enter the aviation field, Wisconsin was not much slower than the rest of the country. In 1916, American manufacturers produced only about 400 aircraft, far fewer than homebuilders were cobbling together in their back-yards.

With well-established industries producing woods products, machinery and gasoline engines, Wisconsin was in a good position to diversify into aviation. A hundred woodworking mills in cities as large as Milwaukee and Oshkosh or as small as Algoma and Park Falls were well able to cut and assemble the framework for aircraft fuselages and wings. Wisconsin woodworkers also could have easily shaped and balanced propellers, built light-weight, watertight pontoons or hulls for flying boats, but most did not. One exception was the Hamilton Manufacturing Company of Two Rivers, a maker of fine cabinetry, which produced framing for DH 4s in 1918.

The war did bring university technologists into aviation. The University of Wisconsin's Forest Products Laboratory began research in the use of wood in aircraft. University people studied the kiln drying of aircraft spruce, devised adhesives for assembly and lamination, and concocted coatings to preserve propeller blades. Some of this work would pay big dividends, but not until after the war.

Accordingly, the same Wisconsin companies that were building tractors, trucks and motorcars, plus gasoline engines of all sizes, might have switched to aircraft engines and other parts had the American involvement in the war lasted more than twenty months.

In short, the aircraft industry of Wisconsin was a casualty of peace. Yet, as always in history and in life, there were exceptions, and in Wisconsin very impor-tant and flamboyant exceptions they were.

Thomas F. Hamilton was born in Seattle, Washington in 1894, A genuine boy aviator, he built and flew his own aeroplane when he was 16 years old in 1910. He was the first person to fly an aeroplane in the state of Washington and probably the youngest person anywhere to organize an aeroplane manufacturing business. The first Hamilton Aero Manufacturing Company was founded in Seattle in 1910. It was a genuine family business. Young Tom built the aeroplanes and Tom's Mom placed ads in avia-tion periodicals, took orders, shipped flying machines to customers and paid the bills. Before he was twenty years old, Tom Hamilton was build-ing and selling aeroplanes and flying boats of his own design, as well as marketing aircraft motors and propellers by mail throughout the United States and Canada and even as far as New

Zealand. Imaginative, inventive and hard working, Tom Hamilton started out a success and remained successful throughout his life.

After the British Empire, including Canada, went to war in 1914, the Canadian market for avi-ation equipment mushroomed. Hamilton opened a second aircraft factory in Vancouver, British Columbia, and incorporated the Hamilton Aero Manufacturing Company of Canada. He continued to design and build aeroplanes and flying boats and ran a flight training school for the Royal Flying Corps, but developed a special interest in propeller design and manufacture. By the time the United States entered World War I, Hamilton was a recog-nized authority in the field.

In Milwaukee, the Matthews Brothers Manufacturing Company ran a lumber and mill-work operation. Matthews had made a few air-plane props prior to the war and saw that the war would give them an opportunity to expand. They created an Aircraft Department and hired Tom Hamilton to manage it. With his reputation as a prop designer, and as a patriot who had been help-ing America's ally for several years, Hamilton had little trouble obtaining a War Department contract to build propellers in Milwaukee.

The first twelve-cylinder OX-5 Liberty engines went into mass production in August 1917. Two

Propellers destined for U. S. Navy aircraft at Matthews Brothers Manufacturing, Milwaukee, 1918. (George Hardie)

months later the U. S. Navy tested its first Liberties in a Curtiss HS-1 Flying Boat and soon approved the engines for use on its aeroplanes. In short time, the Aircraft Department of Matthews Brothers Manufacturing was making propellers specifically for U. S. Navy Liberty engines. Compared to the JN-4 or the DH 4, only a small number of Flying Boats were built and

Above: Pontoons designed by Tom Hamilton at Matthews Brothers, 1918. (George Hardie)

Right: Brochure depicting the military trainer designed and built by Alfred Lawson that might have gone into production had World War I not ended in November, 1918. (WAHF)

Hamilton/Matthews produced no more than 1,000 propellers. Nonetheless, it was the largest and most successful aviation-related war industry in Wisconsin.

When the war ended, Tom Hamilton decided to stay in Milwaukee. He bought out the Matthew Brothers Aircraft Department and started his third Hamilton Aero Manufacturing Company. In the 1920s, Hamilton Aero became one of the largest wooden propeller makers in the country.

Also during the war, Tom Hamilton continued to experiment with pontoons. Based on his work with wooden floats, he designed one of the first successful all-metal pontoons and, just before the war ended, convinced the Navy to use it. After the war, Hamilton's work with metal pontoons led to the development of the first all-metal airplane licensed in the United States.

By the time Tom Hamilton arrived in Wisconsin, Alfred Lawson was already here. Born in London, England in 1868, Lawson migrated with his parents to Detroit, Michigan in 1873. He spent his youth and teen years there, growing up tall and thin, with a wiry arm that proved to be

good on the pitcher's mound. In 1888, he hit the road as a professional baseball player and knocked around the Midwest and East, playing in a number of cities, including Appleton, Wisconsin. Organized baseball was in its formative years at the turn of the century and Lawson the pitcher soon found himself as a manager, team owner and league organizer. By the time he left the sport in 1907, after failing to establish the Union League as the third major league, he could claim that he had organized more baseball leagues than anyone else in the country. He also claimed to have invented night baseball, since he designed a portable electric powerplant that traveled with his team and lit the field for evening games.

Imaginative and eccentric, passionate and persuasive, Alfred Lawson has been described as "a cross between a crackpot and a genius" and also as "one of the dynamic figures of the pioneer days of aviation." In 1907 he witnessed the flight of a dirigible and "That was the spark that set me afire and forever afterward I was unable to extinguish the aeronautical blaze that burned within me."

In October, 1908, one month after the Wright Brothers exhibited their machine for the United States Army, Alfred Lawson published the first issue of *Fly* Magazine at Philadelphia. Although not the first aviation publication, it was the first aviation magazine targeted at a general audience and was a success with both readers and advertisers. In the pages of *Fly*, Lawson displayed his enthusiasm for aviation and brought into general use the term *aircraft*. He seems to have been so taken with the term that he sold his interest in *Fly* and immediately brought out another magazine, entitled *Aircraft*, with offices in New York City. This periodical printed articles by Glenn Curtiss, Ferdinand von Zeppelin and many other aviation luminaries. It was wonderfully illustrated with color artwork depicting Lawson's fanciful conceptions of the aircraft of the future. Great *air-liners* (another term Lawson all but invented) resembling ocean-going ships and powered by banks of spinning propellers floated through the heavens or hovered at sky ports waiting for passengers to board. In his magazines, Lawson presented a vision of aviation as technologically exciting and gloriously romantic.

Aircraft surpassed *Fly* in popularity and profitability and made Alfred Lawson one of the most well-known Americans in the field of aviation. He helped form the Aeronautical Manufacturers Association, assembled a glossary of aviation terms for the National Press Association and—in typically flamboyant style—purchased a Thomas Flying Boat that he piloted on commutes to and from his home in New Jersey and his office in Manhattan. Alfred Lawson was a successful aviation journalist, but words alone would not contain his "aeronautical blaze." What he really wanted was to see the aircraft of his dreams become real flying machines. Several times he attempted to organize partnerships with men of means or expertise to build airplanes, but they never worked out. One plan in 1913 called for the construction of a monoplane of Lawson's design that would fly across the Atlantic, with Lawson in the pilot's seat, of course.

World War I gave Alfred Lawson his chance to build airplanes. With the War Department committed to using warplanes manufactured in the United States and with his eminence in the aviation world, Lawson thought he had a good chance to obtain a government contract. Financing was still his bugbear. He was unable to convince investors or bankers in Philadelphia or New York to put their money behind him—which explains why he turned up in Green Bay, Wisconsin in the spring of 1917.

Green Bay, like other northern and central Wisconsin cities, had witnessed the demise of its pioneer sawmill industry and had yet to complete the transition to papermaking that would become its next industrial base. Green Bay money was old lumber money looking for a new venture when Alfred Lawson spoke at a meeting of the local Association of Commerce. The United States had just entered the war, the Green Bay businessmen were anxious to participate, and the eloquent Lawson struck the match to an aeronautical blaze.

The Lawson Aircraft Corporation was organized with a modest initial investment of $10,000. The principal stockholders came from the ranks of Green Bay's woods products and papermaking families. George Ellis, of the Britton Cooperage, was president, William Hoberg of the Hoberg

Paper Company was treasurer. Other leading investors were banker George Richardson and F.E. Burrall of the Oneida Motor Truck Company. Alfred Lawson served as vice-president and general manager. As described by the *Green-Bay Press Gazette,* "These officers are all young men and hustlers."

Since they were challenging the most formidable airplane builder in the United States, the Green Bay men would need all the youth and energy they could muster. The War Department had authorized Lawson to build one prototype each of a primary and a secondary military training plane. If these planes were as satisfactory or better than other machines, the Department would, most likely, contract with Lawson to build hundreds, maybe thousands more. The plane the Green Bay manufacturers had to match or surpass was the Curtiss JN, which had been in production since 1914, which the War Department had already ordered by the thousands, and for which the Curtiss Company had recently built the largest aircraft factory in the

Boys at an air
show in Wausau
in the 1920s.
World War I
placed aviation in
the forefront of
public awareness
and created
enthusiasm for
the "golden age"
that followed.
(Robert Wylie)

world. Lawson in Green Bay versus Curtiss in
New York was surely a match between David and
Goliath.

Lawson recruited some very able aircraft
designers and engineers and went to work in
Green Bay. Lawson Aircraft's $10,000 in start-up
capital was just about enough to lease the former
Key-Calk Horseshoe Company building, assemble
one machine and buy one motor. Work began on
the MT-1 on May 10th, 1917, less than a month
after the American declaration of war. On
September 10, the prototype rolled out the factory
door. It looked very much like a JN-4, with its
lower wing shorter than its upper. Unlike the JN,
the MT-1 sported a nose wheel to keep the prop
off the ground on student landings. The motor was
a 100-horsepower Scott-Hall, a bit larger than the
JN-4's 90-horsepower OX-5 engine.

When the time came for a test flight, the pilot
who stepped forward was none other than Alfred
Lawson. When one of his partners suggested that
the flight might be risky, Lawson replied,
"Gentlemen, whose life would a man risk if not his
own?"

The gesture was typical of Alfred Lawson,
who seemed to be fearless when it came to testing
his aircraft. On the other hand Lawson was an
experienced pilot, probably just about as experienced as anyone else in Green Bay at the time.

With Lawson at the controls, the MT-1 flew as
well as expected, ascending to 500 feet, circling
and landing with ease. To George Ellis, the flight
showed that "we can build just as good a machine
in Green Bay as in any city in the country." After
a few more trials, in which the plane proved it
could fly as fast as 75 MPH and take off and land

in rough farm fields, the MT-1 was turned over to the army for its evaluation.

The success of the MT-1 encouraged Lawson and his backers to build a new plant across the street from the horseshoe factory on the corner of Pearl and Howard Streets in Green Bay. With space for up to 500 workers, the Lawson plant was dubbed, "one of the most modern factory buildings to be found in Green Bay or the state of Wisconsin." It was to be the first component of a huge industrial compound that would eventually turn out a large percentage of the "200,000, if not then 500,000," airplanes that Lawson declared the Allies should use in the war.

Work also began on the MT-2, which was an advanced trainer with a top speed of 90 MPH that could also be used for observation and aerial photography. Completed in May 1918, the MT-2 was tested by the army and pronounced to be a superior flying machine and an excellent training plane. Throughout the summer of 1918, Lawson and his partners waited for the War Department order to start production. The stakes were large, since each trainer could be sold to the army at about the same price as a fully-equipped JN-4, or about $8,000.

In the meantime, Alfred Lawson spun out more grand designs. When asked how he would deliver to Europe the hundreds of thousands of planes he wanted to build in America, he proposed the "trans-oceanic float system." He would build a fleet of flat-topped ships from which airplanes could land and take off and station them at intervals in the Atlantic. Planes on their way to the front could stop for fuel and service as needed and arrive on time to help win the war.

Lawson also proposed another new airplane, the Armored Battler, also known as "The Groundhog." This plane was a two-seat pursuit machine with a top-speed of 175 MPH, faster than any plane then flying. The Battler would be armed with six machine guns so at least one could be brought to bear in any direction. The bottom of the Battler's fuselage was protected with armored plating so bullets fired from the trenches below could not hit the pilot, observer, engine or fuel tank. Had it been built and had it lived up to Lawson's expectations, the Battler would have been the ideal plane for the coordinated air-armored-infantry invasion of Germany that Billy Mitchell planned for 1919.

Mitchell's offensive did not occur, nor was the Armored Battler built, nor more MT machines. The war ended before the army could place the order that would have made Green Bay an aviation manufacturing center. Alfred Lawson wanted to shift the company's efforts to the manufacture of

passenger aircraft and he had his usual collection of grand designs, but his Green Bay partners were not interested. They wrote off their investment and Alfred Lawson moved to Milwaukee, where he found new partners to finance his next aeronautical dream.[7]

WAR'S OUTCOME

It has been said that war is the price humans pay for material progress. While the accuracy and morality of that statement can be debated endlessly, it does possess a kernel of truth. The will, effort and treasure that nations pour into warfare has brought about much material, technological and scientific progress and perhaps no where more so than in aviation.

Before World War I, aviation in the United States was not much more than a plaything for millionaires, a pastime for backyard tinkerers and a good venue to fill the grandstand at the county fair. After the war, the United States had an aircraft industry employing tens of thousands that had already manufactured airplanes by the thousands and would continue to mass produce more and better machines. Instead of a handful of pilots and mechanics, by war's end the country had thousands of trained flyers and technicians, with many more willing and able to learn.

The war also made aviation glamorous and noble. Even though, or perhaps because, warfare had become a grim, grinding death machine, the aviators of World War I became "knights." Wisconsin's two World War I aviation authors, Bennett Molter and Lester Maitland, both entitled their books *Knights of the Air.* They were not alone, as evidenced by the postwar popularity of books and movies on the war in the air. The idea of single pilots flying alone into combat evoked romantic images of noble knights in armor jousting man to man in a fair fight, as opposed to the reality of a war where death was an arbitrary visitor that sneaked in with a whiff of poison gas, chattered blindly out of the barrel of a machine gun or pounded out of an artillery shell fired by an unseen enemy many miles away.

As a result of World War I, the United States had the infrastructure and the people to make aviation a part of everyday life for millions of people. The war also gave young men and, to a lesser degree, young woman, another aspiration, another worthy calling for their life's work. Out of the war, came aviation's golden age throughout the country and in Wisconsin.

Paul Culver was born in Eau Claire in 1890 and was working in Ashland in 1911 when two of the most important events of his life occurred. First, he met Edith Dodd. Second, he saw Beckwith Havens fly a Curtiss pusher at the Ashland County Fair. Culver was hooked on Dodd, whom he married, and on aviation, which became his life's work. Edith Dodd was also hooked, by Culver, and by aviation. She shared her husband's experience as a pioneer military aviator and left invaluable accounts of their experiences.

After obtaining his degree from the University of Wisconsin, Culver was one of the first to enlist in the Aviation Section of the Reserve Signal Officers Corps. In 1916, he trained at the Curtiss School in Newport News, Virginia, where he soloed in a Curtiss F-Boat, and witnessed Billy Mitchell's solo flight. Already a commissioned lieutenant when war was declared, he was assigned as a flight instructor in the cadet program at Princeton University, then to Ellington Field, Texas. In May 1918, he was awaiting orders dispatching him to France when a War Department telegram arrived telling him to report to Hazelhurst Field in New York for duty with "the aerial mail service."

Except as a promotional stunt during fairs and long distance flights, the mail had yet to be delivered by air. In March, however, President Wilson had proposed an experiment with regularly scheduled air mail service to and from selected American cities. Congress had appropriated $100,000 and authorized Secretary of War Newton Baker to use Army Air Service pilots in the trial runs.

The plan called for Army pilots to fly a route connecting Washington D. C., Philadelphia and New York City. Six army pilots were chosen for the initial flight and Paul Culver was one of them. The planes selected for the flight were customized Curtiss JN4H Models with 150 Horsepower Hispano-Suiza motors. The controls, seats and instruments were removed from the front cockpit of each Jenny to make an compartment for roughly 150 pounds of mail per plane.

Service was scheduled to begin from Washington on May 15, 1918. Lieutenant George Boyle would fly the inaugural leg of 128 miles from Washington to Philadelphia, where Culver would take over and complete the 90-mile leg to New York. At the same time Boyle took off, Lieutenant Torrey Webb would leave New York for Philadelphia, where he would turn his pouches over to Lieutenant James Edgerton, who would fly them to Washington. Money was appropriated for the army pilots to fly the route daily except Sunday for two months, at which time the Post Office would assess the results and decide whether or not to continue.

It has been said that the U. S. postal service is jinxed with bad luck and the inaugural day of air mail service could be offered as proof of it. May 15 dawned warm and clear with fine weather for flying. President Wilson, the First Lady, several Cabinet officers, foreign dignitaries, and representatives of the press all appeared on time for the takeoff at Potomac Park in Washington. Major Reuben Fleet, the officer in charge of the operation, had already flown the route from New York and

Philadelphia and made sure that everybody and everything was in apple pie order. He had gone over the route with Boyle and had personally helped tape a railroad map to the pilot's leg so he could follow the route to Philadelphia.

A few minutes before the 11:00 AM takeoff, Lieutenant Boyle's Jenny was rolled onto the runway. A Post Office truck wheeled dramatically into the park and screeched to a halt next to the plane. Four bags of mail, including one letter personally cancelled with President Wilson's signature, were transferred from truck to plane.

The postal workers stepped back, the dignitaries smiled for the cameras, the officers gave the signal to takeoff. Boyle called out "Contact" to his mechanic, who spun the prop. Nothing happened, not even a cough or a sputter. "Contact" Boyle called out again. The mechanic pulled the prop. Nothing happened.

The President looked at the Secretary of War, who looked at Major Fleet, who looked at Lieutenant Boyle, who shrugged his shoulders in puzzlement. Finally, one of the mechanics thought to look in the fuel tank. It was bone dry and, even worse, no one had remembered to bring gasoline to the park. Fortunately, a British airplane was on display nearby as part of a war propaganda exhibit and it had a full tank. The mechanics borrowed what they needed to fuel the Jenny and Boyle took off only a few minutes behind schedule.

The President and the other dignitaries left, but many people stayed in the park to see the New York plane arrive. Lieutenant Culver was ready and waiting in Philadelphia, had already seen Lieutenant Webb land with the mail from New York, but Lieutenant Boyle was no where in sight. After taking off, he had circled Potomac Park and, instead of heading north to Philadelphia, turned south into Virginia. He did not realize his mistake until he had flown twenty-five miles in the wrong direction. Now worried that he did not have enough fuel to retrace his course, he tried to land in a farm field. Things could have gotten worse, and they did. Boyle's landing gear caught on a pothole, the nose of the plane dropped and the prop splintered, stranding the Jenny, Boyle and the U.S. Mail. Now Lieutenant Boyle faced the unpleasant task of finding a telephone, calling his superior officer and telling him that, while on the way to Philadelphia he had lost his way, run out of fuel, cracked up his machine, and left the first shipment of United States Air Mail stranded in a farm field in Virginia.

The other pilots had better luck than the hapless Boyle, who had earned the distinction of being the first pilot to be in the air mail service and also the first to be fired out of it. Despite this wrong-headed start, the Washington-Philadelphia-New York route soon became a milk run. Army Air Service pilots continued to man the planes until August 12, when the initial experiment ended. In that time Paul Culver made 36 flights, clocked just under 48 hours of air time and logged in just over 3,000 miles.

The United States Air Mail was on its way to becoming a regular and reliable service and Paul Culver helped get it started.[8]

WORLD WAR II
The War At Home

THE END OF THE DECADE

For Wisconsin aviation the decade of the 1930s ended as it had begun—with great promise. The economy was rebounding off its mid-1930s low spot and aviation shared in the recovery. The late 1930s saw a noticeable increase in the pace and volume of aviation activity across the state, whether it be in air shows, airline travel or recreational flying.

The introduction of new aircraft also renewed interest in aviation. The new planes ranged from the window-rattling B-17s and the jumbo China Clippers, to handy sport jobs for Sunday pilots like the Piper J3.

The airport situation had also changed. Many marginal operations had reverted to hayfields, but many other airports had and were benefitting from federal public works spending. For example, by the time the Works Progress Administration (WPA) packed up its last shovel in 1943, its workers had constructed eight new airports, ten new hangars and more than twenty miles of new runways in Wisconsin, all built according to federal specifications. In addition, every other publicly-owned airport in the state also received WPA funds for remodeling and improvement that, to name a few projects, graded runways in Green Bay, improved

Waukesha aviators and a new J-3 Cub in 1940: (l-r) Ella Mae Davies Coleman, Olive Priess Crites, Mary Nell Dunlap Frey and Mary Lehman Crites. (WAC)

lighting at Superior and built a seaplane base at Wausau.

To use these new and improved airports, Northwest and other established air carriers, as well as at least one newcomer out of Clintonville, were exploring the possibilities of extending airline service throughout the state. The long-awaited northwest-southeast route connecting Milwaukee, Oshkosh, Wausau and Superior almost became a reality in these years.

Airlines needed pilots and pilots required training, but flight training was still too expensive for many an aspiring flyer. The situation was eased a bit in 1939, when the Civil Aeronautics Authority offered to subsidize pilot training programs at universities, colleges and technical schools. By the spring of 1940, 183 Wisconsin aviation students were in CAA training at Madison, Stevens Point, Whitewater, Oshkosh and Milwaukee.

Federal involvement in airport construction and pilot training stimulated state interest.

Wisconsin's aviation policy, which had been one of benign neglect ever since the days of "Flying Governor" Kohler, became more active in the late 1930s. The legislature created the first Wisconsin Aeronautic Board in 1937 and later authorized the State Planning Board to draw up the state's first airport system plan, which was published in 1940. Having made these first steps, the state pursued a steady course of involvement in aviation.

The threat of a major war, which had already broken out in China in 1937 and Europe in 1939, was a sad but real encouragement to aviation. The Civilian Pilot Training Program, which expanded the earlier CAA program, was fully funded in 1940. It brought thousands of young men into aviation who would soon step into military service.

American support of Great Britain and its allies strained the bonds of strict neutrality, but stimulated war-related industries in state and out. Oshkosh Mayor Ed Oakes and Milwaukee's most aviation-minded business leader, Clarence Muth, admitted that—as long as the U.S. was not involved—a war overseas was not all bad, since it was good for business at home. In August 1940, the *Milwaukee Journal* reported that since the beginning of the war in Europe in September 1939, Wisconsin had received "more than $29,000,000 in direct orders and jobs for 16,900 persons."

"That's what one year of war has meant for Wisconsin industry! And it's only the beginning!" exulted the *Journal*. Since Wisconsin's aviation sector was small, only a few of those jobs were in aviation-related industries, but the positive nature of the turnaround was evident.

Many young Wisconsin aviators, such as Kohler's Tony Brotz, and Milwaukee's Ted Vogel and "Fish" Salmon, would agree with the *Journal* reporter. They were able to leave Wisconsin in the late 1930s to pursue careers with Boeing and Lockheed. Already at Boeing was Stoughton native Claire Egtvedt who helped design the B-17 and who would rise to the top executive position with the company.

In Wisconsin, the threat of war had stimulated the completion of the state military air field at Camp Williams and had encouraged speculation about additional air bases in Madison, Milwaukee, Wausau and Superior. It also prompted the organization of the state's first Air National Guard squadron at Milwaukee, with talk of additional units coming in the future.

So when the Japanese dive bombers and torpedo planes rained out of the sky above Pearl Harbor on December 7, 1941, Wisconsin aviation was, like the rest of the nation, as prepared as it could be for a war that would change everything.[9]

The War At Home
THE HOME FRONT

On the same day that the United States learned of the Japanese attack on Pearl Harbor, the war came home to airport operators. They received telegrams from the Civil Aeronautics Administration warning them not to allow "any Japanese or suspected Japanese to fly or ride in any aircraft." Since neither the actual nor the suspected Japanese population of Wisconsin totalled more than a few hundred people, airport operators had little trouble complying. Subsequent orders were more challenging. In December 1941, the CAA ordered all pilot licenses suspended and all private aircraft dismantled or placed under 24-hour armed guard. Airports were to be guarded round the clock and all operations recorded. The

new restrictions all but shut down general aviation, especially at smaller airports whose operators could not meet the new requirements.

For many aviators, the new restrictions didn't matter, since they enlisted in the armed forces or flew for the military as civilians. Others continued to fly by signing up as flight instructors in military aviation training schools or by enrolling in the Civil Air Patrol.

Organized before the United States entered the war, the Civilian Pilot Training program was reorganized as the War Training Service after Pearl Harbor. The University of Wisconsin at Madison, state teachers' colleges at Whitewater, Oshkosh, Platteville, La Crosse, Milwaukee, Stevens Point, River Falls, Eau Claire and Superior managed CPT/WTS programs, as did vocational schools in communities without a four-year college. The largest WTS program at a Wisconsin teachers college was managed by the Milwaukee State Teachers College in cooperation with the Knaup Brothers at Milwaukee County Airport. Superior State had one of the smallest enrollments but it could claim the most famous graduate in Richard Bong. Potential Navy pilots were trained at the Stout Institute in Menomonie and Carroll College at Waukesha, while Milton and Beloit were involved in glider training.

WTS was part of the Army Air Force Reserve program and trained potential military cadets and men who were ineligible for regular military flight training because of some minor disability or because they were more than twenty-eight years old. After graduation they were expected to become flight instructors or contribute to the war effort as civilian pilots. In addition to WTS, which was phased out in mid-1943, Wisconsin's colleges also participated in regular army and navy aviation training programs.

Steve Wittman managed a large Army Air Force program in cooperation with Oshkosh State. Wittman recalled that under the CPT/WTS program between 1940 and 1943, he trained 103 pilots. In '43 he started the "Army Indoctrination Course" for 699 students who each received ten hours of flight instruction. Wittman later estimated that he and his instructors flew 17,865 hours of training, "equivalent to 1,339,857 miles."

Wittman also said that he "was obliged to furnish my own ships, and assume all responsibility as to maintenance and insurance. Our school had six training ships, and five instructors...

"When the Army Indoctrination Course started in May, 1943, I was obliged to rent training ships from the government and was forced to dis-

Paul Poberezny. He recalled that, "It was the summer of 1942. We flew our Cubs with precision and grass-roots talent; the flight instructors were also learning as they instructed. We did our ground school and bookwork at night and our flying during the day."

The army program at Madison was conducted by the University of Wisconsin in conjunction with Louis Wuillemeir at Royal Airport and Howard Morey at Middleton. Morey began his military training career managing the Army glider program at Janesville City Airport. After supervising the training of about 1,000 glider pilots, Morey returned to Madison and, with the municipal airport he founded now in the hands of the Army Air Force, opened a new landing field in Middleton. Approximately 1,500 pilots graduated from the Morey/Wisconsin training school there.

The glider facility Morey opened at Janesville in conjunction with Art Hodge, Joe Bouzaine, Milton College and Whitewater State Teachers College was one of two glider training sites in Wisconsin. The other was in Antigo, where the Anderson Brothers and Leonard Larson prepared another 1,000 young men for cockpit duty in gliders. Training actually took place in Taylorcraft BC-65 trainers, which substituted for gliders when the engines were switched off. Many graduates of these Wisconsin glider schools put their training to work during the invasion of Normandy in June, 1944.

Madison Municipal Airport became the Truax Field Army Air Field after the war began. Named in honor of aviation cadet Tommy Truax, who died in a crash while on a training exercise in the summer of 1941, Truax Field became the site of a radio training school which turned out approximately 20,000 graduates who manned both land and air-based communication equipment.

Aviation education also took place in high schools and vocational schools where students learned aircraft mechanics and maintenance to prepare for military service. In order to stimulate wartime awareness Wisconsin high schools and youth organizations also sponsored programs in aircraft modeling and silhouette-making. Models and silhouettes were useful tools for the airplane spotters who were part of the Civil Defense program.

By mid-1942, nearly 250,000 Wisconsin men and women were involved in Civil Defense work,

pose of my own ships to make room for the government ships, of which there were eighteen. I assumed all responsibility for the maintenance of these ships and any damage to them.

"I employed fourteen flight instructors, one licensed airplane and engine mechanic besides myself, five mechanics helpers and three line men." Many of the pilots Wittman and his assistants trained went on to combat duty in the war and remained in aviation after the war ended.

The experience of the Army's 97th College Training Detachment at Central Wisconsin State Teachers College in Stevens Point was typical. Instruction began when 350 prospective pilots from all over the country arrived on campus in February, 1943. College faculty conducted courses in English, history, geography, physics, mathematics and other subjects. Flight training took place at the Stevens Point airport under the direction of Al Padags and nine civilian instructors in Taylorcraft trainers leased from the Army. Padags had moved to Stevens Point after closing the Tri-City Airport at Wisconsin Rapids. He was able to keep Stevens Point open with help from the city government, which funded a round-the-clock guard at the field.

The cadets began actual flight training after about ten weeks on the ground and graduated as pilots after twenty weeks. The Stevens Point program continued until mid-1944 and graduated 1,200 Army aviators.

Both the army and the navy went to Carroll College in Waukesha. Under the direction of Carroll College Professor Vincent Batha and the Spring City Flying Service of Dean and Dale Crites, over 1,000 pilots completed training for naval and army aviation, including EAA founder

most of which was related to aerial defense. Nearly every Wisconsin village had a movie theater where images played of bomb-damaged cities in Europe and Asia. They were potent reminders of what air power could do to Wisconsin and they encouraged preparedness—even if the enemy was ten thousand miles away.

The first and most obvious Civil Defense measure was the creation of the Civil Air Patrol, which was organized to serve as an early warning system for potential air raids. Wisconsin also developed a force of over 36,000 air raid wardens, 27,000 auxiliary police and fire personnel, plus a bomb squad of 14,500 people. They trained to search the skies for enemy aircraft, to ring fire bells or—in more up-to-date places—sound warning sirens, should enemy aircraft appear. They would also supervise evacuation programs, fight fires and provide medical care for the injured—should a raid ever take place. Also, and just as in war zones, strategically-important Wisconsin cities as large as Milwaukee and as small as Park Falls, with its two sawmills and one paper mill, held blackouts in which all

lights were switched off to prevent enemy aircraft from finding their targets.

Since the American military was successful in keeping enemy forces well away from the United States, the Civil Defense program turned out to be preparation for an emergency that never occurred. However, starting in the late 1940s and continuing into the 1950s, when the threat of aerial bombardment of Wisconsin entered the realm of possibility, the World War Civil Defense program proved to be a realistic rehearsal to meet a threat as real as a Soviet bomber bearing a nuclear bomb.[10]

The War At Home
WISCONSIN INDUSTRY

Wisconsin industry was well-suited for war work and, unlike the 1917-18 conflict, World War II lasted long enough for the state to make a major contribution. By 1944, with the war effort at its height, the Milwaukee War Production Region, which included Racine, Kenosha and Waukesha, was producing war related material at the rate of

Warren O'Brien and Civil Air Patrol members at Nathan Hale High School, Wauwatosa, 1945. (WAC)

Richard Bong at the Globe Shipyard in Superior in January 1944. He presented an autographed photo to Pat Conners, one of the "welderettes" who selected him as their "pin-up boy" for the duration. (Joyce Bong Erickson)

one billion-dollars a year. By the end of June 1945, with the war over in Europe, Wisconsin had produced more than five billion dollars worth of war material, including $21 million worth of communication equipment and $1.7 billion worth of ordnance, some of which was earmarked for the air forces. In the War Production Board's "aircraft" category, which included air frames, armaments, engines, parachutes, props and pontoons, Wisconsin produced $725 million worth of goods. In the Milwaukee-Racine-Kenosha War Production area, the "aircraft" sector constituted nearly one-third of all war work

Kenosha was the state's largest aircraft contracting county, producing $403 million dollars of goods, with most of the work going to the Nash-Kelvinator Corporation for aircraft engines. Also on the list of Wisconsin aircraft contractors were Milwaukee's Holeproof Hosiery Co, which made hose and parachute assemblies; Allis Chalmers, which produced superchargers for B-24s; J.I. Case, which made wings for bombers; and A. O. Smith, which produced hollow-core, steel propellers, landing gear for B-17s, nose assemblies for B-29s, and

trusses for C-47s. A. O. Smith's armaments department produced casings for 1,000 and 2,000 pound bombs and high pressure vessels that, unbeknownst in Milwaukee, were part of the Manhattan Project to build the first atomic bomb. Milwaukeean Art Vredenburg, who worked at the Milwaukee Metal Spinning Company, recalled that high priority work on B-29s was set aside for top-secret metal working that was also destined for the first atomic bomb.

While heavily-industrialized southeast Wisconsin was the largest producer of aircraft equipment for the war, other parts of the state also contributed. The Kohler Company made aircraft engine valves and piston rings, Green Bay Drop Forge made tail wheel assemblies and bomb noses, La Crosse's Trane Company built cooling systems, Consolidated Water Power and Paper Company in Wisconsin Rapids fabricated plastic aircraft components and Waupun's National Rivet Corporation made rivets, of course.

Wisconsin's wood products industry was also part of the effort for the war in the air. Forest resources had dwindled since pioneer times, but woodworking technology had progressed to make plywood an important war material. Strong and lightweight, plywood had many uses in military aircraft.

Although the plant was in Marinette, Michigan, many northeast Wisconsin residents worked at the re-tooled Ford factory to build approximately 5,000 plywood gliders destined for the Normandy invasion. Parts for those gliders and other aircraft were also fabricated by the Algoma Plywood and Veneer Company in Kewaunee County.

The British-designed Mosquito airplane was designed as a high-speed light bomber that did not need defensive armament because it could outfly its pursuers. Part of the success of the Mosquito was its plywood construction and much of the plywood for the planes came from Wisconsin. The ironically-named Lullabye Cradle Company of Stevens Point was one of the states' largest suppliers of plywood for Mosquito bombers and other aircraft. Lullabye had plants at Stevens Point, Fond du Lac, Butternut in Ashland County and Oshkosh.

The Oshkosh plant produced "Pluswood," a "resin-impregnated, heat and pressure treated plywood...half the weight of aluminum but stronger..." Pluswood was manufactured at Oshkosh and, along with veneer from other Lullabye mills, was shipped to aircraft manufacturing plants in Canada and Great Britain.

The Roddis Lumber and Veneer Company of Marshfield and Park Falls also produced plywood for the Mosquito, and for gliders and Cessna trainers as well. Roddis, which specialized in furniture-grade hardwood veneers and plywood made of lower grade basswood, was also one of two Wisconsin companies involved in the construction of perhaps the most unusual aircraft ever made, the H-4 Hercules, more commonly-known as Howard Hughes' "Spruce Goose."

In 1942, with enemy submarines taking a severe toll on ocean going ships, Hughes designed the 200 ton, eight-engine Hercules to serve as a transport plane to fly men and material overseas. It would be the largest airplane ever built up to that time and for many years afterwards. The War Department specified that he could not use any strategic material such as aluminum for his plane, so Hughes opted for birch-veneer plywood. The largest supplier of veneers for Hughes was the Penokee Lumber and Veneer Company of Mellen, Wisconsin. The predominately female work force at Mellen produced 400,000 board feet of birch plys as thin as 1/10th to 1/85th of an inch that Roddis and other manufacturers glued over a basswood core to make plywood up to 3/4 inches thick.

It took Hughes Aircraft more than five years to build the world's largest airplane, which had a wingspan longer than a football field, a fuselage

Left: Wisconsin's largest air defense contractor, Kenosha's Nash Company built aircraft engines by the thousands. (Aeronautics Bureau)

Below: Worker at the Kohler Company assembling a needle-valve for a B-25 bomber. (Kohler Company Archives)

The job of gathering it fell to rural youngsters who belonged to 4-H.

"School children of America! Help save your fathers', brothers' and neighbors' lives by collecting milkweed pods," read the posters delivered to 4-H agents throughout Wisconsin in the summer of 1944. It took about 800 pods to fill one life vest, but the young people went at it with a will and collected 283,000 "onion" bags of pods, well beyond the state quota of 50,000 bags. Plans were made to gear up for a greater effort in 1945, but the war ended in August. With the coming of peace, the heroic saver of lives at sea became a common weed once again.[11]

WORLD WAR II
WISCONSIN IN THE AIR WAR

Wisconsin aviators took part in every phase of the military effort in World War II. They served in every location where the global war was fought and were in action from the moment the first American targets were under attack. About 332,200 Wisconsinites, including 9,300 women, served during the war. Approximately 50,000 people served in the army, navy or marine air corps. Others served as civilian flight instructors, as Women's Air Force Service Pilots, or in the Civil Air Patrol and air ferry commands.

longer than a hockey rink and stood over seven stories high. The Hercules made its first and only flight in November 1947, and has remained aviation's largest curiosity ever since. An enterprising reporter nicknamed the Hercules "the Spruce Goose," but even that is misnomer, since the plane also contains significant amounts of Wisconsin white birch and basswood. As Wisconsin aviation writer Don Winkler characterized it, Hughes' ill-fated plane was neither a goose nor a lemon, but a Mellen.

Unusual as it was, the Hughes Hercules was not necessarily the oddest aviation-related enterprise to engage Wisconsin people during World War II. The designation for most unusual should go to the project that dispatched thousands of 4-H youngsters to the fencerows and unused farm plots to gather milkweed pods.

Among the strategic commodities lost when the Japanese occupied southeast Asia was kapok, the lightweight and bouyant plant material used to stuff the "Mae West" life vests worn by aviators. With kapok a casualty of war, researchers sought out alternatives and discovered that the silky hairs of the feather-like milkweed seed were hollow and trapped air enough so that a mere twenty-two ounces of milkweed silk could keep a grown man afloat for four days. Since milkweed fluff was such an excellent insulator researchers also proposed that it be used to replace the heavy, non-bouyant sheepskin lining in flight suits.

Milkweed was going to war in Wisconsin and throughout the eastern half of the United States. No Wisconsin farmer worth his oats would leave milkweed sprouting in his fields, but it was plentiful on just about every other patch of ground.

Of 8,149 Wisconsinites who died in the armed forces, 6,500 were killed in action; another 13,600 were wounded. Separate figures for aviation casualties from Wisconsin are not available.[12]

IN THE PACIFIC

For the United States, World War II began in the air, with the Japanese attack on Pearl Harbor on December 7, 1941. "The attack started at 7:55 A.M., Hawaiian time on Sunday morning," recalled Milwaukee native Stewart Yeo. "I was still in bed when the first bombs hit an airfield adjoining Schofield Barracks...When we saw the large red spots, the rising sun, on the wings of the planes we only needed one guess..." For the United States, the war had begun.

On that same morning, Navy radioman James Buchanan of Janesville was serving in PBY Patrol Squadron VP-23, with hangars on the water of Pearl Harbor. By the time he rolled out of bed and arrived at his station, the PBYs were riddled with bullet holes and the buildings were aflame. He saw a veteran ordnance chief struggling to free a machine gun from a damaged PBY and ran to help. They freed the gun, loaded it, and, with his hands wrapped in rags, Buchanan hefted the barrel over his shoulder and pointed it at the sky. The chief fired at enemy planes heading for the anchorage known as "Battleship Row" until bullets from a strafing plane killed him. As the chief went down, Buchanan let the smoking machine gun barrel slide out of his blistered hands. Then he experienced, "the sound and sight of the whole world exploding....there before my terrified eyes forty thousand tons of battleship, the USS *Arizona,* blew up..."

Buchanan survived Pearl Harbor and became number-two man in a Curtiss SB2C "Helldiver" bomber. In April 1945, he was on the carrier *Intrepid* near Okinawa and took part in the attack that sunk the *Yamato,* the largest battleship afloat.

While the battle raged in Hawaii, American bases in the Philippine Islands were also under attack. Lieutenant Robert Jones of Ashland and Portage, had arrived at Clark Field north of Manila in March, 1941. He was assigned to the 2nd Observation Squadron, flying O-46s, O-19s, A-27s and B-10s, all relics of the 1920s and '30s. When new B-17s needed hangar space at Clark in the fall of 1941, Jones moved to Nichols Field so he was not on hand to witness the attack on Clark Field on December 8.

The Japanese planes hit Clark while the B-17s were refueling and the P-40 fighters detailed for security were lined up for take off. Virtually every plane was destroyed or heavily-damaged without having left the ground. Japanese attacks on other American air fields were equally successful. Only one day into the war, and the main strength of American airpower in the Philippines was destroyed on the ground.

The commander at Clark Field was Colonel Lester Maitland and the Milwaukee-born hero of the first flight from California to Hawaii was criticized for lack of preparedness. It was his misfortune to be attacked at the worst possible time. Given a few more minutes, the fighter planes would have been in the air to challenge the Japanese. Maitland did have the foresight—unlike the commanders at other American air fields—to dig slit trenches that saved many lives at Clark. Nonetheless, Maitland's career did not recover from the Clark attack. As Japanese troops occupied the Philippines, American and Philippine combatants retreated to the Bataan Peninsula. Maitland was evacuated to Australia and served in the Air Service Command. In 1943, he commanded the 385th Bomb Group of the Fifth Air Force and prepared air fields in Britain for the Normandy invasion. He retired from the army with the rank of lieutenant colonel in February, 1944.

For Bob Jones, the air war continued in the lopsided fashion in which it had begun. On December 10, the Japanese attacked Nichols Field and, as Jones said, "they really clobbered us. First came dive-bombers and fighters, strafing and drop-ping small bombs. They were really aggressive—right on the deck. We stood outside some ammo bunkers, firing our 45s at them....Then the high-level bombers took over....We didn't have many planes left after that."

By the end of December 10, no more than thirty of the one hundred American fighter aircraft present on the Philippines on December 8 were still in condition to fly. On Christmas Eve, Jones and other grounded flyers boarded a steamer that carried them to Bataan, where he took charge of a platoon of "provisional infantry." In early April, the American forces surrendered. Jones survived the infamous Bataan Death March to spend 41 months as a prisoner of war in Japan.

Upon his release in September 1945, he returned to military duty. He piloted B-47s, B-50s and B-52s for the Strategic Air Command and flew C-123s in Vietnam in the 1960s.

While Bob Jones was grounded in December 1941, Fritz Wolf became one of the first American pilots to be victorious in aerial combat. Born in Shawano and a graduate of Carroll College, Wolf enlisted as a naval aviator in 1939. In the summer of 1941, he was at San Diego, training as a fighter pilot on the old USS Saratoga, a battle cruiser converted into an aircraft carrier.

The Japanese had invaded China in 1938 and had occupied about one half the country by 1941. Although still formally neutral, the United States had agreed to allow agents of the Chinese Nationalist government to discreetly recruit American pilots for an air force commanded by General Claire Chennault. Wolf agreed to resign his commission and go to China for one year.

"Our salary was only $350 a month, which was a lot better than I was making as an ensign," he recalled many years later. He would also get $30 a month for food and a $500 bonus for each Japanese airplane he destroyed.

Wolf and other American pilots were part of the AVG or American Volunteer Group. They were better known as the Flying Tigers, from the distinctive gaping maw of teeth painted on the noses of their P-40s.

On December 19, 1941, Wolf was one of a dozen Flying Tigers who attacked a V-formation of Mitsubishi bombers on their way to assault the AVG air base at Kumming, China. As he recounted the engagement, Wolf "attacked the outside bomber of the V. Diving down below him, I came up underneath, guns ready for the minute I could get in range. At 500 yards I let go with a quick burst....I could see my bullets rip into the rear gunner...At 100 yards I let go with a burst into the

198 Fritz Wolf in the uniform of the Nationalist Chinese Air Force, 1942. (WAHF)

bomber's gas tanks and engine. A wing folded and a motor tore loose. Then the bomber exploded...."
It was one of two bombers Wolf shot down on the first day the Flying Tigers flew in combat.

By the time his contract expired in the summer of 1942, Wolf had contracted a severe case of hepatitis. He chose not to join the 14th Air Force, which inherited the mantle of the "Flying Tigers," and flew in the China-Burma-India theater until the end of the war.

Wolf came home to the United States, cured his hepatitis, then returned to the Navy to train fighter pilots. In 1944, he returned to combat on the carriers *Yorktown* and *Essex*. Shot down during an attack on Taiwan, he spent three hours afloat on the ocean until he was rescued.

Back in the air, he flew close support for the Marines fighting on the island of Iwo Jima. "The soldiers were down below being held back by concrete pill boxes, and we were shooting rockets within 100 feet and it got pretty dangerous...."

After leaving the Navy in April 1946, Wolf became the first paid employee of the new Wisconsin State Aeronautics Commission.

Fritz Wolf got into combat early and survived until the end of the war. Austin Straubel entered early and died early. He had joined the Army Air Corps in 1927 after an outstanding career as a football player at the University of Wisconsin and East High in his home town of Green Bay. At the start of the war, Straubel was a major in command of a squadron of B-17s on its way to Java in what is now Indonesia. The bombers would have encountered Japanese forces had they not flown to Java by way of Brazil, Africa and India. In January 1942, the Japanese were moving south through the Philippines and Indonesia. Straubel led a bombing group in an attack on the Japanese forces at Celebes for which he was awarded the Distinguished Flying Cross. A few weeks later Straubel's bombing group was attacked by Japanese fighters off New Guinea. His B-17 burst into flames and five crewmen died, but Straubel— although badly burned himself—was able to make a forced landing on a small island near Java. He was picked up by friendly islanders who got him to a military hospital where he died the next day.

His remains were returned to Green Bay in 1949, and the airport there is named in his honor.

Green Bay also sent James Flatley into the Pacific air war. A 1929 Annapolis graduate, Flatley was the executive officer of fighter squadron VF-2 on board the aircraft carrier *Lexington* in December 1941. The *Lexington* and her sister ship *Enterprise* were prime targets for the Japanese

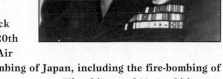

Nathan F. Twining

Few military aviators had as diverse and distinguished a command career as Nathan F. Twining. Born in Monroe, Wisconsin in 1897, Twining spent his teenage years in Portland, Oregon. He served with the National Guard in Mexico in 1916, and graduated from West Point in 1919. He entered the Army Air Corps in 1923, served as engineering officer during the disastrous attempt of the Army Air Corps to deliver air mail in 1933, and was on the staff of the Army Air Force Chief when the U.S. entered World War II. By July of 1943, Twining was in "tactical control" of all Army, Navy Marine and Allied Air Forces in the South Pacific. In January 1944, Twining transferred to Italy where he commanded the 15th Air Force. The B-17s and B-24s of the 15th assaulted targets in Germany and eastern Europe. Their raids on the Romanian oilfields at Ploesti destroyed the Nazi's principal source of gasoline in Europe.

In July 1944, Twining was back in the Pacific in command of the 20th Air Force. The B-29s of the 20th Air Force carried out the strategic bombing of Japan, including the fire-bombing of Tokyo and the first uses of atomic weapons at Hiroshima and Nagasaki in August, 1945.

During the Korean War Twining served as Vice Chief of Staff to Air Force Chief Hoyt Vandenberg. When Vandenberg retired in 1953, Twining succeeded him as Air Force Chief. He was an early advocate of the use of strategic bombing of the Soviet Union as a threat to deter communist aggression. This policy led to the development of the Strategic Air Command, with its long-range bombing capabilities, as one of the three "legs" of American defense in the Cold War years. In 1957, Twining became the first Air Force officer to serve as Chairman of the Joint Chiefs of Staff.

He retired from the Air Force in 1961 and enjoyed a long retirement before passing away in 1982.[13] (WAHF Photo)

raiders on Pearl Harbor, but they were away at sea on December 7. It was one of few Pacific air battles that the *Lexington,* the *Enterprise* or James Flatley missed in the first year of the war.

The *Lexington* was dispatched to relieve the besieged American force on Wake Island, but arrived too late to prevent the island's fall to the Japanese and the capture of two Wisconsin-born Marine Corps aviators—Herbert E. Bartelme, Bowler, and Guy J. Helhofer, Manitowoc.

By May 1942, Flatley had been transferred to the command of squadron VF-42 on the carrier *Yorktown.* He led his squadron as they joined other F4Fs from the *Lexington* at the Battle of Coral Sea. It was the first time in history that two fleets had come together in battle without the ships ever seeing each other. In this four-day battle of naval avia-

A B-25 Mitchell Bomber of the type used to raid Tokyo from the aircraft carrier *Hornet*. (Chuck Marotske)

tors, one Japanese carrier was sunk and two were badly damaged. The Americans lost the *Lexington* and the *Yorktown* was temporarily knocked out of commission.

James Flatley received the Navy Cross for "conspicuous courage in action" at Coral Sea. As his citation continued, "attacking an enemy Japanese carrier...he led a seven-plane division...in a fierce attack...fighting persistently and at great odds, he again led a division of the combat air patrol in a courageous attack against enemy aircraft attacking our surface forces...."

One month later, the hastily-repaired *Yorktown* joined the carriers *Enterprise* and *Hornet* in the decisive victory at Midway Island. In only a few hours, a combination of land-based B-17s and carrier based dive bombers, fighters and torpedo bombers destroyed three Japanese carriers and seriously damaged a fourth. Midway was the decisive battle of the Pacific war. It marked the end of the Japanese offensive and turned the tide in favor of the United States, but not without cost. Among the American ships lost was the Yorktown, which survived two bombing and torpedo attacks before going under.

James Flatley transferred to the *Enterprise,* where he commanded squadron VF 10, known as the "Grim Reapers." As the "Reaper Leader," Flatley flew off the *Enterprise* at the Battle of Santa Cruz and in the Guadalcanal campaign. When a new carrier was built and christened the *Yorktown,*

Flatley transferred to her and was named Air Group Commander. He remained in combat command until mid-1944 when he joined the staff of Pacific Fleet Commander Chester Nimitz.

Flatley remained in service after the war as a carrier captain and air station commander. He attained the rank of Vice Admiral in 1958, shortly before he died of cancer at age 52.

Of all the air battles of the Pacific war, perhaps none so struck the hearts of Americans as the bombing raid on Japan in April 1942. Intended to strike back at the Japanese homeland in return for the attack on Pearl Harbor, the Japan raid was as much a morale-builder as a military assault. It was nonetheless a significant feat of military aviation.

The plan called for a United States aircraft carrier to sail close enough to Japan to launch bombers to hit targets there. No carrier-based naval aircraft had the necessary range for the mission so army air force B-25 bombers were selected, even though no one had ever flown a B-25 off a carrier flight deck. If and when they got airborne, there was no turning back for the B-25s. No plane of that size could land on even the biggest aircraft carrier afloat. Instead the planes would take-off, evade Japanese observation and defense forces, drop their bombs and, if weather and fuel permitted, fly on to safety in that part of China not occupied by the Japanese.

There is a strong Wisconsin connection to the attack, starting with its leader, Colonel James

"Jimmy" Doolittle, a veteran army flyer and protege of General Billy Mitchell. The B-25s used in the raid were nicknamed "Mitchell" bombers. The commanding officer of the aircraft carrier *Hornet,* from which the planes took off, was Captain Marc Mitscher, born in Hillsboro, Wisconsin. There is even a Hollywood link through the Milwaukee-born actor Spencer Tracy, who played Doolittle in the movie version of the raid.

More importantly, three of the eighty crewmen in the sixteen-plane squadron were Wisconsin natives: Sergeant Theodore Laban, flight engineer, Kenosha; Lieutenant Thomas C. Griffin, navigator, Green Bay; Colonel Richard A. Knobloch, co-pilot, Milwaukee. Northland College graduate George Barr also served as navigator on one B-25.

After his plane, "blasted off the deck" of the *Hornet,* Knobloch and his crew "flew on all morning, about 25 feet above the water," for 800 miles. When they reached the Japanese coast, their navigator placed them about 100 miles north of Tokyo. They turned south, came over the mountains separating Tokyo Bay from the sea and saw the city sprawled before them. They rose to 1,500 feet and headed for the docks, where they dropped their four 500-pound bombs. The surprise was nearly complete, no enemy planes scrambled to attack the B-25, and anti-aircraft fire was minimal.

"I didn't have much to do so I put aside a sandwich, got out my camera and took pictures," said Knobloch. "They were the only combat photos to come out of the Tokyo raid."

Now began the real challenge of the mission—reaching China. "We followed the Japanese coastline, rounded the southern tip of the islands then headed due west for China. Because of head winds we never expected to make land. We figured we would run out of gas somewhere over the China Sea."

By 4:00 PM the plane was "lost in fog and darkness." At 10:00 PM, "all four gas tanks registered empty." The crew had no choice but to bail out. "Somewhere below was China or the China Sea, none of us knew which," Knobloch recalled.

"I drifted down silently through the clouds. I looked for the chutes of the other four men in the blackness but couldn't see them. I shouted. Only the occasional swish of the silk canopy above me answered.

"The clouds parted. Below was the most welcome sight a man ever saw—two silver ribbons. They meant land! We had made China after all."

All of Knobloch's crew had landed safely and, after a cold, scary night in the rain, found friendly Chinese to help them. Two weeks later they had

dinner with the Nationalist Chinese dictator and American ally General Chiang Kai Shek. Although his crewmates returned to the United States, Knobloch stayed in China until he flew fifty missions in B-25s.

Thomas Griffin was also fortunate to reach China and land in friendly territory. Ted Laban's B-25 was running short of fuel even before it reached Japan and Captain Ed York decided to head for Soviet-ruled Siberia after the bombing raid. Although an American ally in Europe, the Soviet Union was not at war with Japan and the American flyers were told not to land on Soviet territory. However, Siberia was a better landing place than the China Sea, so there York landed his B-25. The Soviets impounded the plane, imprisoned all five crewmembers and threatened to turn them over to the Japanese. About a year later, the Americans were transferred to a air base near the Soviet border with Iran, from which they were able to escape. In May 1943, they returned to the United States. They were more fortunate than the eight flyers, including Barr, who ended up as prisoners of the Japanese.

As the war in the Pacific progressed, American control of the air increased. American personnel, from pilots to ground crew, were better trained and more experienced. Equipment and material, from fighters planes to fuel dumps, were more plentiful and of superior quality. These facts became evident even to the enemy. After the aircraft of the U.S. Third Fleet, including Admiral Marc Mitscher's fast carrier task force, attacked Taiwan in October 1944 and destroyed over 600 Japanese air craft, one Japanese commander wrote in his journal that, "Our fighters were nothing but so many eggs thrown at the stone wall of the indomitable enemy formation."

In large part due to the success of the Formosa raid, Japanese air power played a minor role in the war's biggest naval engagement which took place two weeks later at Leyte Gulf in the Philippines.

Admiral Marc Mitscher accepted a Wisconsin flag when he visited his home town of Hillsboro in July 1945. (Hillsboro Historical Society)

Once again, the naval air power of the United States, directed by Marc Mitscher, ruled the skies.

Although born in Wisconsin in 1887, Mitscher left the state at age two and did not make much of his roots in the state. He graduated from Annapolis in 1910 and became Naval Aviator No. 33 in 1916. In October 1941, he took over command of the *Hornet* and led her into battle at Midway in June 1942. As part of the Fifth Fleet under Admiral Raymond Spruance and as commander of Fast Carrier Task Force 58, Mitscher gained his greatest fame. Task Force 58 was the most powerful naval striking force yet assembled. It consisted of battleships, cruisers, destroyers and other ships protecting carriers able to launch more than 1,000 aircraft.

There was hardly a naval air battle in the Pacific in which Mitscher, with or without Task Force 58, did not play a leading role: Guadalcanal, Truk, Tinian, Saipan, Guam, Palau, Ulithi, Taiwan, Leyte Gulf, Iwo Jima, Bonin and Okinawa. In the battle for the Marianas, north of Guam, in June, 1944, Mitscher forever etched his memory in the hearts of carrier pilots when he ordered that the strict blackout be broken and

Crew of the B-32 piloted by Wausau's Joe Klein in the Pacific, 1944. (Robert Wylie)

searchlights turned on so late-arriving aircraft could land in the dark. As one of them recalled, "We could have flown anywhere for Admiral Mitscher just to win a battle for him. He was a real aviator who knew about flying and who had a heart for the troubles and dangers of naval aviation."

Mitscher remained in the navy after the war ended. He died of a heart attack while in command of the Atlantic Fleet in 1955.

By the end of 1944, the United States Army Air Force in the Pacific was implementing the long-range bombing strategy of Generals Curtis Le May and Nathan Twining. One of the world's largest airfields had been built on the island of Tinian as a base for the B-29s of the 20th Air Force. From Tinian and other air bases, American army and navy air forces launched the largest air offensive yet known. The "home islands" of Japan were systematically assaulted, including the fire-bombing of Tokyo and the first use of atomic weapons on Hiroshima and Nagasaki.

Not every bomb load was destructive. Bob Wetter of Waukesha was Fire Control Gunner on a B-29 carrying out "prisoner of war missions." In the final months of the war, Wetter's plane was assigned to drop supplies on a POW camp near the Japanese city of Nagoya. "After three hours of searching we sighted the PW camp...We buzzed the camp a couple of times at 200 feet [in a B-29]. I do not know who was more happy to see whom as they were waving so hard and fast I thought they would fly."

The load of medical supplies and food was attached to parachutes and shoved out the bomb bay doors. As the war was drawing to a close, the Japanese, who were not kindly disposed to prisoners in the best of times, were hard-pressed to supply them.

Combat continued even after the atom bombs were dropped. Robert Thomas, a native of Birchwood, Wisconsin, served with the 20th Air Force in the final months of the war. The atomic bombs had been dropped on August 6 and 8, but by August 15, the Japanese had yet to surrender. Accordingly, Thomas and his crewmates on the B-29 they called "The One You Love," set out on one the last aerial bombardment missions of World War II. Their mission was to drop twelve, 1,000 pound mines armed with the explosive Torpex into Japanese seaways.

As late as August 18, even after Japanese Emperor Hirohito had said his nation would surrender, a B-32 piloted by Joe Klein of Wausau was one of four bombers on reconnaissance patrol attacked by Japanese fighters and anti-aircraft batteries over Tokyo. Klein's encounter has been called "the last combat mission of World War II."

The experience of war in the air—the speed,

A restored B-17
Flying Fortress.
(Chuck Marotske)

strained nerves and fear—is difficult to convey in words. One Wisconsinite who did a good job of it was Thurman Fox. He left Oshkosh State Teachers College in May 1943 and became a bombardier with the 13th Air Force in the southwest Pacific. He spent much of the final year of the war making bombing runs in a B-24 from the island of Morotai, south of the Philippines. He wrote home to his family in March, 1945:

"...Do you know what it feels like to make a bombing run over here. ...When you get near the target area you start looking for it, you are fairly calm, and you know what is going on then some one sees it, & shouts there it is 20° left, your heart comes in your mouth, you fall on your knees & start looking through the window for the target, you see it, you check your alt, & air speed, check your sight to see if it is set properly. The Pilot turns on the target, you are now within strafing distance, the nose gun starts firing, the noise & smoke is terrific, you start killing your course, with things running through your mind, ...Your breath comes in short pants, there is a knot in the pit of you stomach, you shake all over from the excitement, and then BOMBS AWAY, ..."

"You live a 1000 lives in 40 secs & then it is all over and you are on your way home, tired by your nervousness, and a calm starts settling over you & you feel at peace with the world."

It was the peace of one who had survived what many others had not.[14]

WORLD WAR II
In Europe

The story of the American air war in Europe is the story of strategic bombing by squadrons of B-17s and B-24s, of P-47 and P-51 fighter escorts, and close tactical support of infantry and armored troops as they fought their way across western, southern and central Europe.

The United States Army's Eighth Air Force made its first attacks on the Continent from England in the summer of 1942. Activity accelerated with the invasion of North Africa in November, 1942 and the organization of the 12th Air Force.

The United States made little use of aircraft carriers in the European theater, but the *USS Ranger* was on station for the North African invasion. Built in 1927, smaller and slower than later models launched during World War II, the Ranger was the first American ship built exclusively as an aircraft carrier. For the North African invasion, the Ranger was commanded by Ashland native Arthur Gavin, who had been a naval aviator since World War I.

In North Africa, the Americans encountered the German Air Force in the open skies over the desert. Among the first in combat was Mark E. Hubbard of Wausau and Green Bay. Hubbard had

Right: Richard Bong wearing the blue ribbon and star of the Congressional Medal of Honor.

Below: Bong in the P-38 which featured the picture of his fiancee, Marge Vattendahl. (Joyce Bong Erickson)

Richard Bong was born on the family farm near Poplar in Douglas County in September 1920. He was the oldest of nine children in a family working hard to make a living in a place where farming was not easy.

As a boy, Dick excelled at sports, loved to hunt and fish, and did well in school. After high school he enrolled in the engineering program at Superior State Teachers College where he planned to spend two years before enlisting in the army aviation cadet program. He hoped to make flying his life's work.

He enrolled in Superior's Civilian Pilot Training program and had completed his primary with Jules Bernt at the Superior Airport when the United States entered World War II. He earned his pilot's wings in January 1942 and in May was taking instruction in P-38s. Powerful, fast and heavily armed, the P-38 proved to be a perfect match for a pilot with Bong's skills. He shipped out for New Guinea in November 1942 and arrived on the big island where the Wisconsin Guardsmen of the 32nd Infantry Division were slugging their way through steaming jungle and tough mountain terrain.

Bong was assigned to the 39th Fighter Squadron and flew as often as he could. By the end of 1942, he had

shot down two planes and by January 8, 1943, he was an ace. "Shot down two of them in my first encounter and got one bullet hole in my plane," he wrote home. "Not bad at all, I would say."

Not bad at all was the way Bong continued to fly and fight. By November 1943, he had twenty-one confirmed kills and was the country's leading ace.

Except for his flying, Dick Bong was as down-to-earth as anyone would expect a son of northern Wisconsin to be. He was hardly prepared for the flood of publicity that engulfed him when he returned home on leave. A clean cut, soft-spoken all-American farm boy turn fighter ace was a public relations dream. Bong dutifully appeared at bond rallies, posed for pictures with his family and answered the same questions over and again at press conferences. He was much more at home in the cockpit of his P-38.

He returned to New Guinea in January 1944 and went back to work. On April 3 he downed enemy number 25 to tie the kill record set by the famed Eddie Rickenbacker in World War I. A week later, Bong shot down another enemy plane to become the all time American Ace of Aces. His assessment of the feat was typically laid back.

"I didn't figure on breaking the record, but they got in front of me so I had to shoot them down."

He merited another leave back home, during which he endured more photo opportunities, press conferences and bond rallies. He did take time out to propose to one of his old Superior State classmates, Marjorie Vattendahl. She said yes.

Bong spent the summer of 1944 in advanced gunnery training. He later remarked that if he had had as much training at the start of his first combat tour, he probably would have shot down twice as many planes. He made up for it when he got back to New Guinea in September 1944. He was assigned as a gunnery instructor who visit-

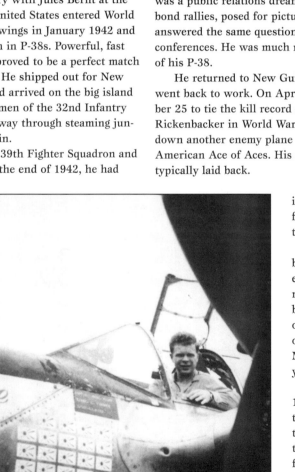

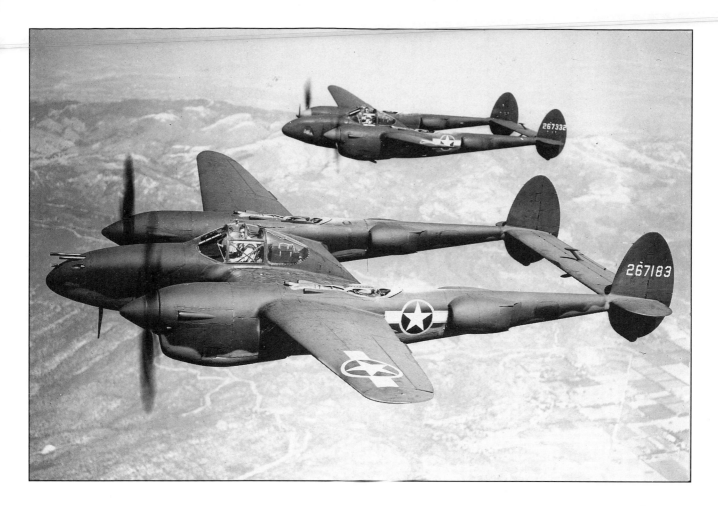

ed squadrons throughout the combat zone. If he chose to he could accompany them into battle, which he did. On October 10, 1944 he became the first American fighter pilot to down thirty enemy aircraft. By the end of November he had 36 victories and had been recommended to receive the Congressional Medal of Honor. While waiting for the medal to arrive, he garnered two more victories.

On December 12, 1944, at Tacloban on the island of Leyte, General Douglas MacArthur presented the Medal of Honor to Richard Bong. "Wear it as a symbol of the invincible courage you have displayed in mortal combat," said General MacArthur at the presentation ceremony. Afterward, MacArthur also said, "Dick my boy, I'm very proud of you."

"Thanks Mac," said Dick Bong.

Although he had every right to retire from combat, Bong returned to battle. He downed two more enemy planes in December 1944, before General George Kenney ordered him back to the United States. When he left the Pacific on December 29, 1944, Dick Bong had flown over two hundred combat missions and shot down forty enemy aircraft—a record no one would match.

Many armchair and genuine aerial combat experts have attempted to assess and explain Dick Bong's abilities as a fighter pilot. Colonel Ken Clark, who flew with him at Tacloban said, "As the days went by at Tacloban, it was readily apparent that Dick's unequaled skill of shooting down enemy aircraft was like that of a top pro-

fessional in any endeavor, a rare combination of physical talent and a cool analytical mind, an ability to concentrate on the job at hand. Dick was not the 'hottest pilot' in the outfit.....He was just exceptionally capable at what he had been hired and trained to do, best the enemy in aerial combat."

Keen eyes, superb coordination, quick reflexes, and the unremitting courage necessary to confront the enemy head on and wait for the opportunity to make the deadly shot—that was Dick Bong at the stick of a P-38.

With his war over at the start of 1945, Bong returned home and married Marge. After an extended honeymoon he reported to Wright Field in Dayton, Ohio for training in jet aviation. He had volunteered to fly as a test pilot in the new Lockheed P-80 and, while the war in the Pacific was drawing to a close, Bong was starting a new career in Burbank, California.

On August 6, 1945, the same day on which the first atomic bomb was dropped on Japan, Bong began to take an P-80 up for a test flight. Seconds into the flight, the plane began leaking smoke. Only four hundred feet into the air, Bong started to bail out, then climbed back into the cockpit. The plane banked to the right then exploded. Bong had been able to eject from the cockpit but was caught in the explosion. He smashed into the ground about one hundred feet from the wreckage of the P-80, his parachute unopened.

The man who had survived 200 combat missions, died as a test pilot, one of the first casualties of the jet age.[15]

The P-38 fighter that helped Richard Bong become America's "Ace of Aces." (Joyce Bong Erickson)

learned how to fly at the Wausau Airport, with his father, Mark C., as flight instructor, and enlisted in the Army Air Corps in August, 1939. By early 1943, he was leading a squadron of P-40 fighters in support of an armored unit advancing against the Germans in North Africa.

A restored B-24 of the type flown by Richard Jerstad on his fateful mission to Ploesti. (Chuck Marotske)

His squadron of twelve P-40s encountered a group of 24 Stuka divebombers escorted by FW and Me fighters. "We caught them completely by surprise." Hubbard said in a newspaper quote.

"Although we came in below 'em they didn't see us until they were about to attack...

"The bombers scattered like ducks...Our boys had targets to burn and fired at everything they saw. The final outcome was that we shot down six airplanes...." Hubbard himself shot down an FW fighter. It was the first of five enemy planes he would destroy in the skies of North Africa.

In early 1944, Hubbard was second in command of a wing of P-51s escorting bombers from England to Germany. He was shot down over Germany and forced to finish the war as a prisoner of war.

As the North African campaign concluded, Allied strategists saw an opportunity to use air power to inflict a crippling blow on German warmaking abilities. In modern warfare, fuel had become as critical as men and arms. For the German war effort, the oilfields of Romania and the massive refinery center of Ploesti were vital resources. Ploesti was one of the most heavily-defended places in Europe, bristling with anti-aircraft batteries and ringed with fighter air bases.

In the summer of 1943, the Army Air Force assembled a fleet of nearly 200 B-24 long-range bombers to assault Ploesti. They had just enough range to make the 2,700-mile round trip from Libya to Romania and could deliver a knock-out blow to the refinery. The planes would fly minus fighter escort since the P-40s and P-38s in use at the time did not have sufficient flying range.

The chief operations officer for the Ploesti raid was Major John J. Jerstad of Racine. Born in 1918, Jerstad was a graduate of Northwestern University and a teacher when he enlisted as an aviation cadet. He had already completed one 25-mission tour as a B-24 pilot and had volunteered for more missions when he joined the staff for Ploesti. "I'm the youngest kid on the staff and it's quite an honor to work with colonels and generals," he wrote his parents.

When the planning was done, Jerstad volunteered to fly the mission as co-pilot for Lieutenant Colonel Addison Baker. His commander tried to keep him on the ground, but Jerstad refused, saying, "Don't worry, sir. Baker and I will make it all right."

The raiders took off from Libya on August 1, 1943. They would fly their B-24s across the Mediterrean, Yugoslavia and Romania at treetop level to avoid detection. Once over the sprawling refinery and its railyards, they would drop their bomb loads and head for safety.

The raid turned out to be a nightmare. Many of the planes lost their way over the Balkans and all were detected by the enemy. Instead of sneaking in at treetop level, they flew through a firestorm of anti-aircraft guns and fighter aircraft. Five miles out from the target, Jerstad's plane hit a barrage balloon cable. A few miles more, and a barrage of flak hit the B-24 in the nose, cockpit and wings. With smoke and flame filling the cockpit and with their wing tanks in flames, Baker and Jerstad could have made a forced landing, but they continued on to the target.

"Their right wing began to drop," reported one witness. "I don't see how anyone could have been alive in that cockpit, but someone kept her leading the force on between the refinery stacks. Baker was a powerful man, but one man could not have held the ship on the climb she took beyond the stacks."

Some crewmembers bailed out, but the plane was too low for parachutes to work. With the cockpit a mass of flames, with pilot and co-pilot still at the controls, the bomber crashed in a clear spot near the refinery. Baker and Jerstad both received the Congressional Medal of Honor for their courage at Ploesti. A total of five aviators were so honored, the largest number of Medals of Honor ever awarded for a single action. John Jerstad was one of two World War II Wisconsin aviators to be awarded the Medal of Honor. The other was Richard Bong.

Ploesti was damaged by the raid but soon repaired and producing as much oil as it had before the bombing. In the spring of 1944, the attacks were renewed, with more bombers than ever accompanied by P-51s that could stay with them all the way to the bombing run. On one raid in August, 1944 a fleet of 1039 B-24s and B-17s dropped 4.5 million pounds of explosives to knock out Ploesti. After the war, German armaments minister Albert Speer declared that it was destruction of the Romanian oil supply in 1944 that won the war for the Allies.

One of the pilots flying a P-51 in escort on those raids was Robert J. Goebel of Racine. He had passed his qualifying test as an aviation cadet in April 1942, and served in North Africa in 1943. He ended up in Italy with the 31st Fighter Group, of the 306th Fighter Wing, 15th Air Force.

Goebel had his first victory in aerial combat over southern Germany in May, 1944: "As I partially rolled out of my turn, I spotted two 109s crossing in front of me, 800 to 900 yards away. Immediately I wrenched my plane into a turn cutting inside to shorten the range as quickly as possible. One, who I took to be a wingman, was lagging behind the other and seemed to be having trouble staying with his leader. I fastened my teeth on him, closing steadily....Then the leader made a sudden, violent turn reversal, which his wingman failed to follow. A bad mistake. I was down to what I judged to be 350 yards. I opened fire, hosing away at nearly 30 degrees of deflection....I concentrated on keeping the sight pipper steady out in front of him....and was rewarded by a few strikes on the forward fuselage. His canopy came off, followed instantly by a dark hurtling figure..."

Goebel would account for at least ten more Me 109s while covering bombers from bases in Italy.

Goebel's 15th Air Force was the powerful air arm of the Mediterrean/Italian battlefront. In western and northern Europe, it was the "Mighty Eighth" Air Force. In January 1943, top British and American commanders ordered the Eighth to begin Operation Pointblank, the day-and-night bombing of targets in Germany. The British bombed by night, the Americans by day.

Lester Rentmeester left the family farm near Green Bay to study engineering at Madison in 1940. Two years later he was a Flying Cadet and,

in 1943, a graduate of B-17 bomber pilot training with a crew on its way to England.

Casualties were heavy in the Eighth Air Force, averaging twenty percent per raid. Losses were so heavy when Rentmeester arrived that, instead of filling in as replacements with experienced crews, the rookies immediately manned their own plane in combat. Veteran pilots told the newcomers that they would have "fighter escort all the way to the target—that our P-47s and RAF Spitfires would accompany us across the English Channel, where the German fighters would then escort us to the target and back to the Channel." The combination of anti-aircraft batteries and unchallenged enemy fighters was deadly for bomber crews.

Rentmeester recorded the sight of a bomber going down: "A B-17 just ahead of us suddenly went into a spin with fire spilling out of it. It looked like a three-dimensional movie—a big four-engine bomber lazily spinning toward white clouds below."

Despite the dangers and like thousands of other soldiers, sailors and aviators, Rentmeester carried on. "One of the things we learned in those last days of 1943 was that the primary motivation driving us during combat was survival, and that in order to survive, we had to carry out our mission successfully. We worked desperately to drop the bombs on target so that we wouldn't have to go back there."

In the beginning of 1944, the situation changed for the B-17s and B-24s of the Eighth Air Force. Squadrons of P-51 Mustang fighters, "the greatest American technical air contribution to World War II," solved the escort problem. In January 1944, Rentmeester took part in the Eighth's last heavy-bomber raid conducted without full fighter escort. In succeeding raids, he was happy to look out of his cockpit and see, "our little friends" flying protective cover nearby.

In 1944, the mission of the Eighth Air Force also grew to include not only the strategic bombing of Germany but the destruction of targets in support of the coming invasion of France.

By the time D-Day arrived, Rentmeester had completed his thirty-mission tour of duty. Of the eighteen men with whom he completed pilot training, only seven others survived the war. Rentmeester attributed his survival to "confidence...hard-won skill and experience...[and] sheer luck." Most important of all was the arrival of the P-51.

The invasion of Normandy required the assembling of the greatest land/sea/air force of the war. One of the participants was James Parsons of

Janesville, who flew a P-47 Thunderbolt in the skies over the beachhead. Parsons patrolled above the Americans landing on Omaha Beach and on dive-bombing missions inside France.

On one patrol, Parsons got on the tail of an Me 109 and—in 45 seconds—fired all 3,600 rounds of his ammunition. The enemy went down, but if any more showed up, Parsons had nothing to shoot at them. He stayed with the other three planes in his Fighter Wing and assisted in the pursuit of another German fighter. When his wingmate also ran out of ammo, they continued to pursue the enemy since, "even if we had no ammo, it was better us chasing him, than him chasing us." Eventually two P-51s with bullets in their guns showed up and downed the 109. Parsons earned a Distinguished Flying Cross for his unarmed pursuit of the enemy plane.

After Allied armies secured the Normandy peninsula, they prepared for the final campaign of the European war. Tactics depended heavily on the principles of air-to-ground support formulated by the strategists of the Ninth Air Force.

The commander of the Ninth, with its 180,000 men and 4,000 aircraft, was General Hoyt Vandenberg. Born in Milwaukee in 1899, Vandenberg and his family moved to Lowell, Massachusetts when he was a teenager. He graduated from West Point in 1923, a member of the first Academy class to which the Air Corps was offered as a career option. Vandenberg joined and quickly became known as one of the army's top young pilots.

He had served as Chief of Staff of the Twelfth Air Force under Jimmy Doolittle in North Africa and on the planning staff for D-Day. Taking over the Ninth Air Force put him in command of the largest tactical air force yet assembled. Here Vandenberg was following the flight-path of his fellow Milwaukee native, Billy Mitchell, who planned and commanded what can be called the first tactical air force in France in 1918.

Cooperation, coordination and communication between ground and air forces were keys to success. As the infantry and tanks of Omar Bradley, Courtney Hodges and George Patton moved across France, they were accompanied by a radar-equipped "air-ground cooperation officer" who kept in constant radio contact with four-ship fight-

er-bomber formations overhead. The planes were an armed reconnaissance force, relaying information to the ground and responding to information sent to them by the troops there.

The system worked so well that it enabled Patton's Third Army to sweep through the German lines, capture Paris and move on. It led Patton to report that, "The cooperation...has been the finest example of the ground and air working together that I have ever seen."

Cooperation couldn't overcome the surprise of the German counterattack in December 1944, but it helped turn the tide in the Battle of the Bulge from defeat to victory. On the crucial four days of the battle from December 23 to December 27, the Ninth Air Force flew 5,291 sorties, concentrating on bombing bridges, roads and railroads to prevent the Germans from reinforcing their troops and on low-level strafing missions on troops, tanks and airfields. A large measure of credit for the victory of the Third Army is shared with the Ninth Air Force.

As the Battle of the Bulge proved, the Allies had won the air war in Europe and winning the air war meant winning the war. Nazi jets and rockets could not make up for the overwhelming Allied superiority in men and material. The war in Europe ended in May, 1945.

Although most American aviators were sent home as soon as possible, Clifford Bowers of Montfort, Grant County, stayed on in Europe until the end of 1945. "All the fighter bases flew all of their fighters —'38s, '47s and '51s in Wattisham [England]. All those pilots were sent home. But, about ten of us stayed and flew them five, six times a day up to Liverpool where they smashed them all up."

The war was over. It was time to beat the swords of aerial combat into the plowshares of peace.[16]

Wisconsin WASPS

Between September 1942 and December 1944, over 1,100 American women flew military aircraft as Women Air Force Service Pilots, or WASPS. The initial women's pilot program was started by Nancy Harkness Love and known as the WAFS, or Women's Auxiliary Ferrying Squadron. As Jacqueline Cochran's larger WASP program developed, the name was extended to cover all women pilots flying for the military.

WASP pilots trained in military aircraft ranging from PT-17s to B-17s, delivered trainers and

Marianne Beard McNutt, in her flight school graduation photo, 1943. (Texas Woman's University)

combat aircraft from factories to shipping points, and towed targets for live anti-aircraft and fighter gunnery practice. The original volunteers were all experienced pilots, with hundreds of hours in the cockpit. Even the women who enlisted later in the program had to have a minimum of thirty-five hours of flying time. By comparison, men joining the air forces did not have to have any flying experience.

At least twenty-five Wisconsin women served as WASPS, including Patricia Hanley, Margaret Bruns, Dorothy Francis and Willette Harkins. Marianne Beard of Milwaukee and Josephine Pitz of Manitowoc were among the first training school graduates in the spring of 1943. They were also among the fifty or so WASPS who also completed training for pursuit aircraft. They could fly any single-engine plane in the American air fleet, including the fast and heavy P-47 and the P-51. In the 18 months they were assigned to the P-47 factory on Long Island, WASPS pilots delivered 2,000 planes to the port in Newark, New Jersey. Jo Pitz herself delivered 142 P-47s in 166 days, including short hops to Newark from Long Island and longer flights from the factory in Indiana.

After eight months ferrying P-47s, Pitz took training in P-40s, P-51s, and P-39s. She also delivered a P-63 to Montana, the first leg of its flight to the Soviet Union.

Although they trained with military instructors and flew military aircraft, the WASPS were rated as civilians. Pay was $150 a month, but the woman paid for their own uniforms, room, board and transportation to and from assignments. They were not covered by government health or life insurance and private companies that had been covering them cancelled their health care coverage and death benefits. The government did offer a $200 funeral allowance and a plain pine box to those who died in service, but prohibited the flag-draped coffin and Gold Star on the window at home accorded to military fatalities.

Pilot training was hazardous and thirty-eight women died as WASPS. One of them was Margaret Seip of Appleton, who died along with her instructor and another student when their UC-78 Bamboo Bomber went into an uncontrolled spin and smashed on impact with the ground.

The risks were real, the pay small, but accepted. Jo Pitz said that she so loved flying P-47s that she would do it for nothing. Marjorie Osborne Nicol of Racine, expressed the spirit of the women pilots when she recalled a song they would sing

Janet Hatch and the TB-26 Martin Marauder she used to tow targets for gunnery training. (Robert Wylie)

when a class completed training:

"You left your mothers and fathers back home on the farms,
You left your husbands and sweethearts in somebody's arms,
You left your love life, your night life, and all such good things—
To get those silver wings."

Nicol and many other WASPS did not get their silver wings before the WASPS were deactivated in December, 1944. By time, the pilot shortage they were helping to fill was over. In addition, pressure to make the women part of the military had increased to the point that even Jacqueline Cochran urged Congress either to "militarize" or disband them. Congress chose to disband them. While many of the WASPS were unhappy, Marjorie Nicol was optimistic. "We are pilots in an overcrowded flying world and the thing is that I can get out now and get a start in commercial flying before the men are released from the army. If I'm lucky I can get something that I can hold on to even after all those hordes of pilots come back to civilian life."

It didn't work out for Nicol. She did not make her career in aviation. Instead, she joined the Marine Reserve, qualified for G.I. benefits and used them to become a college professor as well as the mother of five children.

Other WASP veterans attempted to make careers in aviation after the war. After Eau Claire native Janet Hatch completed her tour as a flight instructor and tow pilot in the WASPS, she moved to Brazil and England and instructed students. She returned to Wisconsin and in the late 1940s was a star on the air show circuit. In 1949, she set a record for consecutive turns in a tailspin at a show in Stevens Point. Flying a 65-horsepower Aeronca Champ, she climbed to 12,500 feet, then made 79 turns before descending to 1,000 feet.

"It took me 45 minutes to get up there, and only 2 1/2 minutes to come down," she said.

The record Hatch broke had been set earlier by another WASP veteran, Jeanette Kapus of Milwaukee. Hatch, Kapus and many WASP veterans continued to fly, but in the postwar years few of them were able to pursue careers in aviation. The abundant supply of male pilots who were war veterans was augmented by new men who used the G.I. Bill to learn to fly. Openings for women were few and far between.

In 1949, commissions in the United States Air Force as officers with non-flying status were offered to WASP veterans. Jeanette Kapus took up the offer and attained the rank of Major before retiring in the 1970s. Many other WASP veterans continued to fly and became active members of the Ninety-Nines.[17]

THE CIVIL AIR PATROL

The Civil Air Patrol was established in 1941, only a few days before American entry into World War II. Its primary mission was to patrol the coast of the United States from Maine to Texas spotting German submarines. CAP pilots flew over twenty-four million miles on anti-submarine patrol, rescued downed pilots and even sunk a few U-boats.

Young John Batten of Racine served in the CAP on the Virginia coast and the experience made a lasting impression. He continued to serve in the CAP and rose to command of the Wisconsin Wing and the Great Lakes Region in the 1950s.

The Wisconsin Wing of the CAP was organized in January 1942, with Seth Pollard of Waukesha as state commander. Group leaders were Archie Towle, Wausau; Henry Lindner, Milwaukee; Frank Lovell, Racine; and Lloyd Graves, Waupun. The state was expected to contribute 500 airplanes and 1,500 pilots, plus trainees. Virtually every person not already in the military who owned an airplane in Wisconsin volunteered for CAP. It was a way to serve during wartime and keep in the air, since the CAP was exempt from the wartime ban on civilian flying and had access to rationed fuel. Since CAP was open to people as young as sixteen years of age it also introduced many a future air corps member to aviation. Furthermore, CAP was open to men and women, and therefore provided a way for females to pursue their interest in aviation.

CAP proved itself to be such a good idea dur-

CIVIL AIR PATROL
WAUKESHA SQUADRON 621-3
OCTOBER 12, 1943

ing the war that it did not die when the war ended. With experienced pilots and surplus aircraft in abundance, CAP expanded in the late 1940s. Squadrons organized in every Wisconsin city from Ashland to Beloit. The recruitment goal for 1951 was to have a squadron in all 57 Wisconsin and Upper Peninsula cities with populations larger than 5,000. However, units were organized in many smaller places, including Stockbridge, Land O'Lakes, Grantsburg and Ladysmith. Headquarters for the Wisconsin Wing in these years was at Racine/Horlick Airport.

One of the new units formed in 1950 was identified as the first all-women CAP unit in the United States. Late in 1949, Wing Commander Colonel Benjamin F. Moeller authorized the formation of a "Women's Flight." By April of 1950, thirty-two women had signed on and the unit was named in honor of Moeller, who had disappeared in the crash of a C-45 in Lake Michigan in March. Staff officers of the Women's Flight were Lieutenants Dora M. Drews, Madison, commander; Nellie Bilstad, Madison, adjutant; Jeanette Kapus, Milwaukee, operations; Elaine Szelstey, Boscobel, communications; Marguerite Brahm, Madison, supply; Mary Heidner, Hartford, public information.

By 1954, 850 adults and more than 1,500 cadets were enrolled in the Wisconsin Wing. They practiced search and rescue operations, prepared to react to a natural disaster or a nuclear attack and, of course, learned how to maintain and fly airplanes. In 1949, five southeastern Wisconsin CAP

personnel received an award for meritorious service for their efforts to save an Air National Guard pilot who had crashed in Lake Michigan. Captains Sarah Lathrop, Milton Bender and Archie Weidner, Lieutenant Isabel Carpenter and Warrant Officer Kenneth Mortag were decorated for attempting to find the downed pilot while flying close to the surface of the frigid lake. Gunshots fired at the CAP planes when they ventured close to shore added a bizarre hazard to the search.

In 1952, under the command of Lieutenant Colonel Stanley Fisher, Racine, the Search and Rescue exercise included fifty airplanes in simulated search for an Air Force C-45 lost somewhere between Racine and Superior. In the midst of the search for the C-45, CAP radios cackled with news of a Piper Cruiser lost out of Fond du Lac. In short time, the "missing" planes, both of which had "crashed," were discovered and CAP first aid kits were dropped over the "wreckage." These two missions were successfully completed when reports were received of a third plane down near Fox Lake. This report wasn't in

Above: Rose Lynch Hoffman flew with the CAP at Wright Field during World War II and later moved to Madison. (Doug Hoffman)

Right: Art Shanley, Waukesha Squadron, CAP. (WAC)

In the Cold War years, CAP also prepared for a nuclear attack on Wisconsin. The CAP would be called on to assist in the planned evacuation of population centers and measure radioactive fallout from a nuclear blast.

With its emphasis on young people and education, CAP made training, student exchanges and scholarships a major part of its program. In the early 1960s, four $1,000 scholarships were available, three for aeronautical engineering open to boys and girls, and one for the humanities, restricted to girls. Although male and female members of the CAP shared the same mission, education and training programs, such as the Jet Orientation Course, were often divided by gender.

In 1961, Milwaukee County built a combination hangar, classroom and office building for the CAP at Timmerman Field. Over 1,000 people attended the dedication ceremonies, enjoyed the military planes on display and applauded the work of the championship Wisconsin CAP Cadet drill team. That same year the entire Wisconsin Wing was rated "Tops" in the Great Lakes Region. It was the one of many such ratings over the years. The Wing led the way in search and rescue, flight safety and communications missions. At that time the Wisconsin CAP had a membership of about 2,000 people who operated 250 aircraft and 400 licensed radio stations.

In the late 1960s and early 1970s, organizations linked to the military became less popular with young people, but CAP held its own. There always seemed to be a core group of young men and women interested in aviation and the opportunities CAP afforded. They were still the "good

the plan, so the pilots and radio people set off again—only to be called back when the report proved to be a false alarm. Search and Rescue CAP operations—SERCAP—were a regular part of Civil Air Patrol training.

On Memorial Day 1956, the Milwaukee CAP made what must have been one of Wisconsin's first aerial traffic reports. Working in cooperation with radio station WRIT, two CAP planes flew over the Milwaukee area and reported on traffic density. The reports were then broadcast over the radio. Years would pass before traffic reports from the air would become a regular broadcast feature in Milwaukee.

In northern Wisconsin, CAP pilots were often called upon to search for lost hunters, with the Superior and Ashland squadrons also called upon to search for boaters or ice fisherman lost on Lake Superior. In 1954, ten aircraft and 100 CAP people from northern Wisconsin groups were called out to search for the wreckage of a plane in which two Illinois women lost their lives. In 1960, the Menominee/Marinette Squadron spotted a man named Harry Poulson clinging to an overturned boat in Green Bay and rushed to land and report its observation. The grateful Poulson later purchased a radio for the unit's plane so it could stay in constant contact with the ground.

samaritans of the airways," as one reporter described them.

By the 1980s, CAP numbers were growing again. Equipment had grown more sophisticated, but the mission was very similar to that of the 1940s. Search and rescue, emergency service, education and training remained at the heart and soul of the operation. Since 1980, the Wisconsin Wing has also volunteered for special duty before, during and after the EAA Convention every year. The Wing even launches a "navy" for the EAA in the form a small boat that patrols Lake Winnebago ready to assist aviators who have trouble on or in the water.

In 1985, after forty years of service, the Wisconsin Wing received state funding. The Wisconsin Division of Emergency Government agreed to allot $20,000 annually to CAP in acknowledgment of the Wing's disaster relief services. In the years since, Wing members added advocacy work with the state legislature to their list of duties. The 1,200 members of the Wing still relied heavily on federal, corporate and private sources. In terms of aircraft, corporate support is very important. The Wisconsin Wing owned fourteen aircraft in 1987, but had access to another fif-

ing, snowshoeing, map and compass skills, ELT location and even aircraft and flight operations out of the Rhinelander airport. CAP Cadets also attended summer camp at Volk Field in cooperation with the Air National Guard.

Just as the CAP offers equal opportunities to men and women, it is also open to people of all ages. It is one of few truly cross-generational institutions, where veterans of World War II spend time with people born almost forty years after the war ended. Families are also involved and have been for years. In the early 1960s, for example, the Wallace and Ruth Federman family of Milwaukee attracted attention because five members of the family belonged to CAP: Wallace and Ruth, and their children Rose, Mary and Rudy. In the late 1980s, the John and Theresa Potterton family, also of Milwaukee, were following in the tradition of

Above: Wisconsin CAP cadets on ground patrol at the EAA Fly-In, Oshkosh. (Don Winkler)
Below: Civil Air Patrol officers and cadets at a weekend training session at Volk Field. (Don Winkler)

teen, including eight Cessna 182s and one Beech T-34.

In 1985, the Wing broke ground for the Alvin Keller Training Center on Pelican Lake near Rhinelander. The 36-acre site was put to use as a training ground for both summer and winter survival skills. The schedule for the winter camp of 1987 included dog team operations, scuba diving, snowmobile operation, first aid, cross-country ski-

the Federmans. John, Theresa, Suzanne and Bill Potterton were all officers in the Mitchell Composite Squadron #9. As Suzanne summarized, "It's a family, not a squadron." The Federmans and the Pottertons are only two examples of many people who have made CAP a family affair.

In 1997 the Wisconsin Wing of the Civil Air Patrol, was made up of 30 squadrons and 1,200 members. Many changes have taken place since CAP was first organized, but much has not. CAP is still a volunteer organization of people who love aviation and are committed to flying.[18]

IN COMBAT
OVER KOREA

Over 132,000 Wisconsin men and women served in the Korean War, more than in World War I. The number who served in the Air Force or in Army and Navy air units is not available, but Wisconsin people took part in all phases of America's first jet air war.

Many World War II veterans returned to active duty for Korea and state Air National Guard units

activated. At first, the planes were more in demand than the people. The F-51s of Madison's 176th Fighter Squadron were shipped overseas not long after the war began in 1950. It was a blessing in disguise for, in 1952, the P-51s were replaced with F-89 Scorpions that made the 176th one of the first Air Guard units in the country equipped with the newest jet aircraft.

Among the Air Guardmen called for active duty were Seymour Levenson, Howard Mattes, Paul Poberezny, Paul Dowd, Thomas Bailey, William Korbel and Jerome Volk. A Milwaukee native, Volk had completed his Air Cadet training in December 1943 and served in the Army Air Force until the end of the war. He joined the 126th Fighter Squadron of the Wisconsin Air Guard early in 1949 and shipped out for Korea two years later. In November 1951, he was killed while flying a mission in an F-80 Shooting Star. He was the first member of the Wisconsin Air Guard killed in the Korean War. In 1956, the Air Guard portion of Camp Williams was rededicated and named in his honor.

One Wisconsin pilot who saw combat service early in Korea was Donne C. Harned. The Madison native was flying F-84Es with the 31st Fighter Group in Georgia. When the call went out for volunteers for Korea in June 1950, Harned raised his hand. He soon found himself on the aircraft carrier *USS Boxer* as it raced across the Pacific, with all available space crammed not with the up-to-date F-84s Harned had been flying, but with World War II vintage F-51s, including a few from the Wisconsin Air Guard.

The F-51s were in demand because—unlike more modern jets they had the flying range to reach Korean targets from bases in Japan. With F-51s in demand, so were pilots who could fly them, like D. C. Harned. By the time Harned took off for his first combat mission in early August, the North Korean forces had pushed the South Korean and American armies into a corner of the peninsula known as the "Pusan Perimeter."

Strategically, it was a "scene of complete chaos," he recalled. The situation was such that Harned and his mates in the 40th Squadron flew "close air support practically right off the runway." So close was the enemy that the ground crew carried rifles, lived in foxholes and risked mortar fire.

Gradually the perimeter widened, the front opened and Harned's mission list came to read like a route map north to the Korean border with China. By October 1950, the 10th was flying along the Yalu River border, when Chinese forces came across. They pushed the South Koreans and Americans back down the peninsula until Harned was again flying out of Pusan.

It was dangerous, hard flying, in close support of ground troops. As Harned said, he was "in the air to mud business," where enemy air forces posed little danger, but ground fire was deadly. "The casualty rate with air to mud guys was pretty high. In the time I was in combat, my 100 missions, we lost 63 pilots, KIA-MIA. The gunners on the ground were effective."

Nonetheless, ground commanders and the soldiers themselves so valued air support, especially air support supplied by F-51s, that the 10th and other F-51 Squadrons were welcome wherever they flew.

D. C. Harned completed his 100 missions then volunteered for duty on the ground as a forward air controller. After the war he served in the Air Force and the Wisconsin Air Guard, where he attained the rank of Brigadier General and Deputy Adjutant General for Air.

On the way he met Ray Matera, whose was also a jet fighter pilot and Korean veteran. He had been with the 35th Fighter Group when the war started and transferred to the 7th Fighter Squadron of the 49th Fighter Wing in Korea. He flew F-80s and F-84s until he was assigned to the front line as a forward air controller whose job it was to direct air support for ground troops.

"My very first FAC mission. The Colonel said 'make sure you get us some good close air support.' I had a radio and two enlisted air force sergeants, a radio Jeep, and an armed personnel carrier."

Matera and his men were as close to the enemy as they could get when the first F-51s came

Above: Many World War II and Korean War pilots trained in T-6 aircraft like this model on duty with the Air Guard at Madison in the 1950s.

Left: Brigadier General D. C. Harned. (Wisconsin Air National Guard)

overhead. He used a white phosphorous flare to mark the target, but "when I shot my white phosphorous guess what else happened? About 40 other white phosphorous shots all over the place. The Chinese weren't so dumb."

When the F-51s arrived, Matera "told 'em they got an awful lot of firepower right in front of that hill. They said right over the air 'they can't hit us and if they hit us they can't hurt us'." Of course "they" could hurt, and two of the four attacking planes were shot down.

They still took out the target and the two remaining planes helped out on the last assault without firing a shot. "As we were going up the hill I asked the last 51s to buzz the hill so [the enemy] would keep their heads down. One guy comes over, turns upside down and flies right over the top."

Ray Matera was fortunate to complete his tour in jet fighters and return to the Air Force and Air Guard. Assigned to Wisconsin after the war, he eventually served as Adjutant General, commander of all National Guard units in the state.

Among the combat veterans returning to duty for Korea was Milwaukee native Paul Hassett. He had flown B-25s in the China-Burma-India theater

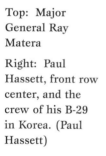

during World War II and now shipped out to fly B-29s off Okinawa in 1952. Editor of the *Dunn County News* in Menomonie when he returned to service, Hassett wrote home regularly and the News reprinted his accounts of the air war in Korea.

"I knew they were going to save this war until our crew got over here," he wrote. "Now our mission No. 6 was the largest raid to date.

"Target for No. 6 was the North Korean capital of Pyongyang, which was hit all day long by the Fifth Air Force and the navy. Then at night we came along with another 1,000 tons of bombs. You could see the flaming city 50 miles away. It was not a pretty sight...

"We were the 932nd plane over the same target that day....No one on the front lines caught it like the city of Pyongyang. Think what it means to have 1,150 planes dropping everything from 100 to 1,000 lb bombs in a raid that lasts 24 hours on a city that looked from the air to cover the same area as Milwaukee."

Hassett also took part in the controversial bombings of hydroelectric dams on the Yalu River, "in the furthest penetration of B-29s in the war," where "intense" and "accurate" flak peppered his plane and "our crew also picked up two purple

Top: Major General Ray Matera

Right: Paul Hassett, front row center, and the crew of his B-29 in Korea. (Paul Hassett)

hearts, with two others pending." Hassett and his crew had to make a forced landing in South Korea, where they met many other combat flyers, "those jet fighters."

"What men they are!," he enthused. "Not all young men either. We talked with several who had their 100 missions in—a mission may last for only 1.5 to 2 hours—but what a fast period of time that is!

"We inquired at what altitude they bomb from, thinking in terms of a low-level drop at 1,000 feet. They told us you get some accuracy at 100 feet, but the best results are obtained at 20."

Hassett survived his tour over Korea and came home early in 1953. He got to know a promising state senator from a neighboring county with an interest in aviation. When that senator—Warren Knowles—was elected Governor in 1964, Hassett accompanied him to Madison where he served as executive secretary until Knowles left office in 1970.

One of the Korean jet fighter pilots Hassett might have been talking about was Navy Lieutenant Gerald "Zeke" Huelsbeck. Born in Menasha, Huelsbeck received his preliminary Naval flight training at Carroll College in Waukesha. In 1953, he was assigned to fly F2H-2 Banshee jets off of aircraft carriers stationed near Korea. He flew 54 combat missions from the *USS Coral Sea, Oriskany* and *Kearsarge.* An inventor as well as a pilot, Huelsback attempted to improve the quality of aerial photography by mounting a small movie camera on the side of his flight helmet. The view finder was mounted on a wire poised in front of his right eye with the camera's switch near his left thumb. As he approached the flight deck for a landing, Huelsback could take a pilot's eye view of a carrier landing.

"It's using your head that counts," he told a reporter.

Huelsbeck continued to use his head after he came home from Korea. He went to work for McDonnell Aircraft and employed the helmet camera as a test pilot in the F3H-Demon. In 1958 he began testing high-speed, high altitude aircraft at Edwards Air Force Base in California. In 1959, he flew an F4H Phantom II fighter to an unofficial altitude record of 96,500 feet during which he became one of a handful of aviators to fly high enough to see the curvature of the earth. In October 1959, Huelsback pushed his Phantom II to Mach 2.2—1,500 MPH—and 44,000 feet, when an engine malfunctioned. The plane burst into flames, slipped into a flat spin and began to fall to the earth. Huelsback was unable to eject in time for

Hoyt Vandenberg

After his success in command of the Ninth Air Force in Europe during World War II, General Hoyt Vandenberg remained in the high command of American air defense. A memorandum he wrote in January 1946, outlined the structure of the postwar Air Force with its Air Defense Command, Tactical Air Command and a new Strategic Air Command with nuclear capability. It was a clear statement of what became the cornerstone of American defense policy for at least another forty years. The United States would rely on strategic air power to maintain peace with other major powers, most notably the Soviet Union and China.

When the independent Air Force was created in 1947, General Carl Spaatz was named first chief of staff and Vandenberg was named vice chief. Spaatz soon retired and Vandenberg moved up, bypassing many officers who were more senior and part of the so-called "Old Guard" of airmen. In fact, if not in name, Hoyt Vandenberg who was born in Billy Mitchell's home town and who chose the Air Corps after listening to Mitchell speak of its potential, was the first commander of the United States Air Force.

Vandenberg encountered his first challenge early in 1948 when the Soviets shut down the roads and rail supply lives to Allied-occupied Berlin. The resulting airlift, in which Air Force supply ships made 275,000 flights and delivered 2.5 million tons of cargo over a ten-month period has been called the first victory for the West in the Cold War.

Victory was harder in the Korean War, which began in June 1950. As Air Force commander, Vandenberg oversaw the operations of a war where—even more so than usual—action was determined as much by politics as by battle. At first an advocate of limiting the war effort, Vandenberg became more bellicose as North Korean and later Chinese troops appeared to be winning. In April 1951, he persuaded President Harry Truman to order the first transfer of atomic weapons to the Air Force. A total of nine bombs and their atomic cores were shipped to American bases on Okinawa. They would be used if the Soviet Army invaded Korea or if the Chinese or Soviets attacked Japan.

Vandenberg also played a role in the controversial dismissal of General Douglas MacArthur. After MacArthur reported that the military situation in Korea had so deteriorated that his forces had to either evacuate or "stand and die," the high command dispatched Vandenberg on an inspection tour. He reported that the situation was serious but not as bleak as MacArthur had portrayed it. Dropping atomic bombs on Manchuria, as MacArthur had suggested, would not help the army in Korea and might trigger another world war. Vandenberg's report aided those who called for MacArthur's dismissal.

When Vandenberg's term as Air Force Chief of Staff ended in 1952 he was fourteen months short of completing a thirty-year career. So the General could fill out his term, President Truman ask Congress to extend Vandenberg's appointment until June 1953. Congress agreed, but Vandenberg's health failed. Stricken by prostate cancer, he was given only a short time to live. In June 1952, General Nathan Twining took over as acting-chief-of-staff. Hoyt Vandenberg died in April 1954 at fifty-five years of age.[19] (U.S. Air Force Photo)

Paul Hassett waving goodbye before a mission in Korea. (Paul Hassett)

his parachute to deploy and died on impact with the earth.

The truce that halted the Korean War began in July 1953. The war had ended a few months earlier for Paul Hassett and his crew who had already made their last bombing run. "We dropped our ten tons of bombs without seeing any searchlights, flak or enemy fighters. Eight minutes after 'bombs away' we were over the Yellow Sea, heading for Okinawa and maybe you don't think we were a happy crew. We sang over the inter-phone all the way home. For me I knew it was the last time I would ever fly in a B-29." And so it was.

"Chalk up combat mission number 8 for us," he wrote in August 1952. "It was another big raid involving 63 B-29s from Japan and Okinawa....the largest B-29 raid on a single building.

"This raid had a little bit of everything, plus plenty of searchlights...Our left wing, my side, was a s bright as a silver dollar.

"We also experienced one of the most unusual sights I have ever seen. We ran through a series of thunderstorms, violent ones...At times lightning would light up the whole dense cloud cover and our props looked like flaming torches. This is called St. Elmo's fire, which I have experienced in lesser form many times, but never so vividly as through those thunderstorms."[20]

In Combat In Vietnam

The air war in Vietnam was as diverse as it was dangerous. No Wisconsin military force was called up as a unit but approximately 165,000 men and women from this state served in the war. The number of Wisconsin men and women who served in Air Force, Army and Naval air units is not available, but a sampling of the experiences of those who did serve has been recorded by the State Historical Society and is recounted here.

The Cold War

The awesome power demonstrated by air power in World War II proved that even the American heartland was vulnerable to attack. After the Soviet Union became a nuclear power in 1949, the catastrophic potential of an aerial attack on the United States became real.

The possibility of Soviet bombers flying over the border from the north had its effects on Wisconsin aviation. General aviation pilots had to file more detailed flight reports and special regulations were enacted for northeastern Wisconsin. The World War II Ground Observation Corps was revived and plane spotters trained to recognize Soviet bombers and fighters. Evacuation plans were made to disperse the population of Milwaukee throughout the state, with movement of one million people supervised in part by the Civil Air Patrol. CAP personnel also took training in how to monitor radioactive fallout from nuclear explosions in Wisconsin and elsewhere.

The Cold War threat helped to keep the Air Force base at Madison even though many residents in the growing city voiced opposition to siting heavily armed military aircraft so close to a population center. At the same time, Maitland Field in downtown Milwaukee was closed and Nike anti-aircraft missiles installed on the site. With a ground-to-air range of about 30 miles, Nikes were sited at eight other locations around Milwaukee. The sleek, pencil-thin white missiles were chilling reminders of the threat of war even in time of peace.

While Maitland Field was closed, the construction of new bases for strategic air forces was considered. Douglas County was on the list, but lost out to sites in Minnesota and the Upper Peninsula. Land was acquired in Kenohsa County to build an air base named in honor of Richard A. Bong, and a runway capable of handling B-52s was built, but further development was cancelled. The land was then put to use as a wildlife area.

By the 1960s, the Cold War was still underway, but it took a back seat to the hot struggle in Vietnam. By the 1970s, the prospect of bombers coming over Canada to Wisconsin was replaced by the threat of nuclear missiles.[21]

WIN YOUR WINGS IN THE

GOC

GROUND OBSERVER CORPS

UNITED STATES AIR FORCE
GOC OBSERVER

All the conventional elements of American air power were exhibited in Vietnam from the most modern carrier and land-based F-4 and F-105 fighter-bombers to propeller driven A-1s, B-52 strategic bombers ranged far overhead while venerable cargo-carrying C-47's, transformed into tactical attack aircraft, swept over the treetops. Observers flew older Cessna O-1s and newly-designed OV-10 observation planes. Helicopters, which had made their combat debut in Korea, came into their own as troop carriers, gunships, search and rescue ships and medical evacuation craft. The Vietnam War was fought in the jungles, on the waterways and in the air.

"The flying is exciting," wrote Navy helicopter gunship pilot John L. Abrams. Born in Milwaukee, Abrams flew light attack helicopters over the Mekong Delta in 1968. "There's no two ways about that," he continued. "It's a certain scarf and goggles and leather helmet-type thing....But it's not all glory. It's excitement, it's all excitement. And a lot of it is being, real, real scared." It was also dangerous, low level flying right on top of the fight zone. It was fatal for John Abrams, who died after his helicopter crashed in combat four months into his tour in Vietnam.

Army helicopter pilot Scott Alwin, Fort Atkinson, was more fortunate than Abrams. He served over three years in Vietnam, flew nearly 4,000 hours, received a battlefield commission and many decorations. "We fly long hours usually and quite frankly under situations that money couldn't pay me to fly," he wrote home in 1967. Yet he con-tinued to serve and when his first tour was over, returned for a second. Alwin flew thousands of hours, ferried troops into combat, carried supplies to forward bases, and returned with the wounded and the dead. He survived the war in Vietnam, but died in auto accident in Wisconsin in 1976.

Although they were well above the tree line where the helicopters flew, fighter-bomber pilots faced equally hazardous situations. Menasha native Frederic Flom flew ninety combat missions in Air Force tactical fighters before he was shot down in August 1966.

"I apparently had amnesia and remember absolutely nothing about the event," he wrote in his journal. "We had a pre-dawn takeoff with 'Baron' as lead. The target was a storage area north of Yen Bai for primary and a similar secondary target. We arrived in the target area just about daybreak under a 1,500 foot overcast...After I dropped my CBUs and was pulling off this target [Baron] saw me take 37 mm in the belly tank. The aircraft immediately started burning and smoking. Baron said I'd better get out and I turned my aircraft to 240 degrees to start heading out. He told me to get out again and then a third time as my aircraft did a violent roll to the right and started coming apart. He saw the canopy come out through the fire and smoke and then the seat. The aircraft flew up with a yellow-orange fire ball like he'd never seen. He said my chute opened immediately...He saw metal debris rip thru the chute and I was hanging limp. He saw me on the ground and I was in the middle of a road on top of my chute just outside a little

Lance Sijan (Jane
A. Sijan)

village and I was not moving."
Flom's wingmate attempted to
keep him in sight in hopes that
a helicopter might be able to
land and rescue him, only to be
shot down himself.

Flom was captured and
spent six and one-half years as a
prisoner of war. He described
his release in 1972. "We came
around the corner in the bus
and saw that C-141 it was beautiful... I was greeted by a flight
stewardess with a kiss and into
the aircraft. Shaking hands with
everyone—-and before I knew it
the rest were aboard and the
engines starting—taxi—take-
off—wheels in well and a sigh
of relief and a big beautiful yell
for freedom." Flom returned to the United States,
flew F-102s with the Air Guard in Madison for a
few years and, in 1997, was piloting commercial
aircraft.

Air Force Captain Lance Sijan received the
Congressional Medal of Honor for his heroism in
Vietnam. The Milwaukee native and graduate of
the Air Force Academy, was assigned to fly a F4C
Phantom out of Da Nang in July 1967. In
November, Sijan's F4C was hit by anti-aircraft fire
over North Vietnam and he was forced to bail out.
Although injured in the jump, and weakened by
hunger and exposure, he eluded capture for six
weeks. When taken by the enemy, he overpowered
a guard and escaped, only to be captured again.
After two weeks in brutal captivity, Lance Sijan
died. For his "extraordinary heroism and intrepidi-
ty" he became one of fourteen American airmen
awarded the nation's highest honor for service in
Vietnam.[23]

THE WISCONSIN AIR NATIONAL GUARD

THE WISCONSIN BLITZKRIEG

The first air unit of the Wisconsin National
Guard was established on July 30 1940, just a bit
too late to take part in the war games known as
"The Battle of Wisconsin." The newly-appointed
Army Chief of Staff, George C. Marshall, had
ordered that a series of maneuvers involving
National Guard and regular army units take place

in several locations around the country in
the summer of 1940. Guardsmen would
be introduced to the new tactics of aerial,
armored and mechanized warfare already
on exhibit in Europe. As a result, 65,000
Guardsmen from Midwestern states set up
camp in west central Wisconsin. Divided
into two armies—the Blue and the Red—
they turned the rolling hills, cranberry
marshes and jackpine barrens of Jackson,
Juneau, Wood and Monroe counties into
practice fields of battle.

In order to give the troops a "glimpse"
of "war from the heavens for the first
time," the Army Air Corps dispatched to
Wisconsin an "air force" of twenty-one P-
36 pursuit planes, twenty-six B-18A light
bombers and C-54 transports, plus eight
B-17 "Flying Fortresses."

"War from the heavens" was much in
the news in the summer of 1940. Using a
combination of infantry, armored and air
forces, the German military had just
defeated both the French and British
armies on the Continent and made the
term "blitzkrieg" familiar throughout the
world. In the Wisconsin war games, the
army's "crack" mechanized Fifth Division
would demonstrate the new tactics of
"blitzkrieg" to the greenhorn Guardsmen of the
Midwest. "Blitzkrieg," minus the air element, that
is. In the "Battle of Wisconsin," the aircraft would
be present as part of the stage setting, but not integrated into the tactical plans of either the Blue or
the Red armies. Indeed, since the military air field
at Camp Williams was still under construction, the
army planes would not even be based near the
maneuvers but at the Madison Municipal Airport.

The ground forces arrived at Camp Williams
and Fort McCoy in a steady stream during the first
weeks of August. The aircraft arrived just in time
to fly in the main battle scheduled for August 24-
25. Optimists predicted that a crowd of 40,000 people would turn out to see the planes land at
Madison on August 22, but rainy weather limited
attendance to 10,000. Bad weather also delayed the
P-36s, the speedy fighter planes affectionately
known as "peashooters," but the bombers rumbled
in on time. The B-17s, already billed as the
"Greatest War Planes in the World," were the most
modern military aircraft yet to fly in Wisconsin
and created quite a stir in Madison. The crews
were treated like celebrities and city officials mustered a legion of police and deputies, including the
Boy Scouts, to manage the anticipated crowds.

Neither the crowd nor the battle turned out as expected. On Saturday, August 24 the bombers were scheduled to take off early to make eight bombing runs over Camp McCoy and Sparta as well as over the Guardsmen in the field. Instead, they were grounded by rain and fog that continued throughout the day and into the next. Only one flight of three bombers got into the air, but not until Sunday afternoon, when "for 92 minutes and more than 300 miles" it flew "through the mist and murk." After nearly colliding with each other over the Monroe County village of Norwalk, the planes were forced to return to Madison where they landed safely despite the soupy fog. The infantry fought its "Battle of Wisconsin," with General Marshall in attendance for part of the battle, but without the aerial blitzkrieg. The Air Corps was bedeviled by bad luck even on the ground in Madison, where the only aviation casualty of the exercise occurred when a Northwest airliner poked its wingtip through the glass nose cone of a B-17 and inflicted damage estimated at fifteen dollars.

Even if the Air Corps had participated more fully, the Battle of Wisconsin would have given Guardsmen no more than an inkling of military air power as it had evolved by 1940. That no more than a few dozen air planes could be mustered for war games involving 65,000 troops was a measure of American military preparedness. This state of unreadiness was not unbeknownst to the War Department and this awareness prompted a military build-up in 1940 and '41. The military budget reached its highest level since World War I, procurement expanded and the first peacetime draft of men took place. In aviation, training programs for civilians were expanded and National Guard air units were organized throughout the country, including the 126th Observation Squadron in Wisconsin.[24]

WISCONSIN'S FIRST GUARD OBSERVATION SQUADRON

No sooner was an air unit proposed for the Wisconsin National Guard than cities began to lobby for the base. Wausau and Superior were briefly in the running, but the race settled down to

F-102s of the Wisconsin Air National Guard in formation take-off. (Wisconsin Air National Guard)

two contenders, Milwaukee and Madison. At stake was a $360,000 federal construction grant, jobs for thirty-one Guard officers and 136 enlisted men, plus civilian spinoffs. As the largest population center in the state and possessed of the largest, most modern airport, Milwaukee was the logical first choice, but Madison argued a strong case. The city had purchased more than enough land for commercial and general aviation and could easily accommodate a military base, while the university offered a pool of eligible manpower. The local business community made a strong pitch for the base and Wisconsin's Adjutant General Ralph Immell also supported Madison.

Site selection was up to Governor Julius Heil, the Milwaukee industrialist who had defeated Phillip La Follette in the 1938 Governor's race. At a stormy meeting in Milwaukee, where five advocates of Madison confronted five Milwaukeeans at the speakers podium, the Governor selected Milwaukee. He based his decision on a recommendation from the chief of the air section of the National Guard in Washington, who preferred Milwaukee because of its proximity to the abundant, uncrowded air space over Lake Michigan and because all the other Guard Observation Squadrons in the country were based in the largest city in their home state. Heil did promise to work for more air units and bases in Wisconsin. "I'll get an air base for Madison and a third one for Superior. But for the first one, it will go to Milwaukee," he said.

While Madison was a political choice, Superior could offer a military rationale for an air base. The iron ore shipping facilities there were among the most strategically important assets in Wisconsin. In 1940, as the battle of Britain began, it was not hard to imagine a Nazi victory and the occupation of Canada by German troops. Consequently, an air base to defend northern Wisconsin was not as far-fetched an idea as it might seem in 1998. After the United States entered the war the location of a Guard air unit

and an Army Air Force base near Lake Superior was resolved with Superior once again losing out to its sister city of Duluth. Madison had better luck, not with the Air Guard, but with the Army Air Force, which opened its base at Madison Municipal Airport in 1942.

With the question of siting the base settled, building an armory and hangar as well as recruiting personnel came to the forefront. Immell projected that it would take six months to build the necessary buildings at Milwaukee and about a year to enlist personnel. "We want men with 300 flying hours behind them and 3,000 ahead of them, not the other way around," he said. On the first day of enlistment, over 1,000 applicants crowded around the sign-up tables at the Plankinton Hotel in Milwaukee.

By September the 126th Observation Squadron had its full complement of men and World War I veteran Major Paul Meyers returned to Wisconsin from New York to take command. His Captains were Myron R. MacLeod, Richard T. Crane, Gordon Hamilton and Raymond F. Kitchingman; First Sergeant was Durban Fisher. Nearly all personnel came from Milwaukee. Ground was broken for the unit's hangar at county airport in late November, 1940, and its first aircraft—three 047, two-seater observation planes—arrived soon after. In the summer of 1941, the squadron was activated for federal service and took part in its first maneuvers at Fort Dix, New Jersey. In September 1941, the Wisconsinites became one of three squadrons comprising the 59th Observation Group of the United States Army Air Force.

Sent to Fort Bragg, North Carolina, the 126th was assigned to the Marston Strip, an experimental runway whose surface consisted of pierced steel planking laid directly on top of the sand. Marston Mat, as it came to be known, was used to create instant landing strips on the islands of the Pacific during World War II and was credited as one of American engineering's most important contributions to victory in the Pacific. While at Fort Bragg, the 126th participated in test landings on Marston Mat by virtually every Army Air Force aircraft from the P-39 to the B-24. Coincidentally, one of the first and largest manufacturers of Marston Mat was the Milcor division of Inland Steel Company in Milwaukee.

The Squadron began anti-submarine patrol duties out of Fort Dix, New Jersey in December, 1941 and remained on active duty until October 1942, when its personnel was transferred to the 519th Bombardment Squadron which flew anti-submarine patrols out of Otis Field in Maine for the duration of the war.[25]

THE POSTWAR AIR GUARD

At the end of World War II, advocates of an aviation arm for the National Guard faced a paradoxical situation. Never had more trained and experienced personnel been available for duty. Never had there been more available aircraft, aviation material or military landing fields. At the same time, the United States was committed to the largest stand down of military power in history. Men and women were demobilized, equipment mothballed and air bases closed or returned to civilian authority. Yet, there was still an air mission for the Guard, still people who wanted to fulfill it and make aviation a part of their lives.

In September 1946, Acting Governor Oscar Rennebohn requested that the War Department assign the 128th Fighter Group, consisting of two squadrons and 1,373 people, to a newly constituted Wisconsin Air National Guard. Two months later Colonel Russell A. Berg reported to Wisconsin Adjutant General John F. Mullen and tried to establish a squadron at Madison. The municipal airport, which had become Truax Field Army Air Base during the war, had been returned to Madison and the city government was reluctant to release the facilities for the Guard. Berg then concentrated his efforts on Milwaukee, where the state's first Air Guard headquarters, training center and hangar had been built at Mitchell Field in 1941 and where he had better results.

The facilities were available, recruiting went well and the Milwaukee unit was established in about six months. In June, 1947 the 126th Utility Flight, 126th Weather Flight, 228th Service Group and the 128th Fighter Group received federal recognition. Lieutenant Colonel Seymour M. Levenson was named the first commander of the 126th Fighter Squadron and Major Paul Fojtik became commander of the 228th Service Group. In July 1947, twenty-two P-51D Mustangs were delivered to Mitchell Field and the Wisconsin Air Guard took to the air.

The Air Guard also returned to Madison, where city government had changed its mind about sharing airport space with a military unit. With Captain Arthur C. Smith in charge of recruitment and a large number of World War II vets and others on hand, the squadron filled quickly. Federal recognition as the 176th Fighter Squadron came in October 1948 followed by a varied collection of aircraft: three T-6s, one C-47, one B-26 and fourteen F-51s.

Both the newly-established Wisconsin Air Guard units faced operational challenges presented by winter weather. In early 1949, the 126th supplied a C-47 and crew for Operation Haylift, the emergency delivery of feed for livestock and wildlife trapped on the northern prairies by an unusually severe storm and extreme cold. The Milwaukee crew flew six sorties a day out of Minot, North Dakota and delivered more tonnage of feed to starving animals than any other Air Guard unit.

Two years later, the Madison unit faced cold weather problems presented by a severe Wisconsin winter. Activated for the Korean War in February 1951, the 176th was not equipped for the below-zero weather that descended on the state that month. "We still did not have that issue of official winter clothing," recalled Brigadier General Ralph Jensen, who was a new PFC at the time. "However we still had 25 P-51s to get combat ready for flight every day."

The new hangar at Madison had room for only eight aircraft, so the Guardsmen had to thaw the others after the planes had spent the night out in temperatures in the -20 degree range. The Guardsmen did what they could to keep themselves warm as well, which meant they wore whatever they had that would do the job. As a result the

---

Wisconsin Air National Guard General Officers

Adjutant General
Major General James G. Blaney 1997-
Major General Jerome J. Berard 1996-1997
Major General Jerald D. Slack 1989-1996
Major General Raymond A. Matera 1979-1989

Deputy Adjutant General for Air
Brigadier General Albert H. Wilkening 1990-
Brigadier General Richard E. Pezzullo 1989-1990
Brigadier General Kenneth G. Stasiewicz 1987-1989
Brigadier General Donne C. Harned 1984-1987
Brigadier General James L. Dawson 1980-1983
Brigadier General Francis G. Linsmeier 1978-1980
Colonel Harvey W. Maher 1972-1978
Colonel Jack C. King 1971-1972
Colonel Arlie M. Mucks, Jr. 1970-1971

Chief of Staff
Colonel Gene Schmitz 1997-
Brigadier General James H. Greshik 1994-1997
Brigadier General Peter L. Drahn 1990-1994
Brigadier General Jerald D. Slack 1988-1990
Brigadier General Ralph C. Jensen 1986-1988
Brigadier General Dale F. Egide 1984-1985
Brigadier General Donne C. Harned 1982-1983
Brigadier General Russell A. Witt 1979-1982
Major General Raymond A. Matera 1971-1979
Brigadier General Oliver S. Ryerson 1970-1971
Major General Collins H. Ferris 1953-1970

ground crews of the 176th looked like a cross between a crowd of spectators bundled up for a December game at Lambeau Field and a gang of hunters at a northern Wisconsin deer camp. Sweatshirts, store-bought parkas, red woolen mackinaws, layers of jeans, ski pants and stocking caps stretched to cover as much bare skin as possible, made up the uniform of the day. Their ragged appearance did not detract from the quality of the work the crews performed. The P-51s were ready to fly everyday, despite the cold.

In fact, their lack of uniforms became a source of pride for the Guardsmen. They were the "raggedy ass militia," citizen soldiers in the tradition of the Minute Men who served at Lexington and Concord in 1775, who answered Abraham Lincoln's call for volunteers to save the Union in 1861, and of the Milwaukee aviators who signed on for duty with the original Wisconsin air unit in 1940. The sentiment survives, as does the phrase, which appeared on the patch of the 176th Tactical Fighter Squadron. While the Madison unit was still equipped with P-51s, the 126th at Milwaukee became one of the first Air Guard units to receive jet aircraft. Twenty-five F-80 Shooting-Stars arrived at Mitchell Field in September, 1949. The unit was then reorganized as the 128th Fighter Wing, with the F-80s assigned to the 126th Jet Fighter Squadron. During the Korean War the unit was assigned to Truax Field, which had again become an active air base, and its personnel deployed as needed throughout the world. While serving in Korea, Captain Jerome Volk of the 126th was killed in action.

Jet aircraft occupied the front line of aerial combat in the Korean War and remained on the front line of defense in the years after. Both the 176th and the 126th Squadrons received their first F-89s in the mid-1950s. While faster than any aircraft Guard pilots had yet flown, the twin-engine F-89 was subject to engine problems because it was prone to "inhale" rocks and other "foreign objects." Indeed, F-89 pilots made so many single-engine landings due to damage from foreign objects that they did not need a practice exercise for it. For other squadron members, the F-89's habit of sucking up runway litter meant that the ramps and runways had to be policed daily.

Along with the F-89s came the Air Defense Command deployment in which the Guard was called upon to help defend the United States from nuclear-armed Soviet bombers flying over the Arctic. In 1960, Guard F-89s carried Genie rockets which could be armed with a nuclear warhead. No longer could a pilot sight on a target with his own eyes. Instead he and his radar officer used the radar to lock on the target then fire on it while it was still four to six miles away.

The same Cold War that required nuclear-capable fighters in Wisconsin also kept the Air Guard on alert, first for fourteen hour days in 1960, then for twenty-four hours during and after the Cuban missile crisis of 1962. The tensions of the times and their status of constant alert made the citizen airmen of the Guard "a real part of the defense of the United States."

In 1960, the Wisconsin Air Guard experienced the most fundamental change since its creation. The Milwaukee unit became one of four Guard groups to shift from fighter aircraft to air refueling tankers. It was not without mixed feelings that many Guard members greeted the arrival of the first KC-97G tanker at Milwaukee in March, 1962,

Wisconsin Air National Guard Units

Madison
Wisconsin Air National Guard, Headquarters
128th Tactical Fighter Wing
176th Tactical Fighter Squadron
115th Consolidated Aircraft Maintenance Squadron
115th Tactical Clinic
115th Civil Engineering Squadron
115th Resource Management Squadron
115th Mission Support Squadron
115th Mission Support Flight
115th Security Police Flight
115th Services Flight

Milwaukee
128th Air Refueling Group
126th Air Refueling Squadron
128th Operations Support Squadron
128th Logistics Group
128th Consolidate Aircraft Maintenance Squadron
128th Resources Management Squadron
128th Logistics Supply Squadron
128th Support Group
128th USAF Clinic
128th Civil Engineering Squadron
128th Mission Support Squadron
128th Communications Squadron
128th Security Police Flight
128th Mission Support Flight
128th Services Flight
126th Weather Flight

Camp Douglas
Volk Field Combat Readiness Training Center
128th Tactical Control Squadron

Left: The first F-89 to serve with the Wisconsin Air National Guard. (Wisconsin Air National Guard)

Below: A Milwaukee-based KC-97 refueling an F-84. (Wisconsin Air National Guard)

but the soldiers accepted their new mission. Refueling duty may not have been as glamorous as fighter combat, but the newly-named 128th Air Refueling Group was combat ready by the end of 1963 and had completed more than 5,100 aircraft-to-aircraft hook-ups in its first year of operation.

A year later the Milwaukee unit participated in its first long range navigation training flight to Europe. It was the first of many flights in the 1960s that would dispatch the Wisconsin tankers to the Azores Islands, Alaska, Hawaii, Japan, New Zealand, Australia and the Caribbean. In 1967, the unit took part in the Operation Creek party in which Guard members were assigned to the Rhein-Main Air Force Base near Frankfort, Germany to set up a KC97S operation. It was the first time an Air Guard unit based personnel and equipment overseas without a national call-up.

Long-range operations continued into the 1970s, with the 128th tankers flying along the Distance Early Warning Line to Greenland and to Germany, England and Nicaragua. In 1977, the venerable KC97s were replaced with modern KC135 tankers in time for the unit to fly them in Wisconsin's first all Air Guard exercise at Volk Field in 1978. Along with the KC135s came the unit's first Strategic Air Command operational readiness inspection, which the 128th passed with flying colors. In the early 1980s, the 128th, led by Major General Ray Matera, the Adjutant General,

and Colonel Kenneth Sweet, convinced the Strategic Air Command to approve the replacement of the KC135's old J-57 engines with JT3D engines. Removed from commercial airliners and overhauled at very cost-effective rates, the JT3D's were capable of revers thrust and allowed the KC135's to use many runways that were too short for the J-57's. In the words of the Air Guard's historian, the replacements gave the Wisconsin Air

Guard, "ten years of improved performance, reduced noise complaints, simplified maintenance and reverse thrust...one of the biggest accomplishments of the first fifty years of the Wisconsin ANG."

All the training and experience paid off at the

Right: Tanker
crew on duty for
the Gulf War,
1991. (Wisconsin
Air National
Guard)

Below: Wisconsin
Air Guard and
Dutch Air Force
personnel taking
part in Operation
Sentry
Independence
exercises at Volk
Field, 1983.
Brigadier General
Ralph Jensen,
kneeling, second
from left.
(Wisconsin Air
National Guard)

onset of the Persian
Gulf crisis in the sum-
mer of 1990. Eleven
hours after the first
call, the 128th dis-
patched its first KC135
to its forward base in
Spain. It was the first
American tanker in the
war. As the United
States enlarged its com-
mitment to defend the
Persian Gulf states
against Iraq so did the importance of air refueling
increase. To reach bases in the Mideast, American
airplanes had to be refueled enroute. To perform
this vital service, the 128th transferred 10 KC135E
tankers along with fifteen crews and 196 support
personnel to Cairo West Air Force Base in Egypt.
Along with other Air Guard units in the 1706 Air
Refueling Wing, the 128th maintained a twenty-
four hour operation from December, 1990 to April
1991, without once cancelling a mission. The
1706th compiled the finest record of any air refueling wing in the area: "more hours, more sorties
more offload and more receivers than any of the
twelve other tanker locations..."

The Wisconsin Air Guard had come a long
way since the days when the "raggedy ass militia"
wore red flannel shirts to keep warm while maintaining P-51s at Madison. The citizen-soldiers had
proven that, given sufficient training, equipment
and support, they could occupy the front line of
national defense.

While Milwaukee
traded its fighters for
air tankers in the early
1960s, the Madison
unit remained a fighter
operation. Madison
received its first F-102s
in 1966. In that same
year the Air Force's
325th Fighter
Squadron was deacti-
vated and the
Wisconsin Air Guard
was able to occupy its quarters at Truax Field.

Just as the air refueling group established its
reputation for excellence in the 1960s and '70s,
Wisconsin's fighter unit made its mark. The first
big splash occurred at the "William Tell" competition in 1972. Led by Lieutenant Colonel Ronald
Skinvik of the 176 Fighter Squadron, who selected
Lieutenant Colonel Phil Brickson as Team Captain,
the Wisconsin team took first place in competition
with other Air Guard units as well as United
States and Canadian Air Force teams. Brickson
added to Wisconsin's accolades when he was
named the contest's "Top Gun." Although called a
"shoot-off," the William Tell competition evaluated the entire Wisconsin team, from pilots to
weapons loaders to maintenance crew. So when
the 176th won William Tell in 1972, it was a victory for the entire Wisconsin Air Guard.

Success at William Tell in 1972 led to a bundle
of awards the following year. The 115th Fighter
Group was declared the Best National Guard
Flying Unit by the National Guard Bureau, the Air
Force Association and the American Fighter Pilots
Association. Despite this success, the unit was
threatened by post-Vietnam War "reduction in
force" measures and scheduled for termination in
1974. With the aid of the Wisconsin Congressional
delegation the unit continued to function, but was
downsized from more than 300 to less than 200
people and with its mission altered to forward air
control and tactical air support.

In 1981, and now part of 128th Tactical
Fighter Wing, the Madison unit received its first
A-10 aircraft. With the A-10s came opportunities
for the Air Guard to take part in large-scale training exercises both in Wisconsin and overseas.

Operation Coronet Giant sent the A-10s on a
13-hour flight across the Atlantic that required five
mid-air refuelings. Once in Germany, the crews
received a "a real opportunity to get an idea of the
problems we'd be dealing with if the 'real thing'
came," as Colonel Michael Jordan said.

Operations Coronet Mercury and Coronet Lariat took the Wisconsinites to England and Germany, while Coronet Cove sent them to Central America to train for the defense of Panama Canal.

Back home, the headquarters and Volk Field staff of the Wisconsin Air Guard managed the Sentry Independence exercises at Volk Field. Beginning in 1983, Sentry Independence evolved to include Air Guard, Air Force, Army and Marine Corps Reserve, the United States Air Force and NATO allies. During the weeks of Sentry Independence, Volk Field became one of the busiest airports in Wisconsin, with military aircraft from all categories—A-10s, F-4s, F-16s, B-52s, C-130s, KC-135s and many others—flying up to 150 missions per day. Wisconsin's 128th Tactical Control Squadron from Milwaukee coordinated all radar control in concert with the FAA's Chicago and Minneapolis Air Traffic Control Centers. This concentration of military air power in central Wisconsin only reinforced awareness of the Air Guard's global mission as it was demonstrated in the Persian Gulf in 1990 and 1991.

In the 1990s, the mission of the Wisconsin Air National Guard ranges from air refueling to tactical fighter squadrons and all the maintenance and mission support functions in between, including the first Air Guard Air Combat Maneuvering System recently installed at the Volk Field Hardwood Range.

Since 1948, twenty-five Guard members have lost their lives while in service. To paraphrase long time Air Guard Commander Major General Collins H. Ferris, they were people who devoted themselves to the high cause of outstanding performance in the pursuit of combat readiness. Those words succinctly state the history of the Wisconsin Air Guard.[26]

1945

These Men Will Supervise

State Aviation Development

By ENAR A. AHLSTROM

A CITY MANAGER, an airport operator, a fruit grower and packer, and two members of the medical profession, comprise the five-man Wisconsin Aeronautics Commission appointed last month by Governor Walter S. Goodland to supervise aviation and its development in the state. The commissioners, however, were not selected because of their occupations or professions alone, but also for their knowledge, experience and interest in aviation. A director of aeronautics, to be hired by the commissioners has not yet been named.

Three members of the new panel, Howard A. Morey, Madison, Dr. A. G. Sell, Ashland, and Dr. L. O. Simenstad, Osceola, also served on the former State Aeronautics Advisory Board. All members but one are fliers, and three, Karl Reynolds, Sturgeon Bay, Morey and Sell, hold licenses and fly their own planes. Dr. Simenstad is a student pilot. Theodore M. Wardwell, Rhinelander, is the only member who is not a flier, though he frequently uses air transport as a means of travel.

Howard A. Morey, chairman of the commission and only representative from the southern portion of the state, was perhaps named to the panel because of his more than 20 years experience as a flier and airport operator. He began his flying career in 1923, did barnstorming during 1925, and a year later established Madison's first airport. In 1927 he expanded his facilities and pioneered the first Madison-Chicago airline, flown daily with the first cabin plane owned in Wisconsin, a J-5 Travelaire which carried five passengers and a pilot.

The Royal Airways Corporation which Morey headed, was sold in 1928. He bought back the corporation's assets in 1932 and since that time has been operating as Morey Airplane Company. He began operation of Madison Municipal Airport in 1939, and continued until the AAF took it over in 1942. He then shifted his business to its present location, eight miles northwest of Madison. During the early stages of the war, Morey also operated an AAF glider school at Janesville. His new port at Madison is rated one of the finest in the state. He has in excess of 7,000 hours of flight and at one time or another has held ratings in most every type of civil aircraft.

Commissioner Karl S. Reynolds, co-owner of Reynolds Brothers Preserving Company, Sturgeon Bay, represents the eastern part of the state on the board. He has long been active in state chamber of commerce activities, is one of Wisconsin's prominent business men and has been a flying enthusiast since 1919 when he made his first hop in a World War I "Jenny." It wasn't until 1937 that he began taking lessons, but under the tutelage of Ed Heeden, pilot for H. F. Johnson, head of Johnson Wax Company, Racine, Reynolds soloed after only two and a half hours of instruction. His enthusiasm was somewhat dampened after a harrowing experience in landing the plane after his initial flight, and he refrained from further

(continued on page fourteen)

MOREY

SELL

SIMENSTAD

WARDWELL

REYNOLDS

CHAPTER IV

State Government in Aviation

THE WISCONSIN STATE AERONAUTICS COMMISSION

The involvement of state government in Wisconsin aviation traces its roots to the legislation passed in 1919 enabling the Milwaukee County Park Commission to establish an airport. In the 1920s, legislative committees examined aviation issues and produced legislation banning stunt flying over crowds and authorizing local governments to build airports but, in keeping with the conservative mind set of the times, the state role was severely limited.

In the mid-1930s, the state acted as a conduit through which federal public works money reached local governments building airports, but the Wisconsin constitution did not allow the state to build a commercial landing field. The state could and did use federal WPA money to build a landing strip and hangar for the Conservation Department at Tomahawk and to construct the "State Military Field" at Camp Williams which—until 1940—consisted of no more than 3,000 feet of mowed grass occasionally visited by U.S. Army aircraft.

In 1937, Wisconsin enacted its first real legislation to regulate aeronautics. All aviators and aviation facilities were subject to registration and liable to supervision by the newly-created Aeronautics Board. The first boardmembers were aviators Howard Morey, Steve Wittman and James King, plus Thomas Pattison of the State Highway Commission and Richard A. Nixon of the State Planning Board and Public Service Commission. The legislature gave the Aeronautics Board broad power to regulate all phases of aviation in Wisconsin but failed to establish the means in which it might do so. The Board had no staff, no

office and no budget other than a ten-dollar-per-day allowance to meet—but only fifteen days a year.

Under these circumstances, Wisconsin's aeronautics agency sat dead on the runway while Governor Julius P. Heil, in response to a federal request, ordered the State Planning Board to draw up the state's first airport system plan. Published in October, 1940 "An Airport System For Wisconsin" assessed Wisconsin's existing airports, laid down criteria for modern facilities and proposed a plan for new construction.

According to "An Airport System For Wisconsin," the state should have 113 airports, with 73 new or substantially enlarged facilities. Milwaukee and Madison would have the largest "Class 4" airports, with Appleton, Green Bay, Oshkosh, Fond du Lac, Menominee/Marinette, Manitowoc, Sheboygan, Watertown, Racine, Kenosha, Beloit-Janesville, La Crosse, Stevens Point, Wausau, Eau Claire and Superior to have "Class 3" facilities. That Wisconsin's largest cities should have improved airports was no surprise, but the 1940 plan also called for the construction of a true state-wide network of airports. The blank spots on the map were to be filled, which meant building airports in places where none currently existed, such as Adams, Amery, Bayfield, Chilton, Cornell, Crandon, Iron River, Mellen, Osceola, Princeton and Wabeno. While it was not stated in the plan, the intention of "An Airport System," was to build at least one up-to-standards airport in every county in Wisconsin.

With the Planning Board doing its job, the Aeronautics Board had less reason than ever to exist and was abolished in 1941. Under the direction of Martin Torkelson, the Planning Board served as the state agency coordinating the flow of federal funds for airport improvements at Eau

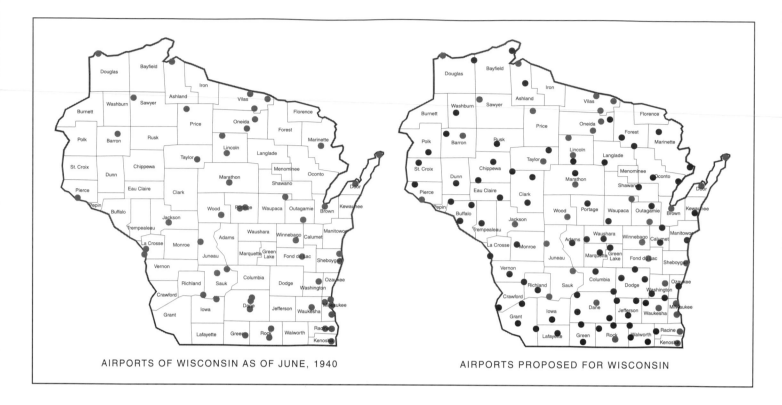

AIRPORTS OF WISCONSIN AS OF JUNE, 1940   AIRPORTS PROPOSED FOR WISCONSIN

The actual number of airports in Wisconsin in 1940 compared to the number projected in the first state airport plan. (WAHF)

Claire, Rhinelander, Clintonville, Sheboygan, Wausau, West Bend and Webster. The Planning Board was also involved in two projects the Civil Aeronautics Administration deemed important to the national defense—the construction of municipal airports at La Crosse and Janesville.

In 1944, with the end of the war in sight, Governor Walter Goodland appointed a Special Aviation Advisory Board of "twenty-eight men prominent in aviation, industry, newspaper publishing, state government and other activities," under the chairmanship of Carlyle Godske. Within a year the Advisory Board recommended that Goodland create an Aeronautics Commission with real power as outlined by the National Association of State Aviation Officials. Early in 1945, Goodland submitted legislation to create and empower a five-member Commission that would hire a director and other employees within the bounds of a budget of $25,000. It was one of four legislative proposals discussed that session, including one to amend the constitution so the state could fund airport construction.

The role of ushering the Governor's bill down the legislative aisle fell to the floor leader of the majority Republican Party, Senator Warren P. Knowles of New Richmond. He presided over hearings in which more than one Wisconsin aviator voiced opposition to a state aeronautics agency. Dr. A. L. Dennis, a pilot from Watertown, said that the state would only duplicate what the federal government was already doing—and charge more

for it. "It seems to me," Dennis said, "that the air has been free for a long time and I think it should continue to be free." The bill did call for the state to license pilots progressively with fees ranging from one to one-hundred dollars.

The counter argument held that the federal government would be spending up to $17 million on Wisconsin airports in the postwar years and that the state needed its own agency to pursue and administer those funds. Curtiss-Wright airport manager Merle Zuehlke testified that "We must...have representation both here and in Washington."

Senator Knowles argued long and eloquently for the aeronautics agency. With the war still underway, he stated that "the men in service do not want to come back to chaos, that they would prefer to have this legislation passed so that airports will be ready for their use when they return." With the United States military about to discharge the largest contingent of trained aviators in its history, Knowles' words were persuasive. The aeronautics legislation passed the Senate on May 10, 1945, two days after the Allies proclaimed victory in Europe, and was signed by Governor Goodland.

The new law created and funded the Aeronautics Commission but left airport regulatory responsibility with the Planning Board for two years in which time the new agency would draw up a plan whereby it would become the sole state aeronautics agency. The Aeronautics Commission held its first meeting on September 28, 1945 with Howard Morey as chair. Karl Reynolds, the flying cherry grower and airport developer from Sturgeon Bay, was vice chair, with Dr. L.O. Simenstad, the flying physician from Osceola, as secretary. Members were Ashland's flying physician, A. G. Sell and Rhinelander city manager Theodore Wardwell.

The first Executive Secretary of the Commission was Thomas K. Jordan, on loan from the Planning Board. When the permanent position of Director was created, it was filled by retired General Lester Maitland. He stayed for two years before moving on to the equivalent job in the state of Michigan. Jordan then came back as Director and remained until 1967.

The first hired employee of the Aeronautics Commission was Flying Tiger war vet and Shawano native, Fritz Wolf. He recalled that his first job was to run education programs but he preferred operations. When the operations job opened, he moved to it, leaving the education position to another young war vet, Carl Guell. Wolf and Guell worked together for thirty-five years and

left a lasting imprint on every feature of state involvement in aviation.

Wolf also recalled that budget limitations forced him to focus on the air marking program, which meant "a sign up on a roof that would be easily seen," by aviators. The sign would identify the place and indicate the whereabouts of the local airport. Wolf was able to persuade the Federal Aviation Administration that adding the longitude and latitude to the sign was unnecessary. "I said that they all have maps who fly around here, so they changed it. We must have saved thousands of gallons of paint."

He also convinced the FAA to switch to chrome yellow and black paint for the air markers

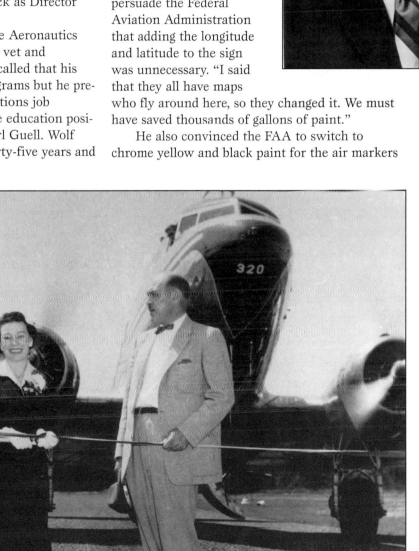

Above: Governor Warren P. Knowles in the 1960s. (Bureau of Aeronautics)

Left: Lester Maitland, Tom Jordan and an unidentified ribbon cutter at the inauguration of Wisconsin Central Airline service to Land'O'Lakes in 1950. After serving as the first Director of the Wisconsin Bureau of Aeronautics, Maitland moved on to a similiar position in Michigan. Jordan then took Maitland's place in Wisconsin. (Robert Wylie)

lease and provided them with an incentive to improve the operation. "The industry got much stronger, and the airports got to be more useful, and they became a good asset for any city looking for new industries."

On the education side of the bureau, Guell developed programs for every level of student from kindergarten to college and beyond. Several thousand veterans used G.I. Bill benefits to enroll in newly-founded flight schools. The peak year was 1948 when 1,155 veterans were training in ninety-five flight schools, seventy of which were no more than two years old. The boom ended as the veterans used up their benefits. By 1953, the number of flight schools in the state had dropped to nineteen.

The extension of G.I. Bill rights to veterans of the Korean War revived veterans flight education programs in the state. The program peaked in the late 1950s with about 250 veterans taking flight training and lasted until Congress altered the Korean vets benefits program in 1965.

World War II had so stimulated popular interest in aviation that some optimists believed that in postwar America not only would every family have a car or two, many would also have an airplane. Guell was able to build on this interest. He pioneered the use of the airplane as an educational tool for teachers and the non-flying public. Milwaukee State Teachers College (now the University of Wisconsin-Milwaukee) became the first state facility to use an airplane for teacher training. With Guell at the controls in 1949, geography teachers in training went aloft to examine the lay of the land before they taught it to their students.

The "aerial field trip" became a popular part of teacher education in Wisconsin and a field trip to

Above: Air marker at La Crosse 1948, part of the successful Aeronautics Commission program.

Right: Aviation educator Carl Guell and an aspiring pilot, 1950s. (Bureau of Aeronautics)

instead of the original orange and white since, "you couldn't see them when it was snowing." In a few years Wisconsin was recognized as the best air-marked state in the Union, with over 1,850 highly-visible yellow and black signs in place by 1955.

Wolf was also proud of his work administering the "tall tower" law and developing the "tower farm" where antennas hazardous to airplanes could be clustered. He also made Wisconsin a pioneer in the strobe lighting of antennas. "We worked on it and then we worked on it and we got the FAA finally convinced. Finally it became a national method of lighting towers."

The number of airports in Wisconsin increased every year in the 1940s and '50s, but the financially perilous condition of many fixed based operators at smaller municipal airports did not improve. In response, Wolf developed a model contract which gave FBOs the security of a long term

the airport part of the curriculum in many state schools. In the course of his work, Guell also became an excellent aerial photographer and pioneered the use of aerial photos in university, high school and elementary education. He gained national recognition for bringing together the aviation and education communities in Wisconsin.

Stimulated by the observation of the Wisconsin centennial of statehood in 1948, Guell also started work with the State Historical Society and began to collect the history of Wisconsin aviation that was the starting point for this book.

One special feature of this work was the "Historical Flight." Pilots volunteered to fly a group of historians, teachers and students from Madison to a selected site in Wisconsin, so the passengers could study its history. Dora Drews, a

State Historical Society Staffer, CAP member and pilot, coordinated the program from Madison. The first historical flight took off for Green Bay in October 1949, with additional flights scheduled to Boscobel, Siren, Madeline Island and Marinette in 1950.

As the Russian and American space programs developed in the late 1950s and early 1960s, the Commission expanded the definition of its role from "aviation" education work to "aerospace" education.

All the work performed by Wolf, Guell and other Aeronautics Commission people was in response to the unprecedented growth of aviation in the first ten years after World War II. All of the numbers were up, starting with airports, which increased from sixty to 116 between 1946 and 1956.

Tall tower "park" on the as yet undeveloped west side of Madison, 1963. (Bureau of Aeronautics)

Right: Teachers from Whitewater ready for an "aerial field trip," 1956. (Bureau of Aeronautics)

Below: The Bureau of Aeronautics's Cessna 170B, 1955. (Bureau of Aeronautics)

The federal government sent Wisconsin $5.1 million for airports in those years. Local government taxes produced an additional $5.4 million and the state contributed $1.3 million. State funding of aviation was increased in 1953, when the legislature mandated registration of all aircraft kept in Wisconsin with fees placed into an airport development fund. Taxes collected on airline property in the state and unrefunded aviation fuel taxes also went into the fund.

To name just a few projects, the tax money was spent to build new airports at Edgerton, Prairie du Chien, Clam Lake, West Salem, Mercer and many other places. It also built new administration buildings at La Crosse, Madison and Wausau, paved the runway at Milwaukee's Curtiss-Wright, graded and drained three grass strips at Phillips, and installed lights at Grantsburg.

Commercial airline traffic also increased. In 1946, Wisconsin had two airlines—Northwest and Capital—serving only Milwaukee and Madison. Ten years later, eight airlines offered regularly scheduled service to thirteen Wisconsin cities, with another four served by airports just over the state line. Between 1948 and 1955, the number of passengers enplaned tripled from 112,256 to 339,390.

The expansion of commercial service required the approval of the federal Civilian Aeronautics Board. Wisconsin was represented in the process by the state attorney general, based on recommendations from the Aeronautics Commission. The expansion of airline service to Milwaukee was the leading concern, but the interests of Ashland, Marshfield, Eau Claire, Wausau, Beloit-Janesville, and other cities were also upheld.

In order to reinforce the links between local governments, business groups and the aviation industry itself, the Commission sponsored the first

Wisconsin Aeronautics Conference in 1956. The meetings quickly acquired a reputation for solid educational and informational programs and for garnering the support of other organizations. The list of co-sponsors over the years has included the Wisconsin Chamber of Commerce, the League of Wisconsin Municipalities, Wisconsin Counties Association, Wisconsin Towns Association, Wisconsin Aviation Trades Association and Wisconsin Airport Managers Association.

Links to other organizations in the aviation community were also maintained through the Wisconsin Aviation Advisory Council, which included the Wisconsin Pilots Association, Wisconsin Aviation Trades Association, the Flying Farmers, Civil Air Patrol and other groups.

General aviation did not experience the phenomenal growth visionaries expected in 1945, but it did expand. Not every Wisconsin family had a hangar in the backyard, but the number of aircraft in the state doubled from 660 in 1945 to 1350 in 1955.

The staff of the Aeronautics Commission also doubled in these years, but was still small enough to fit around a dining room table. The original 1946 trio of Tom Jordan, Fritz Wolf and Carl Guell had been augmented by Airport Engineer William Zutter, Accountant Vincent Scallon and Assistant Secretary Georgia Burdick.

With all signs pointing up, the Commission revised the state airport plan for the 1960s. It now called for sixteen air-carrier airports and ninety-two general aviation airports divided into five classes. The smallest, Class 1, airport would have a landing strip 1,800-2,700 feet long; the largest, Class 5, airport would have a strip at least 5,700 feet long. Every community of at least 10,000 people would have an airport with at least one paved runway, 3,600 feet long. Every county should have at least one secondary airport, "capable of being developed to handle all business and industrial aviation needs, and non-scheduled flying." It was an ambitious program intended to build on the progress made in the 1940s and '50s.[1]

THE DEPARTMENT OF TRANSPORTATION

In the 1960s, the legislature and Governor Warren Knowles acted on the recommendations of the Kellett Commission and reorganized the administrative branch of state government. Many small agencies were consolidated into larger departments, including the Aeronautics Commission, which became a Division of the new Department of Transportation. The five-member Commission itself was reconstituted as the Wisconsin Council on Aeronautics and lost its pol-

icy-making power. Under the new scheme of things, state aviation policy as created by the legislature and the governor would be implemented by the Division staff. The Department would be reorganized internally several times in the following decades, and the Division redesignated a Bureau, but the fundamentals would not change. The job of the state aeronautics agency was to implement state aviation policy in cooperation with federal and local governments.

In 1967, Fritz Wolf became division administrator; Joseph Abernathy, director of airport development; Carl Guell, director of education and safety; Gordon Manke, director of finance and statistics. A year later, James Ash was named director of aviation operations. The new Council on Aeronautics was chaired by publisher and fixed

Bureau of Aeronautics staff members Jim Ash, Gordon Manke, Fritz Wolf, Carl Guell and Joe Abernathy, 1971. (Bureau of Aeronautics)

Robert Kunkel, Director in 1988. (Midwest Flyer)

base operator Harry Chaplin of Plymouth, with Willard Pire, Gordon Leonard, John Conway and John Kachel also on board. The Council would maintain a voice in state aviation policy until it was abolished as part of Governor Tommy Thompson's administrative reorganization in the 1990s.

By the 1970s, the pioneering period of the postwar years was over. Except in a handful of counties, the goal of the 1940 airport plan—that every Wisconsin county should have at least one minimally-improved airport—was met. With the completion of the Kenosha, Sheboygan, Appleton, Fond du Lac and Central Wisconsin airports, all of the state's larger cities were served by new airports or by older airports—such as Madison's or Green Bay's—that had been so improved they were new in all but name.

That the system had matured was made evident by the type of project funded. In the 1950s, for example, aid money went to buy land, grade the first runways and lay down the first layer of asphalt. In the 1970s, aid money went not only to improve runways but also to install up-to-date lighting and navigation aids, improve taxiways and aprons, buy snow removal, fire protection and safety equipment and build bigger maintenance buildings, fuel tank farms and terminals. In the 1980s and '90s, aid money was used to build longer and wider runways at general aviation airports so they could accommodate greater use by business aircraft.

Airports laid as much or more concrete as blacktop. By the end of the decade, for example, the Central Wisconsin airport alone had over forty road miles of concrete surface. Wisconsin had moved from the first to the second stage of airport development. The airport engineering and inspection roles of the Bureau expanded accordingly.

Planning also became an integral part of air-

port operation in the 1970s. A requirement for federal and state funding but also an excellent management tool, airport master plans forced managers and local political leaders to think ahead, take the long view, and look at today's step in terms of how it would affect tomorrow, next year and the next decade.

In 1978, aeronautics bureau personnel expanded planning for their own agency as well. They set out to "compile an exhaustive list of everything that should be done in order to achieve an ideal air transport program....to develop the ideal system." In the process the bureau would define its own role in the future so it could decide, as one planner suggested whether "to lead, follow, or get out of the way." As it turned out, of course, the bureau was required to do all three. Just when to do which was still the important question.

One reason planning was so important is that the amount of money spent on airports had increased at a rate that would astound the most optimistic airport visionary of the 1940s. In the decade between 1945 and 1955 the federal government had sent a total of $5.1 million in airport aid to Wisconsin, and local governments had spent about as much. In the two-year budget for 1972-'73, federal aid totaled $9.8. million. By 1977-'79, that figure had more than doubled; by 1985 it would surpass $30 million and, two years later, cross the $40 million mark. By 1991-1993, the total of local, state and federal money spent on airport development would exceed $90 million.

By then, the system had matured even further, as once again evidenced by the type and location of the projects funded: a radar facility at Central Wisconsin, the relocation of Highway 51 to allow for expansion at Madison, the relighting of runways and taxiways at Timmermann, master plans for virtually every other airport project in the state. All these projects went well beyond the basics of airport development that were so important decades earlier.

In 1981, Fritz Wolf retired as director of aeronautics. He was succeeded by acting director Carl Guell then by Fred Gammon, who held the job until moving to the private sector in 1987. He was succeeded by Dave Strand, who served until 1988. Robert Kunkel, an engineer who had spent his career with the Bureau and had most recently served as chief of airport engineering and deputy director, then moved into the top spot at Aeronautics.

Guiding Kunkel and his staff would be the latest and most ambitious state airport plan. Although it harkened back to the first plan drawn up a half-century earlier, the Wisconsin Airport System Plan, 1986-2010, was a departure from its predecessors. First, it covered a longer time span, unlike previous plans with a lifespan of six years. It also recognized the new realities of an expanding airline industry newly adjusted to and prospering in a deregulated environment. It also noted the growing importance of corporate aviation and the

![Wisconsin Airport System Plan: 1986-2010 — WISCONSIN DEPARTMENT OF TRANSPORTATION, December 1986]

Wisconsin Airport System Plan: 1986-2010

WISCONSIN DEPARTMENT OF TRANSPORTATION
December 1986

demands it would make on the state's mid-sized airports. Finally, it recognized that, even though Wisconsin had been building airports for fifty years, gaps still existed.

The plan projected a state airport system based on 108 publicly-funded airports, plus another 500-some private landing strips, seaplane bases and heliports. The airports on the plan would require an estimated $315 million in improvements in the coming twenty-five years. Assuming that use of Mitchell International and Dane County would grow, the plan called for the immediate designation of Morey Field as a reliever airport for Dane County and the addition of Capitol, West Bend, Burlington and Hartford as relievers for Mitchell. The need for the additional relievers was based on the projection that statewide operations would cross the three million mark by the year 2000 and hit 3.3 million by 2010.

The plan also reported gaps in the state system in Green Lake county and in the Mississippi River counties from Pierce to Trempealeau. It also called for additional study to improve airports in Dunn and Barron counties.

Finally, the plan recogized the development of helicopters and their increased use in the future. It suggested that regular helicopter service could be implemented from Dane County, Mitchell Airports and other large airports to downtown heliports thereby delivering passengers to their ultimate destination in less time than by auto.

The plan presents a good perspective on the role of state government in Wisconsin aviation at the close of the 20th Century. Attention still

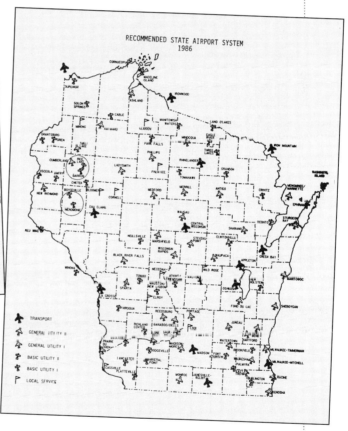

must be paid to the basic goal of building an airport in every county, while maintaining and expanding existing facilities, and keeping an eye on how to meet the needs of the future.

After completing one of the most prestigious careers in the field of aviation education in the United States, Carl Guell retired in 1985. The top aeronautics education job was passed to Duane Esse, who held it until his retirement in 1992. Since the position was not filled due to the state hiring freeze, Esse continued work on a limited basis until January 1998. The programs he, Guell

The current Wisconsin Airport Plan guides aviation development into the next century. (SHSW)

and other Wisconsin people developed over the years gave the state the reputation as having the finest state aviation education program in the country.

In 1992, the Education and Safety Section was consolidated with Airport Operations to become the Aviation Management and Education Section. Headed by Tom Thomas, the Section led Wisconsin aviation education into the space age with the first launch of a Super Loki rocket at Sheboygan in May, 1996. Students of all ages, from elementary to college, participated in 1996 and 1997, with the launch site officially named Spaceport Sheboygan. A third rocket was launched in 1997, with students from Michigan in control.

The Aeronautics Bureau, the Department of Public Instruction, the Wisconsin Aerospace Education Association and interested individuals—aviators and educators—developed a comprehensive set of aviation education and safety programs for the state. They included workshops for teachers in training at the university level and for teachers already in the classroom; supervision of

high school aeronautics courses and aviation career programs, vocational-technical school courses and ground schools; and the supervision and inspection of private flight training programs.

In the late 1980s, Lyle Maves and Mary Millard of Superior organized a committee to work with Duane Esse and other Bureau personnel to establish a university-level aviation curriculum at the University of Wisconsin-Superior. Starting in the fall of 1998, the aviation courses will be part of a transportation studies option offered to students. Committee work continues, but the first steps have been taken to include aviation in university academics.

Safety programs included general aviation pilot refresher programs attended by thousands of flyers; flight instructor refresher courses; flight checks and safety inspections; publication of newsletters, bulletins, the airport directory and the Wisconsin aeronautical chart.

Probably the most satisfying education programs were those involving young people. As of 1989, twenty-nine Wisconsin high schools had avi-

ation courses, with the Madison school system leading the way. Teachers Bud Rogers at LaFollette, Michael McArdle at Madison East and Jim Hein at Madison Memorial used aviation and flight training programs in their own right, and also as a means to introduce students to science. The three-year Madison East program started with an introduction to flight that covered everything from the history of aviation to purchasing an airplane. Year two covered metereology and ground school, followed by independent study that usually led to a pilot's license. Graduates of the programs continued in university aerospace programs then to careers in aviation.

One graduate of the Madison Memorial program was Sherry Pottinger, who went on to become a pilot of the Midway Connection commuter line out of Madison. "The class was fun. It really held your interest," she told a reporter in 1989.

"I'm the last one on the plane and when I close the door people think I'm supposed to sit in the back. Then I walk all the way up to the front and they say, 'Oh, she's the pilot'." Pottinger illustrates the purpose of aviation education programs—to enable Wisconsin people to enjoy aviation, fly safely and to earn a living at it.[2]

AEROSPACE EDUCATION IN WISCONSIN

The Wisconsin Aerospace Education Committee was organized in 1964 by Aeronautics Bureau staff to develop and improve aerospace education efforts in the state. It worked with university educators, teachers-in-training, classroom teachers and students themselves to make aerospace a real part of the school curriculum in Wisconsin.

Responding to a request from the National Aerospace Education Association, the Committee and interested teachers and aviators organized the Wisconsin Aerospace Education Association in 1973. Its goal was "to develop, support and improve aviation/aerospace education in Wisconsin," by concentrating on communication between the aerospace and education communities.

Among the first members were Mary Hodge, Janesville; Carl Smith, Madison; Ed Colbert, Waunakee; Robert W. Heins, Madison; Fred Davel, Shawano; Earl Pingel, West Allis; Bill Menzel, Eau Claire; Duane Esse, Madison; Marie Grimm, Wausau; Hildegard R. Kuse, Stevens Point; Roland

Solberg, La Crosse; Jose D'Arruda, Richland Center, and many others.

In the years since, the efforts and membership of the Council and the Association have overlapped, with the Committee organizing programs and the Association publicizing them through its newsletter, which has been edited by Earl Pingel for all its twenty-five years.

Probably the most intensive aerospace education program in which members of the Committee and the Association participated began in 1976. The Education Outreach Office of the University of Wisconsin-Milwaukee responded positively to a request to offer a three-credit, graduate/undergraduate summer school course for teachers.

In the first week, the teachers took introductory flights in a small plane, a helicopter and a glider. They attended lectures on air navigation, communications, aircraft maintenance and the physical

requirements for pilots. They went behind the scenes at Mitchell International, touring airline operations, airport security, fire protection, international arrivals, air traffic and approach control and a fixed base operation.

The second week featured an educational specialist from NASA who provided an update on space exploration and education projects. The teachers were able to try lessons and activities such as model rocketry and airplanes, then demonstrated the rules of gravity with an egg drop.

In the third week the teachers went on a field trip, which included a flight in a military aircraft usually to the Kennedy Space Center in Florida for

Aerospace Education Association members Earl Pingel, Ellen Baerman and George Henderson at a CAP award ceremony. (Don Winkler)

George Henderson, center, and Bert Grover, Superintendent of the Wisconsin Department of Public Instruction, right, accepting an FAA Award for excellence in aviation education from the FAA's Monte Belger, 1987. (Don Winkler)

teaching at Lancaster school in Milwaukee coordinated a program in which six hundred students participated. The highlight of a week devoted to aerospace school programs was "Helicopter Day" when an Air National Guard chopper parked on the school playground for the children to see, touch and climb on.

In that same year, WAEA was also involved in the "Dream Flight Wausau" program, where teacher Sharon Ryan simulated a space voyage for 140 students. Building a model of the solar system, conducting space science experiments and converting a school bus into space were all part of an imaginative program that drew national attention to Wausau.

The work of teachers like Ryan is recognized through the Aerospace Educator of the Year Award named in honor of Carl Guell. The list of distinguished educators so honored ranges from primary school teacher Ellen Baerman to university professor Jack Kirby and many others in between.

In the words of WAEA co-founder and secretary Earl Pingel, the goal of the Association has been to further "an understanding among fellow educators and the general public that aviation/space education should be represented as a part of the school curriculum." [3]

a special tour of facilities there. It was a tightly structured program providing an introducton to the aviation industry, the military, airlines and general aviation.

The program was directed by Earl Pingel and G. Kenneth Whyte from 1977 to 1981 and with Pingel and Ellen Baerman from 1982 to 1994.

In the early 1990s, the aerospace educators were hard at work on Wisconsin's first Aviation in Education Week. Taking advantage of the observation, Wendy Weiner, a teacher and WAEA member

NATURAL RESOURCES AVIATION

Above: Jack Vilas and his Curtiss Flying boat at Trout Lake, Vilas County in 1915. A Chicago native who made the first airplane flight across Lake Michigan in 1913, Vilas was commissioned as the "official aviator" of the Wisconsin State Forestry board in 1915. He patrolled the northern forests spotting and reporting fires. Vilas's flights were the first use of an airplane for conservation work. (DNR)

Far Left: The first airplane purchased by the Wisconsin Conservation Department, a Stinson 108-2. In the 1920s and '30s, the Conservation Department contracted with many flyers for fire patrol duties in northern Wisconsin. Although it built a landing field at Tomahawk in 1940, the Department did not own an airplane or hire its own pilot until 1947. Jack Wolhaupt was the first WCD pilot. In a career that lasted more than thirty years, he flew a variety of aircraft including a Cessna 180, Beech T34B, and Beaver U-6A. Painted on the fuselage of the 1947 Stinson is "Torchy Timber Loss." The logo was created by WCD employee "Toots" Jaunti and might have gained national renown had it not been replaced by Smokey the Bear. (DNR)

Left: Wisconsin Department of Natural Resources pilot Dave Greene and Conservation Warden Linda Winn preparing for a patrol in the 1980s. Over the years the scope of conservation aviation has increased dramatically. Department of Natural Resources aircraft have been used for aerial photography, fire patrol and supression, wildlife and environmental monitoring and enforcement. (DNR)

WISCONSIN AVIATION FOR TOMORROW

Wisconsin aviation encompasses its past and lays the foundation for its future through educational programs.

Oshkosh Police Officer Jim Busha flew an ultralight to area schools to talk about drug abuse and crime prevention. As Busha reports, it's not hard get a student's attention when you land an ultralight in the school yard.

Students also play close attention to the Rockets For Schools program at "Spaceport Sheboygan." In May of 1996, young people from all over Wisconsin came to Sheboygan to take

part in the launch of a Super Loki rocket. The launch was the climax of a day long program devoted to science and aerospace career education organized by the Wisconsin Aerospace Education Committee. Michelle Ruder, Mosinee, assisted by Allison Thiel of Tomah, pushed the button for lift off. The rocket roared into the heavens and was soon lost from sight, except for the images transmitted to ground monitors from a camera in its nose. Recovery crews hoped to retrieve the rocket after a twenty-five mile flight over Lake Michigan. Instead the Loki hit an air cur-

Above: A Super Loki rocket lifts off at Spaceport Sheboygan. (Milwaukee Journal-Sentinel)

Right: Officer Jim Busha and students at Oshkosh and the ultralight in the schoolyard. (Jim Busha)

rent that carried it all the way to Ohio. The first launch was so successful that more student rocketers came to Wisconsin's only "Spaceport" in 1997 and '98.

Inaugurated in Milwaukee in 1989 and later in Madison, the Aviation Careers Education Program—ACE, also introduces students to a future in aerospace. Targeted at low income and minority students from elementary, middle and high schools, ACE is a partnership that brings together schools, government agencies and aviation businesses. High school age participants work as interns in aircraft maintenance, on ground crews, behind airline ticket counters and elsewhere to gain work experience in aerospace.[4]

Milwaukee ACE Program interns at work with business partners from Signature Flight Services, Midwest Express and Continental America West Airlines. (Dave Greene)

DOUGLAS DC-6

Cruising speed 328 MPH
Ceiling 29,000 ft

1955

Above: Northwest Airlines DC-6 at Madison Municipal
Airport in the 1950s. (Bureau of Aeronautics)
Opposite: Volunteer Manager of the Adams County Airport
for many years, Tom Reise, (second row, right) won a precision landing contest in 1984. (Midwest Flyer)

Modern Aviation

AIRPORT DEVELOPMENTS
1945 - 1998

Adams County

In the years before World War II, Adams County flyers used the infield of the county fairgrounds in Friendship as a landing strip or any convenient farm clearing. The first homegrown flyer on record in Adams County was Everett Erickson who, along with Bob Roseberry, flew a Curtiss Junior and a Piper J-2 off a landing field they cleared in the Town of Strongs Prairie.

In the 1950s, war veteran Don Hollman flew his plane off of a landing strip cut out of the jackpines south of the city of Adams.

The present Adams County Airport began in 1958, when Leslie Flott built an 1,800-foot runway southeast of Adams. That same year a forest fire burned hundreds of acres nearby, including the Memorial Forest planted by the local American Legion Post after World War II.

The Legionnaires donated the burned over ground to the county for airport use. The new Legion Field airport officially opened with a grand fly-in and aerial show in 1962. In the years since, an active airport association, whose Father's Day Fly-In was a major summer event in the 1980s and '90s, and the county government, have improved the facility. Naval air veteran Tom Reise was the volunteer manager of the airport for many years. He played a key role in developing the airport that is currently scheduled to receive its first instrument approach procedure using satellite technology.

Adams County has also been home to the Clearwater Ranch landing strip. Now closed, the 2,600-foot asphalt runway was part of a 1960s vacation home development managed by Cessna 205 owner Ed Tangney.[1]

Ashland County

One of Wisconsin's island airports is in Ashland County on Madeline Island. Work on the airport began in the years after World War II, with a $20,000 appropriation of federal, state and town funds. Governor Oscar Rennebohn was scheduled to attend the dedication in August 1949, but the event had to be postponed when two local men, Vincent O'Brien and Jim Russell, were killed in a crash one day earlier.

Despite this inauspicious beginning, the Madeline Island Airport was established. The runway was surfaced with asphalt as part of a general improvement program that began in the late 1960s. The airport serves

local people and the large number of vacationers who visit every year.

In the 1980s and '90s the Island's best-known aviator was ultralight pilot Wayne Nelson. He used his plane for sport to chase seagulls and for serious purposes, such as assisting in the rescue of boats stranded on the ice of Lake Superior. In 1994, Nelson flew his ultralight from Madeline to Thunder Bay, Ontario, 100 miles across Lake Superior.

A new airport for the city of Ashland went on the state drawing boards in 1956 and opened for business in 1959. Flyers out of Ashland in these years flew equipment and supplies to logging crews working on the Apostle Islands and other isolated sites. They also car-

Ashland Airport Terminal, 1968. (Bureau of Aeronautics)

possible," he wrote.

In 1945, Rice Lake purchased 160 acres north of the city limits and moved airport headquarters there. In the words of local aviation historian, Bob Heffner, "that began the long odyssey to provide the type and size airport the city desired, a journey that was to take 51 years." In the meantime, as many as ten different sites were considered, as well as ownership by the county, the city, or some combination thereof. Rice Lake flyers used several different fields on the south, southwest and north sides of the city, as well as a seaplane port in town, before concentrating on the privately-built Arrowhead Airport on the south side.

By the early 1990s, after overcoming obstacles presented by landowners reluctant to sell, town zoning ordinances, voter opposition at the polls, bald eagle nesting sites, a natural gas pipeline and pioneer archeological diggings, a site was selected in the Town of Stanley near Cameron. Ground was broken in 1994 and operations began in 1995.

The Rice Lake Regional Airport was named Carl's Airport in honor of long time city airport manager Carl Rindlisbacher. Local aviator and airport commissioner Jim Conn used Carl's Airport to prepare for his attempt to circumnavigate the globe via the North and South Pole in 1994.

ried commercial fishermen out on the frozen lake, and a few hardy sportsmen who bobbed for trout on the ice.

Dr. A.G. Sell of Ashland served on the state Aeronautics Commission throughout the 1940s and '50s. Ashland also had a very active Civil Air Patrol squadron, which in 1955 alone, participated in over fifty search and rescue operations in the woods and waters of the north country.

In September 1963, helicopters carrying President John F. Kennedy and his entourage landed at the Ashland Airport after a tour of the Apostle Islands. Two months later Kennedy died, and shortly after the Ashland Airport was named in his honor.

The Glidden airport opened in 1951 and provided local service until it was deactivated in the 1980s.[2]

Barron County

Before World War II, Barron County had public airports at Rice Lake, Barron, Dallas and Chetek. The Dallas field closed during World War II and did not reopen but, in 1946, operations began at Cumberland.

As early as 1943, state aeronautics administrator Tom Jordan had cautioned Rice Lake aviators that the airport site they had been using on the south side of the city was inadequate to meet the needs of the future. "The airport at Rice Lake should be a Class III with....sufficient land available so that expansion to a Class IV airport with runways of 4,800 feet is

The Barron airport began in the 1930s when Oscar Ormson and Harry Carlsteen rebuilt a crash-damaged Pietenpol and flew it off a hayfield on the east side of the city. After World War II the city purchased the 27-acre site which has been used over the years by local flyers Ed Chermack, Maurice Peterson and others. The city mows the grass in summer,

Breaking ground at Rice Lake: Dick Leitner, Jess Miller, Jack Blom, Barbara Rindlisbacher, Jim Conn. Acting locally and thinking globally, in 1994 Jim Conn attempted to fly around the world by way of the North and South Poles. (Bob Heffner)

plows the snow in winter, while operations are managed by the Barron Flying Club.

The Chetek Airport began with a donation of 34 acres of land, with 300 feet of lake frontage, by Fred Southworth in 1937. Not a aviator himself, Southworth saw the need for an airport in his home town and supplied the land.

Activity at Chetek was sparse until the 1970s, when two local physicians, David Pierpont and Fred Bannister, purchased forty acres adjacent to the original airport and extended the runway. Chetek became the home of "flying octogenarian" John Hendricks, who celebrated his 83rd birthday in 1995, by taking a flight.

The Cumberland airport got its start when I.N. Toftness and Clarence Burton decided they didn't want to drive to Rice Lake to fly

CARL'S FIELD DEDICATION
SEPTEMBER 2, 1995
CARL RINDLISBACHER
October 29, 1923 - November 24, 1992
Weather Observer, USAF 1941 - 1945
Rice Lake Airport Manager 1957 - 1992

WEATHERMAN EXTRAORDINAIRE AND PILOT'S FRIEND

Flying Fields are usually named after great pilots. Carl was not a pilot-but he was great. Greatness is often associated with national prominence. Carl was not nationally prominent but he was deeply respected and loved by those of us in aviation who knew of his dedication to his weather and to his pilots whom he served in countless ways over many decades. Carl's Field is the fulfilled vision of Carl's dream, a safe new airport for Rice Lake and all of the pilots who fly in and out of this wonderful area of Northwestern Wisconsin.

Dedication plaque for the Rice Lake Airport, 1995. (Bob Heffner)

their airplanes. In 1946, they purchased eighty acres southwest of the city and cleared a runway. In the 1970s and 1980s, with generous support from I.N. and Louise Toftness, both pilots, the airport was improved. In 1988-89, it had about 9,500 operations.

Also in Barron County is the 2,500 asphalt strip built by Bud Kennan at his "Tagalong" resort on the shores of Red Cedar Lake near Birchwood.[3]

Bayfield County

Bayfield County has been served by local service airports at Cornucopia, Iron River and Drummond, and the public airport at Cable.

Work on building an airport at Cornucopia started in 1958 after St. Paul pilot Hale O'Malley decided to stop using State Highway 13 for landings and takeoffs on visits to his weekend cottage on Lake

Libby Parod welcoming an airplane to Cable. (C. Reynolds)

Superior. O'Malley located the right piece of land, persuaded the owner—Nekoosa-Edwards Paper—to swap it for another parcel owned by the Town of Bell, then got the local Men's Club involved. O'Malley then persuaded building contractor Al Brevak to donate some labor and equipment, the Men's Club put in some more effort, and the landing strip was scraped out of the forest. It took nearly ten years of effort, but the airport opened for business in 1967. Perched on the Bayfield Peninsula, Cornucopia is the northernmost airstrip in Wisconsin.

Air service in the Eau Claire Lakes region near Drummond began in the early 1950s at Sorenson's Airport. Pilot Lee Sorenson cleared a grass strip and promoted the airport as a fast and easy means to reach the many resorts in the area.

In the late 1940s, the countryside near Cable in southern Bayfield County was a busy place. An innovative entrepreneur named Tony Wise was building what was then a new and different kind of resort at Mount Telemark. Within walking distance of the lodge, Tony and Libby Parod cleared a stretch of ground and called it an airport. "We were actually pioneering," recalled Libby. "There was nothing."

By 1950, they had a turf runway and, since Telemark was a ski resort, stayed open year round. With help from Racine aviators Sam Johnson and John Batten, the Parods extended the asphalt runway to 3,700 feet by 1962.

Tony Parod passed away in 1959, and Libby became airport manager. She worked as line-person, groundskeeper, and ground crew on the landing strip.

"I do everything that has to be done on the airport," she told an interviewer in 1985. As part of a thriving tourist region, the governments of the Towns of Namekegon, Drummond and Cable all lend support to the airport, which has averaged 6,000 operations since the mid-1980s.

Parod has welcomed visiting aviators with a cup of coffee and her famous brownies for nearly fifty years. "There is a real love for the airport and the people. The pilots they make the whole game. They are wonderful."

Still on the job as this book is written, Libby Parod is the longest-serving airport manager in Wisconsin.[4]

Brown County

Brown County completed its shift of airport operations from Blesch Field to Austin Straubel Airport in 1948. Wisconsin Central began regular commercial service on October 1 that year when two passengers boarded the flight to the Twin Cities and four boarded for Chicago. The airline operated out of a contractor's shack with one employee. By 1956, Green Bay boasted that it had more scheduled flights per day than any city of its size in the country. In 1974, nearly 250,000 airline passengers departed from Austin Straubel, making it a close rival to Madison as the second-busiest airport in the state. North Central Airlines, formerly Wisconsin Central, was still the leading air carrier at Green Bay, but the city was also served by Green Bay Air Service and the Peninsula Air Transport.

A new terminal was built in 1965. It featured passenger and baggage facilities, a restaurant and waiting area, plus space for the weather bureau, the FAA flight service station and a three-story tall control tower. The new facilities were completed in time for North Central to land its first DC-9 jets at Green Bay in 1969.

Brown County Airport, with no neighbors in 1960 (Sky Eye) and on the edge of town in 1990. (Bureau of Aeronautics)

Green Bay continued to be an important mini-hub for North Central until deregulation in 1979. As the airlines reorganized service again and again, Green Bay became less important—but still busy. By 1996, Austin Straubel was served by six airlines with up to forty departures daily.

In the last forty years, improvements at the airport have cost more than $37 million, including terminal expansion and a new tower in 1995.

In addition to commercial air traffic, Austin Straubel has served as an alternative field for B-52s and other military aircraft from K.I. Sawyer Air Force Base in Michigan. The bombers and other military aircraft have attracted a lot of spectator interest over the years—but not as much as Green Bay's most popular airline passengers, the Packers football team. The winning teams of the 1960s and 1990s have brought crowds to the field to welcome the champions home.

As a general aviation site, Austin Straubel has grown over the years from about twelve planes in 1950, to forty in 1965 and over 100 in 1995. Both corporate and privately-owned aircraft use the field.

Brown County's second public airport is Carter Field at Pulaski. It has been considered as a reliever for Austin Straubel. A privately-owned, public-use airport with an instrument approach procedure, it has twenty-seven based aircraft and an active corps of parachute jumpers.

The John Antonneau Memorial Airport is located just north of Green Bay. It has one grass runway with lights for seventeen based aircraft and five ultralights.

In addition to Austin Straubel, Pulaski and Antonneau airports, Brown County has had at least eight private landing fields in the years since World War II. Probably the most active was the old Nicolet Field which Boyd Miller and John Garrity opened at De Pere in 1946. Revived by war vets James Sorenson and Clarence Reentmeester in 1955, Nicolet was home port for a very active flying club. With more than 125 members and ten airplanes in 1956, the Nicolet Club sponsored fly-ins, group flights and other activities that kept the airport busy for a few years. Bev Butler took over as airport manager until 1963, after which activity at Nicolet wound down. In 1970, the airport site was sold and developed into a residential subdivision, but its memory lives on in Butler's entertaining book of memoirs, *Piper Cub Era*.

Nicolet Airport was also home of one of Wisconsin's busiest aerial photographers, Calberne Studios. Managed by George Frisbee, Calberne used three Taylorcrafts and three full-time aerial photographer/pilots.[5]

Burnett County

In the 1940s, the population of Burnett County was a bit more than 10,000 people. Yet, when the Burnett County Airport was dedicated in June 1947, an "estimated 15 thousand or more people" were in attendance. Perhaps the thirty-three army and navy planes in the air show helped bring out the crowd, especially the aerobatics performed by Commander R.T. Keeling, "who zoomed his Hell Cat close to 400 miles a hour. Perhaps it was the "air queens" chosen from Burnett and three neighboring counties, or the invitations to 125 other airports in the state, but the airport dedication proved to be one of the largest events in the history of the county.

Work on the airport had actually begun in 1942, funded by the last round of WPA grants. Burnett County received $87,000 to acquire 200 acres, clear enough ground for two runways and build a hangar. The work was delayed until after the war but the airport was ready to go in the summer of 1947.

The Grantsburg Airport also got its start before the war ended.

The village set aside funds to buy land in anticipation of a $25,000 state grant for runways and hangars. Ground was cleared north of the village, but planes did not land until after the war, when aviators from out of town visited the airport to instruct G.I. Bill students.

In 1949, Grantsburg became a CAA Weather and Communications Station which rebroadcast weather information from Minneapolis. The station remained open until 1961 when it was replaced by automated equipment. Offering flight instruction and other services, Sandberg Aviation has been the FBO at Grantsburg since 1983.[6]

Calumet County

The New Holstein Municipal Airport was constructed in 1958. After the Kohler Airport closed in 1960, Mel Thompson became the manager at New Holstein. In 1968, he retired as airport manager, closing out a sixty-year working career as an aviator.

Born in 1897 near Quarry in Manitowoc County, Thompson built his first airplane by modifying a Heathkit in 1918. He continued his inventive ways at New Holstein, where he developed a special door for parachute jumping that could be installed quickly in a Cessna 180. He continued to fly until 1970 and reluctantly sold his airplane. He died at age 89 in 1986.

At New Holstein, he worked well with limited resources to develop a fine small community airport.[7]

Chippewa County

Chippewa Falls aviators flew off of several fields on the outskirts of the city in the 1930s until settling in at a landing strip a few miles southwest of the city. This Chippewa Falls airport was used mainly for recreational flying, while aviators who hoped to make a living from it worked out of the Eau Claire Airport on the south side of that city.

Charles Wood, whose father Guy had been one of the founders of the Eau Claire Airport and was himself an experienced glider pilot, flew out of Chippewa Falls between 1939 and 1942. He had just returned from Poland where he had been taking instruction at the world famous gliding school at Katowice. When the Nazi armies occupied Czechoslovakia in 1938, Poland participated and Wood decided to come home. Had he stayed in Poland another year, he would have been present when the Nazis turned on their Polish allies and started World War II in Europe.

Wood acquired a Luscombe and barnstormed at picnics and celebrations in Cadott, Stanley, Cornell and other nearby villages. Once, after a day of giving rides at the Chippewa Falls field, he was approached by the man who lived in the farmhouse nearest the airport.

"He came out and asked how we were doing." Wood recalled. "I was kind of naive about it. I pulled out a whole bunch of money out of my pocket and he said 'don't you think you owe some of that to me for rent on that field?'"

Wood and the other flyers who used the airport had assumed that "somebody" was taking care of details like the rent.

When World War II began the Chippewa landing field shut down and did not reopen. Prompted by the presence of the munitions plant during the war, local business leaders—and Charles Wood when he was home on leave—established a new airport on the northern edge of Eau Claire. Although it is actually in Chippewa County, the airport was built by the city of Eau Claire and is now owned and operated by Eau Claire County. (Its story is told on Page 132).

Charles Wood with his Chevy and his Luscombe at the Chippewa Falls Airport, 1940.
(Charles Wood)

One of the pilots Chuck Wood met in Chippewa County was Robert Jahnke. He was living on the family farm near Cadott in 1936 when he built a plane that he called the "Jahnke Eagle." The Eagle flew but Jahnke soon moved up to an J-2 Taylor Cub that he used to barnstorm around the county. He kept the plane at the Stanley airport, which was known as "the world's smallest" because it was only sixty feet wide by six hundred feet long. After World War II Wally Kozlowski used this field to give flight instruction to G.I. Bill students. When the G.I. benefits ran out, so did the students and the "world's smallest airport" closed.

County flyers could move up to the new Cornell airport which was just getting under way in 1947. City leaders selected a site on the road to Brunet State Park. Since the land needed to be cleared, they encouraged citizens to log it. There must not have been a wood shortage in Cornell that year because the prospective airport remained a forest. In 1948, the Aeronautics Commission urged the city to find a site on cleared ground. After a bit of a search a site was found about one mile east of the city and Cornell's new airport was built.

Bob Jahnke was the leading pilot and he instructed many local people, including Joe Reali, Fred Anderson, Vince Squire and Harold Walters. The airport was slowly improved, but in 1968, one pilot remarked that when he landed, "The grass was so high that I didn't need the brakes to stop the plane." This situation was remedied in 1980, when the airport was blacktopped. The airport continues to serve local aviators and transient flyers on their way to the lake country to the north.

Chippewa County also has a private airport for local use at Bloomer, a CAP landing field at Chippewa Falls and numerous private landing strips.[8]

Clark County

Neillsville began work on building an airport in 1944, with the backing of a positive referendum vote. On Labor Day weekend, 1945,

a crowd of 7,000 turned out for the dedication and air show at the landing field six miles west of the city on Wedge's Creek.

The bright hopes faded in the 1950s and the city council voted to abandon the airport in 1956. In 1968, the pendulum swung the other way and the community began to talk about an airport. As many as ten sites were offered before the Aeronautics Division accepted 170 acres, three miles east of the city.

Construction work began in 1973, with help from a $32,570 federal/state grant and $50,000 from Neillsville's Marguerite Listerman Foundation. The new airport was dedicated in July 1974. It featured a 3,000 foot runway and the "only multi-colored hangar" in Wisconsin, courtesy of Harold "Duffy" Gaier, who has served as manager and FBO ever since.[9]

Columbia County

The Portage Airport remains where Bob and Chester Mael established it in 1930. Aviation interest at Portage in the years since World War II followed the familiar course of upswing in the 1940s and downturn in 1950s.

The Maels continued to own the field, which had two 2,800-foot grass runways. In 1960, the city of Portage leased the airport and contracted with Harvey Miller and his Portage Aero Service as FBO. By 1962, the runways were surfaced, seventeen aircraft were kept on the premises and work commenced on a 134-foot hangar.

By the late 1960s, the picture had changed, with local officials discussing whether they should improve the airport, limit development around it, or close it. The airport stayed where it was, with the runways later extended to 3,000 and 3,700 feet. In the years since the airport has been hemmed in by major highway construction on two sides and commercial development on a third.

Portage Municipal, named Mael Field in honor of its founders, is one of three public airports in Columbia County. Local aviators are also served by landing fields at Rio and Lodi.

The Rio airport, also known as Cowgill Field, is an active public-use airport owned by the Rio Flying Club. It has a neat turf runway, with twelve based aircraft. Founded in 1961, it is named in honor of Air Force Major Arden Cowgill.

Although he didn't do much flying there in recent years, Lodi was home to one of southern Wisconsin's most well-known aviators. Robert Neiman was a veteran of the Imperial German Air Force and flew Rumplers, Albatrosses and Fokkers on the Western Front in World War I. He migrated to the United States in the 1920s and worked in Madison.

In his later years, he developed a slide lecture in which he told of his wartime experiences flying for the "other side." With his white "Santa Claus" beard, German accent, and gift for storytelling, Neiman made real the early days of combat aviation. He passed away in 1982, at 89 years of age.[10]

Crawford County

In 1947, Earl Broadhead, Loyal Johnson and Raymond Schultz, who were doing business as Blackhawk Airways, leased twenty-eight acres of land south of Prairie du Chien for an airport.

In 1953, the city acquired the property and received federal and state funding to improve the sod runway to 3,000 feet. It then became involved in a long-running dispute with an aviator who owned property adjacent to the airport and provided flight services in competition with the city's FBO. The Shawano Airport was involved in a similar dispute that resulted in a lawsuit, but Prairie du Chien's situation was resolved without going to court.

In 1969, the runway was surfaced and extended to 3,500 feet with help from an $81,000 federal and state grant. Two years later the Mississippi Valley Airways of La Crosse extended commuter service to the city, but was forced to terminate in 1974.

By the 1990s manager Glen Meyer had "lots of business traffic at the airport." He pointed out that with railroad traffic curtailed and the nearest interstate highways at least fifty miles away, "there is no other way to get stuff in or out of town." Prairie du Chien has two corporate jets, two privately-owned twin-engine planes plus eleven other aircraft and sixteen hangars at the airport.[11]

Louis Wuilleumeier (left) of Four Lakes Aviation. (Don Winkler)

Dane County

In 1993, the Bureau of Aeronautics conducted a census of airport sites in Wisconsin and discovered that no county had more airports than Dane. Ranging from busy, diverse Truax Field to the residential air park at Waunakee, from the helipad atop the downtown Edgewater Hotel to Dave Weiman's private strip in Oregon, Dane County had fifty-one places where aircraft of one sort or another could land and take off.

The big airport is Dane County Regional, which began life after World World II as Madison's Truax Field, still under lease to the United States Army. The history of the airport for the first twenty years after the war is a parallel story of civilian and military use. Even today, the military presence is strong through the Army and Air National Guard.

The Air Force base was deactivated in 1946, which left the military hangar open for occupancy when Wisconsin Central Airlines moved its headquarters out of Clintonville in 1948. The city also used federal/state grants for a new runway lighting system, terminal and hangar expansion. At this time the airport was still laid out with the terminal, hangars and general aviation facilities on the east side off of old Highway 51. The military base occupied the southern portion of the airport and stretched south almost all the way to Highway 151. The western and northern stretches were vacant wetland.

General aviation activity at Truax was still limited. Louis Wuilleumier was still at Royal Airport, where he managed one of the largest G.I. Bill flight instruction programs in the state. Howard Morey was at his own airport in Middleton where he also ran a large flight training program. Army Air Force veteran

Robert Skuldt began his long career as airport manager in 1946.

The scene began to shift at Truax in the early 1950s. In 1951, the Korean War was underway and the Air Force reactivated its Madison base along with the local Air National Guard unit. A squadron of combat-ready F-51 fighters soon appeared at the airport, with Guardsmen to man them. The following year the Air Force reclaimed its hangar and evicted Wisconsin Central. The civilians were not happy to lose the airline since Madison accounted for twelve percent of its traffic. Ironically, airport manager Robert Skuldt was in no position to protest, since he was an Air Force reservist now on active duty.

Some progress was made on the civilian side, when the city accepted Louis Wuilleumier's bid for the FBO contract instead of Howard Morey's. A majority of the city council felt that Morey would be too busy with other work to focus his attention on airport operations. To be sure, he was chair of the Aeronautics Commission and would soon be named President of Wisconsin Central/North Central Airline. By comparison, Wuilleumier had a Piper dealership, booked charters, ran a flight school and maintained aircraft at Madison until the 1980s.

Relations between Madison and the Air Force were not always smooth. By 1955, passenger traffic had increased to 83,500, residential development was moving closer to the airport, yet daily flights by Air Force jets were the order of the day. Some Madisonians thought armed and dangerous military aircraft should not be stationed so

Morey Airport looking southeast towards Madison, 1960. (Bureau of Aeronautics)

close to a city. The situation was not made easier by some disastrous accidents, including one in which two civilians were injured by shrapnel fired from a burning F-51 as it crashed and another in which Lieutenant Gerald Stull was killed when he crashed his F-102 into Lake Monona to avoid populated areas nearby.

Many people felt that Madison needed to build a new airport. The idea led the *Milwaukee Journal* to state that, "The military has gobbled up Truax Field...Speedy military jets taking off and landing at Truax must take precedence over commercial and private planes....So Madison has been looking at two sites...both around eight miles from the Capitol Square."

The solution for the *Journal* was that "the military would be better off eight miles out of town." However, neither the city nor the military wanted to shoulder the expense of a new airport, so both resolved to live together at Truax.

By 1960, the strategic picture had altered, and the Air Force began a protracted phase out at Madison. By 1962, only the SAGE electronic early warning system and the F-86s of the Air Guard remained in Madison. In 1964, the Air Force announced a final phase out to be completed in 1968. The base closing meant the loss to Madison of 1,700 jobs and $20 million. It also opened acres of land that have been used for residential and commercial development as well as a new campus for the Madison Area Technical College.

Civilian development continued in the 1960s and '70s. A major realignment of airport services occurred in 1967, when the new terminal was built on the west side. As a courtesy to the many people who had difficulty finding their way around the new layout the *Wisconsin State Journal* told its readers that, "The important thing to remember is that International Lane runs off Packers Avenue." The information was important to travelers boarding any one of the eighty-two daily flights provided by the five airlines then serving Madison.

In 1970, airport planners proposed building a new runway east of Highway 51, which would have called for relocating the terminal back to the east side and which ignited a storm of public criticism

James Greene, the father who grew up watching air shows at Royal Airport in the 1930s, became a pilot in the 1970s and founded Air-Pool Travel International as a means for pilots and passengers to share the cost of air travel. Dave Greene, the son (center) who became the first Wisconsin native to enter the Tuskegee Institute aviation program. (Dave Greene)

that helped to kill it. Instead, the existing runways were extended and a plan first considered back in 1952 to move Highway 51 eastwards was revived. In 1974, Dane County assumed ownership and the airport was officially named Dane County Regional-Truax Field.

By the time manager Bob Skuldt retired in 1981, the airport had assumed the configuration in which it would remain until a new $25 million runway was built in 1998. By 1990, commercial passenger traffic had crossed the one million mark and a new terminal addition

Bob Kunkel presents a plaque to Delores and Jerome Ripp in honor of their fifty years of ownership of the Waunakee Airport. (Midwest Flyer)

and parking ramp was on the way. Home to airlines, charter services, flying clubs, flight schools, state government and military aircraft, Dane County is as diverse and modern as any aviation facility in the state.

When Howard Morey built his airport in the cornfields of Middleton during World War II, he was well out of town. In the fifty years since metropolitan sprawl has reached the field and prompted concern among local residents.

In the years in between Morey Airport has been a center for aviation instruction. Howard Morey passed his love of flying down to his son Field and daughter Dale, both licensed pilots. Field has managed the airport since the 1970s and acquired a national reputation for his advanced pilot training program. The training leads to an advanced instrument rating

Field Morey, 1985. (Midwest Flyer)

and includes a three-to-five day cross-country flight to Washington state, down the coast to Los Angeles and back to Middleton.

Morey and co-pilot Oliver Smithies set a few records in 1980, when they decided to fly Morey's Cessna Turbo Centurion to Europe. They prepared for the 2,500 mile ocean hop as thoroughly

that they had a testimonial dinner for him only one year after he arrived. In 1998, the airport is home to thirty hangars and about fifty aircraft under the management of Michael Tegtmeier.

The county airport is a relative newcomer to Dodge County aviation. In the 1920s, Eugene Klink used to fly a Jenny out of local hayfields. When he quit flying in the 1930s and opened a tavern at the junction of Highways 60 and 26, he mounted the plane on the roof and called it the "Blew Inn." The building was torn down in 1959, but a new Blew Inn was constructed and stands today.

Beaver Dam had several landing fields in the 1940s—north, northwest and east of the city. In 1945, Glen Knaup, Norm Knaup and Frank Janczak built a quonset hut for a hangar and cleared a landing strip on the east side of town. Bob Schmidt and Paul Baker joined them in 1946 and incorporated Midway Aviation with six J-3 Cubs and two new Taylorcraft BC-12D's. They soon acquired a Cessna 140 and a four-passenger, low-wing Bellanca 1413 for charter work.

Business boomed and Midway took over management of the Watertown Airport, only to slow down when G.I. Bill students used up their benefits. Janczak pulled out and took the Bellanca to Watertown, where he hoped to find more charters. His partners stayed in Beaver Dam and moved into cropdusting. "The Green Giant people were good friends of mine, so I got part of the Green Giant business and practically all of it in the state," Glen Knaup recalled.

Although a veteran pilot, Paul Baker was the chief mechanic for the company. He recalls that Midway Aviation got its first big cropdusting contract after he and his crew stayed up all night building a new dusting hopper and spreader after the one they had purchased malfunctioned.

"We worked all night long, and by the following morning I had made a whole new spreader, a new door, two agitators, instead of one, chain drive, [with] bicycle sprockets.

"The following afternoon it went to work on one of the largest

as any 1930s's pilot, perhaps even more so, since they had the advantages of modern safety and navigation equipment. Nonetheless it was an adventure to set off in a small plane, watch North America recede beyond the tail and see nothing but cold northern ocean ahead. The flight was made via Nova Scotia, Labrador, Greenland and Iceland, with only one stop planned, at Reykjavik, Iceland. The Centurion carried the pilots across the Atlantic in record time and landed with less than three gallons of fuel in the tank. The flight from Reykjavik to Prestwick, Scotland was also completed in record time and with more fuel to spare. When they arrived back in Middleton, Morey and Smithies announced they were ready for a round-the-world flight.

Dane County flyers who preferred to keep aviation right in their back yards were given that option by Jerome Ripp at Waunakee. He also offered a solution to the problem of suburban sprawl. As housing in growing Waunakee approached his airport, he decided to "join 'em" instead of trying to "beat 'em." He laid out extra-long lots with frontage on the runway and sold rights to use it along with the new houses there. Twenty years later, nearly fifty homes front on the runway, most with airplanes in hangars or tied down on the back lawn. In the 1940s, many visionaries believed that the airport subdivision was the future for the United States. The dream became reality in only a few places, such as Waunakee.

Middleton and Waunakee were only two Dane County communities served by a diminishing number of privately-owned, publicly-used airports. Jana Field or Tobacco City Field at Edgerton, Van Hoof Field at Cottage Grove, Slotten's Verona Air Park, and others forced to close, like Gonstead's at Mount Horeb, have all experienced the squeeze of high operating costs, property taxes and liability insurance. Established in 1962, Verona Air Park has served local flyers and crop dusters over the years. In the 1990s, the highway construction cut off one end of the Air Park's runway, but Slotten is currently working on a new alignment. The result is that aviation becomes increasingly concentrated in a few places, as in Dane County with its fifty-one airport sites, but only one very active airport.[12]

Dodge County

In 1961, the Dodge County board voted to convert acreage at the former county asylum into an airport. Two runways were laid out, a terminal was built and Ken Pieper was hired as manager. Paul Baker moved his Beaver Aviation to Juneau in 1965. A series of FBOs came and went until 1983, when Wisconsin Aviation's Bill Helling took over management. He so impressed the local aviation community

fields of unbroken corn that we had in Dodge County. I think it was 100 acres."

Midway Aviation established itself as a crop duster. Glen Knaup remained in the business until the mid-1950s when he sold his operation to Roy Reabe. The site of the Midway Aviation Airport became the Dodge County Fairgrounds.

Paul Baker had already started his own aircraft mechanics operation, called Beaver Aviation, at his own landing field on the east side of Beaver Dam Lake. "The field that I was on was at lake level almost....so in the springtime, if we had much rain or snow and [it] filled up the sod runways, we had soft spots that would make it impossible to let anyone land. They would go over on their backs. And some of them did."

When the Dodge County Airport opened at Juneau, Baker moved to it. "The business kept getting bigger and bigger. We did just marvelously well...We were one of the busiest in the state. I remember I was doing annual inspections at the rate of 130 odd per year."

Baker had hired Chuck Swain and Pat Daraban and, as he approached retirement age, sold them the business, which continues to hum right along.

Paul Baker and his friends in Beaver Dam found themselves in the right place at the right time. They were located just about in the center of one of the largest vegetable growing regions in the United States at a time when the aerial application of pesticides was growing fast and they made the best of it.

Also making the best of it was Roy Reabe. Born on a farm near Iron Ridge, Reabe began flight training with Dean and Dale Crites at Waukesha in 1938. During World War II, he checked out in nearly every fighter aircraft in the Army Air Force and ferried them across the country. When the war ended he wanted to stay in aviation but wondered how he would "fit in." Any place that already had an airport already had an FBO. Many other vets were opening new airports in communities too small to support them and would fail after in year or two.

Reabe looked around for a small city with some industry that didn't have an airport and discovered Waupun. "I went out here in the month of January in 1946 and looking for land I could get ahold of and make an airport out of," he recalled.

He found a piece of land that was near perfectly level and the following spring found his first business client. A local manufacturer contracted with Reabe to deliver parts to Milwaukee five days a week, twelve months a year. When he couldn't fly, he drove the parts to Milwaukee. This single contract was the foundation of Reabe Flying Service. It remained in force for 42 years. It provided the new business with steady cash and an opportunity for Reabe to give students flying time. Reabe flew to Milwaukee as often as the weather allowed, using skis in winter and landing in the grass off the plowed Mitchell Field runway when necessary.

In addition to the delivery service, Reabe also ran a busy flight

Doctor Dan Dorchester (John Enigl)

school for powered craft and for gliders.

Waupun was at the heart of the canned vegetable region and Reabe soon acquired another charter. He would fly samples of cannery products to the Green Giant Company in Le Seuer, Minnesota, every day during the summer and autumn canning season.

"We called it charter work, except it was kind of dependable charter work, we could depend on it every day."

Reabe also found out that he could depend on a growing demand for crop dusting. In 1947, he noticed that the vegetable fields surrounding Waupun were being dusted by aviators from Arkansas. He thought he could compete and "bought ourselves some equipment and trained ourself and started in on crop dusting and that just kept expanding." He started out with a Stearman, then added a J-3 Cub. In a few years he had eight Super Cubs, five Stearmans and "maybe a helicopter."

"That kept expanding after that due to the fact that the canning companies got bigger and they expanded their area, the central sands opened up...so we set up an operation at Plainfield [and] another operation at Plover." As the growth continued, Reabe opened another landing strip near Nekoosa and flew out of Coloma and Wild Rose as well.

Back home, he expanded his airport at Waupun to 360 acres and acreage not used for flying was farmed. It is one of the largest privately-owned airports in the state and remained open to the public until the costs of liability insurance grew too large. By the 1980s, Reabe had the largest agricultural application operation in Wisconsin and, except for the airlines, the military and the EAA, the largest fleet of aircraft in the state.

It is part of an agricultural aviation industry with a dozen companies in the state, close to 100 certified and licensed pilots, and over one million acres of cropland sprayed every year.

The Reabe operation is also a family business. Helen Reabe was the office manager and bookkeeper for decades. When she retired, she was replaced by "eight girls and a computer." Four sons are licensed pilots, three involved in the family business. As Roy Reabe said, "it worked out real good for us."[13]

Door County

Recognizing that the "Air Age" had arrived, the Door County Board of Supervisors purchased Cherryland Airport in 1944. The site had already been used by local flyers, most notably Karl Reynolds and Dr. Dan Dorchester. It also had one of the first female airport managers in the state, Dorothy Cretney, a home economics teacher with a private license who died when her plane exploded in the air after take-off at Curtiss-Wright Airport in September 1942.

In 1943, Merle Zuehlke of Milwaukee's Curtiss-Wright Airport, opened a CPT program and established a charter service called Cherryland Airways. The airport was also used regularly by military people visiting shipbuilding plants at Sturgeon Bay. County ownership made the airport eligible for postwar state and federal aid, which resulted in regular improvements.

In 1945, Lakeshore Publications of Sturgeon Bay published *Badger Flying*, a monthly magazine focussing on aviation in the state. Enar A. Athlstrom was the editor and Victor Schoen the business manager. *Badger Flying* was the official publication of the

Wisconsin Civil Air Corps, the aviation organization founded in Milwaukee in 1935 and led by Gordon Leonard in the late 1940s and 1950s. The WCAC and *Badger Flying* both faded when the post-war aviation boom deflated. By 1949, the magazine had severed its connection with the WCAC, renamed itself *Personal Flying* and moved to Hastings, Michigan.

While still in Sturgeon Bay, *Badger Flying* promoted the Cherryland Aviation Club and its Frigid Fun Fly-Ins. Held on a cold winter weekend, the Frigid Fun included skiing and tobogganing at nearby Potawatomi State Park, a fish boil, and other attractions that brought up to seventy-five airplanes to the airport. Tourist-minded Door County people also encouraged aviators to visit the peninsula in the spring when cherry blossoms were in bloom.

Many Door County flyers came out to the airport in April 1947, when Karl Reynolds landed his new Beechcraft Bonanza. Purchased from Andersen Aviation in Milwaukee, it was reportedly the first Bonanza in Wisconsin. Reynolds, was one of the leaders of the cherry orchard and cannery industry in the state and planned to use the plane regularly for business. He was also a member of the State Aeronautics Commission and committed to airport development in the state. Accordingly, the entire aviation community was shocked when the Bonanza crashed into a forest near Carlsville, killing Reynolds and two passengers.

One of Reynolds' goals had been to bring scheduled air service to Door County. Wisconsin Central Airline evaluated the airport, offered a long list of improvements necessary before it could use the field, but only "approximately sixty percent of the time." A combination of factors, chiefly the weather, but also the condition of the sod strip in spring and fall, persuaded Wisconsin Central not to provide Sturgeon Bay with such "very unreliable service." By 1974, the weather had not changed, but the airport surface, guidance and navigation equipment had improved for Midstate Airlines to begin service.

The first airport manager hired by the county was George Meredith, who held the job until 1972. It was a part time position that Meredith combined with "a little bit of farming." He was succeed by Robert Harris, Gary Richard, George McQueen and Keith Kasbohn as full-time managers.

In the 1980s the county airport committee focussed on increasing the amount of private-funding the airport received through the leasing of land for hangars. By the end of the decade, forty-four hangars were in use.

In 1948 the Village of Ephraim and the Town of Gibraltar built the Ephraim/Fish Creek Airport with state, federal and local funds. Additional land was purchased and an asphalt runway built in 1968.

That an airport was very useful to people who lived on an island has been made evident many times on Washington Island. The airport has been managed by the town government since 1940, but has also benefitted from the support of island service clubs and individuals. Fly-In Fish Boils, for example, have been popular fund-raisers since the 1950s.

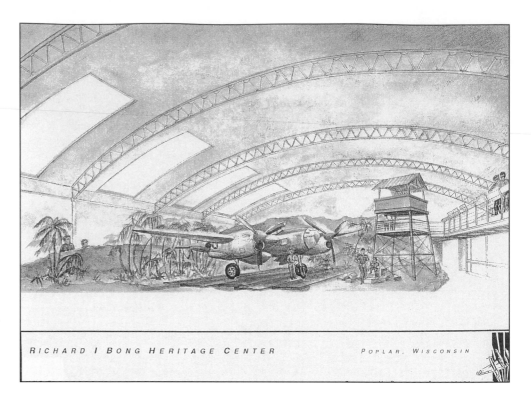

Artist's renditon of the Richard I. Bong Heritage Center proposed for Douglas County. (Bong Heritage Center)

Among the many stories connected with aviation on Washington, two stand out. One is the role the Island played in the Cold War, the second tells of an emergency medical flight.

Perched off the northern tip of Door County, Washington Island was deemed strategically important in the early 1950s. The members of sixty Island families enlisted in the Ground Observer Corps and kept a twenty-four-hour watch on aircraft passing overhead. The Island switchboard, which was still manually operated, was on twenty-four-hour alert for "Aircraft Flashes," which were ultimately reported to the Strategic Air Command. Washington Islanders kept on watch until electronic early warning systems were perfected in the mid-1950s.

A more immediate emergency occurred in March 1946, when 13-year old Dick Bjarnarson was seriously wounded by a firearm in a hunting accident and losing a lot of blood. The Island doctor, identified as Dr. Farmer, was summoned and he immediately called Sturgeon Bay aviator George Meredith to fly north with blood plasma. At the same time, pilot Arnie Arentzen flew over from Escanaba, Michigan. Farmer and the wounded boy climbed in Meredith's three place plane and took off for the Escanaba hospital. It was slightly closer than Sturgeon Bay, and downwind that day. The plane had traveled no farther than nearby Rock Island when the motor began to ice up and Meredith was forced to set down on the ice of Jackson Harbor on the northeast tip of Washington Island. Farmer and Bjarnarson were then transferred to Arntzen's Stinson Cabin plane and the pilot started to take-off from the ice. Before he got into the air, however, he passed over a hole recently cut by ice fishermen and one ski dropped through. Unable to get off the Island and with the boy in danger, Farmer then called Doctor Dan Dorchester. Accompanied by nurse Eunice Isaacson, he flew up from Sturgeon Bay, landed on the ice of Detroit Harbor in the dark by the light of auto headlamps and completed a successful amputation of

Bjarnarson's arm. The boy survived and was still living on the Island in 1997. Such are the hazards and opportunities for heroism involved in Island aviation.[14]

Douglas County

Douglas County is served by two airports, Solon Springs Municipal and Richard I. Bong Airport at Superior.

The Bong Airport has remained in the same location since 1937. The original brick hangar built then is still in use, although many other hangars have been built. The old 3,000 feet sod runway was blacktopped in the 1960s and extended to 4,000 feet in the 1980s. Over the years, the airport has maintained itself as a general aviation airport offering flight instruction, charters, as well as airplane sales and maintenance.

Kathy and Bill Amorde (Amorde Family)

William Amorde has been airport manager since 1969—one of the longest runs of any manager in a publicly-owned airport in the state. He attributes his longevity to staying out of debt, concentrating on what he does best, and to his wife, Kathy, who has shared the work with him every day since 1969.

Amorde began Twin Ports Flying Service in 1963 with one Cessna 150 and a handful of students. He expanded the business by supplying flight instruction under the veteran's program and through ROTC at the University of Wisconsin, Superior and the University of Minnesota, Duluth. He remembers one period in the 1970s when "for nine days in a row I was booked solid twenty-eight days in advance."

Other aviation services were provided by other FBOs who also worked under the terms of a non-exclusive contract. "Each FBO has the privilege to do everything. So that in my mind that has really turned a lot of the airport feuding type problems around."

The final secret to a long career as a public airport manager is a good partner. "It's a mom and pop operation," Amorde says. "With the two of us it has worked out really well."

Over the years Lyle Maves and Mary Millard have also been very active airport supporters, largely responsible for the current runway expansion to 5,100 feet.

Dunn County

The modern airport at Menomonie—Score Field—was built in 1984 by the non-profit Menomonie Airport Inc., as part of a neighboring industrial park. It is now owned by the city of Menomonie and managed by Matt Bainbridge of NAE Inc.

The Boyceville Airport began in 1938, when local flyers rented land that is still part of the airport. During World War II, Pete Peterson, Henry Hanson, Marshall Bolta, Chuck Stone and Lyle Hight owned the property. In 1946, Melvin Simonson organized Boyceville Airways Inc. and two hangars were erected. Interest in aviation was growing until a local pilot and a high school student were killed in what appeared to be an avoidable accident. Part of the airport property was used for a dirt auto race track.

The village of Boyceville purchased most of the property and, in 1981, the Dunn County Board voted to fund $20,000 in improvements. Additional work was funded by public and private contributions from groups like the Airport Booster Club, led by Melvin Sorenson. By the 1980s, the airport had five hangars, ten aircraft and two ultralights.[16]

Eau Claire County

After Charles Wood returned from service in World War II, he went to work at his father's auto dealership in Eau Claire. He fell right in with local business leaders who wanted to develop a new city airport. Northwest Airlines had expressed interest in serving the city in 1941, but the war had intervened. With the return of peace the business community hoped to put Eau Claire on the airline route with help from a new airport.

The city had already purchased 400 acres on the north edge of the city "on the old Chippewa Road" and had applied for federal grants to improve the property. In late 1944, the city moved the

Janice Gill and Ellen Nutschler at Jimmy Doolittle's Cafe in the Terminal at Eau Claire Airport, 1983. (Midwest Flyer)

main hangar from the State Street Airport to the new site and leased it to Steve Williams of Chippewa Falls. George Van Katt constructed a hangar and leased it to George Pettit, who acted as airport manager. He was succeeded in 1947, by Orion Howard, who ran the airport until 1951.

The airport opened for limited operations in the summer of 1945, although two 4,000-foot runways were still under construction. On July 4, 1947, the airport was dedicated with a fine ceremony featuring the DC-3's of Northwest Airlines, which inaugurated service that day. Northwest continued scheduled flights out of Eau

opened a G.I. Bill flight school at Fond du Lac. He was also manager and FBO. He started flying Aeronca Champs then switched to Beech Bonanzas before leaving to manage the Appleton Airport in 1953.

Even before Sagunsky left, it was obvious that the east side airport would be inadequate to meet Fond du Lac's future needs. "It looked absolutely level," Will Haase, Jr., recalled, "but we pitched. From the southeast corner to the northwest corner was an eleven-foot pitch." In addition, the airport belonged to the Haase family, which meant it was ineligible for federal/state aid.

After examining at least six sites in the area, the county board purchased land southwest of Fond du Lac and, in 1957, the Haases moved to it. They brought a few old hangars from the east side and built a new one. In 1958, a federal/state grant helped to pay for two 3,600-feet paved runways and the "Fond du Lac Skyport" was in operation. Will Haase, Jr., became manager and FBO, a position which he held for another three decades. Among the earliest and most important users of the airport were Giddings and Lewis and Mercury Marine.

In 1970, the airport became the site of the International Aerobatic Club Championships. "Mr. Poberezny and entourage came in one day and they said they were contemplating moving out of Rockford with their EAA Fly-In and they needed a satellite airport," said Haase

"We have seen probably all of the world's finest and the U.S. pilots and a lot of other Canadians and Europeans and South Americans perform here....the world's best in world competition."

The aerobatics championship, the world's largest, has taken place in the week following the EAA Fly-In at Oshkosh ever since. Over the years, the contest has brought the world's finest aerobatic aviators to Fond du Lac. One of the most memorable years was 1989, when competitors from the Soviet Union first appeared at the contest. It was yet another sign that the "Iron Curtain" of communism was coming down and sport aviation was part of it.

"The welcome surprised us because it was more than anything we expected," said Alexei Vlassoff, one of the Soviet flyers.

Russian aerobats flying over his airport were only one of the changes Will Haase, Jr. witnessed in his life in aviation. The greatest change was, "the utility of the airplane versus where we started. It was really ninety percent pleasure and ten percent business at that time...[now] it's close to reversing that.

"The main function of the county airport is to provide a base for the based aircraft in the area owned by corporations and to provide

Claire until 1951 when North Central commenced service. Dan Gibson was the airport manager and fixed base operator from the late 1950s until 1975.

In the late 1960s and early 1970s, Charles Wood and other Eau Claire people tried to make the airport a tri-county facility, with funding from Chippewa, Eau Claire and Dunn counties. Dunn balked because its access to the airport was blocked by the Chippewa River. By the time the North Crossing bridge, which provided that access, was completed, Dunn County was no longer interested. Voters in Chippewa Falls supported the tri-county concept, but the Chippewa County Board did not. It made a single appropriation of $200,000 to support a runway expansion in 1975. In the meantime the city of Eau Claire found it increasingly difficult to continue developing the airport. "It's pretty obvious the users come from a wide area and the airport ought to be supported by the tax base of three and possible more area counties," said Eau Claire County Board Chair Lawrence R. Gansluckner in 1978. His county was the only one willing to support the airport and on January 1, 1979, the county acquired ownership. Coincidentally, the airport manager at the time was Guy Wood, son of Charles Wood, and namesake and grandson of one of the three original airport builders in Eau Claire.

Since 1979, the airport grounds have more than doubled, a new modern terminal has been constructed and regular flights serve local travelers.[17]

Fond du Lac County

In the late 1930s business leaders in Fond du Lac tried to convince public officials in Fond du Lac and Winnebago counties to build a regional airport between their two cities. The idea garnered little support and the Fond du Lac Airport remained on the east side of the city, owned and operated by Will Haase, Sr. The airport had a CPT program in 1940-'41 and almost became the site of the glider training operation that ended up in Antigo.

After the war, young Max Sagunsky, fresh out of the service,

an entree [for] the people they do business with. The biggest change I have seen...the county airport almost breaks even [due to] business use of the airport and the airplane. It's just a phenomenal change."[18]

Forest County

In 1955, the Steckert Plywood Company expressed an interest in building a plant in Crandon, if the city had an airport. The following year a $95,000 airport plan was approved by the State Aeronautics Commission and the airport was built. The airport is still in use today and among its regular users are corporately-owned planes delivering people to work on a proposed mineral mine south of Crandon.[19]

Grant County

The oldest airport in Grant County was the air mail landing strip at Boscobel which closed during World War II. After the war a group of local business people organized a stock company and built an airport but responsibility and eventual ownership of the airport fell to Frank Kretschmann. Although managers and operators came and went, Kretschmann remained the patron saint of the airport until his death in 1974. His widow Hilda then sold the property to Ronald Huls, who was able to lease it to the city and qualify for federal/state aid. Huls was still managing the airport, with its 3,700-foot runway in 1998.

Another patron of aviation in Grant County was Bill Nodorft. He learned how to fly in Dubuque in 1945 and soon after opened an airport south of Platteville. By the mid-1960s, three flying clubs were using the grass-strip and over a dozen planes were on site. In 1967, the city of Platteville opened an airport only a few miles away from Nodorft's. With the university providing an ample supply of students and some charter work, both airports were active. By 1980, the second generation of the Nodorft family, Dale and wife Karen, was at the family airport and flying a Piper Aztec twin.

The proximity of the two airports created confusion for pilots, especially when they asked for advisories for "Platteville" on UNICOM. The confusion continued until Homer Lancaster, long time FBO at Mineral Point, moved his operation to Platteville Municipal and suggested that it be renamed Grant County Airport.

The Lancaster Airport started about the same time as Platteville Municipal, when the city purchased acreage five miles south of town. Ken Vesperman was the manager and did his best

Top: Steve Krug's 1929 Bird A at Brodhead. Bottom: Dennis Trone's 1927 Travel Air 3000. (Eric Lundahl)

to keep the field open during the "mudtime" of early spring. In the early 1970s, the runway was surfaced and by the 1990s the airport counted 7,000 operations.

The village of Cassville got in the airport business in 1950 and as President R. J. Eckstein stated a year later, "was well satisfied with the undertaking." For the airport dedication the Aeronautics Bureau organized a demonstration of the ability of aviation to serve in an emergency by organizing an airlift to Cassville. Forty-six airplanes recruited from around the state delivered 5,000 pounds of medical supplies and personnel to show what might happen if, for example, Cassville was isolated by a flood. When the "emergency" work was over, a total of 71 planes flew in for the dedication ceremony and the chicken dinner that followed. Nearly one-half century later, the Cassville Airport runway is surfaced and slightly longer, than in 1950, but is still located midst the bluffs, the river and the powerplant.[20]

Green County

After World War II, Monroe area aviators organized the Badger Aviation Club and flew out of a sod field located on the southwest edge of the city. In 1951, they organized a Sheriff's Aero Patrol, under the direction of Deputy Charles Smith to "investigate aerial mishaps, conduct searches, aid in the capture of fleeing fugitives and other emergency services." In those days, it was customary for a rural county sheriff to have a number of deputies in his county. They were ordinary citizens who, when called out as part of a "sheriff's posse," had police powers. In Green County in 1951, members of the Badger Aviation Club were aerial deputies.

As the 1950s drew to a close, it was obvious that the Badger Airport was inadequate and, as in other places, municipal ownership was required for state and federal funding. A survey of sites was made with Monroe and the Aeronautics Bureau settling on acreage about three miles northwest of the city. The land was acquired and, in 1962, two sod runways were open to the public. Aviation activity was light until the late 1980s when the paved runway was extended to 4,200 feet. By 1997, the number of hangars had increased from five to twenty-one and operations were increasing as aviators were leaving larger airports to the north and south of Monroe.

Green County's other public airport is just south of Brodhead. The first Brodhead Airport was built as an "intermediate" landing field on the air mail route from

Chicago to La Crosse and the Twin Cities. It was located about six miles northwest of the city, had two turf runways and a beacon. It saw little activity as the range of aircraft improved in the 1930s, closed during World War II, and did not reopen after the war.

The modern Brodhead Airport was started after World War II by Bill and Margaret Earleywine who leveled a farm field as best they could, built an office and a hangar and hung out their shingle as Ercoupe and Taylorcraft dealers. The operation was moving ahead until Bill and his brother Derald died in a plane crash.

Wheeler Searles, another veteran flyer who also happened to own the airport site, took over until he passed away in 1971. In the meantime EAA Chapter 431 had formed and taken an active role at the airport. Brodhead became a haven for antique aircraft fans, perhaps because Bill Earleywine's 1946 Taylorcraft BC-12-D was a multiple winner at EAA Fly-Ins in the 1970s.

Antiques became important at Brodhead early in the 1980s when the Wisconsin Chapter of the Antique Airplane Association began its annual Grass Roots Fly-In. For one weekend in the summer, the turf runways at Brodhead host aircraft from the 1940s, '30s and '20s.[21]

Iowa County

In 1961 aviators and business people in Mineral Point organized an airport corporation, bought some land and graded a grass strip about two miles northwest of town. The volunteer group, with some help from the city, maintained the field and blacktopped the runway in 1970. By 1976, twelve planes were in hangars and the corporation, the city and Iowa County began to discuss county ownership. Two years later a joint-ownership agreement was worked out and the Mineral Point Airport became the Iowa County Airport. The "unofficial" manager of the airport was Homer Lancaster until he moved to Platteville Municipal in the 1980s.

The Dodgeville Municipal Airport began as Don Quinn's landing strip adjacent to Quinn's restaurant and resort hotel. A World War II pilot with a flair for self-promotion, Quinn put his business on the map when he purchased a Boeing 377 Stratocruiser in 1977. He planned to park the giant plane along the highway outside of Dodgeville and convert it into a restaurant. Landing one of the largest airplanes ever built on a 2600 x 30 foot runway with an uphill slope was a challenge accepted by pilot Dick Schmidt, co-pilot Tom "Teejay" Thomas of the Aeronautics Bureau, and flight engineer Don Waligorski. The crew had over 5,000 accumulated hours in the KC-97 tanker military version of the 377 when they took off from Madison in October, 1977. The flight to Dodgeville took about fifteen minutes and as they made a low pass prior to their final approach, they noticed a crowd of spectators, television crews and—just in case—emergency vehicles. Thomas described the landing as follows:

1,400 feet of runway and a cloud of dust was all it took to land a Boeing 377 Stratocruiser at Dodgeville in 1977. (Midwest Flyer)

"At our final approach speed of 89 knots we came in over the tops of the trees anticipating meeting up with the last brick at the end of the runway.

"Well, Dick did a superb job of putting the main gear down within ten feet of the approach end.

"The plane hit with a tremendous shudder. Landing uphill at Dodgeville is a combination of you coming down to the earth and the earth coming up to you. The plane skipped briefly into the air and came back down for good about a hundred feet or so up the runway. We were down and she was rolling straight.

"With the props hanging out over the gravel, they blew up a cloud of brown dust in front of us. It was so thick we actually couldn't see the ground from the cockpit.

"As the air began to clear and we placed the engines in forward idle thrust, we noticed that we still had about 1200 feet of runway left."

"We made it!"

After the dust settled the 377 was supposed to begin life as a cafe, but these plans did not work out. Instead the airplane was opened for tours. It had a final few minutes of fame in the 1980s as background for a television commercial featuring actor Farah Fawcett.[22]

Jackson County

Work on a new Black River Falls airport began in 1968 and was completed in 1971. Federal, state, county and city governments shared the $190,000 cost of purchasing and improving the 425 acre site. It was quite different from the old airport which had a 2,400-foot unlighted runway with power lines crossing at the end.

As in other places, aviation revived at Black River Falls after World War II. The Jackson County Flyers Association was formed in 1947, with flying physician Robert Krohn as president. Other officers were Vern Vos, Jerry Hoonsbeen, Bob Iliff, Milo Rozehnol, Lloyd Gilbertson and Art Frederikson. The area also had an active group of Flying Farmers from the 1950s to the 1970s. Veteran pilot Adolph Kosthhryz was president of the local group.

The airport is home to private and business aircraft and serves as a landing strip for aerial sprayers in the growing season.[23]

Jefferson County

Believing that "Civilian aviation is bound to make big strides ahead after the war," the city of Watertown purchased land for an airport in April, 1945. An estimated 5,000 people attended the dedication in August, which featured an air show performed by local pilots Len Drydyk and Dr. Lawrence Dennis. The airport was included in Wisconsin Central's original flight plan but the 2,300-foot grass runway was not improved in time for the airline to land.

The situation changed by the 1980s, when a newly-organized company called Wisconsin Aviation started business at Watertown.

Founder Jeff Baum saw a "bankrupt fixed-base operator and a stagnant municipal airport," in 1981. Combining flight training, charters, maintenance and other services, and with assistance from a major runway expansion and improvement in 1986, Wisconsin Aviation enlivened aviation at Watertown and then expanded. First to the Juneau Airport, then to Milledgeville, Georgia, then to a joint venture across the Atlantic in Germany, the company grew. In the mid-1990s, Wisconsin Aviation purchased one of the best known names in the state, Four Lakes Aviation, and added Madison operations; then expanded again with the purchase of Madison's Coldstream Aviation. By 1995, Wisconsin Aviation was one of the largest and most active aviation operations in the state and Watertown airport was no longer "stagnant."

Ad for Lewis Propellers, 1946. (Badger Flying)

The Fort Atkinson Airport got its start in the late 1940s with what later become known as the Mid-Cities airport between Fort Atkinson and Jefferson. Discussion went on in the mid-1970s to create a county airport but no serious action was taken. Another decade passed until Fort Atkinson voters passed a referendum authorizing a $720,000 expansion and improvement of the city airport.

"This sends a clear message that Fort Atkinson and Jefferson County is a good place to do business," said state assembly representative Randy Radtke at the airport dedication in 1989.

Jefferson County's third municipal airport began in 1954 in the Town of Palmyra, where it remains today. A master plan study began in 1997 and the single grass runway now has thirty-four hangars and fifty-seven based aircraft. Adam Pancake served as manager until 1975 when he was succeeded by Don Agen.[24]

Juneau County

The original Mauston Airport used by flyers in the 1930s was located on the south edge of the city where the consolidated high school was later built.

In 1968, the cities of Mauston and New Lisbon combined efforts to built an airport to serve both communities. They purchased acreage about halfway in between the two cities and laid out a grass runway. In 1994, the runway was rebuilt and resurfaced with help from the Air National Guard while community volunteers built a new operations building. Although publicly-funded, the airport has relied heavily on volunteers who were led for many years by Bill Post and Ron Brunner.

In 1997, the airport covered one hundred acres, with a paved, lighted 3,500-foot runway, fourteen hangars, fifteen based aircraft and one ultralight.

Juneau County is also served by municipal airports at Necedah and a privately-owned, public-use airport at Elroy.[25]

Kenosha County

In 1947, the editor of the *Kenosha News,* was upset that the civic leaders of "the fourth-largest city in Wisconsin" could think of no better way to meet the city's need for an airport than to "leave it to the Walravens." He thought that Kenosha should, like many other Wisconsin cities at the time, build and maintain a municipal airport.

Ruth Harman had been managing the Kenosha airport since 1940 and was joined by Herbert Walraven when they married in 1943. Kenoshans must have been happy with them because talk about building a city airport did not get serious until after Herb died and Ruth moved to California in 1950.

The idea of sharing an airport with Racine was suggested and soon rejected by both communities. In 1952, Aeronautics Commission Director Tom Jordan told the Chamber of Commerce to persuade the city to "get a petition ready," for a site survey, which it did.

In 1955, the city purchased 242 acres at the junction of Highways 192 and 158 and began work on a $360,000 airport, which was ready for operation one year later. In 1959, the city granted a fifty-year lease to FBO Robert Brackett by which he would pay two cents

Kenosha Airport, 1954 and Kenosha Airport, 1989. (Bureau of Aeronautics)

Top: La Crosse Airport on French Island, 1950. Above: La Crosse terminal, 1954. (Bureau of Aeronautics)

per square foot for hangar rental and two cents for every gallon of aviation gas he sold. Despite his lease, Brackett left the airport and Wisconsin in 1975.

Although annual operations were approaching the 100,000 mark, the Kenosha Airport was behind its neighbors at Racine and Waukegan. This condition was remedied by nearly $9 million in local money and federal/state aids that went into the airport in the 1980s.

In 1987, an estimated 30,000 people showed up for the runway dedication and air show. It was the largest aviation event southeastern Wisconsin had seen in many years. At the time the airport was making an estimated $40 million impact on the county economy, a good return on the investment of public funds.

The airport also made a good return on public funds through its participation in aviation education. In the 1960s, Gateway Technical Institute started to develop one of the state's most comprehensive post-secondary aviation programs. The school offered pilot training, aviation management plus A & P mechanics using its own Champion 7ECA and Cessna 305A. Students could also train for commercial pilot and flight instructor certificates as well as single and multi-engine land and instrument ratings. Graduates had little trouble finding jobs even though aviation is often crowded with job-seekers.

In the 1980s, Gateway had a large aviation education program,

as did Blackhawk Tech at Janesville and Milwaukee Area Technical College.

Kenosha County also has the Westosha Airport at Wilmot. It opened to public use in 1972 and is home to the Westosha Flying Club. It has twenty-six hangars and fifty-five based aircraft, listing 22,000 annual operations.[26]

La Crosse County

The dedication of the La Crosse Airport in 1947 was an occasion for great optimism. Managed by Frank Muth, the new airport covered 1,100 acres on French Island and had three 5,300-foot runways. It was on Northwest Airlines' transcontinental route and local aviation boosters touted La Crosse as "a city with the largest airport in the whole northwest, effectively located on a main east-west air line." General aviation was active as well, with G.I. Bill flight instruction, a large group of club flyers, and charter work for local businesses.

Northwest stayed at La Crosse until its initial five-year contract ran out in 1952, then North Central started service with its 21-passenger DC-3s. By 1974, North Central was carrying over 42,000 passengers and a new commuter airline, Mississippi Valley, was struggling to gain a toehold. Mississippi Valley did not survive the late-1970s energy crisis and airport traffic in general declined through the early 1980s. It bounced back in the 1990s and enplanements have remained above the 200,000 mark ever since. The airport underwent a major improvement program in the late 1980s that increased runway length to 8500 feet and enabled it to handle the largest aircraft flying. Occasionally La Crosse is called upon to handle jumbo military jets that cannot land at Fort McCoy. In 1989, for example, an Air Force C-5A, the largest American airplane, landed and took off at La Crosse.

The person with the longest association with aviation in La Crosse was Raymond Bice. A city and county political leader in the 1930s and '40s, he worked hard to build and maintain the French Island Airport. Near the end of his life he reflected on the course of aviation as he witnessed it.

"It has been three-quarters of a century since I witnessed Hugh Robinson's primitive plane land in La Crosse. Last December [1985] I was thrilled to see a huge Lockheed L-1011 land at our airport.

"The automobile has made wonderful progress since the days of the Model T Ford, but no other transportation media in the world can ever approach the phenomenal growth of aeronautics."[27]

Langlade County

Members of the Antigo Lions Club caught the aviation bug going around at the end of the 1920s and contacted federal officials who reviewed possible airport sites for them. The Depression struck and no concrete action was taken until 1941, when the city purchased 180 acres on one of those sites and cleared and graded two runways. The airport was ready for World War II when Anderson Air of Milwaukee set up a glider training school.

After the war the airport was included in the state airport plan and regular improvements ensued. In 1970, Langlade County assumed ownership and commissioned a study for commuter air service which did not materialize. Five years later Karl Kerstetter began his long career as airport manager and FBO. With a 4,000 foot runway the airport serves general, commercial and agricultural aviation over a wide area.[28]

Lincoln County

The first airport at Tomahawk was developed by the city in the mid-1930s and was identified as the "State" airport on the 1938 federal directory. The "State" designation comes from the fact that the airport was used by the Wisconsin Conservation Department for fire

patrol work. The Conservation Department, which had its regional fire control headquarters in Tomahawk, built a 3,300-foot turf runway and a two-story brick hangar as a WPA project in 1937, even though it did not own any aircraft. The department had been hiring pilots and planes in season for mapping and fire spotting since the 1920s, but they did not necessarily fly out of Tomahawk.

The airport all but shut down during World War II but reopened after the war. When the Conservation Department acquired it first airplane—a Stinson 108—in 1947, the volume of traffic increased at Tomahawk. Jack Wolhaupt, the first Conservation Department pilot, recalled that flying at Tomahawk was made interesting by the railroad line that crossed the runway about two-thirds down its length. He learned to keep his eyes open for steam puffing off the tracks because it meant that a train was on its way across the runway—not something he wanted to meet in a Stinson.

Pilot Ed Marquardt also kept his eyes open for steam on the tracks. He had been flying in the Tomahawk area since 1928 and was employed as a pilot by Owens-Illinois in the 1950s and '60s. In 1968, the new Department of Natural Resources left the Tomahawk Airport and requested that it be removed from the state directory. It was, but Tomahawk still needed an airport.

Marquardt, Bob Wallis, Tony Werner, Allen Kainz and other local people organized an airport commission and located a site. They obtained funding from the city of Tomahawk and the neighboring towns of Bradley, Wilson, Skanawan and Tomahawk as well as federal and state grants. In 1972, work began on a 4,000-foot, black-topped runway and the airport was operating the following year.

"It serves our purposes pretty well here," Marquardt said in 1978.

The Merrill Airport operated by Ed Baesemann in the late 1930s closed for World War II, but was reopened by Stan and Bill Hurst after the war. In 1947 Victor Estill and Charles Ercegovac started Merrill Airways to operate the airport. They hoped that other veterans

Upper left: Wisconsin Conservation Department pilot Jack Wolhaupt. (Department of Natural Resources) **Left: The Conservation Department landing field at Tomahawk, and the railroad tracks that crossed it.** (Robert Wylie) **Above: Tomahawk's Tony Werner and his Aeronca "Scenic Sedan."** (Robert Wylie)

would continue to fly, and a few did, but not enough to support two families.

"In truth, not even one," wrote Ercegovac many years later. "We didn't have much money, but we met a lot of good people. And we had wonderful sunsets."

The Ercegovacs enjoyed those sunsets until 1960, when Charles was forced to find a better-paying job.

Operators came and went until 1962 when John Hatz became airport manager and FBO. Hatz was a crackerjack mechanic and one of the most successful home aircraft builders in Wisconsin, if not the United States. By 1959, he had already built dozens of planes, including a Velie Monocoupe on display at the EAA Museum, when he started work on his own "Hatz Biplane." Nine years passed, but when it was finished in 1968, the plane was described as "strictly for those who love flying for its own sake." Jack Cox of the EAA

Merrill's John Hatz and his biplane. (Robert Wylie)

described the Hatz model as "sort of like a Cub with open cockpits and two wings."

John Hatz won many accolades for his airplane before his death in an auto accident in 1989. Probably the most meaningful compliments have come from the 400 other home-builders who have completed or are working on Hatz Biplanes thirty years after he took the first one up from the runway at Merrill.

Hatz resigned as the airport manager at Merrill in 1973. Among those who followed were Gene and Jan Dalessandro, Bob Gehring and Beverly Cornelius.[29]

Manitowoc County

After the demise of the Invincible mid-wing airplane in 1929, aviation activity at Manitowoc was slow. As one of the state's larger communities and an important industrial center, Manitowoc/Two Rivers attracted the attention of the CAA and the State Planning Board. In 1942, the Board surveyed the area's aviation potential and urged the cities of Manitowoc and Two Rivers to built a large airport to meet their anticipated needs. Neither Manitowoc nor Two Rivers was interested in building a new airport on any of the three sites the Planning Board suggested.

When activity picked up after World War II, the city asked Manitowoc County to buy the airport, but the county refused. In 1949, the city received federal and state funding to lengthen, surface and light the main runway. The work was completed in 1953 and the airport was dedicated with an air show that brought out 10,000 spectators.

The air show and other activities at

A crowd came out for the fly-in that marked the inauguration of North Central Airline service to Manitowoc in 1953. (Bureau of Aeronautics)

Manitowoc were organized by Airport Manager Louie Kakuk and the Manitowoc Aviation Club. Organized shortly after World War II by Robert King, Karl Klackner and other local flyers, the Club was known for the aviation contests it sponsored. Spot landing, bomb dropping and precision parachute competitions were held every summer in the late 1940s and early 1950s.

The biggest event occurred at the 1953 dedication, which was timed to salute the airport improvement work and the inaugural flight of North Central Airlines. North Central would make one stop at Manitowoc on its daily run from Green Bay to Chicago.

The city of Manitowoc still considered the airport to be a burden larger than it could handle and petitioned the county to buy it. The county again refused, but did agree to lease the airport as long as the city agreed to build a new terminal.

In the 1960s Wisconsin was in the midst of its airport consolidation debate, with lively discussions taking place between Appleton and Oshkosh and among Marathon, Wood and Portage counties. The airlines, which meant North Central in most of Wisconsin, wanted fewer and better airports in order to serve Wisconsin's smaller cities without having to make short hops between them.

North Central was still serving Manitowoc in the early 1960s, and was not interested in landing a few minutes later in Sheboygan, even though the new county airport there opened in 1960. Accordingly when Manitowoc completed its new terminal in 1963, the sign on the building designated the port as Manitowoc-Sheboygan Airport. Manitowoc was happy with the designation but, to no one's surprise, Sheboygan was not. A "dehyphenation" suit was filed and continued into the mid-1970s. By the time it was settled, neither Manitowoc nor Sheboygan had airline service.

In 1975, Manitowoc County finally accepted the city's thirty-year old request to purchase the airport. Improvement work was continued, including further acquisition of land and a runway extension to 5,000 feet. Although Manitowoc and Sheboygan did not consolidate their airports, they have been managed by the same companies since the late 1960s, including Chaplin Aviation and Magnus Aviation.[30]

Marathon County

The waning months of World War II were a busy time at Wausau Airport, with a total of 157 transient pilots landing between April and June, 1945. The increase in activity, along with expected growth after the war ended, led some supervisors to propose that the county buy into Alexander Field and share the cost of improvements, but no action was taken. It was an idea whose time had not come.

Instead a new airport came to town—or near it at least. In 1946,

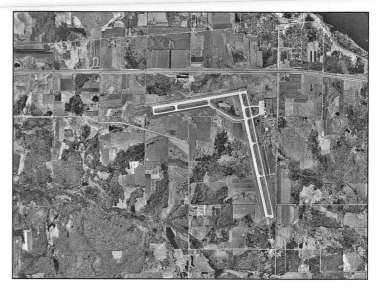

Above: The Central Wisconsin Airport, the state's first regional airport. (Robert Wylie) Left: Wausau's Margaret and Archie Towle and Marie Towle Grimm, the first members of an extended family of fifteen aviators. (Robert Wylie) Bottom: Air Force One, which brought Secretary of Defense Melvin Laird to the dedication of the Central Wisconsin Airport in 1970. (Robert Wylie)

With eight daily flights out of the airport in 1952, Wausau-area business people flew Wisconsin Central/North Central planes heading south to Milwaukee and west to the Twin Cities.

Airport management continued to be a family affair, with Lyle and Marie Towle Grimm taking up where Marie's father Archie left off when he died in a crash at the airport in September 1945. Over the years 24 members of the Towle-Grimm family have made aviation their life's work.

In 1961, the federal government commissioned a study of the need for airport consolidation in Wisconsin. With a number of small cities in relatively close proximity—Wausau, Stevens Point, Marshfield, Wisconsin Rapids—central Wisconsin was a leading candidate for consolidation. Since World War II the federal government had put millions of dollars into municipal airports in these cities. Now, as airplanes were growing bigger and faster and the new interstate highway system was making

Donald Heide, Phil Reidy and WASP veteran Evelyn McNulty opened the Wisconsin Valley Airport, seven miles south of Wausau. Banking on the anticipated postwar boom, they acquired a Cessna 140 and an Aeronca Champ, then offered flight instruction and charters in competition with Lyle and Marie Towle Grimm at Wausau. The newcomers had a tough route to fly especially since their operation was not certified for the G.I. Bill students who were filling classes with paying students at Wausau.

The Valley Airport was on its last legs in 1948 when the State Radio Council tried to erect a public broadcasting antenna on Rib Mountain that would create a hazard for pilots at Alexander Field. The owners offered the Valley Airport as a replacement for Alexander since it was well out of the way of Rib Mountain, but neither Wausau nor Marathon County was interested. The Wisconsin Valley Airport survived on a diminishing basis throughout the 1950s.

With federal and state aid, Alexander Field was improved and enlarged, with a new terminal completed in 1952. Wisconsin Central had made Wausau one of its first stops and airline service continued throughout the 1950s.

Archie Becher, aviation promoter and airport engineer. (Robert Wylie)

auto travel easier, the need for airports in every city of 20,000 people was questioned. In Wisconsin consolidation seemed logical in Winnebago and Outagamie counties, Manitowoc and Sheboygan, Eau Claire, Chippewa Falls and Menomonie, and Marathon, Wood and Portage counties.

Federal logic failed in all these places because local interests, pride and reality prevailed. Since Wausau accounted for seventy percent of airline traffic and ninety percent of air freight in central Wisconsin, locating an airport more than a convenient drive from Wausau was a mistake. At the same time southern Wood County would not be well served if a regional airport was located north of Stevens Point. At the same time, Marshfield was not interested in any airport farther away than its own.

Accordingly, Wood County voted not to support a regional airport proposed for Mosinee in 1963. Wausau hesitated at first, then choose to support the Mosinee site instead of another possibly worse site, as did Stevens Point and Portage County. Located just outside of Mosinee, thirteen miles south of Wausau and nineteen miles north of Stevens Point, the new airport was named the Central Wisconsin Airport in 1965. The project remained in the talking state until the end of 1966, when $716,000 of federal money was pledged on the condition that local governments would raise the rest of the $2 million estimated cost of the airport. Led by county board chair and airport supporter Leroy Jonas, Marathon County voted to spend $950,000 in county money on the airport, while Portage County promised $370,000. Jonas was named chair of a new regional airport committee to oversee the project.

Land was purchased and a design plan drawn up by Becher-Hoppe Associates of Schofield was accepted. The new 1,092-acre airport was dedicated in May 1970 and North Central immediately began landing its DC-9 jets on the 6,700-foot runway.

The airport's first decade was one of steady growth with passenger enplanements increasing from 30,000 in 1971 to 90,000 in 1980. The deregulated 1980s saw numbers zig-zag all over the chart, but continue upward to exceed the

Milwaukee's lakefront airport, Maitland Field. (Bureau of Aeronautics)

120,000 mark by 1990. Of Wisconsin airports with airline service in the 1990s, Central Wisconsin operations fall in the middle range, behind Milwaukee, Madison, Green Bay and Appleton, but ahead of La Crosse, Eau Claire, Oshkosh and Rhinelander. As commuter airlines came and went in these years, service continued to be concentrated in fewer places. By building a regional airport, Marathon and Portage counties insured that their people would have airline service, something that Wausau and Stevens Point could not deliver on their own.

In Wausau, the immediate impact of the new airport, was a call to close Alexander Field. It occupied choice waterfront real estate that could be developed into houses worth $25,000 - $30,000 "to spread the tax base and stem the tide of rising taxes" said one mayoral candidate in 1968. Concerned about this possibility, airport manager Lyle Grimm consulted with Fritz Wolf of the Aeronautics Commission who assured him that, "the use of Alexander Field will increase steadily." Airline service would diminish, but general and corporate traffic would increase since most of these flyers travel to ground destinations no more than five miles from the airport.

So Wausau kept its airport, as did Stevens Point and Marshfield. Airline service is restricted to Central Wisconsin Airport while the other airports are busier than ever with general and corporate traffic. The outcome of the decades old discussion of regional versus local airports is that communities need both of them. [31]

Milwaukee County

The fate of Milwaukee's downtown airport was much-debated in the years after World War II. Critics said it was too small for commercial aircraft, too close to downtown buildings and too often socked in by lake fogs. Maitland also occupied a prime piece of real estate at a time when Milwaukee was expanding its lakefront drive and park system. On the other hand, corporate aviation was expanding, many Wisconsin businesses had headquarters downtown and an

airport nearby was an economic plus for the city.

The airport boosters won the argument in 1951, when the city built a new administration building, resurfaced the runway, landscaped the grounds, and contracted with Anderson Air Services as FBO. At the dedication ceremonies in June 1951, fifty aircraft landed at Maitland, including a DC-3. A representative from the city of Chicago told Milwaukee Mayor Frank Zeidler that he hoped Chicago's Meigs Field would someday look as nice as Maitland.

No matter how it looked, Maitland struggled to attract enough traffic to justify city support. By 1954, airport use peaked at twenty aircraft movements per day, all business-related.

In 1955, the Defense Department presented the final argument for closing Maitland. It was an ideal site for short-range Nike missiles designed to defend Milwaukee from Soviet bombers. The missiles were installed and Maitland became a casualty of the Cold War on May 31, 1956. After the Nikes were removed, the site sat idle for

Above: Bill Lotzer and his Cessna 170. (Lotzer Family)
Right: Milwaukee's Curtiss-Wright Airport, with the large Miller Brewing Co. hanger in the late 1940s. (George Hardie)

a few years before it was developed as part of the Milwaukee Summerfest grounds.

In the late 1930s, Timmermann Field was still known as Curtiss-Wright Airport and was struggling financially. In 1939, Merle Zuehlke became manager and turned the place around. Born in Appleton, Zuehlke learned to fly with Leonard Larson in a J-1 Standard and progressed from there. Taking advantage of new federal pilot training programs, he made Curtiss-Wright one of the largest flight schools in the state, and opened another school at Sturgeon Bay. He also started a crop dusting service in 1939 that was among the first of its kind in the state. During the war years, he continued flight training services and maintained an active CAP unit. At the end of the war Zuehlke's Fliteways, Inc. purchased the airport for $125,000 and ran it until Zuehlke fell ill in 1947, when Milwaukee County bought it for $349,800.

One of Zuehlke's flight instructors was a young Naval aviation veteran named Bill Lotzer. Born in Fond du Lac, Lotzer was studying law at Marquette University when World War II started. He signed up for CPT training with Zuehlke at Curtiss-Wright and was a licensed pilot when he entered the Navy Aviation Cadet program and became a flight instructor. Lotzer's war time experience led him to

organize the first chapter of the Flying American Veterans of World War II in 1949.

After the war he went to work for Zuehlke, but also organized Gran-Aire Aviation in partnership with long time Milwaukee aviator Montford Obrecht. After the county bought the airport in 1947, Gran-Aire became FBO and Lotzer the airport manager. Obrecht retired out of Gran-Aire in 1953 but Lotzer continued at Timmermann until 1973, when he passed the operation down to his children John, Tom and Margaret.

In 1959, the county named the airport in honor of Supervisor Lawrence J. Timmermann, who had long been an advocate for aviation in Milwaukee. Lotzer later said that he recognized all that Timmermann had accomplished, but wished the name had not been changed. Of the eleven Curtiss-Wright airports in the country, Milwaukee's was the only one that did not have to give up the name when it was sold. "We lost a powerful name in aviation," Lotzer said.

The name was important to Lotzer because he appreciated the business value of positive publicity. He became the largest-selling Cessna dealer in the state, ran one of the largest flight schools, and had a mechanics operation capable of converting a war surplus B-24 bomber for civilian use by Fred Miller of the brewing family. In 1955, traffic at Curtiss-Wright approached the 128,000 mark, making it one of the busiest general aviation airports in the country.

Lotzer loved air shows and he organized his first National Air Pageant in 1950. The 1951 Pageant had 25,000 paying customers plus another 30,000 onlookers beyond the fences. The theme for the 1953 show was the 50th anniversary of powered flight and Lotzer's

show featured an auto versus airplane race put on by the Hales Corners Flying Club, high speed precision aerobatics by Steve Wittman, a helicopter square dance by U.S. Army flyers, and the Cole Brothers Air Show. A little-noticed additional feature was a fly-in of home built aircraft by a new organization, the Experimental Aircraft Association, which had been organized at Lotzer's hangar earlier that year.

A licensed seaplane instructor, Lotzer made vacation flights to the northern Wisconsin lake country. In 1954 he purchased land on Sumac Lake near Woodruff and laid out a subdivision for seaplane owners. "In the deed it had to be a plane owner or a pilot who could own the property and that's still in the deed," he said. "I don't know if ever it would hold up in a court of law..." In fact, the lots on what became known as Prop Wash Bay were all owned by pilots.

Throughout the Bill Lotzer years and afterward, Timmermann remained one of Wisconsin's busiest airports and the largest general aviation field in the state. In the 1970s, more than ninety hangars were in use, with many more built since then. In 1993, over 85,000 operations took place at the field.

The Hales Corners airport began in November 1945 when Bob Moody rented some land off Highway 100 and local flyers tied down their planes there. The Hales Corner Flying Club had a hangar and meeting room there and, in 1948, sponsored a big air show featuring the Cole Brothers. Club members included Frank Preston, Gene Due, Romona Rolfson, Wayne Rowles, Cindy Gerth, Erv Matti, Ray Anderson, Gil Pitt and Ray Klips. In 1954, there were as many as 23 airplanes on the field.

Many of these flyers were early members of the Experimental Aircraft Association which had its headquarters in the basement of the Poberezny home on Forest Park Drive for nine years. When the operation out grew the house, the EAA built a building at 113th and Forest Home which served as its first museum. "We certainly thought at the time the museum would stay there forever," Paul Poberezny wrote in a 1988 history of Hales Corners.

Hales Corners is also important to Wisconsin history because it is the home of Wisconsin's premier aviation historian, George Hardie. Also one of the early members of the EAA, Hardie's research and writing is the cornerstone of aviation historical work in this state.

Occupying valuable suburban real estate, the Hales Corners Airport became a residential subdivision and closed in September 1977. The closing was marked by a wake attended by aviators from far and near who shared warm memories around a bonfire made of wood scrapped from the old hangars.

At the end of World War II, Ed Rediske opened Rainbow Airport in the fields near Franklin. Rainbow was the home of the West Allis Flying Club, which shared many members with the Hales Corners group. The headquarters of the EAA were also briefly located here. The airport remained open until 1996, when it fell prey to suburban park devel-

Historian George Hardie, center, examining a document, 1960. (WAHF)

opment.

In the years since World War II, Milwaukee's Mitchell Field developed from a regional airport into an international air transportation facility. To do so the airport had to accommodate itself to growing and changing passenger demands. It had to handle new, larger and more challenging aircraft and master the latest in advanced aviation technology. It also had to adjust to a regulatory climate that shifted from strict control over air carriers by federal authorities to one driven by the marketplace. Local and state politics also played a role, since a publicly-funded facility had to respond to conflicting public demands for less noise, less construction, lower taxes and more and better service.

Finally, Mitchell Airport had to live with a basic historical fact about Milwaukee. It is only ninety miles from Chicago. Just as its proximity to the Illinois city affected the development of Milwaukee as a lake shipping and railroad center, it would affect it as an air transportation hub. In the

Right: Ad for flight training at Anderson Air, FBO at Mitchell Field, 1945. (Badger Flying) **Below: Northwest Airlines Boeing Stratocruiser, the largest airliner of its day, at Milwaukee in 1949.** (George Hardie)

Get Your Water Rating Now in the
Republic Seabee

Be a "Complete" Pilot - - - Learn to Fly on Water as Well as Land. All the thrills of boating plus flying, await you in this new 20 hour course for private and commercial pilots.

Approved under the G.I. Bill of Rights

Seabee

ANDERSON *Air Activities*

years after World War II, Chicago's airports—Midway in the 1950s, O'Hare in the decades after— were the nation's busiest. It was a fact and Milwaukee's airport always had to compete and live with it.

In 1945, Mitchell Field was served by Northwest Airlines flying DC-3s with room for twenty-one passengers. When Wisconsin Central inaugurated service to Milwaukee in 1947, it sent its best and biggest plane, a Lockheed 10—with the 10 standing for the num-

ber of passengers it could carry. By the 1980s, DC-9s and Boeing 737s were carrying passengers by the hundreds and even commuter aircraft were larger and faster than front line commercial airplanes of the 1940s.

Bigger, faster aircraft required a bigger airport and the need to expand was a constant litany heard at Mitchell Field. New runway

Above: Modern gate at Milwaukee in 1968 when the airport was making the transition to jet airliners. (Bureau of Aeronautics)
Top right: Dedication of the new air traffic control tower, 1986.

construction or major expansion took place in every decade from the 1940s to the 1990s. Bigger and faster airplanes meant an increase in passengers from 500,000 in 1955 to 5,000,000 in 1995. New terminals, parking facilities, and access roads had to be built to handle the load. A chicken-and-egg cycle occurred, as each improvement triggered more use and more use required additional improvement.

In the late 1960s, for example, as North Central became the leading airline at Milwaukee, it asked the county to build a new "banjo" style loading pier with eight gates. The county built the shell of the pier for $94,000 and the airline finished the interior. While this cooperative venture was successful, ten years later the county board was presented with plans for another expansion with a $26 million price tag. Reluctant to levy taxes for the expansion, the county supervisors and the airlines worked out a 25-year lease agreement whereby the air carriers would pay all the cost of airport operations and the terminal expansion.

Airport neighbors were sometimes harder to accommodate, as in the late 1960s runway expansion across Howell Avenue. Auto traffic

was directed under the runway by means of an 800-foot long tunnel. Residents in the homes adjacent to the runway extension were unhappy about the jet noise and exhaust and sued the airport. The case was settled when the federal government funded the purchase of the houses. The property then became the site of a new air cargo center.

Airport operations depend on more than runways and terminals. Everything from the relatively low-tech item of snowplowing to high-tech navigation and communication systems are also part of the mix. The 90-foot tall control tower built in 1955 was replaced thirty years later by one 200-foot tall. Its job was to control air traffic within a fifty-mile wide circle, with radar first locating aircraft from about fifty miles out and air traffic controllers taking over as the plane comes closer to the airport. Even this system was improved in 1995, when Milwaukee was authorized to receive a $2 million ground radar system.

Until the 1980s, when new airlines wanted to serve Milwaukee, they had to win the approval of the Civil Aeronautics Board. In the mid-1950s, seven airlines used Mitchell Field and three more were waiting for CAB approval to begin service. In the late 1960s, twelve airlines applied for new routes, five of which included Milwaukee and some of them using it as a hub from which they could fly to many other destinations. The airlines were seeking a way to solve the congestion at Chicago's O'Hare by diverting more traffic to Milwaukee. The Chicagoans, not wanting to lose any traffic instead proposed building a new airport at various sites in Illinois, including one in Lake Michigan. By the time Mitchell was approved as a hub, the airlines chose not to leave Chicago.

The situation was very different after deregulation. In 1984, a record number of new airlines started using Mitchell Field, including TWA, Midwest Express, Delta, Continental and Frontier. Although many of these and many others have come and gone in the years since, deregulation proved that Milwaukee could thrive in the airline marketplace. As a result, air fares declined and passenger traffic set new records.

The chicken-and-egg cycle continued into the late 1980s. A new concession lobby, with the Gallery of Flight Museum and an expanded parking facility, in addition to more flights and lower fares, brought more travelers to the airport. This increase helped prompt airport planners to propose additional runway expansions, which stimulated heated negative response in neighboring communities. One county supervisor suggested the county build an entirely new airport with a price tag near the $1 billion mark. Instead, after much deliberation and discussion, the county adopted a much less costly runway expansion and noise abatement program.

The projections for Mitchell International are for more of the same—further expansion of facilities that increases demand for air travel which requires more and better services. The future is the past, only more of it.[32]

On January 26 1953, at the Curtiss-Wright Airport near Milwaukee, a few more than thirty men gathered to organize a club to fly and build airplanes. The meeting was called by Milwaukee native and World War II veteran Paul Poberezny, who had been flying since the late 1930s and building his own aircraft since the late 1940s.

Poberezny and his friends had a lot in common. Most of them had started out as "airport kids," who had hung around a landing strip, trading chore work for airplane rides. As a teenager Poberezny had spent many hours at Milwaukee-area airports where he met Bob Huggins, Irv

Above: Paul Poberezny's Baby Ace at Curtiss-Wright, 1955. (George Hardie)

Right: Paul and Audrey Poberezny in the EAA office in their home. (EAA)

Opposite: Paul Poberezny and his first home-built, Little Audrey. (George Hardie)

Miller, Al Luft, Dean and Dale Crites, Harold and Oscar Gallatin, as well as other men who built their own aircraft.

Also like him, most of the men at Poberezny's meeting were young family men who had flown during World War II and never lost their love for it. They could not afford to own and operate a factory-built airplane and support their families, but they had come from families were men worked with their hands as well as their heads. They could build their own.

As Harold Gallatin remembered it, Poberezny had started talking about an organization to rescue general aviation from the "doldrums" it had fallen as early as

1951. Now he and his friends were acting on it. They organized the Experimental Aircraft Owners and Pilots Association and elected Poberezny president. Carl Schultz was the first vice-president; Bob Nolinske, the first secretary-treasurer. Although not elected to any office, Audrey Poberezny, Paul's wife, was the office manager and co-founder of the club.

The name was soon changed to the Experimental Aircraft Association, other officers would come and go, but Poberezny would remain president for another 36 years. In the course of those years, the organization founded in the hangar at Curtiss-Wright would become the most significant general aviation organization in the United States.

"To us it was just another flying club and we had no thoughts other than to help it get started," Poberezny later wrote. "We didn't plan for it to gain worldwide recognition."

The EAA might have remained "just another flying club," had Paul, Audrey and the other pioneers not been so good at making it something more. They published the first issue of their newsletter, "The Experimenter," in February 1953. With help from Ray and Bernice Scholler, it soon developed into a vital source of information for homebuilders. A technical committee was soon organized, with Steve Wittman as its most prominent member, to advise homebuilders on how to design and build safe airplanes that would meet the approval of federal regulators. Early on, Poberezny and the other pioneers worked closely with the Civil Aeronautics Administration, correctly assuming that cooperation would help the EAA more than confrontation. In fact, the first Honorary Member of the EAA was CAA Inspector Tony Maugeri.

As an officer in the Air National Guard, Poberezny met many aviatiors from all over the country and he never failed to talk about the EAA. It became obvious that the club would grow beyond Milwaukee when Chapter #1 was organized in January 1954, not just down the road in Wisconsin, but in Riverside, California. The founder of Chapter #1, Ray Stits, later said that he was convinved back then that in five years the EAA would be the

largest and most active group of aviation enthusiasts in the United States. He was correct.

The EAA had its first official fly-in in September, 1953 as part of the Milwaukee Air Pageant organized by Bill Lotzer at Curtiss-Wright Airport. A total of twenty-two homebuilt aircraft turned out including the latest Poberezny creation, *Little Audrey.*

Soon after the fly-in, Poberezny made a decision that would eventually give the EAA national exposure. He had heard that the remains of the old Corben Sport Plane Company were still in Madison. The owner, former Corben partner E. G. Shoelkopf, let Paul look at crates of wing ribs, jigs, fittings and tubing, plus a completed 2-place Junior Ace airplane, several Ford and Salmson aircraft engines and detailed drawings of Corben planes. It was all for sale for $200 and Poberezny snapped it up. He flew the Corben drawings back to Milwaukee in the machinegun wells of his Air Force F-51, then came back with a pair of farm wagons to haul home the rest.

A few months later, *Mechanix Illustrated Magazine,* contacted Paul and asked if he knew anyone who could write an article about home-built aircraft. He referred the magazine to Steve Wittman and Ray Stits, who were not interested. Then Poberezny agreed to do it himself. The resulting articles, first about the EAA and home-builts, then about the modified Corben Baby Ace Paul later built, introduced the organization to the world. A flood of new membership requests filled the mailbox and advertisers began asking about ads in *The Experimenter.*

The fly-in grew as well, with the 1955 event the first EAA solo convention. In 1956, the organization accepted Steve Wittman's invitation to come to Oshkosh. Attendance topped the 50,000 mark, with 500 EAA members and over 350 aircraft. Since nearly all of the volunteers who ran the fly-in lived in the Milwaukee area, the event was moved backed to Curtiss-Wright Airport in 1957. By 1959, the convention had outgrown Curtiss-Wright and was moved to the airport in Rockford, Illinois. A decade later, with 300,000 people and 10,000 aircraft in attendance, Rockford became too small. The 1970 fly-in was moved to Oshkosh, followed by EAA headquarters, where they have remained ever since.

The EAA has developed into much more than a convention host. It has also, in the words of the Wall Street Journal, "inherited an entire sector of American industry." Since liability laws have all but driven commerical small airplane builders out of business, homebuilding is the only alternative for many people who want to own their own airplane. As the largest organization devoted to homebuilding, the EAA flourishes.

With over 160,000 members, the EAA publishes magazines and books, manages a first class museum, conducts educational and training programs for people of all ages, funds aviation research and speaks for general aviation on a national and international level. Its fly-in convention has become the largest aviation event in the United States, if not the world.

In Wisconsin, the EAA has 34 chapters. They are the most active aviation organization in the state, with programs ranging from the Young Eagles flights to the restoration and maintenance of antique aircraft and providing a corps of volunteers for the annnual fly-in at Oshkosh.[33]

**Wisconsin
EAA Chapters**

931 Adams
60 Beloit/Janesville
431 Brodhead
11 Brookfield
509 Eau Claire
572 Fond du Lac
640 Gleason
875 Grantsburg
651 Green Bay
897 Juneau
217 Kenosha
307 La Crosse
93 Madison
383 Manitowoc
535 Marinette
992 Marshfield
18 Milwaukee
1 Milwaukee Ultralight
1010 Monroe
252 Oshkosh
41 Oshkosh Ultralight
1177 Palmyra
371 Portage
838 Racine
631 Rice Lake/Tony
766 Sheboygan Falls
630 Sturgeon Bay
1015 Thorp
982 Washington Island
320 Watertown
243 Wausau
1158 West Bend
706 Wisconsin Rapids

Vic Bloyer and his Stearman. (Dave Rezin)

Monroe County

Vic Bloyer started flying with the Winnieshiek Flying Club in La Crosse in 1929 and purchased his first J-2 Cub in 1938. He was a flight instructor for Howard Morey in Middleton in 1943 when he and his wife Cora purchased 120 acres of land for an airport in his home town of Tomah. When the war ended, he came home and opened a flight school with a J-3 and a Stearman. Both Bloyers continued to hold full times jobs and run the airport.

In the late 1960s, Tomah debated the option of turning Bloyer Field into a municipal airport. The usual arguments surfaced. Should small town taxpayers support a facility for those "rich enough to own an airplane?" versus the necessity of having an airport for community development and emergency services. The debate in Tomah grew more serious in the summer of 1967 when a visiting pilot, John Rarick, caught the landing gear of his Piper Comanche on power lines at the end of the Tomah runway. The plane flipped, crashed to the ground and a passenger died.

The loss of his friend in an avoidable accident led Rarick to launch a national "Bury the Wires, Not the Pilot" campaign. He started in Tomah with a $2,000 donation. Bloyer, who had been saying for years that either the wires had to be buried or the runway lengthened, decided to close the airport to public use. Since Rarick's $2,000 was not enough to bury the wires a local manufacturer matched that amount, and announced that it could not expand its operations unless the airport was improved. Local aviators sponsored a Vic Bloyer Day where additional money was raised.

The situation prompted the city of Tomah to lease the airport for $3,000 and apply for state and federal money to lengthen and surface the runway. Two years later, John Rarick returned to Tomah and presented Bloyer, the Tomah Flying Club and the city with a

plaque for their efforts to make the airport a safer place. Tomah became one of the first of many airports around the country that Rarick cited. The city completed the purchase of the airport in 1973 and has managed it ever since.

In the 1930's, Earl Leverich opened a landing strip in the Town of Angelo east of Sparta which was used by both civilian and military aircraft. In the 1960s, Sparta purchased the field and maintained two turf runways, eventually adding lights to the longest. In the 1980s, the airport at Fort McCoy was improved and Sparta entered into a joint use agreement with the military and the former Sparta Municipal Airport was abandoned.

The city of Sparta is also home to a museum and archive dedicated to astronaut "Deke" Slayton, who was born and raised nearby.[34]

Oconto County

The Oconto Airport began in 1946 when World War II veteran Robert Jubin agreed to take over management of acreage donated to the city by a local business person. Born in Green Bay, Jubin learned how to fly at Blesch Field before entering the Army Air Force. He started at Oconto with two J-3 Cubs—one used, one new— built a hangar and kept the sod graded for the G.I. Bill students taking instruction.

In 1962, the city offered him $3,000 a year and the title of "act-

Oconto Airport terminal, 1998. (Eileen Duffeck)

ing manager." He declined the offer and recalled that some council members were "surprised to see me give them notice because they thought I was receiving the world with a fence around it."

Instead he moved to Austin Straubel Airport and started a charter service called Green Bay Aviation. In 1974, when he bought a Cessna 310 that he couldn't fly within twenty-five miles of Green Bay, he moved back to Oconto. He worked to improve the airport, but stayed there only a few years before moving back to Green Bay. In the late 1960s and early 1970s the Green Bay Packers hired him and his Twin Beechcraft D-18 to carry coach Vince Lombardi and some of the players who wanted to avoid the attention they would attract on a commercial flight. He would fly Lombardi to Chicago or Minneapolis where the coach would board an airliner. In the off-season Jubin also flew the Packers players basketball team to play at fund-raising events.

After Jubin left, Oconto continued to upgrade its airport and has one 3,000-foot blacktopped lighted runway. In 1967, Fritz Wolf visited Oconto and convinced the city to establish an airport commission. One of the first airport supporters, Doug Bake has served as airport commissioner for over thirty-six years.

Oconto county is also served by privately-owned airports at Suring and Lakewood. [35]

Deicing facility at Rhinelander/Oneida County Airport, 1998. (Becher-Hoppe Associates)

Oneida County

In 1941, Rhinelander City Manager Ted Wardwell persuaded the Oneida County Board to turn over to the city 106 acres at the county poor farm for an air field. Wardwell, who became one of the first members of the State Aeronautics Commission, continued to press for improvements and convinced Oneida County to become a joint owner of the airport. By 1946, the airport was enlarged to 590 acres.

The airport manager was Steve Shelbreck, who began flying in 1928 when the airport was at the county fairgrounds. Shelbreck managed that airport through times thick and thin, moved to the new facility when it opened and stayed there until his retirement in 1959. He was followed by Ed Miller, Frank Priebe, Rod Elg, Andy Creglow, Jack Chmiel and Joe Brauer.

Wisconsin Central Airlines began scheduled service from Rhinelander in 1948 with Lockheed 10A Electras. Rhinelander saw Wisconsin Central and its successor airlines send DC-3s, Convairs and DC-9 fanjets to its airport.

Rhinelander was able to accommodate DC-9s because it completed an ambitious expansion plan in the 1970s. Building a jetport in a city of 8,000 was challenging, to say the least. In 1975, Airport Commissioner Robert Heck and county supervisor Judson Mangerson twice presented crucial resolutions that passed the board by no more than one vote. The $7 million, 6,800-foot runway was ready for takeoffs and landings in 1978, fol-

lowed by a new terminal in 1979, which also houses several county offices.

In terms of acreage, Rhinelander airport is one of the largest in Wisconsin. "We built with an eye on projections of traffic growth in the future," said Bob Heck at the time. "I don't believe we have any wasted space at all."

The Three Lakes Airport was built by the town government in 1953 for a total of $26,000. It was used to build a small hangar, drain some wetland and grade the turf. Still in use in 1998, the airport has one 3,740-foot, lighted, turf runway. [36]

Outagamie County

World War II had yet to end when Appleton civic and business leaders attempted to build a new airport. They wanted to buy 245 acres southeast of the city in Calumet County but the citizens said no in a referendum vote. Over the next decade, the old Ballard Road airport was improved several times and North Central provided airline service throughout the 1950s.

Led by attorney Karl Baldwin, the city entertained several schemes, including a combination rail and air terminal to be built west of Appleton and a joint Outagamie-Winnebago County Airport west of Neenah. The Winnebago County Board adamantly opposed replacing the Oshkosh Airport and Outagamie decided to proceed on its own. The county appropriated $2.8 to purchase 1,302 acres in the Town of Greenville and built a new airport which opened for business in 1963.

The airport land purchase was huge for its day. No other civilian airport in Wisconsin occupied as much space, yet Outagamie had its eyes on the future. The Fox Cities metropolitan area was

Right top: Air Wisconsin founders, Karl Baldwin, Kathy Comins, Preston Wilbourne, 1978. Above: Air Wisconsin commuters ready for take off. (Kathy Comins)

about to begin the greatest period of growth in its history. With plenty of space for expansion, the airport could grow along with its community. The land would also act as a buffer to prevent suburban sprawl from hemming in the airport.

The wisdom of acquiring the land was confirmed in the 1980s, when Outagamie became the fastest growing airport in Wisconsin. In 1989, the airport served 300,000 passengers, moved 5.5 million pounds of freight, had 1,000 employees and made an economic impact of $200 million. Only Milwaukee, Madison and Green Bay had more commercial traffic than Outagamie.

Midwest Express founder Tim Hoeksema, 1995. (Midwest Express)

Among the reasons why the Outagamie airport was developing so well is that it was the home of one of the state's largest aviation service companies and the nursery for two airlines. Max Sagunsky's Maxair was located at Outagamie and Air Wisconsin and Midwest Express Airlines were born there.

Sagunsky started as airport manager at the old Appleton Airport in 1953 and moved to the new facility when it opened. His aircraft maintenance and general aviation service company continued to operate at the airport after he retired in the mid-1970s.

Air Wisconsin was born with the Outagamie airport in 1963. Faced with the pullout of service by North Central, Appleton business leaders began to sell stock in what was to be the first publicly-held commuter airline in the United States. Called Fox Cities Airline at first, the corporation was renamed Air Wisconsin by the time it made its first flight in 1965. Air Wisconsin had two nine-passenger DeHaviland Doves, three pilots and seventeen employees, with Preston H. Wilbourne as general manager.

Starting with daily commuter flights to Chicago, Air Wisconsin acquired more routes and aircraft. By 1983, it was serving seven Great Lakes states from Pennsylvania to Minnesota, carrying over 700,000 passengers and flying 100-passenger British Aerospace 146 jets. In the late 1980s, Air Wisconsin consolidated its offices and maintenance facilities in Appleton. Shortly after the airline was acquired by United Airlines as part of its United Express commuter service.

Just as Air Wisconsin was reaching its peak, another airline was born at Appleton. Midwest Express began as an idea in the offices of Tim Hoeksema chief pilot of K-C Aviation, the corporate air service of Appleton's Kimberly-Clark Corporation. K-C had been operating a regularly scheduled shuttle between Appleton and a major facility in Georgia that was often complimented by experienced executive travelers.

Hoeksema saw a market for high-quality service among business travelers and suggested that K-C Aviation start an airline. "Many Kimberly-Clark people were experiencing difficulty with air travel at the time," Hoeksema recalled. "Service was lousy, schedules were skimpy. It was easy to figure out that if we were unhappy, lots of other people probably were too.

"When you have an industry with dissatisfied customers, you have a business opportunity."

Taking advantage of that opportunity, Kimberly-Clark started Midwest Express with Hoeksema at the helm. Service began in 1984 with two airplanes flying to four destinations. Ten years later, Midwest Express, which had registered a profit after two years of operation and every year since, had a fleet of sixteen DC-9s serving twenty-three cities from its Milwaukee hub. Plans for future growth included marketing itself and Mitchell Airport to business travelers from northern Illinois weary of dealing with giant O'Hare Airport.

Midwest Express has consistently been heralded as the "best" airline in terms of traveler satisfaction. It has built its success on the simple philosophy that quality service is good business.[37]

Ozaukee County

Ozaukee currently has seven private airports and one heliport. Although there are no publicly-owned airports in the county, aviation interest dates back to World War II, with Ozaukee included in the State Airport Plan of 1947.

Ray Karrels opened his airport near Port Washington to the public and called it the Ozaukee County Airport. The name stuck, even though the county never funded the airport in any way. Ray was active in the EAA and owned a number of anitque military planes which he flew off his grass runways.

The airport was closed to the public in 1982 and, when the Karrels family offered to sell it to the county in 1984, the offer was turned down. As one county highway commissioner reportedly remarked at the time, "No one has requested it, and West Bend Airport is near by." So Ozaukee remains one of eight Wisconsin counties without a public access airport.[38]

Pierce County

The River Falls airport is a privately owned field built by local business people who organized the River Falls Airport, Inc. in 1959. It covers fifteen acres and has a single 1,560-foot sod runway.

The Red Wing, Minnesota, Municipal Airport is located across the Mississippi River near Bay City, Wisconsin. It has a 4,000-foot surfaced runway. Seifert Airways has been the FBO since the early 1970s.[39]

Polk County

In 1962, at the Wisconsin Aeronautics Conference in Stevens Point, the state aviation community came together to honor one of its most respected members. Dr. Otis L. Simenstad was honored by the Wisconsin Aviation Trades Association and the Aeronautics Commission for his many years of service to aviation in the state.

Champion airplanes on the line at Osceola, 1968. (Bureau of Aeronautics)

"All the things I've done I've just fallen into. The reason that I went into aviation is that I wanted an airport for the town," Simenstad told a reporter in 1967. As World War II was drawing to a close, that interest led Simenstad to contact the state planning board about state funding. The request caught the eye of Governor Walter Goodland who was then creating the advisory committee that was the predecessor of the Aeronautics Commission. Simenstad found himself on the committee and, when the Aeronautics Commission was formed, one of its first members. He would hold a seat on the Commission until his retirement in 1962, longer than anyone else.

Since he was an aeronautics commissioner, he thought he should learn how to fly. After completing flight instruction with Bob Hammond of Eau Claire, Simenstad soloed in a Piper J-3 in 1944. The first plane he owned was a Cessna 170 and his last was a Cessna 421.

The new pilot was not only Osceola's doctor, he was also village president, which enabled him to take the lead on the airport question. In 1947, Osceola received one of the first Aeronautics Commission grants for airport construction. Development was slow at first, but picked up considerably in 1955.

The venerable Aeronca Manufacturing Corporation of Ohio had been acquired by the Champion Aircraft Corporation of St. Paul. Champion was looking for a place to build its own version of the Aeronca 7AC Champion and Simenstad invited them to come to Osceola. He created a financing package for a factory plus a new paved runway at the airport and Champion moved to Osceola. Over the next twenty-five years four lines of airplanes were built at Osceola—the Champion, Challenger, Lancer and Citabria.

In 1970, things started to go bad. Champion merged with Bellanca, but continued to make airplanes in Osceola—until the plant was destroyed by fire in 1971. The village rebuilt the factory, but then Bellanca went bankrupt. By 1979, Osceola's run as an airplane manufacturer was over. Doc Simenstad passed away in 1975, after practicing medicine in Osceola for over fifty years. Appropriately, the airport was named in his honor.

The village sponsored a $300,000 improvement program in the late 1980s. Use continued to grow as an increasing number of businesses and private pilots from the Twin Cities kept aircraft there.

In addition to its airport and airplane factory, Osceola also had an Air Force base. The 674th Aircraft Control and Warning Squadron was set up to detect Soviet aircraft coming over the Canadian border to attack the United State. The Osceola base joined eight additional sites in Michigan and Minnesota to form the "Pine Tree Line." About 125 military and civilian personnel were assigned to the base between 1950 and its closing in 1975.

In 1969, pilots in the Amery area organized a corporation to build an airport. The Amery Flyers, Inc. raised enough money to purchase thirty-six acres and built a 2600-foot turf runway. The city of Amery took over the airport in 1972 and, with federal and state aid, surfaced the runway and lengthened it to 3,100 feet. In 1980, Roger Olson was appointed to the airport commission. Under his leadership, a homing beacon, instrument approach procedure and a 4,000-foot runway became reality at the airport.[40]

Portage County

As an Army Air Force training center, the Stevens Point Airport was a busy place during World War II. The activity continued in the 1940s with G.I. Bill students keeping FBO and flight instructor Al Padags busy certifying new pilots. He also started an airline called the "Indian Trail Route," which never got farther than a few promotional flights with local businessmen on board.

Stevens Point Airport terminal, 1953. (Bureau of Aeronautics)

A major improvement program took place in the late 1940s. Runways were extended and lighted in time for the first Wisconsin Central airline to touch down in February 1948. Stevens Point would be one of the airline's regular stops for many years.

As early as 1957, business people from Stevens Point, Marshfield and Wisconsin Rapids, talked about joining with Wausau to build a "tri-county" airport. Stevens Point and Portage county people were willing, as were Wausau and Marathon county, but Wood county was not interested.

Wisconsin Central continued to serve Stevens Point until the Central Wisconsin Airport opened at Mosinee. After Wisconsin Central left, Midstate Airlines moved in. Founded by Roy Shwery in Marshfield in 1964, Midstate was one of the first and most successful commuter airlines in the country. It did very well carrying business travelers from cities the size of Stevens Point to Milwaukee and Chicago. Midstate was also the FBO at Stevens Point from 1968 until 1979, with Greg Parsons as airport manager. Sentry Aviation Services, which purchased Midstate in 1981, then followed as FBO, offering instruction and charters, as well as keeping the aircraft owned by Sentry Insurance in the air.

Ken Barlow was one of the most memorable people associated with the airport. A mechanic, aircraft builder and restorer, Barlow worked at Stevens Point from the 1950s to the 1980s.

The Portage County area seemed to have more than its share of "pilotless" planes. In 1946, an Aeronca Champ took off from Marshfield on its own and ascended to 6,000 feet before crashing into a farm field near Milladore. The following year

The flight line at Phillips/Price County Airport, 1946. (Charles Kudrna)

another plane took off at Plainfield, buzzed the village, then crashed into a power line. In 1986, Mike Feltz, a flight instructor for Sentry Aviation at Stevens Point, "talked down" a passenger flying with a pilot who had a heart attack. Feltz was able to keep the plane circling until he could get close enough to give the passenger instructions to make a safe landing over the radio.[41]

Price County

Aviation in the Phillips area began in 1931 when Ed Marquardt of Tomahawk landed an Aeronca 3-C in a clearing near the Kudrna family farm east of town. Steve and Otto Kudrna were hooked. They purchased a Waco 9 and took flying lessons from visiting pilots. They were ready to perform at the first Phillips air show, which they organized in 1933. About twenty planes participated along with parachute jumper Roger Ray, who mesmerized the crowd.

Leo Heikkenen using one of his knuckle-boom loaders to move rocks at the Prentice Airport. (Dale Heikkenen)

The Kudrna farm served as the local airport until 1945, when the city of Phillips purchased acreage on "the old sheep farm" north of town. It was a level spot that had been cleared and planted in pasture grass for a large sheep-raising operation that failed in the 1930s and made a great airport site.

In 1960, Price County leased the airport from the city and the following year hired Bob White as manager. He spent the next twenty years improving the facility where traffic was doubling every four years. In 1983, the airport underwent an $800,000 upgrade and in 1997 completed a new $3.8 million north-south runway project.

Park Falls was a reluctant participant in the aviation age. The private landing strip at the golf course north of the city was kept open in the 1950s by the efforts of Jack Tomczak. He built a hangar, installed gas pumps and laid out a 1,440-foot runway. By 1954

"progress had inched its way along," with four planes present. The Park Falls field must have looked a bit unusual from the air. Since it was treated with sulfite "binder" from the Flambeau Paper Company, the runway would not support a crop of grass. In 1963, the city purchased the airport so it would be eligible for federal and state funding and it has been improved several times.

Leo Heikkinen was the man who invented the "Prentice" hydraulic log loader that is as well-known in Wisconsin's forest as tractors are in its corn fields. Elected president of his home village in 1967, he turned his considerable skill and energy into building an airport. A 2,000-foot grass runway was cleared and, just for good measure, a nine-hole golf course laid out around it. It seemed to be all the airport Prentice needed until Omark Industries, the company to which Heikkinen had sold his loader manufactory and the employer of more than one hundred local people, announced that it needed a airport able to handle twin-engine planes or it might have to leave town.

Price County already had two airports in the state airport plan, so a third gaining eligibility for federal/state funding was unlikely. So, led by Leo Heikkinen, the people of Prentice built an airport. Local contractors loaned equipment, volunteers cleared the ground of trees, stumps and rocks. To finance surfacing a 3,250-foot runway, the village created a Tax Incremental Finance District. Instead of leaving the community, Omark expanded and made more jobs. When the ribbon was cut on the new runway in 1981, Governor Lee Dreyfus told the audience, "You didn't sit back and wait for a grant; you pitched in and helped this airport." And so they did.[42]

Racine County

The Racine Airport is known as the "airport that executives built." In the late 1940s, when the prospect of federal/state funding encouraged just about every city, village and county in Wisconsin to consider developing an airport, civic leaders in Racine looked the other way. When Horlick Airport manager and owner Carlisle Godske wanted out of the business end of flying in 1949, neither the city nor county of Racine acted to keep the airport open. Accordingly, eleven city businesses, led by aviators Sam Johnson of Johnson's Wax and John Batten of Twin-Disc Clutch, organized the Racine Commercial Airport Corporation. As a tax-paying corporate property, the Racine Airport has grown into one of the busiest privately-owned, public use airport in the United States.

As in real estate, location is important for airports. In Racine's case, the airport is fortunate to be located in a city with a very aviation-minded business community. In the 1950s, more than a dozen local companies had multi-engine aircraft at the airport. Recognizing its roots, the airport was named John H. Batten Field after its co-founder passed away in 1989.

Corporate aviation was still important in the 1990s. In 1996, Johnson Wax kept four jets and a helicopter at the airport. "If a senior management person is being paid several hundred dollars an hour, you don't want them sitting around a hub airport waiting for a connecting flight," said Michael Parker, head of corporate services for Johnson Wax and president of the airport board. In this sense, having a corporate air fleet and a good airport nearby makes good business sense.

Racine has also benefitted from proximity to Mitchell and O'Hare airports. As a federally-designated reliever airport for both of its neighbors since 1982, Racine has received approximately $14 million in federal/state money so it has runways, navigation and communication equipment to handle any business aircraft flying today.

In its nearly fifty years, the airport has had only three managers, John Sullivan, William Zlevor and Dave Mann. They were

Above: Fern Fisher and J-4 Cub Coupe, 1940. (Fern Fisher) Below: Racine Airport Manager John Sullivan and his Taylorcraft, 1940. (Elmo Halverson) Left: Carlyle Godske's Airport west of Racine, 1940. (Bureau of Aeronautics)

both assisted by Fern Fisher, who spent forty-five years at Batten Field. A licensed pilot and mechanic in 1940, Fisher was the second pilot to land at the airport—then known as Horlick Field—in 1941. She stayed to help run the airport as well as local and state units of the Civil Air Patrol. "I was around airplanes all my life. The airport was the first love of my life," she told a reporter in 1996.

Ford Tri-Motor wrecked by a big wind at Burlington, 1973. (Bureau of Aeronautics)

The Burlington Airport had its beginnings in the mid 1950s when citizens cast their ballots in favor of a city airport—until a recount discovered that they had actually voted against it. In 1960, the city council voted to build an airport and the first hangar was built a year later by Bill Shattuck, B.E. Pippin and Robert Southey. In 1973, the airport was the scene of a freak accident involving the Ford Tri-Motor owned by the EAA. Although the plane was tied down as securely as possible, tornado-force winds lifted it about fifty feet into the air, then dropped it, nose down into the ground.

The Ford stayed on its back at Burlington for a few months until the insurance claims were settled, then restoration began. Dick

Wagner of Wag-Aero in nearby Lyons, and Dr. Pete Williams, headed up a team of volunteers who put hearts, heads and money into bringing the plane back to life. In 1985, the Ford was the star of the EAA Fly-In where it still flies today.

In the late 1980s, the manager and FBO at the Burlington Airport was Jerry Mehlhaff. He had built his own landing strip—the Foxair Airport—on his farm near Rochester and set up a busy maintenance operation specializing in Piper, Mooney and Ercoupe aircraft. In 1988, he purchased the remains of the American Champion Aircraft Company, formerly located in Osceola, and began manufacturing airplanes. By 1990 he turned out his first Super Decathalon

Model and exhibited at the EAA Convention. He set up a factory with eighteen employees and went into production. By 1995, the company was on a firm footing and making over forty airplanes per year. It was the only production aircraft builder in the state and is still going strong with seventy employees building over fifty aircraft a year.[43]

Richland County

In the 1930s, aviation in the region where Sauk, Richland and Iowa counties meet was centered on the Lone Rock Airport. As an "emergency" landing field on the air mail route, Lone Rock was a cut above other local airports in terms of lighting and radio facilities.

Barnstormers visiting Richland Center in the 1920s landed in a farm field north of the city. When local people—Dr. B. I. Pippin, Harry Brewer, Gerald Denman, Phil Leyda—started to fly in the 1930s they used Lone Rock or "the Perkins farm" southeast of the city. Brewer built on his local experience to become an army flight instructor, Air Ferry Command flyer, one of the first pilots for Wisconsin Central Airlines and a CAA/FAA flight inspector.

Above: Dwight Woodard working on the rotary engine of his restored Thomas-Morse Scout at Richland Center. Right: The finished product. (WAHF)

The others stayed in Richland County. Pippin owned a Monocoupe and Leyda had a Piper J-2 that he used to start the first flying club in the area. By 1940, Leyda was flying a Cessna Airmaster with a 145 HP Warner engine that could climb at 1000 feet a minute and hit speeds of 165 MPH. It was the county's top performing airplane.

Towards the end of World War II, the State Aeronautics Commission helped a group of Richland Center businessmen who had formed an airport corporation select a new airport site near the village of Sextonville. The city acquired ownership in the late 1940s and the field has been a municipal airport ever since.

Among the pilots flying out of the Sextonville field were A. E. Weiland with his Taylorcraft L-2 and L-3; Albert Muckler and his Aeronca L-3; Dwight Woodard, who was the first FBO and who rebuilt a World War I-vintage Thomas-Morse Scout that he flew in a Hollywood movie; Dick Young, with his PA-12; Mike and Leslie Meadows, with the four-place American Yankee; and many others.

The Richland Center Airport also had a memorable cafe run by Hilda Lang and Betty Schlafer that filled up at mealtimes with diners who did not fly and with pilots the rest of the time. An Illinois National Guard unit discovered the place on its way to and from Fort McCoy. Every summer for a few years, as many as two-dozen Guard helicopters were parked at the airport while the crews chowed down at the cafe. When Lang and Schlafer retired in the early 1980s, the cafe closed.

In the 1960s and 70s, Richland Center had about twenty airplanes at the airport. By the early 1990s only two planes were in Sextonville, as local pilots concentrated at the Lone Rock Airport. In 1995, a new $1.4 million, 3,200-foot runway and adjoining taxiway revived Richland Center. By 1998, the field had six based aircraft, four ultralights and a new restaurant. [44]

Rock County

The story of Wisconsin's airports in the half-century since World War II is one of progress. There seems to more of everything and everything seems to be bigger, safer, faster and more advanced. Yet not everyone was carried along by the upward tide. As millions of dollars were poured into Wisconsin's publicly-owned airports, privately-owned airports struggled to survive and most did not make it.

Rock County well illustrates what happened. In the years immediately after World War II the "Rock County Airport" managed by Russ and Marge Van Galder was the leading airport in the county. Two years later, when the county-owned "Rock County Airport" was fully up and running, the fate of the Van Galder operation was obvious. They could not compete with a county airport that was exempt from local taxes and the recipient of a million dollars in federal aid. By the mid-1950s, the Van Galders' Beloit Airways was out of business and Russ was working at the MacChesney Airport in Illinois.

"99's"

The first Wisconsin chapter of the Ninety-Nines was organized in Madison in 1940 by Melba Gorby Beard. A charter member of the Ninety-Nines, she had spent nearly all her flying career in California. Finding herself in a place without a Ninety-Nines Chapter, she organized one. When she left the state in 1941, Beard's Madison group merged with the Milwaukee chapter just started by Caroline Iverson. No sooner did Iverson get the Milwaukee group off the ground than the American entry into World War II grounded it. Iverson herself became an editor for *Life* magazine who specialized in covering the air war. The Ninety-Nines revived after the war, as women pilots got together for both hangar and genuine flying. The landing strip of Pearl Nelson, who flew her Beech Staggerwing off the family farm near Stoughton, became an unofficial picnic grounds for female pilots. Regular monthly fly-in meetings were held at various places throughout the state, with as many as forty pilots attending in the early 1950s. For a few years in the 1950s, the state had two chapters, one at Madison, the other at Milwaukee.

After learning how to fly in 1946, Milwaukee's Eugenia Rothrock "Deedo" Heise, became one of the most well-known Ninety-Nines in the state. In 1949, she won the Ninety-Nine's All-Women's Transcontinental Air Race (AWTAR) between Cleveland and New York. It was then known as the "Powder Puff Derby." Heise logged thousands of hours in the air as a Ninety-Nine and also as one of the founders—along with husband Herman Heise—of the Flying Physicians in Wisconsin. Dr. Heise, like all the spouses of Ninety-Nines, was known as a Forty-Nine and One-Half.

Over the years many other Wisconsin women participated in AWTAR, including Anne Roethke and Dorothy Parks of Madison, Lois Truchinski of Wisconsin Rapids and Dora Fritzke of Milwaukee in the 1950s and '60s. In the 1970s, Joan McArthur of Baraboo, Carolyn Arnold of Beloit, Joyce Donner of Oshkosh, Tanya Cunninghan, Terri Martin and Caroline Morey of Madison all competed in the AWTAR. In 1979, Cunningham and Morey flew a

Cessna 182 RG to a fifth place finish in the 2,600 mile race from California to Milwaukee. Wisconsin women have also flown in the Michigan SMALL race, the Illi-Nine and in their own Wis-Sky Run.

The Ninety-Nines have also been committed to education and service. Ramona Huebner, Fond du Lac, made many flying visits to Wisconsin schools and, in 1976, Diane Gorak, Helen Kelly and Marie Grimm headed a committee to collect and publish the history of aviation in Wisconsin. In the 1960s, the women conducted "Magic Carpet" flights in which they took physically handicapped

A gathering of 99's in Milwaukee about 1946. Front l-r, Jeanette Kapus, Deedo Heise, unidentified. Sitting on couch, l-r, unidentified, unidentified, Margaret Bruns, Ruth Craine, Dora Fritzke, Necia Patterson. Standing, Elsie Peter. (Milwaukee County Historical Society)

people up for their first rides aloft. Marie Grimm also shared management of the Wausau Airport with her husband Lyle, one of many husband-wife FBO teams in the state. Florence Toney, who started flying in 1944, managed the Capitol Drive Airport near Milwaukee for many years. In the 1980s and '90s membership in the Wisconsin Chapter of the Ninety-Nines averaged around sixty active members. They still meet for monthly fly-in meetings, usually in the southern half of the state where most of the members live. Once a year they gather at Watertown for a big pancake breakfast fund-raiser.[45]

Rock County Airport, 1947. (WAHF)

Progress continued at the county airport, where new runways were paved, a terminal and tower built. Passenger service from North Central/Republic, Apex, Mississippi Valley, Midstate and American Central Airlines came and went. Managers and FBOs changed, until Joan and Dick Wixom's Blackhawk Airways settled in. They celebrated their twenty-fifth anniversary in 1995.

The airport became the site of Wisconsin's largest vocational-technical aviation education program. Archie Henkelmann started the program in the mid-1950s, at what was then the Janesville Vocational School. When the state technical college system was organized in the 1960s, Henkelmann transferred to Blackhawk Technical Institute. By the mid-1970s, he was supervising pioneering courses in airframe and powerplant mechanics and aviation electronics. To celebrate the 75th anniversary of the Wright Brothers Flight, Henkelmann's students built a replica of the Wright Flyer. Completed in the 1977-78 school year and involving as many as five hundred students, Blackhawk Tech's Wright Flyer ended up on permanent display at the EAA Museum in Oshkosh.

Perhaps a greater measure of success is the number of students who have earned their two-year degrees and stepped directly into good jobs in the aviation industry. Archie Henkelmann continued to produce people prepared for aviation careers until he retired after thirty-three years in 1989.

Rock County is also served by the privately-owned, public-use Beloit Airport. It has a 3,300 foot paved runway and thirty-one based aircraft.[46]

the winter in the deer yards, we even did prairie chicken counts."

In the late 1940s, the Conservation Department was implementing modern and controversial deer management practices. Heavy winter kills of deer in the northern counties attracted a lot of attention and made the winter counts more important than they might otherwise have been. Counting deer by air was easier and more accurate than trying to count while slugging through snow-filled winter woods.

The prairie chicken counts required some fancy flying. "That prairie chicken counting is very interesting because you have to fly fairly low to flush them and they only flush after you've flown over them," Doughty said, "so both guys have to be looking back, one out the left and one out the right. One with the counter and one calling and you hope that the guy that is supposed to be watching ahead doesn't run into anything."

Doughty also flew fire patrol for the Conservation Department. In "1948, the big fire season, the towers couldn't see because of the smoke and both my airplanes flew from light after dark, because the towers couldn't see fires. We found many, many fires..."

Archie Henkelmann, with Blackhawk Tech alumni Ed Alft and John Feeney, 1987. (Midwest Flyer)

Rusk County

In 1946, the Rusk County Board built an airport on 160 acres southeast of Ladysmith. Hal Doughty, who had grown up and learned to fly in nearby Bruce, had just been discharged from the Army Air Force. He came home and bought into a flying service already underway at the airport and eventually became its sole operator. "We started with three Cubs, two 65 horse Lycomings and one 40 horse [which] was good for zilch except solo. Then we had just Aeronca Champs."

Making a living as an airport operator in rural Wisconsin was not easy, but Doughty did all right. "We had some good contracts with the DNR for game surveys," he recalled. "We did deer counts in

He also located many a lost hunter, berry picker and dairy cow, even found his own car after it had been stolen and the county sheriff had abandoned the search. He took up shooters who wanted to collect wolf bounties by bagging animals from the air. "I told them what the restrictions were," Doughty said to one wolf hunter he was about to take up in a Piper Cub. "I didn't want him to shoot the floor, or the prop, or the wing struts and I told him how to shoot the wolf." Since the plane was traveling faster than the animal, Doughty told the hunter to aim for the wolf's tail and he would hit the body. Although other factors were involved, legal hunting of wolves from airplanes contributed to the disappearance of the animals from Wisconsin in the 1950s.

Doughty also assisted loggers who relied on airplanes to reach remote sites. He recalled one case where a logger bogged down his D-4 Cat and needed a heavy chain to yank it out of the mud. A pilot himself, the logger used one of Doughty's Aeroncas to fly the chain up to the stuck Cat. Of course there was no place to land, so the pilot decided to shove the chain out the plane's door. He thought it would land in the middle of a clearing. Instead it dropped into the woods and onto the hood of the Cat operator's car. "It dropped the engine right out of it," he said.

Hal Doughty's colorful life as a north woods aviator came to a conclusion in 1951. He was called up for service in Korea not long after a tornado destroyed most of the hangars and planes at the airport. He left Ladysmith and stayed in the military for thirty years.

Rusk County built a new airport near Tony and hired Elmer Wisherd to manage it. He concentrated on flight instruction in an Aeronca 7AC. Since many of his students were cash-shy, Wisherd took tools and equipment in trade. "I have always tried to help people out if they wanted," he said. "I have taken in boats, outboard motors, guns, I couldn't afford to buy one anyway. I did a lot of horse trading."

It must have worked, for Wisherd continued as airport manager for the better part of three decades.

Also located at Rusk County is Pedersen Aircraft. Started by H.L. Pedersen and now operated by his son Dick, the company specializes in custom maintenance of Beech Bonanzas.[47]

Above: The Lone Rock Flight Service Station was one of the oldest air mail stations in the state. (Bureau of Aeronautics)

St. Croix County

The city of New Richmond purchased land for an airport in 1962 and work began to build a 3000-foot blacktopped runway the following year. The airport faced considerable opposition, especially from the editor of the *New Richmond News*, who identified it as that "damned Idle Field" in his editorials. Despite the editor, the airport was built and improved many times. By the 1990s, it had a 4,000-foot surfaced runway, four FBOs and, in 1997, listd seventy-four based aircraft, one helicopter and three ultralights.[48]

Sauk County

Sauk County has two of the oldest public airports in the state at Reedsburg and Lone Rock/Tri-County, one of the newest at Sauk-Prairie and one that set a precedent for public-private airport management at Baraboo/Wisconsin Dells.

The Reedsburg Airport revived after World War II, with flight instruction offered by Lloyd Bell and William McBoyle. In the 1960s Reedsburg was the headquarters of the N.E. Isaacson Company, builder of lakes for second-home developments. Isaacson used a float plane to visit his projects throughout the state and, since Reedsburg is not itself on a lake, built a "water runway" for himself. It was a long narrow flooded channel on which he could land. When Isaacson left the city, the runway was filled.

In the 1970s the Reedsburg Flying Club was a going operation of pilots who flew a Piper Cherokee, Cessna 150, Cessna 172 and a Piper Warrior. The club had about one dozen members and survived into the late 1980s.

As one of Wisconsin's oldest city airports, Reedsburg has been improved many times since World War II. Its two asphalt runways run for 4,900 and 2,600 feet.

Sauk County's other old airport is Lone Rock. At the junction of two air mail routes, the Lone Rock Airport was used by air mail carriers as early as 1920. As an air mail airport, Lone Rock had beacons, runway lighting and radio earlier than most of the other airports in the state but its runways remained unsurfaced.

At the end of World War II, the Civil Aeronautics Administration sent war veteran Ben Silko to manage the Lone Rock Flight Service Station. It provided weather reports and traffic control for southwestern Wisconsin, including Madison. It was from this weather station on January 30, 1951 that Silko recorded the record temperature of -53 below

Marge Van Galder, Lloyd Bell and State Senator Earl Leverich discuss the plight of private airport owners, 1953. (Marge Van Galder)

zero, thereby giving Lone Rock boosters the opportunity to call their town "the coldest spot with the warmest heart" in the country.

In 1954, the CAA relinquished control of the airport, but continued to maintain the Flight Service Station. Silko remained in charge until his retirement in 1977. He was succeeded by Rosemary Baker, who had started working at the Station in the late 1940s and who stayed until it was closed in 1984. At that time the small station building was moved to the EAA's Pioneer Airport at Oshkosh.

Back in Lone Rock, the CAA's pullout as airport owner in 1954 raised the question of what to do with the field. A group of aviators rallied support and convinced the supervisors of Sauk, Richland and Iowa counties to create and fund a Tri-County Airport. The first members of the Tri-County Airport Committee were Leon Peck, Al Anding and C.L. Porter. This action set the stage for a long struggle with state aviation agencies to make Tri-County eligible for state/federal aid as part of the state airport plan.

The Zech Family, Darin, Donna, Aaron, Austin, Judy. (Zech Family)

In the 1960s, Phil Leyda, who had started flying at Richland Center in the 1930s and who had helped start that city's airport at Sextonville after World War II, became the leading advocate for Tri-County. In 1968, he organized the Tri-County Airport Improvement Corporation to raise public and private funding to build a "jetport" at Tri-County. About the same time a group of investors organized the Wisconsin River Development Corporation which announced ambitious plans for a multi-million dollar resort and residential development on the Iowa County side of the Wisconsin River across from the airport.

The airport was destined to play an integral role in this development and—so its supporters argued—should be in the state airport plan. The state Aeronautics Division was forced to point out that Tri-County was not near the population center of any of the three-counties it served and if it received state plan funding, then the Sextonville airport in Richland County could not. In 1976, the state opted for Sextonville. By this time, it was apparent that the resort development would not be as large as announced. By the 1990s, development on the scale planned was prohibited along the Lower Wisconsin.

Tri-County continues to serve as a fine small airport and was added to the State Airport System Plan in 1985.

Aviation activity was also going on a few miles upstream of Lone Rock at Sauk Prairie. In 1952, Milton Zech built a landing strip on the family farm outside of Prairie du Sac. Volunteers made improvements but the airport hardly changed for nearly thirty years. In the late 1980s, with public support, the airport was improved with the completion of a 2,900-foot asphalt runway. In 1998, it had twenty-five hangars, twenty-three aircraft and an active FBO.

In the 1940s, J. William McBoyle, a colorful veteran of World War I, operated out of the old Lake Delton Airport established by William Newman in the late 1920s. Using the Ryan Brougham that once belonged to Governor Walter Kohler, McBoyle gave aerial tours of Dells' scenery. In 1956, after it became obvious that his airport would not receive state/federal aid, McBoyle closed his airport to the public.

One of the reasons William McBoyle shut down was the airport started by Lloyd Bell in 1945. He opened the Baraboo-

Wisconsin Dells Airport on eighty acres about three miles north of Baraboo with three grass runways and about 100 flight students. He experienced the familiar surge of interest from G.I. Bill pilots in the years immediately after the war, followed by the ebb in the early 1950s. He found a way out of the dilemma by persuading the cities of Baraboo and Wisconsin Dells to lease the airport then contract with him as manager. The arrangement enabled Bell to stay in business and the area to have an airport. It was the first lease of its kind in the state and opened the door to similar arrangements between municipalities and small airport operators around the state. In the years since, the airport has come under municipal ownership of four local governments.

In more recent years, the airport has also made another unique accommodation to its status. It is the only airport in the state which asks pilots to cooperate with avian neighbors by maintaining a no-flyover zone above the International Crane Foundation, which is located a few miles away from the airport.[49]

Sawyer County

In the early 1930s aviation in the Hayward area was in the hands of Bill Leithold who wintered in La Crosse, but came north when the lakes thawed. He flew a Stinson Cabin plane on floats to carry tourists and light freight from lake to lake. He soloed Dan Schmidt and Oscar Johnson, who were among the first local men to become pilots. When Leithold left Wisconsin in 1936, he took most of the aviation at Hayward with him.

Flyers who did pass by landed at the county fairgrounds until 1944 when Jim Wilson and Joseph Szumowski began to clear ground northeast of Hayward for an airport. In September 1944 they held a dedication ceremony for a site with two runways, a repair shop and a hangar with room for two aircraft. The airport was ready when pilots returning from the war needed it. In 1946, about a dozen of them acquired a 1946 Taylorcraft and organized the Hayward Flying Club. Dick Toutant was president, Les Schultis, secretary. Wilson owned the property and attempted to sell it to the county or the city of Hayward, neither of which expressed any interest. The property remained in private ownership with the Hayward Chamber of Commerce leasing and operating the airport.

In 1959, Sawyer County acquired ownership and the airport became eligible for state and federal aid. In the late 1960s and early 1970s, Midstate Air Commuter supplied regular commuter service to Hayward, with twelve flights a week to and from Milwaukee and Chicago. Midstate made Hayward the smallest community in the state with regular commuter service. By the end of the 1970s the airport was upgraded to General Utility 2 with a 5000-foot runway to accommodate small jet aircraft.[50]

Ad for Gumaer's Resort at Shawano, 1946. (Badger Flying)

Shawano County

In 1939, Gumaer's resort on the shore of Shawano Lake opened a landing strip and seaplane base for tourists that saw some use in the final summers before U.S. entry in World War II. The field shut down during the war, then reopened in 1945 as a municipal airport.

Jack and Dorothy Wussow took over as airport managers in 1946 and kept a high profile in state aviation activities. Jack was president of the Flying Farmers, led the local Civil Air Patrol Squadron and organized a Ground Observer Corps unit that kept an eye out for enemy aircraft from the tower above the administration building built in 1952.

Aircraft have been used to carry all kinds of cargo, but in the late 1940s Jack Wussow delivered cargo that—at first thought—was odd. However, considering he was in Wisconsin, perhaps it wasn't so unusual.

In the years after World War II, Wisconsin dairy farmers adopted artificial insemination to improve their dairy herds. The Badger Breeders Cooperative in Shawano was a leader in the field and served farmers from twenty-three distribution points in northeastern Wisconsin and Upper Michigan. Semen deliveries had to be made on time if the cow was to impregnated, even if winter weather closed the roads. Then Badger Breeders called on Wussow and his airplanes—a PA-12 Super Cruiser or Cessna 170 to make deliveries.

"It takes two automobiles nine hours to cover 620 miles," he told a reporter for Flying Farmer Magazine in 1948. "I can fly the delivery in four hours and reduce the mileage to 303 miles."

Not all of the stations were located near airports, so Wussow delivered his cargo by parachute. The semen was packed in a padded box attached to a small chute and dropped over the delivery point. It was fast and safe, although cold flying, since Badger Breeders only called on Wussow when the weather made auto delivery impractical. Sometimes, of course, air travel wasn't practical either. Then Wussow made a forced landing on skis in a farm field.

He continued to make his winter deliveries until 1954, when he gave up cold weather flying and Shawano to manage an airport in Louisiana.

Al and Emily Dimeo moved to Shawano from Racine that year and managed the dedication of the airport that summer. The field was named in honor of Shawano World War II hero Wilmer Zeuske. The keynote speaker at the event was Shawano native and Flying Tiger vet Fritz Wolf of the Aeronautics Commission.

The Shawano airport still has a seaplane base, plus two turf and one 3900-foot asphalt runways.[51]

The Chaplin Family, 1951: baby Wanda, Carol, Dennis and Harry on couch with Harry, Jr., and Jolenn Maria on floor. Both Harry, Sr. and Wanda served on the Wisconsin Council for Aeronautics. (Carol Chaplin)

Sheboygan County

The Sheboygan area continued to be served by the Kohler Airport, with Mel Thompson as FBO throughout the 1940s and '50s. Kohler Company and other corporate aircraft used the airport, but the atmosphere was less exciting than it had been in the days of the "Flying Governor."

In 1945, Harry Chaplin came home to Plymouth after spending three years as an aircraft and powerplant mechanic in the Army Air Force. He had taken his first airplane ride—along with his ninety-

Above: The masthead of Harry Chaplin's newsletter. (WAHF) Left: When the Road America auto races are held at nearby Elkhart Lake the Sheboygan Airport sees many corporate and privately-owned aircraft. (Sheboygan County Airport)

year-old grandmother—in Governor Kohler's old Ryan Brougham before the war and had decided that aviation was his future.

He opened Chaplin's Aeropark on the outskirts of Plymouth in 1946 and purchased several Piper J-3s. He planned to expand operations and build additional hangars but needed a bank loan. "The banker wanted to review the thing, and decided to visit the airport over the weekend," Chaplin recalled. When asked about the loan the next day the banker said "he could not give us a loan because there was not any activity. At that point we owned five airplanes, and all of them were out flying and out of sight. This was bad to him because there were no airplanes sitting around. To us it was great..."

Chaplin didn't get the loan, but he built a successful aviation enterprise without it. He offered flight instruction and charters at Plymouth until 1949 when he moved to Waupaca as airport manager. At Waupaca, Chaplin started the Badger Airway Beacon, "to fill up the time." Starting as a simple typewritten newsletter, the Beacon became the voice of general aviation in the state until Chaplin stopped publishing in the mid-1960s.

Chaplin returned to Plymouth from Waupaca in 1955 because, "we had a an idea at that time that Sheboygan County was going to be building an airport."

As early as 1953, Aeronautics Commission Director Tom Jordan had attended public hearings in Sheboygan where residents spoke of the need for an airport. In 1959, businessman Dick Stiles stated that "Sheboygan, during the past 15 years, has very conveniently hid its head in the sands of Lake Michigan, refusing to realize what the airplane can do for this community..."

Heads came out of the sand very soon. By the end of 1959, Sheboygan County had acquired 504 acres of land in the Town of Sheboygan Falls and had broken ground for an airport. The $700,000 cost of constructing two 3000-foot runways, office and hangar was shared by the federal and county governments, with a smaller portion coming from the state.

The first manager of the airport was Harry Chaplin, who moved his operations there in November 1960. The opening of the county airport closed the book on the Kohler Airport. The stage for some of Wisconsin's best aviation stories, and the home of some of its most important aviators, was turned back into farmland. Kohler manager Mel Thompson shifted his operation to the county airport, then moved on to finish his career at New Holstein.

Chaplin's aviation company expanded at Sheboygan County and so did the airport. His company assumed management of the Manitowoc Airport in 1969 and Dells-Baraboo in the 1970s.

Joshua Sanford, veteran of World War II in China in whose honor the Hillsboro Airport is named.
(Rosemary Sanford)

Sheboygan County was served by several commuter airlines in the 1970s and 1980s, including Commuter Airlines, Air Wisconsin, and Midstate. The airport also acquired one of the largest fleets of corporate aircraft in the state, with Kohler, Vollrath, Aero-Metric, Donahue and others keeping planes there. By the 1990s, on the strength of its corporate fleet, Sheboygan County claimed to be the "second-busiest" airport in Wisconsin.

By then Harry Chaplin had completed his career in aviation. He had retired as airport manager in 1987, having filled out one of the longest aviation resumes in the state. In addition to managing three airports and publishing a magazine, he had served as the last chair of the Wisconsin Aeronautics Commission and the first chair of the Aeronautics Council, president of the Wisconsin Aviation Trades Association and the Wisconsin Aerospace Education Association,

and numerous other organizations from the aviation committee of the American Legion to the Flying Farmers.

Harry Chaplin's story is one of a successful aviation business. Back in the 1940s, when pilots by the thousands attempted to make a living in civilian aviation, Chaplin realized that "aviation had progressed where you had to be something besides just the pilot, you had to be the business person." He was and succeeded at it.[52]

Taylor County

In the late 1930s, the Taylor County Aviation Club used a landing field located south of Medford. In 1938, they sponsored a big air show featuring Archie Towle and his "Aces of Wausau," "The Mystery Ship of Rhinelander," and a spot-landing contest between Merrill's Ed Basemann and Medford's Johnny Cullen.

Local interest in aviation faded during the war years and did not revive until the 1960s when Taylor County built the present airport three miles southeast of Medford. In the mid-1970s a terminal was built and navigation aids installed. In the late 1980s, plans were first discussed to further expand the airport, but work was delayed by opposition from neighboring landowners. At the same time, support for an improved airport came from Medford's major employers, Weather Shield windows, Tombstone pizza and Phillips Plastics. A much debated proposal to extend one runway to 5,000 feet to accommodate new corporate aircraft was acted on in 1996.[53]

Vernon County

Vernon County was a relative latecomer to the airport field, with both the Hillsboro and Viroqua Airports opening in the 1960s. The Hillsboro Airport was built by the Kickapoo Oil Company in the 1960s and purchased by the city in 1985. After basic improvements were made the airport was named in honor of Joshua Sanford.

Born in Friendship and a member of the Ho-Chunk nation, Sanford flew over 100 combat missions with the 14th Air Force, "Flying Tigers" in China during World War II. After the war ended Sanford moved to Hillsboro, married teacher Rosemary Berts and settled into the community. In 1956, Sanford was named manager of the Reedsburg Airport and in 1961, Civil Defense director for eleven southwestern counties. He died of a kidney ailment in 1962 at age 43. The Hillsboro Airport keeps his memory alive.

At Viroqua the city purchased land in 1963 and volunteers have built an airport. A graded runway, administration building and other improvements have come about through a combination of public and private efforts. The airport is managed by a commission headed by Dwain Munyon and, with state aid, now has a 3,300 foot paved runway.[54]

Vilas County

Aviation is important to a county that has depended on tourism for a century and is located hundreds of miles away from the region's largest population centers. In the last twenty years, Vilas County has also attracted many aviators who have retired from their jobs but continue to fly. They have also contributed to an active aviation scene. The extent of the growth of aviation in the county is illustrated by comparing the number of operations at Lakeland/Noble Lee Airport in 1960—2,925—and in 1990—23,550, a ten-fold increase.

Vilas County has four municipal airports plus a state-owned field at Boulder Junction, which is open in the summer. The Eagle River airport established in the 1930s continues to operate in the post war years. A steady stream of improvements occurred throughout the 1950s, culminating with a 5,000-foot runway in 1988 and an award-winning terminal building in 1995. The last decade has seen thirty new hangars built at Eagle River. They are a sign of the increased pace of development that has occurred in Vilas County in the 1980s and '90s.

The Land O'Lakes airport began in the 1940s as part of the King's Gateway resort. With the landing field right out the back door, pilots were encouraged to taxi up to the dining room and come

a landing strip that Noble and his two brothers were clearing out of the woods south of Minocqua. By 1947, they were running a flight school and Noble was taking visitors for rides over the lake country in an Aeronca and a Piper J-C.

In 1950, the Lees moved to the Arbor Vitae Airport, where Noble became manager and FBO. "When we got there," Virginia recalled, "all we had was the east-west runway of around 2,000 feet. And it was strictly a mud hole in spring."

Left: The opening of regularly scheduled service to Land O'Lakes by Wisconsin Central Airlines, 1950. (WAHF) Above: Lakeland Airport, 1965. (Bureau of Acronautics) Below: The new terminal at Eagle River, 1995. (Bureau of Aeronatuics)

in for dinner. In 1950, Wisconsin Central Airlines began to provide summer service to Land O'Lakes, making it the smallest community in Wisconsin with a scheduled airline. In the last decade or so, several northern Wisconsin airports have built striking log-cabin-style terminal buildings. Land O' Lakes had one nearly fifty years ago in Wisconsin Central's flight operations building. The structure is still in use, but as the club house at the Gateway Golf Course.

The resort deeded the airport to the Town of Land O' Lakes in 1951 and federally-funded improvements began. In 1954, the airport was dedicated with Wisconsin Aeronautics Director Tom Jordan and Michigan's Lester Maitland in attendance. The progress continued under the management of Karl Kerscher, who has served as manager since the 1980s.

The Lakeland/Noble Lee Airport is located in Vilas County, although funded in part by towns in Oneida County as well. The airport was first built by the Standard Oil Company in the 1930s, to bring clients and executives to a company-owned lake resort. In 1945, Standard sold the field to the Town of Arbor Vitae. The following year, Noble and Virginia Lee moved north from Milwaukee to

It was difficult for only one town to support an airport, so Noble made it part of his job to bring the towns of Woodruff, Minocqua and Lac du Flambeau to join Arbor Vitae in a joint airport commission. He succeeded in 1958 and the field began operations as Lakeland Airport. With a larger base to draw on and increased use, the airport was improved over the years, culminating with completion of the 5,150-foot runway in 1994.

Noble Lee served as airport manager for thirty-two years. After his death Lakeland Airport was named in his honor.[55]

Walworth County

Walworth County is served by a number of small privately-owned airports linked to the summer home and resort industry, with the longest runways at Lake Geneva and Delavan.

The East Troy municipal airport was built in the late 1950s to replace a privately-owned landing strip the school district wanted for an athletic field. The field saw a number of major improvements in the late 1980s, with a paved 3,900-foot runway to accommodate

Inside the workshop at Wag-Aero. (Wag-Aero)

12,500 pound twin-engine aircraft. The paved runway sparked a boom in hangar construction with twenty structures going up in the 1990s. As the East Troy area continues to attract more residents, more hangars are likely to be built.

One of the state's most noted home airplane builders flies at East Troy. In the late 1960s, Ron Scott built what is "considered to be the first fiberglass/wood composite example using fiberglass as a structural component in the entire airframe, including landing gear." Scott's "Old Ironsides" was featured in Sport Aviation in 1971 and 1992, as well as many other publications. As writer Jack Cox said, "Good ideas are timeless."

Although it does not have a municipal airport, Lyons has made its mark in aviation. It is the home of Wag-Aero, one of the nation's busiest aircraft kit and parts distributors, which was established by Dick and Jackie Wagner on land adjacent to their private landing strip.[56]

Washburn County

The Shell Lake airport was constructed in 1945 with three sod runways used by G.I. Bill students and flight instructor Bill Hensley. By 1950, activity fell off and the only plane at the airport for several years belonged to Chuck Lewis. By the end of the 1950s, activity resumed and the Lake Point Aero Club was organized.

Major improvement work began in the 1980s with the runway enlarged and free space cleared around the landing field. As in all small airports, volunteers are very important at Shell Lake. Chuck Lewis donated space in his hangar for use as a public terminal with furnishings from the local bank and a weather information computer terminal donated by a local insurance firm.[57]

Washington County

The Hartford Airport began when World War II veteran Jim Miles came home and, with help from friends, cleared two grass runways on the Hilmer Schuaer farm two miles north of town. Although Miles was able to attract a few students, he was not able to continue in business and the field fell into disuse. In 1957, the city purchased the field and slowly improved it. With Martin Zivko as manager in the 1960s, a terminal and hangars were built. By the 1990s, one 3000-foot runway was paved and Kettle Moraine Aviation

was the FBO. As the Hartford area continues to grow and more corporate aircraft use it, the Hartford airport may expand, but a recent referendum vote on the issue failed at the polls.

During World War II, Al Haen and Floyd Gessert ran the West Bend city airport. When Earl Stier came home from Air Force duty he joined Haen and Gessert and opened the West Bend Flying Service. "We had three J3 Cubs, a PA 12 Super Cruiser, an old J5 Super Cruiser, and then we had the run-of-the-mill military surplus Stearman and an old BT-13," Stier recalled.

He trained dozens of G.I. Bill pilots and bought a Fairchild 24 for "what we called charter work."

In 1959, the city applied for a federal/state grant to pave one runway and, in the following year, hired Stier as manager. He stayed at it until his retirement in 1988. His work was made easier because, as he said, "The city has been more air minded than most communities and they have never turned us down on any project where we could show just cause."

Karl Schaarschmidt gliding over Washington County. (WAC)

The city's attitude was helpful when Stier inadvertently turned West Bend into one of Wisconsin's leading sites for soaring aircraft. Stier recalled that in the late 1960s a visitor told him about a "sailplane" for sale in Rockford. "So we went down and bought it...the guy towed it up here and landed it out here and there it laid like a ruptured duck....[until] we put a tow hitch on a Tri-pacer and started dragging this thing around the air and it sort of caught on fire. I use that term caught on fire because it went like the dickens cause people wanted to fly it. So a couple guys started bringing more sailplanes on the field and it turned out to be a good fill in. Right now [1989] we have sixteen sailplanes on the field."

One of the "guys" who started bringing sailplanes to West Bend was Gunther Voltz. A World War II veteran of the German Air Force, Voltz migrated to Wisconsin, made his home in Whitefish Bay and took up soaring. The sport blossomed at Rochester, Watertown, Hartford, Capitol Drive and Aero Park, where Karl Schaarschmidt was the Wisconsin Governor for the Soaring Society of America, and West Bend, where Al Steele opened a school.

Post 309 of the Boys Scouts to give young people a chance to soar. "Soaring seems made to order for Explorers," said advisor Paul Hammersmith in 1963. "It's dynamic, educational and timely; and the safety factor is such that 14-year-olds can fly as students and 16-year-olds can become licensed glider pilots." One of the most active members of the Soaring Explorers was Gunther Voltz's son, Gordon.

Gunther himself became an internationally renowned member of the soaring fraternity who is just likely to be found soaring in Europe as in Wisconsin.

"We have only one-half year for soaring in Wisconsin," he said. The heavy air traffic out of Chicago and Milwaukee limits the airspace for soaring, so does Lake Michigan. There are no thermals for a sailplane to ride over the lake itself and the cooling effect of wind blowing off the lake inhibits inland soaring as well. But when the weather is right, the experience of soaring is unforgettable—at least for Gunther Voltz and other member of the soaring community.

As a measure of the popularity of the sport in one place at one time, in the 1980s, Earl Stier was giving "3,500 to 4,500" tows a season at West Bend. "Now mind you some of these flights are only four or five minutes long, [but] we will put on 150 or 200 hours on each sailplane a year." [58]

Waukesha County

Since the airport was already county-owned, Waukesha did not have to go through the process of converting from a private to a public operation in order to obtain federal/state grants in the years after

World War II. Grant money was used to build an administration addition on the hangar in 1952 and the first blacktopped runway in 1955. Improvement and expansion continued throughout the 1960s, '70s, '80s and '90s, including larger runways, apron areas, a fuel farm and two control towers.

The physical improvements were necessary to keep up with the growth of aviation in the area. Located in the heaviest-populated part of the state, in a steadily growing suburban community, Waukesha County Airport experienced heavy use and steady growth in flyers and aircraft in all the years since World War II. While other commununites saw boom years in the 1940s, followed by a lull in the 1950s, Waukesha County saw steady progress. The number of aircraft on the field doubled in the 1950s and, led by growth in the corporate sector, doubled again by the 1990s.

Above: Florence Toney in the cockpit. (Midwest Flyer) Left: Karl Schaarschmidt at his Aero Park. (WAC) Below: Dale Crites flying his home-built Curtiss Pusher on the lake in Hammondsport New York, where Glenn Curtiss tested his first model. (WAC)

The people involved in aviation at Waukesha were among the most active in the state. Dale Crites was airport manager until 1969 and his Spring City Flying Service the FBO. After retirement Dale and his brother Dean built three Curtiss Pusher replicas which Dale first flew at Waukeska. Virtually identical to the planes flown by Lincoln Beachey, Arthur Warner and John Kaminski eighty-five years ago, one Crites Pusher now hangs in the EAA Museum in Oshkosh, the other is in the terminal at Mitchell International. Dale also took one of his replicas to the Curtiss Museum in Hammondsport, New York, mounted it on floats, and flew it off the water, as did C.C. Wittmer, Hugh Robinson and other pioneer aviators in Wisconsin.

The "official cranker" for the Pusher was Charlie Dewey, who was a Crites flight student in the mid-1930s. Dewey had his own plane, a Waco 10, in a few years and has been flying ever since. Having sat at the controls of many OX-5 powered aircraft, Dewey qualified for membership in the OX-5 Aviation Pioneers and was elected national president in 1992.

The airport is home to the Waukesha Aviation Club, founded in 1931 and still going strong nearly seventy years later. Among the many people who made the club go over the years were Chuck Faber, Art Vredenburg, Harland Sedgewick, Warren O'Brien, Russ Schuetze, Ray Crowley, Norm Shuff, Robert Larson and Art Shanley. President in 1997-'98 was Elizabeth Schuetze, who followed in her father's footsteps as a pilot and club officer.

Though its roots are deep, the club has recently directed much of its attention to young people. It has sponsored an aviation education scholarship since 1962 and currently supports the 4-H, Explorer

Scouts and other programs. "Today most of our work is aimed at youth," said President Dan Michalski in 1996. "This is in the interest of perpetuating our species." The club has been working on either converting the old 1938 hangar/museum or building a new youth education/meeting center.

Karl and Sophie Schaarschmidt opened their Aero Park in Menominee Falls in 1946 and were still in business when Karl passed away in 1996. The Schaarschmidts were able to keep their pri-

himself couldn't use that field. See if you can do something about getting it improved."

Higgins was the advertising manager for Four Wheel Drive and knew infinitely more about ad copy than airports, but he jumped right into the policy and politics of airport building in 1941-42. The federal WPA public works program was in its final year of existence so Higgins tried to put Clintonville on its funding list. State planning commission and Wisconsin WPA director M.W. Torkelson told the Civil Aeronautics Administration that "there is very great local interest...I think we are going to get this airport built."

Then the war intervened, WPA was suspended and Torkelson was forced to tell Higgins that there

The 1938 hangar at Waukesha is likely to be demolished in a few years. (WAC) Right: The Clintonville Airport under construction in 1944. (Bureau of Aeronautics)

in 1996. The Schaarschmidts were able to keep their privately-owned airport open by diversifying with the times. They started a flight school in 1946, and trained hundreds of pilots who marked their solos by having their shirt collars cut off and mounted on the wall of the airport lounge. In the 1950s, Karl opened the airport to glider pilots and organized a club in which members could purchase a share of the plane for $100. An accomplished glider flyer himself, Schaarschmidt instructed others and encouraged many aspiring gliders to take to the air. When sky-diving started to become popular, the Schaarschmidts welcomed the jumpers to Aero Park. Although operating without government aid, the Schaarschmidt's kept Aero Park humming for their entire working lives.

Reuben Miller started the Capitol Drive Airport in the late 1930s. After closing during World War II, it reopened under the management of Bob Huggins and Florence Toney. Huggins is credited as the first airplane builder and pilot in Waukesha County, while Toney took her training as part of the Civil Air Patrol in 1944. She was the FBO at Capitol until 1979 and probably would have spent her entire life there had illness not forced her to retire. After logging over 1100 hours in small aircraft and loving every minute of it, Toney contracted multiple sclerosis and was grounded.

Lois and Wally Mitchell purchased the airport after moving from Hales Corners when it closed in 1977. Under their management Capitol Drive has been named as a reliever for Mitchell International and, with eighty-two based aircraft, one helicopter and two gliders, is now the busiest private airport in the state.[59]

Waupaca County

The Clintonville Airport owes its beginnings to the desire of Walter Olen and Francis Higgins to supply air transportation to their home town. The need was very simple. At a time when rail service to its home town of Clintonville had all but disappeared, Olen's Four Wheel Drive Company was expanding. Even before the United States entered World War II, demand for the company's products was increasing. In 1939, Olen purchased a four-place Waco to carry clients, executives and sales people to and from Clintonville. Now he needed an airport for it.

"We got an airplane," he told Francis Higgins, "but Lindbergh

was "no promise of federal aid." He didn't quit, just turned to local resources. The city of Clintonville bought land, Waupaca County and Four Wheel Drive put up funding, and highway department equipment from Waupaca and Shawano County went to work on a new "mile-square" airport. Without federal or state funds, but with the cooperation of several local government and business organizations, Clintonville got an airport.

"You fellows in Clintonville certainly know what you want and how to go after it," Torkelson wrote Higgins in May, 1944. The airport had to be ready because that very same month, Olen, Higgins and Green Bay engineer Herbert S. Foth incorporated Wisconsin Central Airlines. It was obvious to them that if a business traveler in Clintonville needed air transportation, so did travelers in other cities. Northwest and other carriers had talked about extending their routes to smaller Wisconsin cities, but the war had prevented their start up. But the war would end someday and the Clintonville airline would be ready when it did—or so it founders thought.

They spent nearly four years raising capital, finding suitable aircraft and securing CAA approval before launching their first scheduled flight. By then, they were forced to leave Clintonville for Madison, if for no other reason than to find adequate hangar space for the Lockheed 10As that made up Wisconsin Central's original fleet.

After its move to the old Air Force hangar at Madison, Wisconsin Central went on to become one of the most successful regional air carriers in the country. In the late 1940s and early

Wisconsin Central DC-3 at Wausau, 1953. (Robert Wylie) **Right: Map of airline routes across Wisconsin approved by the FAA in 1947 included Wisconsin Central as a "feeder line."** (Badger Flying)

1950s it brought airline service to Wisconsin, Minnesota and Michigan communities that had never know it. Eau Claire, Wausau, Oshkosh, and Madison were on the initial route, and so were Sturgeon Bay, Rhinelander, Manitowoc, Sheboygan, Portage, Watertown and Waukesha. Service to some of these cities depended on their upgrading their airports, which many did, since having airline service appealed to their sense of civic pride. Consequently, Wisconsin Central shares a measure of credit for the development of the airport system in Wisconsin, not just in Clintonville, but in Manitowoc, Rhinelander, Marshfield and other places as well.

In 1952-53, the airline made several important moves. President Francis Higgins was replaced by Howard Morey, whose tenure lasted only about a year. The Air Force reclaimed its Madison hangar, prompting the airline, now renamed North Central, to move its headquarters to Minneapolis-St. Paul. North Central's success continued through three decades of mergers and acquisitions that resulted in its absorption by Northwest. That the basic premise with which Olen and Higgins founded their airline was sound was proven over and again by successors like Midstate and Air Wisconsin. Smaller cities needed air transportation in the 1940s, the 1980s, and beyond.

After Wisconsin Central left, the Clintonville airport assumed its role as a small municipal airport. In the 1970s, the Jet-Air Company developed one of the most extensive jet aircraft mainte-

Feeder line routes which were approved last month by the Civil Aeronautics Board in Washington to serve the Wisconsin area are shown on this map.

nance facilities in the country. Currently, Airtronics is a nationally-known avionics FBO, which has operated at Clintonville for nearly two decades.

Clintonville was a busy place in the late 1940s, and so was Waupaca. The Association of Commerce optioned 200 acres in 1944 and soon sold it to the city. In 1949, Harry Chaplin became airport manager and also printed his Badger Airway Beacon in Waupaca. The airport was managed by Joe Pollack for many years, and also by Maxair from Appleton. [60]

Right: Volunteers at work improving Idlewild Airport at Wild Rose, 1982. (Don Gunderson)

Waushara County

In 1945, Ernest Kotke and a few of his neighbors decided to build an airport near Wild Rose. They purchased farmland northeast of the city and graded two grass runways. The airport was named Idlewild after a long gone pioneer settlement, although a few people couldn't help pointing out that another city also had an Idlewild Airport—New York City.

Wild Rose's Idlewild was a busy place with four hangars and airplanes to fill them. By the early 1950s, however, interest was lagging and by 1966, the hangars and landing strip were disappearing into the sand. The airport remained inactive until 1982 when several pilots, led by Don Gunderson, decided to revive Idlewild. They spent hundreds of hours clearing brush, acquired surplus equipment, installed lights and radio. By 1988, six new hangars were standing

and a crop duster operated out of the port. Idlewild is municipally owned, on the state airport plan and supported by an active Airport Association.

Waushara County is also served by the Wautoma Municipal Airport with one 3,300-foot paved runway. It is used by many aerial applicators working for the area's vegetable growers. [61]

Winnebago County

Winnebago County has perhaps the richest aviation history of any county in the state. It starts with Roy and Leonard Larson, moves to aviation lawmaker Florian Lampert, to trans-Atlantic hopeful Clyde Lee, then on to Steve Wittman, Bill Brennand, and the Experimental Aircraft Association.

In the years after World War II, Leonard Larson continued to operate out of his home landing field until a power line crossing made it a "land at your risk" field. Nonetheless Larson Field remains the oldest airport in continuous operation on the same site in Wisconsin.

One of the pilots Leonard Larson instructed was Louis "Red" Strehlow, who opened his own airport on the Bill Ginnow farm near Omro in 1944. Strehlow had a flock of aircraft on the 1,800-foot landing strip he carved out of Ginnow's woodlot—two Aeronca Champs, one Aeronca Chief, a Stinson 108 and a Cessna 120. He used them for a G.I. Bill flight school and for charter work.

In 1950, he met WTMJ radio personalities Higg Murray and Gordon Thomas. They broadcast a farm-oriented early-morning show that was popular throughout the state. As part of the give and take of the show, Thomas and Murray had a contest to see who could pull more seeds out of a gourd. The prize was flight instruction with Red Strehlow. Thomas won, but he defaulted to Murray who showed up one morning at the Ginnow Airport and told Red to teach him to fly.

Strehlow kept his word, Murray took the course and got his private certificate—all the while giving his teacher daily publicity on his radio show. When the course was complete, Murray invited any pilot within listening range to a celebration fly-in. "We had about eight-five or ninety airplanes," Red recalled. Thomas and Murray continued to feature Strehlow on their show until he quit flying in 1955.

At that time Bill Brennand was bringing his career as a member of the Steve Wittman racing team to a close. He became a pilot for the Marathon Corporation and logged many miles in D-

Winnebago County Airport in the pre-EAA 1960s. (Bureau of Aeronautics)

18 Beechcrafts and Lockheed 18s. In 1968, he opened his own airport west of Neenah, where he bought, sold and refurbished airplanes with his partners Byron Frederickson and Chuck Andreas. The trio's biggest job was what Brennand called a "basketcase trimotor Stinson" which Frederickson trucked back from Alaska in pieces. They let it sit for a few years then, between 1977 and 1981 concentrated on rehabilitating it. After many hours of work the

supervisors voted against a joint airport and in favor of a $1.8 million terminal at Wittman Field. When it opened in 1970 the terminal looked like a white elephant, especially since Oshkosh had just lost its last airline service.

The dark clouds had a silver lining placed there by the smiling face of Paul Poberezny, who brought the EAA Fly-In to Oshkosh, followed by its headquarters and museum. Recalling the negotiations with the EAA, county supervisor James Coughlin, recalled that his aviation committee was ready to give the EAA "whatever they wanted" to come to Oshkosh.

Bill Brennand and a Pitts #8 racer. (Bill Brennand)

As it turned out, Oshkosh already had much of what the EAA needed: a lightly-used airport large enough to accommodate the thousands of aircraft of all sizes that attend the fly-in; vacant, buildable land nearby and a city large enough to host the hundreds of thousands of people that were already attending the event. From 1970, the EAA and Oshkosh have become synonymous as the center of American aviation's largest organization and fly-in. The money and effort put into the airport in the 1960s and early '70s proved to be well-used.

By 1994, Wittman Field was one of only five airports in the state with an 8000-foot runway capable of handling virtually any aircraft that flies.

Stinson took to the air again and has been a hit at air shows ever since.

The man who introduced Brennand to flying remained at the center of aviation in Winnebago County until his death in 1994. Steve and Dorothy Wittman managed the county airport until they retired in 1969. With Steve often away on the racing circuit and working on aircraft when he was home, much of the day-to-day operation of the airport fell to assistant manager Warren Basler.

The 1960s were an important decade for the airport and for the city it represented. For a century Oshkosh had been the premier city of the Fox River Valley, but in the years since World War II, the Neenah-Menasha-Appleton area had grown enough to overtake it. Surprisingly, a survey of passenger traffic at the Oshkosh Airport in 1960 found a larger number of travelers came from Neenah-Menasha than from Oshkosh. This fact was used by proponents of a joint Winnebago-Outagamie County Airport which was to be built outside of Neenah, but was ignored by the Winnebago County board. The

One of the people working on aircraft at Oshkosh was Warren Basler. After growing up on a farm a few miles from the airport he went to work for Steve Wittman, then for the Knaup brothers in Milwaukee, but his favorite boss was himself. He acquired a Beechcraft franchise and sold many Bonanzas, Barons and King Airs.

He also developed a charter business that required the purchase of a DC-3 that he used to fly large fishing parties as far as the Arctic Circle in Canada. The business grew so popular that he needed bigger planes and switched to Martin 404's. By the 1960s Basler Air was the only 121-certified air carrier in Wisconsin that was not an airline. As such he carried presidential candidates Richard Nixon and Barry Goldwater when they campaigned in Wisconsin and neighboring states, as well as numerous college and professional sports teams.

Of all the people connected to aviation in Wisconsin perhaps none is more well-known than Steve Wittman. As an airplane designer and builder, as an inventor and innovator, as a racing pilot and airport manager, Wittman enjoyed one of aviation's longest and most diverse careers.

He was born in the Fond du Lac county village of Byron in 1904 where he enjoyed flying homemade kites more than school work. By 1924, he was at the original Fond du Lac airport on the east side of

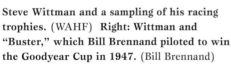

Steve Wittman and a sampling of his racing trophies. (WAHF) Right: Wittman and "Buster," which Bill Brennand piloted to win the Goodyear Cup in 1947. (Bill Brennand)

the city, sharing ownership with Perry Anderson of a OXX-6 powered J-1 Standard biplane. A local man who said he had been a World War I pilot promised to teach Wittman and Anderson how to fly but, as it turned out, barely knew his way around the airplane. Wittman and Anderson tossed a coin and Wittman won the honor of being the first to fly the plane.

He climbed in the cockpit, took off, made his way around the field, landed safely, then did it again. In less than a week after "soloing," he was taking passengers up for $3.00 a ride. It was his beginning as a professional aviator. As he said, "That was the only way I ever made a living."

In short time he had built his first airplane, a single seat biplane powered by a 14-horsepower Harley-Davidson motorcycle engine. He obtained his pilot's license in 1928 and became the "test pilot" for Tom Meiklejohn's Pheasant Aircraft Company.

Flying his J-1, he placed second in his first air race at the Milwaukee Air Derby of 1926. In 1928, he flew a Pheasant in transcontinental races; in '29 he made his first appearance at the Cleveland Nationals with a Pheasant H-10.

In 1931, he became airport manager at Oshkosh and shifted into high gear. He designed and built the Cirrus-90-powered Chief Oshkosh and took it to the Cleveland races before he had the chance to correct its tendency for aileron flutter at high speeds. "A mile before entering the course we had to be level and hold it level through three kilometers," he recalled. "About this time...all hell broke loose! Everything shook."

It was not a very auspicious introduction for the first Wittman-designed racer. After the Cleveland race, Wittman took the "Chief" home, fixed the flutter and took five firsts at the very next racing event. In 1932, he installed a larger engine in the Chief and flew it to victories in Cleveland and Miami. In 1933, he first piloted the Nicholas-Beazley Pobjoy Special. "Everybody thought I was going up to kill myself and they were there to witness it. Low and behold, I fooled them." He went on to master the Pobjoy, win races with it, then develop his own version of the plane.

By 1935, he had his second original design, "Big Bonzo" ready for the Cleveland races. In the Thompson Trophy race Wittman and Bonzo hit 218 MPH to finish second behind Harold Neumann's 220 MPH. Nonetheless, Wittman was one of the top money winners at Cleveland that year. He would need it. In 1936, Bonzo was all but destroyed by fire while enroute to the Los Angles Nationals and Chief Oshkosh was seriously damaged when a prop flange sheared off and the plane crashed.

By 1937, Wittman had patented the flat spring landing gear that became a common feature on Cessna and many other aircraft and he had rebuilt both Bonzo and Chief Oshkosh. He focused on the Thompson Trophy at Cleveland, leading the qualifiers with a speed of 259.108 MPH. Sad to say, but the big prize eluded him, as he fell back to fifth place in the finals. A few weeks later at Detroit he set a world's speed record of 237 MPH in the Chief.

In the next two years, which proved to be the last years of the

Bill Brennand, Herman "Fish" Salmon, Steve Wittman, Bevo Howard, 1947. (Bill Brennand)

so-called "golden age" of air racing, Wittman and his planes consistently finished high in the rankings but did not pull down the top prizes at Cleveland. At the end of the 1939 season, the damaged Chief Oshkosh was stored in a corner of the Wittman hangar and Bonzo was stored in the rafters, never to fly again.

During the war years, Wittman conducted an extensive flight training program clocking over 25,000 hours of instruction in the air. In 1941, he married Dorothy Rady, who became his partner at the airport on the race course and at home.

After the war Wittman and Bill Brennand, a farm boy who had been hanging around the airport, starting restoring the Chief Oshkosh. Air racing had also revived, with plenty of war surplus planes and powerplants available. In 1947, Wittman and Brennand rebuilt the Chief into a new plane they called "Buster." The fabulous story of the youngster from Oshkosh flying the plane designed and financed by Wittman against world famous race pilots backed by big money is a classic hero's tale. But also a true one. Brennand qualified for the $25,000 Goodyear Race, won all his heats and the final, to bag the trophy and the prize money. For the rest of the 1940s and into the early 1950s, Brennand and Wittman were one of the top

Dorothy and Steve Wittman in the 1940s. (WAHF)

racing teams in the country.

In the 1950s, Wittman and Bonzo began their decades-long competition with Bill Falck and his Rivets. Race after race turned into a contest between the quick-starting, tight-turning Bonzo and the wide-swinging, powerful Rivets. By the 1970s, at an age when most people are thinking about retirement, Wittman began another racing career. He built his Witt's V airplane to compete in the latest Formula V races and flew in his first race in 1971, at age 67. He won national championships in 1977, 1978, 1979 and 1981 and placed third in his last race at Daytona in 1989, when he was 85 years old. "I have always maintained that it will kill you or keep you young," he told one interviewer. Racing kept him young. Steve Wittman placed second in his first race in 1926 and third in his last race in 1989—not much of a decline over sixty-three years of racing. He raced longer and in more races than any other pilot and won more races than any pilot. No one is more deserving of the title of world's greatest racing pilot. He continued to fly after his racing career ended. He died flying home from Florida in April 1995, when the homebuilt plane carrying him and his wife Paula crashed in Alabama. He ended his days as he loved to live them, in the cockpit of an airplane.[62]

The 1970s fuel crisis put a crimp in Basler's charter work, but he diversified into aircraft modification. He pioneered the modified DC-3 with a completely overhauled airframe and new PT-6 A-67R engines. The result is a dependable airplane with a useful load capacity of 13,000 pounds. "There are just not any being built today at about three times the cost that would haul what this airplane would haul or go in and out of the places it will go in and out of," he said. Basler developed a unique operation and his modified DC-3s are flown all over the world.

After flying them for decades, the DC-3, modified or not, remained Basler's favorite aircraft, "because of all the other airplanes I've flown, large ones, the DC-3 still seems like its a pilot's airplane. You really are wearing it when you fly."

Doing what he loved helped Warren Basler build the biggest aviation business in Wisconsin, with a $90 million dollar gross in 1990. Warren Basler was doing what he loved best when he made his final flight in the cockpit of a Bonanza which crashed after a mid-air collision with one of his modified DC-3s on a "routine" aerial photo run.[63]

Wood County

After housing German prisoners of war during World War II, the Tri-City Airport fell on hard times. "Nothing more than a weed patch," according to local historian Marshall Buehler. In 1959, activity revived when the Nekoosa Edwards Paper Company resurfaced the landing strip with sulfite binder and parked a Beechcraft Super 18 in a refurbished hangar.

The airport came into municipal ownership when owner John Alexander gave it to surrounding cities, villages and towns in 1961. Renamed Alexander Field, the airport was now eligible for state/federal aid and improved accordingly. When Roy Shwery started his Midstate commuter airline in 1964, he stopped at Alexander Field on the way to Milwaukee and Chicago. Midstate soon became FBO at Alexander and managed the airport for many years. In the 1970s and '80s, the airport saw increased use by corporate aircraft and one runway was

Top: Steve and Paula Wittman, Warren and Pat Basler, 1994. (Basler Family) **Above: Roy Shwery, whose Midstate Airways was one of the nation's first commuter air carriers.** (Roy Shwery)

extended to 5,500-feet to accommodate the larger planes.

Marshfield moved forward in aviation by purchasing 120 acres southwest of town in 1944 and improving it for an airport. In 1947, the city was one of several in Wisconsin targeted for a concentrated marketing effort by Milwaukee's Anderson Air Activities. Anderson dispatched a fleet of Beechcrafts, Ercoupes and Republic Seabees to Marshfield, paraded them down Central Avenue and gave eighty local people rides. The theme of the event was that everyone could fly and should. Local aviators agreed, but most other people did not, so Anderson's promotion did not result in a flood of aircraft sales in Marshfield.

A more significant event for aviation in Marshfield and Wisconsin occurred when Roy Shwery arrived in town. The Janesville native, a student of Art Hodge and Joe Bouzaine, had completed his military service and come to Marshfield to work as an instructor for airport operators Roy Kinlund and Leo Van Ert. By the end of the 1940s, the G.I. Bill student boom was over, and Shwery was flying a Navion for charters.

Work was slow and Shwery signed up to fly for American Airlines, when two opportunities came his way. The Roddis Plywood Company said it was looking for a pilot with an airplane for steady charter work and a Twin Engine Beechcraft came up for sale for $40,000. With a contract from Roddis that he could take to the bank, Shwery was able to buy the Beech, put about $13,000 worth of new radio and other equipment in it, and go to work. As Marshfield Airways, he operated the equivalent of a corporate airline for Roddis but, since he was an independent contractor, was also able to do other charter work. He flew patients to and from the Mayo Clinic in Rochester among other places.

In the early 1960s, opportunity presented itself once again. Roddis sold its Marshfield operation to Weyerhaeuser, which did not need Shwery's regular charter work, and North Central Airlines halted service to Marshfield. After about six months of planning, Shwery's Marshfield Airways made its first round trip flight to

The Twin Beech that was Midstate Airways first aircraft. Alice Shwery's home made box lunches gave the airline a reputation for serving great food. (Roy Shwery)

Milwaukee and Chicago. He also stopped at Wisconsin Rapids, Marshfield's rival city, and was told that passengers there might be reluctant to fly on a "Marshfield" airline. Shwery then changed the name to Midstate. It was a wise choice, since Wisconsin Rapids eventually became Midstate's busiest stop.

Midstate became a fast success and gained fame as the "Ma and Pa Airline," after Alice Shwery started packing picnic lunches for travelers to unwrap and enjoy on their own. By 1965, Midstate was flying six Beech 18s; by 1968 the fleet included four Beech 99s, with Swearingen Metroliners coming on in 1977. Midstate concentrated on what it did best, delivering business travelers to big city airports in fast and friendly fashion. The company was on the verge of anoth-

er expansion in 1980, when Shwery sold the operation to Sentry Insurance. In the years since, other commuter airlines have attempted to serve Marshfield, but none have succeeded.

"When we started there were only five to ten operations in the country, that is, commuter airlines," Shwery recalled. "It was very interesting, the developing stages, you might say we were pioneers in the commuter airline industry." [64]

Out Of State

Wisconsin aviators are also served by out-of-state airports in Menominee, Iron Mountain and Ironwood, Michigan; Duluth and Winona, Minnesota; Dubuque, Iowa; and Rockford, Illinois.

Above: Mark Lee
Right: "Deke"
Slayton
Below: Dan
Brandenstein
(NASA)

Mark C. Lee

A colonel in the United States Air Force, Mark C. Lee was born in 1952 in Viroqua, where his parents Charles M. and Ruth Lee still reside. He was educated at Viroqua High School, the U.S. Air Force Academy and the Massachusetts Institute of Technology. He is married to astronaut Jan Davis.

Lee entered the space program in 1984 and made four flights on space shuttles between 1989 and 1997. He has traveled over 13 million miles, circled the globe 517 times and spent 33 days in orbit. His missions have included deployment of the Magellan-Venus planetary probe, life science and materials processing experiments, and the second Hubble Space Telescope maintenance mission. On the Hubble missions he logged in 19 hours and 10 minutes of extra-vehicular activity.

Curtis F. Michel

Born in La Crosse in 1934, and a graduate of the California Institute of Technology, Curtis F. Michel entered the space program in 1965 as one of its first scientists. He did not make a space flight before leaving NASA to pursue his academic career. In 1997, he was Andrew Hays Professor of Astrophysics at Rice University in Texas.

Leroy Chiao

Chiao was born in Milwaukee in 1960, but considers Danville, California, to be his hometown. He earned a doctorate in chemical engineering from the University of California, Santa Barbara in 1987 and became an astronaut in 1991. A veteran of two space flights, Chiao has logged 567 hours, 55 minutes, 41 seconds in space, including two spacewalks totaling just

over 13 hours. His most recent flight was the shuttle Endeavor in January 1996.

Daniel C. Brandenstein

Dan Brandenstein was born and raised in Watertown and received his undergraduate degree from the University of Wisconsin, River Falls. He entered the U.S. Navy flight program in 1965 and flew 192 combat missions from aircraft carriers in Southeast Asia.

He entered the space program in 1979 and completed four space shuttle missions between 1983 and 1990. He was the pilot on the Challenger when it made the first night launch of a shuttle spacecraft. He commanded the orbiter Discovery on its seven-day mission in 1985 and the and orbiter Columbia for twelve days in 1990. As Commander of the shuttle Endeavor in 1992, Brandenstein took part in the successful retrieval and redeployment of the non-functioning Intelsat satellite in 1992.

After logging more than 1,000 hours in space, Brandenstein became chief of the astronaut office in 1992.

Donald K. Slayton

"Deke" Slayton had the "right stuff" to be one of the original seven Mercury Program astronauts chosen to be the first Americans in space.

He was born in Sparta in 1924 and grew up on the family farm nearby. Impatient to serve in World War II, he entered the Army Air Force at age 18 in April 1942. He flew B-25s in fifty-six combat missions in Europe and seven over Japan, then left the service in 1946. He was recalled to active duty in 1951, served in Germany, then became a fighter test pilot. He entered the space program in 1959 and was scheduled for one of the early orbital space flights in the Mercury Program.

His plans to get into space were indefinitely postponed when it was discovered that he had a heart murmur. He stayed with NASA and became the first chief of the Astronaut Office in 1962. Grounded from space by his heart problem, Slayton watched while his comrades Alan Shepard, Gus Grisson, John Glenn, Walt Schirra, Scott Carpenter and Gordon Cooper made history in space.

He did not lose hope and stayed with the space program. In the early 1970s, Slayton's medical status was reviewed. Qualified for space once again, he piloted the Apollo Docking Module in the first Soviet-American joint space mission, the Apollo-Soyuz Project. In 1975, the American Apollo spacecraft rendezvoused and docked with the Soviet Soyuz. It was the first time two spacecraft met in space and exchanged crew members.

At age 51, Slayton was then the oldest person to travel in space. He had waited sixteen years for the chance

and was ready for more. He had hoped to qualify for the Shuttle Program, but was not scheduled for a flight. He retired from NASA in 1982, one year after the first shuttle flight.

Deke Slayton died of cancer in 1993 at 69 years of age. His memory is kept alive in Sparta at the Deke Slayton Museum, the state's only museum dedicated to the manned space program.

James A. Lovell

Born in Massachusetts in 1928, Jim Lovell was raised in Milwaukee and married Milwaukee native Marilyn Gerlach. He entered the Naval cadet program at the University of Wisconsin, Madison, in 1946 and was admitted to the Naval Academy at Annapolis in 1948. Upon graduation, he became a naval aviator and test pilot.

He volunteered for the Mercury Program, but was not admitted. He did make the second call for astronauts and entered the Gemini program along with Frank Borman, Buzz Aldrin and Neil Armstrong. In 1965 he flew on the Gemini 7 mission and the Gemini 12 in 1966. At the end of 1968, Lovell joined Frank Borman and William Anders on the epic Apollo 8 journey into lunar orbit on which they became the first humans to leave the gravitational influence of the earth. Apollo 8 was the final mission before the lunar landing in the summer of 1969.

Lovell made what has become probably the most well-known space flight during one dramatic week in April 1970. On Apollo 13, Lovell was to become the second American to walk on the moon. Instead, a failure in the oxygen system in the Service Module forced the astronauts to alter the flight plan and make a very tense return to earth. The heroic story of Apollo 13 was all but forgotten until a movie version was made in 1995.

After Apollo 13, Lovell left the space program holding the record for time in space at 715 hours. It stood until the American and Soviet space station programs, which were intended to keep people in space for weeks and months at a time.

As of 1998, the Lovells reside in northern Illinois and are frequent visitors to the Milwaukee area.[65]

Carl Guell with Deke Slayton when the astronaut was inducted into the Wisconsin Aviation Hall of Fame. (WAHF)

Below left: Jim Lovell (NASA)

CHAPTER VI

Wisconsin Aviation Chronology

■ 1845

The Milwaukee Sentinel announces that the "Balloon Ascension that was to have taken place last evening at Woodward's garden was postponed to this evening." There is no confirmation that this or any other balloon flight took place in 1845, but this notice—three years before statehood—is the first mention of an aircraft flight in Wisconsin.

■ 1856

"Professor" Joshua Pusey makes a balloon ascension at Milwaukee; Mrs. Theodore Reis offers to accompany him but only "if the wind blows from the lake."

■ 1859

"Professor" Brooks launches his balloon at Madison and travels south-east for nearly one hour before landing about 25 miles away near Fulton.

A "smoke" balloon bursting before liftoff at Burlington, 1911. (SHSW)

"Professor" John J. Steiner, "with his mammoth balloon," makes an ascension at Wisconsin's third State Fair.

■ 1860

In his big balloon called the *Europa,* Professor Steiner ascends from the corner of Huron and Broadway in Milwaukee, rises to 12,000 feet, then nearly crashes into Lake Michigan before traveling 103 miles and landing near Grand Haven, Michigan.

■ 1863

Professor Steiner, in his new balloon *Hercules,* goes aloft for a flight from downtown Milwaukee over the lake to North Point.

While touring the United States, the young German noble-man, Ferdinand von Zeppelin, travels to Superior, Wisconsin, by lake steamer; he then canoes down the Mississippi River and travels to St. Paul where, in August, he takes his first balloon ride, piloted by John Steiner.

■ 1867

"Professor" Cummings sends up two balloons at Janesville.

■ 1870

At Quentin's Park, Milwaukee, balloonist H. L. Denniston ascends 600 feet above the city, then drops to the rooftops, falls out of his gondola and lies stranded on a roof while his balloon blows away.

■ 1871

Professor Steiner flies his balloon, *The City of Milwaukee,* 150 miles across Lake Michigan and lands near Kalamazoo, Michigan.

■ 1872

"Professors" Garwood and Reno launch a balloon at Janesville and descend on a house in the city.

■ 1874

Delavan "enjoys" a balloon ascension which is a "complete success," including the trapeze acrobatics performed by "Mr. Palmer" while aloft.

At Eau Claire, "Professor" Denniston promises to launch his balloon accompanied by a live bear in the gondola.

■ 1875

As a test flight for a future trip across the Atlantic, Professor Steiner flies his new 100,000-cubic-foot balloon at Milwaukee.

■ 1878

At Oshkosh, "Signor Pedanto" performs acrobatics from a trapeze beneath his balloon which flies south along Lake Winnebago for about five miles.

At Lake Mills, a balloonist/acrobat rises into the clouds and goes "floating away."

■ **1879**
At Reedsburg, "Professor" Rosa makes a successful ascension and flight of about 1.5 miles.

■ **1881**
Flying for the Army Signal Corps, balloonists Samuel King and Private J. G. Hashagan launch the balloon *A. J. Nutting* in Chicago and travel 550 miles before crashing in the woods near Chippewa Falls, Wisconsin.

■ **1892**
Three daily balloon ascensions and parachute drops are featured at the Sheboygan County Fair.

■ **1893**
After filling his balloon from a Milwaukee city gas main, Captain Otto Eiermann ascends from Schlitz Park and out over Lake Michigan before going down. After two hours in the water, he is rescued by a schooner and carried to St. Ignace, Michigan; out of contact with land for a week, Eiermann is feared lost.

■ **1895**
At Whitefish Bay, "Professor" Burt Curtis is injured when his balloon crashes into a tree.

■ **1898**
Balloonist/parachutist Ed Freeman of Beaver Dam makes his first performance at the Dodge County Fair.

■ **1899**
When Ida Leroy makes a balloon ascension and parachute jump at the State Fair, she lands in the path of an oncoming locomotive which manages to stop just in time.

■ **1900**
Oshkosh's Charles Wetterhan announces the completion of "The Common Sense Flying Machine," but the balloon-like device slips away from its moorings and floats away before ever carrying a passenger.

■ **1903**
December 17, 1903
At Kitty Hawk, North Carolina, Orville and Wilbur Wright make the first flights in a heavier-than-air machine; the longest is Wilbur's flight of 852 feet in 59 seconds. On December 19, the *Milwaukee Sentinel* runs a description of the flight received via special dispatch.

Fond du Lac machinist Thomas Abel tells a local reporter that he has been working on a flying machine for the last twelve years;

Abel refuses to show the machine to the reporter and no further word is heard of him.

Milwaukee machinist John Stierle makes a "hop" of a few seconds in his home-built airship at 37th and Vliet in Milwaukee.

■ **1906**
In New York City, Beloit manufacturer Arthur P. Warner meets with other businessmen interested in building flying machines.

Major Henry Hersey and Lieutenant Frank P. Lahm win the first Gordon Bennett Trophy race in a balloon that flies over 400 miles from Paris to Scotland.

High winds and engine failure force William Matteray to make a 250 mile dirigible flight over Lake Michigan from Oconto to Michigan.

Orville and Wilbur Wright at Kitty Hawk, 1903. (WAHF)

The State Fair features Charles K. Hamilton, who flies his dirigible from West Allis to Milwaukee and circles city hall. It is the first controlled flight by an aircraft in Wisconsin.

■ **1907**
The State Board of Agriculture votes to allow "Dr." Rudolph Silverston to use the horse barn at the State Fairgrounds to build his "air-motor" flying machine.

■ **1908**
In Philadelphia, Alfred W. Lawson publishes

Fly, the first magazine dedicated to the science of mechanical flight.

The Milwaukee Aero Club is formed and elects John H. Moss president at its first meeting.

Albert Q. Dufour of Milwaukee attempts flight in a glider towed by R.C. Chidester's 60-HP Packard, reputedly the most powerful car in the city.

Glenn Curtiss flies his *June Bug* airplane, which serves as a model for many of the machines flown in Wisconsin over the next five years.

Frederick H. Fielding, summer resident of Winneconne, Wisconsin, sets a record for distance of 786.5 miles in 23 hours, 15 minutes, in a Chicago Aero Club balloon race.

Cheered on by thousands, Captain Jack Dallas flies a dirigible 2,000 feet over Milwaukee.

The Wright Brothers make a public demonstration of their flying machine in France. About a month later, they demonstrate for the U.S. Army at Fort Meyers, Virginia; among the spectators are Eugene Stout, a native of Cameron, Wisconsin, and Lieutenant William "Billy" Mitchell. At the State Fair, the flight of Silverston's "Vacu-Aerial Flying Machine" is a flop when the crankshaft breaks before the first take-off.

1909
Using a Wright-inspired design, Wisconsin Dells native Ashley Bennett makes the first attempt to get a flying machine into the air in Minnesota.

The *Chicago Tribune* reports on the dubious escapades of Dr. A.R. Silverston in Milwaukee. The State Fair Board rescinds its permission for Silverston to raise a building on the grounds in order to rebuild his plane, and orders his machine off the property.

The State Agriculture Board instructs its secretary "to correspond with noted aviators" to exhibit at the fair.

■ November 9, 1909
At Beloit Arthur P. Warner makes Wisconsin's first aeroplane flights. The longest flight is about one-quarter mile and the highest altitude is 50 feet. He is the sixth American to fly and the first in Wisconsin.

A balloon/parachute act thrills the crowd at the Marathon County Fair when the balloon disappears into low-lying clouds and the parachutist is feared lost.

Young sawmill operator Walter Moldenhauer, Granton, builds his own plane and rumor has it that he "went several hundred feet and had the machine under perfect control."

■ 1910
Otto Brodie, believed to be a Wisconsin native, becomes Chicago's first pilot.

Beloit native Trenton Fry is in Chicago working for the E.B. Heath Aviation Vehicle Company.

In New York, Alfred Lawson publishes *Aircraft Magazine,* thereby first bringing the term "aircraft" into common use.

In a Voisin machine, Appleton-raised escape artist Harry Houdini makes Australia's first aeroplane flight.

Federal court rules that aviators in litigation with the Wright Brothers can fly their machines, thereby opening the era of exhibition flying at air meets and fairs throughout the United States.

The State Fair Board contracts with the Wright Brothers organization to provide an aerial exhibit at the fair. Arch Hoxsey, the

second person to fly an aeroplane in Wisconsin, makes a 17-minute flight in a Wright Flyer that awes the crowd.

Wausau native John Schwister brings his new aeroplane home to Wausau. The home-built biplane resembles a Curtiss, although about 100 pounds heavier, and cost Schwister approximately $3,000.

The Warner Instrument Company, Beloit, advertises its Aero-Meter, which "accurately indicates speed of the wind...in miles per hour" as "The First Aeroplane Accessory."

■ 1911
Glenn Curtiss develops the hydro-aeroplane to take off and land on water.

John Schwister exhibits, but does not fly, his *Minnesota-Badger* aeroplane at the Roller Rink in Grand [Wisconsin] Rapids. Next he builds a hanger near the village park in Rothschild—the first building in Wisconsin specifically erected for an aeroplane.

The Grant County Fair Association advertises for an aviator to appear at the county fair in September.

The Commencement program for Green Bay High School is titled "Aeroplane."

The Aero Club of America issues the nation's first pilot's license to Glenn Curtiss.

■ June 23, 1911
Having test-flown the Minnesota-Badger by towing it behind an automobile, John Schwister makes his first powered flight. As reported, the machine rises "gracefully in to the air, skimming along at an elevation of about twenty feet for quite a distance." This is the third powered flight in Wisconsin and the first flight of an aeroplane designed and built by a Wisconsin native.

Jesse Brabazon of Delavan is so inspired at the Chicago air meet that within a year he sells everything and moves to Cicero Field to learn how to fly.

In Kenosha, Curtiss aviators Cromwell Dixon and Jimmy Ward fly at the "first aviation meet in state."

C.C. Wittmer flies a hydro-aeroplane in De Pere, which is partly wrecked and sinks while attempting a landing on the Fox River.

At Appleton, Galbraith Perry "Cal" Rodgers stars in the first truly successful aviation

exhibition to take place in Wisconsin; he makes several flights and wins a race down College Avenue with an automobile; he takes about a dozen paying customers for rides—the first to pay for an aeroplane ride in the state—including his sister-in-law, Elizabeth Whiting, the first female Wisconsin resident to fly. Rodgers also completes the first cross-country flight in Wisconsin made by a machine designed and built by Orville and Wilbur Wright. The flight north from Appleton lasts about 25 minutes and covers about 25 miles.

John Schwister becomes Wisconsin's first "professional" flyer when he makes two flights at the Langlade County Fair in Antigo and is paid for it.

Injured in a crash, Harry Powers is unable to perform at the Dunn County Fair in Menomonee and is replaced by French pilot Rene Simon. Simon's seven-minute flight in a Moisant model marks the first successful flight in Northwest Wisconsin and the first by a monoplane in the state.

Walter Moldenhauer of Granton exhibits his home-built biplane, featuring a 25-foot wing-spread mounted on a tricycle landing gear and powered by a two-cylinder engine, at county fairs in Marshfield and Neillsville.

The first successful aerial exhibition in Milwaukee County is performed at State Fair Park by Lincoln Beachey, who makes several flights—including his signature "Death Dip." On September 16, he flies to an unheard of altitude of 10,250 feet.

In Manitowoc, Beckwith Havens makes six flights, reaching an altitude of 2,000 feet during a two-day exhibition. Havens also flies at Ashland.

The Grant County Sheriff holds Lincoln Beachey's Curtiss Flyer for failure to complete three flights contracted for at Lancaster.

Lincoln Beachey and C.C. Wittmer fly a successful exhibition at Sheboygan.

Eighteen-year-old Peter Christman of Green Bay builds a monoplane which he will exhibit at the Winnebago County Fair in Oshkosh.

German flyers Hans Gericke and S. O. Dunker win the Gordon Bennett Trophy when their *Berlin II* balloon flies 468 miles from St. Louis before landing near Holcombe, Wisconsin; second-place winner is the *Buckeye,* flown by U.S. Army pilot

Lieutenant Frank P. Lahm and J. H. Wade, which travels 365 miles before landing at La Crosse.

Hugh Robinson, flying down the Mississippi on a promotional tour, makes Wisconsin's first "under-bridge" flight when he passes beneath the Winona bridge. He repeats the stunt in La Crosse for 10,000 spectators before landing to make the first delivery of mail by air in the state. He then flies on to Prairie du Chien to complete a flight of 160 miles.

With $50,000 capital, Eleanor Silverston, Henry Feldhus, Louis Jensen, Lester A. Loewenbach and A. R. Silverston incorporate the Milwaukee School and College of Aviation to train pilots and manufacture flying machines; one of the first students is John "Jack" Knight from Waukesha County. It is the first flight school and, arguably, the first airport in Wisconsin.

John Schwister makes the longest flight yet recorded, in Wisconsin, in an airplane built in Wisconsin: 27 miles in 34 minutes on four gallons of gasoline. This is also the first flight higher than a few hundred feet made by a Wisconsin pilot.

Young John Kaminski of Milwaukee leaves to attend pilot training at the Curtiss school on North Island in San Diego Bay, California.

■ 1912

Mazomanie native Walter Lees leaves the University of Wisconsin and heads to Florida where Otto Brodie charges $150 to teach him to fly. By November he solos in a Benoist XII with dual stick controls at St. Louis.

John G. Kaminski of Milwaukee becomes the first licensed aviator in Wisconsin when he is issued license No. 121 by the Federation Aeronautique Internationale, Aero Club of America. At age 16, he is also the youngest licensed pilot in the country and possibly the world.

Farnum Fish, "The Boy Pilot," sets records: he makes the first-ever flight from Chicago to Milwaukee in a Wright biplane. He delivers the first aerial advertising, the first air freight, the first "air mail," and also claims a record for the longest over-water flight yet made. A few days later, he flies *Milwaukee Journals* from Milwaukee to Waukesha, Oconomowoc and Watertown, making the first delivery of a daily newspaper by air. Fish brings Herbert Hazzard along on his 45-

mile return trip from Watertown and claims a record for the longest flight made with a passenger.

The *Milwaukee Journal* sponsors a "3 Ring Aerial Circus" at the State Fairgrounds featuring "Flying Fish" Farnum, "Birdgirl" Julia Clarke, and "Milwaukee Boy" John Kaminski. The Post Office sets up a substation and "air mail" is flown one half-mile to the West Allis Post Office.

At the state convention of the Fraternal Order of Eagles at Janesville, exhibition pilot Nels J. Nelson takes motion pictures while he flies; he manages the plane with one hand and turns the crank on the camera with the other.

John Schwister is severely injured at Fort Snelling, Minnesota, when the engine of his newest home-built plane stalls and he crashes 200 feet to the ground.

French aviator Franco Castory fills exhibition dates at Stevens Point and Wausau; he competes in races with motorcycles and automobiles in his radio-equipped Curtiss-type biplane. His plane is wrecked in Wausau when it falls from 200 feet but he is not seriously injured.

Curtiss pilot Harry Powers makes a number of flights in his hydro-aeroplane around Oshkosh, Waverly Beach, Appleton and Berlin.

Topeka aviator A.K. Longren entertains crowds at the La Crosse fair with aerial stunts.

Green Bay teenager Harry Tees builds an aeroplane based on the Curtiss design, flies it briefly, then smashes it in a crash. He is the second Wisconsin native to build and fly his own aeroplane.

Three hours weekly, Professor Charles S. Slichter gives a course in aerodynamics to advanced students of mathematics, physics and engineering at the University of Wisconsin—Madison.

Jimmy Ward made the first airplane flight in Marshfield, 1912. (Dan Maurer)

The widow of Cal Rodgers sells the damaged but salvageable Vin Fiz to Wisconsin aviator Jesse Brabazon. He flies the Vin Fiz at the Chicago Air Meet. Among others on the program are top-rated pilots Glenn Martin, Katherine Stinson and Hugh Robinson.

Chicago aviator Jimmy Ward makes Marshfield's first flight, circling the city five times and traveling as far as Ebbe, Hewitt, McMillan and Klondike.

In Chilton, Nels J. Nelson gives an exhibition despite a 40-mile gale which blows over the hangar.

Wright exhibition flyer Louis Mitchell flies at the Rock County Fair in Evansville; on one flight, he takes up Miss Eunice Kuelz, "one of Evansville's most popular young ladies," who says "the sensation of being carried through the air so swiftly and smoothly was one impossible of description."

At the State Fair, Lincoln Beachey thrills crowds during three flights and reaches an altitude of 4,000 feet.

An exhibition flyer from Los Angeles, Harold S. Sjolander, connects with a wire fence while making a landing at the Washington County Fair, West Bend.

Floyd Barlow flies at the Oneida County Fair, Rhinelander.

Milwaukee exhibition flyer Horace Kearney performs at the Gays Mills Agricultural Fair, then flies 37 miles to Prairie du Chien to catch a train to Springfield where he'll perform with Farnum Fish at the Illinois State Fair.

■ 1913

Spectators are thrilled to witness Miss Blanche Stuart Scott take flight at the Dane County Fairgrounds. The New York native is the first woman to pilot an airplane in the state of Wisconsin. She and her *Red Devil* aeroplane do suffer an accident but are not seriously injured.

Chicago aviator P.C. Davis dies of tetanus several days after being injured in a plane accident at the Juneau County Fair in Mauston. His passing was the first aviation fatality due to an accident in Wisconsin.

Jack Knight joins John Kaminski's exhibition tour as mechanic to form the first all-Wisconsin professional flying team.

Dr. Silverston abandons his school in West Allis and the Vacu-Aerial machine and heads to Cuyahoga Falls, Ohio, where he finds new investors and starts a flight school, an airfield and an aircraft manufacturing operation. John Kaminski serves as flight instructor for a few months.

Leland Knowland of Green Bay successfully flies the hydro aeroplane he and Harry Tees built at Bay View Beach. The Curtiss-type biplane is fitted with a Grey Eagle motor and floats and is the first home-built floatplane designed and built in Wisconsin.

Logan "Jack" Vilas flies the first aeroplane across Lake Michigan, 64 miles from Chicago to St. Joseph, Michigan.

Louis Gertson gives an exhibition in Watertown, including a 34-minute flight over the city. The next week he entertains Portage and Fond du Lac.

Jimmy Ward makes "two pretty flights" at Madison and, later in the year, a "remarkable

aeroplane flight" at Green Bay's Perry Centennial in Hagemeister Park. Green Bay people "are now convinced that aeroplane flights scheduled will actually take place."

Floyd Barlow flies his Wright/Bleriot biplane during exhibitions at Durand and Sparta but fails to make dates at Friendship and Menomonie. He later turns "a complete somersault over the grand stand," and thrills 7,000 spectators at the Elroy Fair.

When an aviator named Crossley attempts to fill a date at the Jackson County Fair, his crash on take-off is "a great disappointment to the crowds."

Chicago aviators Max Lillie and M.M. McGuire exhibit "feats of racing, altitude climbing, etc." at the Monroe County Fair.

In Antigo, Wright pilot Oscar Brindley is the Langlade County Fair's 3-day feature. Tom L. Timmons and Trenton Fry build Beloit's first home-built aeroplane, a tractor-style biplane, and fly it out of a farm field south of the city.

Jack Vilas on forest fire patrol, Vilas County, 1915. (WAHF)

At Sturgeon Bay, Louis Gertson makes two flights daily for the Door County Fair Association. His fee is $1,050, the largest single expense for the fair.

Exhibition flyer Frank Champion makes two daily flights at Richland Center in his Bleriot.

Driving rain and bitter cold don't prevent George Mestach from flying his Borel-Somerville monoplane at Mondovi.

■ 1914

Wright pilot Joseph De Riemer assembles his machine at Menominee, Michigan, in order

to make flights over Green Bay from an ice-covered inlet he calls a flying field.

■ April 15, 1914

For the first time in American history, damages are awarded in a suit related to an aeroplane exhibition which resulted in injury to a spectator. In Milwaukee, Irene Morrison takes home $4,000 for injuries suffered during Arch Hoxsey's crash at State Fair Park in 1910.

In Milwaukee, airplane builder Paul Gnauck, Wisconsin Aero Club President Otto Hagemann, and pilot Jack Vilas successfully fly the Aero Club's flying boat off the Lake Michigan Beach. By Memorial Day, Gnauk tries to fly over the lake, but he and an unidentified crew member crash into Lake Michigan. The first Wisconsin aeroplane to attempt a Lake Michigan crossing is lost and the two flyers rescued by members of the Milwaukee Yacht Club.

Balloonist M. L. Tinney provides a "genuine thriller" for the crowds at Sheboygan's Lake View Park with a night ascension featuring fireworks while aloft and then roman candles launching while he parachutes into the lake.

At the Sheboygan County Fair in Plymouth, Chicago pilot Fred A. Hoover, "The German Flyer," announces that he will race against "a monster racing car flying so close to the car that he will touch the head of the driver with front wheel of the landing gear." However, the flight "proved a fizzle," with the plane rising about 150 feet than dropping "softly" into a nearby corn field.

At Beloit on Friday the 13th, Lincoln Beachey defeats Barney Oldfield in an aeroplane-versus-auto race and blows up a miniature battleship. He also survives the "Death Drop" in which he falls from 5,000 to 2,000 feet with a "dead" motor, and performs his signature "loop-the-loop" maneuver, concluding upside-down.

Mr. and Mrs. Clair G. Horton bring their Curtiss hydro-aeroplane to Madison and offer to take passengers aloft "for a consideration."

■ 1915

From Trout Lake, Jack Vilas pilots the first aircraft in the world used to patrol large areas of forest and detect fires. He is commissioned "official aviator" by the Wisconsin State Board of Forestry. The Board later reports that "the experiment proved of no little value," and "that eventually the aeroplane will be a practical device for patrolling great areas of land."

Temporary mail service from State Fair Park to the Milwaukee Post Office is part of the show provided by the Patterson Aviators. Pilots are O.E. Williams of Scranton, Pennsylvania, and Farnum Fish, Chicago. For the first time, prizes are awarded for the best model airplane exhibited at the State Fair.

■ 1916
The American aircraft industry produces approximately 400 airplanes.

Selmer Gjestvang, Abel Jostad and Wendell McEldowney of West Salem build an aircraft in McEldowney's garage.

Paul Culver is one of the first to enlist in the Aviation Section of the Reserve Signal Officers Corps.

Exhibition flyer Charles "Do Anything" Niles dies after his monoplane comes apart during stunts at the Winnebago County Fairgrounds, Oshkosh.

Major Billy Mitchell takes flight lessons at the Curtiss flight school at Newport News, Virginia; one of his instructors is Mazomanie native Walter Lees.

■ 1917
United States enters World War I on the Allied side with Britain, France and Russia; American Navy, Marine and Army air forces number about 100 planes and flying officers.

Major William Mitchell disembarks in Europe as the first American military observer for aviation.

The University of Wisconsin's Forest Products Laboratory conducts research in the use of wood for aviation.

Alfred W. Lawson forms the Lawson Aircraft Corporation in Green Bay to manufacture aircraft for the U.S. Army. Authorized by the War Department, Lawson Aircraft begins work on its first military trainer, the MT-1. After Lawson pilots its successful test-flight in September, work begins on the MT-2 and, in November, a three-story Lawson Aircraft Corporation building, with room for 500 workers, is completed on Pearl and Howard Streets in Green Bay.

The first 12-cylinder OX-5 Liberty engines go into mass production. Under the management of Thomas Hamilton, Milwaukee's Matthews Brothers Manufacturing is soon making propellers specifically for U.S. Navy Liberty engines. This is the largest and most successful aviation-related war industry in Wisconsin.

■ 1918
Returning home from the Army Air Service, Harold Bretting flies an army plane from Illinois to Ashland to make the first north-south flight across Wisconsin.

Rodney Williams flies a Sopwith Camel pursuit plane for the "17th Americans," a squadron stationed with British units in Flanders. In July he becomes the first member of the 17th to down an enemy aircraft. Eventually downing a total of four aircraft and one balloon, Williams becomes Wisconsin's only World War I pilot to earn the distinction "ace."

Heath Parasol, Waukesha. (WAC)

Under Billy Mitchell's command, the first American Air Service pilots go into combat in France.

With presidential authorization, the U.S. Post Office inaugurates air mail service between Washington, Philadelphia and New York. Six army pilots fly the route in Curtiss JN-4Hs, with Eau Claire native Paul Culver covering the Philadelphia-New York leg.

Bennet Molter publishes *Knights of the Air,* the first book on aerial warfare published by a Wisconsinite.

The *Milwaukee Journal* receives news by "aero mail" from New York. Two army pilots fly the mail to Chicago, but it is delivered to Milwaukee by rail.

Under the command of General Billy Mitchell, American aviators play a key role in the defeat of the German army at Chateau-Thierry, St. Mihiel and the Argonne-Meuse, where American pilots log approximately 25,000 hours of combat zone flying.

■ November 11, 1918
The firing halts with the signing of the armistice and World War I ends in western Europe.

By war's end, the United States has had 25,000 men in aviation ground school, 9,000 in primary training and more than 3,000 commissioned pilots or observers.

By war's end in Europe, the United States has 740 airplanes, 744 pilots and 457 observers who downed 704 enemy planes while 187 American flyers died.

During the war, the United States produces more than 16,000 airplanes, up from approximately 400 in 1916.

■ 1919
World War I pilot Rellis Conant comes home to Westfield and begins purchasing war-surplus planes to refurbish and offer for sale. His landing field is the Marquette County fairgrounds.

Milwaukee investors put up $100,000 to finance the newly-formed Lawson Airline

Transportation Company; it will build "airliners" to carry passengers across the country.

Waukesha County teenager Bob Huggins, Honey Creek, builds and flies his own glider. Huggins will later get into powered flight by converting a JN-4D fuselage and an OX-5 engine into a high-wing monoplane.

Mel Thompson, a farm boy from Quarry in Manitowoc County, builds his first plane from a kit and flies it safely to the county fairgrounds.

Captain Norman Moll, a World War I veteran, leases vacant land on the far south side of La Crosse from the Salzer Feed Company. His landing field becomes known as Salzer Field, La Crosse's first airport.

Lieutenant Dave Behncke is discharged from the Army Air Service and goes to work as an independent flyer out of Checkerboard Field. By June he is delivering Society Brand clothing to Janesville and Madison, attracting large crowds to Vilas Park.

Madison's Susie Mae Potter purchases her own Jenny and begins booking air shows. By the end of 1919 she has lost two Jennies, flown by other pilots.

The Wisconsin Conservation Commission announces plans to use two or three airplanes to patrol for forest fires in the upper half of the state.

Two U. S. Navy "flying boats," christened *Victory* and *Peace,* arrive at Milwaukee to promote Liberty war bond sales; they take aerial photos of the city, drop leaflets, then land in the lake at McKinley Beach. A forced landing delays the departure of the *Peace* on its tour to Manitowoc, Sturgeon Bay, Green Bay, Appleton, Neenah-Menasha, Oshkosh and Fond du Lac; the *Victory* flies on to Madison and takes aloft bond purchasers.

Giles Meisenheimer lands "the first commercial aeroplane to enter Wisconsin" on the golf course at Lake Park; the war vet and Milwaukee native flew a war surplus Curtiss "Jennie" from Chicago.

U.S. naval pilots make the first trans-Atlantic flight via the Azores to Portugal; Captain Marc Mitscher, born in Hillsboro, Wisconsin, is the pilot of one of the planes that fails to complete the flight.

The Milwaukee County Park Commission spends $25,000 to purchase 165 acres for a future aircraft landing site.

The first publicly-financed airport in Wisconsin, Milwaukee County Airport is established where Currie Park is now located. It is also the first facility in Wisconsin created specifically as a general purpose, municipal airport.

The new Lawson airliner takes off from the new Milwaukee County Airport on its initial test flight. It is the first flight of an airplane expressly designed to carry passengers.

Senator John A. Conant, Westfield, flies to Madison and becomes the first state legislator to fly to a legislative session.

The U.S. Air Service's "Round-The-Rim" Martin bomber stops at Milwaukee on its 9,800-mile patrol of the borders and coast lines of the country.

On a promotional tour, Wrigley Company planes *Spearmint 1* and *Spearmint 2* make the "first delivery by aeroplane of chewing gum" in the Fox River Valley.

Ruth Law exhibits stunt flying at the Big Badger Fair at Platteville; the newspaper reports that "No bird is more free in the air than she is."

The airplanes of the U. S. Air Service's Pathfinder Squadron include Milwaukee as a stop on their 4,000 mile flight through 171 American cities. The tour is accompanied by a support team of 39 trucks, a complete machine shop, and a 300-million candlepower searchlight.

Giles Meisenheimer's Wisconsin Curtiss Airplane Company leases space at the county airport and erects a hangar. Meisenheimer is Milwaukee's first airport manager and fixed base operator.

◾ 1920
Rellis Conant, Westfield, enlists his JN-4D in the Republican primary contest for governor, touting Conservative Roy P. Wilcox over Progressive James Blaine; Blaine wins.

Thomas Hamilton establishes the Hamilton Aero Manufacturing Company to build wood and metal propellers and pontoons. He purchases 56 acres of farmland south of the city and east of Layton Ave. and opens Hamilton field.

The Wisconsin Air Derby is sponsored by the *Milwaukee Journal,* Hamilton Aero Manufacturing and the Green Bay Aero Club. Its 264-mile course makes it Wisconsin's first long-distance air race of the post-war years.

Richard Lutz and Florian Miller establish the first Oshkosh airport.

Norman Moll opens a flying school and agency for Curtiss airplanes in La Crosse.

Charles Lindbergh leaves his home in Little Falls, Minnesota, to study engineering at the University of Wisconsin.

Elwyn West takes up flying after Rellis Conant gives him a ride at the Waupaca county fair.

Pete Galles brings a Jenny to Kenosha and holds a christening ceremony. The Mayor and other officials help name Galles' plane *Kenosha.*

James Pugh organizes the Black River Falls Aeronautical Company and purchases a Curtiss JN.

Army pilot Walter Smith flies a twin-engine Martin Bomber and 86 pounds of mail on a test flight to establish an air mail route from Chicago to Minneapolis/St. Paul, with a stop at Salzer Field, La Crosse.

For Opening Day at the State Fair, Governor S. R. McKelvie of Nebraska has a prize pig flown to Wisconsin Governor Emmanuel Philipp. Newspapers calls the pig the First Porker of flight.

A 300-mile Aerial Derby is featured at the State Fair; the course is from West Allis to Kenosha, Milwaukee, Green Bay, Fond du Lac and back. The *Milwaukee Journal* sends reporter Muriel Kelly along and claims she is the first "Girl Reporter" to fly in an air race.

The U.S. Post Office awards its first large air mail contract, worth $685,000, to the Lawson Company, provided Lawson can deliver mail on three routes—Pittsburgh-St. Louis; New York-Pittsburgh-Chicago; New York-Washington-Atlanta—by March 15, 1921. Lawson tries, but will not meet the deadline.

With Hamilton Lee flying from Minneapolis and William T. Carroll from Chicago, the first regularly scheduled air mail is delivered from Chicago to Minneapolis. La Crosse is established as a refueling/mail pickup stop, and Lone Rock as an emergency field.

◾ 1921
Robert B. Hill, Arthur Rowe and William T. Carroll crash and die at La Crosse while flying a JL 6 on the Minneapolis-Chicago air mail route.

Stevens Point native Paul F. Collins begins flying air mail for the United States Post Office.

Secretary of State Herbert Hoover points out that aviation is "the only industry that favors itself regulated by the government."

The Post Office cancels air mail service from Minneapolis, La Crosse, Milwaukee and Chicago, and the cancellation becomes permanent in July when Congress fails to appropriate money for it.

On its maiden flight, Alfred Lawson's *Midnight Liner* crashes on a makeshift landing field outside the South Milwaukee factory. The Lawson Airplane Company declares bankruptcy within a year.

Seventeen spectators are injured when Dallas Spears crashes his JN into the grandstand at State Fair Park. Spears was attempting the stunt of transferring a man from a racing automobile to his plane via rope ladder when the ladder hooked on the car's exhaust pipe; the car crashed, followed by the plane.

Demonstrating aviation's military potential, General Billy Mitchell's bombers sink the battleship *Ostfriesland.*

■ **1922**
Encouraged by friend Delos Dudley, Charles A. Lindbergh leaves the University of Wisconsin to take flight lessons at the Nebraska Aircraft Corporation of Lincoln, Nebraska.

The U.S. Supreme Court ruling on the Wisconsin Railroad Commission case sets a precedent useful to aviation: if the federal government can regulate railroad operations inside a state, it can also regulate aviation operations there.

Two Standard J-1 airplanes and their Hall-Scott motors arrive by freight train at Larsen in Winnebago County. By the end of summer, the four Larson brothers have the planes assembled and lay out a runway in the hayfield.

Twelve balloons are launched from Milwaukee's Borchert Field for the National Balloon Races, hosted this year by the Wisconsin Aero Club. The winner is U. S. Army Major Oscar Westover who flies 911 miles. This is the last event of its kind in Wisconsin.

General Billy Mitchell attends the Balloon

Races at Milwaukee in May, and returns again in June with German aircraft builder A. H. Fokker, who wants to see if he should establish an airplane factory and airline in Milwaukee.

After taking lessons in Chicago, Anton Brotz takes delivery of a Curtiss JN-4D, clears ground for a landing field, and begins flying at Sheboygan.

■ **1923**
Rellis Conant and Montford Waushaver make the first flight across Lake Michigan in an airplane without floats; the pair fly from Milwaukee to Holland, Michigan in a fog and cross the lake at its widest point in 57 minutes.

The Post Office begins installing 289 signal beacons at 25-mile intervals to light the air mail route from Chicago to Cheyenne, Wyoming.

Guy Wood, Leo McDonald and M. A. Sine organize the Eau Claire Airplane Corporation and lease 80 acres for an airport along State Street. U.S. Navy veteran Virgil Grace serves as pilot.

Marshfield auto dealers Walter Miner and Henry Peil buy a Curtiss and establish an airport on Highway 13 at the Wood-Marathon County line.

The Larson brothers build a hangar with space for four airplanes.

■ **1924**
Progressive Wisconsin Congressman John H. Nelson, Madison, charges that the legislation to regulate aviation proposed by the Calvin Coolidge Administration is the work of an "aircraft trust" wishing to monopolize commercial aviation.

A Ku Klux Klan convention descends on Oshkosh and hires Elwyn West to fly over the city with a lighted cross on the underside of his plane. After two flights, West refuses to fly again.

The University of Wisconsin offers courses in naval aviation as part of its naval reserve program.

Presidential candidate Robert M. La Follette hires Roy Larson to fly to Progressive Party rallies during his campaign.

Waunakee's Robert Reeve registers at the University of Wisconsin—Madison.

■ **1925**
Progressive Wisconsin Congressman Florian Lampert, Oshkosh, chairs a select Congressional committee to conduct a full review of American aviation.

At Land O'Lakes, a group of resort owners and real estate developers clears 120 acres of stumpland west of the village for an airport. Because of its proximity to the Canadian border, the airport becomes best known as a good landing spot for "rum-runners."

Rellis Conant and a student are killed when the student freezes at the controls of a Standard biplane and crashes.

M.B. Brunkalla, Max Berghammer, Walter Miner and Henry Peil incorporate Ski-Hi airways in Marshfield.

In Sheboygan, fire destroys Anton Brotz's hangar and the two planes he stores inside. Brotz rebounds by purchasing a Woodson Express, one of the first airplanes with an all-wood fuselage.

With partners Frances Lamb, Albert March and Arthur Leupold, Richard Lutz purchases 100 acres on the southwest edge of the city and organizes the Oshkosh Airport, Inc.

The United States Post Office inaugurates regular night air mail delivery between Chicago and New York City; the airway route is marked by beacon lights erected at 25-mile intervals; many of these beacons are powered by Kohler Automatic electric generating plants.

Billy Mitchell publishes *Winged Defense.*

Attempting to fly from California to Hawaii, a Navy PN-9 seaplane and five crewmen are missing and presumed dead for one week.

In Ohio a severe storm destroys the Navy's rigid airship Shenandoah and claims the lives of 14 crewmen; the *Shenandoah* was scheduled to visit the Minnesota State Fair in St. Paul, then fly over Menomonie, Eau Claire, Black River Falls, Wautoma, Oshkosh, Fond du Lac and Milwaukee.

Billy Mitchell issues a press statement blaming the PN-9 and Shenandoah accidents on "the incompetency, criminal negligence and almost treasonable administration...by the Navy and War Departments."

The court martial of Colonel Billy Mitchell begins in October and ends in December with his conviction.

The Lampert Committee's review of American aviation concludes that no "aircraft trust" exists and recommends that a "bureau of Air Navigation" be created in the Commerce Department and that army, navy and air forces be combined into a single department of defense.

■ 1926
The U. S. Post Office awards the contract for the Chicago-Twin Cities mail route, CAM 9, to Charles Dickinson. Dickinson Airlines, whose motto is "Celerity, Certainty, Security," will offer regularly-scheduled air mail service on the CAM 9 route between the Twin Cities and Chicago, with stops at Milwaukee and La Crosse. Inaugural flights are disastrous; only two of six pilots make it to their destination. Minneapolis pilot Elmer Partridge crashes and dies soon after take-off, while three others—including Dan Kiser— are forced down in various locations. After losing four of his five planes by mid-August, Dickinson is out of business.

With Charlie Dickinson out of business, the air mail contract is awarded to the newly-incorporated Northwest Airways and service returns to CAM 9 by October 1.

President Calvin Coolidge signs into law the Air Commerce Act.

Manitowoc's Arnold Schwarz brings home $100 in prize money from his first race, the Wisconsin News Air Derby.

John Wood and George R. Turner found Wausau Airplane Service Company and fly out of an airfield north of Wausau.

In Waukesha, village photographer Warren O'Brien starts taking aerial shots while standing half-in and half-out of the cockpit of a Jenny.

Wausau locals Irvin Hall and Mark Hubbard are flying out of a farm field north of town.

The Rhinelander airport begins operation at the Oneida County Fairgrounds.

In Madison, Howard Morey, Daniel Egan and Edgar Quinn establish the Madison Airways Corporation. They lease land on the Weber farm south of Lake Monona, make a deal with the Pennsylvania Oil Company, and name the new airport Pennco Field.

Former Eau Claire pilot Virgil Grace is one of Hollywood's first stunt pilots. Grace performs four spectacular crashes in the movie

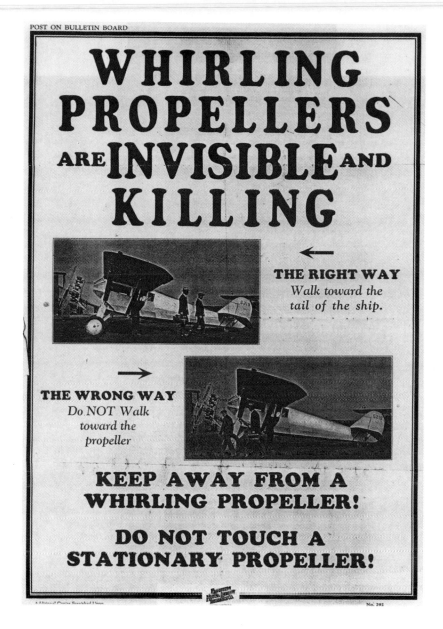

A poster for airports published by Employer's Mutual Insurance, Wausau, late 1920s. (Robert Wylie)

"Wings," helping it to win the first Oscar awarded for Best Picture.

The Curtiss-Wright Corporation builds an airport in Milwaukee.

The Wisconsin Conservation Department authorizes the first use of aerial spraying to control forest insects; Les W. Smith of Decatur, Illinois, pilots a clipped-wing Standard and dusts trees in Peninsula State Park with calcium arsenate.

The Second Annual "Commercial Airplane Reliability Tour" sponsored by the Ford Motor Company makes stops in 14 Midwestern airports, including Milwaukee's Hamilton Field.

Milwaukee county gives up on its inadequate airport and appropriates $150,000 to purchase the 126-acre Hamilton Field.

Floyd Bennett brings Admiral Richard Byrd's polar flight airplane, Josephine Ford, for a visit to Milwaukee. Byrd will be in Milwaukee himself in about a month.

Dr. George Ross builds "Air City" near Sturtevant.

■ 1927
Charles Lindbergh makes the first non-stop solo flight from New York to Paris in his custom-made Ryan monoplane; the flight ignites interest in aviation throughout the United States. On his post-flight tour, Lindbergh vis-

its Milwaukee and Madison and flies over many other Wisconsin cities, dropping messages of greeting.

Lt. Lester J. Maitland of Milwaukee, with Lt. Albert F. Hegenberger navigating, makes the first airplane flight from California to Hawaii.

The Oconomowoc landing field is established by the federal Aeronautics Bureau as a stopping point on the Milwaukee-La Crosse-Twin Cities Airway.

Lt. Vilas R. Knope, Stevens Point, and his crew members are lost at sea during the Dole Pineapple Race from California to Hawaii.

land from Ed Gengler and develops an airport on Brown Deer Road.

Wausau City Council accepts the offer of Ben and J. S. Alexander to lease land for an airport on the river south of the city.

Wausau's John Wood finishes fourth and earns $1,000 in the coast-to-coast National Air Derby race.

A 1,000 watt beacon to guide aviators is mounted atop Rib Mountain.

Wisconsin aviation pioneer John Schwister dies, apparently still the victim of injuries he suffered after falling 200 feet in a plane crash in Minnesota in 1912.

Governor Fred Zimmerman, flying in a Stinson Tri-Motor on loan from the Standard Oil Company, tours north central Wisconsin to study and promote conservation of natural resources.

Air mail service along the Chicago-Twin Cities route begins at Madison.

President Calvin Coolidge presents the Howard Schiif Memorial Trophy to Ashland native Lieutenant Arthur Gavin, who attained the greatest number of flying hours without an accident in 1927.

At Wausau, John Wood, Harry Lilige, Ben Alexander and Wells Turner start Northern Airways; aircraft for passenger service are a Waco OX-5 and a Ryan Whirlwind, with round trip fare to Milwaukee at $135.00.

Neenah realtor H.H. Held sets aside 40 acres of land and builds a hangar on the corner of Commercial and Cecil Streets.

At Milwaukee County Airport, Ed, Ray and Jim Knaup organize Midwest Airways as a charter service, flight school and dealer/distributor of Mahoney/Ryan airplanes.

U.S. Army Tri-Motor on "Arctic Patrol," Wausau, 1929. (Robert Wylie)

The Department of Commerce lays out Wisconsin's first "air highway." The "Great Aerial White Way" labeled U.S. Airway No. 9, will guide night flyers between Milwaukee and Chicago.

Hamilton Field is renamed Milwaukee County Airport.

The City of Superior begins construction of an airport near Billings Park.

Along with the local American Legion Post, the city of Rhinelander starts maintaining a landing field at the county fairgrounds.

Milwaukee's Hamilton Metalplane, the *Maiden Milwaukee*, places second in the Ford Reliability Tour.

In his Waco 10, Wausau's John P. Wood takes fifth place in the third Ford Reliability Air Tour.

At La Crosse, Bill Leithold, Barney Root, ten other men and one woman organize the Winneshiek Flying Club.

When unlucky Anton Brotz loses another hangar and his Woodson to a big wind, he gives up on Sheboygan and moves his operation to Kohler.

In Green Bay, Eddie Kersten brings a plane to Blesch Field and builds a hangar.

Flying takes a quick hold on Washington Island when Arnie Arntzen flies over the bay from Escanaba, Michigan.

Northwest Airways puts three Stinson Detroiter's into regular service, inaugurating passenger service out of Milwaukee County Airport.

Major Herbert J. Dargue, commander of the "Good Will" flyers who flew across South America, visits Madison, Milwaukee and Wausau.

Arnold Schwarz buys forty acres on the northwest edge of Manitowoc and opens the city's first airport, with Frank Shoblaska as manager.

In Milwaukee County, Bill Williams leases

■ **1928**
Howard Morey flies Governor Zimmerman to New York City to welcome the Bremen flyers.

In Sturgeon Bay, cherry grower Karl Reynolds builds a landing field on his property and christens his single-plane operation Cherryland Airways.

In Rhinelander, Ed Bruso solos future airport manager Steve Shelbreck.

Beloit's American Legion Post and Commercial Club organize Beloit Airways and open an airport—the Beloit Legion-Civic Airport—east of the city.

Jim Knaup, Ed Knaup and Elmer Leighton are deputized by the county sheriff to act as an "air patrol" in the skies over Milwaukee. They are to "search for bandits traveling the highways in high-powered automobiles."

The Reedsburg City Council rents (and later purchases) 69 acres northeast of the city to accommodate Cecil Hess' new OX-5 Waco, *Miss Fortune.* The city is one of the first small communities in the state to own an airport.

Janesville service station owner Herman Krause purchases an OX-Travel Air and opens a landing field to be known as Janesville City Airport.

Madison's Pennco Field is renamed Royal Airport when Howard Morey makes a deal with Royal Transit to begin regular air passenger service from Madison to Chicago.

Delos Dudley and Willet Kempton open an airport and the "Wisconsin Air College" on the highway between Janesville and Beloit.

300 copies of the *Chicago Daily News* are flown daily during the summer season to vacationers in the Eagle River area.

The City of Kenosha leases property for an airport on 22nd Avenue and 80th Street, the later site of Anderson Park.

The Pheasant Aircraft Company moves from Memphis, Missouri, to Fond du Lac. The new owners—Tom Meiklejohn, Andre Bechaud and Florian Manor—hire Steve Wittman as test pilot.

The city of La Crosse purchases Salzer Field as a municipal airport.

Roy Larson dies when a student he is instructing freezes at the stick and drives his biplane into the ground.

World War I veteran Harold Bretting organizes the Ashland Aeronautical Association to build an airport.

The Brown Deer Airport is transformed into the Holterhoff Airport when Bill Williams leaves to become chief test pilot for the Invincible airplane in Manitowoc.

In Eagle River, the Otter Rapids Field opens as part of McCullough's Otter Rapids Golf Course.

Nellie Zabel Willhite and "Pard," Kohler, 1929. (Kohler Co. Archives)

Howard Dessert, Warren Winn and J. J. Altenberg incorporate the Mosinee Airport Company, secure an option on 35 acres of land and build a hangar.

Eric Lindberg, Karl Hagen, H.A. DeBaufer, George Schmidt and Fred Schlintz organize North American Airways and lease 100 acres of the Michael Wittman family farm on the edge of Menasha for an airport. Neenah industrialist Frank A. Whiting donates $5,000 for a hangar and the airfield is named Whiting Field in honor of Frank's father.

Clinton Berry opens Berry's Dells Airport on sixty acres of land near Wisconsin Dells.

The newly-organized Stevens Point Airways Corporation purchases 67 acres northeast of the city for an airport and builds a hangar.

The Kohler Company takes delivery of a Ryan Brougham monoplane, "sister ship" of Lindbergh's *Spirit of St. Louis.*

With Stan La Parle as pilot, Walter J. Kohler travels to the Republican National Convention in Kansas City in his new Ryan Brougham airplane; the flight takes 6.5 hours.

Milwaukee's Alonzo Cudworth American Legion Post sponsors its second Commercial Airplane Tour, with stops scheduled at 20 Wisconsin cities.

At Wausau, Alexander Airport is formally opened; visitors include the American Legion Tour, Governor Fred Zimmerman and William P. McCracken, first head of the Department of Commerce's Bureau of Aeronautics.

Charles Lindbergh receives an honorary degree from the University of Wisconsin—Madison.

Max Berghammer and Herman Dickoff organize the Marshfield Aerial Service Company and purchase 79 acres from the Gessert family.

■ June 30 - July 28, 1928

Flying a Waco 10, John Wood of Wausau wins the Fourth Annual Ford Reliability Air Tour; the tour is 6,304 air miles from Michigan to Texas, California and Washington, then back east to Wisconsin and Michigan. Wausau is one of the final stops and Wood is greeted with fireworks, sirens and a crowd of fans at Alexander Field.

Walter Kohler starts using his plane, piloted by Werner Bunge, extensively in his successful campaign for Governor of Wisconsin—covering 7,200 miles and visiting 46 of Wisconsin's 71 counties.

The Nekoosa-Edwards Paper Company purchases a $48,000 Ford Tri-Motor and names it the *NEPCO.* NEPCO manager John Alexander then organizes Tri-City Airways Corporation, and purchases 330 acres on the southern edge of Wisconsin Rapids to be known as Tri-Cities Airport, "the largest all weather, all way airport in the state."

President Calvin Coolidge spends a month at the Cedar Island Lodge on the Brule River in Douglas County; army air corps pilots fly the President's mail into and out of Superior.

Four Hamilton Metalplanes go into service on Northwest's air-to-rail passenger and mail route.

On Washington Island, the Island Holstein Breeders Association is entertained by the new Cherryland Airways plane from Sturgeon Bay during their annual picnic. Later in the year, the Washington Island Airport Company is incorporated and prepares a 55-acre site north of Detroit Harbor for an airport.

As a test pilot for Packard Motors, Walter Lees pilots the first diesel-powered airplane, a Stinson "Detroiter," on test flights at Utica, Michigan.

Walter J. Kohler is the first licensed pilot to be elected Governor of Wisconsin.

Racine pilot Ed Hedeen, in his OX 5-powered Waco 10, sets a world record when he completes 283 barrel rolls at Air City near Racine.

Northwest Airways extends service from Milwaukee to Fond du Lac, Oshkosh, Appleton/Menasha and Green Bay; fare from Green Bay to Milwaukee is $17.

Brown County takes over maintenance of Blesch Field in order to accommodate Northwest Airways.

■ 1929
Packard Motors engineer Lionel Woolson and pilot Walter Lees fly their Stinson Detroiter from Detroit to Langley, Virginia, and make the first long-distance flight powered by a diesel engine.

Hamilton Metalplane becomes a division of Boeing Airplane Company. The Milwaukee Metalplane operation is moved to Wichita, and Hamilton Aero Manufacturing is merged with the Standard Steel Adjustable Propeller Company in Pittsburgh.

Governor Walter Kohler names Lester Maitland and John Wood as military aides; Maitland is promoted to Colonel and Wood to Major. John Wood is also named to the Civilian Advisory Committee of the Wisconsin Legislative Interim Committee on Aviation.

With Irl Beach as pilot, the Invincible Metal Furniture Co. of Manitowoc test flies its first four-place cabin monoplane.

The City of West Bend leases 96 acres for an airport after learning that it will be on the Milwaukee-Green Bay Airway.

Northwest Airways expands service to Madison's Pennco Field.

Pan-American Airways makes its first order of hundreds of Kohler electric plants to power aviation beacons around the world.

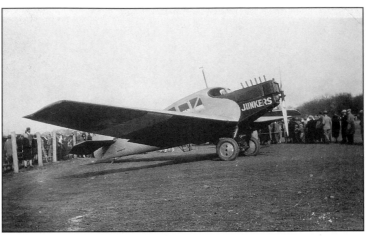

German Junkers monoplane, Milwaukee, 1929. (George Hardie)

With the purchase of a Waco 10, Howard Bibbey is the first person in Rice Lake to own an airplane.

Steve Shalbreck becomes Rhinelander's first airport manager.

The Antigo Lions Club forms a committee to investigate airport requirements and sites.

The Wisconsin Winnebago Indians adopt Governor Walter Kohler into the tribe and, since he is the "Flying Governor," christen him "Red Bird."

J.R. Davis, E.R. Hamilton and John Simpson organize a new Eau Claire Airways.

At Fond du Lac, Steve Wittman charges Wilbur Moersch $15 per flying lesson. Moersch and some friends organize the "3F — Fond du Lac Flying Club," and pool their money to buy one of the three Pheasant biplanes built in Fond du Lac.

With his purchase of a Pheasant aircraft, Vic Cartwright becomes the first Stevens Point pilot to own an airplane.

The Milwaukee Air Terminals Company is incorporated at the Curtiss-Wright airport.

Lee Mulzer runs the Tri-City Flying School at the Tri-City field in Wisconsin Rapids. Among its many students will be "the first Wisconsin priest to learn flying," and Virginia Whittlesey, who becomes the second female transport pilot in the U.S. Milwaukee County airport manager Chris Setvate is killed in a plane crash. Major Stanley Piasecki is appointed his successor.

The federal government reports that more than one half of the 10,700 miles of night air mail routes in the United States are lighted by beacons powered by electric plants manufactured by Wisconsin's Kohler Company; over 600 units are in operation, with the 2 KW model the most popular.

John Wood finishes fourth in the St. Louis-to-Indianapolis Gardner Trophy Race.

South Dakota "aviatrix" Nellie Zabel Willhite flies from Kohler to the new airport at Watertown, South Dakota, to deliver a message from Governor Walter Kohler to South Dakota Governor Bulow.

Governor Walter Kohler flies to Ripon to attend the 75th Anniversary celebration of the Republican Party, along with his newly-appointed military aviation aide, John P. Wood.

Chris Priebe carries Rhinelander's first "air mail" shipment to Oshkosh. His home-built biplane is powered by a 90-horsepower engine designed and built by locals Frank and Al Tank.

In Superior, the Billings Park airport used by local pilots is officially dedicated as the Superior Municipal Airport.

Regular Weather Bureau Stations in Wisconsin are located at La Crosse, Madison, Milwaukee, Green Bay, Wausau and Port Edwards.

The Security National Bank, Sheboygan, mounts a 24-inch, 8 million candlepower rotating beacon on its roof with a 24-inch directional beacon pointing west to the Kohler Airport.

With Charles W. Rouse as pilot, Universal Airlines uses a Fairchild 6-passenger cabin plane to carry anglers to and from Chicago and Rhinelander for weekend fishing trips in the summer.

The Ashland City Airport, two miles south of the city, is dedicated with a fly-in.

Kohler Aviation flies its first passengers in Loening Amphibians from Milwaukee's Maitland Field to Grand Rapids and Detroit, Michigan; Kohler's slogan says the airline is "The Bridge That Spans Lake Michigan."

Ten members of the 120th Field Artillery Band go aloft in the NEPCO tri-motor at Wisconsin Rapids and "play the first band concert ever broadcast from an airplane."

The Airways Communication Station at La Crosse is operating and broadcasting regular weather reports at 45 minutes after the hour, every hour, to pilots on the Chicago-Twin-Cities Airway.

The 32-city Ford Reliability Tour includes stops at Wausau and Milwaukee; 6,000 spectators turn out to watch 37 planes arrive at Milwaukee County Airport.

When Admiral Richard Byrd completes the first flight over the South Pole, news of the flight is reported by Kohler-powered radio.

The Wisconsin American Legion climaxes its membership drive by enlisting twelve aviators to fly the names and dues of 20,000 members from all over the state to Milwaukee.

In Cleveland, Steve Wittman flies a Pheasant H-10 in his first National Air Race.

Lightning strikes his new Lockheed Vega while Wausau aviator John P. Wood is flying home from California; the plane comes apart and Wood dies.

■ **1930**
Wisconsin has 175 licensed and 94 identified aircraft, plus 199 licensed pilots and 88 licensed mechanics. There are also 40 airports: 12 municipal, 22 commercial, 5 intermediate and 1 auxiliary.

Work is completed on the fields and beacons for the "cutoff" to Madison on the Chicago-Twin Cities Airway.

Northwest Airways inaugurates passenger and air mail service from Chicago to Madison with stops at Beloit and Janesville.

The Aeronautics Branch of the Department of Commerce publishes its first Strip Maps of

the Chicago-Milwaukee and Milwaukee-Twin-Cities Airways.

Led by Jack Miller and Warren O'Brien, the Waukesha Aeronautical Association is organized.

Al and Frank Tank move from Rhinelander to Milwaukee, found Tank Aero Engine and begin manufacture of air-cooled V-8 engines modeled on the Curtiss OX-5.

The City of Manitowoc takes over Arnold Schwarz's Manitowoc Airport.

The Milwaukee Glider Club starts to make regular flights from Prospect Hill in Waukesha.

Max Conrad, Jr., of Winona, Minnesota, announces the start of regular air service from Superior/Duluth to the Twin Cities.

Governor Kohler hosts the Mid-West Air Parley at Milwaukee to discuss federal and state aviation policy and coordinate states' policy.

The Wisconsin Conservation Department awards the contract for fire patrol in north-central Wisconsin to the NEPCO tri-motor Ford.

Northwest Airways inaugurates air mail service from Minneapolis to Duluth/Superior, using a Sikorsky amphibian to land in the harbor.

Rhinelander's Ed Bruso and passenger Harry Baldwin are killed in a crash near Green Lake.

The First Wisconsin Air Show is held at Madison and Governor Kohler sponsors an air race from Madison to Kohler; Howard Morey wins the Governor's Cup by flying the 180-mile round trip in 87 minutes; Mel Thompson is second and Madison's Reginald Jackson, third.

Stunt pilot Virginia Whittlesey, Wisconsin Rapids, is the featured attraction at Legion Air Show in Stevens Point.

Northwest Airways pilot Mal Freeberg prevents a serious railroad accident; by dropping his landing flares on the tracks, he signals the engineer of a passenger train to stop before reaching a trestle in flames ahead on the tracks.

Pilot Nellie Zabel Willhite delivers a message from the Governor of South Dakota, accompanied by a hunk of granite from Mt.

Rushmore, to Governor Kohler; dropped from Willhite's plane, the cargo lands safely via parachute at Kohler Airport.

Wisconsin American Legion sponsors an air show and the "Superior-to-Sheboygan" air race as part of its annual convention at Kohler.

On Wisconsin Day at the National Air Races in Chicago, Governor Walter J. Kohler receives a certificate of appreciation "for his indomitable enthusiasm in the cause of aviation" signed by Charles and Anne Lindbergh, Jimmy Doolittle and many other famous aviators.

Steve Wittman flies a Pheasant H-10 in the Chicago Nationals.

Elsie Kamler and Harold Weist, who have both just completed pilot training, exchange marriage vows in a six-passenger Stinson over Superior.

The 30-city Ford Reliability Tour stops in Wausau and Eau Claire; at Eau Claire local radio station WTAQ airs "the first land-air two way radio communication" with the "flying radio station" accompanying the tour.

■ **1931**
After two failed attempts in March and April, Walter Lees and Floyd Brossy set an endurance record of 84 hours, 32 minutes in the air. The plane is a Packard diesel-powered Bellanca 9, and the record will stand until 1986.

David L. Behncke, a native of Cambria, Wisconsin, and four other pilots found the Air Line Pilots Association in Chicago.

The federal government lists 62 airports in Wisconsin, ten with partial or full lighting and with eight more proposed; Milwaukee has five airports, Eagle River three, Madison and Janesville each have two.

Oscar H. Morris, Milwaukee, represents Wisconsin at the National Conference on Uniform Aeronautic Regulatory Laws in Washington, D. C.

The Waukesha Aeronautical Association is reorganized as the Waukesha Aviation Club. In 1931, the Club holds a winter air show, a summer "Air Circus" which attracts 5,000 spectators, and sponsors the visit of Lewis Yancey and his Autogyro.

The Waukesha Flying Club No. 1 is organized and soon purchases its first plane, a Waco 10.

Steve Wittman leaves Fond du Lac's nearly bankrupt Pheasant Aircraft Company to manage the Oshkosh airport. Florian Manor is the new Fond du Lac airport manager.

In Madison, The North Street Airport becomes the home of the Corben Sport Plane Company when Orland "Ace" Corben is hired as airport manager.

A federal survey reveals that Wisconsin has spent $1,087,000 on airports, one of 21 states to surpass the $1 million mark.

Ashland native and Navy Lieutenant Commander Arthur Gavin arranges a stop at the Ashland Airport. Flying a Navy Tri-Motor escorted by five naval pursuit planes, Gavin is en route to Chippewa Falls to deliver Assistant Naval Secretary E.L. Jahnke to the American Legion Convention.

Leo Salkowski of Kewaunee purchases an airplane and begins to lobby civic leaders to build an airport to replace the hayfield currently in use.

Russ Schuetze builds an "Irwin" biplane with a motorcycle engine at his family's church pew factory in Waukesha.

The Janesville City Airport hosts Wiley Post, Harold Gatty and the Lockhead Vega they had flown around the world, the Winnie Mae. The men were invited by Parker Pen executive and aviation enthusiast Ken Parker, who keeps his own planes, including the Parker Duofold, at the airport. Parker purchases his first Stinson this year, and becomes fast friends with Eddie Stinson.

Stiles Whipple reopens the old Beloit Legion-Civic Airport.

The Depression downturn forces Nekoosa-Edwards to sell its tri-motor to pilot and airport manager Lee Mulzer for $1 and his promise to maintain air service at Tri-City Airport.

German air force veteran William Ehrengart starts Land O'Lakes Flying Service on Lake Nagawicka, Delafield, with three floatplanes.

On an experimental flight at Kohler, Anton

Kohler Aviation Amphibian after crashing in Lake Michigan, Milwaukee, 1932. (Debbie Salmon LoGuercio)

Brotz, Sr., takes his open-cockpit Woodson up to 17,050 feet without the aid of oxygen tanks.

Sponsored by the Waukesha Aviation Club, the first ground school at Waukesha Vocational School holds classes.

The dirigible *Akron* flies over Kenosha, Racine and Milwaukee.

Fog blankets the state, grounding most of the planes participating in the American Legion membership flight; Wisconsin Rapids pilot Rodger Davy dies when his plane crashes near Coloma thirty minutes after take-off.

■ 1932
Federal and state officials unveil a 150-foot stone monument atop Kill Devil Hill near Kitty Hawk, North Carolina, to commemorate the first flight of Orville and Wilbur Wright in 1903; floodlights illuminate the monument and an electric beacon is mounted on tip the pillar, reserve power is supplied by a Kohler Company electric power plant.

In Milwaukee, 75,000 spectators watch the "greatest military demonstration ever witnessed in the city," including a mock attack by 50 airplanes fired upon by anti-aircraft batteries.

Clyde Lee saves Oshkosh from a major banking crisis when he flies half a million dollars from Milwaukee to Oshkosh to feed a run on the bank.

The American Legion cancels its 1932 Air Round-Up, but Racine's Carl Godske flies his community's memberships to Milwaukee anyway. Godske also starts the Racine Flying Service at his own airport on the west side of Sturtevant.

Students at Wausau high school design their yearbook on an aeronautics theme. They solicit and receive letters from aviation notables including Amelia Earhart and Dr. Hugo Eckener, the German engineer and builder of the *Graf Zeppelin* airship.

In Janesville, the city airport hangar housing nine planes and a glider—including Ken Parker's Stinson—is destroyed by fire.

Fred Holterhoff dies in an automobile crash; partner Carl Koeffler remains as manager of the Weeks-Holterhoff Aircraft Company.

Eighteen-year-old Ruth Harman decides to give flying a try. By March 1932 she has her private pilot's license and by 1936, transport and instructor's ratings.

The federal government reports that monthly fees for a heated hangar at Milwaukee County Airport start at $40 for small Cessna, Eaglerock, Pheasant, Stearman, Travel Air and Waco airplanes; increase to $60 for larger Laird, Fokker-Universal and Fairchild machines; and grow to $80 for a Ford Tri-Motor, Fokker F-10 and Sikorsky Amphibian; space in an unheated hangar rents for about one-half.

Steve Wittman films the departure of Clyde Lee and crew, setting off on the first leg of their flight across the Atlantic to Norway. Twenty days later, Clyde and co-pilot John Bochkon are in Newfoundland, taking off to cross the Atlantic; they may have reached Great Britain, but no trace of the men or the plane is ever found.

A Kohler Aviation Amphibian, with seven on-board, crashes in Lake Michigan shortly after take-off at Maitland Field; no one is injured and the plane is recovered and towed ashore.

The Goodyear Blimp is at Milwaukee.

Kohler Aviation flies the winner of the college football score forecasting contest to Detroit to watch Marquette's squad play the Detroit University team.

In an event sponsored by the Waukesha Aviation Club, air racer Jimmy Haizlip takes the Waukesha county board for airplane rides to lobby for their support of a county airport.

The Air Marine Terminal in Milwaukee, later known as the Seadrome, is completed in time to be used briefly by Kohler Airways amphibian planes. Although the Seadrome does replace the adjacent Maitland Airport, Milwaukeeans continue to refer to both of the facilities as "Maitland Airport."

■ 1933

Wisconsin enacts legislation empowering villages, cities, towns and counties to regulate airports, landing fields, aircraft, aeronauts, air traffic and schools of aeronautics; local park or harbor commissions may acquire land for airports, build and lease hangars and facilities for amphibian aircraft; and all pilots and aircraft must have a federal, but not a state, license.

In 1933, the Aeronautics Bureau counts 231 aircraft in Wisconsin and 304 pilots.

Northwest Airways pilot Mal Freeburg receives the first Congressional Air Mail Medal of Honor after he safely lands a Ford Tri-Motor minus one engine and one landing wheel at Durand.

In Janesville, Art Hodge, Joe Bouzaine, Floyd Stone, Dee MacFarland, Pete

In Portage, the old Aeronautics Bureau landing field has been phased out and is replaced by the Bob and Chester Mael strip north of the city.

Northwest Airways pulls out of Appleton and the Whiting Airport closes.

Stiles Whipple moves over to the Wisconsin Air College Field and reopens it as the Rock County Airport.

With Joe Doerflinger as pilot, Kohler Aviation makes the first "cross-the-lake" air

Craycraft is in the lake again—he and Pat Gossett spend eight frigid hours perched on the wing of their airplane, forced down about 50 miles out from Grand Haven, Michigan.

In its *Spirit of 3.2%* airplane, Midwest Airways flies three of the first cases of Milwaukee beer brewed since the repeal of Prohibition to President Franklin Roosevelt in Washington; thanks to Midwest, the Milwaukee beer is the first to arrive in the capital.

Northwest Airways pulls out of La Crosse after the city refuses to improve the airport. The federal aeronautics bureau soon follows by removing its weather and radio gear. Local pilot Roy Pfafflin saves the day by developing an airport on French Island, which is later leased by La Crosse County.

The Chicago World's Fair blimp is featured at the state fair; it carries passengers from the fair to downtown Milwaukee for a fare of $3.

Taking advantage of a $14,796 federal work-relief grant and $5,000 in county money, the Waukesha county board votes to build an airport.

■ 1934

An estimated 12,000 spectators attend the big September air show at Curtiss-Wright Field; featured are stunter Ruth Harman, who makes "10 perfect turns" while in a tail spin; "Buck" Leighton, who does aerobatics in a Ford Tri-Motor; Virginia Whittelsey, who executes a perfect dead stick landing; "Farmer" Dick Granere performing comedy stunts; and fledgling parachutist Herman "Fish" Salmon, making his second leap from an airplane.

Stoughton native Clairemont Egtvedt begins design work for Boeing on the plane that will evolve into the B-17.

■ February 9, 1934

U.S. Post Office cancels air mail contracts with private carriers and employs army pilots.

■ May 8, 1934

After twelve army pilots die carrying the mail, the Post Office again contracts with private carriers.

Top: U. S. Army Curtiss Condor bomber, La Crosse, 1934. Above: Curtiss P-6, Milwaukee. (George Hardie)

Tumelson and Owen Higgins revive the City Airport and organize the Eaglet Aero Club.

Brown County takes over the privately managed Blesch Field and renames it Brown County Airport.

In Madison, the Mid-west Air Transport Company is out of business.

mail flight from Milwaukee to Detroit; passengers on first flight are Kohler President John B. Kohler, vice-president William Pabst Jr., and board member Joseph Johnson.

Kohler Aviation pilots Roy Pickering and Ben Craycraft spend seven hours afloat in their Loening after engine failure forces it down in Lake Michigan. Later in the year,

Pennsylvania Airlines purchases Kohler Aviation and expands service to New York City.

Kewaunee receives a federal grant of $11,000 to improve the forty acres it purchased north of the city for an airport.

In La Crosse, Ken Reed and Jack Fanta start the Fanta-Reed Air Service, move to Pfafflin Airport and build a hangar.

Felix Waitkus trains pilots while he and Anton Brotz prepare a Lockheed-Vega, formerly flown by Jimmy Doolittle, for a trans-Atlantic flight to Lithuania.

The Curtiss-Wright airport in Milwaukee hosts an air show featuring locally and nationally known aviators including Art Gobel, Jimmy Haizlip, Frank Hawkes, Steve Wittman, Roscoe Turner and Wisconsin Rapids' Virginia Whittlesey, "the only licensed girl transport pilot."

With the help of a federal public works grant, Outagamie County appropriates $11,000 to purchase 110 acres for a county airport northeast of Appleton on Ballard Road.

The Aeronautics Bureau reports that Wisconsin has only three radio-equipped airplanes, all of them one-way.

■ 1935
United States Senator Bronson Cutting, New Mexico, dies in an airline crash in Missouri; the tragedy prompts a 3-year Congressional investigation of the Bureau of Air Commerce and results in the Civil Aeronautics Act of 1938.

Three local men die, including pilot Oscar Chapin, when their Waco biplane crashes near Chippewa Falls.

The new Corben "Super Ace," is featured on the cover of *Popular Aviation Magazine.*

Stevens Point receives a federal grant to build a hangar and make other improvements, in response to which the city purchases the Stevens Point Airways Corporation airport.

The new Kewaunee airport opens on Memorial Day weekend with a huge celebration featuring a squad of Army Air Corps and an estimated 25,000 people.

Employed by the S.C. Johnson Company, Air City manager Ed Hedeen flies their new

Sikorsky S38 amphibian off the company's seaplane base inside Racine harbor.

At Fond du Lac, Wilbur Moersch and Al Devoe are the new airport managers.

A lakefront air show in Milwaukee is offered during the Midsummer Festival; stunters are Dick Granere and Buck Leighton with Fish Salmon performing a "delayed" parachute jump in which he free falls 8,000 feet before opening his chute.

Four Chicago-area flyers die when their plane crashes at Curtiss-Wright in late July.

The new French Island Airport at La Crosse is officially dedicated by Governor Phil La Follette.

Felix Waitkus crosses the Atlantic and damages his plane while landing in a field in Ireland; the goal of the flight was for Waitkus, an American of Lithuanian heritage, to complete the first non-stop flight from the U.S. to Lithuania.

Legislation to reinstate former General Billy Mitchell is introduced into Congress but will die in the House Military Affairs Committee.

In a benefit air show at Racine for injured pilot Ed Russell, Dean Crites of Waukesha steals the show when he executes "the hazardous and extremely difficult maneuver of picking a handkerchief from the ground with a wing tip."

The federal Works Progress Administration announces an aviation improvement program for Wisconsin.

Pilots Carlyle Godske, Racine; J. B. King, Kenosha; H. A. Robinson, Madison; Archie Towle, Wausau; and Lee Promen will fly to 18 Wisconsin airports to gather memberships for the Wisconsin American Legion and deliver them to the state convention at Beaver Dam.

Guided by radio beacons powered by Kohler electric plants at Hawaii, Midway, Wake, Guam, Manila and Canton, the first Pan-American Airways China Clipper makes its first trans-Pacific flight from the U.S. to China.

■ 1936
Billy Mitchell dies and is buried in Milwaukee.

Alexander Field becomes the Wausau Municipal Airport.

Amelia Earhart speaks to students and faculty at the Teacher's College in Wausau, and Kenosha pilot Ruth Harman helps welcome Amelia Earhart to her local high school.

The city of Merrill opens an airport. Frank Shoblaska, manager of the Manitowoc Airport, dies when his plane hits an "air pocket" while stunt-flying at Livingston.

The new Eagle River Municipal Airport is dedicated.

The Fond du Lac Airport sponsors an air show featuring a night flight in Howard Morey's 12-passenger Ford Tri-Motor and Fish Salmon's "415th Successful Parachute Jump."

Eight aviators deliver a record number of memberships to the Wisconsin American Legion convention at Milwaukee.

■ 1937
The airship *Hindenberg* explodes, with heavy loss of life, while mooring at Lakehurst, New Jersey.

The federal government lists 53 airports in Wisconsin, 18 of them full or partially lighted, along with 204 aircraft, 7 gliders and 209 pilots.

The legislature creates, but does not fund, the Wisconsin Aeronautics Board.

Archie Towle becomes manager of the Wausau Municipal Airport.

The Jackson County Flyers Association is organized; officers are Dr. Robert Krohn, Vern Voss and Jerry Hoonsben.

Former Governor Walter Kohler sells his Ryan-Brougham to his long-time personal pilot, Mel Thompson. Thompson also acquires Anton Brotz's Woodson and becomes airport manager at Kohler.

The new Superior Municipal Airport, on the south side of the city near the fairgrounds, is dedicated and prompts the city to alter its motto from "Where Sail Meets Rail" to "Where Air and Sail Meets Rail."

Wisconsin has 130 licensed and 74 unlicensed aircraft in the state, plus seven gliders. There are 208 licensed pilots: 92 transport pilots, 76 private, 25 limited commercial and 15 amateur.

After significant bickering between the county and Ray Pfafflin, the La Crosse County board votes to abandon the airport on French Island. Within a few months, however, the federal government leases the field and begins to improve it. Another airport, called Brice's Prairie, opens north of Onalaska as well.

■ 1938

Aviators from all over Wisconsin take part in observance of National Air Mail Week, May 15-21.

Lucille and Felix Gauthier open the McDill Airport on 78 acres southeast of Stevens Point.

Local aviators rent some farmland and Boyceville has its first airport.

The Madison Municipal Airport is completed on the northeast edge of the city. Howard Morey becomes the first manager of Madison's new Municipal Airport.

Outagamie County builds three grass runways and a hangar at its Ballard Road Airport.

Ben Towle, one of Wisconsin's first Piper Cub dealers, and his Badger Airways are in residence at the Brown Deer/Holterhoff Airport in Milwaukee County.

Will Haase, Sr. and his son Will, Jr. come into Fond du Lac in their "flying coffin." The Chicagoans will eventually buy the Fond du Lac Airport and lead the effort to relocate the operation to the west side of the city.

A $38,000 stone and steel hangar, with room for up to 14 airplanes, is built as a public works project at Waukesha County.

Ten planes take part in the American Legion Armistice Day Round-Up.

■ 1939

Nazi Germany invades Poland and World War II begins in Europe.

Glider pilot Ted Bellak sets a record for over-the-water gliding when he soars from Sturgeon Bay in Door County, across Lake Michigan to Frankfort, Michigan.

Walter A. Olen, President of Clintonville's Four-Wheel Drive Corporation, trades a truck for a four-place Waco airplane for business travel. With help from the Four-Wheel-Drive Corporation, Waupaca County and Clintonville improve the airport; Olen then purchases a Howard monoplane.

Vic Bloyer's Piper J-3 Cub, Tomah, 1940. (Dave Rezin)

Louis Wuilleumier buys a Waco 10 and begins barnstorming in Dane and surrounding counties.

The King's Gateway Resort opens in Land O'Lakes; its landing field will eventually replace the old Land O'Lakes Airport.

Ed Baesemann inaugurates his Merrill Flying Service with an air show featuring fifteen airplanes.

Dean and Dale Crites open a Piper Cub dealership in Waukesha. In a year they'll organize the Spring City Flying Service.

Northwest Airlines begins serving Milwaukee County Airport with DC-3s that can carry 21 passengers and cruise at 170 MPH.

Alexander Ward leaves Eau Claire and the State Street Airport all but closes.

Russell Van Galder obtains his limited commercial license and joins Stiles Whipple as co-manager of the Rock County Airport.

The Wisconsin Division of the NAA holds its annual convention at McDill Airport near Stevens Point.

■ 1940

Civilian Pilot Training Programs begin through out Wisconsin, with Milwaukee's Midwest Airways one of the largest CPT contractors in the state. Louis Wuilleumier starts a CPT program at Madison's Royal

Airport, and programs get of the ground in Janesville, Stevens Point, Superior and Beloit as well.

While inactive through much of the 1930s due to the Depression, the West Bend Municipal Airport is now home to about 15 planes.

Stiles Whipple leaves the Rock County Airport to become an airline pilot. Co-manager Russell Van Galder and his wife Marge, who will become a ground-school instructor, are now the sole managers.

The Town of Washington purchases the airport on Washington Island.

Fifty airplanes and 96 visitors attend the "breakfast flight" fly-in at Waukesha County Airport.

James Anderson buys the city airport when Kenosha balks at renewing its lease. Named manager, Ruth Harman is the first female airport manager in the state.

Sheboygan native, World War I vet and former Kohler Company pilot Werner Bunge pilots DC-3s for KLM, Royal Dutch Airways. Facing the threat of Nazi invasion the Dutch government moves its gold reserves to Britain via Bunge's DC-3.

The Sturgeon Bay chapter of the National Aeronautics Association sponsors an air show at their Cherryland Field.

Former "Flying Governor" Walter Kohler passes away, aged 65.

The federal public works project completed at Milwaukee County Airport this year includes a new, two story brick administration building to replace the converted farm house in use since 1927.

Northwest Airways considers restoring passenger service to Green Bay, but the war will intervene before the plan is implemented.

Governor Julius Heil selects the Milwaukee County Airport over Madison as the base for the newly-formed 126th Observation Squadron of the Wisconsin National Guard.

Wisconsin Adjutant General Ralph Immell names Captain Paul Meyers to command the 126th Observation Squadron.

Opening day of the state fair is "Aviation and Defense Day" and features an overflight in formation of 75 airplanes.

At Camp McCoy, 65,000 National Guard and Army units take part in the largest peacetime military maneuvers since World War I; flying out of Madison Airport, a total of 56 Army

Air Corps machines are scheduled to take part, including P36 pursuit planes, B-18A light bombers and B-17 Flying Fortress heavy bombers.

The infamous Armistice Day storm grounds the American Legion Membership Round-Up.

■ **1941**
The State Planning Board is assigned responsibility for airport development under executive direction.

Rhinelander City Manager Ted Wardwell convinces the Oneida County Board to transfer to the city 106 acres of former county poor farm land for use as an airport.

The City of Antigo purchases 180 acres for an airport and lays out a north-south and east-west runway.

The Superior Municipal Airport is named in honor of retiring Mayor and aviation advocate, Bryn Ostby.

The Milwaukee County Board adopts a resolution naming the airport General Mitchell Field.

The Rock County Board appropriates $45,000 to purchase 377 acres for an airport.

The Waukesha Aviation Club hosts 57 airplanes and pilots of the Wisconsin Civil Air Corps to the last large "breakfast flight" held before American entry into World War II.

■ **December 7-8, 1941**
Japanese forces attack Pearl Harbor, the Philippines and other American military bases in the Pacific; the United States enters World War II.

Stringent restrictions on non-military flying are enacted, all but halting non-commercial, civilian aviation.

The Civil Aeronautics Administration prohibits all "Japanese or suspected Japanese" from flying in the United States.

The federal government notifies air port managers that the "emergency requires immediate organization Civil Air Patrol."

■ **1942**
U.S. Army Air Force begins training 200 pilots in gliders at Fond du Lac; the program is later moved to Antigo.

Tornado damage, Tomah, 1948. (Dave Rezin)

Using a federal grant the City of Eau Claire purchases 400 acres of land just north of the city for an airport.

While piloting his B-18 bomber over Java in the western Pacific, Lt. Colonel Austin Straubel is shot down by Japanese fighters; a day later he dies of wounds suffered in the engagement.

The Douglas County Town of Highland proposes construction of a military air base, two miles square, to protect the strategically valuable head of the lakes region.

From the decks of the U.S.S. Hornet, General Jimmy Doolittle launches his air raid bombers on Tokyo. Wisconsin native Admiral Marc Mitscher commands the Hornet and Doolittle's B-25 Mitchell Bombers are named in honor of General Billy Mitchell.

The U.S. Army Air Force leases General Mitchell Field for training and other war purposes.

■ 1943
The Penokee Lumber and Veneer Company, Mellen, begins milling birch into plywood as thin as "1/85th" to be used on the world's largest airplane, built in California by Howard Hughes.

The Legislature abolishes the Aeronautics Board and assigns Aeronautics functions to the State Planning Board.

The War Department officially designates the Milwaukee County Airport as Billy Mitchell Field.

Captured Italian and Japanese airplanes are among the war-related displays at the state fair.

■ 1944
Alexander Field, Wisconsin Rapids, and Mitchell Field, Milwaukee are among the airports used to house German prisoners-of-war.

Governor Goodland appoints a Special Aviation Advisory Board to recommend to the 1945 Legislature the best course for the state to follow in air transportation.

With the Four Wheel Drive Corporation as the majority stockholder, Wisconsin Central Airlines is organized at Clintonville; Four Wheel Drive executive Francis M. Higgins is named president.

Variety Show at the state fair includes a "Salute to Victory" ending with a fireworks display entitled "Bombing Berlin."

Poplar native Richard Bong achieves aerial victory number forty to become America's "Ace of Aces."

■ 1945
The Legislature establishes the State Aeronautics Commission with Howard A. Morey, Middleton, Chairman; Karl S. Reynolds, Sturgeon Bay, Vice Chairman; Dr. L.O. Simenstad, Osceola, Secretary; Dr. A.G. Sell, Ashland and T.M. Wardell of Rhinelander as Commissioners.

The atomic bomb is dropped on Hiroshima and Nagasaki; Wisconsin Dells native Leon Smith serves as back-up weaponer on the Nagasaki mission.

Japanese government accepts Allied peace terms, bringing an end to World War II and a boom to civilian aviation in the United States.

Major Richard I. Bong is killed in a test flight of a Lockheed F-80; the Superior Airport is renamed in his honor.

■ 1946
The Aeronautics Commission begins work; hires its first employees, F.E. Wolf, and Carl Guell; initiates the air marker program that will make Wisconsin the best air-marked state in the nation; starts broadcasting aviation weather reports over the state network; and publishes its first official airport map

U.S. Congress enacts the Federal Airport Act authorizing grants-in-aid beginning July 1, 1946, for construction of airports included in the National Airport Plan.

Units of the 126th Fighter Group become the first squadron of the Wisconsin Air National Guard.

The Civil Aeronautics Board certifies Northwest Airlines to serve 1,400 route miles and 43 cities with metropolitan terminals at Chicago, Milwaukee, Green Bay, Minneapolis/St. Paul and Duluth-Superior.

A.E. Padags attempts to launch "North Central Airlines" at Stevens Point; dubbed "The Indian Trail Route," the airline makes only one promotional flight to Milwaukee.

■ 1947
General Hoyt Vandenberg is named chief of staff of the United States Air Force.

The State Planning Board prepares a State Airport Plan for the Aeronautics Commission and the legislature appropriates $500,000 for airport aid.

Oneida County begins joint ownership of Rhinelander Airport and La Crosse's French Island Airport is dedicated.

Howard Hughes briefly flies the 200-ton, "Spruce Goose", substantial parts of which are made of birch plywood from Mellen, Wisconsin.

Flying Steve Wittman's Buster, Bill Brennand wins the Goodyear Cup.

■ 1948
Wisconsin has a total of 157 airports, including 56 municipal and 91 commercial airports.

The Janesville School of Vocational and Adult Education conducts the first FAA approved aircraft and engine school in Wisconsin.

Wisconsin Central Airline purchases six Lockheed Electra 10As, moves to Madison and adopts "Herman" a mallard duck painted blue as its logo, whichs gives the airline the nickname, "The Blue Goose."

When Wisconsin Central Airlines flies summer visitors there, Land O' Lakes, population 400, becomes the smallest community in the nation with regular airline service.

Thirty-four passengers and three crew members die when a Northwest Airlines Martin 2-0-2 crashes near Fountain City in Buffalo County; at the time it is the worst aircraft accident in Wisconsin history

■ 1949
The Madeline Island Airport is dedicated.

Wisconsin Civil Air Patrol members take to the air to search for an Air Force pilot down in Lake Michigan; CAP members Archie Weidner, Milton Bender and Kenneth Mortag of Milwaukee plus Isabel Carpenter and Sarah Lathrop, Waukesha, later receive awards for Meritorious Service during the search.

■ 1950
North Korean forces invade South Korea and the Korean War begins.

The Aeronautics Commission inaugurates its Soil Conservation Air Tour Program for county farm agents and farmers.

Twenty-five Wisconsin pilots organize a

Women's Flight of the CAP; officers are Lieutenants Dora M. Drews, Nellie Bilstad, Jeanette Kapus, Elaine Szelesty, Lois Joyce.

The Wisconsin Cessna Air Caravan, eighteen aircraft and fifty-two people, flies to Guatemala.

Wisconsin Central Airlines purchases six DC-3s.

■ **1951**
Wisconsin has 1382 active aircraft and 716 inactive aircraft.

Fifty-one thousand people attend the Wisconsin Air Pageant organized by Bill Lotzer at Curtiss-Wright Airport.

Beloit native, West Point grad and Air Force pilot Colonel Fred Ascani, sets a world record in the 100 kilometer race at Cleveland when he flies an F-86 Sabre Jet at 605.69 MPH.

The Aeronautics Commission publishes its first annual Pilot's Guide, which lists all operating airports in Wisconsin.

Led by Howard Morey, twenty Wisconsin Cessna owners make a Caravan flight to Los Angeles to board a commercial flight to Hawaii.

Arthur P. Warner, Wisconsin's first aviator, passes away.

■ **1952**
General Nathan Twining succeeds Hoyt Vandenberg as chief of staff of the United States Air Force.

Thirty-one Wisconsin airports plow snow off the runways; four pack it down with rollers.

Wisconsin Central Airlines changes its name to North Central, merges with Lake Central Airlines, elects Howard Morey President and moves its offices from Madison to Minneapolis.

Led by Lloyd Bell and Marge Van Galder, the Wisconsin Airport Owners Association is organized.

Eight OMNI air navigation stations are erected in Wisconsin.

■ **1953**
In a hangar at Curtiss-Wright Airport, thirty local aviators join Paul Poberezny to organize the Experimental Aircraft Association; the

First EAA Fly-In, Curtiss-Wright Airport, Milwaukee, 1953. (George Hardie)

organization holds its first fly-in at Bill Lotzer's Milwaukee Air Pageant.

Northeastern Wisconsin takes part in an experimental flight reporting program to distinguish civilian from potential enemy aircraft.

Wisconsin passes a new aircraft registration program to take the place of the personal property tax; fee for a J-3 Cub is $16; Cessna 170, $28; Bonanza 35, $34.

Madison's Four Lakes Airport closes.

■ **1954**
A U.S. Air Force helicopter tours the state to promote enlistment.

Howard Morey resigns as President of North Central Airlines and is succeeded by Hal N. Carr.

With private airport owners uninterested, the Wisconsin Airport Owners Association disbands.

Twelve Wisconsin airports are Unicom communication stations.

Aviation pioneer Alfred Lawson dies.

■ **1955**
The Airport Zoning Act is passed, protecting navigable airspace and authorizing the Aeronautics Commission to control the erection of tall structures in the state.

The Defense Department proposes stationing Nike anti-aircraft missiles at nine sites in southeastern Wisconsin, including Maitland Field.

Five thousand people attend Aviation Progress Day and help dedicate the new 3,000 foot runway at Waukesha County Airport.

Narrated by Carl Guell of the Aeronautics Commission, the instructional film "Airplanes are for Susan and Billy" is available for elementary schools.

■ **1956**
New airports are scheduled for Kenosha and Ashland, part of a $353,333 federal aid package for Wisconsin.

Milwaukee's Maitland Field closes as Nike anti-aircraft missiles are installed on the site.

Wisconsin Air National Guard Captain Paul Poberezny safely lands a B-25 with one engine out on the 3,000-foot runway at Waukesha County Airport.

Capital Airlines 44-passenger Viscounts are the first turbo-props at Mitchell Field.

■ **1957**
Land is purchased by the Fond du Lac county board for a new airport southwest of Fond du Lac.

Business people from Stevens Point, Marshfield and Wisconsin Rapids begin talks about joining with Wausau to build a "tri-county" airport. Stevens Point and Portage county people are willing, as are Wausau and Marathon county, but Wood county is not interested.

■ **1958**
Nekoosa-Edwards Paper Company purchases a Beechcraft Twin Bonanza and resurfaces the old Tri-City airport with sulfite road binder.

Hale O'Malley begins work on Wisconsin's northernmost airstrip at Cornucopia.

The Adams County Airport is established when Leslie Flott builds an 1800-foot runway southeast of Adams.

■ **1959**
The EAA fly-in outgrows Curtiss-Wright Airport and moves to Rockford, Illinois.

Steve Shalbreck ends his 31-year career as manager of the Rhinelander Airport.

Appleton aviator Karl Baldwin proposes that Outagamie County construct a combination air, rail and bus terminal southwest of Appleton.

The new Ashland Municipal Airport opens.

North Central Airlines begins regular service to Outagamie County Airport.

■ 1960

Airline passenger traffic in Wisconsin increases 10.7 percent to 586,522.

The Portage County Board votes in favor of sharing a regional airport with Wood County.

The Wood County Board votes against sharing a regional airport with Portage County.

Fox Cities business and political leaders propose that Outagamie and Winnebago counties build a regional airport in northern Winnebago County west of Neenah.

Earl Pingel's Sky-Eye publishes the first Wisconsin airport guide to feature aerial photos of airports.

■ 1961

Flying for Northwest Airlines at Milwaukee, Boeing 720Bs are the first jet airliners to serve Wisconsin.

Accepting John Alexander's donation of the land and improvements, five municipalities incorporate the Municipal Airport Commission for Alexander Field-South Wood County Airport and take over management of the former Tri-City Airport.

Winnebago County Board rejects the proposal for a joint airport with Outagamie County.

The Sheboygan County Airport opens with Harry Chaplin as FBO.

■ 1962

Outagamie County purchases 1,302 acres and begins work on a new county airport.

Adams County Legion Field Airport is dedicated.

The runways at the Portage airport are surfaced and seventeen aircraft are now based on the premises. Work is started on a 134-foot hangar.

Two sod runways are open to the public at the new Monroe airport.

■ 1963

The Fraser-Nelson Shipyard, Superior, donates the pilot house of an ore carrier to the Superior Aviation Club for use as a club house at the airport.

In September, helicopters carrying President John F. Kennedy and his entourage land at the Ashland Airport after a tour of the Apostle Islands. Two months later Kennedy dies, and shortly after the Ashland Airport is named in his honor.

A North Central Airlines DC-3 takes 1,000 passengers aloft during an Air Show at Stevens Point.

■ 1964

An 800-foot-long tunnel carries Howell Avenue beneath the new 8,000-foot runway at Mitchell Field.

With a modified Twin Beech, Roy Shwery begins Midstate Air Commuter service from Marshfield.

■ 1965

The new $2.8 million Outagamie County airport is dedicated; the airport is served by Max Sagunsky's Maxair, a feeder line to Milwaukee and Chicago, by North Central Airlines and the newly-incorporated, publicly-held Air Wisconsin Airline.

A new terminal is built at the Austin Straubel Airport with 40 aircraft now based there.

Appleton business leaders sell stock in the first publicly held commuter airline in the United States. Called Fox Cities Airline at first, the corporation is renamed Air Wisconsin.

■ 1966

For the first year, one million passengers use Mitchell Field.

Wild Rose's Idlewild, once a busy airport, closes.

Nine crewmen die when an Air Force B-52 on a training mission crashes near Hauer in Barron County.

■ 1967

The Department of Transportation is organized.

Fritz Wolf is appointed first Administrator of Aeronautics.

The Aeronautics Commission continues as an advisory body to the Department of Transportation under the name "Council on Aeronautics."

The runway at Stevens Point is extended to 6,000 feet to accommodate jet aircraft.

The estimated cost of the new Central Wisconsin Regional Airport is $3 million, with Marathon County paying 72% and Portage County 28% of the local share.

■ 1968

Air Force Captain Lance Sijan, Milwaukee, is shot down over Viet Nam; Sijan's heroism will win him the Congressional Medal of Honor.

Phil Leyda organizes the Tri-County Airport Improvement Corporation to support the Lone Rock Airport.

Mauston and New Lisbon purchase land between the two cities and build a grass runway to serve both communities.

■ 1969

Funding of State Airport projects under the Upper Great Lakes Grant is begun.

The Central Wisconsin Airport, Mosinee, opens as the first regional airport in Wisconsin.

A new airport is constructed at Baraboo/Dells.

■ 1970

Astronaut Jim Lovell is the command pilot on the Apollo 13 space flight.

The EAA moves its fly-in to Oshkosh.

The Division of Aeronautics initiates Air Transportation services for other departments of state government.

Langlade County assumes ownership and management of Antigo City Airport.

A new airport is constructed at Black River Falls.

■ 1971

The new $190,000 Black River Falls Airport is dedicated; Jim Southward, Bloomer; Vic Bloyer, Tomah; and Eldon McDaniel, Merrimac, perform aerobatics for the 5,000 spectators.

The Bellanca plant in Osceola is destroyed by fire.

■ 1972

Thirteen people die in a mid-air collision between North Central Convair and an Air Wisconsin de Haviland Otter over Lake Winnebago.

Work begins on a 4,000-foot, blacktopped runway at the Tomahawk airport.

Jerry Ritz and EAA Chapter 243 attempting man-powered flight, Antigo, 1976.

The city of Amery takes over the local airport and, with federal and state aid, makes improvements.

■ 1973

An embargo on oil from the Middle East prompts an energy crisis in the United States.

The Wisconsin Aerospace Education Association is organized.

■ 1974

The number of passengers using Mitchell Field exceeds the two million mark for the first time.

Nearly 250,000 airline passengers depart from Austin Straubel Airport, narrowing Madison's lead as the second-busiest airport in the state.

Dane County assumes ownership of the airport now officially named Dane County Regional-Truax Field.

■ 1975

After a sixteen-year wait, Deke Slayton makes his first space flight and, at age 51, becomes the oldest person yet to fly in space.

Manitowoc County purchases the Manitowoc airport, accepting the city's thirty-year old request to do so.

Osceola mourns the loss of Doc Simenstad, who practiced medicine in the area for over fifty years and built the village airport.

■ 1976

Instead of the Lone Rock Airport, the Sextonville airport in Richland County receives state funding for a master plan study

■ 1977

Rhinelander/Oneida County Airport builds a new 6,800-foot east-west runway at a cost of $7 million.

Ben Silko retires as manager of the Lone Rock Flight Service Station.

Restauranteur Don Quinn purchases a Boeing 377 Stratocruiser and pilot Dick Schmidt, co-pilot Tom Thomas and flight engineer Wally Waligorski land the plane on the 2600-foot runway at Dodgeville.

Bill Brennand, Byron Frederickson and Chuck Andreas start rehabilitating a tri-motor Stinson which Frederickson trucked back from Alaska in pieces a few years earlier.

■ 1978

The federal Airline Deregulation Act changes commercial aviation throughout the U.S.A.

The Aeronautics Bureau begins an aerial photographic survey of Wisconsin; completed in 1980, the survey requires 30,000 photos shot at 10,000 feet to cover the entire state.

Rhinelander's new $7 million, 6800-foot runway is ready for use.

■ 1979

The Aeronautics Bureau reports 3,962 Wisconsin-based aircraft, 347 airports and 14,213 pilots.

Tanya Cunningham, Madison, and Caroline Morey, Middleton, place fifth in the 2,600 mile Hughes Airwest Air Race Classic from California to Milwaukee.

Dave and Peggy Weiman, Oregon, publish the first issue of Wisconsin Flyer Magazine; a year later, it is renamed Midwest Flyer.

North Central and Southern Airlines merge to form Republic Airlines.

After a collision between an airliner and a small plane kills 150 people at San Diego, the Milwaukee county board transportation committee considers a ban on general aviation at Mitchell Field.

■ 1980

The international oil crisis results in reduced supplies and much higher prices for aviation fuel in Wisconsin.

Lakeland Airlines begins commuter service between Rice Lake and Minneapolis.

Led by Edgerton's Sy Jana, private owners of publicly-used airports seek state tax relief.

The West German Aerobatic Teams uses the Langlade County Airport to practice before the World Championships at Oshkosh.

Herman "Fish" Salmon dies, in the crash of a Constellation at Columbus, Indiana.

■ **1981**
Fritz Wolf retires as director of the Bureau of Aeronautics; Carl Guell serves as acting director.

The 1,683-foot television tower at Rhinelander, tallest tower in the Midwest, is equipped with six up-to-date white strobe lights.

The Dunn county board votes to fund $20,000 in improvements at the Boyceville airport.

■ **1982**
Fred Gammon is named director of the Bureau of Aeronautics.

Economic recession prompts a 23 percent drop in airport operations in Wisconsin; local general aviation falls by one-third.

Green Bay becomes one of the first new FAA automatic Flight Service Stations in the United States.

Several pilots, led by Don Gunderson, revive Wild Rose's Idlewild airport, dormant since 1966.

Robert Neiman, Lodi's Santa Claus and World War I veteran, passes away.

■ **1983**
Watertown's Daniel C. Brandenstein pilots the space shuttle Challenger.

Air Wisconsin is serving seven Great Lakes states from Pennsylvania to Minnesota and carrying over 700,000 passengers.

The Price County Airport undergoes an $800,000 upgrade.

■ **1984**
The Weathermation computerized information system goes on line at 19 locations in the state.

Midwest Express Airlines is founded at Appleton.

The Lone Rock Flight Service Station closes. After sixty-two years as a pilot, Appleton's Elwyn West retires.

■ **1985**
Wisconsin has 596 airports—including 392 private use fields—4,427 active registered aircraft—including 40 seaplanes, 27 sailplanes, 57 rotorcraft, 52 balloons and 172 hangliders/ultralights—flown by 12,174 active pilots.

The Wisconsin Aviation Hall of Fame is organized.

The Hillsboro Airport, built by the Kickapoo Oil Company, is purchased by the city; the airport is later named in honor of Joshua Sanford.

Left: Peggy and Dave Weiman on the cover of their new magazine, 1979. (Midwest Flyer)

Thirty-one people die as a Midwest Express DC-9 crashes at Milwaukee.

■ **1986**
The Aeronautics Bureau publishes its Wisconsin System Airport Plan, 1986-2110.

Republic Airlines merges with Northwest. The National Ercoupe Owners Convention is held at Mt. Telemark Resort and the Cable Union Airport.

Mel Thompson, who built and flew his first airplane in 1919, dies at age 89.

■ **1987**
The FAA recognizes the Wisconsin Aerospace Education Committee as the "most outstanding organization in the United States committed to the infusion of aerospace education..."

Fred Gammon leaves the Aeronautics Bureau and Dave Strand is named director.

Mike Feltz of Sentry Aviation, Stevens Point, is recognized for heroism after he "talks" passenger Ralph Flanders to land a plane at Volk Field after the pilot dies of a heart attack.

Wisconsin's first General Aviation Expo is held at the annual Aviation Conference.

Wisconsin's first medical emergency helicopters services are available at Appleton, Madison and Milwaukee.

Door County's Cherryland Airport is the first airport in the country to use the new runway "lead-in-light" system.

■ **1988**
Robert Kunkel is named acting director of the Aeronautics Bureau.

425 members of the North American Trainer Association attend the 50th Anniversary celebration of the AT6/SNJ airplane at Kenosha's Flightfest.

■ **1989**
Robert Kunkel is named director of the Aeronautics Bureau.

Competitors from the Soviet Union appear for the first time at the aerobatics championship in Fond du Lac.

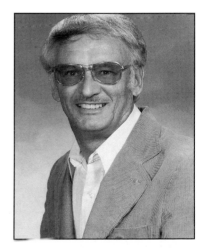

Stunt pilot Art Scholl, who died in 1985. (WAHF)

The Outagamie airport is the fourth busiest airport in the state, behind Milwaukee, Madison and Green Bay, serving 300,000 passengers and moving 5.5 million pounds of freight.

■ 1990
At Dane County Regional-Truax Field, commercial passenger traffic crosses the one million mark.

A $4.2 million renovation project is completed at the Watertown Airport.

■ 1991
The Wisconsin Air National Guard serves in the Middle East during the Gulf War.

Blackhawk Technical College receives a CT39-A Sabreliner jet for use in its aviation education program.

■ 1992
One of the state's most noted home-builders, Ron Scott, and his plane, "Old Ironsides" are featured in Sport Aviation.

Charlie Dewey, a Crites flight student in the mid-1930s, is elected national president of the OX-5 Aviation Pioneers.

The Bureau of Aeronautics consolidates the Aviation Education and Safety Section with the Airport Operations Section to form the Aviation Management and Education Section.

■ 1993
A Aeronautics Bureau census finds that Dane county has more airports than any other county in the state.

Timmermann Field in Milwaukee remains one of Wisconsin's busiest airports with over 85,000 operations taking place at the field.

At the EAA Fly-In in Oshkosh, the Bureau of Aeronautic demonstrates the world's first use at a public airport of a three dimension approach using satellites and a ground station, i.e. GPS.

■ 1994
Passenger traffic at Mitchell International crosses the five million mark.

Wayne Nelson, La Pointe, becomes the first person to fly an ultralight airplane across Lake Superior from Madeline Island to Thunder Bay, Ontario.

Local Rice Lake aviator and airport commissioner Jim Conn attempts to circumnavigate the globe via the North and South Pole.

The Air National Guard rebuilds and resurfaces the runway at the Mauston/New Lisbon Union Airport while community volunteers build a new operations building.

Flight for Life, which began helicopter ambulance service, Milwaukee, 1985.

■ 1995
At Mitchell Field yearly passenger rates increase from 500,000 in 1955 to 5,000,000.

Austin Straubel Airport improvements include expansion of the terminal and a new tower.

Operations begin at the new Rice Lake Regional Airport, named Carl's Airport in honor of long time city airport manager Carl Rindlisbacher.

Jerry Mehlhaff, who in 1988 purchased the remains of the American Champion Aircraft Company, formerly located in Osceola, is producing over forty airplanes per year and is the only production aircraft builder in the state.

Steve and Paula Wittman are killed when Wittman's home-built airplane comes apart in the air and crashes in Alabama.

■ 1996
Austin Straubel Airport is served by six airlines with up to forty departures daily.

Built after World War II, Ed Rediske's Rainbow Airport near Franklin closes.

Wisconsin enters the Space Age with the launch of a Super Loki Rocket at what the students involved have christened "Spaceport Sheboygan."

■ 1997
Fritz Wolf, Wisconsin aviation's first civil servant, passes away at age 81.

Pete Drahn, director of the Dane County Regional Airport, is named President of the American Association of Airport Executives.

The Monroe Municipal Airport now has 21 hangars and operations are increasing as aviators leave larger airports to the north and south of Monroe.

Super Bowl-bound-Packer fans jam Austin Straubel airport prior to departure; then fill the terminal to greet the winning team when it returns.

Two Super Loki rockets are launched at Spaceport Sheboygan.

■ 1998
Don Cammack, airport engineer, retires after thirty-four years with the Bureau of Aeronautics; Cammack earns the distinction of having served as airport engineer longer than anyone else and of working at the Bureau longer than anyone except Carl Guell.

Rhinelander Airport begins operation of the first infared de-icing facility in the country.

The Aeronautic Bureau installs a GPS system in its photo plane to serve as the primary source for locating sites and taking aerial photos.

The Wisconsin Aviation Hall of Fame publishes its history of aviation in Wisconsin.

The Wisconsin Aviation
Hall of Fame

Carl Guell and Ben Silko presenting Governor Tony Earl with a charter membership in the Wisconsin Aviation Hall of Fame

Founded in 1985, the Wisconsin Aviation Hall of Fame is committed to preserving the history of aviation in this state and honoring the people who made it.

The Hall of Honor is located in the atrium of the Experimental Aircraft Association Museum in Oshkosh.

Members of the Board of Directors 1985-1997: **Stuart C. Herro, Charles W. Marotske, Carl E. Guell, Ben D. Silko, Richard Jaye, David Duax, Earl Pingel, Richard Wagner, Kenneth Kuenn, Robert D. Sather, La Fonda Kinnaman, Archie Becher, Jr., Anita M. Kapp, Keith Glasshof, David M. Greene, Duane E. Esse, John M. Dorcey, James Hein.**

Inductees

The first aviators inducted in the Wisconsin Aviation Hall of Fame were Paul Poberezny, General Billy Mitchell and Steve Wittman. At the induction ceremony Mitchell was represented by his niece, Harriet Pillsbury.

1986
Brig. General William Mitchell
Milwaukee (1879-1936)
Paul H. Poberezny
West Allis (1921-)
S.J. "Steve" Wittman
Oshkosh (1904-1995)

1987
Major Richard I. Bong
Poplar (1920-1945)
Brig. General Lester J. Maitland
Milwaukee (1899-1990)
Howard A. Morey
Middleton (1903-1995)

1988
Leonard Larson
Larsen (1903-1991)
Donald K. Slayton
Sparta (1924-1993)
General Nathan F. Twining
Monroe (1897-1982)

1989
Dale E. Crites
Waukesha (1907-1991)
Dean G. Crites
Waukesha (1907-)
Fritz E. Wolf
Shawano (1916-1997)
General Hoyt S. Vandenberg
Milwaukee (1899-1954)

1990
Harry R. Chaplin, Sr.
Plymouth (1922-1988)
Carl E. Guell
Fond du Lac (1919-)
James R. Lovell, Jr.
Milwaukee (1928-)

1991
William J. Lotzer
Fond du Lac (1917-)
George A. Hardie, Jr.
Hales Corners (1912-)
Robert C. Reeve
Waunakee (1902-1980)

1992
Alfred W. Lawson
Milwaukee (1869-1954)
Roy P. Shwery
Marshfield (1023)
Daniel C. Brandenstein
Watertown (1943-)

1993
Warren Basler
Oshkosh (1926-1997)
Col. Robert J. Jones
Ashland (1919-)
David L. Behncke
Cambria (1897-1953)

1994
Louis R. Wuilleumier
Madison (1906-1995)
Art Scholl
Milwaukee (1931-1985)
Archie H. Henkelmann
Janesville (1931-)

1995
William Brennand
Oshkosh (1924-)
Libby Parod
Cable (1914-)
Herman R. "Fish" Salmon
Milwaukee (1913-1980)

1996
Clairmont L. Egtvedt
Stoughton (1892-1975)
Timothy E. Hoeksema
Appleton (1947-)
Tom Poberezny
Oshkosh (1946-)

1997
Brig. General Richard A. Knobloch
Milwaukee (1918-)
Noble F. Lee
Minocqua (1916-1989?)
Preston H. Wilbourne
Appleton (1925-)

History Book
County Volunteers

Adams, Gary Miller; **Ashland**, David Ochsenbauer; **Barron**, Kris Wells, Richard Nelson, Glenn Anderson; **Bayfield**, Captain Harlan Hess Hespen, Glenn Anderson; **Brown**, Clete Cisler, James Sorenson; **Buffalo**, Ron Hurlburt; **Burnett**, Carl G. Hedlund; **Calumet**, David Cooley; **Chippewa**, Rick Bowe, Glenn Anderson; **Clark**, Tom Jabconicky; **Columbia**, David Marks, Steve Johnson, George Bindl; **Crawford**, William L. Adamany; **Dane**, Carl E. Guell, Bridagier General R.C. "Bud" Jensen, USAF(Ret.), Tom Lenox, Louise M. Yeazel, Patricia Pagliaro, Duane Esse, Jim Hein, Bud Rogers, George Bindl; **Dodge**, Earl Pingel; **Door**, Wesley Hakari; Douglas, Bernie Tanski, Bill Amorde, Captain Harlan Hess Hespen; **Dunn**, Charles Thomas, Glenn Anderson; **Eau Claire**, Steve Dickoff; **Florence**, Robert Larsen; **Fond du Lac**, Paul Morin, Ben Owen; **Forest**, Gary Bradley; **Grant**, Harold Beals, Jack Kirby; **Green**, Patti Gibeaut; Phyllis Badertscher; **Green Lake**, Earl E. Pinkall; **Iowa**, Jim Middagh; **Iron**, James Butterbrodt; **Jackson**, Larry Lunda; **Jefferson**, Jim Schumacher, Bob Stockdale; **Juneau**, F.G. Lesavage; Ronald Brunner; **Kenosha**, Ivan R. Ginter, Trista Fowles, Lieutenant Colonel William G. Butler, USA(Ret.), Larry G. Fitzgerald; **Kewaunee**, Wesley Hakari; **La Crosse**, Becky Brockman, Tim Colgan; **Lafayette**, Jack Hanifan; **Langlade**, Cory Haupt, Gerald Nonnenmacher, Marland Malzahn; **Lincoln**, Margo Tsatsa, Alice F. Krueger; **Manitowoc**, Pat Koppa; **Marathon**, Syd Cohen, Bob Wylie; **Marinette**, James LaMalfa, Earl J. DeHart, Jr., Norman Wesolowski, Major Roy Ihde, USAF(Ret.); **Marquette**, Dan McNamara, Donald Cacic; **Menomonee**, Wayne Towne; **Milwaukee**, Earl Pingel, Erv Siegel, Jim Szajkovics, Jerome Hoppe, Doug Drescher, Jerry Theimer, K. Erik Anderson, La Fonda J. Kinnaman, Tim Hoeksema, William Brown, Howard Pergande, Gregory Gorak; **Monroe**, F.G. Lesavage, Paul Amberson; **Oconto**, Eileen Duffeck; **Oneida**, Mark Golomski, Rod Anderson; **Outagamie**, Randy Kroll, Robert Oudenhoven, Joyce Baggot; **Ozaukee**, Ralph L. Zaun; **Pepin**, Ron Hurlburt; **Pierce**, Robert Moody, Rob Seifert; **Polk**, Steve Nuebel, Scott Gray Roger Waterman; **Portage**, Ken Bigelow, John Kamla; **Price**, Nathaniel Nez, Dale Heikkinen; **Racine**, Quentin Rench, Richard Reich, Donal W. Poisl; **Richland**, Mike Kaufman; **Rock**, Marge Van Galder, Simon K. Smith, Dave Hedgecock; **Rusk**, Bill Towle; **Sauk**, Vic Vickmark, Mike Olah, Kirk Olson; **Sawyer**, Cathy Schimke, Daniel Leslie; **Shawano**, Marty Westphal; **Sheboygan**, Gary D. Houk, Judith Meyer; **St. Croix**, Sue Young, Michael Demulling; **Taylor**, Terri Anderson; **Trempealeau**, Mike Berg; **Vernon**, Valdo Geary; **Vilas**, Irene Lotzer, Larry Hanna; **Walworth**, Robert Mick, Dave Hedgecock; **Washburn**, Charles Lewis; **Washington**, Robert Gehring, Marilyn Peters; **Waukesha**, Joanne Murphy, Pete Wormley, G. Kenneth Whyte, Craig Hoaglund, Chris Pasbrig, James Bruno, Charles Dewey; **Waupaca**, Richard Merkley, David Niven, Dennis Kubczak; **Waushara**, Tim Freudenthal; **Winnebago**, Kerry Fores, Larry Marks, Rodger Cavanaugh, Ben Owen, Lloyd Zellmer; **Wood**, Don Winch, Donald Cacic, Michael Pinney.

Wisconsin Sesquicentennial
Corporate Sponsors

This project has been funded in part by the Wisconsin Sesquicentennial Commission, with funds from individual and corporate contributors and the State of Wisconsin.

TRAILBLAZER CONTRIBUTORS

AT&T,
SC Johnson Wax,
The Credit Unions of Wisconsin

VOYAGEUR CONTRIBUTORS

Firstar Corporation;
Harley-Davidson, Inc.;
Marshall & Ilsley Corportation;
Outdoor Advertising Association;
Philip Morris Companies:
Miller Brewing Company, Kraft Foods/Oscar Mayer Foods Corp., Philip Morris USA;
W. H. Brady Co.;
Wisconsin Manufacturers & Commerce

FOUNDER CONTRIBUTORS

ANR Pipeline Company; Blue Cross/Blue Shield United Wisconsin; Color Ink, Inc.; DEC International, Inc.;General Casualty, Home Savings; John Deere Horicon Works; Johnson Controls; Kikkoman Foods, Inc.; Kohler Co.; Marcus Theaters Corporation; Michael, Best & Friedrich; Midwest Express Airlines; Nicolet Minerals Company; Northwestern Mutual Life Foundation; Promega Corporation; Robert W. Baird & Co. Inc.; Snap-on Incorporated; Time Insurance; Weber-Stephen Company; Weyerhaeuser; Wisconsin Central Ltd.; Wisconsin Power & Light Foundation; Wisconsin Public Service Foundation; Wisconsin State Cranberry Growers Association

BADGER CONTRIBUTORS

3M; Aid Association for Lutherans; Allen-Edmonds Shoe Corp.; A.O. Smith Corporation; Badger Mining Corporation; Briggs & Stratton Corporation; Case Corporation; Consolidated Papers, Inc.; Dairyland Power Cooperative; Edgewater Hotel; Eller Media Company; Fort James Corporation; Frazer Papers; Green Bay Packaging, Inc.; International Paper; Jockey International, Inc.; Jorgensen Conveyors, Inc.; Kimberly-Clark Corporation; Mann Bros., Inc.; Marathon Communications; Marcus Corporation; Marshfield Clinic; Modine Manufacturing Company; National Business Furniture, Inc.; Oscar J. Boldt Construction Co.; Pizza Pit, Ltd.; Rockwell Automation/Allen-Bradley; Rust Environment & Infrastructure; ShopKo; Stevens Point Brewery; Twin Disc, Incorporated; United States Cellular; Wausau and Mosinee Papers; Wisconsin Counties Association; Virchow, Krause & Company, LLP

Bureau of Aeronautics
Aviation Award Winners

Person of the Year Award

1969	S. J. Wittman
1970	Howard Morey
1971	Francis Higgins
1972	no conference
1973	T. K. Jordan
1974	Ed Williams
1975	Marie Grimm
1976	Robert Heck
1977	Paul Poberezny
1978	Roy Shwery
1979	Dave Duax
1980	Basil Arvey
1981	Marilyn Hardacre
1982	Joe Liebergen
1983	Wally Mitchell
1984	Preston Wilbourne
1985	Fred Gammon
1986	George McQueen
1987	LeRoy Jonas
1988	James Ash
1989	Art Borchardt
1990	Timothy Hoeksema
1991	Charles E. Swain
1992	Tom Poberezny
1993	Lyle Maves
1994	Dennis Eiler
1995	James Conn
1996	C. Barry Bateman
1997	Peter Drahn

Lifetime Service Award

1981	Robert Skuldt
1982	Libby Parod
1983	Fritz Wolf
1984	Bob White
1985	Carl Rindlisbacher
1986	Charles Wood
1987	Harry Chaplin
1988	Carl Guell
1989	Paul Poberezny
1990	Phil Leyda
1991	Earl Pingel
1992	Walter Mayo
1993	Howard Morey
1994	Robert Acker
1995	Warren Basler
1996	Field Morey
1997	Duane Esse

Carl E. Guell Aviation Educator of the Year Award

1977	Earl Pingel
1978	Roland Solberg
1979	Dr. Charles Thomas
1980	Dr. Larry Hapke
1981	Buddy Rogers
1982	Robert McMahon
1983	Ellen Baerman
1984	Tom Teschendorf
1985	Carl Guell
1986	Larry Scheckel
1987	Melba Sullivan
1988	Robert Clarke
1989	Roy Grade
1990	Dr. Paul Flagg
1991	Charles Larsen
1992	Dr. Jack Kirby
1993	Michael R. McArdle
1994	Sydney Cohen
1995	Sharon Ryan
1996	Beverly Cox
1997	Karen Scharrer-Erickson

Airport Engineering Award

1983	Thomas Janssen
1984	Joe Abernathy
1985	Leo Bussan
1986	Al Fawley
1987	Bill Green
1988	James Foley
1989	Dave Dyrstad
1990	Keith Lindsley
1991	Mike Hinz
1992	Leroy Gilhausen
1993	Andrew Platz
1994	Roy Eckrose
1995	Mike Kirchner
1996	Phil Ramlet
1997	Roy Gilhausen

Notes

PHOTO CREDITS: Photos credited WAHF are from the collection of the Wisconsin Aviation Hall of Fame; WAC identifies photos from the Waukesha Aviation Club; EAA credits photos from the Experimental Aircraft Association, Oshkosh.

CHAPTER I - First Flights - Pages 10-51

1. A. P. Warner's, reminiscences as compiled in his *Making Things,* pps. 19-23; Wright Brothers flight reported in *Milwaukee Sentinel,* December 18, 1903; Warner biography in Joseph J. Rhodes, *Sparks from the Flaming Wheel,* pps. 78-81; material on Curtiss and Herring and their first aeroplanes in Sherwood Harris, *The First To Fly,* pps. 74, 132 and Bill Robie, *For the Greatest Achievement,* pps. 43-45 and C.R. Roseberry, *Glenn Curtiss,* pps. 109, 192-193, 223-225, 228; Warner's first flight reported in *Beloit News,* November 4, 1909; an alternative version is offered by Harold E. Morehouse in *Flying Pioneer Biographies;* ad for Warner's Aerometer in *Aero,* December 3, 1910; Lincoln Beachey recalled in *Beloit News,* December 12, 1953.

2. Allard and Sandvick, *Minnesota Aviation History,* pps. 11-12.

3. Otto Brodie in Morehouse Papers, Curtiss Museum; *Young and Callahan,* pps. 47-48; *Chicago Tribune,* December 5, 1909, April 20, 1913; Certificate and Record of Death, Cook County, Illinois, April 21, 1913.

4. Tom Abel in *Fond du Lac Reporter,* December 12, 1903; John Stierle in *Milwaukee Journal,* June 1, 1969; Wright quote in C.R. Roseberry, p. 65; Albert Dufour in *Milwaukee Sentinel,* May 24, 1908; Moldenhauer in *Marshfield News,* December 16, 1909; Rudolph Silverston in *Minutes of the State Board of Agriculture,* 1907, 1908, 1908, also *Milwaukee Journal,* September, 10, 1908, *Chicago Daily Tribune,* February 18, 1909, *Aero* Magazine, November 26, 1910, and Burbach's *West Allis A City of Marvelous Growth,* p. 140; Hoxsey in *Minutes,* 1910, 1911 and *Milwaukee Journal,* September 13-17, 1910.

5. Schwister in *Wausau Daily Record-Herald,* July 10, 1910, March 6, March 30, April 13, May 20, May 26, June 23, July 1, July 3, July 7, August 8, August 10, August 22, August 23, October 16, October 20, 1911; *Antigo Daily Journal,* September 18, September 22, September 23, 1911; *Aero,* July 15, 1911; *Wausau Pilot,* February 10, 1927.

6. Milbourne Christopher, *Houdini A Pictorial Life,* pps. 61-82.

7. Blanche Stuart Scott in *Madison Capital Times,* June 1, 1913; Stevens, Peter, pps. 218-222.

8. Dixon and Ward in *Kenosha Evening News,* August 28, 1911; Wittmer at De Pere and Green Bay, *Green Bay Gazette,* August 25, 17, 30, 1911, September 16, 1911, also *The Brown County Democrat,* September 1, 1911. Rodgers in Ellen Lebow, *Cal Rodgers and the Vin Fiz,* pps. 78-81, also *Appleton Daily Post,* September 2, 5, 1911. Beachey in *New York Times,* June 28, 1911, *Aero,* September 16, 30, 1911 and *Portage Daily Register,* September 19, 1911; Rene Simon in *Dunn County News,* September 7, 14, 1911; Havens in Edith Dodd Culver, *Talespins,* p. 74 and *Chippewa Falls Daily Independent,* September 23, 1911; Robinson in George L. Vergara, *Hugh Robinson,* pps. 74-75, 88-93; Tees in Scrapbook of Mrs. Howard Tees Larson, Milwaukee County Historical Society; Brabazon in unpublished reminiscences, Brabazon Papers, State Historical Society of Wisconsin Archives.

9. Fish in *Milwaukee Journal,* May 24, 25, 27, 30, 31, 1912 and Thomas J. O'Sullivan *The Pioneer Airplane Mails of the United States,* pps. 121-124, 131-135. Kaminski in Kaminski Papers, Archives, University of Wisconsin, Milwaukee.

10. Castory in *Stevens Point Daily Journal,* July 21, 1912; Powers in *Appleton Daily Post,* September 19, 1912; Nels Nelson in *Janesville Daily Gazette,* June 20, 1912, *Ashland Daily News,* July 3, 1912, *Evansville Review,* August 29, 1912, *The Chilton Times,* September 7, 1912, *Monroe Journal Gazette,* September 13, 1912; Kearney in *Prairie du Chien Union,* October 10, 1912; Mitchell in *Evansville Review,* September 5, 1912; Horton in *Wisconsin State Journal,* September 20, 1914; Barlow in *Pepin County Courier, Dunn County News* and *Mondovi Herald,* September 12, 1913 and *Elroy Tribune,* October 10, 1913; Mestach in *Mondovi Herald,* October 3, 1913; Hoover in *Sheboygan*

Press, July 4, 7, 8, 1914; Davis in *Mauston Star,* September 11, 14, 18, 1913 and *Chicago Record-Herald,* September 17, 1913; Niles in *Oshkosh Daily Northwestern,* July 28, 1979; Fry and Timmons in *Beloit Daily News,* September 14, 1914; McEldowney, Gjestvang and Jostad, in McEldowney's unpublished reminiscences in Collection of Wisconsin Aviation Hall of Fame; Wisconsin Aero Club in Gnauk File, Milwaukee County Historical Society; Beachey in *Beloit Daily News,* September 14, 1914.

11. Ferdinand von Zeppelin in Rhoda R. Gilman's "Zeppelin in Minnesota, A Study in Fact and Fable," *Minnesota History,* v. 39, n. 7, 1965 and "Zeppelin in Minnesota: The Count's Own Story," *Minnesota History,* v. 40, n. 6, 1967, also in Tom Crouch, *The Eagle Aloft,* pps. 282-285. John Steiner in Crouch, pps. 230-235, and *The Milwaukee Sentinel,* July 9, 16, 19, 23, 1860; July 7, 1863; July 7, 1871; June 5, 14, 16, 19, 1875; July, 3, 7, 9, 1875. Joshua Pusey in *Milwaukee Sentinel,* September 4,1856. Samuel King in Crouch, pps. 459-462. Professor Denniston in *Milwaukee Sentinel,* July 25, 1870, and *Eau Claire Free Press,* August 25, 1874. Signor Pedanto in *Oshkosh Northwestern,* September 28, 1878. Ida LeRoy in *Milwaukee Sentinel,* September 14, 1899. Ed Freeman in *Centennial History,* Beaver Dam, Wisconsin, p. 156. William Matteray in *Milwaukee Sentinel,* September 8, 9, 1906. Charles Hamilton in *Milwaukee Sentinel,* September 9, 11, 1906. Milwaukee Aero Club in Crouch, p. 539, *Milwaukee Sentinel,* March 17, July 4, 8, 1908. Frederick Fielding in Crouch, p. 542.

CHAPTER II - Golden Age of Aviation - Pages 52-160

1. Blesch Field in Steve Milquet, manuscript of *Transportation-Aviation* section of Ashwaubenon Anniversary History Book, pps. 46-63. Mitchell in *Milwaukee Sentinel,* April 23, 1919. Meisenheimer in *Milwaukee Journal,* April 26, 1919. Milwaukee County Airport in Hardie, *General Mitchell International Airport,* pps. 3-5. Round the Rim in Maurer Maurer, *Aviation in U.S. Army, 1919-1939,* pps. 170-172 and *Milwaukee Journal,* September 11, 1919. Pathfinders in Maurer, pps. 172-173 and *Milwaukee Journal,* September 9, 12, 15, 16, 19, 1919. Norman Moll in Dom Terpstra, *Chronology of La Crosse Aviation,* unpublished, 1985 and *La Crosse Tribune,* undated 1919 and 1920; Martin Bomber mail flight in O'Sullivan and Weber, *History of United States Pioneer and Government-Operated Air Mail Service, 1910-1928,* pps 131-132. Conant in *Marquette County Tribune,* July 19, 1979, May 22, 1986, May 18, 1995 and *Wisconsin State Journal,* September 4, 1919. Pugh in *Black River Falls Banner Journal,* May 8, 15, 1991. Larson Brothers in Kripenne, *Wingwalker,* pps. 43, 55, 71, 113, 116, 230. Anton Brotz in *Sheboygan Press-Telegram,* May 12, 1923, *Kohler of Kohler News,* April 1926, September, 1930 and transcript of interview with Ralph Brotz, August 7, 1985. Eau Claire Airport in *Eau Claire Leader-Telegram,* May 31, 1986 and transcript of interview with Charles Wood, 1985. Wausau Airport in *Wausau Daily News-Herald,* May 3, 1926. Oshkosh Airport in *The Wisconsin Magazine,* December 1950, p. 7. Howard Morey in *Rice Lake Chronotype,* November 5, 1986. Hamilton Airport in Hardie, pps. 10-13; Airports in "Descriptions of Airports and Landing Fields in the United States," *U.S. Department of Commerce Airway Bulletin,* n. 2, September 1, 1931.

2. Levine, *Mitchell, Pioneer of Air Power,* pps. 322-333, 343-355, 364-368, 391; Hardie, *General William Mitchell, Air Power Pioneer.*

3. Hopkins, pps. 13-19, 33-47, 56-62, 93-100, 149-163.

4. Crash at LaCrosse in Allard and Sandvik, *Minnesota Aviation History,* pps. 160-161. Air Commerce Act in Nick A. Komons, *William P. MacCracken, Jr., and the Regulation of Civil Aviation,* pps. 37-47. Dickinson and Northwest Airways in Mills, *A Pictorial History of Northwest Airlines,* pps. 13-23, Allard and Sandvik, pps. 159-163 and *Air Commerce Bulletin,* v. 1, n. 5., September 2, 1929. Joe Bednar in

Dom Terpstra Transcript of Interview with Joe Bednar, March 3, 1975. *Domestic Air News*, November 1, 1927, January 15, June 15, 1929. Chicago-Twin Cities Airway in *Wisconsin News*, February 22, April 27, 1927 also "General Airway Information," *Airway Bulletin*, No. 1, September 1, 1932, "Descriptions of Airports and Landings Fields in the United States," *Airway Bulletin*, n. 2, September 1, 1931; "America's Airways," *Air Commerce Bulletin*, v. 1. n. 8, October 15, 1929; "Weather and Communications," *Air Commerce Bulletin*, v. 1 n. 5 September 2, 1929; "Radio and the Nation's Airways," *Air Commerce Bulletin*, v. 1, n. 10, November 15, 1929; "Aeronautic Licensing and Inspection Service," *Air Commerce Bulletin*, v. 1 n. 12. "Status of Aircraft, Gliders, Pilots and Glider Pilots," *Air Commerce Bulletin*, v. 4 n. 21, May 1933 and v. 8, n. 10, April 15, 1937. Kohler Airways in *Wisconsin News*, December, 28, 1933 and various *Air Commerce Bulletins*.

5. Dickey, *Aviation at the Head of the Lakes*, pps. 8-10.

6. Geiger, George L., "Governor Finds Airplane Indispensable," *Airway Age* v. 10, n. 4, April 1929; Cassagneres, Ev, *Ryan B-1 S/N 108 Historical Report*, November, 1982, unpublished paper in Archives of Kohler Company; *Kohler of Kohler News*, July 1925; August, November 1928; July, August, September, November 1929; February, March, September, October 1930; February 1931; March 1933; September 1935; November 1939.

7. Society Clothes Aero Express in *Madison Capital Times*, June 3, 7, 9, 10, August 2, 5, 6, 1919 and *Wisconsin State Journal*, August 2, 1919. Harriette Wheaton's plane ride in *Madison Capital Times*, June 12, 1919. Susie Mae Potter in *Madison Capital Times*, April 19, June 11, 17, 27, July 5, 25, 1919. Wrigley Flying Squadron in *Appleton Crescent*, September 9-10, 1919 and *Wisconsin State Journal*, September 13, 15, 1919. Flying Circus in *Milwaukee Journal*, September 4, 7, 9, 11, 14, 1919 and *DePere Journal-Democrat*, August 28, 1919. Wisconsin Air Derby in *Milwaukee Journal*, August 30-31, 1920. Wisconsin News Air Derby of 1925 in *Wisconsin News*, July 13, 14, 15, 16, 17, 18, 19, 20, 1925 and Hardie, p. 8; of 1926, *Manitowoc Herald Times Reporter*, May 31, 1996 and *Insight, Milwaukee Journal*, April 4, 1976. 1926 Ford Tour in *Milwaukee Sentinel*, August 9, 1926 and Lesley Forden, *The Ford Air Tours, 1925-1931*, pps. 23-26, 40-41, 47, 60-62. Hamilton Metalplane in newsclips in *Hamilton Scrapbook*, Milwaukee County Historical Society. John Wood in Forden, pps. 63-80, "The National Air Tour," *Aviation*, August 4, 1928 and *Wausau Record Herald*, July 20, 21, 26, 28, August, 3, 9, 1928 and August 31, September 4, 5, 7, 9, 1929. 1930 Air tour in Forden, pps. 132-133 and *Eau Claire Leader*, September 12, 13, 14. Wisconsin Air Tours in *Milwaukee Journal*, September 22, 1927 and *Aero Digest*, March, 1928. Legion Round-Ups in *The Badger Legionnaire*, November and December, 1929-1941.

8. NC-4 flight in Turnbull and Lord, *History of United States Naval Aviation*, pps. 164-169. Mitscher in *Current Biography, 1944*, pps. 476-480. Maitland in Maitland, *Knights of the Air*, pps. 318-327, *Wisconsin News*, July 19, 20, 1927, *Milwaukee Journal*, June 27, 1952. Lindbergh in Lindbergh, *Autobiography of Values*, pps. 24-25, Brock, "Lindbergh and Madison," *Historic Madison*, v. 12, 1995, *Wisconsin News*, July 20, 1927 and *Oshkosh Northwestern*, September 1, 1974. Collins in Collins & Clark, *Tales of an Old Air-Faring Man*, pps. 23, 25, 37, 59, 69, 87, 91, 99, 104, 114, 121, 131, 133, 134, 135, 155, 160. Robert Reeve in Day, *Glacier Pilot*, pps. 29-37, 40-49, 56-57, 96-97, 284-292. Atlantic Flyers in Beatty, *The Water Jump*, p. 58, also Lueneburg, *The Brown Deer Airport*, p. 5. Clyde Lee in Kripenne, *Wingwalker*, pps. 75, 104, 124, 166, 167, 171, 193-196, 199-203. Felix Waitkus in Waitkus "Trans-Atlantic Flight," *The Wisconsin Engineer*, March, 1939; also *Kohler of Kohler News*, October, 1930, May, 1935, October, 1935, January, 1936, and Baumgartner, "Transatlantic Heroics for Lithuania," *Aviation History*, January, 1996. Walter Lees in Cooper, *Pioneer Pilot*, pps. 82, 91, 101, 105-115, 121-147 and "Voyager Revisited", *Sport Aviation*, December, 1996.

9. Van Galder, pps. 15-21, Transcripts of WAHF Interview with Les Borer, June 1975; Krippene, p. 82; WAHF Interview with Russ Schuetze, February 1997; *Wisconsin Rapids Tribune*, August 30, 1929,

September 2, 1930, *St. Petersburg Times*, December 21, 1929; WAHF Interview with Dean Crites, May 1997; Schuette, p. 95; WAHF Interview with Art Hodge, June 1975; Fish Salmon Scrapbook: Van Galder, pps. 18-21.

10. Hardie, "The Airline That Might Have Been," *Historical Messenger*, Milwaukee County Historical Society, v. 27, n. 1, March, 1971, "Milwaukee's First Airliner," *Historical Messenger*, v. 15, n. 4, December, 1959; Henry, *Zig, Zag and Swirl*, pps. 85-110.

11. Hamilton in *Milwaukee Journal*, April 12, 1928, January 17, 1929, *Chicago Herald-Examiner*, August 16, 1928, November 11, 1928, *Seattle Alaska Weekly*, November 23, 1928, *Milwaukee Sentinel*, November 24, 1928, January 15, 1929, February 7, 1929, *Milwaukee Leader*, December 14, 1928, *Wall Street News*, August 8, 1929 as found in *Hamilton Scrapbook*, Milwaukee County Historical Society, Milwaukee.

12. Corben in *Corben Aircraft*, 1936 Catalog; Feeny, "The Madison Years," *Plasticorner*, Journal of the Madison Plastic Modelers Society, November/December, 1985; Chase, "Corben Super Ace," *Vintage Airplane*, June 12, 1985.

13. Transcript of Carl Guell interviews with Steve Wittman, 1985, Geoge Moersch, July 19, 1985, and Tom Meiklejohn, Jr., July 20, 1985.

14. *Manitowoc Herald-News*, February 6, April 2, 13, 19, 25, 26, 1929; *Aero Digest*, July, 1929; *The New Master of the Air*, brochure, Invincible Metal Furniture Co., Manitowoc, 1929; O'Brien, p. 23.

15. Fox Cities airports, in *Post-Cresent*, June 12, 1983, April 10, 1984, November 6, 1986, *Outagamie County Airport Dedication*, June 1983. Mills, pps. 22, 23.

16. Ashland in *Ashland Daily Press*, January 31, 1959.

17. Phone interview with Town of Athelstane Clerk, April 5, 1997.

18. Transcript of WAHF interviews with Neil Poland, Pete Tumelson, Ralph Tumelson, Stiles Whipple, 1989, and Art Hodge, 1975; Parker material in records of Parker Family, courtesy of Geoffrey Parker; Van Galder in Van Galder, pps. 1-6, 25-26, 35-36, 57-58, 102-103.

19. *Black River Falls Banner Journal*, May 8, May 15, 1991; September 14, 21, 1994.

20. "America's Airways," *Air Commerce Bulletin*, v. 1 n. 8, October 15, 1929 and "General Airways Information" *Airway Bulletin*, n. 1, September 1, 1932. Kenneth L. Rogers, *Short Personal History*, typescript, 1995.

21. "America's Airways," *Air Commerce Bulletin*, v. 1 n. 8, October 15, 1929 and "General Airways Information" *Airway Bulletin*, n. 1, September 1, 1932. "An Airport System for Wisconsin, *Bulletin 11*, Wisconsin Planning Board, October, 1940.

22. Lueneburg, *The Brown Deer Airport*, pps. 1-8.

23. Eau Claire in Barland, *The Rivers Flow On*, pps. 259-260 and *Eau Claire Airways*, brochure, 1930.

24. *Fond du Lac Commonwealth Reporter*, August 22, 1927; *Ourselves, Special Aviation Issue*, v. 6, n. 8, Giddings and Lewis Machine Tool Company, November, 1953; Transcript of Interviews with Wilbur Moersch, Wilbert W. Haase Jr., July 19, 1985.

25. Milquet, pps. 46-57.

26. "America's Airways," *Air Commerce Bulletin*, v. 1 n. 8, October 15, 1929 and "General Airways Information" *Airway Bulletin*, n. 1, September 1, 1932.

27. Transcript of WAHF interview with John Sullivan, 1985. *Southport Newsletter*, Spring 1997. *Kenosha News*, September 15, 1931, September 1, 1936, April 29, 1940, September 1, 1979, July 19, 1991; *Wall Street Journal*, August 23, 1942.

28. *Kewaunee Enterprise*, August 10, 1923, September 15, 1924, May 25, 28, 31, June 1, 1935. *Luxemburg News*, January 1, 1934.

29. *Kohler of Kohler News*, November, 1926; January, July, August, September, 1929; June, August, September, 1930, August, 1931. Transcript of WAHF interview with Ralph Brotz, August 7, 1985. Mel Thompson chronology in WAHF archives.

30. *Vilas County News-Review*, June, 1924, Interview with Karl Kerscher, September, 1996.

31. Transcripts of WAHF interviews with Les Borer and Ken Reed, June 1975 and Ken Reed, April, 1986; *La Crosse Tribune*, December 3, 1974.

32. Transcript of WAHF interview with Louis Wuilleumier, April 22, 1986. *Wisconsin Blue Book*, 1937, p. 553. *Rice Lake Chronotype*, November 5, 12, 1986; *Madison Capital Times*, October 2, 1974, July 17, 1991; "Airplane Schedule," Royal Airways Corporation, Madison, 1928.

33. Manitowoc in *Manitowoc Herald Times Reporter*, May 31, 1996. O'Brien, p. 23.

34. Marshfield in *Marshfield News-Herald*, July 25, 1920, September 6, 1923, July 6, 1925, June 21, 22, 1928, October 3, 1929, May 28, 1930, July 3, August 3, 1932 and "Sales Contract," Curtiss Aeroplane and Motor Corporation, and M.B. Brunkalla, July 14, 1920.

35. *Milwaukee Sentinel*, November 27, 1927; Hardie, *General Mitchell International Airport*, pps. 26-36; *Wisconsin Blue Blue*, 1940, p. 179.

36. *Milwaukee County Airports*, p. 11; *Aero Digest*, July, 1929; *Aviation*, December 7, 1929; *Scrapbook*, compiled by Herman Salmon, WAHF archives.

37. Hardie, *General Mitchell Airport*, pps. 3-45; *Badger Flying*, July, 1946.

38. Oshkosh Airport in *The Wisconsin Magazine*, December 1950. Articles of Incorporation of Oshkosh Airport Incorporated, October 5, 1927. Steve Wittman, "A Summary of Mr. S. J. Wittman's Activities at the Winnebago County Airport, Oshkosh, Wisconsin, undated typescript in files of Wisconsin Aviation Hall of Fame. Krippene, pps. 171-188, 127-131. *Oshkosh Northwestern*, July 16, 17, August 13, 1940; "Oshkosh Starts Move For Seaplane Base," *Wisconsin National Guard Review*, v. 17, n. 6, September, 1940.

39. *South Central Wisconsin Press*, May 7, 1997.

40. Transcript of WAHF interview with John Sullivan, 1987; *Racine Sunday Bulletin*, December 19, 1965, January 11, 1970; *Professional Pilot*, April 1989.

41. *Madison Capital Times*, October 18, 1975.

42. *Rhinelander Daily News*, June 12, 1990, March 1, 1993; Mangerson, pps. 1-5.

43. Kamla, pps. 1-15.

44. Proceedings of the Supervisors of Door County, 1937, 1938, 1939, 1940, 1941, 1942, 1943, 1944. *Door County Advocate*, June 16, 1939, December 7, 1948.

45. Dickey, *Aviation at the Head of the Lakes*, pps. 1-25, *Program of Opening and Dedicaiton of Superior Municipal Airport*, August 21, 1937; *Superior Evening-Telegram*, July 5, 1929.

46. Berquist, "Milestones in Island Aviation," chronology in the Washington Island Archives. *Door County Advocate*, August 3, August 24, November 2, 1928; December 15, 1941; *The Island Reporter*, June 8, 1933.

47. Transcript of WAHF interview with Dale Crites, 1985 and Dean Crites, 1996. *Waukesha Freeman*, May 19, 1929, December 6, 1969, February 28, April 8, 1981, January 22, 1987; O'Brien, pps. 16, 17, 22, 23, 28-33, 54, 57, 58, 67, 73-75, 79-85, 105, 110-111.

48. *Wausau News Herald*, August 3, October 7, 1927, June 11, 1928, May 10, 1938; May 8, June 19, December 27, 1939; *The Deseret News*, February 19, 1934. Transcripts of WAHF interviews with Irvin Hall, Archie Towle, Marie Towle, Larry Towle and Lyle Grimm, 1985.

49. *Wausau Record Herald*, May 28, 1928; Goc, *Others Before You*, pps. 191-195. Adolphson, *Cold Water Canyon*, pps. 31-32, 37.

50. *Wisconsin Rapids Daily Tribune*, October 20, 1928, September 12, October 10, 1929, April 23, 1930; *Milwaukee Journal*, October 21, 1928; Buehler, pps. 79-85. *Master Plan: Alexander Field*, pps. 6-8.

CHAPTER III - Wisconsin Aviators at War - Pages 170-227

1. John Mitchell in Levin, pps. 101, 110-112 and *Liberty Badger*, v. 34 p. 19.

2. Aviation statistics in Gorrell, *The Measure of America's World War Aeronautical Effort*, p. 25. Mitchell biography in Levin, *Mitchell, Pioneer of Air Power*, pps. 22-88; Mitchell's solo in Culver, *The Day the Air Mail Degun*, pps. 90-95, Hennessey, *The United States Army Air Arm, April 1861 - April 1917*, p. 186 and Mitchell's *Memoirs of World War I*, p. 10; Quotes on bombing and flying over the front in Levine, pps. 91 and

92. Plans for 1919 in Levine, pps. 148-149. Maitland quote in Maitland, *Knights of the Air*, p. 276.

3. Kaminski in Kaminski Papers, State Historical Society Archives, University of Wisconsin-Milwaukee.

4. Collins in Collins, *Tales of an Old Air-Faring Man*, p. 2. Molter in Nordhoff and Hall, *The Lafayette Flying Corps*, p. 360; Sloan, *Wings of Honor*, pps. 47, 51; *Wausau Daily Record Herald*, January 12, 1916, July 21, 1917; *New York Tribune*, December 23, 1917. Lehr in Nordhoff and Hall, p. 311, Rasmussen, *Manderson Lehr A Beloit College Hero*, pps. 2-8 and letter from T. Carles in *Beloit College Round Table*, January 7, 1919. Williams in Clapp, *A History of the 17th Aero Squadron*, pps. 23-25, 37-39, 55-71, 102, 157, Sloan, pps. 201-204 and *U.S. Air Service Victory Credits*, p. 58. McGilvary in Fitch, *Wings in the Night*, pps. 114, 100-103, Sloan, p. 299 and *Liberty Badger*, v. 34, 1919, p. 388.

5. Collins in Collins, p. 2. Tobey in *Wahiscan*, p. 93. Conant in Sloan, p. 357. Buckley in *Liberty Badger*, v. 34, p. 11 and Sloan, p. 291. Meyers in Sloan, pps. 140, 145, 154 and *Liberty Badger*, v. 34, p. 389. Kelty in *Liberty Badger*, v. 34, pps. 18, 385. McMurray in Sloan, p. 259, *Liberty Badger*, v. 34, p. 388, *Victory Credits*, p. 37, and Holt, *Glacier Pilot*, p. 33. Reis in *Liberty Badger*, v. 34, pps. 359, 407, *Wisconsin Blue Book*, 1929, p. 544, confidential report found in the Alvin Reis collection of the State Historical Society of Wisconsin Archives, "Elect Judge Alvin C. Reis to the Supreme Court of Wisconsin," pamphlet. Quote by Rowe in *Brodhead's Tribute to her Men of the Service, 1914-1918*, pps. 122-123.

6. Robie, Bill, *For The Greatest Achievement*, p. 90.

7. Lawson in Henry, *Zig, Zag and Swirl*, pps. 57-59, 61, 79-83, *Green Bay Press-Gazette*, September 11, November 15, 1917; *Aerial Age Weekly*, October 1, 1917; Bowers, *Curtiss Aircraft*, p. 145. Hamilton in *Morehouse Biography*, pps. 1-2, *Hamilton Propellers*, brochure, p. 1 and *U. S. Naval Aviation*, p. 33.

8. Dodd, *The Day The Air Mail Began*, pps. 34-59 and Lipsner, *The Airmail, Jennies to Jets*, pps. 4-24.

9. *Wisconsin Blue Book*, 1940, pps. 177-183; *Decade of Progress*, pps. 7-8; *WPA Program*, pps. 113-115; *Milwaukee Journal*, August 25, 1940; *Aerosphere*, pps. A-128 and A-144.

10. Van Galder, pps. 61-66; *Wisconsin Blue Book*, 1944, pps. 105-106; O'Brien, pps. 98-100; Wittman's *Summary*, pps. 1-2; Kamla, p. 15; Paul, pps. 82-84; Poberezny, p. 137; Morey, *Historical Information*, p. 4.

11. War production entries in *Summary of War Supply and Facility Contracts*, November 1, 1945; Mosquito Bomber in Goc, *Native Realm*, p. 130, *Oshkosh Northwestern*, June 10, 1943; Roddis in Maurer, p. 50; Mellen in Winkler, *Midwest Flyer*, June 1984; "When Milkweed Went to War," *Wisconsin Trails*, Fall, 1980.

12. "Wisconsin's Military Manpower," *Wisconsin Blue Book*, 1962, p. 255 and Stevens, *Letters from the Front*, p.73.

13. Twining in *Current Biography*, 1953, pps. 629-631.

14. Yeo in *Letters from the Front*, p. 75; Buchanan, pps. 36-41, 289-291; Jones in *Journal of American Aviation Historical Society*, Fall, 1990, pps. 215-225; Maitland in *U.S. Air Force Biographical Dictionary*, pps. 158-159; Wolf in WAHF Interview, December 1985 and Jablonski, *Airwar*, pps. 32-33; Straubel and Flatley in *Voyageur*, winter/spring, 1992, p. 15-18; Laban, Griffin and Knobloch in *Doolittle's Tokyo Raiders*, pps. 195-215, 217-226, 247-261; Mitscher in Buchanan, *The Navy's Air War*, pps. 194-204 and *Current Biography*, 1944, pps. 476-480; Wetter in "A B-29 Experience," *Landmark*, summer, 1995, p. 23; Thomas in *Rice Lake Chronotype*, August 2, 1995; Klein in *Chicago Tribune*, August 19, 1945; Fox in *Letters from the Front*, p. 131.

15. Murphy, *Heroes of World War II*, pps. 247-251; Bong, *Dear Mom*, pps. 176, 354, 437, 451, 510-513; Bong, *Ace of Aces*, pps. 2, 94.

16. Buchanan, *The Navy's Air War*, pps. 15-16; Hubbard in *Wausau Record-Herald*, February 2, July 22, 1943, April 7, July 25, 1944; Jerstad in Wolff, *Low Level Mission*, pps. 91, 93, 118, 145, 179 and Murphy, *Heroes of World War II*, pps. 127-132; Rentmeester in "Big Brothers and Little Friends: A Memoir of the Air War Against Germany," *Wisconsin Magazine of History*, autumn, 1990; Parsons in *Wisconsin State Journal*, June 7 1944; Vandenberg in Meillinger, *Hoyt S.*

Vandenberg, The Life of a General, pps. 2, 10, 15, 31, 50, 51, 52, 57; Bowers in Mark Van Ells, Interview with Clifford Bowers, *Wisconsin Veterans Oral History Project,* June 7, 1994.

17. Chun, "The Origin of the WASPS," *Journal of the American Aviation Historical Society,* v. 14, n. 4, 1969. Granger, *On Final Approach,* p. 255; Gott, *Women in Pursuit,* pps. 97-104; Nicol, *Extracts from Letters,* pps. 1, 38; Johnson, "The WASP of World War II," *Aerospace Historian,* v. 17, n. 2 & 3, summer 1970; *Eau Claire Leader,* July 14, 1949; *History of the Ninety-Nines,* p. 214.

18. *Wausau News-Herald,* January 1, 1942; *Badger Airway Beacon,* April 22, 1950; February 6, August 21, 1952; January 21, November 4, 1954; June 7, September 20, 1956, December, 1960; August, 1961; O'Brien, p. 123. *Wisconsin Flyer,* January, 1980; *Midwest Flyer,* October, 1984; October, 1985; February, 1986; *Wisconsin Wing Review,* May, June, July, October, November, December, 1987; January, February, March, 1988.

19. Jackson, *Air War Over Korea,* pps. 9, 61; Meilinger, *Hoyt S. Vandenberg,* pps. 2, 10, 62-64, 95-101, 175-179, 180-182, 190-202.

20. *Dunn County News,* July 30, August 5, August 6, August 13, September 17, October 20, October 27, November 26, December 17, 1952. Letter on Gerald Zuelsback from Robert Little of McDonnell Douglass Corporation, August 1, 1990 and scrapbook from W.W. Huelsback in WAHF Archives.

22. *Badger Airway Beacon,* June 28, 1956.

23. Stevens, *Voices From Vietnam,* pps. 91-97, 100-102, 110-112, 157-162; Schneider, *Air Force Heroes in Vietnam,* pps. 1, 14-16, 22-24, 32-34, 43-45, 54-58, 77.

24. Doherty, *Blitzkrieg for Beginners,* pps. 92, 101; *Sparta Herald,* August 12, 1940; *Wisconsin State Journal,* August 22, 23, 24, 25, 26, 28, 1940; *Guard Review,* v. 17 n. 6, September, 1940, v. 18, n. 6, July, 1941; *Wisconsin's Finest,* p. 27.

25. *Milwaukee Journal,* August 9, 1940; *Wisconsin National Guard Review,* v. 17, n. 6, September, 1940, v. 18, n. 6, July 1941; *Wisconsin's Finest,* p. 27-31.

26. *Wisconsin Blue Book,* 1948, p. 346; *Wisconsin's Finest,* pps. 3, 4, 34-35, 42, 47-52, 57-66, 72-79, 90-93, 130-134, 147-158, 166-172, 174-188, 238-242, 280-286.

CHAPTER IV - State Government in Aviation - Pages 228-243

1. *Wisconsin Blue Book,* 1937, p. 553; 1940, p. 273; 1944, pps. 250-252; 1946, p. 263; *An Airport System For Wisconsin,* pps. 40-46; Associated Press, Madison, March 10, 1944, February 2, March 19, March 22, April 26, 1945. WAHF interview with Fritz Wolf, July 10, 1985; *A Decade of Progress in Aviation in Wisconsin,* 1946-1956; Annual Reports, Wisconsin State Aeronautics Commission, 1957-58, 1961, 1962, 1963, 1964, 1965-66.

2. *Wisconsin Blue Book,* 1968; WI DOT, Biennial Report, 1972-73, 1975-77, 1977-79, 1981-83, 1983-85, 1987-89, 1991-93; WI DOT, *Wisconsin Airport Development Program, Completed Projects as of August 26, 1997*; WI DOT, *Wisconsin Airport System Plan: 1986-2010.*

3. "Aeronautics Report," *Midwest Flyer,* September, October, November, December, 1987, February, March, 1988; *Midwest Flyer,* November, 1985; *Wisconsin State Journal,* May 10, 1989.

4. *Wisconsin Aerospace Education Association Newsletter,* June, October, 1973, June-July, 1975, October, 1976, March, 1985.

CHAPTER V - Airport Developments - Pages 244-293

1. *Adams County Times,* June 13, 1984; *Friendship Reporter,* January 26, 1983; *Midwest Flyer,* August, 1983, p.16.

2. *On The Rock,* pps. 62, 74, 80, 83, 85, 87, 100, 104; *Midwest Flyer,* April, 1983; *Minneapolis Star-Tribune,* February 21, 1988; *Ashland Daily Press,* January 31, 1959, September 23, 1963; *Badger Airway Beacon,* June 20, 1951.

3. Heffner, pps. 31-96, 103-107, 117-123. WAHF interview with Carl Rindlisbacher, 1985; *Midwest Flyer,* August 1982, p. 14.

4. Correspondence of Hale O'Malley and Wisconsin State Aeronautics Commission, et. al. August 12, 1963-September 12, 1965; *Duluth News-Tribune,* September 1967. *Badger Airway Beacon,* June 16, 1955. WAHF Interview with Libby Parod, 1985, *Midwest Flyer,* December, 1982.

5. Milquet, *History of Ashwaubenon, Wisconsin Airline Service Study,* 1977, p. 103. *Wisconsin Aviation Activity, 1983; Badger Airway Beacon,* August 20, 1953, May 10, 1955, May 31, 1956.

6. *Journal of Burnett County,* June 25, 1942, August 17, November 7, 1944, May 9 1946, June 26 1947.

7. *Manitowoc Herald Times Reporter,* June 27, 1973.

8. Bonnie Selmer, *Cornell Municipal Airport,* unpublished ms.; Bureau of Aeronautics, *Airport Sites in Wisconsin,* 1993.

9. *Clark County Press,* August 21, 1947, December 11, 1956, June 20, 1974. Neillsville Municipal File, Aeronautics Bureau.

10. Portage Airport in *Portage Daily Register,* July 18, 1962. Robert Nieman in *Midwest Flyer,* December, 1982.

11. Prairie du Chien Municipal File, Aeronautics Bureau, *Badger Airway Beacon,* August 6, 1953, WAHF Interview with Glen Meyer, January, 1998.

12. Dane County Airport in Bureau of Aeronautics, *Airport Sites In Wisconsin,* 1993; *Madison Capital Times,* June 1, 1951, June 3, 1952, January 30, 1962; *Milwaukee Journal,* August 27, 1956; *Wisconsin State Journal,* September 10, 1952, May 6, 1958, November 20, 1964, May 26, 1965, July 23, 1967; *Midwest Flyer,* February 1982. *History of Dane County Regional Airport,* timeline, 1995. Morey Airport in *Wisconsin State Journal,* July 7, July 17, 1991, May 9, 1993, May 16, 1996, *Wisconsin Flyer,* July, 1979, *Midwest Flyer,* December, 1980.

13. Letter from Michael Tegtmeier on history of Dodge County Airport, *Midwest Flyer,* July, 1984; WAHF Interview with Glen Knaup, January, 1990, Paul Baker, February, 1990, Roy Reabe, August, 1991.

14. Peterson, *Cherryland Airport History; Door County Advocate,* September 25, 1942, April 4, 1947; *Badger Airway Beacon,* February 2, 1956; Letter to Russell Austad on Cherryland Airport from J. S. Zimmermann, Civil Aeronautics Administration, December 12, 1949; Goodwin Berquist Papers, Washington Island Archives; *Door County Advocate,* March, 1946.

15. WAHF Interview with William Amorde, July, 1989.

16. Menomonie Airport in *Score Field-Menomonie.* Boyceville Airport in Jim Nosker, *Airport History.*

17. WAHF Interview with Charles Wood, June, 1990; Barland, *The Rivers Flow On,* pps. 259-260; *Eau Claire Leader-Telegram,* February 1, 1945, July 5, 1947, August 17, 1961, December 28, 1978, May 31, 1986.

18. WAHF Interview with Will Haase, Jr., July, 1985; *Fond du Lac Reporter,* July 17, 1959, August 10, 1989.

19. *Badger Airway Beacon,* July 7, 1955, October 25, 1956.

20. Boscobel Airport in *Boscobel Dial,* August 27, 1945, August 23, 1958, November 28, 1974. Platteville Airport in *Platteville Journal,* November 6, 1958, *Wisconsin State Journal,* January 1, 1980. Lancaster Airport in *Grant County Herald,* April 10, 1951, March 5, 1970, November 10, 1976. Cassville Airport in Eckstein, *The Cassville Municipal Airport,* 1951, *Badger Airway Beacon,* November 6, 1950.

21. Monroe Airport in *Badger Airway Beacon,* January 22, 1951, WAHF Interview with Nate Klassy, January, 1998. Brodhead Airport in *Wisconsin Flyer,* April, November, 1980, September, 1981, October, 1983.

22. Mineral Point Airport in *Dodgeville Chronicle,* November 4, 1976, April 13, 1978. Tom Thomas in *Wisconsin Flyer,* June, 1980.

23. *Black River Falls Banner Journal,* July 14, 1971, September 14, 21, 1994.

24. Watertown Airport in *Watertown Times,* April 10, August 27, 1945; Wisconsin Aviation *Talewinds,* July-September, 1996.

25. Barb Brunner, *Mauston/New Lisbon Union Airport,* 1997.

26. Kenosha Airport in *Kenosha News,* May 28, 1947; *Kenosha Messenger Courier,* August 19, 1987; *Midwest Flyer,* November, 1987. Education in *Midwest Flyer,* February, 1988. Westosha Airport in WAHF Interview with Mike Ruggles, December, 1997.

27. La Crosse Airport in *La Crosse Municipal Airport Master Plan Study,* December, 1975; *La Crosse Tribune,* March 21, 1976, August 3, 1986;

Goc, *Where The Waters Flow*, p. 49.

28. Kerstetter, Carl, *Chronological Listing of Events and Activities Related to the Development of Langlade County Airport*.

29. Tomahawk Airport in *16th Biennial Report of the Wisconsin Conservation Commission, 1937-38*; *Tomahawk Leader*, July 6, 1978. Merrill Airport in Letter to WAHF from Charles Ercegovac, January, 1997; WAHF Nomination from Leroy Jonas, June, 1987; *Wausau Record Herald*, May 13, 1968; *Midwest Flyer*, May, 1984.

30. Donohue and Associates, *Airport Master Plan for the Manitowoc Municipal Airport*, 1975; *Badger Airway Beacon*, July 3, 1952, October, 15, 1953, May 31, 1956; WAHF interview with Carl Klackner, November 1996.

31. *Wausau Daily Record Herald*, February 9, 1944, September 4, 1945, August 12, 1946, February 18, 1948, April 13, 1952, July 19, 1961, May 21, 1970; Bureau of Aeronautics, *Wisconsin Air Activity*, 1995; Fritz Wolf letter to Lyle Grimm, April 17, 1968.

32. EAA in *Experimental Aircraft Association Chronology*, EAA 1998; Parnall and Poberezny, pps. 199-200, 219, 259-329; *Wall Streey Journal*, December 11, 1991.

33. Maitland Field in *Badger Airway Beacon*, July 5 1951, April 21, 1955, May 31, 1956. Timmermann Field in *Milwaukee Journal*, April 27, 1941, June 23, 1967; *Badger Airway Beacon*, March 15, 1956; *Milwaukee County's Airports*, p. 11, WAHF interview with William Lotzer, July, 1987. Hales Corners in Shepherd and Weiler, *Hales Corners Wisconsin*, pps. 42-43, *Badger Airway Beacon*, October 2, 1952. Rainbow Airport in *Badger Airway Beacon*, February 4, 1954, *Midwest Flyer*, January, 1985. Mitchell Field in Hardie, *General Mitchell International Airport*, pps. 42-48, 68-70, 76-78, 101-103, 106-109, 165-169.

34. Tomah Airport in *Tomah Journal*, August 3, 1944, June 3 1945, June 14, 1973, April 27, 1989, *AOPA Pilot*, June 1969. Sparta Airport in *Monroe County, Wisconsin Pictorial History*, 1976, pps. 15, 120, 250.

35. WAHF Interview with Robert Jubin, July, 1989.

36. Rhinelander Airport in Mangerson, *Rhinelander/Oneida County Airport*. Three Lakes Airport in *Badger Airway Beacon*, December 3, 1953.

37. *Appleton Post-Crescent*, June 12, 1983, *Wisconsin Aviation Bulletin*, July, 1990, July 13, 1992. Air Wisconsin in *Appleton Post-Crescent*, September 8, 1968, Kort, *The Fox Cities*, 1985. Midwest Express in *Midwest Express Magazine*, May/June 1994, *Frequent Flyer*, June 1994, *Chicago Tribune*, February 18, 1996, *Milwaukee Journal Sentinel*, April 20, 1996.

38. Aeronautics Bureau Municipal File, Ozaukee County; *Port Washington Herald*, October 16, 1957; *Port Washington Ozaukee Press*, January 26, 1984.

39. Howard Needles Tammen & Bergendoff, *Airport Feasibility Study, River Falls, Wisconsin*, 1985. Red Wing Airport in *Midwest Flyer*, July 1989.

40. *Osceola Sun*, September 2, 1986; *Osceola, A Village Chronicle*; *Badger Airway Beacon*, March, 1962. R. Dixon Speas, *Master Plan, Amery Municipal Airport*, 1976.

41. Kamla, *STE 1928-1988, A History of the Stevens Point Airfield*.

42. Phillips Airport in Kudrna, *Phillips History in Aviation*, *Phillips Bee*, September 15, 1983. Park Falls Airport in *Badger Airway Beacon*, June 19, 1952, July 8, 1954, July 24, 1955. Prentice Airport in *Phillips Bee*, October 1, 1981, *Midwest Flyer*, November, 1987.

43. WAHF Interview with John Sullivan, February, 1987, *Racine Journal Times*, April 1, 1996. Burlington Airport in *Kenosha News*, April 5, 1957, *Burlington Standard-Press*, September 8, 1960, October 12, 1961, *Midwest Flyer*, October, 1985, July, 1986, *Racine Journal Times*, August 20, 1990.

44. Weiland, *Fifty Missions Over Sextonville*.

45. *History of the Ninety-Nines*, pps. 214-215; *Badger Airway Beacon*, 1951-1960; *Midwest Flyer*, 1980s; *Wisconsin State Journal*, May 10, 1977, June 3, 1979.

46. Rock County Airport in *Beloit Daily News*, June 6, August 2, August 5, 1995, Van Galder, *Taming The Blue*, pps. 102-106. Henkelmann in *Midwest Flyer*, April, 1987.

47. WAHF interviews with Hal Doughty, May, 1989, Elmer Wisherd, March, 1985; phone interview with Dick Pedersen, January, 1998.

48. *New Richmond News*, February 13, 1962, April 25, 1963, July 11, 1963, November 21, 1963. Wisconsin Department of Transportation, Bureau of Aeronautics, *Wisconsin Airport Directory*, 1995-1996.

49. Reedsburg Airport in Schuette, *Reedsburg Remembers*, pps. 94-95. Lone Rock Airport in *Badger Airway Beacon*, December 16, 1954, *Wisconsin State Journal*, May 24, 1968, *Dodgeville Chronicle*, November 13, 1969, October 5, 1972, July 26, 1979, *Spring Green Home News*, October 5, 1983, November 7, 1984, *Milwaukee Journal*, November 23, 1984, *Midwest Flyer*, May, 1990. Sauk Prairie Airport in *Sauk City Prairie Star*, April 25, 1963, April 13, 1977, June 25, 1987. Baraboo Dells Airport in *Baraboo News-Republic*, August 14, 1945, March 12, 1954, April 29, 1965, *Badger Airway Beacon*, April 19, 1956.

50. *Sawyer County Record*, November 13, 1953; WI DOT, *Survey of Public Airports Serving Recreational Areas*, 1972; *Wisconsin Airport System Plan: 1986-2010*, 1986.

51. *Badger Airway Beacon*, August 25, 1950, November 6, 1952, July 2, 1953, February 4, 1954.

52. WAHF Interview with Harry Chaplin, July, 1987. *Badger Airway Beacon*, December, 1960; *Sheboygan Press*, August, 1957, December, 1959, December 8, 1969, February 22, 1988, February 28, 1991.

53. Terri Vetter, *The Taylor County Airport*.

54. *Hillsboro Sentry-Enterprise*, June 3, 1993. Viroqua Airport in letter from Dwain Munyon, December, 1997.

55. Eagle River Airport in *History of Eagle River Airport*. Land O'Lakes Airport in WAHF interview with Karl Kerschner, January, 1996. Lakeland/Noble Lee Airport in WAHF interview with Virginia Lee, May, 1986.

56. WAHF Interview with Bob Washburn, January, 1998. *Midwest Flyer*, August, 1988; *Sport Aviation*, November, 1971, May, 1992.

57. Chuck Lewis, *History of Shell Lake Airport, 1945-1995*.

58. Spellman, *History of Hartford Airport*. West Bend Airport in WAHF Interview with Earl Stier, March, 1989, WAHF Interview with Gunther Voltz, September, 1997.

59. Waukesha Airport in *Waukesha County Airport 60th Anniversary*, 1995, *Milwaukee Journal*, October 30, 1992, *Waukesha Freeman*, July 29, 1996. Aero Park and Capitol Drive Airports in O'Brien, *History of Aviation in Waukesha County*, pps. 145-148. Capitol Airport in *Waukesha Aviation Club 50th Anniversary*, p. 30, *History of the Ninety Nines*, 1979, pps. 511-512.

60. Clintonville Airport in Serling, *Ceiling Unlimited*, pps. 1-25; Letter from M. W. Torkelson to CAA, July 20, 1942 in Clintonville Municipal File, Aeronautics Bureau. Waupaca Airport in *Waupaca Post*, November 1, 1944, July 22, 1971.

61. Wild Rose Airport in *Wisconsin Aviation Bulletin*, October, 1988.

62. A. L. Osmundsen & Associates, *Progress Report of the Winnebago County Airport 1940-1961*; Goc, *James P. Coughlin in County Government*, p. 23. *Wisconsin Flyer*, November, 1983; WAHF Interview with "Red" Strehlow, April, 1986, with Bill Brennand, August, 1985, with Warren Basler, September, 1989.

63. King, "Steve Wittman–One of the World's Greatest Race Pilots" in *The Golden Age of Air-Racing*, pps. 382 - 407. WAHF interview with Steve Wittman, 1974.

64. Perry-Carrington Engineering, *Master Plan Report: Alexander Field*, 1962. Maurer, *Aviation History of Marshfield*, WAHF interview with Roy Shwery, July, 1989. *Reader's Digest*, January, 1968.

65. *NASA Astronaut Fact Book*.

Wisconsin Aviation History Bibliography

Books

Books in bold type are either about Wisconsin aviators or written by Wisconsin authors.

AAF, The Official Guide to the Army Air Forces, A Directory, Almanac and Chronicle of Achievement, Simon and Schuster, New York, New York. • *Air War-Vietnam*, Arno Press, New York, 1978. • Allard, Noel E. and Sandvick, Gerald N., *Minnesota Aviation History, 1857-1945*, MAHB Publishing, Inc. Chaska, Minnesota, 1993. • The Aviation History Unit, *The Navy's Air War, A Mission Completed*, Harper & Brothers Publishers, New York, 1946. • Barland, Lois, *The Rivers Flow On*, Eau Claire County Historical Society, 1965. • Beachey, Betty K., *Abraham Beachey, 1783-1850, Ancestor of Barnstormer Lincoln Beachey*, Amundsen Publishing, Decorah, Iowa, 52101. • Bice, Raymond C., *Years To Remember*, Readmore, La Crosse, Wisconsin, undated. • Bilstein, Roger E., *Flight In America, 1900-1983, From the Wrights to the Astronauts*, The Johns Hopkins University Press, Baltimore, 1984. • **Bong, Carl and Mike O'Connor, *Ace of Aces: The Dick Bong Story*, Champlin Fighter Museum, Mesa, Arizona, 1985.** • **Bong, Carl, *Dear Mom, So We Have a War*, Burgess Publishing, 1991.** • Bowers, Peter M., *Curtiss Aircraft, 1907-1947*, Putnam & Company Ltd., London, 1979. • Briddon, Arnold E., Champie Ellmore A. and Marraine, Peter A., *FAA Historical Fact Book, A chronology 1926-1971*, Department of Transportation, Federal Aviation Administration Office of Information Services, Washington, D. C., 1974. • Buehler, J. Marshall, *The Nekoosa Story, A Commemorative History of Nekoosa Papers Inc.*, Nekoosa Papers Inc. Port Edwards, Wisconsin, 1987. • Burbach, Julius, *West Allis, A City of Marvelous Growth in A Decade, June 28, 1902-June 28, 1912*, West Allis, 1912. • Burnham, Frank A., *Hero Next Door*, Aero Publishers, Inc., Fallbrook, California, 1974. • Burnham, Guy, *The Lake Superior Country in History and Story*, Ashland Daily Press, Ashland, Wisconsin, 1930. • **Butler, Beverly M., *The Piper Cub Era at Nicolet Airport*, Airport Owners Association, Iola, Wisconsin, 1991.** • Chappelle, Ethel Elliot, *Around the Four Corners*, Chronotype Publishing Co., Inc., Rice Lake, Wisconsin. • Christopher, Melbourne, *Houdini, A Pictorial Life*, Thomas Y. Crowell, New York, 1976. • The Civics Club, *Brodhead's Tribute to her Men of the Service, 1914-1918*, The Civics Club, Brodhead, Wisconsin, 1921. • Clapp, *A History of the 17th Aero Squadron*, reprinted, The Battery Press, Nashville, 1990. • **Clark, William L. M. H., ed., *Tales of an Old Air-Faring Man: A Half Century of Incidents, Accidents and Providence, The Reminiscences of Paul F. Collins*, University of Wisconsin-Stevens Point Foundation Press, 1983.** • Class of 1918 of the University of Wisconsin at Madison, *The Badger*, vol. XXXII, 1917, University of Wisconsin, Madison. • Class of 1919 of the University of Wisconsin at Madison, *The Badger*, vol. XXXIII, 1918, University of Wisconsin, Madison. • Class of 1920 of the University of Wisconsin at Madison, *The Liberty Badger*, vol. XXXIV, 1919, University of Wisconsin, Madison. • Cooke, James J., *The U.S. Air Service in the Great War, 1917-1919*, Praeger Publishers, Westport, Connecticut, 1996. • **Cooper, Jo, ed., *Pioneer Pilot, Based on Walter Lees' Journal, 1911-1931*, Converse Publishing, San Marino, California, 1995.** • Crouch, Tom D., *The Eagle Aloft, Two Centuries of the Balloon In America*, Smithsonian Institution Press, Washington D.C., 1983. • **Culver, Edith Dodd, *Talespins, A Story of Early Aviation Days*, Sunstone Press, Santa Fe, New Mexico, 1986.** • **Culver, Edith Dodd, *The Day The Air Mail Began*, Cub Flyers Enterprises, Kansas City, Kansas, 1967.** • Cutler, Thomas J., *The Battle of Leyte Gulf, 23-26 October 1944*, HarperCollins Publishers, New York, 1994. • Dawes, William and Clara Dawes, *History of Oshkosh, 1938*, 1938. • **Day, Beth, *Glacier Pilot: The Story of Bob Reeve and the Flyers Who Pushed Back Alaska's Air Frontiers*, Henry Holt and Company, New York, 1957.** • Dorr, Robert F., *Vietnam: Combat From the Cockpit*, Motorbooks International Publishers & Wholesalers Inc., Osceola, Wisconsin, 1989. • DuPre, Col. Flint O., USAFR, *U.S. Air Force Biographical Dictionary*, Franklin Watts, Inc., New York, 1965. • **Faunce, Cy, Q., *The Airline and its Inventor*, Rocheotel Publiishing Co., Columbus, Ohio, 1921.** • Fausel, Robert W., *Whatever Happened To Curtiss-Wright*, Sunflower University Press, Manhattan, Kansas, 1990. • Federal Aviation Administration, *Pilot's Handbook of Aeronautical Knowledge*, Arco Publishing Company, Inc., New York, 1978. • Fitch, Willis S., *Wings in the Night: Flying the Caproni Bomber in World War I*, The Battery Press, Nashville, Tennessee, 1989. • Francis, Charles E., *The Men Who Changed A Nation, The Tuskegee Airmen*, Branden Publishing Company, Boston, Massachuttes, 1988. • Futrell, Robert Frank, *The United States Air Force In Korea, 1950-1953*, Duell, Sloan and Pearce, New York, 1961. • Glines, Carroll V., *Doolittle's Tokyo Raiders*, D. Van Nostrand Company, Inc., Princeton, New Jersey, 1964. • Goc, Michael J., *Stewards of the Wisconsin, The Wisconsin Valley Improvement Company*, New Past Press Inc., Friendship, Wisconsin, 1993. • Goc, Michael J., *Where The Waters Flow*, New Past Press Inc., Friendship, Wisconsin, 1991. • Goc, Michael J., ed., *Others Before You The History of Wisconsin Dells Country*, New Past Press Inc., Friendship, Wisconsin, 1996. • **Goebel, Robert J., *Mustang Ace: Memoirs of a P-51 Fighter Pilot*, Pacifica Press, Pacifica, California, 1991.** • Granger, Byrd Howell, *On Final Approach: The Women Airforce Service Pilots of W.W. II*, Falconer Publishing Company, Scottsdale, Arizona, 1991. • Griffin, Fern Bauer, Bonnie Fritsch Brandt, ed., *Historical Collections of Washburn County and the Surrounding Indianhead County*, vol. 4, J.B. Duncan and Associates, Inc., Shell Lake, Wisconsin, 1994. • Harris, Walt, *The Chequamegon Country, 1659-1976*, Walter J. Harris, Fayetteville, Arkansas, 1976. • **Heffner, Bob, *Cleared For Landing, A History of Barron County Aviation*, Bob Heffner, Rice Lake, Wisconsin, 1995.** • Hennessy, Juliette A., *The United States Army Air Arm, April 1861 to April 1917*, Office of Air Force History, United States Air Force, Washington, D.C., 1985. • Highway Planning Survey, ed., *A History of Wisconsin Highway Development, 1835-1945*, Madison, Wisconsin, 1947. • Historical Office of the Army Air Forces, *The Official Pictorial History of the Army Air Forces*, Arno, New York, 1979. • Hopkins, George E., *The Airline Pilots, A Study in Elite Unionization*, Harvard University Press, Cambridge, Massachusetts, 1971. • *Flying the Line, The First Half Century of the Air Line Pilots Association*, The Air Line Pilots Association, Washington D. C. 1982. • Hunt, N. Jane, ed., *Brevet's Wisconsin Historical Markers & Sites*, Brevet International, Sioux Falls, South Dakota, 1974. • Iron County Board of Supervisors Advertising Committee, *Iron County Wisconsin*, Diamond Jubilee, Iron County, Wisconsin, 1968. • Jackson, Robert, *Air War Over Korea*, Charles Scribner's Sons, New York, 1973. • Jane, Fred T., ed., *Jane's All The World's Airships 1909* Reprint, Arco Publishing Co. Inc., New York. • Jane, Fred T., ed., *Jane's All The World's Airships 1913* Reprint, Arco Publishing Co. Inc., New York. • **Jasiunas, Edward, *The Second Transatlantic Flight of Lithuania America*, Felix Waitkus Album Committee, Chicago, 1986.** • **Kamla, John D., *A History of the Stevens Point Airfield*, John D.**

Kamla, Stevens Point, Wisconsin, 1989. • Keil, Sally Van Wagenen, *Those Wonderful Women in Their Flying Machines: The Unknown Heroines of World War II*, Four Directions Press, New York, 1990. • Komons, Nick A., *Bonfires to Beacons: Federal Aviation Policy Under The Air Commerce Act, 1916-38*. United States Department of Transportation, 1978. • Kort, Ellen, *The Fox Heritage, A History of Wisconsin's Fox Cities*, Windsor Publications, Inc., Woodland Hills, California. • **Krippene, Bernice Lee, *Wingwalker, From Wisconsin To Norway, The Larson Brothers and Clyde Lee*, New Past Press Inc., Friendship, Wisconsin, 1995.** • Kronenwetter, Michael, *Wisconsin Heartland, The Story of Wausau and Marathon County*, Pendell Publishing, Midland, Michigan.Krug, Merton Edwin, *History of Reedsburg and the Upper Baraboo Valley*, Merton Edwin Krug, Madison, Wisconsin, 1929. • Laabs, Joyce, *A Collection of Northwoods Nostalgia from the Pages of the Lakeland Times*, Royle Publishing Co., Sun Prairie, Wisconsin, 1978. • Lafayette County Bicentennial Committee, *1776-1976, The Lafayette County Bicentennial Book*, Windmill Publications, Inc., Mt. Vernon, Indiana, 1976. • Langill, Ellen D. and Jean Penn Loerke, ed., *From Farmland to Freeways, A History of Waukesha County Wisconsin*, Waukesha County Historical Society, Inc., Waukesha, Wisconsin, 1984. • Latton, Arthur J., *Reminiscences of Early Taylor County*, 1947. • *Lawson, Aircraft Industry Builder*, **Humanity Publishing Company, Detroit, Michigan.** • Lawson, Alfred W., *Historical Documents Aircraft History: Congressional Record Recommendations to Congress, January 22, 1918 to September 17, 1918*, **Humanity Benefactor Foundation, Detroit, Michigan, 1982.** • Lebow, Eileen F., *Cal Rodgers and the Vin Fiz, The First Transcontinental Flight*, Smithsonian Institution Press, Washington, D. C. • Levin, Isaac Don, *Mitchell, Pioneer of Air Power*, Arno Press, New York, 1972. • Lipsner, Benjamin B., *The Air Mail, Jenny to Jets*, Wilcox and Follett, 1956. • **Maitland, Lester, *Knights of the Air*, Doubleday, Doran & Co., Garden City, New York, 1929.** • Manitowoc County Centennial Committee, *The Manitowoc County Story of a Century, 1848 - 1948*, Manitowoc County Centennial Committee, Manitowoc, Wisconsin, 1948. • **Meilinger, Phillip S., *Hoyt S. Vandenberg, The Life of a General*, Indiana University Press, Bloomington and Indianapolis, Indiana, 1989.** • Mitchell, William, *Memoirs of World War I, From Start to Finish of Our Greatest War*, Greenwood Press, Publishers, Westport, Connecticut, 1975. • Monroe County Wisconsin Bicentennial Committee, *Monroe County, Wisconsin: Pictorial History, 1976*, Tomah Journal Printing Company, Inc., Tomah, Wisconsin, 1976. • Munson, Kenneth, *The Pocket Encyclopedia of World Aircraft in Color: Bombers, Patrol and Transport Aircraft, 1939-45*, The MacMillan Company, 1969. • Neuenschwander, John A., ed., *Kenosha County in the Twentieth Century: A Topical History*, Carthage College, 1976. • Nielson, Dale, ed., *Saga of the U.S. Air Mail Service, 1918-1927*, Air Mail Pioneers, Inc, 1962. • Northwest Airways, *A Million Miles Without an Accident*, Mainstreet Antique Mall of Hopkins, Inc., Hopkins, Minnesota, 1991. • **O'Brien, Warren S., *The History of Aviation In Waukesha County*, Waukesha Aviation Club Inc. Waukesha, Wisconsin, 1956.** • Osceola Historical Society, *Osceola A Village Chronicle*, Osceola Historical Society, Osceola, 1994. • O'Sullivan, Thomas J., *The Pioneer Airplane Mails of the United States*, The American Air Mail Society, Cinnaminson, New Jersey, 1985. • O'Sullivan, Thomas J., and Weber, Karl B., *History of the United State Pioneer and Government-Operated Air Mail Service, 1910-1928*, The American Air Mail Society, Philadelphia, 1973. • Ragsdale, Kenneth Baxter, *Wings Over The Mexican Border, Pioneer Military Aviation in the Big Bend*, University of Texas Press, Austin Texas, 1984. • Paul, Justus F., *The World Is Ours: A History of the University of Wisconsin, Stevens Point, 1894-1994*, Foundation Press, Stevens Point, Wisconsin, 1994. • Parrish, Wayne W., ed., *Who's Who in World Aviation*, vol. 1, American Aviation Publications, Inc., Washington, D.C., 1955. • Pellegreno, Ann Holtgren, *Iowa Takes to the Air, Volume II (1919-1941)*, Aerodrome Press, Story City, Iowa, 1986. • Pisano, Dominick A., *To Fill the Skies with Pilots: The Civilian Pilot Training Program, 1939-46*, University of Illinois Press, Urbana and Chicago,1993. • Powell, William J., *Black Aviator, The Storyof William J. Powell: New Edition of William J. Powell's 1934 Black Wings*, Simthsonian Institution Press, Washington, D.C., 1994. • **Rhodes, Joseph W., *Sparks from the Flaming Wheel*, Beloit Historical Society, Beloit, Wisconsin, 1984.** • Robie, Bill, *For The Greatest Achievement, A History of the Aero Club of America and the National Aeronautical Association*, Smithsonian Institution Press, Washington D. C., 1993. • Roseberry, C. R., *Glenn Curtiss, Pioneer of Flight*, Doubleday & Company, Inc., Garden City, New York, 1972. • **Rosholt, Malcolm, *Flight in the China Air Space, 1910-1950*, Rosholt House, Rosholt, Wisconsin, 1984.** • Schuette, William C., editor, *Reedsburg Remembers 150 Years, A History of Reedsburg, Wisconsin, 1848-1998*, The Sesquicentennial History Committee, 1997. • Seeley, Charlotte Palmer, compiled by, *American Women and the U.S. Armed Forces*, National Archives and Records Administration, Washington, D. C., 1992. • Schneider, Major Donald K., *Air Force Heroes in Vietnam*, Airpower Research Institute, Air War College, Maxwell Air Force Base, Alabama, 1979. • Sellinger, Philip, ed., *A Guide to Sheboygan County and the Fair, Past and Present*, Centennial Celebration History Committee, Sheboygan, Wisconsin, 1952. • **Serling, Robert J., *Ceiling Unlimited, The Story of North Central Airlines*, Walsworth Publishing Co., Marceline, Missouri, 1973.** • Shiner, John F., *Foulois and the U.S. Army Air Corps, 1931-1935*, Office of Air Force History, United States Air Force, Washington, D.C., 1983. • Smith, Henry Ladd, *Airways, The History of Commercial Aviation in the United States*, Alfred A. Knopf, New York, 1942. • Spanier, John W., *The Truman-MacArthur Controversy and the Korean War*, The Belknap Press of Harvard University Press, Cambridge, Massachusetts, 1959. • Stare, Fred A., *The Story of Wisconsin's Great Canning Industry*, The Wisconsin Canners Association, Madison, Wisconsin, 1949. • Stevens, Michael E., editor, *Letters From the Front, 1898-1945: (Voices of the Wisconsin Past)*, State Historical Society of Wisconsin, Madison, Wisconsin, 1992. • Stevens, Michael E., editor, *Voices from Vietnam: (Voices of the Wisconsin Past)*, State Historical Society of Wisconsin, Madison, Wisconsin, 1996. • Stevens, Peter F., *The Mayflower Murderer And Other Forgotten Firsts In American History*, William Morrow and Company, Inc., New York, 1993. • Thayer, Lt. Lucien H., *America's First Eagles, The Official History of the U.S. Air Service, A.E.F. (1917-1918)*, R. James Bender Publishing, San Jose, California and Champlin Fighter Museum Press, Mesa, Arizona, 1983. • Treadwell, Mattie E., *United States Army in World War II, Special Studies, The Women's Army Corps*, Office of the Chief of Military History, Department of the Army, Washington, D.C., 1954. • Turnbull, Archibald D. and Clifford L. Lord, *History of United States Naval Aviation*, Yale University Press, New Haven, 1949. • *United States Naval Aviation, 1910-1970*, Washington, D.C., 1970. • **Van Galder, Marge, *Taming The Blue*, Plum Tree Publications, Beloit, Wisconsin, 1991.** • Van Goethem, Larry, *Not Long Ago*, Larry Van Goethem, 1979. • Vergara, George L., *Hugh Robinson, Pioneer Aviator*. • Verges, Marianne, *On Silver Wings: The Women Airforce Service Pilots of World War II, 1942-1944*, Ballantine Books, New York, 1991. • Winton, Kay Brown, ed., *Historical Collections of Washburn County and the Surrounding Indianhead County*, vol. III, Washburn County Historical Society, 1983. • Wolff, Leon, *Low Level Mission*, Doubleday & Company, Inc., Garden City, New York, 1957. • Wolk, Herman S., *Toward Independence: The Emergence of the U.S. Air Force, 1945-1947*, Air Force History and Museums Program, 1996.

• Young, David and Callahan, Neal, *Fill The Heavens With Commerce, Chicago Aviation, 1855-1926*, Review Press, Chicago, 1981.

Articles

"Arpin Centennial," *Histories of Wood County (and area), Wisconsin Communities*, Helbach Printing, Inc., Amherst, Wisconsin.

Ayotte, Lieutenant Colonel John U., "Blue Meets Red," *Infantry Journal*, vol. XLVII, no. 6, November-December, 1940.

Badger Airway Beacon, various issues from April 22, 1950 through March 1962.

Badger Flying, various issues from vol. 1, no. 1, September, 1945, through vol. II, no. 12, August, 1947.

Baumgartner, "Transatlantic Heroics For Lithuania," *Aviation History*, January 1996.

Becker, Terry Biwer, "The Biwer Beacon," *Landmark*, vol. 37, no. 3, Autumn 1994, Waukesha County Historical Society, Inc., Waukesha, Wisconsin.

Brock, Thomas D. "Lindbergh and Madison," *Historic Madison*, vol. 12, Madison, Wisconsin, 1995.

Buehler, J. Marshall, "A Recent History of Alexander Field, South Wood County Airport," *Master Plan Report: Alexander Field, South Wood County Airport*, Municipal Airport Commission, Wisconsin Rapids, Wisconsin, 1962.

Collins, Paul F., "The Flying Postman," *Liberty Magazine*, vol. 6, no. 11, March 23, 1929.

Collins, Paul F., "When the Air Mail," *Liberty Magazine*, vol. 6, no. 15, April 20, 1929.

Custer, Frank, "The birth of aviation in Madison: And the contribution of a University of Wisconsin drop-out named Lindbergh," *Madison*, September 1981.

Doherty, Thomas, "Blitzkrieg for Beginners: The Maneuvers of 1940 in Central Wisconsin," *Wisconsin Magazine Of History*, vol. 68, no. 2, Winter, 1984-1985.

"The Eagle's Mitts," *Landmark*, vol. 18, no. 1, Winter-Spring 1975, The Waukesha County Historical Society, Waukesha, Wisconsin.

Gilman, Rhoda R., "Zeppelin in Minnesota: A Study in Fact and Fable," *Minnesota History*, vol. 39, no. 7, Fall, 1965.

Hardie, George Jr., "The Airline That Might Have Been," *Historical Messenger of the Milwaukee County Historical Society*, vol. 27, no. 1, March, 1971.

Hardie, George Jr., "Milwaukee's First Airliner," *Historical Messenger of the Milwaukee County Historical Society*, vol. 15, no. 4, December, 1959.

Henry, Lyell D., Jr., "Alfred W. Lawson, The Forgotten "Columbus of the Air"," *Journal of American Culture*, vol. 7, no. 1 & 2, Spring & Summer, 1984.

Keller, Fred H., "Anecdotes of War, On the Home Front," *Landmark*, vol. 34, no. 4, Winter 1991, Waukesha County Historical Society, Waukesha, Wisconsin.

Ketter, Fred H., "WWII in the Tail of a B-29," *Landmark*, vol. 36, no. 1, Spring 1993, Waukesha County Historical Society, Waukesha, Wisconsin.

Kuntz, Jerrold P., "The Jersey Superplane That Almost Was," *New Jersey History*, vol. XCIX, No. 3-4, Fall-Winter, 1981.

Langeswiesche, Wolfgang, "Here Comes The Mini-Airliner" *Reader's Digest*, January, 1968; condensed from *Air Facts*, November 1967. (Roy Shwery)

Lembke, Ruth C., "Grounded Pilot Wins," *Landmark*, vol. 17, no. 1, Winter-Spring 1974, The Waukesha County Historical Society, Waukesha, Wisconsin.

Midwest Flyer, various issues from vol. 2, no. 11, October, 1980 through vol. 19, no. 4, June/July, 1997.

Milquet, Steven R., "Region's Role in Early Stages: From Here to World War II," *Voyageur*, vol. 8, no. 2, Winter/Spring 1992.

Mueller, Arthur E.A., "Air Service for Main Street, U.S.A., *Addresses*, The Newcomen Society in North America, New York, 1961.

Nolan, Libbie, "Waukesha Wings Over Wisconsin," *Landmark*, vol. 14, no. 3 and 4, November 1971, The Waukesha County Historical Society, Waukesha, Wisconsin.

O'Brien, Warren S., "History of Aviation in Waukesha County," *Landmark*, vol. 1, no. 1 and 2, January and April 1958, Waukesha County Historical Society, Waukesha, Wisconsin.

O'Brien, Warren S., "Seventy Old Bold Pilots of Waukesha," *Landmark*, vol.13, no. 2, Spring 1970, The Waukesha County Historical Society, Waukesha, Wisconsin.

O'Brien, Warren S., "More Old Bold Ones . . .," *Landmark*, vol. 14, no. 1, Winter 1971, The Waukesha County Historical Society, Waukesha, Wisconsin.

O'Hara, Bob and James Scott, "Wings of Steel," *Air Classics*, March, 1966.

Parkinson, Russell J., "United States Signal Corps Balloons, 1871-1902," *Military Affairs*, vol. 24, no. 4, winter, 1960-'61.

Personal Flying, various issues from vol. 3, no. 1, September, 1947 through vol. 4, no. 12, August, 1949.

Rodgers, Calbraith P., "The First Trans-continental Aeroplane Flight," *Scientific American*, vol. 106, no. 16, April 20, 1912.

Servais, Larry and Dean, Jill, "The Flight of the Great Northwest," *Yarns of Wisconsin*, Wisconsin Trails/Tamarack Press, Madison, Wisconsin, 1979.

"The Special Service of the University to the War," *The Wisconsin Alumni Magazine*, Madison, Wisconsin, vol. XIX, no. 4, February 1918.

"Those Great Old Boathouses!" *NewMonth*, March/April 1995.

von Zeppelin, Count Ferdinand, "Zeppelin in Minnesota: The Count's Own Story," Translated by Maria Bach Dunn, *Minnesota History*, vol. 40, no. 6, Summer, 1967.

Waitkus, Felix, "Flight to Lithuania," *The Wisconsin Engineer*, March, 1938.

Winkler, Don, "Not a Lemon, but a Mellen," *Midwest Flyer*, vol. 6, no. 6, June 1984.

Wisconsin Flyer, various issues from vol. 1, no. 1, 1979 through vol. 2, no. 10, September, 1980.

Pamphlets

Hamilton Propellers, Since 1909, The Standard of Fine Performance, Hamilton Propellers, 1929.

Travel By Air, Northern Airways Inc., Wausau, 1928.

Making Things, A. P. Warner, ed. by Susan Fulton Welty, Beloit, 1954.

Public Relations Department, Wisconsin State Fair Park, *A Brief History of the Wisconsin State Fair*, Milwaukee/West Allis, 1992.

Souvenir Program and Centennial History, Beaver Dam, Wisconsin, Historical Committee, Beaver Dam Centennial, Inc., Beaver Dam, Wisconsin, 1941.

Brooks-Pazmany, Kathleen, *United States Women in Aviation, 1919-1929*, Smithsonian Studies in Air and Space.

Oakes, Claudia M., *United States Women in Aviation, 1930-1939*, Smithsonian Studies in Air and Space, no. 6.

Douglas, Deborah G., *United States Women in Aviation, 1940-1985*, Smithsonian Studies in Air and Space, no. 7.

Newsletters

The Badger Legionnaire, Official Publication of the American Legion, Department of Wisconsin, Appleton, Wisconsin, various issues, 1928 - 1941.

Kohler of Kohler News, Kohler, Wisconsin, various issues, 1927 - 1945.

Wisconsin National Guard Review, vol. 17, no. 5, August 1940, through vol. 18, no. 8, November 1941; vol. 19, no. 1, January 1942, through vol. 23, no. 3, May 1946; vol. 23, no. 6, November 1946, through vol. 27, no. 1, January 1950; vol. 27, no. 3, May 1950.

Activities Progress Report, State of Wisconsin Conservation Department, various issues, January 30, 1948, no. 3 through December 29, 1949, no. 23.

Wisconsin Aerospace Education News, Wisconsin Aerospace Education Association, West Allis, Wisconsin, various issues, vol. I, issue 1, June 1973, through vol. XXV, issue 1, 1996-97.

Wisconsin Aviation Bulletin, Wisconsin Department of Transportation, Bureau of Aviation, Madison, Wisconsin, varioius issues, Winter, 1984, no. 1 through Spring, 1998, no. 52.

Manuscripts, Scrapbooks

Aviation History, scrapbook of photos of Milwaukee's celebrations for Lester Maitland and Charles Lindbergh in 1927; also photos of first air mail planes and pilots of Dickinson Airlines.

Dickey, Rev. Norris C., Ph.D., *Aviation at The Head of the Lakes,* unpublished manuscript transcribed for The Superior Public Library by W. P. A. Project #11068, the original is filed at Superior Public Library.

Gallatin, Harold A., notes, letters and newsclips of EAA founding member (#20) who built a Corben Baby Ace airplane in Milwaukee in 1930-32.

Gnauck, Johanna, *They Built And Flew Wisconsin's First Flying Boats,* Archives, Milwaukee County Historical Society.

Hamilton, Thomas F., *Biography and Scrapbook,* microfilm, University of Wisconsin-Milwaukee Area Research Center.

Kerstetter, Carl, *Chronological Listing of Events and Activities Related to the Development of Langlade County Airport, 1929-1977,* Langlade County Airport.

Lewis, Charles H., *History of the Shell Lake Airport, 1945-1995,* reminiscences, newsclips, newsletter and excerpts from the Proceedings of the Shell Lake Village Board.

Lueneburg, Fred, *The Brown Deer Airport, 1927-1939.* Property of Fred Lueneburg.

Mangerson, Judson W., JUD, Rhinelander/Oneida County Airport, history, reminiscenses of and collection of newsclips on Rhinelander Airport.

Milwaukee County Parks and Airport, scrapbook of newsclips, Archives, Milwaukee County Historical Society.

Nosker, Jim, *Boyceville Airport History,* typewritten history of Boyceville airport, 1938-1984, Nor-Wes Aviation, Boyceville, Wisconsin.

Outagamie County Airport, *Chronology,* 1996.

Salmon, Herman, "Fish," collection of newsclips and photos of Salmon's career as parachute jumper and pilot in Wisconsin in the 1930s and as a test pilot for Lockheed, 1940s-1960s.

Service Record Book of Men and Women of Westfield, Wisconsin and Community, American Legion Post No. 244, Westfield, Wisconsin, c. 1946.

Tees, Harry, scrapbook of photos, captions and newsclips of Green Bay's first aviator; also contains a copy of 1911 Green Bay High School Commencement Program titled, "Aeroplane." Archives, Milwaukee County Historical Society, Milwaukee.

Whiting, Barbro M., typewritten account of flight of Galbraith Perry Rodgers in Appleton in 1911 and relation of Rodgers to Neenah's George Whiting Family.

Wright, Burt, *History of the Chippewa Valley Regional Airport,* in the files of the Manager, Chippewa Valley Regional Airport, March 27, 1995

Documents

Map 4/14, Sc. 210, *Maps, Plans for Airports, 1927-1930,* Aeronautics Branch, Air Information Division, United States Department of Commerce, from Wisconsin State Historical Society Archives.

Airport Management, Aeronautics Bulletin Number 17, July 1, 1932, Aeronautics Branch United States Department of Commerce.

Air Navigation Maps, Aeronautics Bulletin Number 10, April 1, 1932, Aeronautics Branch, United States Department of Commerce.

State Aeronautical Legislation Digest and Uniform State Laws, Aeronautics Bulletin Number 18, January 1, 1936, Aeronautics Branch, United States Department of Commerce.

Aviation Training, Aeronautics Bulletin Number 19, July 1, 1935, Aeronautics Branch, United States Department of Commerce.

Scheduled Air Transportation, Aeronautics Bulletin Number 23, July 1, 1932, Aeronautics Branch, United States Department of Commerce.

The Federal Airways System, Aeronautics Bulletin Number 24, July 1, 1936, Aeronautics Branch, United States Department of Commerce.

Lists of Airports and Landing Fields, Aeronautics Bulletin Number 5, October 15, 1931, Aeronautics Branch, United States Department of Commerce.

Descriptions of Airports and Landing Fields in the United States, Airway Bulleten No. 2, June 1, 1933, September 1, 1934, January 1, 1936, January 1, 1937 and January 1, 1938, Bureau of Air Commerce, United States Department of Commerce.

Final Report on the WPA Program, 1935-43, Work Program Association, 1994.

National Airport Plan for 1949, U.S. Department of Commerce and Civil Aeronautics Administration.

Civil Aeronautics in the United States, Aeronautics Bulletin Number 1, January 1, 1937, Aeronautics Branch, United States Department of Commerce.

Aeronautics Trade Directory, Part I Commodities, Part II Activities, Aeronautics Bulletin Number 3, July 1, 1932, Aeronautics Branch, United States Department of Commerce.

Statistical Review, Vol. 1, No. 1, Works Progress Administration, State of Wisconsin, January, 1936.

Gregory, John G., *Wisconsin's Gold Star List, Soldiers, Sailors, Marines and Nurses from the Badger State Who Died in the Federal Service During the World War,* State Historical Society of Wisconsin, Madison, 1925.

Wisconsin Blue Books: 1919, 1921, 1923, 1925, 1940

Annual Report of the State Board of Agriculture, 1907; 1908; 1910; 1911.

Biennial Report of the State Conservation Commission, 1915-16; 1931-32; 1935-36; 1937-38; 1943-44; 1945-46; 1947-48; 1949-50; 1951-52; 1952-54.

Annual Reports of the Wisconsin State Aeronautics Commission, 1957; 1958; 1961; 1962; 1963; 1964; 1965; 1966.

Biennial Report of the Wisconsin Department of Transportation, 1972-73; 1975-77; 1977-79; 1981-83; 1983-85; 1987-89; 1989-91; 1991-93.

Toward a Six Year Investment Plan for Aeronautics, Wisconsin Department of Transportation, July 10, 1978.

Airports in Use in Wisconsin as of June, 1940, State Aeronautics Commission, 1940.

An Airport System Plan For Wisconsin, Wisconsin State Planning Board Bulletin No. 11, 1940 and No. 12, 1941, The State Aeronautics Commission and the Civil Aeronautics Authority.

Air Traffic in Northern Wisconsin, June-July, 1956, Wisconsin State Aeronautics Commission.

Wisconsin Illustrated Directory of Airports, Sky Eye, Inc., 1960.

An Airport System Plan for Wisconsin, July, 1961, Wisconsin State Aeronautics Commission.

Wisconsin Airport System Plan: 1986-2010, Wisconsin Department of Transportation, December, 1986.

Wisconsin Aviation Activity, 1979, Wisconsin Department of Transportation, Bureau of Aeronautics, April, 1980.

Wisconsin Aviation Activity, 1985, Wisconsin Department of Transportation, Bureau of Aeronautics, May, 1986.

Wisconsin Aviation Activity, 1988, Wisconsin Department of Transportation, Bureau of Aeronauatics, March, 1989.

Wisconsin Aviaiton Activity, 1992, Wisconsin Department of Transportation, Bureau of Aeronautics, April, 1993.

5-Year Airport Improvement Program, Wisconsin Department of Transportation, Bureau of Aeronautics, February, 1996.

Wisconsin Department of Transportation Accomplishments, 1987-1993, Wisconsin Department of Transportation.

Wisconsin Department of Transportation 1993 Accomplishments, Wisconsin Department of Transportation.

Wisconsin Department of Transportation 1996 Achievements, Wisconsin Department of Transportation.

Catalog of Aviation Motion Pictures, 1951, Wisconsin State Aeronautics Commission.

A Decade of Progress in Aviation in Wisconsin, 1946-1956, The Wisconsin State Aeronautics Commission, 1956.

Wisconsin Airport Development Handbook, Wisconsin Department of Transportation, June, 1995.

Wisconsin Airport Development Program, Completed Projects as of August 26, 1997, Wisconsin Department of Transportation, Bureau of Aeronautics.

Proceedings Second Wisconsin Aeronautics Conference, Wisconsin State Aeronautics Commission, February 26, 1948.

Survey of Public Airports Serving Recreational Areas in Wisconsin, Division of Planning, Wisconsin Department of Transportation, 1972.

Briefing Paper on Aeronautics Revenues, Wisconsin Department of Transportation, May 7, 1980.

Airport Sites in Wisconsin, 1993, Wisconsin Department of Transportation, Bureau of Aeronautics.

Wisconsin Air Activity, 1995, Wisconsin Department of Transportation, Bureau of Aeronautics.

Wisconsin Airport Directory, 1995-1996, Wisconsin Department of Transportation, 1995.

The National Airplane Fund, information sheet sent by the Aero Club of America to the Roberts Motors Company, February 24, 1916. Rheinhardt Ausmus Collection, Rutherford B. Hayes Presidential Center Library, Fremont Ohio.

Letter from Harry G. Slater, Secretary, Wisconsin Legislative Committee on Aviation to Major John P. Wood, Wausau, July 17, 1928.

Air Commerce Bulletin, Aeronautics Branch, United States Department of Commerce, v. 1, no. 1, July 1, 1929; v.1, no. 2, July 15, 1929; v. 1, no. 3, August 1, 1929; v. 1, no. 4, August 15, 1929; v. 1, no. 5, September 2, 1929; v. 1, no. 6, September 15, 1929; v. 1, no. 7, October 1, 1929; v. 1, no. 8, October 15, 1929; v. 1, no. 9, November 1, 1929; v. 1, no. 10, November 15, 1929; v. 1, no. 11, December 2, 1929; v. 1, no. 12, December 16, 1929; v. 1, no. 13, January 2, 1930; v. 1, no. 14, January 15, 1930; v. 1, no. 15, February 1, 1930; v. 1, no. 16, February 15, 1930; v. 1, no. 17, March 1, 1930; v. 1, no. 18, March 15, 1930; v. 1, no. 19, April 1, 1930; v. 1, no. 20, April 15, 1930; v. 1, no. 21, May 1, 1930; v. 1, no. 22, May 15, 1930; v. 1, no. 23, June 2, 1930; v. 1, no. 24, June 15, 1930; v. 2, no. 1, July 1, 1930; v. 2, no. 2, July 15, 1930; v. 2, no. 3, August 1, 1930; v. 2, no. 4, August 15, 1930; v. 2, no. 5, September 2, 1930; v. 2, no. 6, September 15, 1930; v. 2, no. 7, October 1, 1930; v. 2, no. 8, October 15, 1930; v. 2, no. 9, November 1, 1930; v. 2, no. 10, November 15, 1930; v. 2, no. 11, December 1, 1930; v. 2, no. 12, December 15, 1930; v. 2, no. 13, January 2, 1931; v. 2, no. 14, January 15, 1931; v. 2, no. 15, February 2, 1931; v. 2, no. 16, February 16, 1931; v. 2, no. 17, March 2, 1931; v. 2, no. 18, March 16, 1931; v. 2, no. 19, April 1, 1931; v. 2, no. 20, April 15, 1931; v. 2, no. 21, May 1, 1931; v. 2, no. 22, May 15, 1931; v. 2, no. 23, June 1, 1931; and v. 2, no. 24, June 15, 1931; v. 3, no. 1, July 1, 1931; v. 3, no. 2, July 15, 1931; v. 3, no. 3, August 1, 1931; v. 3, no. 4, August 15, 1931; v. 3, no. 5, September 1, 1931; v. 3, no. 6, September 15, 1931; v. 3, no. 7, October 1, 1931; v. 3, no. 8, October 15, 1931; v. 3, no. 9, November 2, 1931; v. 3, no. 10, November 16, 1931; v. 3, no. 11, December 1, 1931; v. 3, no. 12, December 15, 1931; v. 3, no. 13, January 2, 1932; v.3, no. 14, January 15, 1932; v. 3, no. 15, February 1, 1932; v. 3, no. 16, February 15, 1932; v. 3, no. 17, March 1, 1932; v. 3, no. 18, March 15, 1932; v. 3, no. 19, April 1, 1932; v. 3, no. 20, April 15, 1932; v. 3, no. 21, May 2, 1932; v. 3, no. 22, May 16, 1932; v. 3, no. 23, June 1, 1932; v. 3, no. 24, June 15, 1932; v. 4, no. 1, July 1, 1932; v.4, no. 2, July 15, 1932; v. 4, no. 3, August 1, 1932; v. 4, no. 4, August 15, 1932; v. 4, no. 5, September 1, 1932; v. 4, no. 6, September 15, 1932; v. 4, no. 7, October 1, 1932; v. 4, no. 8, October 15, 1932; v. 4, no. 9, November 1, 1932; v. 4, no. 10, November 15, 1932; v. 4, no. 11, December 1, 1932; v. 4, no. 12, December 15, 1932; v. 4, no. 13, January 13, 1933; v. 4, no. 14, January 16, 1933; v. 4, no. 15, February 1, 1933; v. 4, no. 16, February 15, 1933; v. 4, no. 17, March 1, 1933; v. 4, no. 18, March 15, 1933; v. 4, no. 19, April 1, 1933; v. 4, no. 20, April 15, 1933; v. 4, no. 21, May 1, 1933; v. 4, no. 22, May 15, 1933; v. 4, no. 23, June 1, 1933; v. 4, no. 24, June 15, 1933; v. 5, no. 1, July 15, 1933; v. 5, no. 3, September 15, 1933; v. 5, no. 4, October 15, 1933; v. 5, no. 5, November 15, 1933; v. 5, no. 7, January 15, 1934; v. 5, no. 8, February 15, 1934; v. 5, no. 9, March 15, 1934; v. 5, no. 10, April 15, 1934; v. 5, no. 11, May 15, 1934; v. 5, no. 12, June 15, 1934; v. 6, no. 1, July 15, 1934; v. 6, no. 2, August 15, 1934; v. 6, no. 3, September 15, 1934; v. 6, no. 5, November 15, 1934; v. 6, no. 6, December 15, 1934; v. 6, no. 7, January 15, 1935; v. 6, no. 8, February 15, 1935; v. 6, no. 9, March 15, 1935; v. 6, no. 10, April 15, 1935; v. 6, no. 11, May 15, 1935; v. 6 no. 12, June 15, 1935; v. 7, no. 1, July 15, 1935; v. 7, no. 2, August 15, 1935; v. 7, no. 4, October 15, 1935; v. 7, no. 5, November 15, 1935; v. 7, no. 6, December 15, 1935; v. 7, no. 7, January 15, 1936; v. 7, no. 8, February 15, 1936; v. 7, no. 9, March 15, 1936; v. 7, no. 10, April 15, 1936; v. 7, no. 11, May 15, 1936; v. 7, no. 12, June 15, 1936; v. 8, no. 1, July 15, 1936; v. 8, no. 2, August 15, 1936; v. 8, no. 3, September 15, 1936; v. 8, no. 4, October 15, 1936; v. 8, no. 5, November 15, 1936; v. 8, no. 6, December 15, 1936; v. 8, no. 7, January 15, 1937; v. 8, no. 8, February 15, 1937; v. 8 no. 9, March 15, 1937; v. 8 no. 10, April 15, 1937; v. 8, no. 11, May 15, 1937; v. 8, no. 12, June 15, 1937; v. 9, no. 1, July 15, 1937; v. 9, no. 2, August 15, 1937; v. 9, no. 3, September 15, 1937; v. 9, no. 4, October 15, 1937; v. 9, no. 5, November 15, 1937; v. 9, no. 6, December 15, 1937; v. 9, no. 7, January 15, 1938; v. 9, no. 9, March 15, 1938; v. 9, no. 10, April 15, 1938; v. 9, no. 11, May 15, 1938; v. 9, no. 12, June 15, 1938; v. 10, no. 1, July 15, 1938; v. 10, no. 2, August 15, 1938; v. 10, no. 4, October 15, 1938; v. 10, no. 5, November 15, 1938; v. 10, no. 7, January 15,

1939; v. 10, no. 8, February 15, 1939; v. 10, no. 9, March 15, 1939; v. 10, no. 10, April 15, 1939; v. 10, no. 11, May 15, 1939; v. 10, no. 12, June 15, 1939; v. 11, no. 1, July 15, 1939; v. 11, no. 2, August 15, 1939; v. 11, no. 3, September 15, 1939; v. 11, no. 4, October 15, 1939; vo. 11, no. 5, November 15, 1939; v. 11, no. 6, December 15, 1939.

National Airport Plan for 1949, Civil Aeronautics Administration, United States Department of Commerce.

Airworthiness Requirements For Aircraft Components And Accessories, Aeronautics Branch, United States Department of Commerce, Aeronautics Bulletin No. 7-F, March 1, 1933.

School Supplement of Air Commerce Regulations, Aeronautics Branch, United States Department of Commerce, Aeronautics Bulletin No. 7-B, January 1, 1931.

Parachute Supplement of Air Commerce Regulations, Aeronautics Branch, United States Department of Commerce, Aeronautics Bulletin No. 7-D, January 1, 1931.

The Wisconsin Warden, 100 Years of Conservation Law Enforcement History, Wisconsin Conservation Warden.

Annual Forest Fire Report, Forest Protection Division, Wisconsin Conservation Department, 1955-1966.

Airworthiness Requirements For Engines And Propellers, Aeronautics Branch, United States Department of Commerce, Aeronautics Bulletin No. 7-G, January 1, 1933.

Airworthiness Requirements For Aircraft, Bureau of Air Commerce, United States Department of Commerce, Aeronautics Bulletin No. 7-A, October 1, 1934.

Air Commerce Regulations, Aeronautics Branch, United States Department of Commerce, Aeronautics Bulletin No. 7, January 1, 1934.

Notes On Airport Lighting, Aeronautics Branch, United States Department of Commerce, April 15, 1929.

Semi-monthly Report on Prisoners of War as of 1 August 1945, Restricted Headquarters Army Service Forces, Office of the Provost Marshal General, Washington, D. C., August 1, 1945.

Establishment of Prisoner of War Camps, War Department, Prisoner of War Circular, Washington, D. C., No. 21, April 11, 1944.

Aviation in the U.S. Army, 1919-1939, Office of Air Force History, United States Air Force, Washington, D.C., 1987.

Use of Prisoners of War Located Near Army Air Forces Installations, War Department, Prisoner of War Circular, Washington, D. C., No. 16, March 14, 1944.

Batten, Colonel John H., CAP, *History of Coastal Patrol Base No. 6, Civil Air Patrol, World War II, St. Simons Island, Georgia*, CAP National Historical Committee Monograph Series, no. 7, 1988.

Summary of War Supply and Facility Contracts by State, Industrial Area and County, War Production Board, Program and Statistics Bureau, Militsary Division, Procurement Reports Branch, November 1, 1945.

USAF Credits For the Destruction of Enemy Aircraft, Korean War, USAF Historical Study No. 81, Office of Air Force History, Headquarters USAF, 1975.

Domestic Air News, Department of Commerce, Office of the Assistant Secretary of Commerce for Aeronautics, Air Information Division, Washington, D. C., no. 11, September 1, 1927; no. 14, October 15, 1927; no. 15, November 1, 1927; no. 16, November 15, 1927; no. 18, December 15, 1927; no. 19, January 1, 1928; no. 20, January 15, 1928; no. 21, January 31, 1928; no. 22, February 15, 1928; no. 23, February 29, 1928; no. 24, March 15, 1928; no. 25, March 31, 1928; no. 26, April 15, 1928; no. 27, April 30, 1928; no. 28, May 15, 1928; no. 29, May 30, 1928; no. 31, June 30, 1928; no. 44, January 15, 1929; no. 45, January 31, 1929; no. 46, February 15, 1929; no. 47, February 28, 1929; no. 48, March 15, 1929; no. 49, March 30, 1929; no. 50, April 15, 1929; no. 51, April 30, 1929; no. 52, May 15, 1929; no. 53, May 30, 1929; no. 54, June 15, 1929.

Newspapers (Alphabetical By City)

Algoma

"Red Letter Day for Ace and Plywood," *Algoma Record-Herald*, August 6, 1943.

"40 Missions Completed to Enemy Targets, Bob Beck Comes Home," *Algoma Record-Herald*, September 15, 1944.

"Here Today, Maryland Tomorrow, That's the Story of Plywood Panels," *Algoma Record-Herald*, August 2, 1946.

"You've Heard and Wondered About Our Plywood Boats? Here's How!" *Algoma Record-Herald*, August 9, 1946.

Antigo

"Was Not Schwister's Flying Machine," "Special Fair Attraction," *Antigo Daily Journal*, September 18, 1911.

"Big Day At The Fair," *Antigo Daily Journal*, September 22, 1911.

"Record Breaking Crowd At Fair," *Antigo Daily Journal*, September 23, 1911.

"Crowd of 12,000 People Attended Fair Wednesday," *Antigo Daily Journal*, September 4, 1919.

Appleton

"Airship Here This Afternoon," "Co-Operation Makes a City," *Appleton Daily Post*, September 2, 1911.

"Aviation Meet Successful Every Way But Financially," *Appleton Daily Post*, September 5, 1911.

"Powers Crosses Lake in Hydro-Aeroplane,"*Appleton Daily Post*, July 19, 1912.

"Large Crowds Witness Flights at Waverly," *Appleton Daily Post*, July 22, 1912.

"Bullock's 'Fake' Airship Story Did Not Add To His Pelf," "Airplane Here," *Appleton Daily Post*, April 28, 1919.

"Crescent Delivered By Plane,First in Valley by Air Route," *Appleton Crescent*, September 8, 1919.

"Crescent is Delivered by Airplane," *Appleton Crescent*, September 9, 1919.

"Planes are Stuck in Mud at Neenah," *Appleton Crescent*, September 10, 1919.

"Whiting Field Forerunner to Present County Airport," *Appleton Post Crescent*, June 12, 1983.

"Flyer Finally Touches Down," *Appleton Post-Crescent*, April 10, 1984.

Ashland

"The Eagle Will Scream and the Hydroplane Will Soar at Ashland Tomorrow," *Ashland Daily Press*, July 3, 1912.

"Glorious Fourth Celebrated in Grand Style at Ashland Yesterday," *Ashland Daily Press*, July 5, 1912.

Beaver Dam

"A Rascally Humbug," *Beaver Dam Argus*, June 11, 1870.

"First Appearane of Winter Takes Big Toll," *Beaver Dam Daily Citizen*, November 12, 1940.

Beloit

"Warner Makes Seven Flights of Quarter Mile 50 Feet High," *Beloit Daily News*, November 4, 1909.

"Beachey Gives Crowd Thrills; Oldfield Speedy," *Beloit Daily News*, September 14, 1914.

"Three Hurt When Plane Falls," *Beloit Daily News*, August 28, 1928.

"Beloit Man Wants To Fly With Airmen," and "Birdmen In Big Flights," *Beloit Daily News*, August 5, 1911.

"Ward Flies To South Beloit," *Beloit Daily News*, August 7, 1911.

"Inaugurate Air Mail Service Here Monday," *Beloit Daily News*, August 27, 1930.

"300 Pounds of Airmail is Sent on Inaugural Flight," *Beloit Daily News*, September 11, 1930.

"Fish Poles and Baling Wire, But It Flew," *Beloit Daily News*, January 23, 1940.

"T. L. Timmons Built Beloit's First Homemade Airplane, but Gave Up Flying 26 Years Ago," *Beloit Daily News*, February 3, 1940.

"A. P. Warner, Beloit, Was First Individual to Buy an Airplane, in 1909; Flew Craft on Morgan Farm," *Beloit Daily News*, December 12, 1953.

"Beloit's First Commercial Airport Was Organized Here in 1928; Roy Reed Compares Then with Now," *Beloit Daily News*, December 17, 1953.

"Several Young Rock County Flyers Served During World War II; Howard Packard Won Decorations," *Beloit Daily News*, December 21, 1953.

"First Flights Day Observed at Rock County Airport On May 15, 1950; North Central Provides Service," *Beloit Daily News*, December 23, 1953.

"Beloit Man, Jess C. Brabazon, Has Vivid Memories and Many Mementos of His Early Days of Flying," *Beloit Daily News*, December 24, 1953.

Black River Falls

"Looking Back Jackson County Part I, Part II," *Black River Falls Banner-Journal*, May 8, 1991.

"Several Thousand See Airport Dedicated," *Black River Falls Banner-Journal*, July 14, 1971.

Bloomington

"Fair Prospects Are Extra Good," *Bloomington Record*, September 10, 1919.

Cambria

"Airmail Pilot Thrills His Family, Flying Over Farm Home Each Trip," *The Cambria News*, March 25, 1927.

Chicago

"Vision of Airship Magnet for Gold," *Chicago Daily Tribune*, February 18, 1909.

"Fall Kills Aviator Brodie," *Chicago Tribune*, April 20, 1913.

"Aviator Brodie Killed in Plunge From Plane," *Chicago Record-Herald*, April 20, 1913.

"Another Local Airman Dies," *Chicago Daily Tribune*, September 17, 1913.

"Aviation Costs Another Life," *Chicago Record-Herald*, September 17, 1913.

Chilton

"But One Day's Fair," *The Chilton Times*, September 7, 1912.

Chippewa Falls

"Bird Men At Fair," *Chippewa Falls Daily Independent*, August 1, 1911.

"Shaft Breaks, the Aeroplane Takes a Dangerous 'Header,'" *Chippewa Falls Daily Independent*, September 23, 1911.

"Three Men Killed in Plane Crash," *Chippewa Herald-Telegram*, June 10, 1935.

"1911 Fair Visitors Saw County's First Recorded Aeroplane Crash," *Chippewa Falls Daily Independent*, July 24, 1959.

Delavan

"The balloon ascension on Saturday afternoon last was a complete success notwithstanding the unfavorableness of the weather, as it was almost raining at the time." *Delavan Republican*, April 30, 1874.

De Pere

"Brown County Fair A Success," *The Brown County Democrat*, September 1, 1911.

"County Fair Again Goes 'Over the Top,'" *Brown County Journal*, August 28, 1919.

Dodgeville

"Old Man River Fails to Give Up His Victim," *Dodgeville Chronicle*, November 21, 1940.

"Body of Harold Steffenson is Found Sunday," *Dodgeville Chronicle*, November 28, 1940.

Duluth

"Winged Mail," *Duluth News*, May 16, 1948.

Durand

"Visit the Inter-County Fair at Durand, September 3-4-5," *Pepin County Courier*, August 29, 1913.

"Inter-County Fair Closed Last Week," *Pepin County Courier*, September 12, 1913.

Eau Claire

"Grand Balloon Ascension," *Eau Claire Weekly Free Press*, July 2, 1874.

"'Von' Grand Humbug," *Eau Claire Weekly Free Press*, July 9, 1874.

"Aeronautic," *Eau Claire Weekly Free Press*, August 26, 1874.

"Active Patriotism Needed in Future, Says Norenberg," *Eau Claire Leader*, November 12, 1940.

"Several Others Believed Dead in Mississippi," *Eau Claire Leader*, November 13, 1940.

"Lives of 17 Aboard Novadoc Spectacularly Saved," *Eau Claire Leader*, November 14, 1940.

Elroy

"The Big Fair is Great Success," *Elroy Tribune*, October 3, 1913.

Evansville

"Green County Fair," "The One and Only Rock Co. Fair," *Evansville Review*, August 29, 1912.

"Immense Excitement," "Big Crowds, Great Enthusiasm, Big Show," *Evansville Review*, September 5, 1912.

"Rock County Fair," *Evansville Review*, September 12, 1912.

Fond du Lac

"Making Flying Machine in His Workshop Here," *Fond du Lac Daily Reporter*, December 22, 1903.

"County Fair Now Ready for Visitors," *Fond du Lac Daily Commonwealth*, August 27, 1912.

"Prospects Remain for Banner Fair," *Fond du Lac Daily Commonwealth*, August 28, 1912.

"The First Flight Ends in Disaster," *Fond du Lac Daily Commonwealth*, August 29, 1912.

"Thousands See Seaplane Soar Over The Town," *Fond du Lac Daily Reporter*, April 28, 1919.

"Seaplane Is Attraction For Sunday Crowds," *Fond du Lac Daily Commonwealth*, April 28, 1919.

"Dedication Recalls History of Old Airport East of City," *Fond du Lac Reporter*, July 7, 1959.

Fort Atkinson
"The Little Lady's Daughter and the Balloon Man," *Jefferson County Union*, September 27, 1878.

Friendship
"The County Fair," *Friendship Reporter*, September 25, 1919.

Grand Rapids
"Aeroplane Made in Minneapolis," *Wood County Reporter*, March 23, 1911.

Green Bay
"Flight By Aviator Will Be Feature of Brown County Fair," *Green Bay Gazette*, August 25, 1911.
"County Fair Open Today, Hydro-Aeroplane To Fly," *Green Bay Gazette*, August 27, 1911.
"Birdman and His Machine in River," *Green Bay Gazette, August 27, 1911*, August 30, 1911.
"Wittmar to Make Flight on Sunday," *Green Bay Gazette*, September 16, 1911.
"Feature of the Day Another Failure," *Green Bay Gazette*, September 18, 1911.
"Tees Ready to Fly," *Green Bay Press-Gazette*, July 27, 1912.
"Knowlan Flies And Later Has Accident," *Green Bay Semi-Weekly Gazette*, May 28, 1913.
"Aviator Ward in Successful Flight," *Green Bay Semi-Weekly Gazette*, August 16, 1913.
"Lawson Makes Initial Voyage with Airplane," *Green Bay Press-Gazette*, September 11, 1917.
"Magnificent New Plant," *Green Bay Press-Gazette*, November 15, 1917.
"Seaplane 'Peace To Be Here Today; Arrival Delayed," *Green Bay Press-Gazette*, April 26, 1919.
"Brown County Falls Down in Victory Liberty Loan," *Green Bay Press-Gazette*, April 28, 1919.

Janesville
"Balloons," *Janesville Gazette*, July 5, 1867.
"Gratuitous Balloon Ascension!!" *Janesville Daily Gazette*, June 1, 1872.
"The balloon which went up from the circus enclosure this afternoon landed on the roof of Dr. Harvey's house in its descent," *Janesville Daily Gazette*, June 3, 1872.
"Nichols Re-elected As State Secretary," *Janesville Daily Gazette*, June 20, 1912.
"Convention Crowds Have All Departed," *Janesville Daily Gazette*, June 21, 1912.

Kenosha
"Birdmen Tuning Up," *Kenosha Evening News*, August 26, 1911.
"Birdmen Disappoint," *Kenosha Evening News*, August 28, 1911.
"Gertson Makes Flight," *Kenosha Evening News*, August 31, 1912.
"Kenosha's Woman CPT Instructor Keeps Class of Navy Pilots Flying," *The Milwaukee Journal*, July 26, 1942.
"Aeronautics Now A Safety Program Too," *Kenosha Evening News*, April 25, 1940.

La Crosse
"Locate Five Bodies, Seek Many Others," *La Crosse Tribune and Leader-Press*, November 12, 1940.

"Warmer Weather Forecast Friday," *La Crosse Tribune and Leader-Press*, November 13, 1940.
"Experimental Air Mail Flight Made Here in 1911," *La Crosse Tribune*, June 8, 1958.

Lancaster
"Fair Turned Out Well Despite Bad Weather," *Grant County Herald*, September 24, 1913.

Luxemburg
"Approve Plans for $11,000 Airport at Kewaunee," *The Luxumburg News*, January 5, 1934.

Madison
"Airship Crosses Lake Mendota And Attempts To Stop In Madison," *Wisconsin State Journal*, September 23, 1910.
"Red Devil Falls; Woman Driver In Close Call," *Wisconsin State Journal*, June 1, 1913.
"Air-Water Boat is Here," *Wisconsin State Journal*, September 20, 1914.
"Hydroaeroplane Demonstrations Over Lake Mendota," *Madison Democrat*, September 20, 1914.
"President Van Hise Takes a Flyer in Hydroaeroplane," *Madison Democrat*, September 22, 1914.
"Fine Flying Weather Doped For Seaplane," *Capital Times*, April 26, 1919.
"Fifteen Air Rides Go To Loan Buyers," *Wisconsin State Journal*, April 27, 1919.
"Trial Flights Of Hydroplane This Afternoon," *Capital Times*, April 28, 1919.
"Ready For Air Flights Over Tenney Park," *Capital Times*, April 29, 1919.
"Watch The Skies Is Hint To Public," *Wisconsin State Journal*, April 29, 1919.
"Toby Curtis To Fly Over The Sierra Nevada," *Capital Times*, May 6, 1919.
"Senator Conant Arrives in Aero," *Wisconsin State Journal*, September 4, 1919.
"'Greatest War Plane in the World' Visits Madison," "Weather 'Defeats' 21 Pursuit Ships," *Wisconsin State Journal*, August 25, 1940.
"Rain, Wind Sweep City; Cold Due," "Seven City Area Youths Named Flying Cadets," *Wisconsin State Journal*, November 11, 1940.
"State Journal Speeds to Hunters' Rescue," "Voters' League to Hear Lecture on Aviation," *Wisconsin State Journal*, November 12, 1940.
"Duck Hunters," "Chimneys, Trees Fall In High Wind Here," *Madison Capital Times*, November 12, 1940.
"Sad Father Aids Search for Lost Son," "City Air Travel Zooms During Year," *Wisconsin State Journal*, November 15, 1940.
"Aeronautics Board Named," *Associated Press-Madison*, March 10, 1944.
"Aeronautics Bill Causes Stormy Board Session," *Associated Press-Madison*, February 2, 1945.
"No Compromise In Sight on Aviation Bills," *Associated Press-Madison*, April 26, 1945.

Manitowoc
"Bird Man Made Trip of 75 Miles in 55 Minutes," *Manitowoc Herald-News*, April 28, 1919.

Mauston
"Flying Machine at the Fair," "Program for the Juneau Co. Fair," *Mauston Star*, August 28, 1913.

"Flying Machine Wrecked at Fair," *Mauston Star*, September 11, 1913.

"Aviator Davis Flies at Fair," *Mauston Star*, September 14, 1913.

"Aviator Davis Dies at Chicago," *Mauston Star*, September 18, 1913.

Menasha

"Aeroplane Is: Not Coming," *Menasha Record*, April 26, 1919.

"Seaplane Here Sunday Morning," *Menasha Record*, April 28, 1919.

Menomonie

"Everything Ready for Fair Next Week That Will Break All Records,""Flight Announcement of Curtiss Biplane," *Dunn County News*, September 7, 1911.

"Monoplane Makes Great Flight at Dunn County's Record Fair," *Dunn County News*, September 14, 1911.

"Barlow Meets with Accident," *Dunn County News*, September 5, 1913.

"All Pleased with the Fair," *Dunn County News*, September 12, 1913.

"Barlow Left for Sparta on Sunday," *Dunn County News*, September 16, 1913.

Merrill

"Appeal to Citizens of Merrill," *Merrill Daily Herald*, July 3, 1913.

"Statement of the Reasons for Non-Flight," *Merrill Daily Herald*, July 5, 1913.

Milwaukee

"The Balloon Ascension," *Milwaukee Sentinel*, August 19, 1856.

"Balloon Ascension," *Milwaukee Sentinel*, September 4, 1856.

"The Balloon Ascension," *Milwaukee Sentinel*, September 17, 1856.

"Balloon Ascension During the Fair," *Milwaukee Sentinel*, September 17, 1859.

"The Balloon Ascension," *Milwaukee Sentinel*, October 1, 1859.

"The Balloon Ascension," *Milwaukee Sentinel*, October 4, 1859.

"Prof. J. H. Steiner," *Milwaukee Sentinel*, June 23, 1860.

"A Balloon Race," *Milwaukee Sentinel*, June 28, 1860.

"Balloon Ascension on the Fourth," "Prof. Steiner," *Milwaukee Sentinel*, July 3, 1860.

"Safe Return of Professor Steiner," "Professor Steiner and His Ascension," *Milwaukee Sentinel*, July 6, 1860.

"Professor Steiner and His Ascension," *Milwaukee Sentinel*, July 6, 1860.

"Narrative of Prof. Steiner's Eighty-Ninth Ascension in the Balloon 'Europa'," *Milwaukee Sentinel*, July 9, 1860.

"A Willow Boat For Professor Steiner, the Aeronaut," *Milwaukee Sentinel*, July 19, 1860.

"A Novice in a Balloon Sensations," *Milwaukee Sentinel*, July 7, 1863.

"Unfortunate," *Daily Wisconsin*, August 21, 1863.

"At Janesville on the 4th a 'Prof.' Cummings will make several balloon ascensions," *Milwaukee Sentinel*, June 28, 1867.

"The Beaver Dam Citizen says that Prof. Niebling, with his monster balloon 'Great Eastern,' will make an ascension from the fair grounds in that city, Tuesday, June 7th." *Milwaukee Sentinel*, May 26, 1870.

"Balloon Ascension," *Milwaukee Sentinel*, July 25, 1870.

"Balloon Ascension Fourth of July," *Milwaukee Sentinel*, June 15, 1871.

"The Balloon Ascension," *Milwaukee Sentinel*, June 28, 1871.

"The Balloon Ascension," *Milwaukee Sentinel*, July 1, 1871.

"Sky-High," *Milwaukee Sentinel*, July 7, 1871.

"A Balloon Wedding," *Milwaukee Sentinel*, August 31, 1872.

"Aeronaut Steiner has hinted that he would be pleased with a contribution of one thousand dollars to enable him to test a new airship," *Milwaukee Sentinel*, February 21, 1873.

"Delavan enjoyed a balloon ascension, Saturday." *Milwaukee Sentinel*, May 2, 1874.

"Voyage Through the Air," *Milwaukee Sentinel*, June 5, 1875.

"Two Sunsets in One Day," *Milwaukee Sentinel*, June 14, 1875.

"All Above the World so High," *Milwaukee Sentinel*, June 16, 1875.

"The Balloon Ascension," *Milwaukee Sentinel*, July 2-3, 1875.

"Balloon Ascension by Prof. Steiner and Some Wellknown Citizens," *Milwaukee Sentinel*, July 5, 1875.

"Steiner," *Milwaukee Sentinel*, July 7, 1875.

"Sailing the Air," *Milwaukee Sentinel*, July 9, 1875.

"Hasn't Come Down Yet," *Milwaukee Sentinel*, September 4, 1893.

"The Aeronaut Still Missing," *Milwaukee Sentinel*, September 5, 1893.

"No Tidings From Him," *Milwaukee Sentinel*, September 6, 1893.

"Dropped in the Lake," *Milwaukee Sentinel*, September 7, 1893.

"Capt. Eiermann is Safe," "His Balloon Safe, Too," *Milwaukee Journal*, September 7, 1893.

"Fall of an Aeronaut," *Milwaukee Sentinel*, July 29, 1895.

"Mlle. Ida's Close Call," "Scientific Road Building," *Milwaukee Sentinel*, September 14, 1899.

"Aero Club Asked to Compete at Berlin," *Milwaukee Sentinel*, July 2, 1908.

"Ten Balloons to Start in a Race to Ocean," "Will Provide a Balloon," *Milwaukee Sentinel*, July 4, 1908.

"Gift of a Balloon for the Aero Club," *Milwaukee Sentinel*, July 8, 1908.

"Boy Builds Aeroplane from Journal Instructions," *Milwaukee Journal*, July 29, 1910.

"Wrecks $3,000 Biplane," *Milwaukee Sentinel*, July 3, 1911.

"Sees Aero Press Lure," *Milwaukee Journal*, August 5, 1911.

"Atwood A-Wing on Long Trip," *Milwaukee Journal*, August 14, 1911.

"Watch for Aviator Fish in His Biplane and the Advertisements He Will Scatter in His Flight Over the City Saturday," *Milwaukee Journal*, May 24, 1912.

"Curtiss-Wright Aviation," *Milwaukee Journal*, May 30, 1912.

"In Aerial Circus," *Milwaukee Journal*, May 31, 1912.

"Aviation Only Sideshow in Milwaukee," Says Arch Hoxsey,' *Milwaukee Journal*, September 13, 1910.

"A Few Sidelights on the State Fair," *Milwaukee Journal*, September 14, 1910.

"State Day Success at the Fair," *Milwaukee Journal*, September 14, 1910.

"An Automobile Stolen," "Crowds are in Awe," *Milwaukee Journal*, September 15, 1910.

"Aeroplane Falls Upon Fair Crowd," *Milwaukee Journal*, September 17, 1910.

"Aviator Flies to Milwaukee," "Flyer Hurled to the Ground," *Milwaukee Journal*, May 25, 1912.

"Tuesday's Journal Goes By Aeroplane," "Will Fly With School Children," "Free Souvenir of the Record-breaking Aeroplane Trip Made by Aviator Fish from Chicago to the Boston Store," *Milwaukee Journal*, May 27, 1912.

"Getting Ready for the Airship Meet," "Weather Man Delays Journal Air Delivery," "Journal Auto Racing with Young Fish's Aeroplane as it Speeds Over the City from South," *Milwaukee Journal*, May 28, 1912.

"Tries Bravely to Deliver the Journal by Aeroplane," *Milwaukee Journal*, May 29, 1912.

"Thousands See Amazing Feat," "See Air Visitor," *Milwaukee Journal*, May 30, 1912.

"Master Fish Starting on Record Aeroplane Flight," and "Journal Man Takes Remarkable Picture," *Milwaukee Journal*, May 31, 1912.

"Long Trial Flights Made by an Airship," *Milwaukee Daily News*, August 28, 1912.

"Airship Thrills Race Spectators," *Milwaukee Journal*, October 2, 1912.

"Airship Flight is to be Made if Practicable," *Milwaukee Journal*, October 3, 1912.

"Fish is to Fly Again Saturday," *Milwaukee Journal*, October 4, 1912.

"Flying a Thriller," *Milwaukee Journal*, October 5, 1912.

"Most Remarkable Photographs Ever Taken---Pictures From Sky; An Airship Going 60 Miles an Hour, Showing Grand Prize Racer Going 72 Miles an Hour," *Milwaukee Journal*, October 7, 1912.

"Journal Gets Airship Pictures of Auto Race," *Milwaukee Journal*, October 7, 1912.

"Aviator Ducked in Lake," *Milwaukee Sentinel*, July 15, 1914.

"Herewith the Journal Gives You 'News From the Heavens,'" *Milwaukee Journal*, September 7, 1918.

"Sees Peace-time Work for Planes," "Big Planes Boost City's Loan Drive," *Milwaukee Sentinel*, April 23, 1919.

"Thousands Are Thrilled By Journal Flier," "Plane to Take Movie of City," *Milwaukee Journal*, April 26, 1919.

"First Official Naval Photos of Milwaukee Taken 5,600 Feet Above City," "Belgian Veterans Will Boost Loan," *Milwaukee Sentinel*, April 29, 1919.

"Airplane Landing Field Here Urged," *Milwaukee Sentinel*, April 30, 1919.

"Assisted In Building Planes Rapidly," *Milwaukee Journal*, September 7, 1919.

"Flying Circus Gets in Bad," *Milwaukee Journal*, September 9, 1919.

"Bombing Plane Unable to Leave Milwaukee Port," "City Flocks to State Fair," *Milwaukee Journal*, September 11, 1919.

"'Around Rim' Flyers to Give Exhibitions Here," *Milwaukee Journal*, September 12, 1919.

"Lawson Plane Lands in N. Y.," "Oconto Falls May Yet See 'Flying Circus,'" *Milwaukee Journal*, September 13, 1919.

"City May Become Base Air Port," *Milwaukee Journal*, September 15, 1919.

"Circus All Set At Friendship," *Milwaukee Journal*, September 16, 1919.

"Rain Maroons Air Men Here," *Milwaukee Journal*, September 19, 1919.

"Eight Flyers on Way to Green Bay in Second Lap of First Badger Air Derby," "Pig Sent Here by Airplane," *Milwaukee Journal*, August 30, 1920.

"Journal Plane, Gardner Pilot, Wins Air Race," "Girl Reporter, Passenger in Air Derby, Not a Bit Scared," "Illinois - Interurban Day at Badger Fair Breaks All Records," *Milwaukee Journal*, August 31, 1920.

"Stunt Flyer Drops, 17 Hurt in Fair Park," *Milwaukee Journal*, May 30, 1921.

"Plane Hits Crowd Here, 16 Hurt; 7 Die In Washington Air Crash," "Mitchell Fights for Life in Air," *Milwaukee Sentinel*, May 30, 1921.

"Meisenheimer Has A Narrow Escape," *Milwaukee Sentinel*, May 31, 1921.

"State Has Its Day at Big Fair," *Milwaukee Sentinel*, August 31, 1921.

"Milwaukee, Chicago Air Line Is Opened," "Champions Race in Biggest Air Derby," "City Is Host to Aerial Derby," *Milwaukee Journal*, May 28, 1922.

"Pilots Await Signal for Start of Classic," "Love of Thrills Draws Men to Pilot Balloons," "Gen. Patrick Favors Large U.S. Air Force," *Milwaukee Journal*, May 31, 1922.

"First 'Air Mail' Arrives," "15 Planes Looping Over City Give Thousands Thrill," "Predicts Mail by Air Here," "Army Airplane Falls Into Lake," *Milwaukee Journal*, May 31, 1922.

"Breeze Freshens, Skies Clear Before Jump-Off," *Milwaukee Journal*, May 31, 1922, Final Edition.

"Ten Flyers Still Battle to Win Race," *Milwaukee Journal*, June 1, 1922, Final Edition.

"Army Balloon Leads Flyers," "Journal Men Recount Struggles in Air," "Honeywell Bag to Win, Belief," *Milwaukee Journal*, June 2, 1922.

"Navy Pilot Is Still Missing in Air Derby," *Milwaukee Journal*, June 3, 1922.

"Navy Balloon Pilot Safe; Fourth, Belief," *Milwaukee Journal*, June 4, 1922.

"Fokker Sees Great Air Future for U.S.," *Milwaukee Journal*, June 27, 1922.

"Fokker to Decide Soon as to Locating Here," *Milwaukee Journal*, June 28, 1922.

"Here is the Derby Route the Fliers Will Take," *Wisconsin News*, July 18, 1925.

"Great Air Derby Thrills Half Million Spectators," *Wisconsin News*, July 20, 1925.

"Great Aerial 'White Way' is Laid Out," *Wisconsin News*, April 27, 1927.

"Lake Airport Used by Plane," *Milwaukee Journal*, May 26, 1927.

"State's First Air Highway Laid Out," *Wisconsin News*, June 22, 1927.

"12 Planes on Badger Air Tour," *Wisconsin News*, October 11-13, 1927.

"Increase Air Committee to 35," *Wisconsin News*, October 13, 1927.

"New Airport on Harbor is Being Planned," *Milwaukee Sentinel*, November 27, 1927.

"Big Air Show Planned for Sept. 29,30," *Wisconsin News*, September 29-30, 1934.

"Big Ship Plunges to Water in Mist," *Wisconsin News*, August 28, 1932.

"Giant Airship Is at Airport Here," *Wisconsin News*, September 18, 1932.

"All Aboard, Football Fans!" *Wisconsin News*, October 24, 1932.

"They're Off! First Milwaukee-Detroit Airmail," *Wisconsin News*, March 2, 1933.

"Plane Forced Down on Lake," *Wisconsin News*, March 3, 1933.

"'Spirit of 3.2' Flight is Dry-Ver-ee Dry," *Wisconsin News*, April 10, 1933.

"Sick Boy Finally Gets Away by Air," *Wisconsin News*, April 17, 1933.

"Flyers Rescued From Lake," *Wisconsin News*, December 28, 1933.

"Make First Hop," *Wisconsin News*, July 10, 1934.

"14 Milwaukee Fliers to Seek African War Jobs," *Wisconsin News*, July 1935.

"4 Killed as Plane Crashes in Field Near Airport Here," *Wisconsin News*, July 27, 1935.

"Air Show to be Held at Markesan 2 Days," *Wisconsin News*, July 28, 1935.

"50,000 Parcels of Mail Land Here In Mass Flight," *Milwaukee Sentinel*, May 21, 1938. (Steve Shalbreck)

"Seek quick Release of $360,000 for Air Base Here," *Milwaukee Journal*, August 9, 1940.

"Paul Meyers Named to Run Air Base Here," *Milwaukee Journal*, August 12, 1940.

"Swell Factory Activity Here," "Defense Jobs Eyed by Many," "Barrack Bags Used as Trap," *Milwaukee Journal*, August 25, 1940.

"Wrecked Army Plane and Body Are Found," "Furious Wind Delays Trains," *Milwaukee Journal*, November 12, 1940.

"Wind Storm Death Toll 17; Ferry Ashore; 1 Unreported," *Milwaukee Sentinel*, November 12, 1940.

"UW Man to Tell Alumni His Part in Tokyo Raid," *Milwaukee Journal*, January 31, 1944.

Wills, Robert H., "Ken Cook Spurns Wheels for His Printing Firm's Deals," *Milwaukee Journal*, February 28, 1959.

"Plaque to Honor First State Pilot," *Milwaukee Journal*, November 17, 1963.

"75 Years of Service, Milwaukee County's Airports," *Milwaukee Journal*, November 13, 1994.

Mondovi

"'Flying is my business and I have to take chances to stay at the top of my profession' said Barlow in Chicago during the recent aviation neet there." *Mondovi Herald*, September 12, 1913.

"The fair, September 24th and 25th was spoiled by rain so that but little of the official program could be carried out." *Mondovi Herald*, October 3, 1913.

Monroe

"Fair Opens Under Most Favorable Conditions," *Monroe Journal-Gazette*, September 13, 1912.

Big Crowd at Fair Today," *Monroe Daily Journal*, September 13, 1913.

"How the Fair Panned Out," *Monroe County Democrat*, September 18, 1913.

Neenah

"Sea Plane Made Flying Visit Here," *Neenah Daily Times*, April 28, 1919.

"Whiting Field," *Twin City News-Record*, November 14, 1984.

Neillsville

"The Big Fair and Soldiers Reunion," *Neillsville Republican and Press*, September 18, 1919.

"Last Saturday the Editor of this paper had the pleasure of having his first aeroplane ride." *Neillsville Republican and Press*, September 25, 1919.

New York

"Navy to Lend Aeroplanes," *New York Times*, June 25, 1915.

Oshkosh

"Balloon Ascension," "No Balloon Ascension," *Oshkosh Daily Northwestern*, September 27, 1878.

"The Wind Up," *Oshkosh Daily Northwestern*, September 28, 1878.

"Airplane To Come To City Tomorrow At Noon For Loan. Flies In County," *Oshkosh Daily Northwestern*, April 25, 1919.

"Seaplane May Come Tomorrow Morning Whistle Will Warn," *Oshkosh Daily Northwestern*, April 26, 1919.

"Lake Ideal Here For Hydroplanes," *Oshkosh Daily Northwestern*, April 28, 1919.

"Wings over Oshkosh," "Schedule of EAA Activities," *Oshkosh Daily Northwestern*, July 28, 1979.

Phillips

"County Airport Construction Completed," *The Bee*, Phillips, September 15, 1983.

Platteville

"One Plane to Eight At Airport," *Platteville Journal*, January 1, 1980.

Portage

"Wittmer is Here, Flights Tomorrow," *Portage Daily Register*, September 18, 1911.

"The Aviation Day Attracts Throngs," *Portage Daily Register*, September 19, 1911.

Prairie du Chien

"Gays Mills Fair a Big Success," *Prairie du Chien Courier*, October 8, 1912.

"Gays Mills Fourteenth Annual Fair," "Aviator Kearney Has Another Fall," *Prairie du Chien Union*, October 10, 1912.

Racine

"Thousands Witness Events on Program at Air Circus Here," *Racine Journal-Times*, October 14, 1935

"2 Planes Crash During Storms," "Storm Cancels Legion Flight," "Prospective Aviators to Begin Training Course Here Tonight," *Racine Journal-Times*, November 11, 1940.

"Violent Gale Causes Damage In All Parts of Racine County," "Wind, Rain,Snow Lash City on Armistice Day," *Racine Journal-Times*, November 12, 1940.

"Rescue Crews Continue Their Search For Victims of Violent Storm on Lake," *Racine Journal-Times*, November 14, 1940.

Reedsburg

"The Balloon Ascension," *Reedsburg Free Press*, September 11, 1879.

Rice Lake

"Attendance Record Broken at 1919 Barron County Fair," *Rice Lake Chronotype*, September 4, 1919.

Richland Center

"Rain Marred the Fair," *Richland Center Republican Observer*, October 2, 1913.

St. Louis

"Old, Bold Pilot Refutes Rule," *St. Louis Post-Dispatch*, May 21-22, 1967.

"Stafford Lambert Funeral Service," *St. Louis Post-Dispatch*, October 4, 1976.

Salt Lake City

"Aviators to be Met by Ogden Citizens," *Salt Lake City Semi-Weekly Tribune*, May 9, 1919.

"Notable Trip Made in Curtiss Airplane," *Salt Lake City Semi-Weekly Tribune*, May 16, 1919.

San Francisco

"Sacramento Aviators Reach Elko, Nevada," *San Francisco Chronicle*, May 9, 1919.

"Flight to Utah Ends in Disaster," *San Francisco Chronicle*, May 10, 1919.

"Sacramento Flyers Start Return Trip," *San Francisco Chronicle*, May 13, 1919.

"First Night Flight Made Over Sierra," *San Francisco Chronicle*, May 15, 1919.

Sheboygan

"Dare Devil Air Stunts at Plymouth," *Sheboygan Press*, July 3, 1914.

"Tinney Has a Thrilling Experience," *Sheboygan Press*, July 6, 1914.

"Local Boys Furnish All The Interest," *Sheboygan Press*, July 13, 1914.

"Is Real Flying Governor," *Sheboygan Press*, January 10, 1929.

"Sheboygan To Have Future As Aviation Port," *Sheboygan Press-Telegram*, May 12, 1923.

Sparta

"65,000 Soldiers Come To McCoy For Army Maneuvers,"*Sparta Herald*, August 12, 1940.

Stevens Point

"Tomorrow's Events," *Stevens Point Daily Journal*, July 19, 1912.

"Will Fly Tomorrow," *Stevens Point Daily Journal*, July 20, 1912.

"The Aeroplane Flew," *Stevens Point Daily Journal*, July 22, 1912.

Sturgeon Bay

"The Fair Faces a Deficit," *Sturgeon Bay Advocate*, September 25, 1913.

"Hydroplane Day Late," "The people of Sawyer are indignant over the way they are treated by the powers that be in collecting toll across the municipal bridge when occasions of public interest draws large numbers of its citizens to the east side." *Door County Advocate*, May 2, 1919.

"A Great County Fair," *Door County Advocate*, August 22, 1919.

"County Fair Winner," *Door County Advocate*, September 12, 1919.

Sun Prairie

"Industrial Fair Outshines Many of Our County Fairs," *Sun Prairie Countryman*, August 22, 1912.

Superior

"Here's a map of the vital defense area that the proposed two-mile square army air base in the town of Highland would...," *The Evening Telegram*, April 8, 1942.

"Richard I. Bong Airport," *The Evening Telegram*, January 17, 1945.

"Flying Club Gets Pilot House," *The Evening Telegram*, February 13, 1963.

Tomahawk

"Balloon Ascension A Feature," *Tomahawk Leader*, June 28, 1912.

"Balloon Stunt A Success," *Tomahawk Leader*, July 5, 1912.

"Tomahawk In Readiness To Celebrate The Fourth," *Tomahawk Leader*, July 3, 1914.

"Aviator Takes A Tumble," *Tomahawk Leader*, July 10, 1914.

"Flying Event, Crash 'Fireworks' for 1914 Fourth," *Tomahawk Leader*, July 2, 1996.

Watertown

"May Hold Fair On Saturday Owing To Rain," *Watertown Daily Times*, September 18, 1919.

Wausau

"Marshfield Aviator Drops 600 Feet and Suffers Slight Cut," *Wausau Daily Record-Herald*, July 24, 1925.

"Will Fly Over Wisconsin Cities on Way to West," *Wausau Daily Record-Herald*, August 17, 1925.

"Col. Mitchell Has a Narrow Escape in Fall," *Wausau Daily Record-Herald*, August 31, 1925.

"Commander of South America Good Will Fliers Coming Here," *Wausau Daily Record-Herald*, May 7, 1927.

"Good Will Flyers Come To Wausau Saturday, June 18," *Wausau Daily Record-Herald*, June 3, 1927.

"Wausau Will Welcome Flyers Next Saturday," *Wausau Daily Record-Herald*, June 14, 1927.

"Good Will Flyer Here" and "Big Amphibian Plane Lands On Lake Wausau With Its Noted Aviator," *Wausau Daily Record-Herold*, June 18, 1927.

"City Must Build Landing Court Or Be Off The Map," *Wausau Daily Record-Herald*, June 20, 1927.

"Reliability Tour Plane Will Visit Wausau In Week," *Wausau Daily Record-Herald*, July 7, 1927.

"Wisconsin Takes to Air With Great Enthusiasm; Cites Planning Fields," Associated Press article in *Wausau Daily Record-Herald*, July 15, 1927.

"An Airport For Wausau," *Wausau Daily Record-Herald*, August 3, 1927.

"Aviators Will Visit Wausau In National Tours," *Wausau Daily Record-Herald*, August 16, 1927.

"Lieutenant Wood and 'Miss Wausau' In Endurance Test," *Wausau Daily Record-Herald*, September 20, 1927.

"Holman, Myers A And B Winners In Aerial Derby," *Wausau Daily Record-Herald*, September 9, 1927.

"Ten-Plane Fleet To Tour State To Aid Aerial Trade," Associated Press article in *Wausau Daily Record-Herald*, September 22, 1927.

"Beacon Lights To Guide Planes To City Airport," *Wausau Daily Record-Herald*, September 29, 1927.

"10 Planes Ready To Start Badger Commercial Tour," *Wausau Daily Record-Herald*, October 10, 1927.

"Governor Zimmerman Flies to Wausau," *Wausau Daily Record-Herald*, November 4, 1927.

"Governor Lays Cornerstone of Airport Hangar," *Wausau Daily Record-Herald*, November 7, 1927.

"Northern Airways Company Carries on Increased Business," *Wausau Daily Record-Herald First Aviation Edition*, June 11, 1928.

"Wausau Will Greet Flyers At Program At Alexander Field," and "Referee Concedes Wood is Winner of National Air Tour," *Wausau Daily Record-Herald*, July 24, 1928.

"Welcome Plans Are Made For Aviators in Reliability Tour," *Wausau Daily Record-Herald*, July 25, 1928.

"Throngs Greet Airmen," *Wausau Daily Record-Herald*, July 26, 1928.

"Wisconsin Youth Wants to Fly Across Ocean in Attempt to Bring Peace," *Wausau Daily Record-Hearald*, September 7, 1939.

West Bend

"County Fair Next Week," *West Bend News*, September 11, 1912.

"Rain Mars the Fair," *West Bend News*, September 18, 1912.

Index

FIRSTS